STATISTICS

STATISTICS

Fourteenth Edition

by

A. R. ILERSIC
M.Sc.(Econ)., B.Com., F.I.S.

*Professor of Social Studies in the
University of London*

and

R. A. PLUCK
B.Sc.(Econ)., F.I.S.

*Lecturer in Social Statistics at
Bedford College (University of London)*

HFL (PUBLISHERS) LTD
9 BOW STREET, COVENT GARDEN
LONDON WC2

The first eleven editions of this book were published under the title of
Statistics and Their Application to Commerce

Twelfth edition completely revised under the title of *Statistics* 1959

Twelfth edition	*1959*
(Second impression)	*1962*
(Third impression)	*1963*
(Fourth impression)	*1963*
Thirteenth edition	*1964*
(Second impression)	*1968*
(Third impression)	*1969*
(Fourth impression)	*1970*
(Fifth impression)	*1973*
Fourteenth edition	*1979*

This edition © HFL (Publishers) Ltd 1979

ISBN 0 372 30033 2

Printed in Great Britain by
THE STELLAR PRESS HATFIELD HERTS

PREFACE TO THE FOURTEENTH EDITION

For those teachers and students who have used earlier editions of this book a brief outline of the changes in this new edition may be helpful. Most chapters have been substantially rewritten, in particular the chapters on economic and social statistics, and new material introduced into the text. Each chapter on statistical method is concluded with a selection of examination questions, together with worked answers and comments thereon to guide the prospective examinee. The exposition of sampling theory and statistical inference has been considerably expanded. A new chapter on elementary probability and a fuller treatment of the Normal distribution as well as of significance tests has been introduced. In these chapters, and in the earlier chapters on elementary statistical method, every effort has been made to meet the needs of the reader whose study of arithmetic and algebra stopped at G.C.E. Ordinary level if not before.

To the new reader some explanation of the scope and form of this text is also due. It is intended primarily for students taking examinations leading to a professional qualification and for undergraduates reading for degrees in the Social Sciences in which some understanding of basic statisical method is required.

Many such students find considerable difficulty with this subject; some even approach it with trepidation and fear arising from their earlier and often unsuccessful efforts to understand simple mathematics. It is with such students in mind that this book has been written. For those with the requisite mathematical understanding there is no need for new textbooks, a sufficient number of excellent books is available. It is not possible to learn even basic statistics without some facility in calculation, but it is too often forgotten that a great deal of statistical work requires no real mathematics at all and, for the tyro, the present-day pocket calculator has greatly reduced the burden of calculation.

For such reasons this text seeks to emphasise the importance of interpretation and the evaluation of statistical data rather than the mechanical application of formulae to improbable data. To meet the special needs of the less numerate reader, numerous worked examples are included with extended commentary and explanation. Some readers not so handicapped may find the repetition of basic points unnecessary. I can only answer that in many years of interviewing graduate statisticians for employment I have never ceased to wonder, not so much at the gaps in their knowledge, but their often very limited grasp of elementary principles. Much of what appears in these pages is due to that experience.

The foregoing comment applies particularly to the chapters on economic and social statistics. I have met honours graduates just down from University who apparently believe all data comes from a computer; certainly they have never seen, much less opened, a Blue Book or any other published source of statistical data. Students in the social sciences may actually have opened a copy of *Social Trends* or the *Monthly Digest of Statistics* but, all too often, their essays are unsullied by any evidence that some basic facts on say, the balance of payments or the birth rate, might improve the essay. More than half of the average professional statistician's time is spent in collecting his data and a knowledge of key sources is indispensable. I can only hope that the contents of the two chapters on official statistics will provide a readable introduction to a neglected area of statistics for the average student.

While the needs of the prospective examinee must be paramount in a text such as this, I would feel I had failed in my task if this was the sole purpose which the book served. Throughout I have sought to emphasise what the subject is about and why statistical method finds such extended application in so many fields of study. In particular, by the time the reader has worked his way through these pages he should be aware that, even if there are no 'damned lies', there can often be half-truths. If the reader has recognised this simple fact and knows what to look for when he comes across the printed or spoken statistic, then this book will have served its purpose.

It is with pleasure I acknowledge the assistance given me by various people. First, I owe a very real debt to my colleague Mr R. A. Pluck who, at short notice, took on the task of rewriting the extended chapters on Economic and Social Statistics. Without that help this edition would not have appeared and in the circumstances, I feel it is only right that his name should appear on the title page. I am most grateful to a fellow examiner in the University, Mrs Myra Woolf, who helped me revise the chapters on sample design and sample surveys, as well as to Miss Lilian Button of the University of Exeter who made many helpful suggestions for simplifying the exposition of elementary probability and the Normal curve.

I acknowledge with grateful thanks the kindness of various bodies in allowing me to reproduce copyright material, in particular Oliver & Boyd Ltd for the reproduction of part of Table No. 3 in the late Sir Ronald A. Fisher's work *Statistical Methods for Research Workers*; the editor of *Barclays Bank Review*, the Confederation of British Industry and, not least, the Controller of Publications at H.M. Stationery Office. I acknowledge too, with grateful thanks, the kind permission given by the following examining bodies to reproduce questions from past examination papers: The University of London Examinaticns Department, the Local Government Examinations Board, the Institute of Chartered Accountants, The Institute of Statisticians, the Chartered Institute of Public Finance & Accountancy, the Rating & Valuation Association, and the Institute of Health Service Administrators.

Lastly, I take this opportunity to thank the many teachers and students who have written to me in the past drawing attention to both the virtues and limitations of the previous editions. I shall be grateful if they will continue to do so.

A. R. Ilersic

TABLE OF CONTENTS

ix

PART I
THE SCOPE OF STATISTICS

CHAPTER I

THE NATURE AND PURPOSE OF STATISTICS

According to a memorandum prepared by a committee of the Royal Statistical Society,[1] 'the science and methods of *statistics* in the modern sense range from the mere recording and tabulation of numerical data to subtle processes of inductive reasoning based on the mathematical theory of probability'. To allay any fears that may be aroused in the reader's mind, it can be stated that this study stops well before the latter stage. Statistics as defined in the latter part of the above quotation is a relatively recent development. Most of the significant advances in statistical techniques were developed in this century.

It would be a mistake, moreover, to assume that only a mathematician can become a competent statistician. The bulk of statistical work has little to do with mathematics. Indeed, most statisticians such as those in Government departments or the research departments of stockbroking firms or industrial and commercial organisations, spend most of their time on the collection and interpretation of statistics relevant to the interests or activities of those departments. This is not to assert that they do not need mathematical skills. From time to time new problems of analysis will arise such as a reconstruction of a complicated index number, a new design for sampling the population, or simply a more effective technique of analysing some experimental research results. To meet such needs, the statistician will require a good understanding of mathematical statistics, or at least enough for him to recognise the need for consulting a specialist in that field and to be able to discuss the problem with such a person.

But, a major part of the work is concerned with collection and classification. This may sound mundane and even boring. In fact, however, as will be seen later, such work is of the utmost importance in ensuring a successful outcome to any enquiry. Before ever data are collected, there must be full and careful consideration of the problem to a solution of which the statistical information and analysis is to contribute. Furthermore, it is not always easy to obtain just the information required. A lot of thought must be devoted to definitions, to trying to frame the questions people have to answer to ensure that the questions will elicit the correct information yet not require a lot of time to answer.

Even the basic analysis and interpretation may not require complex

---

[1] Memorandum on Official Statistics. By a committee of the Council of the Royal Statistical Society, 1943.

statistical techniques. For example, William Farr was a medical practitioner who joined the newly formed General Register Office which was responsible for the decennial census of population from 1841 on. His annual reports for much of the rest of the 19th century on the statistics from the registration of births, deaths and marriages are classics and it was he who, by simple comparison and matching of the mortality statistics for the new industrial towns and other parts of the country, clearly demonstrated that bad living conditions, infected water supplies, etc., were responsible for the abnormally high death rates of such places. Such work needed no more mathematics than an ability to add up and multiply; but it needed intelligence and judgement as well. Whereas the *Journal* of the Royal Statistical Society, which was founded in 1837, nowadays contains predominantly articles mathematical in character, for most of the 19th and early 20th century it contained many papers dealing with social problems in which the authors did little more than assemble the data they had painstakingly collected and make a series of comparisons which brought out the discrepancies and anomalies in the data which required explanation.

To make this point is not to decry the value of mathematical statistics. Rather it is to drive home the fact that even with a very limited understanding of mathematics and the laws of probability which underlie modern statistical theory, it is still possible to do good statistical work and learn how to interpret information presented in numerical form. Above all, a sound knowledge of basic principles ensures that you will not be taken in by spurious and irrelevant statistics which proliferate in political speeches and reports or in partisan evidence to bodies of enquiry. Finally, because of the expansion of the applications of statistical techniques to an ever-widening field of human activity, whether one is a doctor, economist or accountant, to mention but three diverse occupations, the professional journals will contain numerous statistical articles which may, or may not, be useful contributions to knowledge. A sound grasp of what statisticians can do – and cannot do – will enable an assessment of such articles and papers to be made. Likewise, with the emphasis on numerate management and the growth of operations research as a management aid, it becomes essential for the prospective executive to be able to understand, at least in general terms, what such people are talking about.

The term 'statistician' has until recently been very widely defined, the more so since there existed no recognised professional statistical qualification. In lieu thereof, graduates with degrees in mathematics or economics with some training in statistics formed the main source of statistical workers. After the last war, a new professional body, the

Institute of Statisticians, established such a qualification while the universities have been extending the scope and scale of their teaching and granting degrees in which statistics is the dominant, *i.e.* honours, subject. The undoubted importance of statistics is reflected in the large number of professional bodies which now set a paper in statistics at some stage of their qualifying examinations. For this purpose, the student is required to learn the basic ideas and principles of the subject and it is, in the main, with such fundamentals that this book is concerned.

Definitions of 'Statistics'

The term 'statistics' is somewhat loosely employed to cover two separate concepts: (1) descriptive statistics (2) statistical method. 'Descriptive statistics' covers the collection and summaries of numerical data, popularly known as the 'facts'. Examples of this type of statistic are encountered every day in the national Press; one reads, for example, that the 'total working population of Great Britain in mid-June 1976 totalled 25.9 million of whom some 15.9 million were male and 10.0 million were female. Figures relating to United Kingdom overseas trade and balance of payments appear regularly in the press. For example: exports in the third quarter of 1975 totalled £5,252 million compared with imports of £5,779 million, so that for that quarter there was an excess of total imports over total exports, termed the visible balance, of £527 million.

Such quotations from published statistics are good enough to provide an indication of the magnitudes involved. After all, the figure of 26 million for the working population, with a division of 16 and 10 millions for men and women is good enough as an indication of the size and structure of the labour force. The same is true of the import and export statistics indicating that exports usually fall short of imports in total and that there is a deficit on what is termed visible trade. Beyond such simple generalisations, however, one cannot go. The point is that it is not the absolute accuracy of the figures which is important, but rather the degree of accuracy which is required. For example, provisional figures of the population are published on the basis of the previous full census and then estimated in the intervening years until the next decennial census. As an indication of the size and structure of the working population and its age distribution the annual estimates between censuses are reliable enough. If, however, figures were needed from which one could measure the decennial change in the mortality of different occupational groups, then clearly, it would be necessary to wait for the census figures. Also it would then be necessary to check that the latest revised figures were compiled on the same basis as those for the preceding periods or dates.

In the case of the overseas or external trade figures it should be noted that the quoted values may have been seasonally adjusted, *i.e.* they are not the crude totals of the goods actually passing through the ports, but are based upon the average figures prepared by the Customs. Also, if one is trying to make an estimate of the results for balance of payments of these trade figures then it must be borne in mind that the export total quoted above is given 'free on board'. Imports are now also stated f.o.b. but this is after deducting freight and insurance charges which provide a valuable contribution to what are known as this country's 'invisible' exports. In other words, figures are seldom what they appear to be; definitions affect them and it is therefore of the utmost importance that such definitions be checked before using or quoting the statistics.

Descriptive statistics are very often not exact or accurate in the arithmetic or accounting sense. Some data may be; for instance in Great Britain the number of Civil Servants and their salaries can be given precisely, but on the other hand no one can state *exactly* how many people there are in Great Britain at any date. This is true even for the census day itself, because errors due to omissions and mis-countings are inevitable when enumerating 53,827,550 persons living in Great Britain. This figure is based on the number of persons enumerated in the 1971 census of population and is taken from the *Advance Analysis* of the 1971 census published a full year after the census. It can be stated with every confidence that even the census day total so recorded is inaccurate; not everyone who should have made a return will have done so, not to mention mistakes in the returns such as omissions of young children or a lodger, and mistakes made in processing the data for publication. In fact, the mid-year estimate for 1971 gives the population as 54.1 million. An exact figure is certainly not possible several years after that date, although the registration system, which should record every birth and death between the censuses, is very efficient. On the other hand the figures for emigrants from and immigrants into the United Kingdom are only estimates.

A good example of the difficulty of producing both accurate and meaningful statistics was provided by the controversy over the monthly totals of unemployed published until November 1972. In consequence of a report from an Inter-Departmental Working Party entitled *Unemployment Statistics*[1] the count of unemployed was changed quite significantly. According to some Labour back-benchers the revised figures were a 'fiddle' or, more precisely, 'the long-stand-ing method of presentation of unemployment statistics had been altered in order to obscure the intolerably high level of unemploy-

[1] Cmnd 5157

ment'. The point at issue turned on the definition of 'unemployed'; when the 'long-standing' method of counting was used then the unemployed were those registered with the local employment exchanges as being unemployed, *i.e.* not at work on the day they signed the register. Thus, when on the second Monday of the month the unemployment register was totalled for the monthly unemployment figures, that figure included all those so registered. But, among those so registered were the 'temporarily stopped', *e.g.* by virtue of short-time working or because of industrial strikes outside their own organisation affecting supplies, their work had ceased. As soon as the difficulties were over, their firm would re-open and the men would start full-time work again. Thus, in the strict sense of the term, such people were not without jobs and it was the opinion of the Inter-Departmental Working Party that the inclusion of their numbers exaggerated the magnitude of the problem. Henceforth they should be excluded from the 'unemployed' as published in the monthly count. Whether or not the decision is right or wrong is here irrelevant; the point to note is that when published statistics are used, make sure you fully understand the definition, *i.e.* what does the total refer to; what is the unit?

Thus, while it is perfectly all right to give an exact figure in such cases, it should not be forgotten that the appearance of accuracy can be misleading, especially if for some reason the registration system is at all unreliable or temporarily affected by extraneous factors. Thus, the figures of monthly imports and exports are completely distorted by a dock strike. Furthermore, in some of the under-developed countries registration of births is incomplete partly because not all births are registered. But the result may also be misleading since female children are sometimes ignored and not registered. Persistent under-notification can be detected since the sex ratio of registered births should not differ significantly from the expected ratio of about 51 male to 49 female births. It is essential, when handling and studying statistical data, to ensure that the source of the original data is reliable and that the data collected are relevant to the question to which an answer is sought. Whenever any statistics are consulted, the first question is not, 'To what unit or place of decimals are these figures reliable?' but 'Where were the figures obtained, by whom, and why?' If satisfactory answers to these questions can be given, it is then time to consider the accuracy of the data.

Interpreting the data

Statistical data in their raw state are by themselves of little value. It may be interesting to the managing director of a company to learn that the sales of a particular product in one country total £500,000 last calendar month, but the information only becomes statistically significant when related, for instance, to the fact that a turnover of only £300,000 was achieved in the corresponding month of the preceding year. The essence of statistics is not mere counting, but *comparison* – and provided this fact is always borne in mind – careless and consequently useless compilation of data may be avoided. Comparisons are valid only when they are between quantities expressed in identical terms, *e.g.* a direct comparison of weekly earnings as an indication of living standards between two periods is invalidated if in the first the working week was 45 hours and in the second only 40 hours.

A good example of careless and consequently irrelevant comparison was provided after the war by a Board of Trade Press notice concerning the tobacco shortage. After pointing out that more tobacco was reaching the shops, it continued: 'Against this is the fact that more persons are smoking than before the war, the United Kingdom population having risen from 47,700,000 in 1939 to 50,000,000 at the end of 1949.' Since the population can only expand by immigration and by new births, and the former was relatively insignificant in this period, it might be assumed that the infants were tobacco addicts at an early age! The relevant figures were, of course, those of the *adult* population which, due to the changing age structure of the whole population, had increased.[1]

On the other hand, too much should not be read into a comparison of such data. The results should be scrutinised because there is a difference. The question to be asked is then not so much 'how big is the difference', but 'why is there a difference'. The following illustrations may bring home the point. An examination of the marriage rates in the United Kingdom show occasional but sharp fluctuations between the relative numbers of marriages registered in the first and second quarters of the calendar year. Such fluctuations are largely attributable to the fact that the date of Easter varies and occasionally falls within the first quarter. A further influence, before the tax law was changed, was the attraction of an income tax refund if the marriage took place before 6th April. Comparisons of quarterly births in the United Kingdom have not always been straightforward. After 1941 the number of births registered in the final and first quarters of successive years had to be adjusted to provide a true comparison with previous years. Previously, births were often registered up to six weeks after the event, as allowed by law. In consequence December births were often registered in January, thereby inflating the following quarter's total. But, with the introduction of ration

---

[1] Even this needs qualification, since it assumes that the smoking habits of the average adults are unchanged, or at least that the *per capita* consumption has not decreased.

books, the arrival of a new baby – subject to registration – meant a new and extra ration book. The elimination of the delay between the two events markedly affected the official statistics, yet at the time there was a very simple explanation of the sudden change in the birth pattern! Similarly, the sharp increase in the number of divorce petitions in the immediate post-war period gave rise to much public comment and suggestions that family life is disintegrating. Further reflections indicated that although the number of petitions had greatly increased, the increase could be explained largely by the fact that the war had led to an accumulation of petitions which would normally have been spread over the war-years thus avoiding the marked post-war accumulation of divorce proceedings.

The continuing increase in the divorce rate has revived public fears about the breakdown of family life. Despite the increase in the number of divorces, see the chart on p. 87, two important facts must be borne in mind in interpreting the situation. First, more people than ever before are now married so, even if the attitude to divorce had not changed over the past half century, one would have expected more divorces. Also, changes in the law relating to divorce and the extension of legal aid has made it possible for many people, in particular, wives, to apply for divorce when, in earlier times, they simply had neither the legal right nor the resources to seek a dissolution of their marriages. In other words, when reviewing the trend of divorce figures, while no doubt social influences and attitudes have played an important part, it is worth asking what would the rates have been in the 1930s, for example, had legal aid existed, the new laws applied and the same opportunities for women in the labour market existed then as now? Tiresome the repetition may be, but it must be remembered that the statistics tell only half the story! The important other half can be made up only by a combination of knowledge of the background, common-sense and judgement.

The collection of statistical data and their verification regarding source and definitions used, form only the first part of the statistician's work. The statistics themselves prove nothing; nor are they at any time a substitute for logical thinking. There are, as pointed out above, many simple but not always obvious snags in the data to contend with. Variations in even the simplest of figures may conceal a compound of influences which have to be taken into account before any conclusions are drawn from the data. For example, it was contended by the civic authorities that the reduction in the number of street accidents in Birmingham during the first half of 1963 was due to the success of their experiment of persuading drivers to use dipped headlamps while driving in the city. No doubt the scheme was helpful, but how can one attribute the entire difference in the number of accidents to this single factor when other factors undoubtedly played a part? In particular, the exceptionally bad weather at the time would tend to keep people at home, hence there would be fewer pedestrians crossing the streets at night. Fewer cars would be out, particularly on pleasure, *e.g.* from cinemas, dance halls, and hotels, so that there would be less traffic, less dazzle from on-coming lights, etc. Also, many of the drivers out in such weather would tend to be those whose profession necessitated driving a great deal and these would tend to be above-average drivers in skill whose accident rate would be lower than that for weekend drivers and others. Finally, the number of accidents fluctuates from time to time even if road conditions remain constant; to what extent was the difference accounted for by such fortuitous fluctuations?

Another case of dubious use of statistics was provided by the controversy which followed the assertion that the high toll of road accidents in Christmas 1963 was attributable to drivers who had been drinking. It was argued by the motoring correspondent of one newspaper that it was false to assert that drink causes as many accidents as the public seemed to believe. Statistics of convictions for road accidents showed, he argued, only a small proportion of cases in which the driver was convicted for driving under the influence of drugs or alcohol. This is true, but the inference is not justified that drink was a minor factor in those road accidents, any more than the number of convictions measures the extent to which drivers drink too much. After all, even if at other times of the year the number of accidents caused by drunken drivers is relatively low, is it not highly probable that the proportion will rise substantially at a time when drinking is widespread and intensive? In other words, it is wrong to infer, as did the motoring correspondent, that the average for the year corresponds with the figures for one short public festival when vastly different conditions prevail.

Statistical Methods

As indicated in the quotation in the opening paragraph, statistical methods range from simple numerical processes to 'subtle processes of inductive reasoning based on the mathematical theory of probability'. These processes are also covered by the term *statistics*, but to distinguish this meaning of the term from our first definition – descriptive statistics – they are usually referred to as *statistical method*. The simpler methods which involve little more than elementary arithmetic are discussed in the chapters which follow. The really fascinating developments in technique, which have made statistical science one of the most powerful tools in the hands of the modern research worker, are of relatively recent origin, mainly in the last fifty years. In industry, particularly since the war, statistical methods have been extensively employed to control the quality of the product and to ensure that faulty goods are not sent out. A brief description of this technique, known as *quality control*, is given later.[1] Another important development has been that dealing with the design of experiments and their subsequent analysis, which is of course determined by the actual design. Modern designs are much more efficient in that they enable much more information to be extracted from a given amount of data. These techniques, however, require a statistical ability of no mean order and are only mentioned in this text to emphasise the applications of statistical method.

Perhaps the most useful and generally applied technique devised by the statistician is known as *sampling*. Most readers will be familiar with the election forecasts of the public opinion polls; many will have heard about market research whereby manufacturers learn what the consumer thinks of a product by posing specially designed questions to a selected few people. Fortunately, although this branch of statistical method is complex in application, the lay reader can acquire an understanding of the principles underlying sampling techniques which will enable him to appreciate what the statistician terms the 'significance' of his results from an analysis of sample data.[2] Information and conclusions based upon sample data, although they are reported with all their limitations, are later often misquoted and bandied about with a complete disregard for their limitations which the statistician has so carefully emphasised. It is hardly surprising that the statistician so often hears the dictum, 'lies, damned lies and statistics' quoted at him. Yet it is not the statistician who is at fault; it is the individual who quotes – often selectively to support his own tenuous arguments – the statistical results without any of the qualifications with which the statistician has surrounded his conclusions. For this reason the quip has been made that some people use statistics in the same way as a drunk uses a lamp-post, more for support than for illumination!

Statistics in Business

Every businessman appreciates the importance of regular reports on the financial progress and position of his business; accountants are nowadays much less concerned with the routine auditing of business accounts than with providing management information. Unfortunately, there are still many business people who do not believe that statistical information, as well as the profit and loss account plus balance sheet, can be an invaluable aid to management. Part of

[1] Chapter XIX
[2] Explained in Chapter XIV

the trouble lies in the fact that many such businesses are required periodically to provide the government or their trades associations with statistics and this 'useless form-filling' has generated a lot of hostility which has affected attitudes towards the end-product. The Business Statistics Office is part of the Government Statistical Service and, quite apart from its responsibility for collecting information from industry and business, is also trying to get across to such people that the information produced by the statistical departments of the government can be valuable.[1] Such published statistics enable a business to assess its share of the market; to assess its potential market and to learn what people spend their money on; the extent to which some towns have more shops of particular kinds than others; to learn the extent of overseas competition in the home market; to assess trends in the economy; to compare the results of one's own business with those of the industry at large. No doubt there are still many men who run businesses by 'hunch' or from 'the seat of their pants' and, no doubt, in many lines of business hunches and good guessing about the future are invaluable. But, no ship's captain sails without a compass or charts; likewise no businessman can be sure that he is making the most of his assets unless he studies the conditions which affect his business.

Most large businesses have their own research departments, some may have one or two people attached to the managing director's office to keep him informed of extraneous developments. Clearly, as British industry now finds itself in the European Economic Community, it is unthinkable that we should not try and find out something about the size, structure, distribution of competing industry in Europe. All modern governments produce voluminous statistics relating to their economic life and there is a lot to be learned from studying them. It tends to be forgotten that the demand for statistical information on overseas countries' economies, foreign trade, etc. did not come initially from the government departments. The forerunner of the Confederation of British Industry, the Association of British Chambers of Commerce founded in 1860, spent a large part of the latter half of the 19th century requesting the governments of the day to improve the Board of Trade and its information service to industry! No industrial trades association, which is of any use to its members, can function efficiently and usefully without a fact-gathering section. Ministers and senior Civil servants, any more than Members of Parliament, are not impressed by woolly appeals from industrial interests for various forms of assistance. To be effective any such memorandum must be fully documented with relevant

---

[1] See the publication *Facts from your figures*, published by the Central Statistical Office 1977.

statistics and rational argument. Such papers are not the product of one-man bands!

In recent years the Confederation of British Industry has collected information from member firms for its Industrial Trends Enquiry. A copy of the schedule used is reproduced on page 32. The purpose of the survey, which takes place every four months, is to ascertain variations in the level of industrial activity and manufacturers' exports, together with industrialists' expectations regarding the immediate prospects for their firms and industries. Increasing attention is being paid by both industry and the government to such 'forward-looking statistics' as well as in reducing the time-lag between the event and publication of relevant statistics which, in the case of so many series, has been such as to reduce the usefulness of the data. The Association of British Chambers of Commerce conducts a similar enquiry relating to the level of orders, stocks and expectations of merchants and export agencies. In all these cases the data are supplied by the member firms of the organisations.

It is much easier and probably more important for the larger undertaking to assemble and prepare statistical data relevant to their problems. This does not mean, however, that the smaller firm can derive no benefit from the simpler statistical techniques outlined in later pages. The mere assembly of data relating to the financial and production activities of the firm in tabular form and simple charts can often bring to light facts and trends which were hitherto not fully appreciated or not apparent from a scrutiny of the bare figures themselves. Given some knowledge of even the simpler methods, errors in the interpretation of such statistical data can often be avoided.

Government Statistics

Most of these data are the product of government activity in the social and economic spheres which has brought with it the need for positive and constructive legislation in economic affairs. The acceptance by all parties of responsibility for the maintenance of economic stability, which was acknowledged in the White Paper on Full Employment,[1] necessitates the collection and preparation by the responsible Government departments of statistics covering the whole vast complex of the nation's economy. Many of these data can only be obtained from the business and industrial community, and this involves the generally disliked task of form filling. There is scope for much education on both sides in this matter. The Government statisticians responsible for the preparation of the forms and the presentation of the results will perform their tasks more efficiently given reasonable co-operation from their informants just as the sim-

[1] Employment Policy. Cmnd. 6527.

plification of the questionnaires will facilitate their completion.

Statistical techniques enable the Government Actuary to estimate the potential demand for pensions, sickness benefit and unemployment allowances. The B.B.C. has, since October 1936, maintained a statistical department for audience research in order that programmes should as nearly as possible meet the demands of the public. The Budget, which influences every side of the economic life of the community, is itself based on estimates of the probable consumption of taxed commodities, prospective income levels and mortality rates (for estate duty receipts), all of which owe their accuracy to statistical techniques. There is little doubt as to the importance attached by the government to reliable and up-to-date statistical data on the economic scene. The Central Statistical Office is expanding continuously its output of economically significant series such as hire-purchase statistics and estimates of investment outlays by large firms in the United Kingdom. Much is being done to improve the economic industrial and commercial statistics needed for economic planning. In 1957 Mr Macmillan, then Chancellor, likened the then available data to 'looking up the trains in last year's Bradshaw'. Economic planning is impossible without accurate statistics published with the minimum of delay. The material condensed into Chapters XVII and XVIII will later give the reader some impression of the tremendous volume of statistical information produced in connection with the economic situation as well as on social conditions.

The contents of the following chapters may at times appear to be far removed from these important and fascinating problems; but just as a prospective mathematician has first to learn the multiplication tables, so the potential statistician must first acquaint himself with the elementary principles of statistical analysis. If after finishing this book, the reader is still interested in the subject, then a brief bibliography offers him additional material for study.

CHAPTER II

STATISTICAL DATA:
DEFINITIONS AND SOURCES

Statistical method consists of two main operations; counting and analysis. The analysis may entail no more than a simple comparison, *e.g.* at last Saturday's football matches there were 40,000 spectators at Chelsea and 60,000 at Manchester United. From these data at least one conclusion can be drawn, *i.e.* there were 50 per cent more spectators at one match than at the other. The ensuing question, 'why this was so?' requires more information than is given here. At more advanced levels statistical analysis is very much more complicated and is based on specially designed mathematical techniques. But to whatever type of analytical technique the data are to be subjected, the first stage of any statistical enquiry is the collection of the facts and this means counting. The statistician has no use for information that cannot be expressed numerically, nor generally speaking, is he interested in isolated events or examples. The term 'data' is itself plural and the statistician is concerned with the analysis of aggregates.

The data themselves may be of any kind as long as they can be counted. They must, however, be susceptible to classification as well as to counting. In the statement that there are nearly 56,000,000 people in Great Britain, the unit of counting is a person, just as in the figure of unemployed quoted earlier the unit is a person registered at the local Employment Exchange as unemployed. The actual process of counting, whether it be the decennial census enumeration of households and the persons in them, or the number of insurance cards lodged at the Employment Exchange on a given day each month, is easy enough, although with very large aggregates mistakes will occur. But the latter are, generally speaking, insignificant in relation to the absolute figures in the totals. A much more serious consideration for the statistician is to be certain that not merely have all the units been counted, but that only the units relevant to his enquiry are included. For example, the characteristic of the unit in a count of the unemployed is the fact of being both unemployed and registered as such. The Department of Employment publishes, among other analyses, totals sub-divided by sex and age (actually as between men, youths, women and girls) by the duration of unemployment as well as the location. All these analyses depend on classifications which in turn depend on the definitions employed. Clearly, some definitions are easier than others, *e.g.* male and female, men and youths – the latter being defined as under 18 years of age.

It is a good rule to remember that the first step in analysing any statistical data, whether it be culled from an official publication or a report prepared by someone else, is to check the definitions used for classification. How often do we hear radio news items recounting the number of road accidents. For most listeners this conjures up a scene of two cars colliding head-on. Yet this collision is not classified as an accident unless personal injury has been sustained. When we learn a few days after the Christmas holiday that sixty people have been 'killed' on the road, we think of the people who died at the time of the accident. In the road accident statistics, however, a person is classified as 'killed' if he dies within thirty days of the accident; thus early announcements of the Bank Holiday road deaths are usually under-statements. To take another example, most of us have a clear idea of what 'murder' is. The official statistics classify murders according to the number of victims, which is not the same thing as the number of murderers. Several people, *e.g.* a gang, may commit one murder; one person may kill several people, *i.e.* multiple murders. The distinction is very important if one is researching into the cause of 'murder'.

Some classifications, however, are more arbitrary since the definition of the unit is itself arbitrary. For example, suppose we sought to classify a group of women by the colour of their hair or eyes. Inevitably there will be some colours which will be difficult to determine although if the same women were classified by height, the classification would be simple. The basis of classification depends on the nature of the characteristic by which units are being identified and counted, *e.g.* women over 16 years of age in the United Kingdom are either single, married, widowed, separated or divorced. The characteristic in this case is described as an *attribute*. The same women can be classified by age; in this case the classification is based on a characteristic which is known as a *variable*. The distinction between 'attribute' and 'variable' is important but quite simple. The former describes a characteristic which is not capable of numerical definition, *e.g.* colour of eyes, houses condemend as 'unfit for habitation', recruits classified as 'grade one'. A variable is a characteristic which can be expressed in quantitative terms. *e.g.* height in inches, salary in pounds, or marks in an examination.

The point of the foregoing paragraph is to emphasise the fact that the statistician is usually concerned with groups and 'populations'. The term 'population' in the statistical sense is not restricted to the people within a given area. It describes any aggregate of units which the statistician is studying, *e.g.* the number of shops in England and

Wales, the number of motor cars licensed. Such populations consist of units possessing a common characteristic, although the statistician may compare such groups which are dissimilar in one particular respect. For example, in the pre-election polls it is usual to classify the respondents (*i.e.* those who have been interviewed) by their political party to ascertain how far allegiance to a party affects their attitudes to particular problems of the day. But, it should be noted, all the units in the 'population', *i.e.* the list of electors from which the respondents were chosen, share a common characteristic, *i.e.* the right to vote, and it is for this reason that they have been interviewed.

The significance of precise definition becomes apparent when information is being collected. This is especially true of what are termed 'secondary' statistics, *i.e.* statistical data available in published form such as the Annual Abstract of Statistics.[1] Especial care must be taken in using published data to ensure that over the relevant period of time the definitions or coverage of a series of data have not been altered. For example, it is impossible to compare pre- and post-war living costs simply by comparing the pre-1947 Cost of Living Index with the current Index of Retail Prices. Similarly, the published official estimates of the 'working population' at the present time are compiled in a different way from the figures published at the end of the war so that comparisons of 'total working populations' in 1947 and 1977 can only be made after adjusting certain figures to a common basis. And such adjustments are at best approximate.

Such considerations are especially relevant when it is learnt that by far the most important and prolific source of published statistical data is the government. Each department produces a great deal of statistical data, primarily as a by-product of its administrative functions. For example, the Home Office is responsible for the preparation of the Annual Report on 'Criminal Statistics' which gives information on the extent and type of crimes committed, the activities of the police in clearing up such crimes and the punishment meted out to the convicted offenders by the Courts. The published statistics on crime are especially interesting in view of their chequered history.[2] For example, the only crimes which officially exist are those known to the police. Thus, it is probable that the extent of blackmail and sexual assaults is understated in the annual returns, since the victims are often unwilling to run the risk of publicity if they were to charge the offender. Fluctuations from year to year in the published figures may reflect not so much changes in the incidence of a particular crime, but

A compendium of official statistics compiled by the Central Statistical Office and published annually. The Abstract for 1977 is the 116th in the series.

[2] See Chapter XVII for references.

mainly the fact that the police have at intervals undertaken a major drive against it. This, for example, probably explains the apparent increase in homosexual offences between 1955 and 1965. It is unlikely that the extent of such practices among the male population had changed as much as the publicity given to court cases would suggest. The increased number of convictions merely indicates that the police have become more active in trying to suppress these practices. Thus, a *Police Review* article commenting on the extent of homosexual practices notes that in Manchester in 1955 there was only 1 prosecution for importuning, 0 in 1956 and 1957, 2 in 1958. In 1959 the number rose to 30, with 105 in 1960, 135 and 216 in the next two years. A new Chief Constable had been appointed at the end of 1958 and the *Police Review* rightly comments that the local Watch Committee ought to have considered the figures for 1955-58 more closely.[1] Contrasting rates of crime, *i.e.* of certain types of offence in different areas of the country, may merely reflect local police directives or the attitudes of the local bench of magistrates. For example, where the bench is reputed to be lenient towards certain types of offence, *e.g.* speeding, the local police will be more reluctant to charge the offender than in another area where the bench is not so inclined.

One of the most important social issues of our times is the need to relieve poverty. Given the declared intention of governments to deal with this problem it will come as surprise to the average reader to learn that estimates of the extent of poverty in Britain range from 2 to 5 million persons.[2] The reason for such different estimates is partly due to the different definitions of 'poverty' which can be used and partly from the fact that no count of people living in 'poverty' is complete. For example, people can be said to be living in poverty if their incomes are less than the sums to which they would be entitled if they were in receipt of what was known as 'social security'. Alternatively, a poverty line could be worked out whereby the sum required to provide a minimum living standard could be matched against the actual take-home pay of a worker. This is basically the same as using the social security scales, but views will differ as to what represents the 'minimum'. When Seebohm Rowntree undertook his study of poverty in York at the turn of the century he devised a minimum standard of consumption for a household, varying it according to its composition and age. The standard he used was so incontestibly meagre that his findings were not seriously disputed. Just before the first World War Professor Arthur Bowley used a similar technique but with a more generous standard of life to assess poverty in some of our industrial towns. In more recent

---

[1] Quoted in the *Observer*, Sept. 1, 1963.
[2] 'Poverty in Britain and the Reform of Social Security'. A. B. Atkinson, 1969.

times both private investigators and the government have used much the same technique for similar purposes.[1] It will be self-evident that, quite apart from the problem of obtaining a full count, the results of any such survey will be a reflection of the standards and criteria of poverty used.

In brief, the greatest care must be exercised in using any statistical data, especially when it has been collected by another agency. At all times, the statistician who uses published data must ask himself, by whom were the data collected, how and for what purpose? Many official statistics, *i.e.* government produced, are reliable and complete. But this is not true of all published data, least of all that covering a long period of time. There has been a great improvement in the quality of official statistics since the last war. Thus, some years ago the 'working population' was differently classified by the Board of Trade, the Registrar-General and the Ministry of Labour as these departments were then known, thereby making comparisons of similar data collected by these three government departments virtually impossible. Since 1948 a Standard Industrial Classification, since revised, has been used to ensure a measure of comparability between statistics collected by different agencies. Yet, even with the substantial improvement that has undoubtedly taken place, published statistics can sometimes be quite misleading. For example, a few years ago a small town was largely dependent for employment on one major undertaking which, due to inadequate orders, was only working alternate weeks. Since the count of unemployed each month took place on the second Monday, if that happened to be in a working week there were virtually no unemployed. If next month it coincided with the weekly lay-off, then unemployment would be substantial. Thus, anyone studying the monthly data without a knowledge of this background would be sorely puzzled by the periodic sharp jump in registered unemployed in that town.

With these provisos and warnings regarding the use of published data, some indication of the scope and extent of published statistics can be given. Published sources can be divided into two categories. The *first* and most important are the official statistics prepared by the government. These are of two kinds: those which are the administrative by-product of a department's daily work and those which are collected at intervals for specific purposes. An example of the first type are the figures prepared by the Customs and Excise department. The bulk of these appear in the annual report of the department. Some of these annual reports, *i.e.* Blue Books, contain a wide range of statistical information. For example, apart from such routine

[1] 'The Poor and the Poorest', B. Abel-Smith and P. Townsend, 1965; 'Circumstances of Families', Ministry of Social Security, 1967.

statistics as the amount of tax collected and number of assessments made, the annual report of H.M. Commissioners of Inland Revenue has been considerably expanded in recent years and is now a mine of information regarding the size and distribution of income and wealth. Examples of the second type of official statistics are the various censuses, *e.g.* the decennial population census and the census of production. Apart from information of a statistical character contained in Blue Books and special census reports, there are the annual publications such as those on the Balance of Payments and the General Household Survey. These are prepared by the appropriate department, but since the war the Central Statistical Office has been responsible for co-ordinating the statistical information produced by the various departments so that, for example, with a Standard Industrial Classification introduced in 1948 and last revised in 1968, all departments now classify data (where this is appropriate) under the same industrial headings and not as before the war, as was pointed out above, on their own classification. Second, the C.S.O. as it is usually termed, is responsible for bringing together the economic statistics needed for the formulation of policies designed to maintain economic stability. Many of them are published in the *Monthly Digest of Statistics* and *Economic Trends*. The more important of the United Kingdom economic statistics are discussed more fully in Chapter XVIII.

The *second* category of published statistics is not so large, nor is it so well known. Local authorities publish annually a wide range of statistical information relating to their financial and social activities, as do the various nationalised industries, *e.g.* the National Coal Board. Some of the City institutions produce statistical studies of matters which are of especial interest to them. For example, the Midland Bank has long published a series of statistics showing the amount of capital raised in the capital market by governments and companies. In recent years the need for the independent collection of economic statistics has been greatly reduced by the government's recognition of its responsibilities in this field. There remains, however, one branch of statistical work of the utmost importance for the private investigator, either individual or, more usually, corporate. This is the carrying out of surveys among special groups of the population to obtain information which is not otherwise available. Thus the Department of Applied Economics in Cambridge has conducted local surveys into family budgets and the Institute of Economic and Social Statistics at Oxford was responsible among other surveys for a pioneer enquiry into personal savings in the United Kingdom. Another private organisation conducted a national enquiry into the conditions of life among the 'over-seventies', while a professional body carries out sample enquiries into the reading habits of the community. Although initiated and developed by non-government bodies, the technique of sample enquiries has been adopted by the government since the war. It has its own survey organisation known as the Social Survey Division of the Office of Population Censuses and Surveys. Large scale sample surveys have formed the basis of the Retail Price Index which serves as a cost of living index in the United Kingdom. Using similar methods, there is a continuous survey into the food consumption habits of the community, the findings of which are published in the annual reports of the National Food Survey.

If it is proposed to use statistical data which have been obtained from a sample survey carried out by some other party, then it is imperative that the report of that survey be read, special attention being paid both to the sample design, *i.e.* the informants and whether they were representative of the larger population, and to the questionnaire. Any survey report which lays claim to serious attention will give the reader such information within its covers.

Similar considerations arise when the statistician is forced to collect his own data direct from a group of respondents. Questions must be carefully phrased so that they are unambiguous and mean the same to all respondents. It will often be necessary to define certain terms. For example, 'household income' covers all wages and salaries before tax, as well as pensions and tax-free spare-time earnings. Respondents in the Household Expenditure Survey of 1953-4 and its annual successors, known now as the Family Expenditure Survey sometimes gave their net incomes after deduction of tax and national insurance contribution, as well as omitting cash receipts from any spare-time activities.[1]

The importance of paying attention to the precise definition of statistical units and sources of data collected by others becomes evident when it is recalled that the conclusions derived from the enquiry can only be as good as the original data upon which they are based. You cannot make, runs the old adage, a silk purse out of a sow's ear. It is equally true that an ill-classified collection of ill-defined data from misguided informants will not provide reliable data for any useful statistical study.

Even when definitions and sources have been checked, the mere extraction of the data must be done with care and a clear appreciation of what the published figures mean, quite apart from the question of what can be inferred from them. Thus, a government publication entitled *The Influenza Epidemic in England & Wales 1957-58*[2] analysed

[1] For a detailed account of these matters see 'Family Expenditure Survey'. W. F. F. Kemsley, published by the Government Social Survey, 1969.
[2] H.M.S.O. 1960.

the extent and incidence of that disease between June 1957 and April 1958. It concluded that 'almost certainly at least 7,500,000 persons suffered some incapacity from influenza during the course of the epidemic'. Since influenza is not a notifiable disease such as typhus, smallpox, etc., how can such a statement be made? Note, however, the careful qualifications to the figure, 'almost certainly' and 'at least', suggesting that some estimation is involved. It was. The total of $7\frac{1}{2}$ million was derived partly from estimates of the number of new claims for sickness benefit during this period in excess of the corresponding period in each of the preceding five years. Since not every adult is insured under the National Insurance scheme further estimates had to be derived for this very large non-insured section, predominantly female, of the population. It was in fact assumed that the incidence of the disease in this group was the same as in the first. Then, for children of school age, estimates were derived from records of local medical officers of health which related to absences of children from school. Lastly, the incidence of influenza among the under five's and those over 64 years also required a further rough estimate. The official report explains these facts very clearly, but such figures tend often to be quoted as if they were accurate to the last unit, particularly in abbreviated press reports. While there is no excuse for such mistakes or misinterpretations in real statistical work, it is idle to pretend they do not arise.

CHAPTER III

COLLECTING THE DATA

So far the emphasis has been laid on statistical information which is available in government reports and from other published sources. Whatever the subject matter of the statistician's current enquiry he can usually be certain that someone has done some work on that problem before. Such work, if it can be traced, should always be consulted. It may produce the answer for which the statistician is searching. More likely, it will give him a few ideas and even draw his attention to points which so far had escaped his notice. It may even contain some mistakes in technique or interpretation from which valuable and important lessons may be drawn for the enquiry projected by the statistician. In other words, before embarking upon a project which necessitates the collection of information and statistics, start by consulting all the known statistical sources and examining earlier survey material. This done, the statistician will know what additional or new information he must obtain. An important benefit from such work is that it helps him to clarify the issue, as well as the precise nature of the problem, in his own mind.

The emphasis on the need to clarify the problem, quite apart from obtaining all the relevant information, is justified by the fact that unless this is done, the survey may well prove unsatisfactory. Once the precise nature of the enquiry or survey has been defined, it becomes possible to consider how it may best be carried out. This will enable the statistician to decide how much information he needs to collect, from how many and which people, what questions will produce the information he needs. If it is important to be able to generalise about the sample data, *i.e.* the information collected from a sample of respondents, then he may need a larger sample than would be the case if he is merely concerned with collecting information for local use. Alternatively, his financial resources may be limited and he must consider the advantages of asking a smaller sample more detailed questions compared with asking a larger number of people fewer and simpler questions. After all, he cannot hope to interview all the people selected in his sample by himself; this is the task of specially trained interviewers and such work costs money.

In brief, too much time cannot be spent on these initial stages of considering all aspects of the enquiry. It is a commonplace among market research organisations and business consultants that when their client firms first come to them, very few have a really clear notion of the nature of their problem. The first part of such work is for the specialist to uncover the facts and help clarify the problem. Once that is done, they can consider how their organisation can best help the client. No survey organisation worth its salt will undertake a sample survey for a client company just because some senior director of that company thinks it would be a good thing. The first question is always, how and in what way is a survey likely to contribute to a solution of the problem as defined. This said, let it now be assumed that the statistician needs further information beyond that available to him.

Collection of Data

There are three basic methods of collecting the information needed:

1. The investigator may interview personally everyone who is in a position to supply the information he requires. Such a procedure will be possible in very few cases indeed, since most statistical enquiries cover a wider field than any single investigator could possibly examine personally within any reasonable time. An interesting example of such an enquiry is that conducted by Professor Zweig who personally interviewed 400 people.[1] The task of interviewing informants may be delegated to selected agents who are provided with a standardised questionnaire and explicit instructions as to the mode of its completion and, quite often, the names and addresses of the persons to be questioned. The main problems in this case are the selection of suitable agents and the cost involved in interviewing. Against the disadvantage of high cost and the difficulties of obtaining suitable agents must be set the very considerable advantage that the information received will probably be highly reliable. Such interviewers are nowadays employed by all research organisations such as the Government Social Survey and the market research offices.

2. An increasingly important method of collecting information is to use an observer(s), either outside or living within the group or community, who notes any aspect of their activities which are relevant to the enquiry. This method is discussed in Chapter XVI.

3. The last method is by questionnaire addressed to individual informants. This method, at one time extensively employed, possesses the apparent advantage that a very large field of enquiry may be covered at relatively low cost, and the larger the coverage the less significant will be occasional errors in the filling up of individual forms. This method of collecting information is not

[1] *Labour, Life and Poverty*, F. Zweig, Gollancz, 1948.

often satisfactory due to the low proportion of returns. The government uses it for various census enquiries, *e.g.* population, electors, production, but in these cases the return of the form is compulsory. If it is voluntary, only those individuals, generally speaking, who are particularly interested in the subject matter of the enquiry will trouble to return the questionnaire. Then the investigator may merely have a collection of biased data. Nevertheless, some recent enquiries have shown that good results may be achieved with postal surveys.[1]

Drafting the Questionnaire

The old adage about asking silly questions and getting silly answers is probably engraved on most statistician's memories, if not their hearts. Most practitioners will be able to recall one or more such incidents in their professional careers. The simple fact is that a survey is as good as its questionnaire; it cannot be better although it may be worse because of other additional defects in the design or organisation of the enquiry. Although the subject of questionnaire and schedule design is discussed in Chapter XVI, some of the more obvious points are worth making even at this early stage in the study of statistics. First, the distinction between questionnaire and schedule. Usually the former describes the form sent *by post* or delivered some other way to the respondent and which is then completed by him unaided. The term 'schedule' is usually kept for the form which is filled up by an interviewer, whose job it is to contact selected persons and ask them to answer the questions which the interviewer then puts as set out on the schedule.

A number of questionnaires and schedules have been reproduced at the end of this chapter and in Chapter XVI. They show the layout and the type of question asked, as well as indicating how the interviewer or respondent should complete the form. The best way of learning how to design such forms is by studying the work of the professionals. In the meantime, here are a few simple and apparently obvious points to bear in mind. It is worth remembering that the more obvious something is, the easier it is to overlook!

1. Few people enjoy form-filling or answering questions. Keep it as short as possible.

2. Complicated and long-winded questions sometimes irritate and often confuse the respondent and result in careless replies. Make the individual questions short and simple.

3. Answers such as 'Probably', 'Fairly good', 'Average', mean nothing to a statistician, since they signify different degrees to

---

[1] See Chapter XVI for a discussion of postal enquiries.

different individuals. Ensure that all questions may be answered as far as possible by either 'Yes' or 'No', or by a name or figure. Some readers may, however, have encountered the type of questionnaire circulated by the Audience Research section of the B.B.C., in which the listener is asked to indicate whether he or she considered a particular programme excellent, good, fair, or poor. This survey is concerned with estimating the number of listeners who 'thought' the programme was good, *i.e.*, the listener's *subjective* assessment of the programme. If 90 per cent. of the listening public answered 'excellent', then as far as the B.B.C. producer is concerned, the programme was outstandingly successful. There is no attempt here to arrive at an impartial, objective assessment of the *quality* of the programme, since it is clearly impossible to do so. In short, the questions and their answers depend on the purpose to be served by the enquiry.

4. The questions should follow a logical sequence, so that a natural and spontaneous reply to each is induced. Thus it is clearly politic to enquire whether a woman informant is married before asking her how many children she has!

5. Few people willingly provide intimate facts about themselves. Many resent such questions, which should be avoided as far as possible. In some cases where private information of this nature is needed, the method of personal enquiry may be most likely to yield results. Generally speaking, highly personal questions should be kept to the end of the interview, when the informant may feel more at ease with the interviewer.[1]

6. When public opinion on a particular issue is being assessed, it is important to ascertain from the respondent whether he has any knowledge of the subject, before asking his opinion on it! Opinion polls, as compared with factual enquiries, give rise to a host of very complicated problems in questionnaire design, some of which are discussed in Chapter XVI.

7. Remember that even the best questions, however well phrased they may appear, do not always elicit the true answer. This may be due to honest misunderstanding of the question, or a desire on the part of the respondent not to disclose the truth. Thus, in the 1951 census of population, householders were asked if they had the exclusive or shared use of amenities such as piped water, cooking stoves, baths and lavatories. All the evidence goes to show that this question was misunderstood and the tabulated answers worthless.[2]

[1] The extent to which people will supply information, even of the most intimate nature, is demonstrated by the enquiry into attitudes and practices of birth control among persons married since the First World War by the Population Investigation Committee. See 'Birth Control in Britain' by G. Rowntree and R. M. Pierce in *Population Studies*, July 1961.

[2] 1951 Census, General Report.

In the Family Expenditure Surveys householders are asked to state their outlay on tobacco and alcohol. Comparing the aggregate answers with the information available from the Customs and Excise relating to consumption of these commodities, it is obvious that there is considerable under-statement.

It need hardly be added that once the questionnaire has been drafted, it should first be tested on a small number of individuals, to assess the probable reaction of the wider public to be covered later. The advantages of such a pre-test are considerable. This policy was pursued by the Board of Trade in the 1948 Pilot Census of Distribution. It was proposed to carry out the first-ever full enumeration of shops and service establishments in 1951, but the Department undertook initially a sample survey of a few selected areas and trades representing the whole country. The lessons drawn from the many criticisms and suggestions made enabled improvements in the questionnaire to be introduced, thereby facilitating the task of the informant and ensuring more accurate and prompt replies.[1] Before the 1966 and 1971 censuses of population the General Register Office · pre-tested a number of questions which it anticipated might create difficulties. The mere fact that the census is enforced legally does not help the statistician very much; he is much more anxious to obtain a fair sample of accurate replies than a mass of carelessly compiled and often inaccurate information from an unrepresentative group of respondents.

Technique of Sampling

As already explained, it is frequently physically impossible to obtain a really wide coverage of information from all those individuals who might come within the scope of the enquiry. This is especially true where, owing to the nature of the enquiry or survey, it has been decided to use agents interviewing their subjects personally. Examples of such surveys are the annual Family Expenditure Surveys of some 7,000 household budgets and the Ministry of Social Security's enquiry into the financial circumstances of large families. Many surveys are carried out by the Social Survey on behalf of various Government Departments, not to forget the publicised political polls which are discussed regularly in the daily press. In these cases only a small part of the field may be covered; estimates of national public opinion are often based on a sample of less than 1,000 informants. Yet it is true to say that in most cases, provided that the survey has been conducted with due regard for statistical technique and principles, the results should differ only to an insignifi-

[1] In view of the widespread protests and even hostility encountered with the Pilot survey, it is clear that as a result of the lessons learnt, a great deal of expense was avoided.

cant extent from those which would be derived from a census.[1]. The validity of this contention has been proved in the past by careful checking, repeated sample enquiries, and in some cases by a full-scale enquiry where the field to be covered was not impossibly large.

This system of selection of a part of the whole, known in statistical method as 'sampling', may be explained by a simple analogy. The practice of sampling is frequently encountered in the world of commerce. Thus a small sample of tea or grain, of cloth, or of many other commodities, is frequently the only means whereby a prospective buyer can assess the quality of the bulk. The principle underlying the process is the assumption, generally borne out in practice, that the part is genuinely representative of the whole. Thus the Public Analyst bases his report on the quality of a product on a few tested samples, while the assayer assesses the mineral content of an area on samples of ore selected at random.

Ideally, any sample from a population should be selected by what are known as *random* methods of selection. In this particular context 'random' has a rather special meaning. The simplest definition is that a sampling procedure is random if *every* item in the group from which the statistician is making his choice has an equal chance of selection. The group or aggregate of the sampling units, *e.g.* all the households in Great Britain, all the farms in England and Wales, all boys in the Sixth form of grammar schools, etc.; all these aggregates are usually referred to as *populations*. In other words a statistical population is the total number or aggregate of all the units which, by virtue of a common characteristic, may be classified as belonging to the population. Thus, we can refer to the 'population' of people who regularly attend symphony concerts; all the women who do not use cosmetics or those who drink only 'Lyons' tea. Obviously, some of these populations can hardly be counted or listed without the expenditure of a great deal of time and money in enumerating them.

It does not follow that because a sample is random, it represents accurately the characteristics of the population. But, it enables the possible extent of non-representativeness to be estimated. Sometimes its representativeness can be checked against other information. For example, if the distribution of the sample by, say, social class, reflects the known social-class composition of the population as shown in the figures prepared by the Office for Population Censuses and Surveys, as far as that particular characteristic is concerned, this is evidence that the sample is a replica of the population. Usually,

---

[1] A complete enumeration of the entire field is known as a 'census'. A limited enquiry based on part of the field is usually described as a 'sample survey'. These are discussed more fully in Chapter XV.

there is information about the population, *e.g.* sex, age structure, ownership of homes or cars, which can be compared with the corresponding characteristics of the sample. If the distribution of such characteristics is similar for both the sample and the population, then it can be inferred that the sample is probably representative. There can be no *certainty* that the sample, although drawn by random methods, is representative. This is where what is known as sampling theory comes in and in Chapters XIII and XIV the reader may learn how the statistician can nevertheless generalise his sample results for the population with considerable confidence.

Samples drawn by methods which are not random seldom yield reliable data. So well understood is this maxim, *i.e.* all samples must be random, that the statistician seldom prefaces the word 'sample' with the adjective 'random'. For him, all statistical samples are random. If not, then they rarely have interest for him. The methods used to select samples in various types of surveys are discussed in Chapter XV. At this stage it is pertinent to point out that 'sample design' as it is known to statisticians is a highly complex technique. The purpose of good sample design is to ensure the maximum of information from the sample drawn. Contrary to a widely held belief, the size of the sample in a survey is quite independent of the size of the population from which it is drawn. For example, a random sample of some 2,000 voters would give a reliable estimate of the probable outcome of an election involving either three or thirty million voters. The only relevance that the size of the sample has is that the larger it is, the more confident the statistician may be about his conclusions from the data. But, as will be seen later, this does not alter the fact that quite small samples are big enough for most purposes depending on the complexity of information required.

Sample Schedules and Questionnaires

The subject of schedule design is discussed in more detail in Chapter XVI, but the points and observations made already may be better impressed on the reader's memory by the opportunity to study some illustrations of good questionnaires and schedules. The first questionnaire was used in the Family Census in 1946, which was undertaken on behalf of the Royal Commission on Population. Although this is an old questionnaire it provides an excellent example of good lay-out. The form was sent to some 1·7 million married women together with the accompanying letter. The form is exceptionally well-designed to facilitate its correct completion; note for example the three clear sub-divisions of the questions relating to the woman, her children and her husband. Note too the footnote stressing the need for an accurate description of the husband's occupation. Questions relating to work or occupation are often inaccurately answered; either the description is too vague for classification or the respondent up-grades himself! In view of the subject matter of the enquiry, the stress laid on its confidential nature in the letter is noteworthy, while the heavy black type at the head of the questionnaire 'strictly confidential' is almost a stroke of genius on the part of the designer. The letter is well phrased and the reader will observe how the benefits of the enquiry are conveyed to the respondent in the opening paragraph with its references to housing, family allowances and social welfare, all topics in which the average respondent would have a considerable interest. The ultimate response rate was 87 per cent., a very good result when it is recalled that unlike most government enquiries, the return of the questionnaire was voluntary.

The second illustration shows the questionnaire distributed by the Confederation of British Industry to a sample of its member firms. The object of this four-monthly enquiry is to obtain an indication of industrial opinion on the current state of the economy and industrialists' views regarding the immediate prospects, e.g. during the next four months. The form is well designed and quite simple to complete. Note that the answers required are not in terms of figures, but merely an indication of the respondent's views of the trend. It is easier to complete such a questionnaire; in any case most firms would be unwilling to give actual figures, even if they were prepared to go to the trouble of extracting them from their books. The whole point of this particular enquiry is simply to evaluate business and industrial opinion, which is a highly important factor in the economic situation at any time. This type of enquiry is a relatively new development in the field of what is usually termed 'forward-looking' statistics. In other words, instead of the economic statistician concerning himself solely with past events, he is here endeavouring to make some estimate of the future trend of the economy. Inevitably, any deductions drawn from such data must be somewhat tentative, but a study of the results derived from this enquiry during the first six years after its introduction concluded that the information had been helpful to government economists in formulating policy.[1] A particular virtue of the C.B.I. enquiry is the speed with which the data are processed and the results published.

The final example is of a schedule used by interviewers in a survey undertaken by Research Services Ltd on behalf of the Independent Television Authority and reproduced in the report *Parents, Children*

---

[1] National Institute Economic Review. Nov. 1963.

ROYAL COMMISSION ON POPULATION

FAMILY CENSUS

Dear Madam,

You will probably have seen in the newspapers, or heard on the wireless, that the Royal Commission on Population are trying to find out how family size has been changing during the past generation. At present it is not known how much childlessness there is, or how many families there are with one, two, three or other numbers of children. These and similar facts are needed urgently, so that the Royal Commission can give to the people and the Government a sound basis for understanding the population problem and its bearing on housing programmes, family allowances, social insurance and other measures of social welfare.

To collect the facts a 'Sample' Family Census is being held. A *strictly confidential inquiry* is being addressed to one tenth of the women in this country who are or have been married. If your name has incorrectly been included in our lists and you are not or have not been married, please disregard the questions on the form. Just write 'SINGLE' in the space against Question I and give the form back to the Royal Commission enumerator who calls to collect it.

If you are or have been married, the Royal Commission are very anxious for you to answer the questions on the form. If you wish to fill up the form yourself, please do so and give the completed form to the Royal Commission enumerator who calls for it. If you have difficulty with any of the questions, please tell the enumerator, who may be able to help you.

When your form is filled up and collected, it will be sent to the Royal Commission, where it will be dealt with together with many thousands of other forms. All these forms will be treated with the utmost confidence. The information on occupation and family size will be put on special cards for study, *but your name and address will not be used in any way.*

This Family Census is of the greatest importance to the country. If the results are complete and trustworthy, they will throw much light on problems of family and population, problems in which, as the Royal Commission know, men and women throughout the country are taking a keen interest. The Commission need your co-operation in this inquiry and they ask you to do all you can to ensure that it is a success.

Yours truly,
SIMON,
Chairman,
Royal Commission on Population.

ROYAL COMMISSION ON POPULATION

FAMILY CENSUS — Strictly Confidential

If you care to fill up this form yourself, please do so and give it completed to the Royal Commission Enumerator who will call to see you. If you prefer it, the Enumerator will be glad to fill up the form for you or help you with any difficulties you may have.

For Official Use Only

F.O.......................

YOURSELF

Please write clearly and in full

S.N.......................

Are you now **Married or Widowed** – or was your last marriage ended by Divorce? } *Please state which*

| 1 | M 1 |

2 When were you born?

Month Year

M 2

MM 3

For those who have been **Married Once Only:** Month Year

MM 4

(*a*) When were you married?
(*b*) If your marriage has ended – when did it end?
(*By death of your husband, or divorce – NOT separation*)

W 5

W 6

4 For those who have been **Married More Than Once:** Month Year

(*a*) When were you **First Married?**

| 2 | 1 P | WM |

(*b*) When did your **First Marriage End?**

2 E   7 F

YOUR CHILDREN

Month Year

3 OA   8 AW

(a) Number of **Children Born Alive**   1st child

4 S   9 L

Beginning with your FIRST BORN child – enter, in order of birth, the date of birth of EVERY LIVE BORN CHILD you have had– *whether or not the child is still living.*
Do NOT include still-births or miscarriages.

2nd „

3rd „

5 WE   X AF

4th „

| 3 | L.C. |

In the case of twins or triplets, use a separate line for every child born alive.
Step-children or adopted children should NOT be counted.

5th „

6th „

(b) **No Children**
If you have NOT borne a living child, write NIL in this box.

7th „

| 4 | T.C. |

8th „

9th „

Note: For those who have had more than 10 children there are more spaces on the back.

10th „

INTERVIEW DATE

6 Of your children **Alive** today, how many have NOT yet reached their Sixteenth birthday?
(*Only children BORNE BY YOU and under 16 – even if they are living away from you*)

YOUR HUSBAND   *If possible discuss this section with your Husband*

7 (a) What is your **Husband's Occupation?**

(*If he is retired, out of work, or dead – state*)
 or
(*If he is temporarily in the Services – state former occupation. If no former occupation – put 'Armed Forces'*)
(*If he is a regular Sailor, Soldier or Airman – state which, and his rank*)
(*If you have been married more than once – the answer should refer to your FIRST husband*)

Note: Please describe the KIND of work your husband does in as much detail as possible. For example: if your husband is an Engineer, it will help us if you can say EXACTLY which kind he is.

(b) Is Your Husband –

1 An employer of 10 or more people?
 or
2 Working for himself or employing LESS than 10 people?
 or
3 Employed and earning a monthly salary?
 or
4 Employed and earning a weekly or other wage?
PLEASE PUT A RING ROUND THE NUMBER WHICH APPLIES

(c) Employer's Business –

(*If your husband is NOT himself an employer or working for himself*)

and Television.[1] In this survey only parents aged between 30 and 49, with children aged 5 to 13, were interviewed. The reader should note the classificatory data relating to family composition on the first page of the schedule and the additional information on the same subject placed at the end of the schedule. Such information, usually collected at the end of the interview, permits a more thorough analysis of the information collected, in this case parents' attitudes by reference to their social class, occupation, education, etc. The codes on the right hand side of the questions are used when the information is being transferred from the schedules to punched cards, the appropriate code for the answer having been ringed by the interviewer. The lists referred to in Q.10 to 13 are not reproduced here, but they consist of two lists of children's programmes throughout the week; one for B.B.C. and the other for I.T.V. The main value of such lists is to enable the respondent to recall just which programmes her child or children did view. Note also the use of the pre-coded question, *e.g.* Q.4, 5, 20 etc. sometimes referred to as 'multi-choice' or 'cafeteria' questions. The advantages of this are obvious. The interviewer merely marks off the appropriate response, thus saving time and facilitating the classification of the respondent's answers. To the extent that the respondent's answer may not be expressed so tersely as these pre-coded answers suggest, it is for the interviewer to ring the answer which she feels most closely corresponds to the respondent's opinions. This can be a fruitful source of error, and the subject is discussed in Chapter XVI.

The outstanding characteristic of the foregoing questionnaires and schedules is their relative simplicity. By this is meant not that the questions are simple, but the forms and their layout convey the impression that they will not pose difficulties for the respondent. While this first impression upon the respondent is clearly of vital importance with a postal questionnaire, it is no less important with a schedule which is to be completed by an interviewer. A great deal of care is needed to help the interviewer complete the form so as not to interrupt the smooth flow of questions. Even the size, much less the layout of the form and the way it can be folded and turned over is important, as anyone who has tried reading a newspaper on a windy corner well knows.

A weakness of many questionnaires which the respondent, without the help of an interviewer, is required by law to complete, such as statutory enquiries like the censuses of production and distribution, are the numerous and extensive footnotes to the questions and what are termed 'instructions for completion'. While such instructions may be used extensively on schedules to be completed by an

[1] H.M.S.O., 1959.

CBI Industrial Trends Survey   Number 71   January 1979

Please tick appropriate answers: If question not applicable, tick N/A

Please use space overleaf for any comments you would like to make on points not covered by your replies.

1 Are you more, or less, optimistic than you were four months ago about
   THE GENERAL BUSINESS SITUATION IN YOUR INDUSTRY

More	Same	Less

2 Are you more, or less, optimistic about your EXPORT PROSPECTS
   for the next twelve months than you were four months ago

More	Same	Less	N/A

3 Do you expect to authorise more or less
   capital expenditure in the next twelve months
   than you authorised in the past twelve months on: a. buildings
                                                        b. plant & machinery

More	Same	Less	N/A

4 Is your present level of output below capacity (i.e., are you working
   below a satisfactory full rate of operation)

Yes	No	N/A

5 **Excluding seasonal variations**, do you consider
   that in **volume** terms:

   a. Your present total order book is

   b. Your present export order book is

   *(firms with no order book are requested to
   estimate the level of demand)*

Above Normal	Normal	Below Normal	N/A

   c. Your present stocks of finished goods are

More than Adequate	Adequate	Less than Adequate	N/A
1	2	3	4

Excluding seasonal variations, what has been the
trend over the PAST FOUR MONTHS, and what are
the expected trends for the NEXT FOUR MONTHS,
with regard to:

Trend over PAST FOUR MONTHS				Expected trend over NEXT FOUR MONTHS			
Up	Same	Down	N/A	Up	Same	Down	N/A

6 Numbers employed

7 **Volume** of total new orders

   of which: a. domestic orders

               b. export orders

8 **Volume** of output

9 **Volume** of: a. domestic deliveries

                    b. export deliveries

10 **Volume** of stocks of: a. raw materials and brought in supplies

                               b. work in progress

                               c. finished goods

11 Average costs per unit of output

12 Average prices at which: a. domestic orders are booked

                              b. export orders are booked

13 Approximately how many months' production is accounted for by your present order book or production schedule.

Less than 1	1-3	4-6	7-9	10-12	13-18	More than 18	N/A
1	2	3	4	5	6	7	8

41

14 What factors are likely to limit your OUTPUT over the next four months. *Please tick the most important factor or factors. If you tick more than one factor it would be helpful if you could rank them in order of importance*

Orders or Sales	Skilled Labour	Other Labour	Plant Capacity	Credit or Finance	Materials or Components	Other

42-48

15 What factors are likely to limit your ability to obtain EXPORT ORDERS over the next four months. *Please tick the most important factor or factors. If you tick more than one factor it would be helpful if you could rank them in order of importance*

Prices (compared with overseas competitors)	Delivery Dates	Credit or Finance	Quota & Import Licence Restrictions	Political or Economic Conditions Abroad	Other

49-54

16 Factors likely to limit your CAPITAL EXPENDITURE AUTHORISATIONS ON BUILDINGS, PLANT AND MACHINERY over the next twelve months.

Please tick those statements with which you agree: if you tick more than one reason in section b or c it would be helpful if you could rank them in order of importance.

a. I have adequate capacity to meet expected demand ☐ 55

b. Although I have adequate capacity, I have also capital investment opportunities which would be profitable at the present cost of finance, but I shall not be undertaking some of them for the following reason or reasons:

(i)   Shortage of internal finance ☐ 56
(ii)   Inability to raise external finance ☐ 57
(iii) Shortage of managerial and technical staff ☐ 58
(iv)   Shortage of labour ☐ 59
(v)   Other *(please specify)* ☐ 60

c. My capacity is not adequate to meet expected demand but I do not intend increasing my capacity. This is for the following reason or reasons: ☐ 61

(i)   Not profitable because of the cost of finance ☐ 62
(ii)   Shortage of internal finance ☐ 63
(iii) Inability to raise external finance ☐ 64
(iv)   Shortage of managerial and technical staff ☐ 65
(v)   Shortage of labour ☐ 66
(vi)   Other *(please specify)* ☐ 67

d. None of the above is applicable ☐ 68

Please enter here the code number of the *main* manufacturing activity covered by this return *(See Standard Industrial Classification circulated previously).* ☐ 69-73

How many EMPLOYEES are covered by this return

(a) 0 – 199 ☐   (b) 200 – 499 ☐   (c) 500 – 4,999 ☐   (d) 5,000 and over ☐ 74

What is the annual ex-works value of your <u>direct</u> EXPORTS

Nil – £50th	£50th – £750th	£750th – £2m	£2m – £5m	£5m – £10m	£10m – £15m	£15m – £25m	£25m – £40m	£40m – £60m	£60m – £100m	Over £100m
0	1	2	3	4	5	6	7	8	9	10

75

Signature ....

Company (Block Capitals) ....

Address ....

Note: If you wish your reply to remain anonymous, please detach this slip and return it under separate cover

The Questionnaire

J.1016   *April*, 1958
                    Research Services Ltd., 91 Shaftesbury Avenue, W.1

Family composition   *Codes*

Relationship to informant	Sex M	Sex F	Age (years)	Office use a	Office use b
Informant	X	Y		c	d
	X	Y		e	f
	X	Y			
	X	Y		g	h
	X	Y		i	j
	X	Y			
	X	Y			
	X	Y			
	X	Y			
	X	Y			

If more than one child aged 5–13 inclusive, questions are to be asked in respect of the child whose birthday comes first after date of interview. *Tick* to show which child.

All informants

1. What time did your child go to bed last night?   Yesterday ....
   (On MONDAYS ask about *both* SATURDAY and SUNDAY)   Saturday ....

2. How much time did he/she spend yesterday playing out of doors?   Yesterday ...... hours
   (On MONDAY ask about *both* SATURDAY and SUNDAY)   Saturday ...... hours

3. How much time did he/she spend yesterday doing homework?   Yesterday ...... hours
   (On MONDAY ask about *both* SATURDAY and SUNDAY)   Saturday ...... hours

J.1016

6. Here are some things which some children occasionally do. (Show list). Supposing your own *Codes*
child were to behave this way, would you please tell me:
    (a) How you would deal with it?
    (b) What would you think might be the cause?
    (c) How would your parents have dealt with you if your had behaved that way?

Behaviour	How informant would deal with	Cause	How inft's parents would have dealt with
(i) Child constantly shouting, breaking things, fighting			
(ii) Child lazy, refusing to help around house, untidy			
(iii) Started stealing money			
(iv) Regularly would not eat meals prepared for him/her			

7. (a) Do you feel that films which children usually see at cinemas are good entertainment
for children or not?

Good	1
Not good	2
Don't know	3

    (b) Why do you feel that way? ....
....
....

8. Do you have a television set in your home?

Yes	1
No	2

If Yes, ask Questions 9-23, then 24-78
If No, go to Question 24
All Parents with TV in Home

9. Does it receive both BBC and ITA
or just the BBC?

BBC and ITA	3
BBC only	4

10. Which of these programmes have you watched in the past week? (SHOW LISTS – ITA **and**
BBC list for ITA and BBC SET owners: BBC list for BBC only set owners)

11. (About each programme watched). Were you watching it along with your child?

12. Are there any programmes on the list which you have encouraged your child to watch – e.g.
by suggesting to him/her that it's good?

13. (a) Are there any on the list which you have discouraged him from watching?
    (b) **If yes:** in what way?
    (c) Why?
    (d) (If not mentioned at 11). Did your child, in fact, watch this programme?
    Record Answers to Questions 10-13 on next two pages.

J.1016

14. How much time did your child spend watching TV yesterday? (On MONDAY ask about *both* SATURDAY and SUNDAY)

Yesterday .... hours
Saturday .... hours

15. During the past week has your child stayed up beyond his usual bed time to see any particular programme? (Here is a list of last week's main evening programmes as a reminder). *If yes:* which?

Yes | 1
No | 2

Day	Programme

	ITA	BBC
16. (a) What is your personal opinion of programmes on Children's Television – those in the afternoon and up till about 6 p.m., (i) on ITA. (ii) on BBC?		
Very good	1	7
Reasonably good	2	8
Not up to much	3	9
Bad	4	0
Don't know	5	X

(b) In what way?
(i) ITA ....
(ii) BBC ....

	ITA	BBC
17. (a) And what about the programmes from 6–7.30 p.m. (i) on ITA. (ii) on BBC.		
Very good	1	7
Reasonably good	2	8
Not up to much	3	9
Bad	4	0
Don't know	5	X

(b) In what way?
(i) ITA ....
(ii) BBC ....

18. Do your children stay at home more or less because of television?

More	1
Less	2
Same	3
Don't know	4

19. Do you spend more time together or less as a family because of television?

More	5
Less	6
Same	7
Don't know	8

20. Would you say that television has made your home life more interesting and happier, or do you think your family life would be better without it, or does it make no difference?

More interesting	1
Better without	2
No difference	3
Don't know	4

21. Would you say that having television has made it easier for you to bring up your children as you would like them to be, or harder? Or does it make no difference?

Easier	5
Harder	6
No difference	7
Don't know	8

J.1016

	Codes

22. What would you say your child did before you got your set with the time he now spends watching television?

....

23. How long have you had a television set? ....

All informants

24. Supposing your child had a couple of free hours with nothing to do, which would you prefer him/her to do:

Go to the pictures	1
Watch television	2
None of these	4
Don't know	5

25. Why do you think that? ....

26. Would you say television is:

Good for children	1
Bad for children	2
Makes no difference	3
Don't know	4

27. In what way? ....

28. With which of these do you agree or disagree:
Watching television makes children:

	Agree	Dis-agree	Don't know
More social and friendly	1	2	3
Better informed and more knowledgeable	4	5	6
Mentally lazy	7	8	9
Better at their school work	0	X	Y
Noisy and disobedient	1	1	3
Better behaved	4	5	6
Violent and cruel	7	8	9

29. Which daily newspaper(s) do you yourself read regularly? (i.e., 3 issues out of 4)

Daily Express	1	Daily Sketch	7
Daily Herald	2	Daily Telegraph	8
Daily Mail	3	Times	9
Manchester Guardian	4	Daily Worker	0
Daily Mirror	5	Other (state)	X
News Chronicle	6	None	Y

Classification:

Sex of informant	Man 1	Age 30–39—3	**Social grade**	AB 5
	Woman 2	40–49—4		C1 6
				C2 7
				DE 8

Occupation of informant ....

Occupation of H/H ....

Education of informant: **Type of school (child):**

Elementary	1	Primary	5	Day ....
Secondary	2	Secondary modern	6	
University or college	3	Secondary grammar	7	Date ....
Other (state)	4	Other (state)	8	

Date of child's return to school ....

Sample	BBC only	1
	BBC and ITA	2
	Neither	3

Name of informant ....

Home address ....

If interviewed at work, business address ....

Quota district ....   Inv. No. ....

interviewer, for statutory returns or postal questionnaires they are most undesirable. The several pages of instructions which accompany these enquiry schedules tend to be somewhat intimidating and discouraging! If they are absolutely necessary then they should be kept as short as possible and preferably printed next to the actual question. In the first three post-war censuses of population the instructions were first printed on the reverse side of the schedule which the respondent was required to complete. That, apart from the mere fact that the instructions covered a whole page, was sufficient to ensure that the average householder would not trouble himself to read the instructions. In the 1961 census the instructions were shortened and printed on the same side as the questions but separately from them. This was an improvement, but it is probable that the instructions were often ignored. In the last census in 1971 the instructions were detachable from the schedule so that they could be read with the questions, a more effective way of endeavouring to ensure accurate answers. Even so there still can be no certainty that all respondents, many of whom will regard the census at best as tiresome and at worst as mischievous prying into private affairs, will actually consider the instructions carefully.

As a general rule, a brief letter accompanying a statutory schedule or questionnaire which explains why the respondent is being troubled with it and indicating how the information he is asked to provide may ultimately be of benefit to him and his fellow citizens, undoubtedly helps. Thus, the letter on p.29 accompanying the Family Census enquiry or that on p.420 on the road safety enquiry are excellent examples of the art. In the enquiry into the financial circumstances of pensioners conducted by the Ministry of Pensions and National Insurance in 1965 those selected in the sample to be visited by the interviewers first received a letter signed by the Minister. This asked in simple language for their help 'because she would like to know just how retirement pensioners manage and what difficulties they experience'. In the next paragraph an attempt was made to anticipate or disarm criticism by stating that the interviewers will 'ask you about some things which people are not always very willing discuss with strangers – about your money affairs for instance. You too may think this sort of thing is no business of ours, but I hope you will understand that we are not just prying into your affairs.' It was hardly surprising that the pensioners approached were, for reasons which are self-evident, quite apart from the effect of the letter, extremely co-operative and the effective response was over 90 per cent.[1]

---

[1] Financial and other Circumstances of Retirement Pensioners. H.M.S.O. 1966, pp. 89-103. Ministry of Pensions and N.I. H.M.S.O. 1967.

This brief introduction into schedules and questionnaires used in sample surveys for collecting information may appear to emphasise the obvious and self-evident. The topic is considered further in Chapter XVI but the essential points have been made. While there is no excuse for overlooking them in the preparation and design of schedules and questionnaires, it is a salutary exercise for the student to examine published survey reports which should always include a copy of the schedule used and consider carefully how far that schedule is well designed to achieve its objects.[1]

[1] A further list of survey reports is appended to Chapter XVI but for the enquiring student with good library facilities some of the following reports will be instructive.

Circumstances of Families. Ministry of Pensions and N.I., H.M.S.O. 1967.

Medical Students' Attitudes towards Smoking. J. M. Bynner. SS. 382, H.M.S.O. 1967.

Children and their Primary Schools. Vol. 2. Research & Surveys. H.M.S.O. 1967.

Small Firms. Cmnd 4811, H.M.S.O. 1971.

Industrial Relations at Establishment Level: A Statistical Survey. C.I.R. Study 2., H.M.S.O. 1973.

PART II

ELEMENTARY STATISTICAL METHOD

CHAPTER IV

TABULATION

The Purpose of Tabulation

In no investigation of any size is the volume of collected data or material so small that it may be rapidly or easily assimilated by a perusal of the completed forms. At best only the haziest impressions may be gathered of the ultimate results, and those impressions may well be the reverse of the truth for it is usually the unusual or freak cases that stick in the memory to the exclusion of the many more 'ordinary' replies. The statistician's first task is to reduce and simplify the detail into such a form that the salient features may be brought out, while still facilitating the interpretation of the assembled data. This procedure is known as *classifying* and *tabulating* the data; *i.e.* extracting from the individual questionnaires or schedules the answers to each question and entering the replies on separate summary sheets. These totals are then transferred to the relevant columns of prepared tables.

Before the summarising is commenced, the questionnaires should have been checked on receipt to ensure that they have been completed reasonably correctly. The person editing the returned forms cannot know if they are *correctly* completed, otherwise there would be no need for the enquiry. 'Reasonably correct' in this context means that there are no obvious mistakes in, or contradictions between, the various answers. Inevitably there will be uncompleted forms, and these it may be possible to complete by further enquiry; in other cases the replies will be useless, as they are either irrelevant or patently false. It requires little imagination on the reader's part to visualise the task involved in sorting several thousands of forms and tabulating their contents without mechanical assistance. The results of many large-scale enquiries would be available only long after the field work had been completed. Fortunately the introduction of mechanical punching and sorting machines has facilitated the task of the statistician. All that is now necessary is for the information on the questionnaires to be transferred to specially designed punched cards, the machines then sort the cards, tabulate and compute the totals at great speeds. There is, of course, the risk that the cards may be incorrectly punched by the operator, but this problem can be overcome with adequate supervision. The cost of such methods is considerable and careful thought must be given to the information to be entered.

on the cards to ensure that the maximum information will be given out by the machines in the minimum space of time. According to an article in the *Journal of the Royal Statistical Society*, the representative of a machine accounting company was able to devise a procedure whereby the first results of the census of the population of Cyprus were available within a few weeks, instead of several months, as is usually the case. More recently, however, punched card installations have been superseded by computers in cases where the volume of work is very large. Even so the data may still be recorded initially on punched cards and then transferred to tape which is then fed into computer. The computer has transformed data processing. It serves as a store for such information and is, upon demand, capable of processing the data contained in its storage units at very high speed. Thus large numbers of combinations of the basic data can be produced in a short space of time. The 1961 Census of Population data was processed on a large computer and it was hoped that this would mean an end to the customary long delay between collection and publication. In the event, a shortage of programmers, *i.e.* persons who are responsible for the computer, as well as the fact that the Census authorities did not have the sole use of the computer, together produced serious delays.

The Basis of Classification

Before the actual tabulation can be undertaken there is an intermediate stage, generally described as classification. The point has already been made that statistics is concerned with aggregates, the individual members of which are homogeneous. That is, all the items comprising the aggregate or what the statistician calls the 'population' are of one type, *i.e.* they possess a characteristic in common. For example, retail businesses may be classified according to turnover, schoolboys according to their heights, shares quoted on the Stock Exchange according to the dividend paid. The 'characteristics' in these cases are: turnover, height and dividends respectively, *i.e.* these constitute the link or basis of comparison between all the items within each group. These groups of individual items are usually termed statistical *series* or *distributions*.

A more precise way of defining a series or distribution is that it comprises a group of items which are related one to the other by the possession of some common characteristic. The term 'series' is usually restricted to data which have been collected over time. The figures of the annual turnover of a firm for the past decade would be described as a *time* series. Data which relate to any characteristic other than time may be classified as spatial or attributive distributions. Whereas the time series indicated the turnover of a group of departmental stores over a period of several years, a *spatial* distribution may be one which classifies the turnover of any period according to the location of the sales. Thus, the turnover may be classified according to the departments of the stores, or on the basis of comparing the annual turnover of the various stores in the different towns. In brief, spatial distributions are concerned with location.

The term *attributive* covers all distributions other than time series and spatial distributions. An attribute is simply a characteristic; data are classified according to their attributes. As already explained (p.14) these fall into two main types, those which are capable of numerical expression and those which are not. Thus, in the example of schoolboys classified according to height, the characteristic can be expressed numerically, *i.e.* so many inches. But if the boys are being graded by the school doctor on the basis of their general health and physique, they could only be classified somewhat as follows: excellent, good, fair, and poor. The first example of an attribute, which can be expressed in quantitative terms, *i.e.* height in inches, is termed a *variable;* the second type of classification is based on the *attribute* itself, *i.e.* a quality incapable of being measured in numerical terms, such as 'good health', and is given that name. These points have been repeated because they are relevant not merely to classification; they also affect the type of tabulation used and, as will be shown later, the form of diagrammatic representation of the data.

The Construction of Tables

The purpose of tabulation is primarily to condense and thereby facilitate comparison of the data. The form of the tables employed varies according to the nature of the data and the requirements of the survey. In consequence, it is not possible to lay down hard and fast rules which may be applied in all cases. It may come as a surprise to the reader to learn that draft tables are drawn up before the enquiry is actually started. More precisely, the frame of the tables is drawn up and this has two advantages. First, it enables the survey team to visualise the sort of data they want and are going to get and second, it sometimes draws attention to other information which would be of interest. Provision for such questions can then be made on the questionnaire. As with so many matters, common sense dictates certain guides which should be borne in mind in the construction of any statistical table if it is to serve the purpose of revealing the basic structure of the data.

In no case should the table be overloaded with detail. A closely-printed and concentrated mass of figures may appear most impressive to the casual observer, but merely compels the reader to do what ought to have been done by the compiler of the table at the outset: namely, to reduce the mass into several sub-tables, each bringing out a separate aspect of the data. The purpose of the table should be immediately apparent, *i.e.* it should have a clear and concise title, although clarity and precision should not be sacrificed for brevity. Occasionally tables are encountered where the main title is amplified by a series of footnotes; wherever possible, this practice should be avoided. Where the individual figures are large, the table gains in clarity far more than it loses by eliminating the '000's' or even '00,000's', *i.e.* the final digits. This is especially true of summary tables which are often inserted in the text in the body of the main report or its conclusions; individuals seeking detailed figures can be referred back to the full tables which are best put into an appendix separate from the main report.

It is highly desirable in any report presenting data collected for that enquiry to precede the information presented in tabular form by a short summary of the methods of collection employed, in order that the reader may obtain some idea as to the probable reliability of the results given in the tables. If secondary data from other published sources are given, say for purposes of comparison, then a footnote should be appended indicating the source of that particular section of the table. Especial care should then be taken to leave the reader in no doubt as to the unit of measurement: whether it be £ sterling or $ Australian, long or short tons, ton-miles of passenger trains, or goods trains, etc. If any heading is at all liable to misinterpretation, a clear definition should be provided as to what information is included under that head. Thus, the statistics published by the Home Office of 'persons proceeded against for drunkenness' do not include those persons charged with 'driving under the influence of drink'; these are incorporated with offences against the Highway Act.

Simple Tabulation

To illustrate the normal procedure in tabulation, the data given in Table 1 relating to the individual outputs of 180 workers producing a certain manufactured article are set out with the smallest output at the beginning of the group, and the largest at the end, *i.e.* in order of magnitude. Such an arrangement of the data is known as an *array*. Inspection of the table reveals that the minimum and maximum outputs are 501 and 579 respectively. The difference between these two quantities is described as the *range*. Apart from the range, it is impossible without further careful study to extract any exact information of any value from the table. By breaking down the data into the form of Table 2 below, however, certain features of the data become apparent. Thus, by setting the number of workers producing each

TABLE 1

GREAT PRODUCERS LTD

INDIVIDUAL OUTPUTS OF 180 FEMALE OPERATIVES IN PLANT 1, IN THE WEEK
ENDING 10TH NOVEMBER, 1978

501	520	534	540	547	555
503	522	535	542	547	557
503	522	535	542	547	557
504	523	535	542	547	557
506	523	535	542	547	559
507	524	536	542	548	559
507	525	536	542	548	559
509	525	537	543	548	559
510	526	537	543	548	559
511	526	537	543	549	561
511	527	537	543	549	561
513	527	537	544	549	561
515	527	537	544	549	563
515	528	538	544	550	563
515	528	538	544	550	563
515	528	538	544	550	564
515	528	538	544	550	565
515	528	538	545	551	565
517	528	539	545	551	565
517	530	539	545	551	567
518	530	539	545	551	567
518	532	539	546	552	567
519	532	539	546	552	569
519	532	539	546	552	569
519	532	539	546	553	569
519	532	539	546	553	572
520	532	540	546	553	574
520	534	540	547	553	575
520	534	540	547	555	577
520	534	540	547	555	579

individual output against that figure, a more intelligible picture is provided. Even a superficial scrutiny of Table 2 reveals that the outputs from 537 to 547 inclusive occur most frequently. Such a table is known as a *frequency distribution*. It is so described because it indicates the frequency or number of times each individual output figure occurs. More precisely, it tabulates the frequency of occurrence of the different values of any given variable. Nevertheless, even after this simplification, there are still too many figures to assimilate. The conventional procedure is next to construct a *frequency distribution* as in Table 3.

The data in this form are sometimes described as a *grouped* frequency distribution.[1] Instead of the 'frequencies' of each single output being shown separately, the range (difference between maximum

---

[1] The term generally used is 'frequency distribution.' *i.e.* the same term is usually used whether the data are grouped or not.

TABLE 2
FREQUENCY DISTRIBUTION OF OUTPUTS DETAILED IN TABLE 1

Output	Frequency	Output	Frequency	Output	Frequency
501	1	527	3	550	4
503	2	528	6	551	4
504	1	530	2	552	3
506	1	532	6	553	4
507	2	534	4	555	3
509	1	535	4	557	3
510	1	536	2	559	5
511	2	537	6	561	3
513	1	538	5	563	3
515	6	539	8	564	1
517	2	540	5	565	3
518	2	542	6	567	3
519	4	543	4	569	3
520	5	544	6	572	1
522	2	545	4	574	1
523	2	546	6	575	1
524	1	547	8	577	1
525	2	548	4	579	1
526	2	549	4		

TABLE 3
GROUPED FREQUENCY DISTRIBUTION. DATA FROM TABLE 2

Output	No. of Operatives
(Units per operative)	
500— 9	8
510—19	18
520—29	23
530—39	37
540—49	47
550—59	26
560—69	16
570—79	5
	180

and minimum outputs) is sub-divided into smaller groups, usually termed 'classes'. In this example each class comprises ten units of output. Thus the first class, 500-509, covers all ten values inclusive. In this class eight operatives had outputs of 500 units or above, but none more than 509. In the fifth class, 540-549, there were 47 operatives, none of whose individual outputs was below 540 or exceeded 549. The reader can and should verify the figures in Table 3 by reference to the previous table.

By grouping the data into such a frequency distribution, the basic structure of the information is prominently revealed. The main body of operatives have outputs falling within the middle classes, and only a few operatives come within the classes at either extreme. In passing, it can be stated that the frequency table or 'grouped' frequency distribution is the most common form of presentation of numerical data, and, as will be seen later, is the basis of most statistical analysis. The figures of output can be referred to as the *value* variable to distinguish that variable from the corresponding frequencies which can be referred to as the *frequency* variable.

The same data can be presented in cumulative form, *i.e.* 86 operatives each produced less than 540 units per week, 133 operatives less than 550; and so on up to the last stage, when 180 operatives each produced less than 580 units. Note that the 'cumulation' may be upward or downward; the upper half of Table 4 is read as '133 operatives produced less than 550 units per week . . .' etc.; the lower half as '94 operatives produced 540 or more units per week'.

TABLE 4

DATA FROM TABLE 3 PRESENTED IN CUMULATIVE FORM

Output (Units per operative)	500–9	510–9	520–9	530–9	540–9	550–9	560–9	570–9
No. of operatives	8	26	49	86	133	159	175	180
	180	172	154	131	94	47	21	5

This table yields the data to answer such questions as 'What percentage or proportion of the workers produce 550 or more units per week?' In this case the answer would be 26 per cent.

(*i.e.* $\frac{47}{180} \times 100$).

The Selection of 'Classes'

The preparation of grouped frequency distributions from the raw data may give rise to difficulties. The greatest of these is deciding the number of *classes* into which the series may be divided: *e.g.* in the above table there are eight classes, 500-9, 510-9, and so on up to 570-9. This problem is directly linked with the second: what is the size, or, more precisely, the range, of each class to be, *i.e.* what is the *class-interval*? Thus, in the above example, the class-interval is ten units. There are no hard and fast rules on these points, but generally it is desirable that the number of classes should not exceed 10 or 15, depending on the range of the value variable and the total frequencies in the distribution, otherwise the purpose of the table, the reduction of the data to manageable size, may be defeated. As to the size of the class-interval, this will depend primarily on the number of classes and the distribution of the frequencies. Sometimes the class-interval is easily determined, *e.g.* if families are being classified according to the number of children in each, then the class interval is clearly one child. The frequency table heading would read:

Number of children per family	No. of Families

There are no set rules which if followed will ensure good tabulation in all cases. The student should at all times bear in mind the two main needs of tabulation work. First the table must be comprehensible in that it reduces the data to manageable proportions, and second, the content of the table should be clearly yet simply defined in the title and column headings. In brief, Table 1 on p.47 may have its uses for detailed analysis of the factory's production performance; but as a means of conveying the state of affairs in the plant Table 3 is far more comprehensible and its content easier to grasp. A frequency distribution should resemble Table 3 rather than Table 1.

It is most important to define the successive classes so that there is no doubt as to which class any single value should be allotted. In Table 3 the classes are 500-509, 510-519, etc., which avoids any uncertainty as to the allocation of terminal values such as 510, or 520, which would arise if the classes had been written incorrectly as 500-510, 510-520, etc. The limits of the class-interval are also affected according to whether the independent variable is *continuous* or *discrete*.

Suppose we are classifying households in a given town by reference to the number of children of school age in the household: then we should get a frequency distribution in which the value variable would take values of 0, 1, 2, 3, 4, etc., according to the number of children in the household. Such measurements are exact, we cannot have less or more than a whole child. The unit is clearly and un-equivocally defined for us. Such a variable is termed *discrete*, as is any other variable which can take only certain restricted values, *e.g.* the distribution of cinema tickets sold during the week classified according to their individual price, *e.g.* 25p, 50p, 75p, etc., the number of living rooms in a house, and so on.

On other occasions, however, the limitations of our measuring rod tend to give approximate values. For example, if we take the temperature of a furnace at one minute intervals, the best readings we get will be rounded to the nearest degree centigrade. If we measure the height or weight of schoolchildren, the recorded heights and weights will be expressed to the nearest unit practicable, *e.g.* $\frac{1}{2}''$ or 1 pound. Two children may in fact be identical in height and weight, yet the records may show one to be $\frac{1}{2}''$ shorter than the other but one pound heavier. The difference is partly explained by the human error in taking these measurements, but it is also partly the fault of our height measures and scales which will give only an approximate result, *e.g.* to the nearest inch or pound. In practice, however, the approximation is quite adequate for most purposes. Where a variable can take any value within the range of its observed minimum and maximum values, it is referred to as a *continuous* variable.

Note that where the variable is discrete, then there will be a clear gap between the lower limit of one class and the upper limit of the preceding class, *e.g.* 520 and 519. This natural break does not arise with continuous variables. For example, if men are classified by height, then the simplest classification is as follows: under 5ft 6in; 5ft 6in and under 5ft 7in, etc. This again ensures that no confusion arises as to the allocation of any individual height to its appropriate class.

Where the individual values to be classified tend to group themselves around particular values, care should be taken when deciding upon the class-interval that such values of the independent variable coincide as far as possible with the mid-points of the classes. For example, if in Table 1 a large majority of the outputs ended with the digit 5, *e.g.* 545, 555, etc., the classification used in Table 3 is excellent. If, however, there were many outputs ending in 9, 0 or 1, then it would be preferable to draw up classes as follows: 505-514, 515-524, 525-534 and so on. The reason for this is that it is customary to regard the middle values of classes as the 'average' value of the items in that class. If, as will be shown in Chapter VI, calculations are to be carried out on the data, any inaccuracy or bias in the grouping within the class intervals may distort the final results. To illustrate the effect

TABLE 5

EFFECTS OF DIFFERENT CLASSIFICATION ON DISTRIBUTION OF DATA FROM TABLE 1

First Grouping	Frequencies	Frequencies	Alternate Grouping
—	—	4	Under 505
500— 9	8	8	505—514
510—19	18	24	515— 24
520—29	23	25	525— 34
530—39	37	46	535— 44
540—49	47	41	545— 54
550—59	26	18	555— 64
560—69	16	11	565— 74
570—79	5	3	575— 84
	180	180	

of using the same-sized class interval (10 units) with different limits, Table 5 has been drawn up showing the data from Table 1 classified in two ways. The differences can be observed by comparing the resultant distributions.

Further reference will be made to this matter when the various averages are discussed, but keeping the above principles in mind, the numerous types of tabulation and classification can be examined. Table 3 above, *i.e.* the frequency distribution, is the basic and most usual form of presenting data. Even the most complex tabulation comprises little more than a number of such tables brought together under one head. Nevertheless, the more information which it is sought to bring into one table, the more important it becomes to ensure that the table remains intelligible and easily read.

Further Examples of Tabulation

A number of tables taken from official publications are reproduced in the following pages together with comments upon their salient features. Table 6 is basically a frequency distribution in the first part of the table which classifies the actual number of trades unions in the United Kingdom by their size. This distribution is supplemented in the second part of the table by information indicating how many trade union members are to be found in each size class. Thus, it is possible to estimate the actual number of members which unions within each size class have on *average*. For example, take the pen-

TABLE 6

TRADES UNIONS IN THE U.K.: ANALYSIS BY MEMBERSHIP, 1960 AND 1970[1]

			Number		Membership (000's)	
			1960	1970	1960	1970
Under 100			130	90	6	4
100 and under	500	..	176	116	45	29
500 ,, ,,	1,000	..	56	50	40	35
1,000 ,, ,,	2,500	..	107	59	169	99
2,500 ,, ,,	5,000	..	67	50	223	172
5,000 ,, ,,	10,000	..	35	30	254	199
10,000 ,, ,,	15,000	..	18	13	219	155
15,000 ,, ,,	25,000	..	26	21	499	403
25,000 ,, ,,	50,000	..	11	13	384	452
50,000 ,, ,,	100,000	..	21	16	1,405	1,111
100,000 and over	..	..	17	23	6,590	8,343
TOTALS[2]			664	481	9,835	11,000

Source: Based on Table 168 Annual Abstract of Statistics 1972

At end of year.
[2] Totals may not agree due to rounding.

ultimate class which in 1960 had 21 unions with memberships ranging from 50,000-100,000 each. Their combined membership in that year was 1,405,000 so that on average each of these unions had about 70,000 members. Rather more important, however, are two other pieces of information which the table provides. The first is the surprisingly large number of small unions; in 1970 of the 481 unions listed 395 had less than 10,000 members apiece, while 52 or just over 10 per cent. of the unions by number had between them over 90 per cent. of the total membership, *i.e.* 9,906,000 out of 11,000,000. The other point of interest is the contraction over the decade 1960-70 in the number of unions, *i.e.* from 664 to 481, equal to a fall in numbers of 27.5 per cent. As far as may be judged from the information contained in the table this reduction in numbers of unions is accounted for by many smaller unions merging (one can hardly talk of take-overs in this context!) with the largest. Note how the aggregate membership of all the unions in the classes below 50,000 has declined while the only classes to increase their membership are the three largest classes. There were, in 1970, six more unions in the largest size class as the result of mergers inflating the membership of unions which, in 1960, had rather less than 100,000 members.

Table 7 provides an illustration of how much information can be put into a relatively small table. As with the previous table it provides comparison over time, *i.e.* the number of taxpayers classified

TABLE 7

DISTRIBUTION OF PERSONAL INCOMES
1959-60 AND 1969-70

Income before Tax £	1959-60			1969-70		
	No. of Incomes	Income before Tax	Tax	No. of Incomes	Income before Tax	Tax
	000's	£m	£m	000's	£m	£m
Under 400 ..	4,738	1,386	41	730	266	4
400—600 ..	4,950	2,494	131	2,568	1,289	79
600—800 ..	4,815	3,343	197	2,674	1,869	176
800—1,000 ..	2,930	2,605	194	2,626	2,360	281
1,000—1,250 ..	1,658	1,830	186	3,243	3,642	480
1,250—1,500 ..	614	833	115	2,959	4,058	574
1,500—2,000 ..	448	764	137	4,216	7,257	1,148
2,000—5,000 ..	443	1,276	351	2,412	6,402	1,418
5,000 and over	82	710	383	255	2,175	986
TOTALS[1] ..	20,678	15,242	1,733	21,683	29,319	5,146

Source: Based on Table 57. *Inland Revenue Statistics* 1972.
[1] Totals may not agree due to rounding.

by reference to their incomes in two tax years, 1969-70 compared with 1959-60. The first set of data constitutes the basic frequency distribution; the value variable is income which is broken up into nine classes. Note the basis of the classification; the first and final classes are *open-ended*, *i.e.* in the first class there is no lower limit shown and in the top class no upper limit is given. This is often done where there are a few odd extreme values at either end of the range of the value variable which would necessitate the addition to the distribution of one or more additional classes containing relatively few frequencies. In the case of the first class in this table, the £400 is a convenient limit for the Inland Revenue for classifying incomes since few below this limit were taxable. As will be seen later in discussing the calculation of averages and other statistics, such open-ended classes may cause problems. For the moment, however, all that matters is to note that they are often used.

Since the words 'under' and 'over' are used in the first and final classes to indicate the class interval, the reader can interpret the rest of the classification correctly. Without that guidance, however, what would one do with an income of say £1,000; does it go into the class £800-1,000 or the next class up £1,000-1,250? Clearly, from the first class in the entire distribution it seems that such an income would go into the class £1,000 to £1,250 since the upper limit of the former class is defined as 'under £1,000'. This matter of defining the limits of classes in a frequency distribution is most important and sometimes overlooked. The Inland Revenue's 97th annual report omitted any indication as to the definition, merely writing £250-500, £500-750 and the consequent confusion was inevitable. In the 105th report they changed the basis to the following, £180-249, £250-499 which is perfectly clear. A report on a *Sample Survey of the Roads and Traffic of G.B.* published by the H.M.S.O. in 1962 used a most curious technique. The width of roads was classified in feet as follows: 8-10, 10-12, 12-14, etc. with a footnote to the title of the table to the effect that '18-20ft for example, includes roads of exactly 18ft but not those of exactly 20ft'. This is not a practice to be recommended; it is better always to define the class interval in the first column of the table in quite unambiguous terms.

Returning to the content of Table 7 it will be seen that apart from the comparison over time, three other quantities are compared for each class of income. The first is the actual number of incomes within each size class; for example, there were 443,000 incomes of between £2,000 and £5,000 and ten years later their number had risen to 2,412,000. The second column of information in each half of the table shows the total income before tax received by the taxpayers within each income class; thus the 443,000 incomes in 1959-60 aggregated £1,276 million out of which sum, according to the final column in the first part of the table, £351 million was paid in tax.

At this stage one or two apparently minor points of interest should be made. First, as with any statistics, there is the obvious question on their accuracy. As far as the information in Table 6 concerning trade unions is concerned there is no reason for doubting these data which are collected by the Registrar of Friendly Societies from information submitted to him by the unions. It should be perfectly feasible to count accurately the number of registered unions and, by giving their aggregate membership to the nearest 1,000, any minor errors due to miscounting, deaths or new members are more than covered. Table 7, however, is not quite in the same class. The data are based upon tax returns made by taxpayers to the Inland Revenue and, while the majority are correct and true, some are not. Furthermore, there are some people who evade their tax liabilities altogether by not making any return. Hence the figure of incomes is not the count of all incomes, but of those actually returned. However, the magnitude of the errors arising from such practices is not likely to affect the overall picture revealed by the actual table. Lastly, there is the matter of 'rounding'. The reader will have noted that in both Tables 6 and 7 there are footnotes to the effect that the 'total may

TABLE 8

DISTRIBUTION OF POPULATION OF ENGLAND AND WALES
BY STANDARD REGIONS IN 1931, 1951, 1971[1]

Standard Region	1931		1951		1971	
	Number 000's	Per- centage	Number 000's	Per- centage	Number 000's	Per- centage
North	3,037	7·6	3,138	7·2	3,292	6·7
Yorkshire and						
Humberside ..	4,307	10·8	4,527	10·4	4,792	9·9
East Midlands ..	2,511	6·3	2,887	6·6	3,385	7·0
East Anglia ..	1,233	3·1	1,382	3·2	1,665	3·4
South East ..	13,537	33·9	15,127	34·6	17,143	35·3
South West ..	2,794	7·0	3,229	7·4	3,771	7·8
West Midlands..	3,743	9·4	4,423	10·1	5,103	10·5
North West ..	6,196	15·5	6,447	14·7	6,729	13·8
Sub-total:						
England[2] ..	37,359	93·5	41,159	94·1	45,880	94·4
Wales ..	2,593	6·5	2,599	5·9	2,724	5·6
TOTALS	39,952	100·0	43,758	100·0	48,604	100·0

Source: Based on Table 11 in Annual Abstract of Statistics 1972.

[1] Census figures. Data for 1971 provisional.

[2] Totals may not agree due to rounding.

not agree due to rounding'. This is a frequent insertion and is necessary because, by rounding figures to the nearest, say 1,000, the rounded figures when aggregated may not add up to the original total which is itself rounded off to the nearest 1,000. There is no need to adjust the total or constituent figures to produce an apparently correct result. This issue is discussed more fully in Chapter VIII.

Table 8 is not a frequency distribution but a compound of facts relating to the population of England and Wales. It gives the populations for each of the nine regions of England and Wales. The latter are termed the *standard regions* and are used for all official statistics which are classified on a regional basis, *e.g.* employment, unemployment, house-building, etc. There is now published by the government an *Abstract of Regional Statistics* wherein all the data are based upon these standard regions. The essence of Table 8 is to provide a comparison over a 40-year period of the change in regional populations. To facilitate this comparison, because any change in the actual figures is a compound of the population growth in the country as a whole and the shift in population between regions, a further column of percentage figures is added. In this way the relevant importance of any region, as far as population size is concerned, is given. Thus, the *actual* population of the Northern region has increased over the 40 years from 3,037,000 to 3,292,000, but its *share* of the total population in England and Wales has declined from 7.6 to barely 6.7 per cent. This may seem a small drop of under one

TABLE 9

ANALYSIS OF DOMESTIC RATEABLE VALUES†

ENGLAND AND WALES, 1ST APRIL 1971

Valuation £		Admin. Counties[1]		County Boroughs		Greater London[2]		All Rating Authorities	
Over	Not over	No. 000's	Value £m	No. 000's	Value £m	No. 000's	Value £m	No. 000's	Value £m
	30	1,337	30	638	16	20	—	1,996	47
30	56	2,591	116	1,625	73	166	8	4,382	196
56	100	3,519	286	1,995	145	1,083	88	6,647	502
100	200	1,197	153	438	55	1,028	133	2,664	340
200	330	97	23	26	6	108	27	231	56
330	—	12	5	2	1	42	23	56	29
TOTALS[3]		8,804	595	4,724	297	2,448	278	15,976	1,170

Source: Based on Tables 94 and 95. Inland Revenue Statistics 1972.

†Excluding agricultural dwellings, caravans and Crown houses.

[1] Excluding London.

[2] Greater London Boroughs incl. City of London.

[3] Totals may not agree due to rounding.

percentage point but, in relation to the base percentage of 7.6 per cent it represents a *relative* fall of almost 12 per cent, *i.e.* 0.9 over 7.6.

The reader will appreciate that this table could be re-arranged on the lines of Table 6 where, instead of the basic division of the table being by reference to time, Table 6 shows the change-over time under the two main headings, numbers and membership. One can read off this information from Table 8 as it now stands but, if it is particularly important to emphasise either the absolute or relative change then it is better to put the actual numbers for the three successive dates in adjacent columns and similarly for the percentages. In that way the eye can take in the alterations more easily. In short, the structure or lay-out of any table depends on what it is designed to do and what information is to be emphasised.

Table 9 is an example of a classification which brings out four different facets of the basic data. First is the rateable value and the reader may care to note the different basis for defining the class-interval from the methods used already and discussed above. Then there is a horizontal classification of total rateable value according to the type of local authority area in which it is sited with a total column at the far right. For each of the three types of rating authority shown in the horizontal breakdown the aggregate rateable value is analysed both by reference to the number of domestic hereditaments (*i.e.* buildings) within each class and for each such class the total rateable value of those hereditaments. The table is most informative and a study of the constituent parts reveals the significant differences between the different classes of authority.

Table 10 is a good illustration of a geographical comparison based on a simple frequency distribution with reference to two characteristics. The frequency distribution is simple, a classification of school classes by reference to the number of pupils. The class intervals are straight-forward and clearly defined with the exception of the final class which is open-ended. The numbers involved in this class are so small that they will not affect any calculations that may be made.[1] This analysis is given for both primary and secondary schools in the public sector, *i.e.* State schools. For each of these two main groupings, the national differences within the United Kingdom are well brought out. The use of percentages facilitates the interpretation of the table; had actual figures been given for each class then, because of the differences in size between the three regions, which is reflected in the final row of figures showing the number of pupils, it would have been very difficult to interpret the data. In short, this is an excellent illustration of the fact that for some data percentage figures are far more readily comprehensible than are the actual data. Generally speaking, when two or more frequency distributions are

[1] This point is discussed in Chapter VI on averages.

being compared, if the size of the distributions varies considerably, then it is helpful to use percentages to show the importance of each class within the distribution. And, as has been done in Table 10, the absolute difference in size can be brought home to the reader by appending the actual number as a final row in the table.

TABLE 10

PERCENTAGE DISTRIBUTION BY SIZE OF CLASSES IN PRIMARY AND SECONDARY
PUBLIC SECTOR SCHOOLS. U.K. 1971

Size of Class	Primary			Secondary		
	England and Wales	Scotland	Northern Ireland	England and Wales	Scotland	Northern Ireland
	%	%	%	%	%	%
1—15 ..	0·9	1·2	} 5·7	11·0	15·9	8·3
16—20 ..	2·6	2·9		12·3	19.9	15·6
21—25 ..	6·4	6·8	9·2	13·7	14·4	14·4
26—30 ..	17·4	17·5	19·3	27·2	15·1	23·0
31—35 ..	35·6	28·4	35·6	25·9	17·4	28·1
36—40 ..	32·5	27·2	25·2	4·9	13·4	9·7
41—45 ..	4·0	13·2	4·3	0·5	3·3	0·8
46—50 ..	0·3	2·7	0·6	0·4	0·4	—
51 and over..	0·2	0·2	0·1	4·1	0·2	0·1
TOTALS[1] ..	100·0	100·0	100·0	100·0	100·0	100·0
No. of Pupils (000's) ..	5,004	628	213	3,107	311	95

Source: Social Trends 1972· Table 84·
[1] Totals may not agree due to rounding.

Table 11 is included as an example of what is sometimes referred to as a two-way classification. Unlike the earlier tables, this table is simply a combination of two frequency distributions. The vertical classification breaks down the total of households in Great Britain by reference to the number of children in the household; thus, there are 227,000 households with five or more children. The horizontal classification shows the same total of households this time classified by reference to the number of persons in each, e.g. there are 437,000 households with seven or more persons. Then, in addition to this information, the cells of the table contain the numbers of households classified by reference to both these characteristics. Thus, of the 437,000 households with seven or more persons, the bulk of them, 379,000, have one child apiece and 52,000 have two children.

TABLE 11

DISTRIBUTION OF PRIVATE HOUSEHOLDS BY NUMBER OF CHILDREN
GREAT BRITAIN 1966 (000's)[1]

No. of children in household	Total No. of house- holds	Number of persons in household						
		1	2	3	4	5	6	7 or more
0	10,263	2,572	5,066	1,830	615	141	32	1
1	2,801		92	1,708	651	258	74	379
2	2,305			54	1,752	327	128	52
3	970				24	743	135	4
4	372					10	282	
5 or more	227						4	
TOTALS[2]	16,937	2,572	5,158	3,592	3,042	1,480	656	437

Source: Based on Table 79. Annual Abstract of Statistics 1972
[1] Figures based on 10 per cent sample.
[2] Totals may not agree due to rounding.

TABLE 12

CONSUMERS' EXPENDITURE IN U.K. SELECTED YEARS 1961-71
ANALYSED BY MAIN COMPONENTS, £m AT 1963 PRICES†

Expenditure on	1961	1963	1966	1969	1971
Food	4,593	4,689	4,848	4,924	4,993
Alcoholic Drink ..	1,161	1,219	1,323	1,447	1,658
Tobacco	1,294	1,286	1,264	1,250	1,206
Housing	2,018	2,161	2,341	2,616	2,698
Fuel and Light ..	856	1,010	1,068	1,227	1,307
Clothing	1,806	1,873	2,026	2,168	2,269
Durable and Household Goods	1,894	2,197	2,372	2,460	2,902
Running Cost of Motor Vehicles	550	682	955	1,196	1,291
Travel	653	633	692	712	722
Entertainment and Re- creation[1]	688	746	856	927	987
Sub-total	15,513	16,526	17,745	18,927	20,013
All other items	3,068	3,278	3,515	3,563	3,663
TOTAL	18,581	19,804	21,260	22,490	23,676
Total expenditure at cur- rent prices, £m ..	17,559	19,804	23,837	28,428	33,960
Price Index of consumer goods and services — 1963=100	94·5	100·0	112·1	126·5	143·6

†*Source: Based on Table 23. National Income and Expenditure 1972.*
[1] Including 'Miscellaneous recreational goods'.

Table 12 is taken from a very important statistical publication, the *National Income and Expenditure Blue Book*, in this case the volume for 1972. This particular table reveals the main components of consumer expenditure which follow closely the classification of household expenditure used in calculating the index of retail prices (discussed in Chapter X and XVI) which serves to measure changes in the cost of living in the United Kingdom. The main feature of this table is the use of fixed prices, *i.e.* those ruling in 1963, to effect a comparison over time. By this method it is possible to compare the figures of any group, *e.g.* food, for any two or more years and measure the change in quantitative terms. If the figures of actual expenditure had been given, as they are in a similar table in the Blue Book, then it is not possible to compare the change in what the statistician calls the 'real' consumption)as opposed to 'money' outlays on each group of items.

The figures are all given to the nearest million £s but the margin of error in each figure varies quite considerably depending on the basic information available to the statisticians for compiling these various totals. For example, the figures on alcoholic drink and tobacco are likely to be much more reliable than those on, say, entertainment and recreation because the former commodities are dutiable and exact records of the alcoholic drink and tobacco released for sale are available from the Customs and Excise authorities. There are no such data for many other goods and services, *e.g.* hairdressing, upon which the modern consumer spends his money. In the future, however, the quality of the data on this respect should improve since the Value Added Tax is now chargeable over a wide range of goods and services. Henceforth the authorities should be able to build up a bank of statistical information relating to spending on all classes of dutiable goods and services. There is a further statistical problem in compiling such a table and this concerns the price index, as it is termed, for converting, say, 1971 prices into those which ruled in 1963. This index is shown on the bottom line of Table 12 and indicates that prices of consumer goods and services in general were 43.6 per cent higher in 1971 than in 1963. To arrive at the actual total expenditure in 1971 it would be necessary to multiply the 1971 total at 1963 prices, *i.e.* £23,676, by 143.6. Even if this conversion of *current* prices into the prices ruling in the *base* year can be done successfully, (some of the problems are discussed in Chapter X) there is always the fact that the quality and type of goods purchased change over time and no index can take such changes into account. On the other hand, while it is easy to point to the various limitations in the quality of a great deal of data published in the Blue Book, the fact is that exact figures are not needed. What is required are series of data over time which can be relied upon to show trends and patterns of consumer expenditure and this, in large measure, is being achieved. This consumers' price index in Table 12 is quite different from the retail price index referred to earlier since it covers all expenditure, whereas the retail price index is based upon the expenditure of selected income groups. On the other hand, it must be remembered there is no such thing as an all-purpose index; each one is designed for a particular purpose and the price index of consumer goods and services cited in Table 12 is designed to measure a very wide range of price changes indeed. How far it achieves that object satisfactorily

TABLE 13

EMPLOYEES' ATTITUDES TO MEASURED DAYWORK (M.D.W.) ANALYSED BY THEIR VIEWS ON EFFECT OF CHANGE TO M.D.W.[1]

	Number in sample (100%)	Employees' attitude				
		Very much for the better	A bit better	No differ-ence	A bit worse	Very much for the worse
	Nos.	%	%	%	%	%
Opinion of establishment:						
Very good ..	168	64	28	4	2	2
Quite good ..	237	41	38	12	5	4
About average ..	169	32	41	11	12	4
Not very good ..	24	8	58	4	17	13
Not good at all ..	14	36	29	0	7	29
Need to work harder:						
Need to work harder now ..	330	37	43	6	8	7
No difference ..	263	52	30	12	5	2
Need to work less hard now ..	19	47	26	11	16	0
Degree of job security:						
More secure ..	119	59	34	5	2	0
No difference ..	349	47	38	9	5	2
Less secure ..	119	21	34	13	16	16
Co-operation from other workers:						
More now ..	148	65	27	5	3	0
No difference ..	363	40	40	9	7	3
Less now	88	22	38	14	11	16
Ease of union representation:						
Easier	159	70	25	3	1	1
No difference ..	235	39	43	11	6	2
More difficult ..	104	14	42	10	15	18

[1]Source: Table 5, Appendix C in "Measured Daywork" by Office of Manpower Economics. H.M.S.O. 1973.

is a matter for debate but, all that need be said at this stage is that whenever the reader encounters a reference to an index number either in a report or in a table it is only common-sense to find out what it purports to do!

Table 13 illustrates the amount of information, not all of it numerical, which can be put into a table. As the title of the table indicates, its content reflects employees' attitudes to measured day work derived from a sample enquiry in various plants and factories. While the bulk of the information is given in percentage terms, these percentages relate to the figures shown in the first column giving the number of respondents in the sample. Whereas it is quite legitimate to provide a percentage breakdown of total figures of several hundred, it is difficult to believe that such a procedure is sound when the basic number of respondents is as low as 14, 19 or 24 to quote three such groups in Table 13. On the other hand, to be fair to compilers of the report and these tables, the fact that some percentages are based upon very small samples indeed is at least disclosed. What is thoroughly reprehensible is to compare percentages for quite different size groups, without disclosing the fact that some of the samples are very small. Thus, the sort of advertising statement that 90 per cent of men questioned said they used such and such a product may merely mean that only 20 men were asked, instead of the much larger number implied by the statement.

Some Simple Rules

The construction of a statistical table does not require profound thought or great skill. Provided attention is paid to the more obvious and simple points, it should not be difficult to produce an intelligible table. The following simple rules will help remind the student of the more prevalent pitfalls.

1. The table should have a title which should be short and self-explanatory. Try to avoid supplementing it with footnotes, although from time to time this is necessary.

2. Always give the source of the data in the table whether it is based upon your own collection of facts, or as is more often likely to be the case, where it is compiled from published sources, *e.g. Criminal Statistics* or the *Monthly Digest of Statistics.*

3. The units of measurement should be clearly shown and, if necessary, defined. What for example are 'metric' tons, as opposed to 'long' tons; or $ Australian compared with £? The column headings should also be clearly shown and explained.

4. Where the data are classified, *e.g.* in a frequency distribution as in

Table 6, the classification must be quite clear, *i.e.* no overlapping of limits of the successive classes.

5. Don't hesitate to round the constituent figures in the columns to the nearest £000 or £m. or 000's etc. This is especially important if there are several columns of data to compare.

6. If the columns of figures are to be aggregated, consider whether their totals should be placed at the top of the column or at the foot. Likewise, if percentages are to be included; should they be shown alongside the actual figures, or kept separate with other percentages? It depends largely upon which comparisons are the most important; the *absolute* changes in the variable, or its *relative*, *i.e.* proportionate, importance.

7. Where there is a considerable volume of data it is better to break them down into two or more tables, rather than try to incorporate them all into a single table. Remember that the primary purpose of a table is to convey information; the simpler the table, the easier it is to understand.

8. Use different thicknesses of column rulings to break up a large table; likewise, italicise some of the figures to make them stand apart from others.

Lastly, before drafting the table be quite clear what it is designed to reveal from the data. As with so many other things in life, practice in drawing up tables is the best means of learning the basic principles. Make a habit of scrutinising any published or printed table and asking whether or not it might have been better laid-out; whether there are any mistakes, *e.g.* in classification; or an excess of footnotes. For a start, look through the numerous tables which are reproduced in the chapters which follow[1] and consider how far they satisfy the criteria set out above.

---

[1] Especially Chapters XVII and XVIII on Official Statistics.

Questions

General

Questions on tabulation or on tabulated data are usually of two kinds. First there is the question which contains a short piece of prose with numerous statistics from which the candidate is required to draw up a table which will bring out the main features of the data. Given the completed table the candidate is then often required to make some comment thereon or perform some calculations. For example, the examiner will often ask for secondary statistics and/or a diagram. Usually the secondary statistics entail no more than the calculation of a few percentages. As far as the diagram is concerned it should be simple and candidates in the examination should avoid spending too much time on that part of the question.

The second type of question presents a table, usually with quite a lot of data. The candidate is then required to write a report on the table, once again being told to calculate any secondary statistics he thinks may be useful for interpreting the tabulated data and sometimes to draw a diagram. Here the diagram is rather more important than in the first type of question but, even so, try to produce a diagram which is as simple as is consistent with the data. Bear in mind that the purpose of a diagram is to reduce the data to their essentials so that the few *main* points of the tabulated data are highlighted.

In both types of question, however, the weakest part of the candidates' answers is invariably the report or commentary on the data. Frequently candidates content themselves with reciting, usually at length, all the figures in the table. This is quite useless. The purpose of the report or your comment is to draw the reader's attention to the significant features of the data. Usually the comparisons between the various components of the totals or the totals at different points of time can be emphasised by means of simple proportions. In short, try to ask yourself the question, what is the table about? Is it the growth in, say, overall expenditure, or is it the changing components within the totals over time etc.?

Note that the report or commentary you write need not be long. It is better if it is concise – but not in note form – and restricted to the main features of the data. Also, start the report by indicating what the data are about, just in case the reader has not got a copy of the table in front of him to read in conjunction with the report.

The eight questions which follow illustrate the two types of tabulation question asked in most examination papers. Some are more complex than others, but in the draft answers attention is drawn to the most important points. Note that the answers which follow are not intended as 'model' answers; they are intended primarily to draw attention to the sort of points which the examiner is looking for in the candidates' answers. It is suggested that before studying the answers below, the reader working for an examination should attempt the questions.

1. 'In 1966 total local authority income amounted to £4,603m, a quarter of which came from the rate support grant while a further 7 per cent came from specific central government grants. The local authorities raised £1,380m by rates and a further £415m by rents. However, local authorities had a borrowing requirement of 21 per cent of their total income. Other local authority sources provided £368m. By 1976 total local authority income had risen to £19,049m of which rate support grant totalled £7,810m and a further 8 per cent came from specific central government grants. The rate contribution to local authority income was 24 per cent while 10 per cent came from rents. The borrowing requirement in 1976 had fallen by 12 percentage points compared with 1966 and other local authority sources provided £1,524m.'

Present the above information in the form of a table and write a short report on its contents.

2. Analysis of rateable value in England as at 1st April, 1975.

Amounts £m
Numbers in 0,000

Classification by type of hereditament	Districts		Metropolitan Districts		Greater London		TOTALS[1]	
	No.	Value	No.	Value	No.	Value	No.	Value
Domestic	9.63	1,794	4.09	646	2.51	705	16.23	3,145
Commercial	1.66	616	0.66	266	0.50	761	2.83	1,644
Industrial	0.05	419	0.03	208	0.02	139	0.10	767
Other undertakings [2]	0.03	171	0.01	67	0.00	77	0.04	316
Entertainment and Recreational	0.05	32	0.01	16	0.01	17	0.07	65
Educational and Cultural	0.03	115	0.01	53	0.00	38	0.04	205
Miscellaneous	0.12	158	0.05	48	0.10	149	0.27	354
TOTALS[1]	11.57	3,305	4.86	1,304	3.14	1,885	19.57	6,496

[1] Totals may not agree due to rounding
[2] Mainly nationalised industries, water undertakings and Post Office

Source: *Inland Revenue Statistics 1976* from Table 116.

Draft a report on the above table preparing such secondary statistics and any diagrams which will, in your opinion, bring out the salient points.

3. 'In the five years, 1935-9, there were 1,775 cases of certain industrial diseases reported in Great Britain. This number was made up of 677 cases of lead poisoning, 111 of other poisoning, 144 of anthrax and 843 of gassing. The number of deaths reported was 10¼ per cent of the cases reported for all four diseases taken together. The corresponding figures were 10·9 per cent for lead poisoning, 6·3 per cent for other poisoning and 12·5 per cent for anthrax.

'The total number of cases reported in the subsequent five years, 1940-4, was 2,807 higher. But lead poisoning cases reported fell by 351 and anthrax cases by 35. Other poisoning cases increased by 748 between the two periods. The number of deaths reported decreased by 45 for lead poisoning, but only by 2 for anthrax between 1935-9 and 1940-4. In the latter period, 52 deaths were reported from poisoning other than lead poisoning. The total number of deaths reported in 1940-4, including those from gassing, was 64 greater than in 1935-9.'

Construct a table from the above information, making whatever calculations are needed to complete the entries. Comment on the changes shown between the pre-war and war periods.

4. In his annual statement, the Chairman of a group of three companies, A, B, C, gave the following analysis of the profit (in £'s sterling) from trading in various parts of the world. 'For Company A the total profit was £130,000; of this sum, £100,000 came from the United Kingdom and £10,000 from trade with the Commonwealth, whereas profit in Europe amounted to £3,000 from the European Free Trade Area (E.F.T.A.), together with £15,000 from the European Economic Community (E.E.C.); profit from the U.S.A. was only £2,000. As for Company B this company made £67,000 in the United Kingdom but had no trade with the U.S.A.; profit from E.F.T.A. and E.E.C. countries was £1,500 and £5,000 respectively which, together with £2,500 from the Commonwealth, made a total of £76,000. Finally, Company C made the lowest total profit £52,800; of this, £40,000 was made in the United Kingdom, the Commonwealth profit being £5,700 compared with £2,100 from E.E.C. and £5,000 from E.F.T.A.'

Tabulate these data, adding any secondary statistics which may be helpful.

5.

Public expenditure summary by programme: actual and planned

United Kingdom Index numbers and £ million

Programme:	Indices (1976-77=100) at constant prices						£ million at current prices		Percentage spent by local authorities
	1972-73	1975-76	1976-77	1977-78	1978-79	1981-82	1976-77	1977-78[1]	1977-78
Social security	84	97	100	104	111	115	11,220	13,217	0
Health and personal social services	89	99	100	101	103	109	7,111	7,942	14.8
Education	92	101	100	96	97	99	7,633	8,124	88.7
Housing	64	101	100	92	97	103	4,823	4,714	50.6
Food subsidies	—	146	100	52	1	—	399	244	0
Environmental services	101	109	100	94	97	99	2,582	2,712	75.2
Libraries, museums, and the arts	87	98	100	99	101	105	311	338	66.7
Law, order, and protective services	81	98	100	101	103	105	1,823	2,025	77.1
Employment services	81	72	100	143	144	132	687	905	3.4
Roads and transport	91	114	100	93	92	92	2,757	2,757	56.5
Trade, industry and agriculture, fisheries, food, and forestry: less food subsidies	113	129	100	46	84	71	3,041	1,512	3.6
Defence, overseas aid, and other overseas services	101	99	100	101	106	114	7,238	8,316	0
Other expenditure on programmes	179	145	100	103	145	141	2,193	1,852	6.1
Northern Ireland	81	99	100	100	104	104	1,672	1,829	14.2
Total public expenditure on programmes	92	104	100	97	103	106	53,490	56,487	29.3
Debt interest	55	70	100	114	120	96	1,423	1,986	..
Total public expenditure	91	103	100	97	105[2]	109[2]	54,913	58,473	..

[1]Provisional   [2]Including contingency reserve

Source: HM Treasury

6. Selected Regional Health Statistics

Standard Regions	Chronic sickness		Standardised mortality ratios (England and Wales=100) 1975		Infant mortality	General medical practitioners average list size (thousands)
	Persons reporting long-standing illness (age standardised percentages) 1974 and 1975		Persons aged 15 to 64			
			Males	Females		
			Deaths from all causes	Deaths from all causes		
	Males	Females			1975	1975
North	24	25	111	108	14.9	2.4
Yorkshire & Humberside	22	25	104	103	17.3	2.5
East Midlands	24	25	97	100	15.1	2.5
East Anglia)	22	22	88	93	14.7	2.3
South East:	21	23	94	95	15.0	
Greater London	21	24	99	96	16.0	2.3
Other South East	21	22	91	94	14.3	2.4
South West	21	21	90	94	14.4	2.2
West Midlands	23	25	103	102	16.9	2.4
North West	23	25	111	108	17.3	2.5
Wales	25	26	109	105	14.5	2.2
England and Wales	22	24	100	100	15.7	2.4

Source: Social Trends No. 8

Write a formal report on the above data for the benefit of a committee concerned with the distribution of health service resources. Define any technical terms used.

7. In a recent survey 7,381 children were studied of whom 219 attended private schools, 78% were the children of manual workers but only 40 of these latter attended private schools, 1 out of every 9 children were only children; among private school attenders the proportion was 20·1% of whom 7 were the children of manual workers. Of the families with only children, 567 came from the manual working class.

Arrange these figures in a table calculating any secondary statistics you consider necessary and comment on the results.

Q. 8 Overleaf

8.   SCHOOL LEAVERS BY DESTINATION 1974-75

	Degree courses at			Teacher training courses	Other full-time further education	Employment	Total sample size (=100%) (thousands)
	Universities	Polytechnics	Other establishments				
Boys (percentages):							
Grammar	24.5	4.0	0.3	2.8	12.8	55.7	28.0
Comprehensive	4.3	0.9	0.1	0.8	7.4	86.6	222.5
Secondary Modern	0.2	0.1	—	0.1	9.3	90.4	67.6
Other maintained secondary	2.8	0.9	—	0.8	8.3	87.2	12.3
Direct grant	41.5	3.6	0.3	1.5	13.9	39.3	7.9
Independent recognised	30.4	3.0	0.2	0.6	21.6	44.2	15.5
TOTAL BOYS (thousands)	24.7	4.1	0.3	2.9	31.7	289.9	353.7
Girls (percentages):							
Grammar	14.8	2.2	0.2	11.5	24.4	47.0	29.8
Comprehensive	2.7	0.4	0.1	3.1	14.2	79.5	212.5
Secondary modern	0.1	—	—	0.4	17.3	82.2	64.3
Other maintained secondary	1.2	0.3	0.1	1.9	18.2	78.3	11.0
Direct grant	28.3	2.5	0.3	8.9	25.4	34.8	8.1
Independent recognised	13.5	1.0	0.2	4.6	38.4	42.5	12.5
TOTAL GIRLS (thousands)	14.2	2.0	0.3	11.9	57.3	252.5	338.1

Source: Statistics of Education, *Department of Education and Science*

Comment on any difference or similarities revealed by the above table, making any further calculations which seem necessary for this purpose.

Answers

Answer to Question 1

LOCAL AUTHORITY FINANCE BY SOURCE 1966 AND 1976

Source	1976		1966	
	£m	%	£m	%
Rates	4,572	24	1,380	30
Rents	1,905	10	415	9
Rate Support Grant	7,810	41	1,151	25
Specific Grants	1,524	8	322	7
Other Revenue	1,524	8	368	8
Total Revenue	17,335	91	3,636	79
Borrowing Requirement	1,714	9	967	21
TOTAL	19,049	100	4,603	100

This is a very easy question. All that needs to be done is to calculate either percentages from the actual figures or derive the actual figure from the percentage given. The division at the bottom of the table which puts the borrowing requirement separately from the other figures is because this is a different type of revenue, capital as distinct from income. Remember to give the table a title and to indicate the measures used, *e.g.* £ millions.

As for the report, there are only a few important points worth mentioning in a *short* report. You could start by drawing attention to the fact that between 1966-76 revenue, excluding the borrowing requirement, increased about 4½ times from just over £3,600m to £17,300m. Note that a rounded figure as in this case will be easier for the reader to assimilate than the actual figures. Within the growth of local authority income, the following changes are important. First, there is the big increase in the *proportion* of income met out of the Rate Support Grant, up from 25 to 41 per cent. Note that although specific grants jumped from £322m to £1,524m the actual increase is not so important as the fact that the *proportion* of total income met from this source remained virtually constant, *i.e.* 7 to 8 per cent. Both these points could be mentioned, however. The second important feature is the fall in the relative importance of the rates; 30 per cent in the earlier year and only 24 per cent in 1976. Lastly, the fall in the relative size of the borrowing requirement between the two years in relation to the other income also merits comment.

Answer to Question 2

It is all too easy with such a table to dwell at length on the mass of figures so that the reader of the report fails to grasp the significant features. Note that, as already emphasised there is no need to cite *every* figure in a table. Only quote the more important ones in terms of size and those where, even if fairly small, marked changes have taken place over periods of time.

Start by indicating the subject-matter of the table, *i.e.* total rateable value (R.V.) in England and Wales in April 1975 and its distribution:

(i) according to the type of local authority in which it is sited; and

(ii) the relative importance of the various types of hereditament in terms of their contribution to the R.V. of each type of local authority.

Of the total R.V. in England and Wales amounting to almost £6.5 billion, just over half (51 per cent) is in District authority control, 29 per cent in Greater London and 20 per cent in the Metropolitan Districts. The distribution of the number of hereditaments differs from the total value in each type of authority; thus the Districts have 59 per cent of all hereditaments and 51 per cent of total R.V.; the Metropolitan Districts 25 per cent of all hereditaments and 20 per cent of the R.V. while Greater London has 16 per cent of the total hereditaments but 29 per cent of total R.V. This suggests that the R.V. of individual hereditaments is highest in Greater London and lowest in the Metropolitan Districts.

Just over half of the total R.V. in the Districts (54 per cent) is accounted for by domestic hereditaments; in the Metropolitan Districts the corresponding percentage is 50 and in Greater London 37. Commercial hereditaments account for 19 per cent of total R.V. in the Districts, 20 per cent in the Metropolitan Districts but 48 per cent in Greater London. The corresponding figures for industrial hereditaments are 13 and 16 per cent in the two types of District but only 7 per cent in London.

A further point which might be worth making is that, if the number of domestic hereditaments is divided into their aggregate R.V. for each type of authority, the mean values are quite similar. Thus, for Greater London the average domestic R.V. is £192, for the Districts the mean is £186 and for the Metropolitan Districts £158. The final point to be made relates to the concentration in Greater London of what are termed Educational and Cultural and the Miscellaneous category. Greater London has over £550m in these categories; the Districts £273m and the Metropolitan Districts £101m. Nevertheless, the contribution to total R.V. in each of these types of authority is virtually the same, *i.e.* about 8 per cent.

The diagrams chosen to illustrate these data should be those which bring out the main features. First, we need to portray the relative sizes of the R.V. totals in each of the three types of authority. This could be done by means of a couple of pie charts or a bar diagram as illustrated in Figures 6 and 7 on 82-3. The distribution of the R.V. within the totals for each type of authority could be shown by using another bar chart sub-divided according to the proportions of, say, Domestic, Commercial and Industrial and All Other.

It would be possible to show the distribution of all domestic, all commercial and industrial, as well as all other R.V. according to the type of authority in which it was sited. The main constraint in an examination is usually time, particularly where diagrams are concerned. Provided the diagram is relevant and properly drawn – it need not be done in various colour inks – the candidate will get his marks.

Answer to Question 3

This is a relatively simple question but the student should read it carefully to make sure he really understands what it is about and how the table should be drawn up. Thus, it is fairly clear that what is being compared is the frequency of four types of industrial disease as between two five-year periods. This gives the framework of the table. Then, for each disease it can be seen that three pieces of information will be given in the table; the number of cases reported, the number of deaths and the percentage of deaths relative to reported cases.

Once that has been done, the completion of the table should be fairly simple. Note that, in the earlier period, the number of deaths needs to be derived from the percentages, whereas in the later period you are given the actual number of deaths and the percentages have to be calculated. Note, too, that the cases reported in the second period need to be derived by the addition to the figure of the earlier period of the change, *e.g.* 'other poisoning cases increased by 748 . . .'. The final table should look something like the following:

INCIDENCE OF INDUSTRIAL DISEASES 1935-39 AND 1940-44

Disease	1935-39			1940-44		
	No. of cases	Deaths	% Deaths	No. of Cases	Deaths	% Deaths
Lead poisoning	677	74	10.9	326	29	8.9
Other poisoning	111	7	6.3	859	52	6.1
Anthrax	144	18	12.5	109	16	14.7
Gassing	843	82	9.7	3,288	148	4.5
TOTALS	1,775	181	10.2	4,582	245	5.3

As for comment, this need only be brief. Despite the substantial increase in cases reported, due largely to the virtual quadrupling of 'gassing' cases, the death rate – as distinct from the number of deaths – was halved. Even so, mortality from anthrax increased, i.e. the proportion of deaths to cases, but 'other poisoning' hardly changed.

Answer to Question 4

This is an easy question in which the only problem is the structure of the table and the derivation of the percentages to facilitate comparison of the figures of each company. As with the previous question, the main need is to read the question and grasp the essential features, in this case three companies with trade in four main areas of the world. As for comment, the only significant point is that the bulk of profits is earned in the United Kingdom and that the one company (A) trades with the U.S.A. and is also more active in the E.E.C. than the other two.

Trading Area	Company					
	A		B		C	
	Amount	% of total	Amount	% of total	Amount	% of total
	£	%	£	%	£	%
United Kingdom	100,000	77	67,000	88	40,000	76
Commonwealth	10,000	8	2,500	4	5,700	11
European Free Trade Area	3,000	2	1,500	2	5,000	9
European Economic Commn.	15,000	12	5,000	6	. 2,100	4
United States of America	2,000	1	—	—	—	—
	130,000	100	76,000	100	52,800	100

Answer to Question 5

Despite the large size of this table and its apparent complexity it is not a difficult table to comment upon. As stated earlier, it is worth spending a little time studying the table and making notes of the more important features, rather than starting to write the report straight away. This ensures first, that the *main* features are picked out and second, the report is marked by some semblance of ordering the main changes in order of importance.

As before, one should start by indicating the purpose of the table, *i.e.* to show the growth in public, *i.e.* government, expenditure, actual between 1972 and 1976-77 and then planned up to 1981-82. The aggregate expenditure is analysed by the major services and the growth therein is measured, not by the annual money outlays but by indices showing the ratio of each year's expenditure to that in 1976-77.

It would be possible to calculate the expenditure in each of the years on any service by taking the appropriate index for the year in question and expressing it in money terms, but at 1976-77 prices using the actual expenditure in 1976-77, given in the central column of the table. Thus, in 1976-77 social security expenditure amounted to £11,220m. Since the index for that item in that year is 100 and the index for 1972-73 is 84, the expenditure in that year but at 1976-77 prices was £9,425m. Looking ahead, it seems that the actual expenditure in 1977-78 is in excess of planned expenditure which should be only four per cent higher than in the previous year.

Attention should be drawn in the report to the main changes. For example, the largest relative increases between 1972-73 and 1981-82, as planned, are on employment services and debt interest. In contrast, the expenditure on education, although much larger in money aggregates, will increase quite modestly over the same period. It would also help if the percentage contribution to the total 1976-77 money outlays from each of the *major* services were to be calculated. For example, education accounts for 14.3 per cent of total expenditure on services. In that way the comparative costs of the individual services would be easier to assess. In picking out the major services it would also be useful to calculate the cash expenditure of the local authorities in 1977-78 on those services. For example, they account for 88.7 per cent of total education expenditure of £8,124m, *i.e.* £7,206m, by far and away the largest single item of expenditure by the local authorities.

Such a question gives a fair amount of scope for differing interpretations as to the more interesting features. For example, from the local government viewpoint, it is the last column which deserves most attention. For the economist it is probably the planned expenditure in relation to 1976-77 and, for the taxpayer, the actual costs in the two years given in the centre of the table. There is no unique correct answer. What the examiner is looking for is the evidence that a candidate can grasp the import of the table, understand how the figures are calculated and discriminate between what is important and that which is less important!

Answer to Question 6

Once again it is essential to consider the purpose of the table and to appreciate the meaning of its contents before starting to draft the report. The main point of the table is, of course, to provide a regional comparison of certain aspects of health in England and Wales. The subject is highly specialised and would not appear in a paper to be taken by general students. Chronic sickness is defined as any long-standing illness, disability or infirmity as disclosed by respondents in the course of a special survey. Both the figures for chronic sickness and the mortality figures in the next column have been standardised for age. In other words, to the extent that age and mortality are correlated, *i.e.* associated, as is chronic illness and age, to achieve a fair comparison between the regions in respect both of mortality and chronic sickness, any distorting effect of the differing age distributions of the regional populations is taken into account. (The technique of standardisation is explained later in Chapter XVII.) Infant mortality is the rate per 1,000 live births of deaths among infants under one year (also explained in Chapter XVII) and is a useful social indicator. The average size of the list of patients of general practitioners provides a rough indication of the extent of medical care available in the region, but as is evident from the table the regional differences are apparently small, although the difference between 2,200 in the south-west and 2,500 in the north-west is 14 per cent, which, in terms of the doctor's case load, may well be significant.

Apart from the explanation of the terms required by the examiner, the actual report is fairly easy to draft. Attention should be drawn in all the columns to the magnitude of the difference between the lowest and highest figures and in the case of mortality, to the contrasting experience between males and females in the different regions. Note too, that a three-point difference in the chronic sickness figures is very different from a three-point difference in the mortality ratios and in the case of infant mortality.

Answer to Question 7

This is a difficult question not least because it is not easy to visualise the framework of the table from a first reading of the question. The correct framework is crucial if the right figures are to be found. There are, to start with, two major classifications of the children; those from manual working-class homes and those from other than such homes. These two main groups are sub-divided into two further groups, those who attend private schools and those at council schools. Within these two latter classifications, there is a further breakdown of each of the two groups of children according to whether they are only children or have brothers and sisters. Then there is a total column dividing the children by reference to the type of home, *i.e.* manual or non-manual working-class.

Once the structure of the table has been established, the actual calculations can be started upon. The total number of children, 7,381 can be entered and divided between the type of home; thus, 78 per cent come from manual working-class homes and the balance – found by subtracting the 78 per cent of 7,381 from that last figure – must be from other than manual working-class homes.

Family background	Private School				Council School				Total	
	Only children		More than one child in family		Only children		More than one child in family		Total	
	Unit	%	Unit	%	Unit	%	Unit	%	Unit	%
Children from manual working-class homes	7	0.1	33	0.4	560	7.7	5,157	69.8	5,757	78.0
Children from other than manual working-class homes	37	0.5	142	2.0	216	2.8	1,229	16.7	1,624	22.0
TOTALS	44	0.6	175	2.4	776	10.5	6,386	86.5	7,381	100.0

The total of those attending private schools was 219 and of these 40 were from manual working-class homes and the balance 179 from non-manual working-class homes. These, however, have to be broken down into:
 (i) only children; and
(ii) more than one child families.
The clue here is that 20.1 per cent of the 219 private school attenders were only children (*i.e.* 44), and of these seven came from manual working-class homes, thus leaving 37 to come from non-manual working-class homes. Since 40 manual working-class children attend private school and seven are only children, this leaves 33 in families with more than one child. Of the above 219, 44 were only children; this leaves 175 in homes with other children of whom 33 (40—7) come from manual working-class homes. This completes the section of the table for Private schools. The Council school numbers are derived by subtraction and addition. Thus, 560 attending Council schools are only children. If 560 is added to the 40 'only' children from manual working-class homes in Private schools we get 600 which, taken from the total number of manual working-class children, *i.e.* 5,757, leaves 5,157. One out of nine children were only children and of these, 44 are in Private schools. Therefore, 776 must be at Council schools, of which number 560 are from manual working-class homes, leaving 776—560= 216 only children from other than manual working-class homes. The final figure, non-manual working-class children from 'more than one child' families attending Council schools is the sum of the Private school children in that non-manual working-class category, 37+142 together with the only children in Council schools, *i.e.* 216. This makes a total of 395 out of the figure in the total column of 1,624 so that the balance is 1,624—395 which equals 1,229.

The secondary statistics required are the percentages corresponding to the absolute figures in the five columns. The only comment is that only children have a better chance of getting a Private school education than those in families with other children. Manual workers' children are less likely to be sent to Private school compared with only children from other than working-class homes.

Answer to Question 8

As with any such fairly large table it is important to spend some time studying the table to ensure that you are clear what it is about and the main points to be drawn from it. This is quite a simple table. It provides two major comparisons. First, it breaks down the population of boys leaving school by type of school attended in 1974-75 and then shows what they do when they leave that school. The same analysis is provided for girl school-leavers and, apart from comparing the inter-school experience of the girl leavers, one may also compare their figures with those of boys.

The more obvious points which merit comment are first, the difference between schools in the proportion of leavers who take a degree course. Thus 41.5 per cent of those attending direct grant schools and 30.4 per cent of those leaving independent recognised schools go on to take such a course at Universities and a further 3.9 and 3.2 per cent at Polytechnics and other institutions. The equivalent percentages from grammar schools are 24.5 and 4.3. These large proportions are in sharp contrast with the handful of boys at comprehensive and secondary schools who go on to study for a degree. The disparity between these particular groups is heightened if 'other full-time education' is taken into account; the former group of direct grant, independent and grammar schools all provide a higher proportion of school-leavers for these institutions than the secondary and comprehensive schools.

The same facts can be looked at in terms of the proportion of school-leavers who take up employment. Thus, among the comprehensive and secondary school leavers the percentage is nearly 90. Of the grammar school leavers 55 per cent go into paid employment compared with only 39.3 per cent of the direct grant school leavers.

The next set of comparisons should be made between the boys and girls. There is the same contrast between the types of schools among the girls as there is among the boys, but the figures for University entry from every type of school are lower than for boys. The attraction of teacher training for girls is marked, 11,900 compared with only 2,900 for boys. As with University entry so with employment, the proportion of girls from each type of school is less than for boys.

If one grouped, say, the comprehensive and secondary schools, one could use the percentages and apply them to the actual population of school leavers and determine how many boys from these schools, compared with the actual number of boys from direct grant or grammar schools, go to University. It is worth noting that 86 per cent of the boys and 85 per cent of the girls attend comprehensive and secondary schools. In other words, only about one in seven of each sex reaches grammar school or direct grant or some similar institution.

CHAPTER V

GRAPHS AND DIAGRAMS

However informative and well designed a statistical table may be, as a medium for conveying to the reader an immediate and clear impression of its content, it is inferior to a good chart or graph. Many people are incapable of comprehending large masses of information presented in tabular form; the figures merely confuse them. Furthermore, many such people are unwilling to make the effort to grasp the meaning of such data. Graphs and charts come into their own as a means of conveying information in easily comprehensible form. It is for such reasons that the government has produced popular versions of important White Papers in the form of multi-coloured booklets full of charts and simple figures. Such pictorial representation admittedly reduces the amount of detail that can be put across to the reader, but very often it is not the detail which is important, but rather the overall picture. For example, few citizens can give figures of the extent of this country's post-war balance of payments position, but most of them have been made aware by publicity employing charts that an expansion of exports is still necessary to pay for our foodstuffs and raw materials.

Diagramatic representation of statistical facts is not only popular with the lay public; it is also extremely useful to the statistician. For example, a few well designed but simple charts showing the trend of sales and costs will be infinitely more eloquent at a board meeting than a mass of detailed monthly figures. Even the statistician himself will employ diagrams to ascertain the pattern or distribution of his data because the character of the distribution will sometimes determine the type of statistical analysis he will employ. There is a large number of diagrammatic forms to choose from; some of the most popular types of chart are reproduced in this chapter. The variety does not arise because statisticians as a class are particularly artistic; the data will usually determine the type of chart used. While there are certain obvious rules regarding the construction of charts, the most important consideration is commonsense. A good policy to adopt is to consider the finished diagram and ask what conclusions can be drawn from it. If they differ substantially from the impressions derived from a brief study of the actual data, then the chart should be scrapped. Some loss of detail is inevitable, but the chart need not be misleading.

A good illustration of misleading design is given in Figures 1 and 2 below. Some years ago during a municipal election, one party anxious to impress upon the electorate its superior performance in house building put up a poster on the hoardings on the lines of the left hand part of Figure 1. By not drawing the base line upon which the vertical bars were drawn from zero, the relative performance of that party was greatly enhanced in the eyes of the casual observer. The fact that the correct figures were inserted in the chart probably did little to counter the first impression. The correct method of drawing this chart is given on the right hand side of the Figure 1. Some criticism

Figure 1

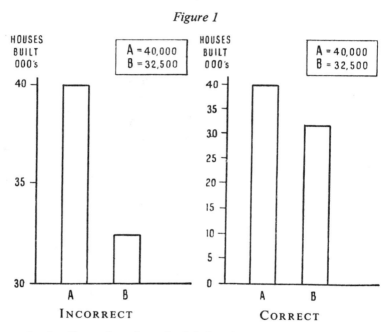

INCORRECT   CORRECT

can also be directed against the left hand chart in Figure 2, which illustrates an advertisement used by one newspaper to demonstrate its popularity *vis-à-vis* its main rival. The vertical axis is clearly marked with the actual circulation figures, but once again, by omitting the base line and the entire lower part of the chart the performance of the advertiser's paper is greatly enhanced. It is undoubtedly true that the one paper had in the space of two years outstripped its rival, but by using a different scale and redesigning the chart, the picture can be made to look rather different. The reader should compare the right hand chart with the original on the left. This is also a bad chart, but

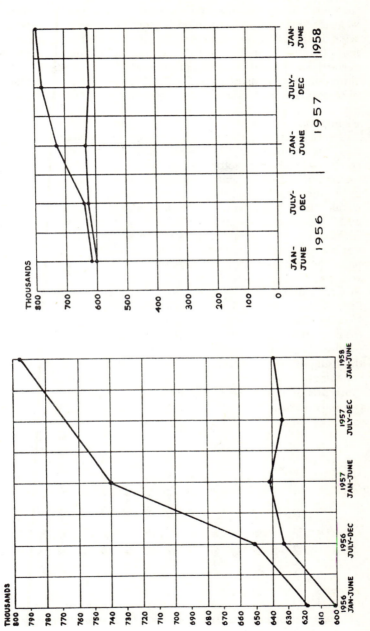

Figure 2

for different reasons. It is badly designed with the bulk of the space wasted. As an exercise the student should draw a new graph. The scale on the left-hand graph is sufficiently detailed to enable approximate figures of circulation to be extracted. In this new graph, the vertical axis should show the origin and at a point slightly above it show a distinctive break as in Figure 11 (page 88) up to the first figure of 600,000 from which point the scale can then be marked off.

Pictograms

Before discussing the various types of diagrams and their uses, a clear distinction should be drawn between the highly simplified and sometimes coloured pictorial diagrams, such as are employed by the Government Departments to explain the economic situation as well as by some leading companies to bring out the main features of their development in the past year to supplement the Chairman's speech, and the graphs employed in statistical work proper. Within limits, the former type, 'pictograms', as they are sometimes called, are most useful. Their main advantage is the immediate visual impact on people who would not normally pay any attention to the more conventional line graph or column diagrams such as are portrayed in Figures 1 and 2. Pictograms are often printed in colour to heighten their impact. Figure 3 illustrates the conventional type of pictogram. Here the information to be conveyed to the reader is the increase in the consumption of light wine in this country between 1938 and 1958. the use of the small glass as the unit of measurement is effective, while the rising number of glasses from left to right indicates the growth of consumption. By placing a figure at the top of each column, a little more precision is given to the inter-year comparison although one can only guess at the precise content of each glass.

Figure 3

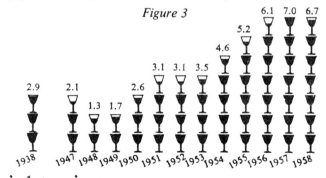

Light wine   Glasses drunk per adult each year

Source: 'Barclays Bank Review', November 1962.

Sometimes, in place of rows or columns of such units, *i.e.* glasses or little men, cars, etc., the same facts, usually a startling increase over a period of time, are conveyed by drawing two similar figures but with the later one drawn several times larger than that for the earlier period. This certainly conveys the message, but such diagrams are considered inferior to the type illustrated in Figure 3, since the relationship between the two units is not always clear. Is it by height or by area or even by volume? As in the above diagram, the appropriate figures are often inserted by the side or even within the unit itself in order to facilitate the comparison.

Simple Diagrams

The conventional method of depicting the information contained in Figure 3 would be to draw thick vertical lines or columns for each year, the height of each bar or column reflecting the change in consumption from year to year. Figure 4 is an example of such a bar or column diagram. It illustrates the changing distribution of medical partnerships between 1961-71 in Great Britain by reference to the number of partners. The height of the bars measured against the vertical scale indicates the number of partnerships of a given size, while the use of two contiguous columns enables a further comparison to be made of the changes in size distribution over the decade 1961-71. The diagram is clear, simple to understand and effective for its purpose.

A popular type of chart is illustrated in Figure 5. This consists of two circles each divided into sectors in order to show the composition of and compare two particular aggregates. The same method of illustration can be used where only one circle is needed. In this particular illustration public sector revenues, *i.e.* governmental revenues, are compared with the corresponding expenditures for the year 1972. The size of each sector within the circle is determined by the ratio of the part of the whole multiplied by 360 degrees. Thus, if income taxes in the left hand circle account for one-third of all revenue, then the sector will be 120 degrees, *i.e.* $\frac{1}{3} \times 360$ degrees. Each sector is labelled by reference to the nature of the revenue or expenditure. In addition to the legend or description of each sector the size of the sector is often inserted, sometimes the actual figure and sometimes the percentage. While this may give the reader useful information, it has the disadvantage of overloading.

There are two major limitations to this type of diagram. The first is that it is all too easy to overload it with information and the clarity of the diagram is thereby diminished. A second weakness sometimes encountered is to use circles of varying size to illustrate, not only the change in composition of two aggregates, but the fact that the aggre-

Figure 4

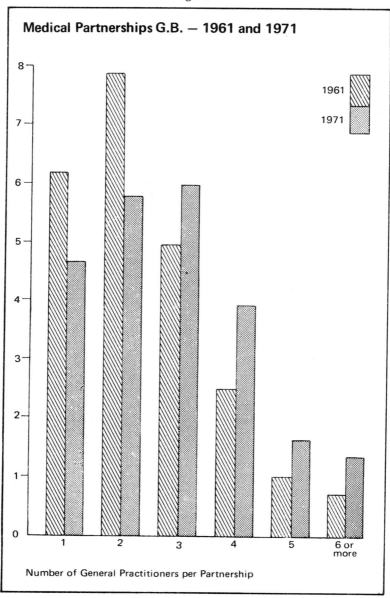

Source: *Social Trends 1973.*

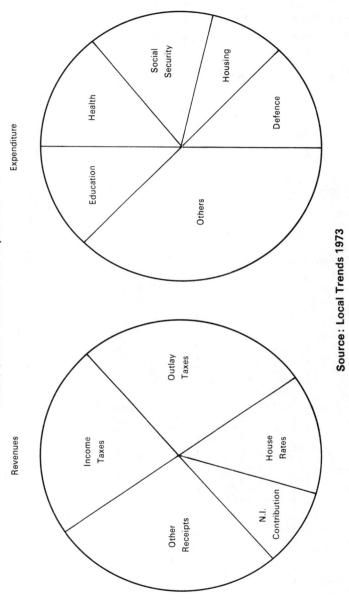

Figure 5

Public Sector Revenue and Expenditure 1972

Revenues

Expenditure

Source: Local Trends 1973

Figure 6

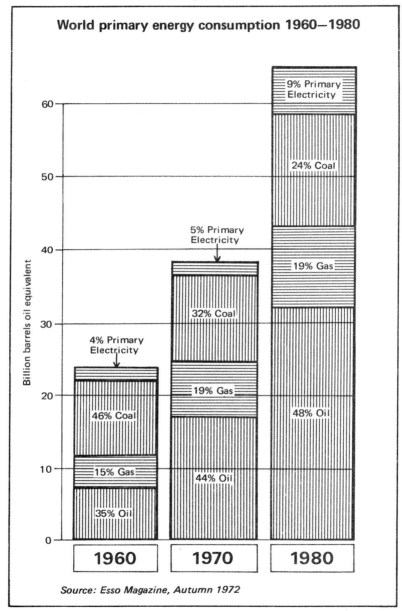

World primary energy consumption 1960–1980

Source: Esso Magazine, Autumn 1972

gates have changed over time. While such diagrams make the point clearly that there has been such a change in the aggregates, it is difficult for the average person to estimate the extent to which the area of a circle has changed in order to judge the change in the total aggregate.

The usefulness of the bar chart is well brought out in Figure 6. The feature of this particular diagram is that it enables comparison over time as well as the changes in the composition of primary energy consumption over that period. For example, quite apart from the obvious increase in total world energy consumption between 1960 and 1980, it can be seen that the relative contribution of each fuel is expected to change. Thus, coal's contribution to the world's energy needs falls from 46 per cent to only 24 per cent whereas that of gas increases from 15 per cent to 19 per cent and oil, at the time of the forecast, would rise from 35 to 48 per cent. The reader will appreciate

Figure 7

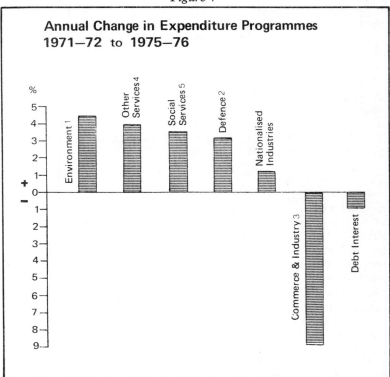

that this is merely a variant on the pie chart in Figure 5 and its limitations are similar. Thus, Figure 6 might be criticised on the score that it seeks to get a little too much information across. After all, the essence of any such diagram is simplicity.

Column or bar diagrams can be adapted in a number of ways; for example, Figure 7 shows both positive and negative changes in the quantities depicted. The vertical bars above the horizontal line at zero indicate increases in expenditure on the specified services, while the two bars falling below the line indicate that expenditure on these services will decline. The extent of the change is measured against the ordinate, positive values being above the horizontal line and those below the zero are negative, as indicated by the plus and minus signs. The diagram is simple and clear.

Figure 8, however, which uses the same principle as Figure 7, is rather less successful. In this case, the extent of the percentage changes is shown on either side of the vertical line; thus, those to the left of that line indicate a reduction and when the bar is on the right it signifies an increase. The actual percentages are read off against the bottom scale which shows the negative and positive values by the appropriate signs. The basic weakness of the diagram is that it tries to do too much. For each category of imports there are three separate bars, each one of which must be read off the legend at the bottom of the chart. In addition, the insertion of percentages for each category of imports specified to the left of the ordinate to show their relative importance within the total of all imports is not really helpful; it may confuse the reader until he has grasped the full significance of the figures, as well as distracting attention from the overall picture presented by the chart.

Time Series Charts

The use of graphical methods for depicting time series is familiar to most people. Cartoonists depicting the business tycoon's office often show decorating the walls, a number of charts illustrating either declining or rising sales. Typical of this type of diagram are figures 10 and 11; both are often referred to as line charts and they represent the most usual way of illustrating time series. Sometimes, however, one comes across a time series which is represented by a succession of vertical bars or columns of varying heights. For example, in Fig. 9 the loans outstanding from financial institutions and local authorities for house purchase are depicted by a series of bars, the height of each indicating the amount of advances at each year-end.

The question arises as to when one uses a bar diagram to represent data collected over time and when a line chart, such as in Figures 10

Figure 8

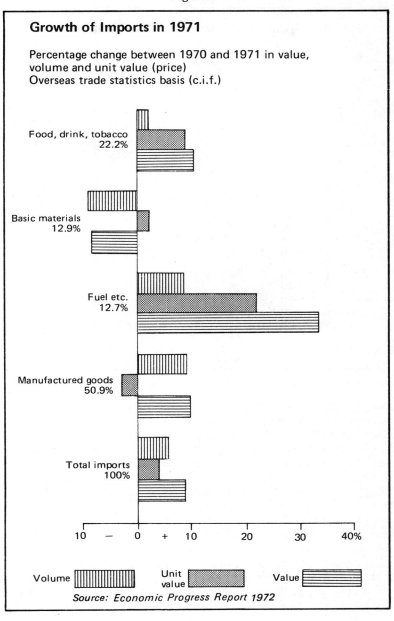

Growth of Imports in 1971

Percentage change between 1970 and 1971 in value,
volume and unit value (price)
Overseas trade statistics basis (c.i.f.)

Source: *Economic Progress Report 1972*

Figure 9

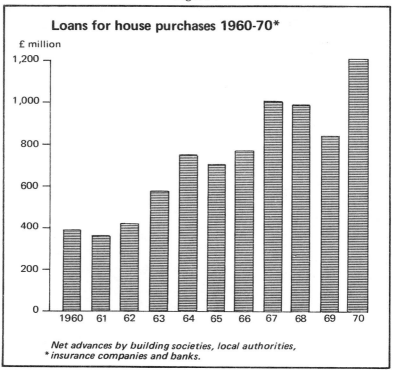

Loans for house purchases 1960-70*

£ million

Net advances by building societies, local authorities,
* insurance companies and banks.

and 11. Generally speaking, this type of bar chart is used when the annual data are measured at a particular single point of time, for example, at the year end or on a particular date, *e.g.* 30th June. The line chart, however, is used to emphasize the fact that the particular series is continuously measured throughout the year as well as between different points of time. In the bar variant of a time series diagram, the bars can be horizontal instead of vertical and the years will then be written along the ordinate instead of along the base line. In the case of the line chart it is the movement between the successive points of time which is significant rather than, as is the case with the bar diagram, the values at particular points of time, although the differences in the height or length of the bars are obviously relevant.

In Figure 10, a simple line chart, the important figure is the number of decree nisi granted, *i.e.* the number of divorces. It is obvious that there will be a relationship between the petitions filed and the

Figure 10

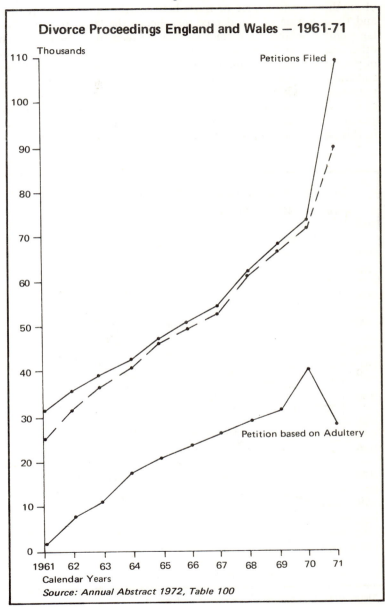

Divorce Proceedings England and Wales — 1961-71

Thousands

Petitions Filed

Petition based on Adultery

1961 62 63 64 65 66 67 68 69 70 71

Calendar Years

Source: Annual Abstract 1972, Table 100

STATISTICS

Figure 12

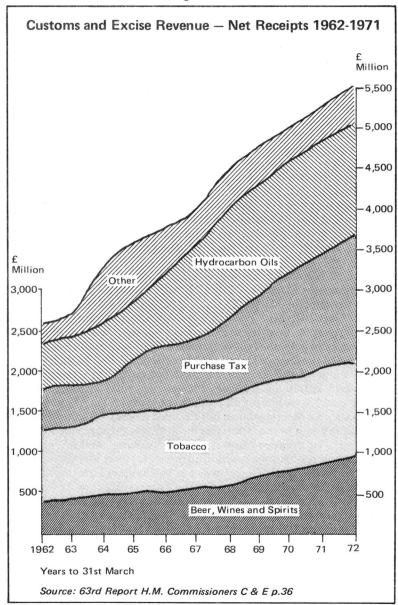

Customs and Excise Revenue — Net Receipts 1962-1971

£ Million

- 5,500
- 5,000
- 4,500
- 4,000
- 3,500
- 3,000
- 2,500
- 2,000
- 1,500
- 1,000
- 500

£ Million

- 3,000
- 2,500
- 2,000
- 1,500
- 1,000
- 500

Hydrocarbon Oils

Other

Purchase Tax

Tobacco

Beer, Wines and Spirits

1962 63 64 65 66 67 68 69 70 71 72

Years to 31st March

Source: 63rd Report H.M. Commissioners C & E p.36

plotted on scales along the ordinate, *i.e.* the vertical scale, in absolute terms. In other words, the space along the ordinate is divided equally into given units; thus, £1,000 occupies the same interval at any stage along the vertical scale. Sometimes, however, it is of greater importance to study the *rates* of the change or the *relative* change instead of the *absolute* change in the series. For example, consider two businesses into which an investor is invited to put his money. Over the past 4 years the first business has earned profits of £25,000, £50,000, £75,000 and £100,000. The alternative business has much larger profits since its capital is larger and, over the past four years, the record is £100,000, £125,000, £150,000 and £175,000. If both these two series were plotted on a line chart the two lines on the graph would run parallel to each other for this interval of four years, the line depicting the first business below the line depicting the second business's profits.

From the investor's point of view, however, the smaller business is more attractive because its profits are increasing very much faster. For example, suppose we call the first year's profit equal to 100; then the successive values for the first business are 200, 300 and 400. Using the same basis of measurement for the second and larger business, the comparable figures are 100, 125, 150 and 175. In other words, the first business has quadrupled its profits in the same time as it has taken the second business to increase its profits by only 75 per cent. For purposes of making such comparisons by diagrammatic methods, the two series can be plotted on a logarithmic scale along the ordinate. The use of logarithms enables the relative or proportionate, as distinct from the absolute, change to be measured. On a conventional scale the space needed along the ordinate to measure the £25,000 annual increase in profits will be the same for the small business when its profits rise from £25,000 to £50,000, as for the larger business with profits increasing from £100,000 to £125,000. On the logarithmic scale the smaller firm's increase of £25,000 will occupy four times as much distance along the ordinate as the same increase for the larger business, reflecting the fact that the former is equivalent to a 100 per cent. increase against only a 25 per cent increase in the second case.

Such logarithmic scale graphs are also useful when the variable which is being plotted is growing very rapidly. This then enables the statistician to judge whether, for all the large absolute increases in annual figures, the annual rate of expansion is being maintained. Consider the data in Table 14 which shows the very rapid increase in the number of passengers using the airports in the London area. Looking down the annual figures it is clear that each year has seen a very large increase. What we want to know, however, is whether the *rate* of growth in this traffic is declining, remaining constant or increasing. This is demonstrated very simply in Figure 13 which uses a logarithmic scale along the ordinate.

TABLE 14

TOTAL PASSENGERS HANDLED AT LONDON AREA AIRPORTS[1]
ANNUALLY 1962-72

Year	Passengers Number	Logarithm	Year	Passengers Number	Logarithm
	(millions)			(millions)	
1962	8·7	0·9395	1968	16·8	1·2253
1963	9·9	0·9586	1969	19·5	1·2900
1964	11·4	1·0569	1970	22·2	1·3464
1965	12·9	1·1106	1971	24·8	1·3945
1966	14·6	1·1644	1972	27·8	1·4440
1967	15·7	1·1959			

[1] Including Heathrow, Gatwick, Luton, Southend, Stansted and Westland Heliport.

Source: Annual Abstract of Greater London Statistics, 1972.

The important feature of such a graph is the *slope of the line* and changes in its direction. For example, the year 1964 witnessed a much faster rate of growth than in the previous year, hence the slope of that part of the line is much steeper; thereafter it levels off slightly. Later the steepness of the line is virtually constant, indicating that the rate of growth is being maintained year by year. If it had begun to fall off in the later years, then the line of the graph would have tended to flatten.

A number of points relating to this graph should be noted. First, it will be seen that there is no origin, *i.e.* a zero value where the ordinate and the base line normally meet. Second, note the way in which the scale has been marked off to help read the values at particular points along the line. The distance between 10.0 and 12.5 is larger than the interval between 12.5 and 15.0 and each successive interval, which in absolute terms is equal to 2.5 mns, is successively smaller reflecting the logarithmic instead of the actual values. Using this scale the intervals measured along the ordinate are same when the *ratio* of the actual numbers is the same. In other words, an increase from 10 mn to 11 mn will require the same distance along the ordinate as an increase from 20 to 22 mn.

Since only the vertical scale in this graph is logarithmic it is customary to refer to such graphs as *semi-logarithmic*, hence the title in Figure 13. It is possible to purchase semi-logarithmic scale paper but it is as well to be able to work without it. All that needs to be done with an ordinary sheet of graph paper is to mark off the ordinate

Figure 13

Total passengers handled at London Area Airports 1962-72

(Data as in Table 14).

Semi-Logarithmic scale

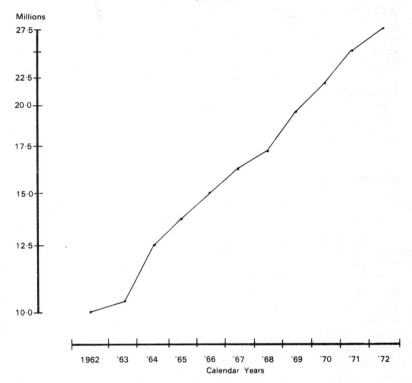

using the logarithms instead of the actual values. Both are shown in Table 14. Those logarithms are then plotted along the ordinate as if they were ordinary numbers. When the line is then drawn, the actual values can be inserted in place of the logarithms. If a slide rule is available, then the quickest way is to lay the log. scale of the rule against the ordinate and mark off the actual values.

Quite apart from the particular advantage of the semi-logarithmic graph in directing attention to the rate of change in the variable as reflected in the slope of the line, this type of graph has the further advantage in that it is possible to depict several series on a single chart even if the absolute values in the various series are widely different. For example, we might have several economic series showing, say, industrial investment in particular industries in tens of millions of pounds, of corporate profits in hundreds of millions, of imports in thousands of millions of pounds and consumer expenditure in tens of thousands of millions. It would be impracticable if not impossible to plot these different series on a single chart using ordinary scales because, if the ordinate scale was large enough to show up fluctuations in the smallest series, then the graph paper would be too small to represent fluctuations in the largest values. If, conversely, the scale were drawn to ensure that consumer expenditure fluctuations were clearly shown, then the fluctuations in the investment series would be so small as to be virtually indecipherable. Using semi-log. paper, which is printed with what are termed 'cycles' of 1 to 10 so that the actual range is then 1 to 1,000 on a single ordinate, it becomes possible to plot all such widely different series on a single sheet and assess the degree to which their movements are related.

The Histogram

If the reader reflects on the diagrams so far described, it may occur to him that they have either been concerned with depicting the make-up of a particular aggregate or with series of data over time. A great deal of statistical data, however, comprises what have been referred to as frequency distributions. Such distributions were illustrated in Tables 3 and 5, or the later tables showing the distribution of taxpayers according to income or trades unions classified by reference to their total membership. Yet none of the diagrams described so far is really suited to depict a frequency distribution of this type, although it is useful to be able to represent such data diagrammatically.

For this purpose the *histogram* is used, and this as may be seen from Figure 14 is a variant on the bar chart. Using the data from Table 3, the workers' outputs are read off along the ordinate. The dependent or frequency variable measures the number of operatives who produce particular outputs which are measured off along the base. The class-interval in the frequency distribution is reflected by the width of the column standing on the base line; the height of the bar measured against the ordinate indicates the frequency of the values within that particular class interval. Thus, referring to Table 3 on page 48 it is evident that the largest single group is within the class-interval 540-9 with a frequency of 47. From Figure 14 this is reflected in the fact that the highest bar is over the values marked 540-9 along the base and drawn to the appropriate height along the ordinate.

The usual method of drawing such a graph, given that the ordinate has been marked off with the appropriate frequencies and the base

Figure 14
HISTOGRAM

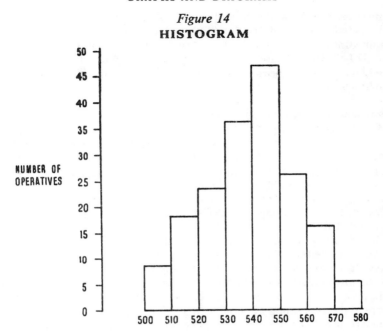

NUMBER OF
OPERATIVES

OUTPUT   IN   UNITS

Source: Data in Table 3.

line dividing the independent or value variable according to the class-interval, is to draw single vertical lines from the mid-point of the class interval. Then, given this succession of lines, the height of each reflecting the frequency appropriate to the corresponding class, a flat line can be drawn across the line equal to the width of the class interval on the base and its extremities joined to the base by two perpendiculars to form the column. The original guide line in the middle of the column can then be erased. The effect is to produce a series of contiguous columns or rectangles and, in a frequency distribution in which the class-interval is constant, the width of all the bars or columns is the same. All that then matters is the height of those columns. Sometimes, however, particularly at the extremes of a frequency distribution, we have either open-ended classes or a class-interval which is twice the size of those preceding it. In that case the height of the column must be adjusted to take account of the double-width of the interval. Thus, if the actual frequencies in the final class within a double class-interval were 50 in number, then it is necessary to draw the height of the column only up to 25. This ensures that the area of that column is proportional to its frequencies. To illustrate, suppose the final class in Table 3 had net read '570-9' but '570-89. In that case, the width of the final column in Figure 14 would have been doubled and its height half that of the last shown in that diagram.

Continuous and Discrete Variables

The importance of this distinction between these types of variable, *i.e.* discrete and continuous, was discussed earlier in the chapter on tabulation. It is also relevant in discussing the appropriate form of graph for depicting certain data. Take, for example, the distribution of households by the number of children per household. A line graph with the frequencies plotted against the ordinate and the values 0, 1, 2, etc., along the base would not make sense. It could be interpreted from such a chart that there were (say) 549 households with 1.6 children apiece because a continuous line implies that a reading can be taken from the line at any point.

As a general rule, line charts and histograms in which the bars are contiguous should be kept solely for plotting the course or distribution of given values of a continous variable. If the variable is discrete, then column diagrams, such as Figure 9, with a gap between each bar or column are conventionally used. In some cases the distribution is such that although the variable is discrete it can be regarded for practical purposes as continuous. The reason for doing this is that if we can assume a variable to be continuous, the statistician can use certain statistical techniques which are extremely useful but which lie beyond our purview. The point can be illustrated by noting the histogram in Figure 14 which relates, strictly speaking, to a discrete variable. After all, a single article produced in a factory can be no more nor less than one unit. But since the differences between successive values of this variable are so small in relation to the value of any single worker's output, *e.g.* 580 units, we are in the same position as with temperature recordings given to the nearest unit which we stated represented a continuous variable. The same is true of frequency distributions of money sums where the difference between successive recorded values of the variable are small in relation to the individual values themselves.

Lorenz Curves

A great deal is heard in political discussion of the need for a greater degree of equality in the distribution of income and wealth in our society. In the industrial field, there is a corresponding measure of criticism of the trend towards monopoly in industry. Now, to discuss rationally such matters it is essential first to agree on the facts. In recent years the Inland Revenue has greatly improved its statistics not only concerning personal incomes but, more especially, of personal wealth. Table 15 shows the distribution of personal incomes before tax; in particular one can read off the number of incomes within each income class and the total income before tax received by each income class. Such data can be adapted to provide a useful measure of the extent to which the actual distribution of incomes departs from, or falls short of, perfect equality.

In Tables 15 and 16 the data in the first two of the three columns in each of the years in Table 7 (p.53) are converted into percentage terms. For example, in the original table 4,738,000 out of the total number of incomes were in the class 'under £400.' In other words, 22.9 per cent of all incomes in 1959-60 were under £400. Collectively these incomes totalled £1,386 which is equal to 9.1 per cent of the total of all personal incomes. Thus, assuming the figures and the arithmetic to be correct, it can be asserted that 22·9 per cent of all income recipients in the United Kingdom in 1959-60 received only 9.1 per cent of total incomes. At the other end of the distribution, *i.e.* the income class of £5,000 and over, a similar calculation reveals that 0.4 per cent of all income recipients enjoyed 4.7 per cent of total incomes. This conversion of the actual figures into percentages can be done for each income class in both years; the results are set out in Table 15. It is, of course, possible to compare the resultant distributions for the two years but the increase in income levels

TABLE 15

PERCENTAGE DISTRIBUTION OF PERSONAL INCOME[1]
(DATA FROM TABLE 7)

Income £	1959-60		1969-70	
	Number of Incomes %	Income before tax %	Number of Incomes %	Income before tax %
Under 400	22·9	9·1	3·4	0·9
400-600	23·9	16·4	11·8	4·4
600-800	23·3	21·9	12·3	6·4
800-1,000	14·2	17·1	12·1	8·1
1,000-1,250	8·0	12·0	15·0	12·4
1,250-1,500	3·0	5·5	13·7	13·8
1,500-2,000	2·2	5·0	19·4	24·8
2,000-5,000	2·1	8·4	11·1	21·8
5,000 and over	0·4	4·7	1·2	7·4
TOTAL[1]	100·0	100·0	100·0	100·0

[1] Totals may not agree due to rounding.

generally, due in greater part to inflation and lesser part to rising living standards, makes the comparison difficult. In particular, it is virtually impossible merely by looking at Table 15 to judge whether over that decade the distribution of incomes has become more equal or not.

To enable such a conclusion to be drawn we use what is known as a Lorenz curve. This is derived from Table 16 in which the data in Table 15 are cumulated, *i.e.* the successive percentages in each column are added together working from the top of the table downward. Thus, in the first column of Table 15 the successive percentages

TABLE 16

CUMULATIVE PERCENTAGE DISTRIBUTION BASED ON DATA IN TABLE 15

Income £	1959-60		1969-70	
	Number of Incomes %	Income before tax %	Number of Incomes %	Income before tax %
Under 400	22·9	9·1	3·4	0·9
400-600	46·8	25·5	15·2	5·3
600-800	70·1	47·4	27·5	11·7
800-1,000	84·3	64·5	39·6	19·8
1,000-1,250	92·3	76·5	54·6	32·2
1,250-1,500	95·3	82·0	68·3	46·0
1,500-2,000	97·5	87·0	87·7	70·8
2,000-5,000	99·6	95·4	98·8	92·6
5,000 and over	100·0	100·0	100·0	100·0

of 22.9 and 23.9, when added together, give the second value in the corresponding column of Table 16, *i.e.* 46.8. By adding the next figure in Table 15, *i.e.* 23.3 to the preceding total of 46.8 we get 70.1. This process of accumulating the successive percentages until they total 100 per cent is carried out for each of the four columns.

Figure 15 shows the Lorenz curves for the 1959-60 and 1969-70 cumulative distribution as derived in Table 16. The two curves are drawn in the following manner. The cumulative percentages of incomes and the share in total income are plotted for the successive income classes against the base line and ordinate respectively. Both of these two lines are marked off from 0 to 100 and each income class in Table 16 has two values which locate the points on the graph. Thus, the first point in the 1959-60 line is given by reading along the base 22.9 and 9.1 along the vertical; the next point is at 46.8 along the base line and 25.5 along the vertical axis.

When all the points have been plotted they are joined by a single continuous line as on the graph for 1959-60; the line for 1969-70 is

Figure 15

LORENZ CURVE of Income Distribution in U.K.
(Based on Data in Table 16)

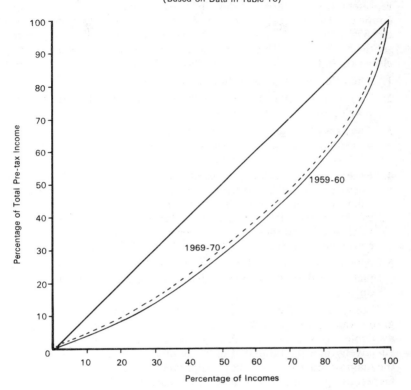

broken merely to distinguish it from the earlier line since the two lines are very close. The diagonal straight line which joins the bottom left hand corner to the top right of the graph represents a perfectly equal distribution of income; thus 25 per cent of incomes have 25 per cent of total income; 50 per cent have 50 per cent of all incomes, etc. The divergence from this theoretical standard of perfect equality is shown by the gap between the diagonal and the curve depicting the actual distribution. Since the curve for 1969-70 is marginally closer to the diagonal than the curve for the earlier year, it follows that over the intervening period there has been a very slight shift towards a greater measure of equality in income distribution.

Summary

The type of diagram to be used for depicting given data does not usually pose serious problems. As with tabulation, diagrammatic representation of statistical data is largely a matter of commonsense coupled with a few rather obvious rules. Since experience shows that these rules tend, all too often, to be overlooked, it may be helpful to set them out below. The charts and graphs in the previous pages and elsewhere in the book can then be assessed in the light of these rules.

1. The title should be brief but self-explanatory.

2. The source of the data plotted should be given so that the reader may consult them for himself.

3. The axes of the graph or chart must be clearly labelled so that the quantities and values to which they refer are immediately apparent.

4. Except for logarithmic graphs, always show the origin. Whenever the values are such that the points plotted will normally lie a considerable distance from the origin and lead to a compression of the scale, then the graph may be 'broken' or 'torn' across the vertical axis and the relevant values marked off along virtually the entire length of the ordinate as in Figure 11.

5. Always bear in mind that graphs are meant to simplify the picture; a detailed or overloaded chart or graph defeats its own object.

Finally, it should not be forgotten that the addition of a diagram or graph among the published data adds nothing to what is already available. Its sole *raison d'être* is that it should drive home more effectively than the tabulated data the main contents of the table. If the diagram does not meet this requirement, then it is better omitted. Generally speaking, diagrams are useful aids to comprehension. The reader interested in time charts will find a varied collection in any issue of *Economic Trends* published monthly by H.M. Stationery Office. In *Social Trends*, an annual publication also published by H.M. Stationery Office, dealing with social statistics (discussed in Chapter XVII) there is an extremely wide variety of diagrams which will help the reader to assess the merits and advantages of each type. Barclays Bank also publishes a quarterly *Review* which contains coloured centre pages of diagrams and charts which merit study.

Questions

General.

Questions in examinations which require candidates to draw a diagram are often linked with some further requirement, *e.g.* a comment on the diagram or reasons for choosing the particular diagram. The comment need not be long nor should the candidate assume that there is only one diagram which is correct. Most data can be illustrated in various ways although, often, one is better suited than the others. However, even if the candidate does not choose the best diagram, it does not follow he will gain no marks. This is especially true where he is required to explain his choice of diagram for the data in the question. Provided he makes sense to the examiner, then marks will be gained.

A frequent shortcoming of answers to such questions is the failure on the part of the candidate to give his diagram a title, or to indicate the units in which distances along the ordinate are measured. If the diagram is of a time series, always remember to put the years along the base and to indicate whether the year to which the data relate is the calendar year or a year ending, *e.g.* 30th June or 5th April etc. Finally, while a diagram should look neat, there is no need to try to make a work of art of it. More marks are to be gained by spending the equivalent time answering some other question. Remember the first few marks out of, say, 20 for the question, are easier to earn than the last five!

The following questions have all been set in various examination papers and, in the suggestions for dealing with the questions, reference is made back to the illustrations in this chapter. The student reader can quickly draft the appropriate diagram and compare his answer with the suggestions made hereunder.

1. The following figures come from the report on the Census of Production for 1958: Textile Machinery and Accessories:

Establishments Nos.	Net Output £000
48	1,406
42	2,263
38	3,699
21	2,836
26	3,152
16	5,032
23	20,385
214	38,773

Analyse this table by means of a Lorenz Curve and explain what the curve shows. *I.C.W.A.*

2. The following table gives the age distribution in 1958 of male teachers in maintained grammar schools in England and Wales who have degrees in science and

Age Group	1st Class Honours	2nd Class Honours	Other Degrees	Total
20-24	23	119	77	219
25-29	68	380	533	981
30-34	34	206	356	596
35-39	57	165	203	425
40-44	104	335	250	689
45-49	160	314	336	810
50-54	147	282	369	789
55-59	72	155	260	487
60-64	41	72	153	266
65 and over	11	13	29	53

Intermediate D.M.A.

mathematics. Compare the advantages of two different diagrams (other than cumulative frequency diagrams) that might be used to illustrate these data. Draw the diagram that in your opinion provides the better illustration.

3. The following table is reproduced from the *Monthly Digest of Statistics:*

Permanent House Building: Construction began. (U.K.)

	All houses	For local housing authorities	For private owners	For other authorities
1958	263,249	119,675	139,076	4,498
1959	324,976	147,721	172,336	4,919
1960	316,741	123,405	186,061	7,275
1961	320,054	120,651	192,950	6,453

Show how this information can be presented in the form of: (*a*) pie charts; (*b*) bar (or column) diagrams.

Comment briefly on the advantages and disadvantages of the two types of presentation.   *I.C.W.A.*

4.   ADDICTS TAKING DANGEROUS DRUGS ON 31ST DECEMBER 1971

Age	Male No.	Male %	Female No.	Female %
16 and under 18	10	1	5	1
18 and under 21	158	14	47	12
21 and under 25	517	46	103	25
25 and under 35	303	27	98	24
35 and over	135	12	156	38
Totals	1,123	100	409	100

(*a*) Draw one diagram to illustrate the main points of this information.

(*b*) Write a short report on these data. Describe, but do not calculate, any additional statistics that you think would be helpful in summarising these data. Give reasons for your choice of any such statistics.

B.Sc. (Sociology)

5.   *Local Authorities' Current Revenue*
                                    (£ million)

	1950	1952	1954	1956	1958	1960
Grants from Central Government ..	298	372	422	521	632	741
From rates	337	392	460	556	649	764
From rents	104	136	185	240	304	362

Represent the information above graphically. Discuss the relative rates of increase.   *B.Sc. (Econ.)*

6. Plot the current and capital expenditure on housing given below, upon a graph, forecast roughly expenditure in 1974-75. Interpret your results, discussing the limitations of your method.

Public Expenditure on Housing
(£ million)

Current

1961-2	1962-3	1963-4	1964-5	1965-6	1966-7	1967-8	1968-9	1969-70
137	126	124	150	174	187	207	233	276

Capital

1961-2	1962-3	1963-4	1964-5	1965-6	1966-7	1967-8	1968-9	1969-70
431	381	532	696	770	825	880	845	800

(Source: Social Trends 1970)   *R.V.A.*

7.   LONDON TRANSPORT ROAD AND RAIL SERVICES 1963-71

	ROAD				RAIL			
Year	Passenger miles[1]	Average journey length[2]	Average receipt[3]	Average cost[3]	Passenger miles[1]	Average journey length[2]	Average receipt[3]	Average cost[3]
1963	4,623	2.13	1.10	1.05	3,075	4.56	1.05	0.98
1964	4,204	2.10	1.26	1.23	3,066	4.55	1.13	1.02
1965	3,786	2.00	1.40	1.46	3,002	4.57	1.18	1.13
1966	3,698	2.11	1.43	1.54	3,054	4.58	1.28	1.18
1967	3,711	2.11	1.43	1.60	3,045	4.60	1.28	1.25
1968	3,701	2.14	1.49	1.63	2,968	4.53	1.34	1.31
1969	3,538	2.23	1.59	1.69	3,187	4.72	1.42	1.38
1970	3,410	2.27	1.85	1.96	3,249	4.84	1.66	1.54
1971	3,315	2.24	2.04	2.27	3,270	5.00	1.91	1.77

[1] millions.   [2] miles.   [3] pence per passenger mile.

1. Prepare suitable diagrams or graphs to illustrate the data and bring out their main features.

2. Draft a brief report on the data and graphs, drawing attention to any features consider significant

C.M.I.

Answers

1.   This is a straightforward question in so far as the examiner has indicated the type of diagram required. Reference to the illustration in this chapter will show the preliminary work required to convert the two series into cumulative percentages. This done, they should be plotted so that the percentages relating to the number of establishments are plotted along the vertical axis and the net output figures, in percentages, along the base. If the Lorenz curve 'fitted' the diagonal on the graph, which it clearly does not, then it could be inferred that the output of textile machinery was evenly spread among all the firms in that industry. In fact, there is a heavy concentration of the output, over 50 per cent thereof in the 23 largest companies. Incidentally, it can be assumed that the establishment frequencies are classified in order of magnitude, probably by the number of those employed.

2.   This is a more difficult question since the examiner has pre-empted the simplest choice, *i.e.* three ogives or cumulative frequency curves. (These are discussed in the next chapter.) On the basis of the diagrams discussed in this particular chapter the best choice is a histogram based upon the total column, with age along the base and the height of the columns reflecting the total frequencies in each age group. The reader may recall that it is the *area* of each column in a histogram which indicates the frequencies of each class. But, where the class-intervals are constant, *i.e.* the same throughout the distribution, then it will be the height which indicates the class frequencies. Note, although the last class is open-ended, it can be assumed the upper limit of the class is 70. Each column can then be split up into three separate parts according to the class of degree gained. An alternative would be to make the age interval on the base line fairly wide and then, within each

interval, draw three columns. They should be contiguous, showing the frequency for each class of degree. Another possibility, but less satisfactory, would be to depict the data in the form of a strata diagram as in Figure 12.

3.   These data are not easy to present either in bar or column diagrams. Such diagrams, especially the former, are best suited to simple comparisons between two years, *e.g.* in this case 1958 and 1961. The main purpose of the diagram is presumably to bring out the changes in the composition of the aggregate of all types of houses, the construction of which has begun. One could equally well use similar diagrams to show the changes in the successive annual totals of each class separately, but it is fairly certain that it is the former aspect of the data which the examiner wants. For the pie diagrams the percentage composition of each year's total will have to be worked out and then converted in the appropriate ratio of 360 degrees. It would seem unnecessary to draw a pie chart for each year; in the examination it would be best simply to draw those for 1958 and 1961; four such diagrams would be too much of a good thing!

The bar diagram would be far better for this purpose. It would be easiest to draw four vertical columns, each relating to one of the four years, and then sub-dividing the column into the component parts. The height of each column is determined by the total number of buildings started. In other words, on the lines of Figure 6.

4.   In so far as the candidate is also required to write a report on the data in the table (this requirement can be ignored for the present purposes) the actual diagram probably carries relatively few marks and too much time should not be spent thereon in such cases. Probably the simplest way of presenting these data is to copy Figure 8, with the age groups against each successive pair of contiguous bars, the length of each bar reflecting the number of cases (male and female) measured off against the base. An alternative or preferably supplementary diagram would be to draw two wide bars of equal length one for each sex, and then sub-divide them by reference to the percentage distribution as in Figure 6. A note could then be appended to the chart indicating the actual number of cases for each sex.

5.   In so far as the examiner asks for a comment on the relative rates of increase in the three sources of funds for local authorities, the most suitable diagram would be a semi-logarithmic scale chart. Figure 13 provides the explanation as to how this may be drawn.

6.   This is a straightforward time series chart with the money values ranging from £124m to £880m marked off along the ordinate and the years along the base. To ensure that the extent of the annual fluctuations are well brought out, it would be simplest to divide the ordinate into two parts, the lower ranging from £120m to £276m and the upper part (there should be a clear gap between them) ranging from £381m to £880m. To ensure the comparative movements are not distorted, it is necessary to use the same scale on each part of the ordinate. The scale could be increased, *i.e.* the distance along the ordinate for each £100m, by drawing ordinates on both sides of the base; the left for, say, current expenditure and the right for capital. The two lines on the chart should be labelled or drawn differently, *e.g.* a dotted line and a continuous line, so that they are distinguishable.

As for the forecast of 1974-75 the best method would be to extend the trend line of the graph for 5 years to provide what would be a very 'rough' forecast!

7.   The method suggested for the previous question can be used for this one. It would be possible to divide the ordinate into two parts but it would be a good deal easier to use the left-hand ordinate for passenger miles, starting with a break above the base line as in Figure 11 so that the entire range of the ordinate is used, *e.g.* from just under 3,000 to just over 4,600 marked off in units of 100 miles. On the right-hand side, the ordinate will relate to the three other figures, average journey length, average receipt and average cost. The range of the variables here is quite small, but the units should be marked off in such a way that even a small change of, say, 0.05p per passenger mile shows up on the chart.

There may be some intersection of the lines and, for this reason, it is important to differentiate between them in the way they are drawn, *e.g.* dotted, dashes, continuous, etc.

The second requirement relating to the report can be ignored at this stage, although there is no reason why the prospective examination candidate should not reflect upon the figures and his diagram and consider what he would say. Note in the case of the road series how receipts and, in particular costs, move inversely with the total of passenger miles. Note too the relative stability in the rail data of the total passenger miles and the fact that average costs have not risen as fast as those of road.

CHAPTER VI

AVERAGES: TYPES AND FUNCTIONS

The Function of Averages

Few people can assimilate a mass of detailed information expressed in numerical form, even when it has been substantially reduced by tabulation. It is helpful, therefore, if instead of merely tabulating the information derived from a specific enquiry and depicting it in graphs or diagrams, it can be expressed in more abbreviated numerical form, yet in such a way that the salient features of the tables are clearly brought out.

For instance, in the case of the firm owning the plant with 180 employees whose outputs were given in Table 1 it may be assumed that this firm controls several such plants of varying size in different parts of the country. The management would be anxious to compare the outputs of the operatives in the various plants. If conditions in each plant are similar, the results should closely correspond. If there are serious discrepancies in their respective production levels, then some explanation must be found. It would be a tedious process comparing all the individual outputs in every plant, finding out the lowest output, the highest, and the most frequent, by such tables and graphs as we have so far employed for illustrative purposes. If all the significant features of the data relating to each plant can be brought out by one or two figures, their comparison is a far simpler task than the detailed scrutiny of the data suggested above. These 'summary figures' may for the moment be described simply as 'averages', illustrated by the following three examples:

1. If, for example, it is stated that the average weekly output of an operative in Plant 1 is 539 units and in Plant 2 with identical working conditions it is 519, such information warrants investigation.

2. If the individual outputs of the operatives in both plants are ranged separately in two arrays, *i.e.*, in order of magnitude as in Table 1, it may appear that the middle worker in the array for Plant 1, *i.e.*, the 91st out of 180, has a weekly output of 540 units, while in Plant 2, with an equal number of operatives, 120 have a smaller weekly output than this.[1] The management confronted with this information would invariably seek an explanation.

[1] To be exact, the *middle* operative in a series of 180 'lies between the 90th and 91st'. This point is discussed later in the chapter and does not affect the present argument.

106

3. Further, if more operatives each produce 539 units per week than any other output in Plant 1, and the corresponding most frequent output in Plant 2 is 515, the apparent conclusion is that the operatives in Plant 1 are for some reason generally more productive.

Given the facts above, together with the ranges of the two distributions, it would be possible for anyone conversant with statistical methods to estimate with reasonable accuracy the general level of productivity in each plant, and even depict the various distributions of outputs as a frequency curve sufficiently accurately to bring out the same essential features as a graph of the complete data. It is because 'averages' summarise the salient features of most data so usefully that they are so widely employed in statistics. In fact, 'statistics' has been described as the 'science of averages', although this is a little misleading in so far as averages form only a part of the techniques employed.

The three specific comparisons made above have now to be considered separately and in detail.

The Arithmetic Average or Mean

'The "average" output of the operatives in Plant 1 was 539 units.' Most people are acquainted with the use of the term 'average' in this context. Thus in cricket, when a batsman has 'averaged' 50·0 runs per innings, no one assumes that exactly 50 runs have been scored in each innings or possibly in any innings; but if the total runs scored are divided by the number of completed innings the result will represent the batting 'average'. Assuming the above batsman completed 30 innings it is clear that his aggregate is 1,500 runs.

Using the data in Table 1, by aggregating the individual outputs and dividing the total by 180, an average output per operative of 539 units is obtained. Reference to the detailed array reveals that only eight workers actually produced this output, and with only this figure as a guide, a somewhat limited picture of the situation would be obtained. This fundamental weakness in this type of average, or arithmetic 'mean' as it is known in statistics, is even more clearly demonstrated by the following example. A prospective investor is informed that three companies, X, Y and Z, have, during the past six years, averaged a net profit of £6,250 each. From this information alone he would conclude that the three investments are equally attractive. An examination of the profits record over the last six years suggests otherwise. The actual figures for each company over the period are as follows and it is assumed for the purpose of this example that the annual profit figures have been adjusted to a common basis in order to eliminate non-recurring and capital items and are therefore comparable.

TABLE 17

COMPARATIVE PROFITS OF COMPANIES X, Y AND Z, 1968-73

Year to Dec. 31st	X Co. Ltd	Y Co. Ltd	Z Co. Ltd
	£	£	£
1968	1,500	8,800	12,000
1969	4,000	7,200	4,000
1970	6,000	6,600	*Loss* 2,000
1971	7,500	6,000	8,000
1972	8,500	5,900	15,000
1973	10,000	3,000	500
	6)37,500	6)37,500	6)37,500
Average Annual Profit	6,250	6,250	6,250

It will be self-evident that confronted with this more detailed information the investor would promptly forget all about the 'average' profits. He would revise his first impression based on the original statement of equal average profits that the investments are equally attractive. In the case of X Company the profits of the past six years show a rising trend; in the Y Company the reverse is true and the two companies are thus poles apart in terms of their attraction to a prospective investor. The last company Z is clearly a highly speculative prospect for the investor, although if the capital were highly geared, *i.e.* a small equity capital and a very large fixed interest loan, so that sharp increases in annual profits would mean disproportionate rises in equity dividends, the investor might be attracted. However, the main point should be clear. The 'mean' by itself can give quite a misleading impression of any series or distribution as it provides no indication of the variation between the actual values within the distribution. Later, in the next chapter, a statistic to meet this need for indicating the range of values will be explained.

Calculation of the Mean

Most people know how to calculate an average, *e.g.* the batsman's average score during the cricket season, or the average annual profits of the three companies illustrated above. In practice, however, the arithmetic mean is not always quite so simple to compute, as is illustrated by the following example. In a certain works, the works staff comprises 100 skilled men, 200 semi-skilled operatives and 50 unskilled men, all of whom are paid on a time basis at £70, £50 and £40 per week respectively. The 'average' or 'mean' wage paid in the works is *not* £53.33 per week computed as follows:

$$\frac{£70+50+40}{3} = \frac{£160}{3}$$

The inaccuracy of this particular result may be easily proved. The total sum required to pay the weekly wages of the factory is £19,000, *i.e.* (£70 × 100, £50 × 200, £40 × 50). The total yielded by multiplying the first mean of £53.33 by 350 workers is £18,666, or £333 short. The correct mean wage is £19,000 divided by 350, *i.e.* £54.28 to the nearest penny.

This type of average is sometimes described as a 'weighted' mean, *i.e.* the separate values or items within the series are each multiplied by the frequency with which each item or value appears. In the preceding example, the weights were the number of employees within each group, 100, 200 and 50 respectively. Such a computation is required when a compound made up of several constituents has to be priced for the purpose of cost accounts or final stock valuation. Thus, if A, B, C and D are four chemicals costing £15, £12, £8 and £5 per cwt. respectively and are contained in a given compound in the ratio of 1, 2, 3 and 4 parts respectively, the resultant compound must be priced out at £(1 × 15) + (2 × 12) + (3 × 8) + (4 × 5) divided by 10, equalling £8.30 per cwt. In the correct statistical sense of the term these figures (numbers of workers or cwt.) are *not* weights – they are simply the frequencies of each value of the independent variable. Unfortunately, the distinction is not always clearly made and all too often the frequency of a single value or group of values is termed its 'weight'.[1]

The calculation of the mean from a *grouped* frequency distribution is different from that employed for the simple series or frequency distribution above. Where the data have been grouped, the exact frequency with which each value of the independent variable occurs in the distribution is unknown. Our knowledge is limited to the fact that, within successive class limits of the independent variable, a certain number of frequencies occur. The procedure for calculating the mean in such cases is illustrated in Table 18. Here it will be seen that for the purpose of 'averaging', the mid-point of the class-interval is selected. This is the same as saying that the average, or 'mean', of the values lying between the limits of each class corresponds with the mid-point of the class-interval. Thus, in Table 18 there are 34 operatives whose individual outputs contain between 36 and 40 rejects. How many there are with 36, 37, 38, 39 or 40, is not known.

---

[1] The main use of weighting is discussed in Chapter X on Index Numbers.

To make any progress at all, however, it is therefore assumed that the mean number of rejects, *i.e*, average, is 38, and corresponds with the mid-point of the class 36-40. Note that in this example the variable is discrete. Hence the mid-point is derived by summing the two limits and dividing by two. This arbitrary procedure is justified on the score that if the number of frequencies is large, the frequencies within each class will probably be spread evenly over the range of the class-interval, *i.e.* there will be as many items below the mid-point as above it.[1]

TABLE 18

REJECTS PER OPERATIVE IN PLANT 4 DURING 4-WEEK PERIOD

(1) No. of Rejects		(2) Mid-point	(3) No. of Operatives	(4) Products of cols. (2) × (3)
21-25	..	23	6	138
26-30	..	28	17	476
31-35	..	33	22	726
36-40	..	38	34	1,292
41-45	..	43	20	860
46-50	..	48	12	576
51-55	..	53	5	265
			116	4,333

Average rejects per operative $= \dfrac{4,333}{116} = 37$ to nearest unit.

It should be noted that the procedure of multiplying the mid-points of the classes within a grouped frequency distribution by the number of items within the respective classes does not provide the mean as such. It produces the mean of all the mid-points of the classes 'weighted' by the frequencies within each class of the distribution. Since, as stated above, the assumption is made that the mean of all the values within each class is equal to the mid-point of that class, the use of the mid-points in order to obtain the mean of the distribution

---

[1] The same arithmetic result will, of course, be obtained if the majority of the frequencies were concentrated on the mid-point of the group as in (2) below and the remainder of the frequencies spread equally over the other four values in the group, *i.e.* two on each side of the mid-point. Using hypothetical figures we get:

(1) Value in units	f	$f.x.$		(2) Value in units	f	$f.x.$
1	16	16		1	5	5
2	16	32		2	10	20
3	16	48		3	50	150
4	16	64		4	10	40
5	16	80		5	5	25
	80	240			80	240

Average $= 3$ Average $= 3$

The student should note that these results arise because the frequencies are distributed symmetrically about the mean.

is permissible. It is, after all, the only rational method of arriving at the value of the mean! Generally, the smaller the class-interval and the larger the number of frequencies in each class, the more likely it is that the 'mid-point' average will correspond to the true average, *i.e.* if the data were given as an array as in Table 1 (p.47) the mean could be calculated exactly.

When preparing the grouped frequency distribution it will be seen whether all the items are dispersed evenly throughout the range of the independent variable. If this is the case, the classes may be taken at the most convenient intervals, *e.g.* multiples of 5 or 10 units as with the data in Table 3 (p. 48). But where, as is frequently the case, there are irregular concentrations at intervals throughout the range of the independent variable, the obvious class-limits may not be suitable. It will then be necessary, as was explained on p. 51, to revise the class intervals in such a way that within each class the mean value will be found around the mid-point. Clearly this is an ideal seldom attainable in practice, but it is important to remember it when a simple frequency distribution such as is given in Table 2 is converted into the grouped distribution shown in Table 3. At some later date someone else may wish to use the grouped data.

Determination of the Mid-Point

Apart from the questions of selecting a suitable number of classes for the grouping of any frequency distribution and the size of the class interval, care must be taken to ensure that no uncertainty can arise in allocating any particular value to its appropriate class. The most common slip is to state the class interval as follows: £10-20, £20-30, £30-40 and so on throughout the range of the value variable. If, after its compilation, a grouped frequency distribution in this form were to be examined, three alternatives concerning the disposition of those units which are multiples of £10, *e.g.* £20, £40, etc., spring to mind. The person responsible for the classification may have had no system at all, sometimes the item was put in the lower class, sometimes in the upper class; *e.g.* £30 could have been put in £20-30 or £30-40. The second course would have been to place it systematically in the upper class, *i.e.* assume that the upper limit of the preceding class was read as 'under £30'. The third alternative would be to assume that the lower limit of the class £30-40 meant all items *over* £30 to be included. The value of any calculations performed on such dubious tables would be problematical to say the least.

The classes quoted above can be written in several ways, and although the differences are not in themselves important, one method may be more suitable than another for a particular distribution. Thus:

(1)	(2)	(3)	(4)
Under £10	£0— Signifying	—£10 Signifying	£0 – £9
£10 and under £20	£10— up to but	—£20 up to and	£10 – £19
£20 ,, ,, £30	£20— not includ-	—£30 including	£20 – £29
	ing £10,	£10, or	
	£20 etc.	£20	

The first is clear enough and can be used for values quoted to the nearest penny. A frequently used alternative to the classification in (1) is given in (2); they are the same. The third example differs from (2) since a value of exactly £10 will fall in the second class in the first example but in the first class in (3). The last grouping is based on the assumption that all the items are given to the nearest pound. The conventional methods for deriving the mid-points of the classes in a distribution differ according to whether the variable is discrete or continuous. If the variable is *discrete*, and the classification written as follows: 1-5, 6-10, 11-15, and so on, the mid-points are clearly 3, 8 and 13 respectively. The method may be summarised by stating that the limits of each class are aggregated and their sum halved, *e.g.* $\frac{6 + 10}{2} = 8$.

Continuous variables are slightly more difficult, since much depends on the correct demarcation of the class limits. If the classes are written as in example (1) above, 'Under £10', and so on, the class limits will depend on the way in which the individual values in the distribution have been expressed. For example, if all are expressed to the nearest penny, the upper limit of the first class is £9.99; the limits for the second class are £10 and £19.99, and so on. Strictly speaking, money values should be treated as a discrete variable, but as for example in the above illustration, the smallest unit of one penny is so very small in relation to the individual values, the error introduced by treating the values as continuous may be ignored. Normal practice with *continuous* variables is to derive the mid-point by halving the sum of the lower limits of two successive classes. Applying this rule to example (3), the mid-point for the second class would be £15. If the values in a continuous distribution are written to the nearest decimal place, the classes could then be written — 10·0, — 20·0, — 30·0, — 40·0, etc., with mid-points of 5·0, 15·0 and 25·0.

When in doubt as to the limits of the class interval the student should consider first the unit of measurement and secondly how the individual values have been defined. For example, if no payment is less than a multiple of a pound then the series is discrete, since the difference between the upper limit of a class interval and the lower limit of the next must be one pound. Such a classification would then read as in example (4). If, however, the values have been rounded to the nearest pound, then clearly a value of £10 in the distribution could represent any value ranging from £9.50 to £10.49. Such a distribution should be treated as a continuous series and the classification should be similar to that given in any of the first three examples. It should be remembered that the grouping of a distribution and the use of mid-points for calculating averages by themselves give rise to possible error in the average. The choice of the class-interval should be as accurate as is compatible with such considerations.

The Short-cut Method

When using the mid-points of successive classes in a frequency distribution to compute the mean, the volume of arithmetic calculation can be reduced in the following ways:

TABLE 19

CALCULATION OF MEAN FROM
GROUPED OUTPUTS OF 180 FEMALE OPERATIVES

Output in Units (1)	Mid-points (2)	Mid-points less 504·5 (3)	No. of Operatives (4)	Products (3) × (4)
500 to 509 ..	504·5	Nil	8	Nil
510 to 519 ..	514·5	10	18	180
520 to 529 ..	524·5	20	23	460
530 to 539 ..	534·5	30	37	1,110
540 to 549 ..	544·5	40	47	1,880
550 to 559 ..	554·5	50	26	1,300
560 to 569 ..	564·5	60	16	960
570 to 579 ..	574·5	70	5	350
			180	6,240

Mean output per operative= 504·5+34·7=539 to nearest unit.

In the example in Table 19, by using the mid-points and subtracting the figure of 504·5 which is common to every mid-point, the arithmetic involved is reduced to very simple proportions.

Such a simple example involving easily manageable figures does not arise very frequently, and a more usual method of computing the arithmetic mean is given in Table 20 below. This method is based upon the simple rule of algebra that the sum of the individual differences between a series of numbers and their mean is always equal to zero. Take for example the following series: 4, 7, 9, 10, 15, 17 and 22. Their aggregate is 84 and the average of the seven figures comprising that total is therefore 12. From this figure, *i.e.* their mean, subtract each of the figures in the distribution in turn. The following result is obtained: —8, —5, —3, —2, 3, 5, 10. When aggregated the differences are equal to zero. The reader may check the rule by testing any selection of values he cares to make. Given this rule the accuracy of an estimated mean may be tested quite simply. Suppose that for the above series we had guessed that the true mean equalled 10. The differences, or as they are usually termed, the *deviations* from the mean, would then be: —6, —3, —1, 0, 5, 7, 12 and their total is 14. Clearly then, if the rule is valid the estimate of the mean is wrong. But if the 'error' is apportioned, *i.e.* 14 units, between the seven constituent numbers, the 'average error' is 2 and if this is then added to the estimated value of the mean, *i.e.* 10, we arrive at the correct value of the mean of the distribution, *i.e.* 12. The student should amuse himself setting out short series of figures and proving to himself the validity of the rule.

The foregoing principle is illustrated in Table 20. The successive stages in the calculation are as follows:

1. Select as the assumed mean the mid-point of the class which contains a high proportion of the units and is nearly central. Since expenditure is given to the nearest penny, the limits of the first class are £54.50-£54.74 and the variable is, strictly speaking, discrete. But, for all practical purposes, this variable may be treated as continuous since one penny is so small a unit and the mid-points are derived by adding together the upper limits of successive classes and halving them.

2. In the column headed 'Deviations from assumed mean in class-interval units', enter 0 against the mid-point to be used as the assumed mean, *i.e.* £55.50-£55.75. Against the mid-points on either side of this latter class enter 1; against the next above and below those mid-points enter 2 and so forth. Where the mid-point is smaller than the selected mid-point representing the assumed mean, the deviation will be negative; thus the upper part of Col. (4) before the mid-point marked 0 will contain all the negative deviations. The reverse applies to the lower part where the mid-points are greater in magnitude than the assumed mean, *i.e.* the deviations are positive. Before inserting the figures, the student should note whether all the class-intervals are of equal size; *i.e.* as they are in Table 20.

3. Each deviation is multiplied by its respective frequency, *i.e.* the frequencies in each class; the negative quantities being kept apart from the positive products to avoid confusion. Both the negative and positive products are then aggregated separately and the balance obtained, *i.e.* + 1,216 —1,461 —245.

TABLE 20

CALCULATION OF ARITHMETIC MEAN OF GROUPED FREQUENCY
DISTRIBUTION OF WEEKLY EXPENDITURE ON FOOD OF 1,783 WOMEN, 1979

Weekly Expenditure		Fre-quencies	Mid-points	Deviations from assumed Mean in Class Interval units	Products of cols. 2 × 4
£	£				
54.50 but under 54.75	..	64	54·62½	—4	—256
54.75 ,, ,, 55.00	..	126	54·87½	—3	—378
55.00 ,, ,, 55.25	..	224	55·12½	—2	—448
55.25 ,, ,, 55.50	..	379	55·37½	—1	—379
55.50 ,, ,, 55.75	..	474	55·62½	0	—1,461
55.75 ,, ,, 56.00	..	227	55·87½	+1	+227
56.00 ,, ,, 56.25	..	108	56·12½	+2	+216
56.25 ,, ,, 56.50	..	74	56·37½	+3	+222
56.50 ,, ,, 56.75	..	31	56·62½	+4	+124
56.75 ,, ,, 57.00	..	43	56·87½	+5	+215
57.00 ,, ,, 57.25	..	19	57·12½	+6	+114
57.25 ,, ,, 57.50	..	14	57·37½	+7	+ 98
		1,783			1,216

Let the assumed mean equal the mid-point of the class £55.50-55.75, *i.e.* £55.62½.

Sum of deviations from the assumed mean = +1,216—1,461 = —245.

True mean = assumed mean + average deviation

$$= £55.62\tfrac{1}{2} + \left(\frac{-245}{1,783}\right)$$

Since the deviations are in class interval units of 25p, the correction to the assumed mean must be converted into pence, *i.e.* $\frac{-245 \times 25}{1,783} = -34.35$p.

∴ True mean = £55.62½—34·35
= £55.28p to nearest penny.

4. The balance, in this case negative, is divided by the sum of the frequencies, *i.e.* 1,783. The result in this example is a *fraction of the class-interval*, not of a single unit. In other words the result is expressed in units of 25p. Reference to columns (3) and (4) will

reveal that the deviations are measured in units of 25p; thus 2 deviations equal 50p as is apparent by subtracting the mid-point of the class £55.50-£55.75 from that of the class £55.00-£55.25. It is important, therefore, that the quotient of —·137 is converted into pence before it is subtracted from the assumed mean, from which the deviations were measured. The result gives the true arithmetic mean of the frequency distribution.

Working With Class Interval Units

The figures entered under the heading of 'deviations from the assumed mean', might have been multiples of 5p instead of 25p, or, for that matter, of any unit always provided the difference between the negative and positive totals expressed in terms of those units is finally converted to the original unit of measurement. If the deviations had been measured in units of 5p instead of multiples of 25p, then the figures in column (4) would have read 0, 5, 10, 15 and so on instead of 0, 1, 2, 3, etc. Equally, the '0', *i.e.* the mid-point assumed to be the mean from which all the deviations are measured, may be placed anywhere in the series, but it simplifies the calculation if put against the class limits between which the largest number of frequencies occur. To exercise his arithmetic and prove this point to his own satisfaction, the reader should re-work the data in Table 20 taking another mid-point as the assumed mean and measuring the deviations in multiples of 5 pence.

It will be realised that there is no need to work in class-intervals, but this is usually the most convenient method when all the class-intervals are equal in size. If, however, they vary, the mid-point method of deriving the mean may still be used. With varying class-limits the differences will be in multiples (sometimes fractions) of the class-interval 'unit'. If, for example, there had been another class at the upper end of Table, say £57.50-£58.25, then the mid-point of this class interval is £57.87½. Had this been the case the deviation from the mean allowed for that class would be 9 and not 8, since the difference between the mid-point of this class and that immediately preceding it is equal to 50p; twice as much as the unit of 25p in which previous deviations have been measured.

Where 'open-end' classes are involved, *e.g.* '£57.50 and over', the difficulty is still greater. If the open-end was necessary there is every reason to assume that one or more of the frequencies did not fall within the limits of any normal class, *i.e.* there is (or are) extreme item(s) which might affect markedly the value of the mean. The usual assumption in the absence of further information is to assume the limits of that class are identical with the others and select a mid-point accordingly. It is probable that the use of this arbitrary mid-point will tend to under-estimate the true mean of the distribution. Since extreme or unrepresentative items distort the mean this compromise avoids that danger, but the method is still unsatisfactory. Sometimes in the case of an open-ended class at the upper end of the distribution, because this indicates some values which do not fall within the range of a single class interval, a compromise is made. This is to assume that the open-ended class has an interval of twice the interval of the other classes in the body of the table. A similar difficulty arises with open-ended classes at the lower end of a distribution, *e.g.* under £54.50. Can we assume that the range of this class is 25p, *i.e.* no value under £54.25, or should it be a double interval on the assumption that all the values fall within the limits of £54 and £54.50?

The only guide is knowledge of the data being handled. For example, if the distribution is concerned with the age of women at marriage, with the first class in the distribution reading 'under 20 years', and the next class '20 but under 25', then knowledge of the law provides the answer regarding the lower limit since no girl under 16 may marry. In practice, the decision about the lower or upper limit of such open-ended classes often depends on the number of frequencies in that class. For example, suppose the top class reads '£57.50 and over'. If only one or two cases are recorded in this class, compared with a marked concentration of frequencies in the body of the table, then it hardly matters whether one takes £58.50 or £60 as the upper limit. This is because it will be swamped in the calculation by the large number of other values in the rest of the distribution. If, however, a large proportion of the total frequencies are in that class, then clearly the choice of the upper limit and the consequent mid-point does matter a great deal. Any error in the choice, *e.g.* a mid-point rather higher than the true mean of that class, will tend to raise the mean of the distribution. In such cases the assumptions used in fixing the lower limit of the bottom class and the upper limit of the highest class should be clearly stated next to the calculation. In examination questions such distributions are often used to test the candidate's understanding of the process and, if he is in doubt, then it is a good practice to write a short footnote explaining the choice of limit made. Some examples of calculations with open-ended classes are given at the end of this chapter and Chapter VII.

Apart from its relative simplicity of computation, the arithmetic mean has other advantages. The statistician considers it a useful measure because it is the result of an arithmetic process and therefore lends itself to further mathematical treatment. In so far as the mean takes into account every item in the series or distribution, it generally provides a reasonably accurate summary of the data, hence its popularity with the lay public who use the term 'average man' to refer to the representative of the majority of the male members of the community. On the other hand this advantage also lies at the root of its outstanding weakness; by including every item in the series the presence of extreme, or even a single non-representative, items may, especially in a short series, so seriously distort the mean that it no longer provides an accurate indication of the nature of the data. Thus, if seven employees receive bonuses of £100, £200, £200, £250, £250, £300 and £1,500 respectively, the mean is £400. In fact, this particular amount is not received by anyone; is in excess of what six out of seven receive and provides no indication whatsoever of the nature of the series on account of the extreme item of £1,500. This weakness occasionally provides one of the reasons for needing other measures which will amplify and even replace the mean. Nevertheless, the latter remains one of the most frequently employed measures in statistical work.

Formulae for the Mean

Reference to the majority of books on statistics will reveal a formidable array of mathematical symbols dealing with the calculation of the mean which convey little to the non-mathematical reader and may even confuse the issue for him. Nor is the beginner helped by the fact that the notation has not yet been completely standardised and statisticians may use slight variations of symbols which are comprehensible to the informed reader but confusing to the student.

Most of the symbols employed are merely 'shorthand' or abbreviations of simple procedures which would be cumbersome if expressed in simple English. The following are typical of the various notations and symbols used.

Thus:

1. The arithmetic mean of a *simple* series, e.g., 2, 6, 9, 12, 15, is

written $\bar{x} = \dfrac{\Sigma x}{N \text{ (or } n)}$. to represent

$$\text{A.M.} = \frac{(2 + 6 + 9 + 12 + 15)}{5}$$

$\bar{x}$ = the arithmetic mean.

where Σ (termed large sigma) = the sum of all x values

x = the individual items.

N or n = total frequencies.

By using Σ the need for the following notation is avoided:

$$\frac{x_1 + x_2 + x_3 + x_4 + \ldots .x_n}{n}$$

where x_1, x_2, $x_3 \ldots x_4$ refer to the individual values of the variable and $n =$ the total frequency.

2. For frequency distributions, such as the wages or chemical compound examples on page 109, the formula may be written:

$$\frac{f_1x_1 + f_2x_2 + f_3x_3 \ldots + f_nx_n}{f_1 + f_2 + f_3 \ldots + f_n} \ i.e., \ \frac{(15 \times 1) + (12 \times 2) + (8 \times 3) + (5 \times 4)}{(1 + 2 + 3 + 4)}$$

which is normally abbreviated to $\frac{\Sigma fx}{\Sigma f}$, the letter f representing the frequencies. Σf, it should be noted, is the same as N or n.

3. The A.M. of a *grouped* frequency distribution is written $\bar{x} = \frac{\Sigma fx}{\Sigma f}$, where $f =$ the number of observations in each class of the distribution. Note that x in this case, *i.e.* in fx, represents the mid-points of the classes.

4. When the A.M. is derived from a frequency distribution by using the *deviations from an assumed mean*, the formula is written $\bar{x} = x' + \frac{\Sigma fd'}{\Sigma f}$, where $d' =$ the deviations from the assumed mean written as x'. (Note: if the deviations are expressed in class-intervals, they must be converted into the original unit values. Thus $\frac{\Sigma fd'}{\Sigma f} \times i$ where i represents the class-interval). This formula applies to the example in Table 20. The student reader may commit these formulae to memory in case they should appear on an examination paper, or more probably, in another text. For practical purposes they are unnecessary at this stage. It is the method, not the formula, which should be learned.

The Median

The nature of the second average employed in describing statistical data was indicated in the passage on page 160: 'If the individual outputs of the operatives are ranged in order of magnitude, *i.e.* as an array, the central figure has a value of 540 units'. The central value, known as the median, divides the distribution into two equal parts. In other words, it is the value which divides a distribution so that an equal number of values lie on either side of it. In this example the one half contains the better operatives and the other the less productive.

Median of Ungrouped Data

In contrast to the mean the task of finding the median is sometimes extremely simple. All that is necessary is to arrange the individual items in order of magnitude; the middle item is then the median. Thus in the following series, 2, 3, 4, 5, 6, 7, 8, 9 and 10 the median value is 6, *i.e.* the fifth figure, with four figures on either side of it. Such is the procedure when the data are given in an array, more usually it is described as *ungrouped* data. It may be located by the formula $\frac{N+1}{2}$ where $N =$ the number of items in the series. When the number of items, *i.e.* N, is odd, then the median is an actual value with the remainder of the series in two equal parts on either side of it. If N is even, then the median is a derived figure, usually half the sum of the two middle values. If these are the same, as they often are, then the median of an even series will also be an actual value.

Median of Grouped Data

More frequently, however, it is necessary to select the median from grouped data. In this case the ranging of the data has already been effected since clearly the classes will be in order. The normal method is to add the class frequencies together cumulatively, as has been done in the example below, and divide the total frequencies into

TABLE 21

DERIVATION OF MEDIAN FROM DATA IN TABLE 20

Expenditure £				Frequencies	Cumulative Frequencies	
54.50 and under 54.75		..	..	64	64	
54.75	,,	,, 55.00 ..	..	126	190	(64+126)
55.00	,,	,, 55.25 ..	..	224	414	(190+224)
55.25	,,	,, 55.50 ..	..	379	793	(414+379)
55.50	,,	,, 55.75 ..	..	474	1,267	(793+474)
55.75	,,	,, 56.00 ..	..	227	1,494	etc.
56.00	,,	,, 56.25 ..	..	108	1,602	
56.25	,,	,, 56.50 ..	..	74	1,676	
56.50	,,	,, 56.75 ..	..	31	1,707	
56.75	,,	,, 57.00 ..	..	43	1,750	
57.00	,,	,, 57.25 ..	..	19	1,769	
57.25	,,	,, 57.50 ..	..	14	1,783	
				1,783		

two halves. The formula for deriving the median from *grouped* data, *i.e.* as in a grouped frequency distribution, is $\frac{N}{2}$. Thus, in the distribution given in Table 21, the median value is located as follows :

$$\text{Median} = \frac{N}{2} = \frac{1,783}{2} = 891\tfrac{1}{2}.$$

The median is located between 793 and 1,267, *i.e.*, in the class with 474 individuals spending at least £55.50 but under £55.75. Therefore the median wage is greater than £55.50 but below £55.75.

$891\tfrac{1}{2}$—793 =98$\tfrac{1}{2}$, thus the median is the 98$\tfrac{1}{2}$th of the 474 items ranged in order of size, these 474 values ranging from £55.50-£55.75.

$$£55.50 + \left(\frac{98\tfrac{1}{2}}{474} \times 25p \right) = £55.50 + 5.3p \text{ or 5p to nearest penny, i.e., } £55.55$$

=median expenditure.

Alternatively the calculation may be carried out by assuming that £55.75 is greater than the median expenditure, and 375 (474—99) in that class spend more than the median amount.

$$\text{Median expenditure} = £55.75 - \left(\frac{375}{474} \times 25p \right)$$

calculated to nearest penny =£55.55.

It will be noticed that the same assumption has been made in the computation of the median as was made in determining the arithmetic mean, *i.e.* that the values within any given class are ranged evenly throughout and, as before, the validity of this assumption will determine the accuracy of the result.[1] This is justified with a continuous series with a large number of classes. If the variable is discrete and the class-interval large, the median may be little better than an approximation, and the result is best given to a round number,

The outstanding advantage of the median resides in the fact that it is not affected by extreme items, as is the mean. Thus if six salesmen take £700, £750, £780, £800, £870 and £1,600 respectively, the median value is £800, which gives a fair indication of the typical salesman's results; the mean on the other hand is over £900 and quite unrepresentative. The median value often corresponds to a definite item in the distribution; the mean seldom. A further important advantage of the median is that it can be located just as easily in a grouped distribution in which the first and last classes are open-ended and the lower and upper units are not available. In contrast it may be virtually impossible to compute the mean of such a distribution with any degree of accuracy, particularly if there is a fairly large number of values in those classes.

---

[1] This assumption need only be valid for the class containing the median, since the median is unaffected by the distribution of values in any other class.

Median by Interpolation

The median can also be interpolated approximately from the *ogive*, *i.e.* the cumulative frequency distribution plotted on a graph as shown in Figure 16. This is true regardless of whether the *ogive* is drawn by cumulating the series upwards or downwards as was explained on p. 49. The reader should cumulate the distribution from

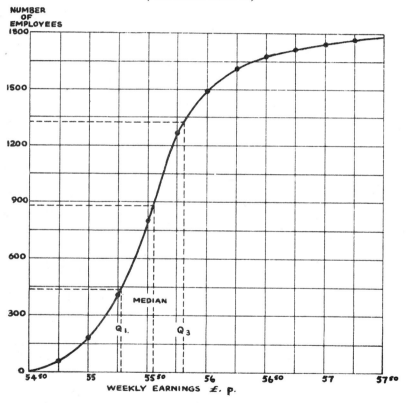

Figure 16

DERIVATION OF MEDIAN AND QUARTILES FROM A
CUMULATIVE FREQUENCY CURVE
(DATA FROM TABLE 21)

the highest value and sketch the corresponding curve. Care is required when drawing either curve that the data are correctly plotted. Thus the curve shown starts at zero frequencies and rises continuously. The first point plotted against the vertical axis, in this case

64 (see Table 21), will be above the upper limit of the class £54.50-£54.75, the next figure 126 against the upper limit of the next class, *i.e.* £54.75-£55.00. Thus, when the frequencies of any given output are read from the curve, they will be interpreted as '190 employees below £55, 64 below £54.75, etc. The student should *not* plot the frequencies over the mid-points of the class-intervals as is done with the histogram (p. 95) otherwise he will read off the wrong results, *i.e.* the values of the independent variable will be too low.

Having drawn the *ogive*, find the mid-point $891\frac{1}{2}$ on the scale representing the frequencies, which in Fig. 16 is the vertical axis. From that point draw a line parallel to the horizontal axis until it intersects the *ogive*. The value of the median will then be read off against the scale along the horizontal axis directly below the point of intersection. The reader can compare the values derived from the graph with those calculated from the data in the example on p. 120. Since both methods of deriving the median are approximate it is not surprising that there are often slight differences between the results.

Quartiles and Deciles

In precisely the same way as is used to obtain the median, it is possible to locate the *quartiles* and *deciles*, the values of which are useful in describing a distribution. As the name of the former suggests, the *quartiles* divide the series into four equal parts, *i.e.* they perform for each equal part of the distribution on either side of the median what the median has done for the whole series. The *deciles*, less frequently employed in practical work than the quartiles, divide the series into 10 equal parts. The method of computing the quartiles of *grouped* data is the same as for the median, except that instead of $\frac{N}{2}$, the denominator is 4, *i.e.* $\frac{N}{4}$. The two quartiles in any distribution are known as the *lower* and *upper* quartiles, the former indicating the smaller value and obtained by $\frac{N}{4}$, and the latter, the higher value in the position $\frac{3N}{4}$. The lower quartile is usually written as Q_1, the upper quartile as Q_3. The calculations for the deciles are similar, the denominator being 10, thus the fourth decile is the observation which is $\frac{4N}{10}$ from the lower end of the range.[1]

---

[1] When the series is ungrouped, the formula for Q_1 is $\frac{N+1}{4}$, and for Q_3 $\frac{3(N+1)}{4}$ if the division yields an odd quarter in the quotient, the answer may be expressed to the nearest unit.

Working on the data given in Table 21, the following results are obtained for the two quartiles:

$$Q_1 = \frac{1,783}{4} = 446 \text{ to nearest unit, } i.e., Q_1 = \text{value of 446th item.}$$

The 446th item lies in the class £55.25-£55.50 containing 379 items, which are assumed to be spread evenly over the class-interval of 25p.

$$\therefore Q_1 = £55.25 + \left(\frac{446-414}{379}\right) \times 25p$$

$$= £55.25 + \frac{32}{379} \times 25p$$

Lower quartile wage = £55.25 + 2.1p = £55.27 to nearest penny

$$Q_3 = \frac{3 \times 1,783}{4} = 1,337 \text{ to nearest unit, } i.e., Q_3 = \text{value of 1,337th item.}$$

1,337th item lies in group £55.75–£56.00 containing 227 items;

$$Q_3 = £55.75 + \left(\frac{1,337-1,267}{227}\right) \times 25p$$

$$= £55.75 + \frac{70}{227} \times 25p$$

Upper quartile wage = £55.75 + 7·7p = £55.83 to nearest penny.

Apart from their value in providing a description of any distribution, the quartiles and deciles are especially useful for comparison of two distributions, *i.e.* contrasting the values in each series at the lower quartile position, upper quartile and so on. As explained above the values of the quartiles or any of the deciles can be estimated from the *ogive*, as was the median in Fig. 16. Note that neither the quartiles nor deciles are averages, they are measures of dispersion and as such are discussed in the next chapter. They are discussed at this stage simply because they are derived by the same methods as those employed in calculating the median.

The Mode

Statements such as 'the average man prefers this brand of cigarettes', or that 'the average woman uses cosmetics', are frequently read and overheard. Used in this context, the term 'average' means the majority and not the arithmetic mean discussed earlier in this chapter. The fact that the mean does not always provide an accurate reflection of the data due to the presence of extreme items has already been stated; similarly, the median may prove to be quite unrepresentative of the data owing to an uneven distribution of the series. For example, the values in the lower half of a distribution range from, say, £20 to £100, while the same number of items in the upper half of the series range from £100 to £5,000 with most of them nearer the higher limit. In such a distribution the median value of £100 will provide little indication of the true nature of the data.

Both these shortcomings may be overcome by the use of the mode, which refers to the value which occurs most frequently within a distribution. This particular 'average' is the easiest of all to find in some distributions, since it is the value corresponding to the largest frequency. Thus in the following distribution which is discrete:

No. of rooms ..	1	2	3	4	5	6	7	8	9	10	11
Frequencies ..	4	9	15	19	24	38	26	18	13	7	1

the modal value or mode is '6', since it appears more times in the series than any other value. The mode is a particularly useful average for discrete series, *e.g.* number of people wearing a given size shoe, or number of children per household, etc.

The Mode by Interpolation

Ascertaining the mode is not always quite so easy as the above simple example suggests, although it is seldom necessary to find it exactly. When, as is frequently the case, it has to be located in a grouped frequency distribution, the mode lies within a given class, *i.e.* within the limits of the maximum and minimum values of that class. The simplest course is to select the mid-point of that particular class; this is no more arbitrary than computing the mean from a grouped frequency distribution by multiplying the frequencies by the mid-points of the corresponding classes. As was pointed out, if the distribution were evenly dispersed throughout its range of values, the result from calculating the mean by this arbitrary method should correspond with the mean derived from a detailed computation.

The assumption that the frequencies in a given class are spread evenly over all the values within the limits of that class is arbitrary but, as stated above, provides in many cases a fair enough approximation to the truth. In some distributions there are more items below the modal value than above it, *e.g.* in the classes below the modal group in value, the number of frequencies may be far greater than the number of frequencies contained in the classes in the upper regions of the table. Such a case is illustrated in Table 22, where the modal class, *i.e.* the largest with 96 cases, lies within the class limits £35-40.

Here, it is found that more salesmen (77) were in the class below the modal class than in the one above, containing 54. Because of this, it is likely that the concentration of the salesmen within the modal class (£35-40) is more marked between, say, £35 and £37.50 than between

TABLE 22

Commission Payments for January 1976					No. of Salesmen
£10 and under £15	..	..	..		6
£15 ,, ,, £20	..	..	..		12
£20 ,, ,, £25	..	..	..		30
£25 ,, ,, £30	..	..	..		53
£30 ,, ,, £35	..	..	..		77
£35 ,, ,, £40	..	..	..		96
£40 ,, ,, £45	..	..	..		54
£45 ,, ,, £50	..	..	..		37
£50 ,, ,, £55	..	..	..		19
£55 ,, ,, £60	..	..	..		8

£37.50 and £40. In other words, had a different class interval been selected for this frequency distribution, it is possible that instead of most frequencies being within the class £35-40, yielding an arbitrary mode of £37.50, *i.e.* the mid-point; the mode would have been located in a new group, say, £35-£37.50, yielding a modal value of £36.25. Such a breakdown of the distribution into smaller or different groups is not possible unless the full data are given elsewhere, and in passing it may be noted that the mode can be markedly affected by the classification adopted in compiling the grouped frequency distributions. The above theory underlies the following formula for estimating the mode which involves a simple exercise in proportions.

$$\text{Mode} = L + \left(\frac{(f_0 - f_1)}{(f_0 - f_1) + (f_0 - f_2)} \right) \times C.I.$$

Where:

L = lower limit of modal group (£35).
f_0 = frequencies in modal group (96).
f_1 = frequencies in group preceding the modal group (77).
f_2 = frequencies in group following the modal group (54).
$C.I.$ = class interval (£5).

Thus:

$$£35 + \left(\frac{96 - 77}{(96 - 77) + (96 - 54)} \right) \times £5$$

$$= £35 + \left(\frac{19}{61} \right) \times £5 = £35 + 1.55$$

$$= £36.55 \text{ to nearest } £ = £37.$$

In this example, the use of the formula does not result in the same modal value as may be obtained by simply taking the mid-point of the modal class, *i.e.* £37.50. This arises because the relative sizes of the two classes adjacent to the modal class, *i.e.* 77 and 54, are unequal. The principle of the theory may be tested by substituting more closely similar figures, *e.g.* 70 and 68 in place of 77 and 54 respectively. The mode derived by using the above formula is then £37.40 which is almost the same as the mid-point, *i.e.* £37.50.

The above formula for estimating the mode is one of several based upon the same principle of proportions. The more complicated formula sometimes encountered represents an attempt to obtain a better estimate. In practice, however, the mode is quite difficult to calculate if some degree of precision is required. The only satisfactory method is to fit a curve to the distribution and determine the highest point of the curve in relation to the independent variable. Even this method can yield only an approximate result; so much depends on the shape of the distribution and the size of the class interval. Hence, in elementary statistical work the mode is not often used except where it is fairly self-evident, or where it is especially appropriate, *e.g.* the modal size in men's shoes is $8\frac{1}{2}$.

Which Average?

While the actual calculation of any of the three averages described above is fairly simple, the choice between them for purposes of describing a distribution is not always so clear-cut. By examining the advantages and limitations of each of the three averages, it is possible to draw up some general rules. What can be said of each of them?

Arithmetic Mean:

i Its main characteristic and virtue is that in its calculation every value in the distribution is used. To this extent the arithmetic mean may be regarded as more representative than the other two.

ii The foregoing advantage also provides its main defect. If in a distribution there are few very large or very small values, these may distort the mean. Thus it may be rather lower than the bulk of the values, or it may be rather higher, and as such becomes unrepresentative.

iii It is basically the simplest of all the averages. Most people understand this type of average. Since it is the result of arithmetic processes it can be used for further calculation. For example, knowing the mean and the total frequency of the distribution, their product gives the aggregate of the entire distribution.

iv Since the mean is often calculated from grouped frequency distributions, the presence of open-ended classes at the extreme ends of the distribution has the result that the mean can only be estimated on the basis of assumptions regarding the size of the class-interval in the open-ended classes. If such classes contain a large proportion of the values, then the mean may be subject to substantial error.

Common sense suggests that the defects and limitations of the mean provide the *raison-d'être* of the other two averages. These too have their merits and shortcomings:

Median:
   i It is a useful average in so far as it divides a distribution into two equal parts conveying the information that the same proportion of values lie above the median value as lie below it.
  ii It is especially valuable for distributions with extreme values or with open-ended classes since it remains unaffected by these values.
 iii To the extent that it does not reflect the distribution in the way that the mean does, *i.e.* by including all values, it needs to be supplemented by other statistics.

Mode:
   i This can be both the easiest average to obtain and also, in the case of a grouped frequency distribution, the most difficult since, strictly speaking, unless it can be easily picked out from the distribution it should be derived by algebraic methods.
  ii When it does not need to be calculated it is an actual value in the distribution and as such forms an important part of the distribution.
 iii It enjoys with the median the advantage that it is not affected by the remainder of the distribution, *e.g.* opened-ended classes or extreme values.

From the above summary it is evident that no single average is preferable at all times to the others. As a rough guide, however, the arithmetic mean and mode are preferable where the frequency curve of the distribution is hump-backed and there are no extreme values in the distribution since, it will be remembered, such values may distort the arithmetic mean. The median is generally the best choice with open-ended grouped distributions especially where, if plotted as a frequency curve, instead of a hump-backed curve one gets a J or reverse J curve. This signifies, in the case of the former, that there are relatively few frequencies at the lower values of the independent variable and many at the upper values. In the latter case, *i.e.* reverse J, the frequencies are concentrated at the lower values of the independent variable and their number declines continuously as one approaches the upper values. Distributions of income and wealth are of this type.

Clearly then, the choice of the average in any given case must be determined by the nature of the data and the purpose to be served by the average. If it is not forgotten that a single average is designed to replace the detail, yet at the same time to provide the outline of that detail, then the selection of the average will be seen to depend on which measure fulfils this requirement most adequately. Since the three 'averages' comprise rather different concepts, the data may be such as to warrant the use of all three, and as will be shown in the next chapter, the relationship between the three measures may be significant. In any case, the chief use of averages is to compare those of one series with the same averages of another but comparable series. In practice, the mean is a firm favourite in so far as it is so readily computed and understood; generally speaking, it should be used instead of the others. But either the median or even the mode will be preferable if the generalisation concerning mid-points in the calculation of the mean is unjustified, or the mean is seriously affected by extreme items.

Questions

General

An examination paper in elementary statistics which does not include a question requiring the candidate to calculate one or more of the averages discussed in this chapter is inconceivable. Most of these questions require not only the calculation of a measure of central tendency, but also of the appropriate measure of dispersion. These are discussed in the next chapter, where further examples of typical examination questions requiring both averages and measures of dispersion are included. But, to ensure that the reader has the opportunity of checking that he has understood the contents of this chapter, several questions involving computation are given hereunder.

Before proceeding to the questions and their answers, two points are worth making for the benefit of the prospective examination candidate. The first is, once the calculation has been completed, to consider whether the answer makes sense. For example, if the arithmetic mean has been calculated and is equal to a value outside the range of the independent variable, or even to one of the extreme values, it is certain that the calculation is wrong. Or, suppose the candidate is required to calculate the mean of a frequency distribution in which the value variable, say, marks awarded in an examination, ranges from 10 to 90. If an answer in excess of 90 or around 10 or 80 is obtained, look again at the calculations.

This may sound obvious or even ridiculous to the reader but, the frequency with which such errors appear on examination papers is such that this warning is entirely necessary. If the frequency distribution has a marked concentration of the frequencies in a particular class, then it is more than likely that the arithmetic average, or median and almost certainly the mode, will be found within that class interval. If, however, the result differs widely from what might be expected, then don't waste a lot of time re-checking the arithmetic. One frequent error is to forget to adjust the mean differences of the deviations for the class interval in which the deviations have been measured. If the error is not quickly to be found and, in your view, the answer does not make sense, then don't hesitate to ring it round with the comment that you believe it to be wrong for one of the above reasons. At least the examiner will know that you have some understanding of what you are trying to do, and not just reproducing a set of calculations from the textbook.

The second point to bear in mind, not least because it is so often overlooked, is to try to keep the columns and figures in line and give yourself plenty of space for corrections which can be read, not least by yourself in the heat of the examination. Time and time again one picks up examination papers in which the columns for calculations are squeezed together, corrections are scribbled in between or over the top of figures which are often almost indecipherable. These generate their own errors because, when the columns come to be added up, the tens column is confused with the thousands, etc. Most examination candidates are short on knowledge, many are left short of time in an examination. But, the one thing that there is more than enough of, is paper. And, don't squeeze up the rough calculations into a corner or margin of the paper, even here it is worth using plenty of space if only because it looks neater! It also means that the examiner can trace the source of any error; it makes a difference to the mark if he can see that the error stems from a mere arithmetic slip rather than a mistake of principle.

Lastly, the bulk of elementary statistics examination papers consists of calculation. There is no royal road to learning how to perform such calculations; the best and most effective method is to practise on past examination papers. Not merely does this ensure that the principles underlying the calculation are understood, but, particularly for examinees, the facility acquired in performing these calculations will stand them in good stead in the examination room.

AVERAGES: TYPES AND FUNCTIONS

1.

Weekly Income (£)	No. of Incomes
Under 10	34
10 and under 12	58
12 and under 14	69
14 and under 16	103
16 and under 18	95
18 and under 20	70
20 and under 24	34
24 and under 30	13
	476

For the above distribution calculate the arithmetic mean and modal income.

Rating and Valuation Association

2. The following table gives the total number of persons dying by homicide in 1960, classified by age last birthday.
   (i) Plot these figures in the form of a histogram.
   (ii) Calculate the mean age at death.
   (iii) If the last class had been specified as '70 and over', what would you consider to be the appropriate measure of central tendency?

Age last birthday		No. of
Not under	*Under*	*Homicides*
—	1	28
1	5	18
5	10	13
10	20	22
20	35	59
35	50	46
50	70	35
70	85	10

Institute of Statisticians

3. *Students admitted to Courses for a First Degree*

Age on Admission (years)	Males	Females
17½–	15	27
18 –	67	73
18½–	67	56
19 –	41	49
19½–	22	20
20 –	11	8
21 –	5	5
22 –	12	2

Calculate from the above data the arithmetic mean age of admission for males and females separately. State precisely any assumptions that you make.

Inter D.M.A.

4. Combine the data of question 3 above into one distribution irrespective of sex. Illustrate this distribution with a cumulative frequency graph. Show how the graph may be used to estimate the following quantities:

(*a*) the median age of admission;
(*b*) the minimum proportion of students who will attain the age of 22 years before graduation, assuming that no student will graduate in less than 2¾ years from admission. *Inter D.M.A.*

5. Distribution of personal income after tax, 1960

Range of income after tax				Number (thousands)	Income and surtax paid (£ million)
£50 and under	£250 ..	..	..	4,540	2
£250 ,, ,,	£500 ..	..	..	7,220	147
£500 ,, ,,	£750 ..	..	..	7,670	391
£750 ,, ,,	£1,000 ..	..	..	4,470	335
£1,000 ,, ,,	£2,000 ..	..	..	2,307	480
£2,000 ,, ,,	£4,000 ..	..	..	262	405
£4,000 ,, over		..	..	31	275

Source: National Income and Expenditure, 1961

Estimate for 1960 the size of the median income and the upper quartile income after tax. What amount of tax would you expect the median and upper quartile incomes to have paid? *B.Sc. (Econ.)*

6. Personal Incomes before tax 1967-68, U.K.

Income Range	Number (thousands)	Income for class (£ millions)
less than £350	903	283
£350 to £450	1,346	539
£450 ,, £600	2,388	1,251
£600 ,, £800	3,058	2,140
£800 ,, £1,000	3,134	2,821
£1,000 ,, £1,200	2,953	3,239
£1,200 ,, £1,400	2,510	3,255
£1,400 ,, £1,750	2,874	4,471
£1,750 ,, £3,000	2,007	4,247
over £3,000	558	3,026
Total	21,731	25,272

(Source: Abstract of Regional Statistics 1970)

Find the mean, median and modal incomes. Which, in your opinion, is the best indicator of the average income? *I.M.T.A.*

Answers

Answer to Question 1

This is a perfectly straightforward question as far as the calculation of the Mode is concerned. In the calculation of the mean, however, attention must be paid to the open-ended class at the head of the table, *i.e.* under 10, as well as the last two classes which have different class intervals from the main part of the distribution. In such cases it is quite a good practice in the early stages of study to include an extra column, before the column headed 'deviations', which gives the mid-point of each class. This makes the derivation of the deviations, particularly when they are to be converted into class interval units, much simpler. In this case the mid-points for the majority of the classes are straightforward. It may be assumed that the variable is continuous and therefore the mid-points of each class will be derived by adding successive lower limits, *i.e.* $\frac{10+12}{2}=11$.

The same method may be used for the penultimate class, *i.e.* 20-24, which, divided by 2, gives a mid-point of 22 and, in the case of the final class 24-30, the mid-point is 27.

The only problem arises with the first class which has no lower limit. Obviously there will not be many incomes of less than £8 and it is not unreasonable to assume that the interval is £8-10. If this gives a mid-point which is higher than the mean of the values within that class (of which the mid-point is an estimate) then it will distort the mean especially if there are a large number of cases within that class. In this class there are only 34 out of 476. The margin of error which the above estimate of the mid-point may involve is not likely to be significant given so small a proportion of the total frequencies in that class.

Weekly Income (£) x	Number of Incomes (f)	Deviations $d_1=2$	Frequencies × deviation f d_1	
Under 10	34	−3	−102	
10-12	58	−2	−116	
12-14	69	−1	−69	
14-16	103	=	=	
16-18	95	1		+95
18-20	70	2		+140
20-24	34	$3\frac{1}{2}$		119
24-30	13	5		65
	476		−287	+419

Mean
$$\bar{x} = x^1 + \frac{\Sigma fd}{\Sigma f} \times c.i.$$

$$= 15 + \frac{419-287}{476} \times 2$$

$$= 15 + \frac{132}{476} \times 2$$

$$15 + .55$$

$$= £15.50 \text{ to nearest 50p}$$

As explained in the text of the chapter, it is easiest to work from an assumed mean which corresponds to the mid-point of the class with most frequencies. In this case, use the mid-point of the class with 103 cases which lie between £14-16; the mid-point here is 15. The deviations are expressed in multiples of the class-interval which is £2. Thus, given that the opening class has a mid-point of 9 and and the mid-point which is taken as the assumed mean is 15, then the deviation from the assumed mean of the opening class is 6 which, in class interval units, is equal to -3. In the case of the class 20-24 with a mid-point of 22, the difference between that mid-point and the assumed mean is 7 which, divided by 2, gives $3\frac{1}{2}$. The rest of the calculations are as in the text.

$$\text{Mode} = L + \frac{f_0 - f_1}{(f_0 - f_1) + (f_0 - f_2)} \times \text{c.i.}$$

$$= £14 + \frac{103 - 69}{(103 - 69) + (103 - 95)} \times 2$$

$$= £14 + \frac{34}{42} \times 2 = £14 + 1.62$$

$$= £15.6 \text{ or } £15.50 \text{ to nearest 50p}$$

Answer to Question 2

This is quite a simple question but note the following points. In drawing the histogram remember that unless the class interval is constant throughout the range of the independent variable, then the width of the columns in the histogram will vary. Since it is the *area* of the columns and not their height which reflects the frequencies, the height of the columns will have to be adjusted to take account of the differing widths. The class interval varies for almost every class; the largest is 20 years, *i.e.* 50-70. Three other classes have an interval of 15 years, while there is one of 10 years, one of 5, one of 4 and the first class interval is only one year. It is easiest to work from the largest class with 20 years as its interval and take the height determined by the actual frequencies. Then, in the classes with 15-year intervals, the height should be 15/20 times the actual frequency in the table and correspondingly for the frequencies based on 10 and 5-year intervals.

The variable class interval also poses some problems for the calculation of the mean. In this case the mid-points of the successive classes have been inserted and this makes the derivation of the deviations from the assumed mean easier. The only problem arises with the second class where the interval is 4 years. There are only 18 cases in this class so almost any figure within reason will not affect the result to any extent. It greatly simplifies the arithmetic if the actual mid-point of 3 is treated as $2\frac{1}{2}$ although, in determining the deviation of the first class, it is assumed that the difference between the mid-points of the first two classes is exactly one class interval unit. The consequent margin of error is negligible, particularly since the mid-points in the lower classes are at best rather dubious estimates of the mean of the values in those classes given that the frequencies are relatively low in number and the class interval is relatively large.

Age last birthday		No. of homicides				
Not under	Under	f	mid-point	$d^1 = 2\frac{1}{2}$	fd^1	
	1	28	$\frac{1}{2}$	-11	-308	
1	5	18	3	-10	-180	
5	10	13	$7\frac{1}{2}$	-8	-104	
10	20	22	15	-5	-110	
20	35	59	$27\frac{1}{2}$	$=$	$=$	
35	50	46	$42\frac{1}{2}$	$+6$		$+276$
50	70	35	60	$+13$		$+455$
70	85	10	$77\frac{1}{2}$	$+20$		$+200$
		231			-702	$+931$

$$\bar{x} = 27.5 + \left(\frac{931 - 702}{231}\right)2\tfrac{1}{2}$$

$$+\frac{229}{231} \times \frac{5}{2}$$

27.5 + 2.5

= 30 years to the nearest year

The third part of the question, which is often asked by examiners, relates to the problem of estimating the mid-point of open-ended classes. The likelihood is that the use of the mid-point as above over-estimates the mean of the ages of the persons in that particular age group. More of the 10 members are likely to be nearer 70 than 85, but since the frequency is less than five per cent of the distribution the resultant possible error is negligible. Had the class-interval been open-ended, *i.e.* 70 and over, it would have been quite sensible to have used the same interval as in the preceding class although since this gives an interval of 20 years it would again lead to an over-estimate of the mean age in that class. In the circumstances, since the mean age of the 10 persons is almost certainly nearer 70 than 85, the best estimate would have been to take a 10-year interval and the mid-point would then have been 75. Whatever the decision, the mean remains the best measure of central tendency. In the circumstances, the answer is given at the end of the calculation as 30 years to the nearest year.

The reader may have noted that, in the various parts of Question 1 and again in this question, all the answers were rounded. Thus, to the nearest year in Question 2, and in Question 1 to the nearest 50p. The same policy has been pursued in the remaining answers. Although arithmetic accuracy is obviously desirable, it must be recognised that there is a substantial element of estimation in the derivation of any one of the measures of central tendency, whether it be the mean, mode or median. The assumption that the frequencies are evenly spread over the class intervals may or may not be true; it is less likely to be true if there are few frequencies than if there are many. Similarly, if the interval is large rather than if it is small. For this reason it is ridiculous to give an answer which may just be correct to the nearest £, to two or three places of decimals. Yet frequently in examination scripts one sees the values for the mean or median which may be accurate only to the nearest £50 or even £100, expressed to three places of decimals, *i.e.* correct to the nearest farthing which was almost 1,000th of a £! The examiner is entitled to conclude that the candidate who does this, does not really comprehend the basis of the method he is using.

Answer to Question 3
This is a perfectly straightforward calculation requiring only an adjustment of the deviations in the lower classes where the class interval is one year and not half-year as in the earlier classes. Note that in this case the two means have been given in the answer to the nearest three months. In all probability this exaggerates the accuracy of the data. It would be more realistic to express the means to the nearest six months, but this would then magnify the difference between the two means to six months, *i.e.* 19 years for men and 18½ for women. It will be noted that the calculation gives a difference of about three months, *i.e.* 18.77 less 18.55 and, on balance, the final figure given in the answer probably reflects the true difference. Note too, that whereas there are only 15 women admitted after their twentieth birthday, the corresponding number for men is 28 and it is this element which creates the difference between the mean ages. The 'tails' of the distributions apart, there is not much to choose between the sexes in the age at admission and thus the approximation to three months gives what appears to be a reasonable result.

	MALES				**FEMALES**	
Age	Number				Number	
$\bar{x}$	f	$d^1=\frac{1}{2}$	fd'		f	fd'
$17\frac{1}{2}-$	15	-3	$- 45$		27	$- 81$
$17-$	67	-2	-134		73	-146
$18\frac{1}{2}$	67	-1	$- 67$		56	$- 56$
19	41	$=$	$=$		49	$=$
$19\frac{1}{2}$	22	$+1$	$+ 22$		20	$+20$
$20-$	11	$+2$	$+ 22$		8	$+16$
$21-$	5	$+4$	$+ 20$		5	$+20$
$22-$	12	$+6$	$+ 72$		2	$+12$
	240		$-246+136$		240	$-283+68$

$$\bar{x} = x' + \frac{\Sigma fd}{\Sigma f} \times d'$$

$= 19+\left(-\dfrac{110}{240}\times\frac{1}{2}\right)$ $=$	$19+\left(-\dfrac{215}{240}\times\frac{1}{2}\right)$
$= 19-0\cdot23$	$19-0\cdot45$
$= 18.77$ years	18.55 years
$= 18\frac{3}{4}$ years to nearest 3 months	$18\frac{1}{2}$ years to nearest 3 months

Answer to Question 4

The data in this question are derived by aggregating the age groups for males and females in the previous question. This substantially increases the number of cases within the relevant classes in which are to be found the median, and the two quartiles. Thus, the median is in a class in which the interval is six months and there are 123 men and women; in the case of the lower quartile 140 cases are spread over a short interval of six months and the upper quartile is in a class containing 90 with a similar interval. The significance of this is the degree of appoximation used for the estimates of the median and the two quartiles. For each, the answer has been given to the nearest month which does not seem unreasonable, not least since if the answers were rounded to the nearest six months, two of them, the median and upper quartile, would coincide.

Age $\bar{x}$	Number f	Cumulative frequencies
$17\frac{1}{2}-$	42	42
$18-$	140	182
$18\frac{1}{2}-$	123	305
$19-$	90	395
$19\frac{1}{2}-$	42	437
$20-$	19	456
$21-$	10	466
$22-$	14	480

$$Me = \frac{n}{2}=\frac{480}{2}=240$$

$$=18\frac{1}{2}+\left(\frac{240-182}{123}\right)\frac{1}{2}$$

$$+\frac{58}{123}\times 6 \text{ months}=2.4 \text{ months}$$

Median $=18\frac{1}{2}+2.4$ months $=18$ years 8 months to nearest month

$$Q_1 = \frac{n}{4} = \frac{480}{4} = 120$$

$$= 18 + \left(\frac{120-42}{140}\right) \times 6 \text{ months}$$

$$+ \frac{78}{140} \times 6 \text{ months} = 3.3 \text{ months}$$

$Q_1 = 18$ years 3 months to nearst month

$$Q_3 = \quad \frac{3n}{4} = \frac{3}{4} \times 480 = 360$$

$$19 + \left(\frac{360-305}{90}\right) \times 6 \text{ months}$$

$$+ \frac{55}{90} \times 6 \text{ months} = 3.7 \text{ months}$$

$Q_3 = 19$ years 4 months to nearest month

The candidate should compare these worked estimates with the estimates he derives from answering this question which also requires the drawing of the cumulative frequency curve as shown in Figure 16. It is quite possible that all three results will differ by three or six months from the calculated answers. If this is the case, check the location of the ogive. Remember that the cumulated frequencies should be plotted over the *upper* limit of the class interval to which they relate. If they are plotted in the middle of the class interval there will be a difference in all three values from the calculated values of three months and, if plotted at the lower end of the interval, then the difference will be six months. The easiest way of avoiding this mistake is to bear in mind, referring now to the above working, that the cumulative frequencies as set down in the above table should be read as 182 below $18\frac{1}{2}$ years, 305 below 19 years, etc.

It should be remembered that *some* difference between a calculated value and an estimated value from the ogive is highly probable. But, where it is consistent and regular for the median and the two quartile values, then the likelihood is that the curve has been incorrectly plotted.

Answer to Question 5

This particular question could be done either by means of the cumulative frequency curve as in Question 4 or by calculation. The reader will note that the question asks him to 'estimate' which term is normally used for deriving the median and quartile incomes from the ogive, instead of 'calculate' which indicates the method shown below. The prospective examinee should practise both methods and compare his results; given the size of the class intervals there could well be some differences.

Most frequency distributions relating to income or wealth usually have open-ended classes at both ends of the distribution; in this case such a class interval is given only at the upper end. However, even if the first class had been described as 'Under 250', *i.e.* open-ended, it would not have affected the calculation of the median and quartile values since these all fall into clearly defined classes.

£	f	cum.
50–	4,540	4,540
250–	7,220	11,760
500	7,670	19,430
750	4,470	23,900
1,000	2,307	26,207
2,000	262	26,469
4,000	31	26,500
	26,500	

$$\text{Me} = \frac{26,500}{2} = 13,250$$

$$£500 + \frac{13,250 - 11,760}{7,670} \times 250$$

$$+ \frac{1,490}{7,670} \times 250$$

48.6, say, 50

$$= £550 \text{ to nearest } £10$$

$$Q_1 = \frac{n}{4} = \frac{26,500}{4} = 6,625$$

$$£250 + \frac{6,625 - 4,540}{7,220} \times 250$$

$$+ \frac{2,085}{7,220} \times 250$$

$$+72, \text{ say, } 70$$

$$Q_1 = 250 + 70 = £320 \text{ to nearest } £10$$

$$Q_3 = \frac{3n}{4} = \frac{3 \times 26,500}{4} = 19,875$$

$$= \quad 750 + \frac{19,875 - 19,430}{4,470} \times 250$$

$$= \quad \frac{445}{4,470} \times 250 = £25$$

$$= \quad £750 + 25 = £775$$

The main problem in this question is the degree of approximation that is needed in estimating the median and quartile incomes. The concentration of frequencies in each of the three classes affected is considerable and, as was noted earlier on this point, where the interval is relatively small and the frequencies within the class large, the estimate can be given with a fair degree of precision. Thus, both the median and lower quartile incomes can be assumed to be within about £10 of the correct figure. In the case of the upper quartile, although there are considerably fewer frequencies within the same class interval as applied to the other two statistics, it would be quite reasonable to assume no greater margin of error in the result.

As for the second part of the question, it is highly doubtful whether any estimate can be derived which is likely to be true. The average rate of tax applicable to incomes rises on a progressive scale. At best one could diivde the number of incomes in each class into the total tax paid by that group of incomes and arrive at a class average. Incomes at the lower end of the interval would normally pay less than those at the upper end of the interval.

Answer to Question 6
The derivation of the mean is greatly simplified by the inclusion in the original data of the total of the 21,731 incomes, *i.e.* £25,272m. The mean income is simply the latter aggregate divided by the number of incomes and can be given exactly. The calculation of the median is straightforward and the estimate of the median income is probably fairly accurate, given the large number of incomes in the class containing the median income. Nor does the mode present any difficulties in calculation.

Income range (£)	No. (000's)	Cumulative frequencies	Income for class (£m)
Less than 350	903	903	
350-450	1,346	2,249	
450-600	2,388	4,637	
600-800	3,058	7,695	See Q6
800-1,000	3,134	10,829	for actual
1,000-1,200	2,953	13,782	figures
1,200-1,400	2,510		
1,400-1,750	2,874		
1,750-3,000	2,007		
Over 3,000	558		
	21,731		25,272

$$\bar{x} = \frac{£25,272}{21,731} = £1,163$$

$$\text{Median} = \frac{n}{2} = \frac{21,731}{2} = 10,865\tfrac{1}{2}$$

$$= £1,000 + \frac{10,865 - 10,829}{2,953} \times 200$$

$$+ \frac{7,200}{2,953} = 2.44$$

$$= £1,002 \text{ or } £1,000 \text{ to nearest } £10$$

Mode $\quad L + \dfrac{f_0 - f_1}{(f_0 - f_1) + (f_0 - f_2)} \times \text{c.i.}$

$$= 800 + \frac{3,134 - 3,058}{(3,134 - 3,058) + (3,134 - 2,953)} \times 200$$

$$+ \frac{76}{76 + 181} \times 200 = \frac{76}{257} \times 200$$

$$+ 59$$

$$\text{Mode} = £860 \text{ to nearest } £10$$

The question as to which is the best measure of 'average' income is more difficult. It is noteworthy that the mean income is considerably larger than the median and, more especially, the modal income. This can be attributed to the effect on the average of the higher incomes which do not affect either the median or the modal income. Given the importance of the higher incomes within the distribution, one must conclude that the mean is a better measure than either the median or the modal income. Note too, that for this distribution where there is no very marked concentration of the frequencies in any class, the usefulness of the mode is greatly reduced.

CHAPTER VII

MEASURES OF VARIATION

Introduction

A brief recapitulation of the content of the preceding chapters may assist the reader in understanding the purpose of the measures to be discussed in this chapter. It may be assumed that the data have been assembled in tabular form so that the initial semblance of order, so necessary to further progress, has been achieved. In the chapter on Tabulation the various forms of presenting the data in full or, more usually, in abbreviated form were discussed. The conclusion was drawn that, helpful as tabulation undoubtedly is in providing some indication of the nature of the data, it is still inadequate to permit rapid comparison with comparable data drawn from other but similar sources. Graphical representation, it was found, was particularly valuable in conveying rapidly and often very effectively, an impression of the nature of the data. They greatly facilitated comparison, although in such diagrams much of the detail had to be sacrificed.

The next stage was to summarise the data from the state of tables and frequency distributions into simple figures which would indicate the characteristics of the series. To this end three averages were discussed in the last chapter, each with its particular advantages and shortcomings. The mean and mode are sometimes referred to as measures of central tendency. The reason will be apparent from the examples already given, since the major part of many distributions appears to concentrate around a central value with the remaining items distributed on either side of that value. It is only because of this tendency, to which further reference will be made below, that the mode and, sometimes the mean, have value as representative items. If all the items in a distribution are widely dispersed and there is no tendency to concentrate around any one value, then clearly no average can adequately summarise the distribution.

These averages nevertheless provide only rather incomplete summaries of any frequency distribution, and important as, say, the central section of any distribution may be, it is also essential to know what form the rest of the distribution takes. (Thus, if the mean age of a group of six people was 25, many varieties of combinations of ages would yield this mean. Thus, 10, 16, 20, 22, 31 and 51 years yield a mean of 25, as do the following: 22, 23, 24, 25, 27 and 29.) Our information is increased if the *range, i.e.* the difference between the maximum and minimum values in the distribution is known. In some frequency distributions the range cannot be given, since the extreme values are unknown. Such an example is given by the income distributions in Table 7, the lower extreme is some unknown quantity 'below £400', while the upper limit is concealed in the group 'over £5,000'. When the range is given, this together with the averages, provides a good deal of information about the frequency distribution. But, since the existence of a single extreme value in a distribution will greatly distort the range, its value in describing the distribution is limited.

For all distributions it is necessary to know how typical, *i.e.* representative, of the distribution the average is; whether most of the values are concentrated around that average or widely dispersed through the range. Clearly, if the intermediate values throughout the range and their distribution can be described in some numerical form, a whole series can be summarised for comparative purposes in a few simple figures. The methods used to this end produce measures of *dispersion* and *skewness*.

The Meaning of Dispersion and Skewness

In Figure 14 the frequency distribution in Table 3 was depicted in the form of a histogram. Instead of drawing a histogram it is easier to draw a *frequency curve*. This is done by linking the mid-points at the top of each column by a continuous line. Where, as is the case with the data in Table 3, there is a marked concentration of frequencies around some central values, such a frequency curve will have a single peak and the frequencies on either side will become fewer and the curve will tail away on both sides. As may be seen from the three examples in Figure 17, the shape of the curve differs according to the pattern of the distribution. The left-hand curve (1) is single-peaked but it is not symmetrical as is the curve (2); curve (3) is also single-peaked but the peak is to the right of centre whereas in (1) the peak was to the left, *i.e.* nearer the ordinate.

If a frequency distribution is of the type depicted in (2), *i.e.* symmetrical about the peak or central value, then the three measures of central tendency discussed in the preceding chapter will all have the same value as measured off along the X axis or base line. The spread of the curve, *i.e.* the distance between the two tails reflects the range of the value variable, while the height of the curve (y) at any point is the frequency of the corresponding value along the base (x). The two curves in (2) have the same mean but the dotted curve is more broadly based than the smooth lined curve. This spread of the values in the distribution reflected in the spread of the frequency curve

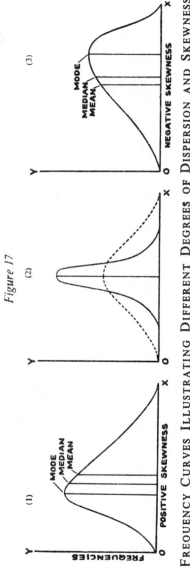

FREQUENCY CURVES ILLUSTRATING DIFFERENT DEGREES OF DISPERSION AND SKEWNESS.

is referred to as the *dispersion*. It can be calculated just as can be the arithmetic mean or median.

When a frequency distribution is no longer symmetrical so that the three measures of central tendency do not coincide, then it is useful to know the extent to which these values diverge. This is done by calculating the measure of what is referred to as *skewness*. That particular value can be either positive or negative; whereas in (1) the peak of the curve, *i.e.* the maximum frequencies, are to the left of the centre of the distribution, then the measure of skewness will be positive. If the distribution is as in (3) then the measure is negative.

It is possible, therefore, to summarise and describe any frequency distribution by these statistics, *i.e.* a measure of central tendency such as the mean, a measure of dispersion and one of skewness, so that with these statistics we have a better picture of that distribution. If similar statistics are calculated for other distributions then they can be compared. With the basic purpose of these measures of dispersion and skewness in mind, the methods of deriving them can now be outlined.

The Range

The first measure of dispersion is the *Range*. This is usually defined as the difference between the smallest and largest values of a distribution or series. The difficulty of ascertaining the range where the classes at the extremes of a frequency table are 'open', has already been mentioned. Where, as is usual, the class-limits are given, by convention the range is taken as the difference between the mid-point of the first class in order of magnitude and the mid-point of the last class. Thus, in Table 24, on page 145, the range of marks awarded is 45, *i.e.* from 13 to 58. This is quite arbitrary, since as a result of the grouping of data the actual value of the smallest and largest items cannot be ascertained. The weakness of the range is almost self-apparent. It requires only one extreme value at either end of the series to render it virtually useless. In brief, dependence on the two extreme items renders the range most unreliable as a guide to the dispersion of the values within a distribution. Its chief merit lies in its simplicity.

The Quartile Deviation

The weakness of the range can be partially overcome by using a measure of dispersion which covers only a restricted range of items so that any extreme values are effectively excluded. The majority of the frequencies of a frequency distribution are often found in the central part, hence, it is natural that the *quartile deviation* should have been evolved. This measures the dispersion of that part of any distribution lying between the two quartiles, *i.e.* upper and lower quartiles.

The formula for the quartile deviation is written $\dfrac{Q_3 - Q_1}{2}$

The reader may wish to refresh his memory on the derivation of the quartiles by re-reading pp 123-4.

The smaller the result given by this formula, the less is the dispersion of the middle half of the distribution about the median. This is the average normally used with this dispersion measure.

The quartile deviation is an absolute measure which is affected by the values of the observations in the distribution. Thus, the Q.D. of one distribution may be much greater than that of another, although the range of values is in fact smaller. This may occur when the central values in the latter distribution are more dispersed than in the former. Alternatively, with a distribution of weights of adult males the quartile values might be 161 and 199 pounds with a median value of 180 pounds. A similar distribution of adult women's weights might give quartile values of 110 and 130 pounds with a median value of 120 pounds. It cannot be inferred from these data that male weight is more widely dispersed than is that for females. The quartile deviation for men of 19 pounds as against 10 pounds for women is due simply to the fact that men are on the whole heavier than women. This illustration will serve as a reminder of the basic rule of statistics; compare like with like.

This measure depends finally, like the range, on only two derived limits, in consequence it is sometimes described as the '*semi-inter-quartile* range'. Unfortunately, it provides no indication of the degree of dispersion or grouping of the other half of the distribution lying beyond the limits of the two quartiles. Consequently, some further measure may be required which will indicate the dispersion of all the items throughout their range.

The Mean Deviation

The mean deviation measures the *average* or mean of the sum of all the deviations of every item in the distribution from a central value (either the mean or median). The mean deviation, therefore, provides a useful method of comparing the relative tendency of the values in comparable distributions to cluster around a central value or to disperse themselves throughout the range.

It will be recalled that in Table 20 on page 115, the calculation of the mean was carried out by use of deviations from an assumed mean. It will be recalled that if the true mean were selected, then the sum of the deviations would equal zero. The difference between the assumed mean and the true mean is given by the average of the sum of the deviations. The same notion is applied in the calculation of the mean deviation. As before, the deviations from the true mean (they may also be taken from an assumed mean, but then a further correction is necessary) are taken and aggregated. To avoid the situation of a zero total, the signs in front of the deviations are ignored. The reason for this is that we are only concerned with measuring the extent of the variation about the mean; not whether more values are above or below it. Having derived the sum of the deviations, it is divided by the total frequencies to give the mean deviation. The principle is illustrated in Table 23, for both the arithmetic mean and the mean deviation.

TABLE 23

(1) Values	(2) Frequencies	(3) Deviations in Class Interval Units from AM=45	(4) F × CI Units	
			with signs	ignoring signs
10 and under 20 ..	2	— 3	— 6	6
20 ,, ,, 30 ..	4	— 2	— 8	8
30 ,, ,, 40 ..	4	— 1	— 4	4
40 ,, ,, 50 ..	8	0	0	0
50 ,, ,, 60 ..	6	1	6	6
60 ,, ,, 70 ..	3	2	6	6
70 ,, ,, 80 ..	2	3	6	6
	29		0	36

$$\text{A.M.} = 45 + \frac{0}{45} \times 10 = 45.$$

$$\text{M.D. (ignoring signs)} = \frac{36}{29} \times \text{C.I.} = 1 \cdot 24 \times 10 = 12 \cdot 4.$$

The computation of the mean deviation is much more complicated where the mean proves to be an awkward number entailing tedious arithmetical calculation in deriving the products of the deviations and their respective frequencies. In such cases an arbitrary origin or assumed mean is selected and the adjustment is made at the end on lines similar to the correction made when calculating the mean from an arbitrary origin as on p. 115. This difficulty usually arises with grouped distributions in which the mean proves to be an awkward fraction for further calculations. Often the mid-point of the middle group is arbitrarily selected as the value[1] from which the deviations may be computed. These points will be illustrated in the examples

[1] Termed the 'arbitrary origin' or the 'assumed' mean.

showing the computation of the next measure of dispersion. The rather complex method of calculating the M.D. from an arbitrary origin is not dealt with here, since this particular measure of dispersion is little used. The mean deviation is nowadays only of academic interest, and in practice has been replaced by the *standard deviation*, which enters into so many statistical formulae.

The Standard Deviation

From the point of view of the mathematician, the practice of ignoring the signs before the deviations when computing the mean deviation is quite unjustifiable and, in consequence, the mean deviation is unsuitable for use in further calculation. On the other hand, to leave the signs in, will, as has already been pointed out, reduce the mean deviation to zero. The standard deviation which is the most important measure of dispersion overcomes this problem by 'squaring' the deviations.

Thus, $(-2)^2$ is 4, just as the square of $+2$ is 4. As with the mean deviation, the sum of the products is divided by the total frequencies. The mean of the sum of the squared deviations is known as the *variance* but, before it can be related to any other statistic, *e.g.* the mean, the square root of the variance must be obtained. This is known as the standard deviation. Table 24 illustrates the principle; the reader should compare the result with the mean deviation computed from the same data above in Table 23. He will note that the standard deviation is larger, owing to the fact that the process of squaring gives relatively greater emphasis to the extreme values in the distribution.

Short Method of Calculating the Standard Deviation

The deviations are usually measured from the mean of the distribution, but if, as is often the case, the mean is not a round number

TABLE 24

CALCULATION OF THE STANDARD DEVIATION

Classes	f	mid-points	d Deviation from A.M. (45)	$f \times d$	$(fd \times d)$ $= f d^2$
10 and under 20 ..	2	15	— 30	— 60	1,800
20 ,, ,, 30 ..	4	25	— 20	— 80	1,600
30 ,, ,, 40 ..	4	35	— 10	— 40	400
40 ,, ,, 50 ..	8	45	0	0	0
50 ,, ,, 60 ..	6	55	10	60	600
60 , ,, 70 ..	3	65	20	60	1,200
70 ,, ,, 80 ..	2	75	30	60	1,800
	29			— 180+180	7,400

$$\text{S.D.} = \sqrt{\frac{\text{Sum of (frequencies} \times \text{deviations squared)}}{\text{Total frequencies}}} = \sqrt{\frac{\Sigma fd^2}{\Sigma f}}$$

$$\text{S.D.} = \sqrt{\frac{7,400}{29}}$$

S.D. $= \sqrt{255 \cdot 172} = 16$ (answer rounded to nearest unit since the original data do not justify greater accuracy).

coinciding with, say, the value of the mid-point of any class, then the calculations could be extremely tedious. Consequently, a method has been evolved to avoid this, which in its essence is the same as the short method for calculating the mean itself.[1] It will be remembered that an assumed mean was chosen and from it the differences for each class worked out in terms of class intervals and the residual or net difference converted and deducted from or added to the value of the assumed mean. To calculate the standard deviation the same procedure is employed with the additional step of multiplying the *products* of the frequencies and deviations, by the deviations. This is the 'squaring' of the deviations required for the standard deviation. Then, as for the mean, a correction is introduced to derive the standard deviation of the distribution from the true mean. Table 25 provides a simple example; the successive steps in the calculations are detailed below.

1. The selection of the mid-points of the classes is relatively simple. The series, is discrete, since the individual values are determinate amounts, *i.e.* one unit is the minimum variation. The mid-points are derived by halving the sum of the limits of the individual class.

TABLE 25

EXAMINATION MARKS AWARDED TO 392 CANDIDATES

Marks	Mid-point of class (2)	Frequencies (3)	Deviations in units of 5 (4)	$f \times d'$ $=fd'$ (5)	$fd' \times d'$ $=fd'^2$ (6)
11 .. 15	13	6	— 5	— 30	150
16 .. 20	18	12	— 4	— 48	192
21 .. 25	23	30	— 3	— 90	270
26 .. 30	28	53	— 2	—106	212
31 .. 35	33	77	— 1	— 77	77
36 .. 40	38	96	0	0	0
41 .. 45	43	54	1	54	54
46 .. 50	48	37	2	74	148
51 .. 55	53	19	3	57	171
56 .. 60	58	8	4	32	128
		392		—134	1,402

[1] If the student reader has forgotten the process he should refresh his memory by reference to p. 115.

2. The deviations are measured from an assumed mean (38, the mid-point of 36-40 group), instead of the true mean, which is unknown. A correction will have to be introduced later to offset the discrepancy this method will introduce into the calculation.

3. The deviations from the assumed mean are expressed, as can be seen in Col. 4, in units of class intervals (multiples of 5) and the result will be expressed in these terms. Sometimes these units are referred to as *arbitrary units* especially when the class intervals are not constant throughout the distribution.

4. Col. 5 gives the products of the frequencies and the deviations (Col. 3 × Col. 4). This column is important since from it is derived the correction to adjust the error introduced by calculating both the mean and standard deviation from an arbitrary origin. The *true* mean equals $38 + \left(\dfrac{-134}{392}\right) \times 5 = 38 - 1{\cdot}7$, or 36 to the nearest unit.

5. Col. 6 gives the results of multiplying Col. 5 (*i.e.* products of frequencies and deviations) by the deviations. This can be verified by squaring all the deviations in Col. 4 and multiplying the squared products by their respective frequencies in Col. 3. The results will be the same as given by the method shown in Col. 6.

The standard deviation from the assumed mean can now be calculated by dividing the total of Col. 6 by the total frequencies and taking from this the correction for the use of an assumed mean. The student should note that the correction fraction $\left(\dfrac{-134}{392}\right)$ is the same for the S.D. as it is for the A.M. except that for the former calculation it is squared. Then the square root of the balance is calculated. The calculations are as follows: the usual symbol for the standard deviation is σ the Greek letter (little sigma), but S.D. will serve equally well.

$$\sigma^2 = \left(\frac{1{,}402}{392}\right) - \left(\frac{-134}{392}\right)^2$$

$$\sigma = \sqrt{\left(\frac{1{,}402}{392}\right) - \left(\frac{-134}{392}\right)^2}$$

It should be noted in passing, that the correction fraction should be squared and subtracted from the other fraction, before the square root is calculated.

$$\sigma = \sqrt{3 \cdot 5765 - (\cdot 3418)^2} = \sqrt{3 \cdot 5765 - \cdot 1169}$$
$$= \sqrt{3 \cdot 4596} \qquad = 1 \cdot 86$$

But σ is still in class-interval units, to convert to the original units $1 \cdot 86$ is multiplied by 5; then σ in original units $= 9 \cdot 3$ or 9 to nearest whole unit.

Characteristics of Dispersion Measures

The major characteristics of the measures of dispersion may be summarised as follows:

Range

 i The simplest to derive and the easiest to comprehend.

 ii Its value as an indication of the variation in the data may be virtually nullified by the existence of one exceptionally large or small value.

 iii It provides no indication as to the distribution of the frequencies between the limits of the range.

Quartile Deviation

 i This measure is not difficult to calculate, but covers only half the items within the distribution. It does eliminate, however, the risk of extreme items which seriously distort the range.

 ii As with the range, its value is based on the values of the two limits, *i.e.* Q_1 and Q_3 with all the attendant disadvantages arising from this fact.

 iii It bears no relationship to any fixed point in the distribution as do the M.D. and S.D.; nor is it affected by the distribution of the individual values lying between the quartiles.

Mean Deviation

 i Unlike the Q.D. it is affected by every value in the distribution.

 ii It indicates the extent of the deviation of all values from a given value, in this case the median or mean of the distribution.

 iii For the purpose of further mathematical treatment the M.D. is unsatisfactory.

Standard Deviation

 i Like the M.D., it includes every value of the distribution.

 ii It is itself the result of correct mathematical processes and thus further calculations may be based upon it.

 iii It is the best measure of dispersion and, as will be seen in the later chapters, is of very great importance for sampling theory.

Coefficient of Variation

It cannot be sufficiently emphasised that all measures of dispersion are in terms of the units in which the original values are expressed.

Thus, the S.D. of the men's heights, weight of cotton bales and sales-men's salaries might be expressed in inches, hundredweights and pounds sterling, respectively. These measures of absolute variation cannot be compared with each other, if expressed in differing units, or if the average values of two distributions in a comparable field are widely dissimilar. Thus, in the case of differing units, if the A.M. and S.D. of one distribution are expressed in centimetres, and for the other in feet, the units must either be converted to a common base, *e.g.* both series in feet, or a standard measure devised which ignores the original units of measurement. Similarly, where the means of the distributions are widely dissimilar, *e.g.* the average levels of remuner-ation received by the administrative and labouring sections of a large organisation respectively, then the dispersions within the two groups can only be compared by relating them to a 'standardising' factor.

This is done by turning the absolute measure of dispersion, *i.e.* the S.D., into a relative measure. More precisely, the S.D. is related to some other measure directly connected with the same distribution, *e.g.* it is frequently expressed as a *percentage* of the mean of that dis-tribution. This new measure is termed the *Coefficient of Variation* normally written as $CV = \dfrac{100\sigma}{\bar{x}}$. Where the distributions being com-pared are expressed in the same unit of measurement and the means are similar, no advantage is to be gained by calculating the coefficient of variation. The S.D. is then quite sufficient.

Measures of Skewness

So far, only the first group of measures of variation have been covered, those which indicate the *dispersion* of the frequencies throughout the range of the independent variable.

The second group was described as measuring the degree of symmetry of any distribution plotted as a frequency curve. Any curve which is not 'symmetrical' may be described as 'asymmetrical', or '*skewed*'. The latter term is generally employed and the statistician refers to measures of skewness. Most 'hump-backed' or uni-modal frequency distributions are skewed (*i.e.* not symmetrical); and to that extent the characteristic of a symmetrical distribution, *i.e.* identity of values of A.M., median and mode, is absent.

It is a logical step, therefore, to develop some measure which shows the degree to which these three measures of central tendency diverge. The difference between them provides the first measure of skewness. This difference, however, could be unsatisfactory on two counts.

1. It would be expressed in the unit of value of the distribution and could therefore not be compared with another comparable series expressed in different units.

2. Distributions vary greatly and the difference between, say, the mean and mode in absolute terms might be considerable in one distribution and small in another, although the frequency curves of the two distributions were similarly skewed.

If the absolute differences were expressed in relation to some measure of the spread of the values in their respective distributions, the measures would then be *relative* and not *absolute* and therefore directly comparable.

The above considerations form the basis of Professor Karl Pearson's formula for deriving what is known as a coefficient of skewness:

$$sk = \frac{Mean—Mode}{SD}$$

The mode was criticised in an earlier chapter as being particularly difficult to determine precisely for many frequency distributions and in such cases a variation of the above formula is used:

$$sk = \frac{3 \ (Mean—Median)}{SD}$$

An alternative measure of skewness was formulated by the late Professor Bowley. This is based on the relative positions of the median and the quartiles. If the distribution were symmetrical then Q_1 and Q_3 would be at equal distances from the median. Then it follows that $(Q_3—Me)—(Me—Q_1)=O$. The more skewed the distribution, the larger will be the difference between these two quantities, which can be re-arranged as follows: $(Q_3—Me)—(Me—Q_1) \times Q_3 +Q_1—2Me$. This measure of skewness is expressed in absolute terms so that if there were two distributions, one highly skewed and the other much less, comprising very different-sized variables, *e.g.* pounds and ounces, then despite the fact that the distribution with the large values was less markedly skewed than the other, the above measure of skewness would yield a larger result. To overcome this weakness, the absolute measure is converted into a relative measure (as in the Pearson coefficient above) by relating it to the quartile deviation, which is itself a reflection of the absolute variation of the independent variable. Thus, we get:

$$sk = \frac{Q_3+Q_1—2Me}{\dfrac{Q_3—Q_1}{2}} = \frac{2(Q_3+Q_1—2Me)}{Q_3—Q_1}$$

Beyond the fact that symmetry (*i.e.* complete absence of skewness) is indicated by O (zero) in both the above formulae, *i.e.* Bowley's and Pearson's, the coefficients of skewness derived by the two measures are *not* comparable.

Formulae for Measures of Dispersion

The mathematical notation of the measures of dispersion like those of the arithmetic mean, given in the preceding chapter, is fundamentally simple.

Only two of the four measures of dispersion are so expressed, the M.D. and the S.D.

The mean deviation calculated from the true mean of an ungrouped series:

$$\text{M.D.} = \frac{\Sigma |d|}{N} \quad i.e., \quad \frac{\text{Sum of the deviations (ignoring signs)}}{\text{number of items}}$$

When the data are in the form of a frequency distribution,

$$= \frac{\Sigma f |d|}{\Sigma f} \quad i.e., \quad \frac{\text{Sum of frequencies} \times \text{deviations (ignoring signs)}}{\text{Sum of frequencies}}$$

The *standard deviation* is usually represented by the sign σ (small Greek letter 'sigma'), but S.D. is often used. For an ungrouped distribution with the deviations taken from the true mean: $\sigma = \sqrt{\dfrac{\Sigma d^2}{N}}$

The S.D. of a grouped frequency distribution computed from the true mean:

$$\sigma = \sqrt{\frac{\Sigma f d^2}{N}} \quad \text{Equally one can write: } \sigma = \sqrt{\frac{\Sigma f d^2}{\Sigma f}}$$

since Σf and N both refer to the total frequencies.

If the S.D. is computed from an assumed mean then:

$$\sigma = \sqrt{\frac{\Sigma f (d')^2}{\Sigma f} - \left(\frac{\Sigma f d'}{\Sigma f}\right)^2}$$

Where the symbol d' denotes deviations from an assumed mean.

If the calculation has been performed with the deviations expressed in class intervals:

$$\sigma = \sqrt{\frac{\Sigma f d'^2}{\Sigma f} - \left(\frac{\Sigma f d'}{\Sigma f}\right)^2} \times i$$

where i = range of class interval or arbitrary unit.

The same comment applies here as was made in connection with the formulae for the various averages. If these processes are really understood, these formulae can always be constructed. Nevertheless, most students prefer, sometimes unwisely, to rely on their memories.

Conclusions

The student has now reached the end of what may be termed 'descriptive statistics'. After collection of the data, all the processes described so far have been in the nature of summarizing with the object of making simple comparisons. Such comparisons can be made between two or more distributions by means of simple tables, or by use of diagrams as was shown in Chapter V. The next stage was to summarise the data still further by means of 'averages' and at the beginning of this chapter it was explained that such averages may describe a distribution very imperfectly. In fact, two widely disparate distributions can have identical means, but whereas in the one case the range of the values is very slight, in the other it is considerable. Hence, it is essential to calculate statistics which will measure not merely averages, but also describe the degree of dispersion of the values within the distribution. In most statistical work, it is not only the tendency for observations or values to conform to an average that is of vital importance. Any tendency for values to diverge from the norm may be of even greater interest to the statistician. Hence, just as we think of Tweedledum and Tweedledee as inseparable, so each measure of central tendency (*i.e.* average) should be quoted with its appropriate measure of dispersion. Thus, the arithmetic mean should always be given with the standard deviation, while the median is linked with the quartile deviation. The student need not worry himself about the calculation of the mean deviation, but he should know what is meant by the range. Likewise, the measures of skewness are of less importance for elementary statistical work; it is the concept which needs to be remembered.

Some Worked Examples

The only satisfactory way of learning how to calculate the measures of central tendency and of dispersion is by practice. Each frequency distribution can pose its own particular problems, *e.g.* uneven class-intervals, or open-ended classes. To provide such practice and to ensure that the reader has grasped the principles involved, the next few pages contain worked examples of the mean and median, quartile and standard deviations. These are the standard fare of all examination papers. The student would be well advised to check that he understands the methods by calculating these statistics from the frequency distributions in Tables 26 and 27 and comparing his working with the answers given.

The first example is really two frequency distributions which offer extra practice. It is suggested that the student works on the data for Great Britain first and compares his working with those overleaf. If he has worked the example correctly, he can pass on to the next example. If, however, he has slipped up and made mistakes, he should work out the same statistics from the second frequency distribution relating to London and South East England.

The next example is more complicated since the distribution in Table 27 contains both irregular class-intervals and open-ended classes. In this particular illustration the student would be well advised to have an extra column in his working to show the mid-points of each class and this will avoid the risk of calculating the deviations from the assumed mean incorrectly.

Note that whatever the assumed mean chosen for purposes of the calculation, the result should be the same. Thus, if in the case of Table 27 one student chose £12 as the assumed mean and calculated all the deviations from that figure, and another reader worked from £25, the true means will still be the same. Thus, if the reader finds on comparing his working with those given below that different assumed means have been selected, this does not mean that his method is wrong. If his working is correct, the results obtained by both methods should agree.

Note, however, the answers will probably disagree with those in the worked example below if different mid-points have been used in the first and last open-ended classes. For example, if instead of assuming for the final class in Table 26 that the upper limit is 70, it is taken as 75, so that the mid-point is 70 instead of $67\frac{1}{2}$, then this will tend to increase the value of the mean. Likewise, in the first class where a lower limit must be assumed, the lower the mid-point of that class the smaller will the mean prove to be. Thus, it is important for the reader, when he compares his workings, if he has used different mid-points or assumed means, to follow through the effects of these differences and judge to what extent they have affected the answer.

TABLE 26

ANALYSIS BY AGE OF EMPLOYED MALES IN GREAT BRITAIN, MAY 1957 (THOUSANDS)

AGE	Great Britain	London and S.E. England
under 20 years ..	1,094	211
20–25 years	1,237	286
25–30 "	1,512	359
30–35 "	1,594	382
35–40 "	1,546	369
40–45 "	1,515	373
45–50 "	1,560	398
50–55 "	1,473	374
55–60 "	1,192	291
60–65 "	880	212
65 years and over	597	164
TOTAL	14,200	3,419

Source: Based on data in Ministry of Labour Gazette, June, 1958

TABLE 27

SAMPLE OF HOUSEHOLDS IN U.K. CLASSIFIED BY INCOMES OF
HEAD OF HOUSEHOLD

Gross Weekly Income	Number of Households
Under £4	350
£4 but under £6	303
6 ,, ,, 10	426
10 ,, ,, 14	896
14 ,, ,, 20	932
20 ,, ,, 25	288
25 ,, ,, 30	109
30 ,, ,, 40	96
40 and more	86
	3,486

Source: Family Expenditure Survey 1960 and 1961.

When answering examination questions, it is good practice to indicate for any open-ended class, what limit has been chosen.

In this distribution there are two open-ended classes, the first and the last. Of the first, the question is what is the lower limit? This is easy. Since no boy may leave school and start work before his 16th birthday, the lower limit is clearly 16. In the case of the last class, the choice is more difficult. Quite a few men work after their 70th year, but most of them retire soon after reaching 65. Bearing in mind that the mid-point is merely the best estimate of the mean of all the members of that class and the majority of them are likely to be nearer

Illustration (1)

CALCULATION OF MEAN, S.D. AND MEDIAN AND Q.D.
DATA for Great Britain from Table 26.

Age	No. of employed males	Mid-point	$d' \div CI$	$fd' \div CI$	$f(d)^2 \div CI$	Cum.f.
under 20 years	1,094	$17\frac{1}{2}$	—5	— 5,470	27,350	1,094
20–25 years	1,237	$22\frac{1}{2}$	—4	— 4,948	19,792	2,331
25–30 ,, ...	1,512	$27\frac{1}{2}$	—3	— 4,536	13,608	3,843
30–35 ,, ...	1,594	$32\frac{1}{2}$	—2	— 3,188	6,376	5,437
35–40 ,, ...	1.546	$37\frac{1}{2}$	—1	— 1,546	1,546	6,983
40–45 ,, ...	1,515	$42\frac{1}{2}$	0	— 19,688	0	8,498
45–50 ,, ...	1,560	$47\frac{1}{2}$	+1	+ 1,560	1,560	10,058
50–55 ,, ...	1,473	$52\frac{1}{2}$	+2	+ 2,946	5,892	11,531
55–60 ,, ...	1,192	$57\frac{1}{2}$	+3	+ 3,576	10,728	12,723
60–65 ,, ...	880	$62\frac{1}{2}$	+4	+ 3,520	14,080	13,603
65 years and over	597	$67\frac{1}{2}$	+5	+ 2,985	14,925	14,200
TOTAL	14,200			(+ 14,587 — 19,688)	115,857	
				— 5,101		

65 than 70, much less 75, it seems reasonable to assume that the mid-point should be $67\frac{1}{2}$, *i.e.* the upper limit is taken as 70. Note that the relative frequency of that class compared with the other class frequencies is small. This means that even if a slight error has been made in determining the mid-point, it will not affect the answer very much. The same applies to the first class which is really 16-20 but, on balance, the error involved in using $17\frac{1}{2}$ instead of 18 as the mid-point is not likely to affect the answer to any significant extent. The mid-point for a continuous series is derived by adding the lower limits of the successive classes and dividing by 2, *e.g.* $(20 + 25) \div 2$.

Working on the figures for Great Britain, the first calculation provides the arithmetic mean. It is simplest to use the short-cut method of working in deviations from the assumed mean ($42\frac{1}{2}$ years, *i.e.* the mid-point of the class 40 and under 45 years) measured in group intervals:

$$AM = 42\frac{1}{2} + \left(\frac{-5,101}{14,200}\right) \times 5 \text{ years}$$

$$= 42\frac{1}{2} + 5(-0.36) \text{ years}$$

$$= 42\frac{1}{2} - 1.8 \text{ years}$$

$$= 41 \text{ years (to nearest year)}$$

The standard deviation is derived from the formula:

$$\sqrt{\left(\frac{\Sigma f d'^2}{\Sigma f} - \frac{\Sigma f d'}{\Sigma f}\right)^2} \times i$$

i.e., working in class intervals from the assumed mean.

Substituting the actual values for the symbols in the above formula

$$S.D. = \sqrt{\frac{115,857}{14,200} - \left(\frac{-5,101}{14,200}\right)^2} \times 5$$

$$= \sqrt{8.1589 - (0.36)^2} \times 5$$

$$= \sqrt{8.1589 - 0.1296} \times 5$$

$$= \sqrt{8.0293} \times 5$$

$$= 5(2.834) = 14.17 = 14 \text{ years to nearest year.}$$

The median from a grouped frequency distribution is derived by the formula $\dfrac{N}{2}$. Thus:

$$\frac{14,200}{2} = 7,100\text{th item which lies in the group 40-44 years.}$$

Thus the value of the median by interpolation

$$=40+\left(\frac{7,100-6,983}{1,515}\right)\times 5 \text{ years}$$

$$=40+\left(\frac{117}{1,515}\right)\times 5$$

$$=40+5(0\cdot077)=40 \text{ years 5 months.}$$

$$=40 \text{ years to nearest year.}$$

The values at the quartiles are derived in the same way

$$Q_1=\frac{14,200}{4}=3,550\text{th item}$$

$$=25+\left(\frac{3,550-2,331}{1,512}\right)\times 5$$

$$=25+\left(\frac{1,219}{1,512}\right)\times 5$$

$$=25+5(0\cdot806)=29 \text{ years to nearest year.}$$

$$Q_3=\frac{3(14,200)}{4}=10,650\text{th item}$$

$$=50+5\left(\frac{10,650-10,058}{1,473}\right)$$

$$=50+5\left(\frac{592}{1,473}\right)=50+5(0\cdot402)=52 \text{ years to nearest year.}$$

The quartile deviation is easily obtained by using the above results in

the formula $Q D=\dfrac{Q_3-Q_1}{2}$

$$=\frac{52-29}{2}\text{ years}=\frac{23}{2}=11\tfrac{1}{2}\text{ years}$$

The coefficient of variation is derived from $\dfrac{100\times\text{S.D.}}{AM}$

$$=\frac{100\times14\cdot2}{40\cdot75}=\frac{1,420}{40\cdot75}=35\%$$

If the reader has performed the above calculations correctly he may omit the next illustration and attempt the third illustration, on page 159.

Illustration (2)

CALCULATION OF MEAN, S.D. AND MEDIAN AND Q.D.
Data for London and South East England from Table 26

Age	No. of employed males	Mid-point	$d \div CI$	$fd \div CI$		$f(d)^2 \div CI$	Cum.f.
under 20 years	211	$17\frac{1}{2}$	-5	$-$	1,055	5,275	211
20–25 years ..	286	$22\frac{1}{2}$	-4	$-$	1,144	4,576	497
25–30	359	$27\frac{1}{2}$	-3	$-$	1,077	3,231	856
30–35	382	$32\frac{1}{2}$	-2	$-$	764	1,528	1,238
35–40	369	$37\frac{1}{2}$	-1	$-$	369	369	1,607
40–45	373	$42\frac{1}{2}$	-0	$-$	4,409	0	1,980
45–50	398	$47\frac{1}{2}$	$+1$	$+$	398	398	2,378
50–55	374	$52\frac{1}{2}$	$+2$	$+$	748	1,496	2,752
55–60	291	$57\frac{1}{2}$	$+3$	$+$	873	2,619	3,043
60–65	212	$62\frac{1}{2}$	$+4$	$+$	848	3,392	3,255
65 years and over	164	$67\frac{1}{2}$	$+5$	$+$	820	4,100	3,419
TOTAL	3,419			$(+$	3,687	26,984	
				$-$	4,409)		
				$-$	722		

The calculations follow the same pattern as for the first distribution and no comment is required.

$$AM = 42\frac{1}{2} + \left(\frac{-722}{3,419}\right) \times 5 = 42\frac{1}{2} + (-0.21)5$$

$$= 42\frac{1}{2} - 1.05 = 41 \text{ years to nearest year.}$$

$$SD = \sqrt{\frac{\Sigma fd'^2}{\Sigma f} - \left(\frac{\Sigma fd'}{\Sigma f}\right)^2} \times i$$

$$= \sqrt{\frac{26,984}{3,419} - \left(\frac{-722}{3,419}\right)^2} \times 5$$

$$= \sqrt{7.8924 - (-0.21)^2} \times 5$$

$$= \sqrt{7.8924 - 0.0441} \times 5$$

$$= \sqrt{7.8483} \times 5$$

$$= 5(2.801) = 14.005 = 14 \text{ years to nearest year.}$$

$$\text{Median} = 1,709.5 = 40 + 5 \left(\frac{1,709.5 - 1,607}{373}\right) = 40 + 5 \left(\frac{102.5}{373}\right)$$

$$= 40 + 5(0.275) = 41 \text{ years.}$$

Quartile deviation: Although fractions are used in the following calculations of Q_1 and Q_3, the reader will readily appreciate that, in practice, it would be simpler and as accurate to use throughout the nearest whole numbers.

Position of $Q_3 = \dfrac{3(3,419)}{4} = \dfrac{10,257}{4} = 2,564\frac{1}{4}$ rank

Value of $Q_3 = 50 + \dfrac{5(2,564\frac{1}{4} - 2,378)}{374}$

$= 50 + \dfrac{5(186\frac{1}{4})}{374} = 50 + \dfrac{931\frac{1}{4}}{374} = 50 + 2 \cdot 489$

$= 52$ years to nearest year.

Position of $Q_1 = \dfrac{3,419}{4} = 854\frac{3}{4}$ rank

Value of $Q_1 = 25 + \dfrac{5(854\frac{3}{4} - 497)}{359}$

$= 25 + \dfrac{5(357\frac{3}{4})}{359} = 25 + \dfrac{1,788\frac{3}{4}}{359} = 25 + 4 \cdot 98$ years

$= 30$ years

Quartile deviation $= \dfrac{Q_3 - Q_1}{2} = \dfrac{52\frac{1}{2} - 30}{2} = \dfrac{22\frac{1}{2}}{2}$

$= 11\frac{1}{4}$ years

Coefficient of variation

$$\frac{\text{S.D.} \times 100}{AM} = \frac{14 \cdot 005 \times 100}{41 \cdot 5} = \frac{1,400 \cdot 5}{41 \cdot 5} = 33 \cdot 74\%$$

It will be noted that several places of decimals have been used in the calculations above. However, in the comparison of results below all the statistics have been rounded to the nearest year as this approximation is adequate for the data involved and any greater degree of accuracy is unobtainable from data classified as in the original tables.

	Great Britain	London and S.E. England
Number in thousands	14,200	3,419
Arithmetic mean	41 years	41 years
Median value	40 ,,	41 ,,
Lower quartile Q_1 value	29 ,,	30 ,,
Upper quartile Q_3 value	52 ,,	52 ,,
Quartile deviation	12 ,,	11 ,,
Standard deviation	14 ,,	14 ,,
Coefficient of variation	35%	34%

Illustration (3)

The data in Table 27 are derived from a government report on family expenditure and show the distribution of incomes of heads of households. As in the preceding illustrations the reader is required to calculate the arithmetic mean, the standard deviation, the median and the quartiles. In this case the insertion of an extra column for the mid-points of each class is essential for accurate working. As the distribution is continuous, the mid-points are derived by halving the sum of the lower limits of the successive class-intervals, *e.g.* £4 + £6 divided by 2. The next problem is to determine the mid-points of the first and last class-intervals which are open-ended. In the first, obviously no one has a zero income so the mid-point would not be £2. At the time pension was over £3 and those who do not have as much as that will usually be supplementing their incomes from the Supplementary Benefits Commission. We can choose either £3 or £3.50 as the mid-point and, since it simplifies the arithmetic, the former will serve. In the final class 'over £40' it can be assumed that the majority of income in this class are nearer the lower limit than over, say, £50. It is also a very small group so whatever mid-point is chosen, within reason, it is not likely to affect the final answer greatly. In the event it is assumed that the class interval is £40 to £50 and the mid-point is then £45.

CALCULATION OF MEAN, S.D., MEDIAN AND QUARTILES. DATA FROM TABLE 27

Gross Weekly Income	No. of House-holders	Mid-Points £	d′	fd′	fd′	Cum. f.
Under £4	350	3	— 14	— 4,900	68,600	350
£4 but under 6	303	5	— 12	— 3,636	43,632	653
6 ,, ,, 10	426	8	— 9	— 3,834	34,506	1,079
10 ,, ,, 14	896	12	— 5	— 4,480	22,400	1,975
14 ,, ,, 20	932	17	—	—	—	2,907
20 ,, ,, 25	288	22½	+ 5½	+ 1,584	8,712	3,195
25 ,, ,, 30	109	27½	+ 10½	+ 1,144½	12,017	3,304
30 ,, ,, 40	96	35	+ 18	+ 1,728	31,104	3,400
40 and more	86	45	+ 28	+ 2,408	67,424	3,486
TOTAL	3,486			— 16,850		
				+ 6,864½	288,395	
				— 9,985½		

$$\bar{x} = £17 + \left(-\frac{9,985\frac{1}{2}}{3,486} \right) = -2.9 \text{ to one decimal place.}$$

$$\bar{x} = £14 \text{ to nearest £.}$$

$$\sigma = \sqrt{\frac{288,395}{3,486} - \left(-\frac{9,985\frac{1}{2}}{3,486} \right)^2} = \sqrt{82.7 - (2.9)^2}$$

$$= \sqrt{82.7 - 8.4} = \sqrt{74.3} = £8.6 \text{ approx.}$$

$$Me = \frac{3,486}{2} = 1,743 = £10 + \left(\frac{1,743 - 1,079}{896}\right)4 = £13 \text{ to nearest } £.$$

$$Q_1 = \frac{3,486}{4} = 871\tfrac{1}{2} = £6 + \left(\frac{871\tfrac{1}{2} - 653}{426}\right)4 = £8 \text{ to nearest } £.$$

$$Q_3 = \left(\frac{3,486}{4}\right)3 = 2,614\tfrac{1}{2} = £14 + \left(\frac{2,614\tfrac{1}{2} - 1,975}{932}\right)6 = £18 \text{ to nearest } £.$$

Since the class interval is irregular it is not possible to work as in the two previous illustrations, *i.e.*, in deviations in class-interval units. The actual differences of each mid-point from the assumed mean are used. The arithmetic is in consequence rather laborious, but there is no alternative unless we are prepared to approximate extensively. Note that in the final calculations there is a small element of approximation; products and quotients have not been worked to several decimal places, etc., and in the case of the mean, median and quartiles, all have been approximated to the nearest £. Any attempt to express these statistics more precisely, *e.g.*, to the nearest penny, would be rather silly in view of the nature of the data, in particular the large class intervals and the assumptions involved in using mid-points.

For the Examinee

While it would be too much to claim that the reader who has mastered all the material in the past seven chapters understands a great deal of statistics, the fact remains that with this relatively limited knowledge one can perform quite a lot of useful statistical work. A large volume of statistical work is concerned with the collection of numerical data, while an understanding of the points made in the final part of Chapter III on schedules and questionnaires is essential if foolish mistakes in collecting data are to be avoided. The ability to present statistical information in simple tables and effective diagrams is not by any means as widespread as it should be. A great deal of statistical work of this kind is prepared for the information and guidance of non-statisticians such as administrators, managers and senior executives. To be effective such material must be well designed and, as far as possible, self-explanatory.

One would look far to find an examination paper in elementary statistics set over the past twenty years which does not contain a question involving the calculation of the mean and standard deviation and, less frequently, the median and quartile deviation. Despite this obvious fact, it is one of the more depressing experiences of examiners to read examination scripts from which it is all too evident that the candidate has not the glimmerings of an idea how such basic questions should be tackled. This is not just carelessness on the part of the candidate, it is downright stupidity to sit the examination without such fundamental knowledge.

There is no royal road to learning how to calculate the mean and standard deviation or any other statistic. Nor is it enough to understand by repeated re-reading what is being calculated. The need for the examination candidate is practice on the sample of questions from past examination papers which follow below, or from any past examination papers he may come across.

Bricks cannot be built without straw; likewise anyone wanting to acquire a sound knowledge of basic statistics really must have the material which has appeared in the last seven chapters at his fingertips if he is to get any further. And this means not only re-reading some of the examples and sections in these chapters, but also taking the trouble to look at some of the numerous statistical publications which provide excellent illustrations of how tables should be compiled and their content graphically presented. Any serious student should, therefore, obtain one or two recent copies of the monthly *Economic Trends*, which is especially valuable in the field of economic and industrial statistics, and also look through the annual publication entitled *Social Trends*. This is especially valuable for social statistics and the numerous charts and diagrams.

Attention to the above points will ensure not merely that the reader will be successful in his examination but, more important, will begin to acquire a useful foundation of statistical expertise upon which he can build.

Questions

MEASURES OF VARIATION

General

As was noted earlier, examination questions involving the calculation of the arithmetic mean usually also require the calculation of the standard deviation, just as examinees are usually expected to derive not only the median value but the quartile deviation as well, either by calculation or by graphical methods. As far as the former question is concerned, *i.e.* on the mean and standard deviation, this is often linked to a further part of the question involving the use of significance tests which are discussed in Chapter XIV. In short, the subject matter of the last two chapters appears regularly in all examination papers and, if there is one topic which the prospective candidate can be virtually certain of meeting in the examination room, it is some form of question involving the mean and standard deviation or the median and quartile deviation.

A selection of typical questions is set out hereunder together with suggested workings and comments thereon. Since there will be further questions on the mean and standard deviation in the chapter on significance tests and, as the reader has already had several opportunities to practise on this type of question, just five more are given below.

1. The following data relate to age at admission to a certain hospital of surgical cases during the past year. Calculate the mean age and standard deviation for both males and females.

Age last birthday	Males	Females
20–24	43	17
25–29	87	43
30–34	40	21
35–39	32	16
40–44	39	24
45–49	25	48
50–54	51	52
55–59	86	40
60 and over	91	12
	494	273

I.M.T.A.

2. The following distribution shows the percentage increases in the rate demands in Scotland between 1974-75 and 1975-76 and the proportion of total authorities imposing such increases.

Percentage increase over 1974-75	Percentage of authorities
Up to 10	13
Above 10 and up to 20	10
,, 20 ,, ,, ,, 30	17
,, 30 ,, ,, ,, 40	11
,, 40 ,, ,, ,, 50	9
,, 50 ,, ,, ,, 60	10
,, 60 ,, ,, ,, 70	8
,, 70 ,, ,, ,, 80	6
,, 80 ,, ,, ,, 90	4
,, 90 ,, ,, ,, 100	3
,, 100 ,, ,, ,, 200	8
,, 200	1

Calculate the mean increase and the standard deviation for this distribution.

3.

Size of school by number of registered pupils	Percentage of Schools in Scotland
Up to 25	15.6
26 to 50	13.1
51 to 100	11.5
101 to 200	13.0
201 to 300	10.4
301 to 400	8.3
401 to 600	17.8
601 to 800	8.6
801 to 1,000	1.5
Over 1,000	0.2

Source: Social Trends 1972.

Calculate the median and quartile deviation for the above data.

Would you expect the mean and the mode to be higher or lower than the median? Give your reasons.

What would have been the advantages of calculating any other measures of central tendency and dispersion?

I.H.S.A.

4. DISTRIBUTION IN 1976 OF WEEKLY INCOME OF A SAMPLE OF HEADS
OF HOUSEHOLDS AGED 25-30

£			Number
Under 20			6
20 and	,,	40	58
40 ,,	,,	60	102
60 ,,	,,	80	168
80 ,,	,,	100	145
100 ,,	,,	120	100
120 ,,	,,	150	68
150 ,,	,,	200	25
200 ,,	over		4
			676

Calculate the arithmetic mean and standard deviation of this distribution.

5. DISTRIBUTION OF OWNERS BY INDIVIDUAL NET WEALTH

Over	Not over	1966	1975
£	£	%	%
	1,000	35.3	14.6
1,000	3,000	31.2	24.4
3,000	5,000	15.3	12.4
5,000	10,000	10.9	22.4
10,000	25,000	5.2	20.7
25,000	100,000	1.8	5.1
100,000		0.3	0.4

Estimate the median value and the quartile deviation for each of the years 1966 and 1975.

Answer to Question 1

This is a straightforward calculation, but the following points should be noted. Often, when the question requires the calculation of such statistics as the mean and S.D. for two distributions, candidates will often write down the two parts of the question in their entirety, thus wasting time. The age distribution is common to both as are the deviations which, incidentally, are in this case given in terms of the class interval which is five years. Do not be misled by the classification 20-24 etc. This means 'from exact age 20 to one day short of the 25th birthday' which is effectively five years. It is, however, often helpful to repeat the column with the deviations in the second distribution adjacent to the frequencies since it is all too easy to misread a column and pick up the wrong number.

Age		Males				Females		
x	f	$d'=5$	fd'	fd'^{2}	f	$d'=5$	fd'	fd'^{2}
20-24	43	-4	-172	688	17	-4	-68	272
25-29	87	-3	-261	783	43	-3	-129	387
30-34	40	-2	-80	160	21	-2	-42	84
35-39	32	-1	-32	32	16	-1	-16	16
40-44	39	$=$	$=$		24	$=$	$=$	
45-49	25	$+1$	$+25$	25	48	$+1$	48	48
50-54	51	$+2$	$+102$	204	52	$+2$	104	208
55-59	86	$+3$	$+258$	774	40	$+3$	120	360
60 and over	91	$+4$	$+364$	1,456	12	$+4$	48	192
			-545				-255	
	494		$+749$	4,122	273		$+320$	1,567
			$+204$				$+65$	

$$\bar{x} = x' + \frac{\Sigma fd'}{\Sigma f} \times c.i.$$

$$= 42 + \frac{204}{494} \times 5$$

$$= 42 + 2.1$$

$$= 44 \text{ years to nearest year}$$

$$\frac{\sigma^2}{c.i.} = \left[\frac{\Sigma fd^2}{\Sigma f} - \left(\frac{\Sigma fd'}{\Sigma f} \right)^2 \right]$$

$$= \frac{4,122}{494} - \left(\frac{204}{494} \right)^2$$

$$= 8.34 - 0.17$$

$$\sigma = \sqrt{8.17} \times c.i.$$
$$= \quad 2.86 \times 5$$
$$= 14.3 \text{ years}$$

$$\bar{x} = x' + \frac{\Sigma fd'}{\Sigma f} \times c.i.$$

$$= 42 + \frac{65}{273} \times 5$$

$$= 42 + 1.19$$

$$= 43 \text{ years to nearest year}$$

$$\frac{\sigma^2}{c.i.} = \frac{1,567}{273} - \left(\frac{65}{273} \right)^2$$

$$= 5.74 - 0.06$$

$$\sigma = \sqrt{5.68} \times 5$$
$$= \quad 2.38 \times 5$$
$$= 11.9 \text{ years}$$

Note that in the case of the means of both distributions the results have been rounded to the nearest year, *i.e.* 44 and 43 for males and females respectively. As far as the calculation of the standard deviation is concerned, the reader should note how the formula has been written down, with the left hand side showing the symbol for the standard deviation squared and divided by the class interval. The reason for this is that it saves writing in the square root sign at each stage of the calculation and, more important because it is so often a cause of error in an examination, it is a reminder the final square root value has to be converted from class interval units into actual units. Incidentally, note that the conversion is not done until the square root has been obtained. In the case of the values for the standard deviations, the answers have been expressed to one decimal place but it is arguable that they should be expressed to the nearest year. Marks are not likely to be lost whichever way the final answer is presented. In case the reader has forgotten, $\bar{x}$ represents the true mean and x' the assumed mean or arbitrary origin. The dash by the deviations symbol, *i.e.* d', indicates the deviations are measured from the assumed mean.

The two distributions merit further study, although the question does not call for any comment as is usually the case where the candidate is required to derive statistics such as the mean for both distributions. Neither of the distributions is particularly well suited for summarising by use of the mean since they are both spread out over the entire range of the independent variable, *i.e.* age. The mode would be quite useless; the median and Q.D. are just as good if not better than the mean and standard deviation.

Note also the concentration in the male distribution of the frequencies at the higher ages. Well over a third, *i.e.* 177 out of 494 cases are in the two top age groups. In contrast, the highest age group is relatively unimportant for the females distribution. This explains the higher mean age for males and also affects the standard deviation which is sensitive to extreme values.

Answer to Question 2

Another simple question in which the only problem concerns the selection of the mid-points in the top and bottom classes. In the opening class, defined as 'up to 10' one can only guess at the actual average increase in areas where the authorities did not increase their rate demands by more than 10 per cent. The mid-point chosen, 5 per cent, is as sensible as any. Perhaps it might be a shade low, since it is more than likely that more of these authorities levied increases above 5 per cent than below. But, there is no information to guide us and the margin of error is not likely to be serious. Thus, even if the mid-point of that class had been taken as $7\frac{1}{2}$, which might be a better approximation to the true mean of those particular authorities' increases, it would not have affected the distribution if the result is rounded to the nearest unit.

% increase	f	$d'=10$	fd'		fd²
Up to 10	13	−5	−65		325
10-20	10	−4	−40		160
20-30	17	−3	−51		153
30-40	11	−2	−22		44
40-50	9	−1	−9		9
50-60	10	=	=		
60-70	8	+1		+8	8
70-80	6	+2		+12	24
80-90	4	+3		+12	36
90-100	3	+4		+12	48
100-200	8	+9½		+76	722
200	1	+17		+17	289
	100		−187	+137	1,818
				−50	

$$\bar{x} = 55 + \left(\frac{-50}{100}\right)10 = 55 - 5 = 50\%$$

$$\frac{\sigma^2}{10} = \frac{1,818}{100} - \left(\frac{-50}{100}\right)^2 = 18.18 - 0.25 = 17.93$$

$$\frac{\sigma}{10} = \sqrt{17.93} = 4.23$$

$$\sigma = 4.23 \times 10 = 42\% \text{ to nearest percentage point.}$$

Slightly more problematical is the treatment of the last two classes. With only 8 per cent of the authorities in the class 100-200 any reasonable guess as to the mean of the group, which is what the mid-point is supposed to represent, will not introduce a significant margin of error into the answer. Thus, we can take the mid-value between 100 and 200 as 150. As for the final class 'over 200' it really does not matter very much what figure is chosen. In this case, it is assumed that the single value might be as much as 250 and the mid-point chosen is therefore 225. The deviations are in terms of class interval units.

It is always worth looking at the result to see whether it looks more or less correct. Sixty per cent of the authorities had rate increases of under 50 per cent, but the remaining 40 per cent were well strung out and these higher increases undoubtedly pulled up the mean. Hence a mean of 50 per cent looks reasonable. It is more difficult to assess the correctness of the standard deviation. When a distribution is characterised by a strong concentration around the central value of the distribution, with the balance of the frequencies'more or less evenly dispersed on either side of that central value, then the standard deviation should be – very approximately – one-sixth of the range of the independent variable. In this case the range is about 250. Actually, this particular distribution is well spread out, but not all that unevenly, and while the foregoing guide is not directly relevant, the result does not look wrong.

Answer to Question 3
This provides an illustration of a distribution which lends itself to the use of the median and quartile deviation rather than the mean and standard deviation, not least because the size of the class interval is so variable. Although there is the same element of estimation in locating the median and quartile values within their respective classes as with the mean and standard deviation, at least the results will not be as distorted as would be, for example, the standard deviation, by the existence of the long tail of this distribution.

x	f	Cumulative frequencies
Up to 25	15.6	15.6
26-50	13.1	28.7
51-100	11.5	40.2
101-200	13.0	53.2
201-300	10.4	63.6
301-400	8.3	71.9
401-600	17.8	89.7
601-800	8.6	98.3
801-1,000	1.5	99.8
Over 1,000	0.2	100.0

Median $=\dfrac{n}{2}=\dfrac{100}{2}=50$

Median value $=100+\dfrac{50-40.2}{13.0}\times100=100+\dfrac{9.8}{13.0}\times100$

$=100+75=175$

$Q_1 \quad =\dfrac{n}{4}=\dfrac{100}{4}=25$

$=25+\dfrac{25-15.6}{13.1}\times25=25+\dfrac{9.4}{13.1}\times25$

$=25+17.9=43$

$Q_3 \quad =\dfrac{3n}{4}=\dfrac{300}{4}=75$

$=400+\dfrac{75-71.9}{17.8}\times200=400+\dfrac{3.1}{17.8}\times200$

$=400+34.8=435$

Note that the upper limit of the preceding class is taken as the point from which the distance along the relevant class interval is measured. This is because, for example, with the median some 9.8 points of the 13.0 per cent spread over the class interval of 100 between 101-200 would lie on the value 101. Thus the true starting point should be 100. The same point applies to the two quartiles. As is usually the case with this type of calculation, where the frequencies are relatively small in relation to the size of the class interval, it is difficult to know to what extent the answer should be approximated. In this case all three values have been given to the nearest percentage point, but the figures should be taken as a guide rather than as precise measures of the median and quartile sizes of Scottish schools.

As far as the rest of the question is concerned, the mode would be a totally unacceptable measure. The modal group is clearly the group in the 401 to 600 class but, with well over half the distribution in schools of 200 or less, the mode is a poor indicator. The mean would be better. At first sight with about 48 per cent of the schools under the median size, even allowing for the effect of the large modal group, it would be surprising if the mean were much different from median. It would probably be higher since 46 per cent of the schools are in classes above the median class and their distribution is such that they probably would offset the concentration of about 53 per cent of the schools in the three lowest classes. On balance the median and quartiles are the most suitable measures for this particular distribution.

Answer to Question 4

This distribution, by virtue of the concentration of the frequencies in the central classes, is eminently well suited for the calculation of the mean and standard deviation. As in Question 2 above, the only problem arises with the determination of the mid-points of the opening class and the last two classes. As far as the first class is concerned, with only 1 per cent of the distribution in it, whatever mid-value is chosen, within reason, will hardly affect the result. The same is true of the final class defined as '200 and over' and it has been assumed here that the mid-value, *i.e.* the mean of the class, is 215. But, even if 250 had been used as the mid-point it would not have affected the result at all, because the relevant frequency is so minute. As with Question 2 the only other query surrounds the degree of approximation to be used in the answers. In the event, given the heavy concentration of frequencies in the three central classes the mean has been given to the nearest £ and the standard deviation likewise. Note how, in this particular distribution, as was mentioned in the comments on Question 2, the range of the independent variable is almost exactly six times the standard deviation, *i.e.* $6 \times 36 = 216$.

£	f	$d' = 10$	fd'		fd'^{2}
Under 20	6	-4	-24		96
20-40	58	-3	-174		522
40-60	102	-2	-204		408
60-80	168	-1	-168		168
80-100	145	$=$	$=$		
100-120	100	$+1$		$+100$	100
120-150	68	$+2\frac{1}{2}$		$+153$	344
150-200	25	$+4\frac{1}{4}$		$+106$	450
200 and over	4	$+6\frac{1}{4}$		$+25$	156
	676		-570 $= -186$	$+384$	2,244

$$\bar{x} = 90 + \left(\frac{-186}{676}\right) \times 20 = 90 + 5.50 = £95 \text{ to nearest £.}$$

$$\frac{\sigma^2}{20} = \frac{2,244}{676} - \left(\frac{-186}{676}\right)^2 = 3.32 - 0.08 = 3.24$$

$$\frac{\sigma}{20} = \sqrt{3.24} = 1.8$$

$$\sigma = 1.8 \times 20 = £36$$

The reason why the mean can be expressed to the nearest £, is that the frequencies in the central classes are so numerous that the element of approximation in choosing the mid-point of the class as the mean of that class is probably quite small. In other words, the mid-point of the class is unlikely to differ, if at all, from the mean of that class.

Answer to Question 5

These distributions of personal wealth as disclosed for estate duty purposes are better suited to the use of the median and quartiles. Note how the class interval varies for each group. Examination candidates often become absent-minded and use the same class interval, or the one which applied to the previous class ! But, because there is likely to be a fair spread of the frequencies within the relevant classes where the class interval is large, *e.g.* as with the upper quartile in 1966 or even more so, the same value in 1975, the degree of estimation is greater. Hence, as may be seen, all the derived values are rounded to either the nearest £50 or £100.

Over	Not over (£)	1966 f.	1966 cum. f.	1975 f.	1975 cum. f.
—	1,000	35.3	35.3	14.6	14.6
1,000	3,000	31.2	66.5	24.4	39.0
3,000	5,000	15.3	81.8	12.4	51.4
5,000	10,000	10.9	92.7	22.4	73.8
10,000	25,000	5.2	97.9	20.7	94.5
25,000	100,000	1.8	99.7	5.1	99.6
100,000		0.3	100.0	0.4	100.0

1966

$$Me = \frac{n}{2} = \frac{100}{2} = 50\text{th value}$$

$$= £1,000 + \frac{50.0 - 35.3}{31.2} \times 2,000$$

$$= £1,000 + 942$$

Median value $= £1,950$ approx.

Q_1 = 25th value

$$= \frac{25}{35.3} \times £1,000$$

$$= 708 = £700 \text{ approx.}$$

Q_3 = 75th value

$$= £3,000 + \frac{75.0 - 66.5}{15.3} \times 2,000$$

$$+ \frac{8.5}{15.3} \times 2,000$$

$$+ 1,111$$

$$= £3,000 + £1,100 = £4,100$$

$$Q.D. = \frac{4,100 - 700}{2} = \frac{3,400}{2}$$

$$= £1,700$$

1975

$$= £3,000 + \frac{50.0 - 39.0}{12.4} \times 2,000$$

$$+ 1,774$$

$$Me = £4,750$$

$$Q_1 = £1,000 + \frac{25.0 - 14.6}{24.4} \times 2,000$$

$$= +852$$

$$= £1,850$$

$$Q_3 = £10,000 + \frac{75.0 - 73.8}{20.7} \times 15,000$$

$$= 10,000 + \frac{1.2}{20.7} \times 15,000$$

$$= 10,000 + 869$$

$$= £10,900 \text{ to nearest } £100$$

$$Q.D. = \frac{10,900 - 1,850}{2} = \frac{9,050}{2}$$

$$= £4,525$$

Certainly there is no justification in such distributions for giving the answer to the nearest £ or, as some candidates prefer, to the nearest penny! Very few statistical data are accurate or exact in the accountancy sense of the term. Remember that mistakes have probably crept in during the processing of the raw data and, in any case, some of that data was probably wrong. Furthermore, the element of estimation entailed in assuming that the frequencies are evenly distributed over the class interval varies according to the number of such frequencies and the range of the class interval. Better rough approximation than spurious accuracy!

CHAPTER VIII

STATISTICAL AND ARITHMETIC ACCURACY

For the layman statistics may often possess a significance far beyond their real importance. For example, a speech containing a large number of statistics is often regarded by audiences as much more impressive than one which concentrates on ideas and principles. Much the same is true of the printed figure, and as many a statistician knows, what was once a hopeful guess in the committee room can all too often later appear to haunt him in a published report. In all probability the latter will be quoted with all the authority of the office from which the guess emanated! There are good statistics and bad statistics; it may be doubted if there are many perfect data which are of any practical value. It is the statistician's function to discriminate between good and bad data; to decide when an informed estimate is justified and when it is not; to extract the maximum reliable information from limited and possibly biased data.

Poor statistics may be attributed to a number of causes. There are the mistakes which arise in the course of collecting the data, and there are those which occur when those data are being converted into manageable form for publication. Still later, mistakes arise because the conclusions drawn from the published data are wrong. The real trouble with errors which arise during the course of collecting the data is that they are the hardest to detect. It is virtually impossible to check whether an interviewer should have ticked *Yes* instead of *No* as the answer to a given question. Like the rest of mankind, interviewers make mistakes; they don't always ask the right questions and they sometimes write down the wrong answers. When the questionnaires and schedules are returned to the Head Office for tabulation a new source of error appears. The answers may be incorrectly transferred from the schedules to the punched cards or tabulations; but good supervision can reduce this risk considerably. Sometimes, however, the answer given on the schedule has to be classified. This is at best an arbitrary procedure and mistakes in classification arise. Once the tables have been prepared detailing the results of the enquiry, their contents are analysed. At this stage, too, a great deal more can be read into some statistics than the people who provided them ever dreamed of!

A weakness frequently encountered in reports which quote published statistics of trade, unemployment and other economic or social subjects, is the failure to consult with sufficient care the source from which a total or figure has been taken. Unemployment figures for Great Britain may be incorrectly related to population figures for England and Wales; pre-1973 unemployment figures may be freely compared with current data yet there is no evidence that the author realises that owing to a re-definition of those statistics, the two totals cover different groups. This is especially true of index numbers which are quoted to measure changes in quantities and values over periods of time. For example, changes in the present cost of living can be measured from month to month by the Index of Retail Prices, but this index cannot be directly compared with either the Interim index for the period 1947-52-62 or the pre-1947 Cost of Living index.[1] Earlier, in Chapter II, great emphasis was laid upon the need for verifying definitions and sources of data taken from published documents; no apology is made for returning to this theme because inaccurate extraction of published data is an extremely prevalent disease.

Most people tend to think of values and quantities expressed in numerical terms as being exact figures; much the same as the figures which appear in the trading account of a company. It therefore comes as a considerable surprise to many to learn that few published statistics, particularly economic and sociological data, are exact. Many published figures are only approximations to the real value, while others are estimates of aggregates which are far too large to be measured with precision. For example, the *Monthly Digest of Statistics* contains many series of economic statistics which are expressed to the nearest million pounds, or hundreds of thousands of yards, or thousands of tons. It would be very satisfactory to know that every figure in that Digest was correct to the nearest unit, but in many cases it would be quite impossible to achieve complete accuracy for some units are always missed out in a count involving hundreds and thousands of units. To achieve such accuracy would also take a great deal of time so that when finally these statistics were published they would be so much out of date as to be useless. In the case of many economic series, early publication is usually more important than precision to the last unit. If action is required on the evidence of these data, the sooner it is taken the better. In many series, it is not so much the aggregates themselves which are of interest as the pattern of change which emerges over a period of months. A good example is provided by the monthly figures of overseas trade which may fluctuate sharply from month to month. Such fluctuations may be a completely unreliable guide to the nation's trade, but over a period of months a trend may emerge and it is this that needs to be watched.

[1] This index is discussed in Chapter X.

Approximate Data

In the chapter on tabulation it was pointed out that a table can be made more comprehensible to the reader if the figures are rounded to, say, the nearest 1,000 or 1,000,000. There are even more important reasons for preferring rounded figures. For example, when the first results of the decennial population census are published the total population is enumerated given to the nearest unit. For example, on the census night in April, 1971, there were 48,603,945 persons enumerated in England and Wales. To express the figure in such precise terms suggests a remarkable degree of accuracy. It is certainly wrong as a measure of the actual population at that date; some people were omitted from the enumeration while others may have died between the time the form was completed at the weekend and the actual day for the count; others have been born in that short interval.

For such reasons it is customary to express population totals as estimates to the nearest 1,000. For example, at the mid-1971 count it is estimated that there were 48,895 thousand persons in England and Wales. That figure is stated to the nearest 1,000, and is probably accurate or, to put it no stronger, is a good enough estimate for any purpose to which such data may be put. For that reason it does not matter too much that the census figure upon which the mid-year estimate is based is wrong; and while the net increase of births over deaths registered by the Registrars throughout England and Wales may be accurate, the figures of migration are certain to be wrong. All such errors of omission and commission, to quote the accountant's phrase, are covered, one hopes, by the degree of estimation used.

The widespread desire for precision is reflected in many reports on economic trends which quote figures in great detail, rather than emphasising the trends and movements reflected in the figures. For example, while it may be true that exports of a particular product rose last year to £20,879,169 from £13,998,372 in the previous year, it is much clearer to state that the value of exports rose from about £14 million to approximately £21 million; alternatively, that this year's figure of almost £21 million was half as large again as that for last year. It is important to distinguish the purposes to which such published statistics are to be put; if they are merely inserted to indicate the course of events or approximate magnitude of the variables, then rounded figures which are immediately comprehensible are infinitely preferable to the exact figures. On the other hand, if a detailed analysis is to be carried out then the results may have to be given to the nearest unit.

The practice, described above, of expressing large figures more simply, *i.e.* by dropping the last few digits, is described as *rounding*.

This is done with the mid-year estimate of the population, the total being expressed to the nearest thousand, and such rounding implies that the last digit in the rounded figure is correct. The following are other methods available. Assuming the original figure to lie within the limits of 82,500 to 83,500, we may write:

(1) 83,000 $\pm$ 500.

(2) 83,000 correct to 0.6 per cent.

(3) 83,000 correct to nearest 1,000.

Often, in order to simplify statistical tables, the practice of rounding large figures and totals is resorted to. Where the constituent figures in a table together with their aggregate have been so treated, a discrepancy between the rounded total and the true sum of the rounded constituent figures frequently arises. As was pointed out earlier in the chapter on tabulation, under no circumstances should the total be adjusted to what appears to be the right answer. A note to the table to the effect that the figures have been rounded, *e.g.* to the nearest 1,000, is all that is necessary. The same remark applies to percentage equivalents of the constituent parts of a total; if they do not add to exactly 100 per cent, leave them. This has been done in several columns of Table 10 (page 57). The error arises here because each percentage figure has been calculated to two places of decimals and then rounded to the nearest first place. Similarly, in Table 6 the columns headed 'Membership' do not add up exactly to the total shown, due to the fact that the numbers in each class have been rounded to the nearest thousand.

Biased and Unbiased Errors

The rounding of individual values comprising an aggregate can give rise to what are known as *unbiased* or *biased* errors. Table 28 below illustrates this. The *biased* error arises because all the individual figures are reduced to the lower 1,000, as in column 3; or as in column 4, where they have been raised to the higher 1,000.

The *unbiased* error is so described since by rounding each item to the nearest 1,000 some of the approximations are greater and some smaller than the original figures. Given a large number of such approximations, the final total may therefore correspond very closely to the true or original total, since the approximations tend to offset each other. This is true of Column 2, which totals 75,000, the same as the true total expressed to the nearest 1,000. It is possible, even if rather unlikely, that the 'unbiased' total may be very different from the true total if most of the approximations are in one direction only, *e.g.* a group of figures each rounded to the nearest '000' where most of them lie just above '500'. The larger the number of values, however, the less likely is the total to differ from their true aggregate since the unbiased rounding of each figure will tend to balance out.

With *biased* approximation, however, the errors are cumulative and their aggregate increases with the number of items in the series. 'Biased' errors may arise in a variety of ways. If a number of women are asked to state their ages, and an average is computed, the latter is quite likely to be lower than the 'true' average, since many of the informants will tend to understate their ages by a year or so. Likewise, an administrative officer in computing his probable staff requirements in a group of offices may, to be on the safe side, over-estimate his needs for each office. Similarly, data based on readings from an inaccurate slide-rule, thermometer, or similar measuring instrument, will be consistently biased in the same direction, *i.e.* either above or below the true figures.

Absolute and Relative Errors

Errors may be measured in two ways: *absolutely* and *relatively*. The *absolute* error is the arithmetic difference between the approximated figure and the original quantity. Thus, in Table 28, the absolute error in the total arising from the 'unbiased' rounding in Column 2 is — 182, *i.e.* the difference between the true total of 75,182 and the rounded total of 75,000.

TABLE 28
EXAMPLE OF ROUNDING AND BIASED ERRORS

Actual Figures (1)	Unbiased (000) (2)	Biased (Lower 000) (3)	Biased (Higher 000) (4)
17,118	17	17	18
613	1	0	1
1,253	1	1	2
8,362	8	8	9
15,443	15	15	16
7,645	8	7	8
11,759	12	11	12
10,509	11	10	11
2,480	2	2	3
TOTAL 75,182	75	71	80

The *relative* error is generally derived by expressing the absolute error as a fraction of the estimated total, *i.e.* 75,000. Thus $\frac{-182}{75,000} =$ — 0·0024. The same calculations have been performed for both the biased errors, where the estimated figures are adjusted downward to the nearest 1,000, *i.e.* in Column 3 the relative error is —·0590, when the figures are adjusted upwards, the error is $+\cdot0602$ (Col. 4). The advantage of relatives is that widely differing quantities can be compared in similar terms. Thus, an error of 100,000 in £10 million is the same as 5 in £500, *i.e.* 1 per cent.

Actual Absolute Error	-182	$-4,182$	$+4,818$
Actual Relative Error	$\left(\dfrac{-182}{75,000}\right)$	$\left(\dfrac{-4,182}{71,000}\right)$	$\left(\dfrac{+4,818}{80,000}\right)$
	$=-0\cdot24\%$	$=-5\cdot90\%$	$=+6\cdot02\%$
AVERAGE, 8,353·5	8,333·3	7,888·8	8,888·8

Absolute Error in Average

$$\left(\frac{-182}{9}\right)=-20\cdot2 \quad \left(\frac{-4,182}{9}\right)=-464\cdot6 \quad \left(\frac{4,818}{9}\right)=+535\cdot3$$

Relative Error in Average

$$\left(\frac{-182}{9}\div\frac{75,000}{9}\right) \qquad \left(\frac{-4,182}{9}\div\frac{71,000}{9}\right) \qquad \left(\frac{4,818}{9}\div\frac{80,000}{9}\right)$$

$$=-0\cdot24\% \qquad\qquad =-5\cdot90\% \qquad\qquad =+6\cdot02\%$$

The *absolute* error in the aggregate of a *biased* series will tend to increase with the number of items. The *relative* error in the total figure will, generally speaking, tend to diminish as the number of items increases.

The remainder of the calculations following Table 28 are simple, involving the calculation of the absolute and the relative errors in the *average*. The results in this case provide an indication of the accuracy, not of the aggregates themselves, but of the *averages* computed from those aggregates. The reader will note by reference to Table 28 that the relative error in both the average and the aggregate is the same. In any series where the individual figures have all been rounded to the same unit, (*e.g.* rounding to nearest '000' means an error ±500), then the *average* of the total is probably more reliable than any of the individual figures.

Calculations with Estimates

Wherever any arithmetical calculation involving approximated figures is carried out, and the degree of error in those figures is known it is possible to estimate the error arising in the final result. Starting with simple *addition:*

Add 56,000, 7,000 and 20,000 correct to 5 per cent, 0·5 per cent, and 0·05 per cent respectively:

56,000	5% of which is	2,800
7,000	0·5% of which is	35
20,000	0·05% of which is	10
83,000		2,845

The aggregate is 83,000 $\pm$ 2,845, *i.e.* correct to 3·43 per cent. Thus, the error in the aggregate is the sum of the absolute errors in the component items.

For *subtraction* the difference will be at a minimum if the estimate of the larger figure is assumed to be below the true figure by the amount of error, and the smaller estimated figure to be subtracted is above its true amount by the amount of error shown. A maximum result is obtained if the reverse of the above case applies. Assuming that 45,000 is to be subtracted from 72,000, and the former figure lies between 44,000 and 46,000, and the latter sum between 71,500 and 72,500, then:

Maximum difference	Minimum difference
72,500	71,500
44,000	46,000
28,500	25,500

The answer is $\dfrac{(28,500 + 25,500)}{2} = 27,000 \pm 1,500$, *i.e.* correct to

5·55 per cent. With subtraction, as with addition, the error in the answer is equal to the sum of the errors in the individual amounts, *i.e.* $\pm$ 1,000 and $\pm$ 500 $= \pm$ 1,500.

When *multiplying* two rounded values together, it is usual to show both the result and the maximum possible error which could have occurred in it. This is derived as follows. The product of two values, 12,500 and 400, is 5 million. Assume that the larger value has been rounded to the nearest 500 and the other value to the nearest 50. Thus the true values might have read 12,749 and 424 which when multiplied together give a product of approximately 5·43 million. The maximum error in the original product of 5 million is thus 0·43 million which is equal to an error of $8\frac{1}{2}$ per cent. Therefore, the answer to the multiplication given above would be written 5 million $\pm$ $8\frac{1}{2}$ per cent.

With *division* the same principle is applied. If the total 300,000 is divided by 500, the quotient is 600. If the dividend had been rounded to the nearest 10,000 and the divisor to the nearest 10 units, then the maximum error in the above quotient of 600 is derived when we divide the smallest possible divisor into the largest possible dividend, *i.e.* 496 into 304,999, which gives 615. In other words, there is a maximum error of $\pm$ 15 in a figure of 600, which is equal to $\pm$ $2\frac{1}{2}$ per cent.

It should not be necessary to memorise the various formulae which are sometimes evolved for these operations, usually remembered at the expense of the principles on which they are based. All that needs to be kept in mind is that the maximum error is always possible. Generally speaking, no amount of juggling with figures can increase the accuracy of the result if the original data are liable to error. The result of any calculation involving approximation can be no more accurate than the least accurate of the figures used in the calculation. Thus, in stating the final result, it may be advisable to give it to at least one significant figure less than found in the least accurate figure employed in the calculations. The same point should be borne in mind when calculating means and medians, etc., from a grouped frequency distribution where the class interval is large.

Use of Ratios

Earlier in this chapter the usefulness of relatives instead of absolute quantities for comparative purposes was mentioned. The main feature to be remembered is that a ratio or percentage expresses the variation in the data, irrespective of its actual or absolute size. Thus an expansion in a firm's turnover from £500,000 to £750,000 is the same in relation to the first value as is a rise from £10,000 to £15,000, *i.e.* 50 per cent rise on the base year, *i.e*, the year in which the £500,000 and £10,000 were earned.

The main danger to avoid in expressing variations in terms of ratios or percentages is the use of two different bases in the comparison, or more generally, of failing to make clear on which base the change has been calculated. Thus, if in Year 1 profits were £25,000, and the chairman made the following statement: 'In Year 1 profits rose 10 per cent, the following year 25 per cent, and last year 33 per cent', the shareholders might be forgiven if they arrived at two very different results:

	Year 1	Year 2	Year 3		Year 4
(i)	£25,000	£27,500	£34,375	and	£45,833
(ii)	£25,000	£27,500	£31,250		£33,333

The first line is calculated on the assumption that each percentage rise is based on the figure of the immediately preceding year; in the second line the percentages are all worked on Year 1 as base year. Whichever method is intended, it should be made clear which is to be the base year.

Such comparative ratios or percentages are a frequent source of confusion. If the two sets of quantities are widely different in absolute size, as in the examples of the sales given above, a mere percentage comparison may be quite misleading in so far as it may tell only half the story, or more seriously, it may suggest that the comparison made is justified when it most certainly is not. Thus, if a school teacher discussing the latest examination results with the head of a large coaching institution, states that 50 per cent of his candidates obtained distinction in all subjects, and the coaching institution only 5 per cent can any conclusions be drawn? The answer is 'no'. It may be that 500 pupils of the coaching institution sat and only six at the teacher's school. In any case it is highly improbable that a direct comparison can be made between the two teaching methods until more is known of the calibre of the pupils, the amount of study done by the students and the numbers of staff. The first rule of statistics, 'compare like with like', has hardly been observed.

The averaging of percentages themselves requires care, where the percentages are each computed on different bases, *i.e.* different quantities. The average is *not* derived by aggregating the percentages and dividing them. Instead of this, each percentage must first be multiplied by its base to bring out its relative significance to the other percentages and to the total. The sum of the resultant products is then divided by the sum of the base values as in (Col. 2) below, not merely the number of items.

Suppose the ratio of equity capital to the total capital for each of six public companies is as follows:

Company	A	B	C	D	E	F
%	100	50	50	40	50	25

The average ratio for all six companies is *not* the average of these ratios, *i.e.* $315 \div 6$, as set out in column (4) below, because this method makes no allowance for the different amounts of the companies' capital as shown in column (2) below. The correct method requires us to work from the actual figures of share capital and equity capital given in columns (2) and (3) below. Then each percentage is 'weighted', *i.e.* multiplied by the figure of total capital, their product added together as in column (5) and that total divided by the total weights. The correct answer is 43·3 %, as compared with the answer of $\frac{315}{6} = 52 \cdot 5\%$ derived by using the incorrect method.

The reason for the difference is simple. In column (4) there is an implied assumption that all the companies are of equal size (in terms of their issued capital) and consequently equal importance has been attached to the percentages for the small and the large firms. In col-

Percentage of Equity Capital in Six Public Companies

(1)	(2)	(3)	(4)	(5)
			Ratio of	Col. 2 ×
	Total Capital	Equity Capital	Col. 3 to	Col. 4
Company	000's	000's	Col. 2	000's
	£	£	%	£
A	50	50	100	50
B	100	50	50	50
C	200	100	50	100
D	250	100	40	100
E	500	250	50	250
F	400	100	25	100
	1,500	650	315	15)650 = 43·3%

umn (5), however, correct importance has been given to each firm; *i.e.* the percentage of equity to total capital has been *weighted* in the ratio of their total capitals one to the other.[1]

The same rules apply to the 'averaging' of averages, *e.g.*:

(1)	(2)	(3)	(4)
	No. of	Average Weekly	Products in
Plant	operatives	Output per operative	00's
A	180	540	972
B	140	530	742
C	50	490	245
D	90	500	450
E	110	510	561
F	160	525	840
	730	3,095	730)3,810
			522 to nearest unit

The average output of all workers in the six plants is not the average of the six plant averages, *i.e.* 3,095 ÷ 6 = 516. This is wrong. The correct method is given in the last column; the products of multiplying columns 2 and 3 together and dividing their sum by the total of operatives, *i.e.* column 2. This has the same effect as adding up the output of every one of the 730 operatives in the six factories and dividing the aggregate output so derived by the number of operatives. The true average per operative is thus found to be 522 per week.

Conclusions

While it is true to assert that much statistical work involves arithmetic and mathematics, it would be quite untrue to suggest that the

[1] The subject of 'weighting' is discussed more fully in Chapter X on Index Numbers.

main source of errors in statistics and their use is due to inaccurate calculations. This happens, of course. Lord Randolph Churchill was not the first man to be confused by those 'damned' dots; nor was he the last to get the answer to the wrong place of decimals. Arithmetic apart, the first lesson to be learned in statistics is that many figures are little better than good estimates. The art of the statistician lies in two related fields. First, he learns how to collect his data in such ways as to minimise the risk of errors; second, he learns to judge the quality and reliability of other people's data, whether they be published in official reports or have been collected by someone else, and thereby minimise the effects of any possible errors.

When using estimated figures, *i.e.* figures subject to error, for further calculation make allowance for the absolute and relative errors. Above all, avoid what is known to statisticians as 'spurious' accuracy. For example, if the arithmetic mean has to be derived from a distribution of ages given to the nearest year, do not give the answer to several places of decimals. Such an answer would imply a degree of accuracy in the results of your calculations which is quite unjustified by the data. The same holds true when calculating percentages. For example, 'of the 49·1 million estimated population in England and Wales at 30th June 1977, 10·9 were under 15 years of age, *i.e.* 22·199 per cent'; this answer is silly. It implies that the original estimates of total population and those under 15 were correct to the last unit, instead of having been approximated to the nearest 1,000. It could well be, if there had been heavy migration that year, that both figures would be subject to an even larger margin of error. At most, given these figures, one could say that 22 per cent of the estimated population are believed to be under 15 years of age.

A great deal of nonsense is talked these days about economic growth. Year-by-year comparisons are made of the rate at which Britain's economy is expanding and the National Economic Development Council has set a target of 3 per cent per annum. How sure can the statisticians be that performance matches the target? The key estimate is the gross national product (G.N.P.) which in 1977 was £123,791 million, subject to an error which is not less than 3 per cent and could be considerably more than 5 per cent.[1] In other words, the error in the estimate is undoubtedly as large as the required annual increase in the gross national product. How much confidence can we have in public declarations by politicians that the G.N.P. this year has risen by 4 per cent, or by 3½ per cent, or any other figure? These data are at best tentative estimates to be used with caution. In the longer run they provide some indication of the trend of the economy. Economic fluctuations from year to year, however, as measured by current

[1] These and other official statistical series are discussed in Chapter XVIII.

statistics, need to be taken with more than the proverbial pinch of salt. The same is true of many other series. Hence, it is not enough for the statistician to know how to manipulate his data; he must also know what the data can stand.[1]

Questions

ACCURACY AND APPROXIMATION

General

Questions on accuracy and approximation do not appear as frequently in examination papers as was once the case. Nevertheless, they can and do pose problems for candidates. They require not so much the routine application of a basic technique but sometimes quite a lot of thought. Question 2 and Question 6 below both require careful thought if mistakes are not to be made. The selection of questions below illustrates the type of question which may appear in examinations.

1.

	Number of cattle slaughtered mln.	Quantity of beef produced thous. tons
1954	0·22	60·9
5	0·21	56·9
6	0·24	65·0
7	0·25	66·6
1958	0·25	66·4

Having regard to the degree of rounding up used in the above figures, comment on the change, if any, over the past five years, in the weight (cwt.) of beef produced per head of cattle. *I.M.T.A.*

2. A motorist whose car has a broken distance recorder and who, therefore, measures his distances by map-reading, wishes to assess his petrol consumption on a continental trip. His petrol gauge indicates his fuel consumption in litres with an error of $\pm 10\%$. He also uses approximate conversion factors of 1 gallon = 4·5 litres and 1 mile = 1·6 kilometres, instead of the more accurate 1 gallon = 4·55 litres and 1 mile = 1·61 kilometres.

(i) Estimate his probable petrol consumption in miles per gallon, giving limits of error, if he claims to be getting 31 miles per gallon after a trip of exactly 615 miles.

ii) If 31 miles per gallon is, in fact, an exact estimate and he states that he has used 95 litres of petrol, within what limits does his true mileage lie?
Institute of Statisticians

3. The table below shows the weekly wage bill and the numbers employed in three subsidiary companies. The figures have been rounded to the nearest £100 for the wage bill and the nearest 10 for the numbers employed.

---

[1] So important is a thorough understanding of the nature of statistical data in all statistical work, that it is debatable whether a firm should engage a statistician to analyse its data, or teach a member of its own staff, who is familiar with the product and production processes, sufficient statistical theory to enable him to analyse the available data. There are good arguments for both policies.

Company	Weekly wage bill £	Numbers employed
A	5,000	530
B	5,200	590
C	8,000	800

Calculate the average wage paid by each company and by the group as a whole. What is the maximum possible error due to rounding in the figures for:

(a) the wage bill;
(b) the numbers employed;
(c) the average wage,

for each of the three companies as well as for the group as a whole? Show in detail how you reach your estimates.   *I.C.W.A.*

4. Two measurements, A and B, are each subject to an error of $\pm$ 10 per cent. Determine the range of possible error of

(i) The sum $(A+B)$,
(ii) The product (AB),
(iii) The difference $(A-B)$,
(iv) The quotient (A/B),

when $A = 375$ and $B = 25$.
In each case express your result both as an absolute and as a relative error.

Institute of Statisticians

5. In a report making use of the following table (but not reproducing it in the text), it was stated only that the mean weight of the particles was 8·49 milligrams with standard deviation 3·891 milligrams.

Discuss the accuracy of these figures and usefulness of the summary statement.

Weight of small chemical particles (in milligrams, to nearest unit)				Number of particles
1	..	..	..	1
2	..	..	..	2
3	..	..	..	4
4	..	..	..	9
5	..	..	..	15
6	..	..	..	20
7	..	..	..	20
8	..	..	..	19
9	..	..	..	18
10	..	..	..	19
11	..	..	..	21
12	..	..	..	20
13	..	..	..	15
14	..	..	..	9
15	..	..	..	4
16	..	..	..	2
17	..	..	..	1
25	..	..	..	1
				200

Institute of Statisticians

6. The data overleaf refer to births and infant deaths in a single year for two areas in which vital registration is defective. The possible error is believed to be within the limits shown. Express the neo-natal death rate for area B as a percentage of that for area A, and indicate the margin of possible error in this result. Do the same for all infant deaths.

	Area A	*Area B*
No. of births ..	$4{,}168 \pm 5\%$	$6{,}285 \pm 7\%$
Neo-natal deaths ..	$392 \pm 6\%$	$614 \pm 4\%$
Post-natal deaths ..	$168 \pm 2\%$	$267 \pm 3\%$

Inter. D.M.A.

Answers

Answer to Question 1

This is a straightforward question in which the main problem is to remember that each calculation, in which the quantity of beef produced is divided by the number of cattle slaughtered, can yield two different answers depending on the basis of the rounding and the figures used as numerator and denominator. Thus, the rounded figures in the first year of 0.22mn and 60.9 thousand tons could have been rounded either upwards or downwards. Then, if the larger figure is taken as the numerator and the smaller estimate of the other figure as the denominator, as is the case in the figures in the column headed 'Maximum', the result will be larger than that derived when the alternatives are used as is shown in the column headed 'Minimum'.

Actual	*Maximum*	*Minimum*
$\dfrac{60\cdot90}{220} = \cdot2768$	$\dfrac{60\cdot94}{215} = \cdot2834$	$\dfrac{60\cdot85}{224} = \cdot2716$
$\dfrac{56\cdot90}{210} = \cdot2709$	$\dfrac{56\cdot94}{205} = \cdot2778$	$\dfrac{56\cdot85}{214} = \cdot2657$
$\dfrac{65\cdot00}{240} = \cdot2708$	$\dfrac{65\cdot04}{235} = \cdot2768$	$\dfrac{64\cdot95}{244} = \cdot2662$
$\dfrac{66\cdot60}{250} = \cdot2664$	$\dfrac{66\cdot64}{245} = \cdot2720$	$\dfrac{66\cdot55}{254} = \cdot2620$
$\dfrac{66\cdot40}{250} = \cdot2656$	$\dfrac{66\cdot44}{245} = \cdot2712$	$\dfrac{66\cdot35}{254} = \cdot2612$

Whichever method is used the resultant series both show a marked downward trend in the average weight of meat produced per head of cattle. Note that, to meet the requirement of the question, the quotients from each calculation have to be converted into hundredweights. This can be done merely by multiplying the quotients by 20. Thus, in the case of the first year's figures, the results would be a mean value of 5·54 cwts, a maximum value of 5·67 cwt and a minimum value of 5·43 cwt. Note that although decimal points have been inserted in the calculations, it is easier to ignore them until the final conversion into hundredweights.

Answer to Question 2

This is quite a difficult question and needs to be read with care before starting upon it. The suggested answer should be self-explanatory. Note that here too a maximum and minimum answer is derived.

A distance of 615 miles getting 31 m.p.g. requires 19·84 gallons. Converting this figure at 4·5 litres=1 gallon he uses 89·3 litres. Given 10% error in the gauge, the estimate of 89·3 litres could represent a consumption as high as $89\cdot3+8\cdot9=$ 98·2 litres or as low as $89\cdot3-8\cdot9=80\cdot4$ litres. If the higher figure is correct, then he used $\dfrac{98\cdot2}{4\cdot55} = 21\cdot58$ gallons; if the lower, then his petrol consumption was

$\dfrac{80\cdot4}{4\cdot55}=17\cdot66$ gallons.

He claims he travelled $615 \times 1 \cdot 6$ miles $= 984$ kilometres. In fact he travelled $\dfrac{984}{1 \cdot 61}$ miles $= 611 \cdot 2$. Given his highest petrol consumption he obtained $\dfrac{611 \cdot 2}{21 \cdot 58}$

$= 28 \cdot 3$ m.p.g. If the lowest, then he obtained $34 \cdot 6$ m.p.g., *i.e.* $\dfrac{611 \cdot 2}{17 \cdot 66}$

Answer to Question 3

As with Question 1 that the error in the mean can be in either direction. Note that the first part of the answer below is merely setting down the information given in the question. The error in the average wage given in the third line of the middle section of the draft answer is derived by taking the difference between the estimated mean and the minimum and maximum values. Thus, in Company B the mean wage is £881 but the maximum possible estimate of the average wage is £897 and the minimum estimate is £865, a range of £32 so that the mean lies within $\pm$ £16 of the mean.

Company	Wage bill £	Numbers employed	Average wage £
A	$5,000 \pm 100$	530 ± 10	943
B	$5,200 \pm 100$	590 ± 10	881
C	$8,000 \pm 100$	800 ± 10	1,000
Total	18,200	1,920	948

	A	B	C	Total
Error on Wage Bill	± 50	± 50	± 50	± 150
Error on Number employed	± 5	± 5	± 5	± 15
Error on Average Wage	$943 \cdot 5 \pm 18 \cdot 5$	881 ± 16	$1,000 \pm 13$	948 ± 15
Maximum	5,050	5,250	8,050	18,350
	525	585	795	1,905
	$= 962$	$= 897$	$= 1,013$	$= 963$
Minimum	4,950	5,150	7,950	18,050
	535	595	805	1,935
	$= 925$	$= 865$	$= 987$	$= 933$

Answer to Question 4

This is a straightforward question. In each case, *i.e.* calculation, two answers are possible, a maximum and a minimum. The absolute error in addition and subtraction is half the range of the difference between those two values. With division and multiplication, take the larger of the differences as the possible, *i.e.* maximum error.

$A+B = 375 \pm 10\% + 25 \pm 10\%$
$\qquad = 375 \pm 37 \cdot 5 + 25 \pm 2 \cdot 25$

(i) Maximum $= 412 \cdot 5 + 27 \cdot 5 = 440$
 Minimum $= 337 \cdot 5 + 22 \cdot 5 = 360$

 Mean $\qquad = 400 \pm 40$ Relative error $= \dfrac{40}{400} = 10\%$

(ii) $A \times B \quad = 375 \times 25 = 9,375$
 Maximum $= 412 \cdot 5 \times 27 \cdot 5 = 11,344$
 Minimum $= 337 \cdot 5 \times 22 \cdot 5 = 7,594$

 Mean $\qquad = 9,375 \pm 1,969$ Relative error $= \dfrac{1,969}{9,375} = 21\%$

(iii) $A - B \quad = 375 - 25 = 350$
 Maximum $= 412 \cdot 5 - 22 \cdot 5 = 390$
 Minimum $= 337 \cdot 5 - 27 \cdot 5 = 310$

 Mean $\qquad = 350 \pm 40$ Relative error $= \dfrac{40}{350} = 11 \cdot 1\%$

(iv) $A \div B \qquad = 375 \div 25 = 15$

$\qquad$ Maximum $= \dfrac{412 \cdot 5}{22 \cdot 5} = 18 \cdot 33$

$\qquad$ Minimum $= \dfrac{337 \cdot 5}{27 \cdot 5} = 12 \cdot 27$

$$\text{Possible error} = 15 \pm 3 \cdot 3 \text{ Relative error } \frac{3 \cdot 3}{15} = 22 \cdot 2\%$$

Answer to Question 5

The bulk of the work in this question entails the calculation of the mean and standard deviation of the summarised distribution. Note the differences between these statistics and the corresponding statistics derived from the original data. As indicated below this would suggest that the rounding has led to some bias in the result.

The mean and standard deviation calculated from the summarised distribution equal 9·09 and 3·75 respectively. These compare with 8·49 and 3·891.

The original statistics were presumably given to three places of decimals, otherwise the mean and standard deviation could not justifiably be given to 2 and 3 places of decimals respectively.

The difference between the estimate of the means is 0·6 (9·09 − 8·49) which seems rather high assuming that by rounding the values to the nearest unit the average error would be 0·5. A possible explanation is that the rounding process tended towards the upper value, *e.g.* 5·55, 15·57, etc. would be rounded to 6 and 16 respectively. This would, if frequent, produce a higher value for the mean of the summarised distribution than the calculation from the full data.

Answer to Question 6

A rather more complicated version of Questions 3 and 4, especially the second part. Note the very large error in the ratio of area B to A. This is an indication of how quite small errors in successive calculations can build up into substantial values.

		Area A	Area B
No. of births	..	$4,168 \pm 5\%$ (208)	$6,285 \pm 7\%$ (440)
Neo-natal deaths	..	$392 \pm 6\%$ (23.5)	$614 \pm 4\%$ (25)
Post-natal deaths	..	$168 \pm 2\%$ (3)	$267 \pm 3\%$ (8)

Neo-natal D/R

	Minimum	$\dfrac{368 \cdot 5}{4,376} = 8 \cdot 42$	$\dfrac{589}{6,725} = 8 \cdot 76$
	Maximum	$\dfrac{415 \cdot 5}{3,960} = 10 \cdot 49$	$\dfrac{639}{5,845} = 10 \cdot 93$

All infant deaths

	Minimum	$\dfrac{533}{4,376} = 12 \cdot 18$	$\dfrac{848}{6,725} = 12 \cdot 61$
	Maximum	$\dfrac{587}{3,960} = 14 \cdot 82$	$\dfrac{914}{5,845} = 15 \cdot 64$

Ratio of B:A

	Minimum	$\dfrac{8 \cdot 76}{10 \cdot 49} = 83 \cdot 5$	
N.N.D.			$= 106 \cdot 7 \pm 23 \cdot 1$
	Maximum	$\dfrac{10.93}{8 \cdot 42} = 129 \cdot 8$	
All infants	Maximum	$\dfrac{15 \cdot 64}{12 \cdot 18} = 128 \cdot 4$	
			$= 106 \cdot 7 \pm 21 \cdot 7$
	Minimum	$\dfrac{12 \cdot 61}{14 \cdot 82} = 85 \cdot 0$	

CHAPTER IX

REGRESSION AND CORRELATION

So far we have been discussing the description and analysis of one variable. For example, the weekly turnover of twenty retail shops can be set out in tabular form as follows and for this distribution it is possible to calculate the arithmetic mean and the standard deviation.

Retail Shop		1	2	3	4	5	6	7	8	9	10
Weekly Turnover	£	150	200	210	230	260	280	300	320	350	370
Retail Shop		11	12	13	14	15	16	17	18	19	20
Weekly Turnover	£	380	400	410	430	460	470	480	500	520	540

A similar tabulation can be constructed to show the gross profit of each of the same twenty shops and the same statistics calculated. There would, however, probably be some relationship between turnover and the amount of profit. We might ask, for example, whether the profit increases constantly with the turnover. In order to answer this question the data can be arranged, as a preliminary to further analysis, in the form of a table such as that above together with the following data relating to profits:

Retail Shop		1	2	3	4	5	6	7	8	9	10
Profit	£	30	35	40	45	50	50	60	65	70	70
Retail Shop		11	12	13	14	15	16	17	18	19	20
Profit	£	80	75	85	90	100	80	90	100	110	115

There are, however, rather too many figures to judge to what extent turnover and profit are directly connected, *i.e.* that a given increase in sales is accompanied by a specific increase in profits. A simple device for examining the data so as to bring out any relationship between the two variables is the so-called *scatter* diagram. This is an ordinary graph on which turnover is measured along the base and the profit against the vertical axis. For each shop there are two values which together locate a point on the graph. The twenty pairs of values are plotted on the graph depicted in Figure 17A. It is immediately

185

apparent that the points plotted form a clear pattern diagonally across the graph from the bottom left-hand corner to the top right. Such a pattern indicates that the amount of profit tends to rise with the sales volume of each shop.

Lines of Regression

It is possible to define the approximate relationship between profit and turnover in mathematical terms by means of an equation. Any straight line conforming to the path of the points plotted in the graph can be defined by an equation of the form $y = a + bx$. Given this equation and the values of a and b, which are termed constants, by substituting in the equation any value of x we can derive a value for y. Unfortunately, in this particular case, the points plotted do not lie exactly along such line. They are scattered about that line, some above and some below.

Now rearrange the data in the form of a frequency distribution so that for any given turnover the average profit is given.

Turnover x	Observed profit y	Average profit	Turnover x	Observed profit y	Average profit
150—	30	30	400—	75, 85, 90	83½
200—	35, 40, 45	40	450—	100, 80, 90	90
250—	50, 50	50	500—	100, 110	105
300—	60, 65	62½	500—	100, 110, 115	108½
350—	70, 70, 80	73½			

For each class of turnover an 'average' profit is derived. If these average profits are now plotted with the mid-points of the corresponding classes of turnover, it will be seen from Figure 17B that the approximation of the plotted points to a straight line is much better. The line that has been drawn on the basis of these points, *i.e.* through the means of each group of y values corresponding to each value of x, is drawn in such a way that the squares of the vertical distances between each of the points and the line under or over the point are at a minimum. A method of calculating the equation of such a line is explained later on p. 190. Such a line is called a *regression* line because it is derived from the equation which defines the regression of y upon x. In terms of our data, it measures the extent to which y, *i.e.* profit changes in relation to variations in the value of x, *i.e.* the turnover.

The rather curious term *regression* needs some explanation since it has no obvious relevance to the data. Regression analysis was introduced by Sir Francis Galton towards the end of the 19th century and

Figure 17
REGRESSION LINES

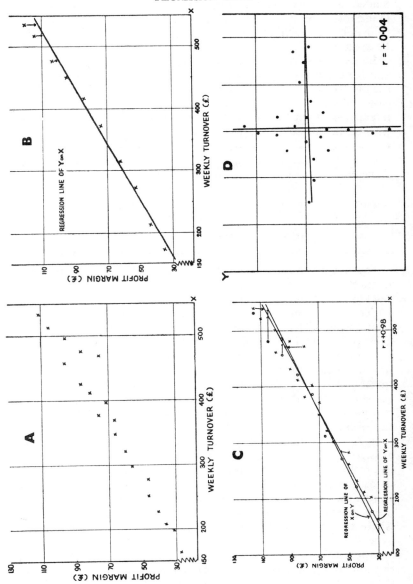

the original data he used related to the heights of fathers and sons. He found that on average tall fathers had tall sons, but the sons tended to 'regress' to the average male height. The term has remained in use for all types of data ever since although the methods now used to define such relationships were developed later by Professor Karl Pearson.

By re-classifying the original data as is done in the table below, another regression line can be derived for which the values for x and y are plotted on the scatter diagram (Graph C) as small circles. In this case, however, it is so drawn that the squares of the *horizontal* differences between the points and the regression line are minimised. This particular line is known as the regression line of x upon y.

Profits x	Observed Turnover y	Average Turnover	Profits x	Observed Turnover y	Average Turnover
30—	150, 200	175	80—	380, 410, 470	420
40—	210, 230	220	90—	430, 480	455
50—	260, 280	270	100—	460, 500	480
60—	300, 320	310	110—	520	520
70—	350, 370, 400	373	110—	520, 540	530

The obvious questions which come to mind are: 'what is the difference between the two regression lines' and when is it preferable to calculate the regression line of y upon x rather than that for x upon y? The answer lies in the fact that the two lines measure different relationships. That of y upon x indicates the extent to which, on average, profits will change as a result of a change in turnover. Using such a regression line it becomes possible to use the equation of that line for prediction purposes. In other words, if we define the relationship between profits and turnover by means of an equation, that equation will enable the value of y to be determined for any value of x. In sum, what profit is to be expected from a shop with a given turnover?

In the case of the second regression line, that of x upon y, this answers the question: 'what is the turnover of a shop likely to be if its profits are y?' This is not such a useful question because, with these data, it is clear that profits are dependent upon turnover. In other words, the independent variable is x or turnover, while y, profits, is the dependent variable. This is also reflected in the scatter diagram where the independent variable is plotted along the base and the dependent along the ordinate. Generally speaking, regression is appropriate where the two variables are linked in some causal relationship as with the above case. While it is perfectly easy to calculate the other regression line, there is not a lot of point to it since profits are so obviously the dependent variable. Suppose, however, there are two series one of which relates to total industrial output and the other to imports of raw materials. While it is self-evident that the volume of imports of raw materials will depend upon the level of industrial activity, *i.e.* output; if the economists are designing an economic model for future growth, it is just as important for them to be able to estimate the imports of raw materials which a projected level of industrial output in a year or two's time will require. In such a case, the regression of x upon y can be as useful as that for y upon x.

Since there is a basic assumption that some relationship exists between the two variables, common sense suggests that the two regression lines are in some way related. Consider the two diagrams 17C and D. In the former the two regression lines are very close; in D, however, they are at right angles to each other. The clue to this contrast is provided by the distribution of the points on the scatter diagram. In C the points of both lines, *i.e.* the little circles for x upon y and the crosses for y upon x are very close to their respective regression lines. Suppose now the points for the regression line of y upon x lay exactly along the regression line; in other words, the relation between x and y is what the statistician terms 'perfect'. Obviously, the vertical distances from the observed points to the line which provide the basis for drawing the line or what is termed, 'fitting' the line, will be zero. The same is true of the horizontal distances which enable the regression line of x upon y to be fitted. In other words, where the relationship between y and x is perfect, there can be only one regression line because the paths of the two lines, y upon x and x upon y, will coincide. At the other extreme, where there is no relationship between the two variables, as is illustrated by the scatter of the observations in 17D, the two lines will intersect each other at right angles.

Where the regression line defines a causal relationship it can be used for predictive purposes. For example, if imports depend on the level of economic activity, it becomes possible to forecast the volume of future imports for the expected level of economic activity. In other cases, however, an association or relationship between two variables may be observed but the relationship is clearly not causal. For example, the prices of fixed interest securities vary with the prices of equity stocks, but there is no direct causal relationship between them. In such cases instead of calculating the equation of a regression line, we calculate the *coefficient of correlation*, discussed below. The value of the coefficient will reflect the intensity of closeness of the relationship. This is in contrast to the regression equation which actually *defines* the relationship in such a way that, given a value of one variable, the corresponding value of the other variable can be derived.

Calculation of Regression Lines

The line of regression of y upon x is given by the equation $y=a+bx$ if the relationship between y and x is linear, *i.e.* when plotted it gives a straight line. We need first to determine the value of the two constants a and b. It is known that when x has its average value, the best estimate of the corresponding value of y is its own mean. Thus, we have two values for the above equation, $\bar{x}=363$ and $\bar{y}=72$.

The value for b, which gives the slope of the regression line, is derived from the equation $b=\dfrac{\Sigma xy}{\Sigma x^2}$ where x and y are the deviations of individual values of x and y from their respective means.[1] The numerator requires the deviations for each pair of x and y values to be multiplied together and their products added. This is done in col. 6 of the table opposite. The denominator in the above equation is the sum of all the squared deviations of x values from their mean as given in column 5. This is done in the same way as if we were proposing to calculate the standard deviation of the series of x values.

Thus if $b = \dfrac{\Sigma xy}{\Sigma x^2}$ then $b = \dfrac{53,780}{254,220} = 0.2115$

We now have three of the four values in the equation $y = a + bx$, *i.e.* $x = 363$, $y = 72$ and $b = 0.2115$. The fourth value a is easily derived:

$72 = a + 0.2115(363)$

$72 = a + 76.8 \therefore a = -4.8$

Therefore, the complete regression equation of y on x as drawn in Figure 17B reads: $y'=-4.8 + 0.2115\,(x)$. The y' symbol indicates that this value of y is a calculated or predicted value, using this equation.

We can test the equation by substituting some of the known values of x, *e.g.* 200, and compare the predicted value of y, which is 37.5 when $x = 200$, compared with an observed value of 35. Thus the correspondence is quite close.

Just as we have calculated the regression line of y upon x, we can calculate the line of x upon y. In this case, the value of b is given by the equation $b=\dfrac{\Sigma\, xy}{\Sigma\, y^2}$. The calculation of Σy^2 is given in column 7 below and the student can repeat the calculations given above to obtain the regression equation of x upon y. The answer is $x=36.1+4.53y$.

Reference has been made to the usefulness of the regression equation for prediction purposes. The method is really very simple;

---

[1] Or in the alternative notation at the top of the columns on page 191 $\dfrac{\Sigma(x-\bar{x})\,(y-\bar{y})}{\Sigma(x-\bar{x})^2}$

CALCULATION OF REGRESSION EQUATION

x	y	$(x - \bar{x})$	$(y - \bar{y})$	$(x - \bar{x})^2$	$(x - \bar{x}) \times (y - \bar{y})$	$(y - \bar{y})^2$
(1)	(2)	(3)	(4)	(5)	(6)	(7)
150	30	—213	— 42	45,369	8,946	1,764
200	35	—163	— 37	26,569	6,031	1,369
210	40	—153	— 32	23,409	4,896	1,024
230	45	—133	— 27	17,689	3,591	729
260	50	—103	— 22	10,609	2,266	484
280	50	— 83	— 22	6,889	1,826	484
300	60	— 63	— 12	3,969	756	144
320	65	— 43	— 7	1,849	301	49
350	70	— 13	— 2	169	26	4
370	70	+ 7	— 2	49	— 14	4
380	80	+ 17	+ 8	289	136	64
400	75	+ 37	+ 3	1,369	111	9
410	85	+ 47	+ 13	2,209	611	169
430	90	+ 67	+ 18	4,489	1,206	324
460	100	+ 97	+ 28	9,409	2,716	784
470	80	+107	+ 8	11,449	856	64
480	90	+117	+ 18	13,689	2,106	324
500	100	+137	+ 28	18,769	3,836	784
520	110	+157	+ 38	24,649	5,966	1,444
540	115	+177	+ 43	31,329	7,611	1,849
$\bar{x} = 363$	$\bar{y} = 72$	0	0	254,220	53,780	11,870

once the equation has been derived it is only necessary to substitute for the x value a figure for which the corresponding value of y is needed. Take, for example, the regression equation of profits (y) upon turnover (x) calculated above, i.e. $y = —4·8 + 0·2115x$. In the table of observed values there is no figure for a turnover of £450 and one may want to know what is the likely profit from such a turnover. The answer is derived as follows:

$$\text{given that } y = —4·8 + 0·2115x$$

if $x = £450$, then y will equal $—4·8 + 0·2115(450)$

$$\text{which equals} —4·8 + 95·17 = \text{approx. } £90.4$$

Alternatively, instead of estimating a value for y which lies within the range of the observed values of x as in the previous illustration, the same technique can be used to make a prediction of what profits would be earned if turnover reached £560. The procedure is as before:

$$\text{given that } y = —4·8 + 0·2115x$$

$$\text{then } y = —4·8 + 0·2115(560)$$

$$= £113.6$$

Having calculated such figures they should be compared with the observed values. The first estimate of £90.6 with a turnover of £450 is probably a little low. For example, the profits for turnovers of £430 and £460 respectively are shown in the table as £90 and £100 respectively and one would have expected the estimate of y for an x value of £450 to be nearer the larger figure. In the case of the second example where the turnover is £560, the predicted profit of £113.6 again seems a shade low compared with an observed profit of £115 on a turnover of £540 and a profit of £110 on a turnover of £520.

These discrepancies should not lead the reader to discount the value of regression for estimation and prediction purposes. Only if the observed values fell exactly along the regression line would a derived value for some intervening figure fit perfectly with all the other values. The 'fit' of this particular regression line is very good but even so, some variation must be expected. Nevertheless, the discrepancy noted is not so large that the result should be rejected. In the case of 'predicting' values beyond the range of the observed values, especial care must be exercised. It cannot be assumed that the linear relationship which apparently describes the relationship between the two variables will continue for values beyond those observed. The derived value in this case seems acceptable but, when time series are discussed and where such 'extrapolation', as it is termed, is frequently used, the dangers of over-enthusiastic prediction by such means will be emphasised.[1]

In the above example it was possible to work out the value of b from the true means of x and y. This is not always the case and just as when calculating the mean or the standard deviation we may have to work from assumed means, so it is possible to derive the regression equations by working from assumed means. In such a case, the

formula for b for the line of y on x reads $\quad \dfrac{\Sigma xy - \dfrac{\Sigma x \Sigma y}{n}}{\Sigma x^2 - \dfrac{(\Sigma x)^2}{n}}$

The corrections $\dfrac{\Sigma x \Sigma y}{n}$ and $\dfrac{(\Sigma x)^2}{n}$ are really the same as we should use when calculating the standard deviations of x and y. Space does not allow us to show all the details, but if the data given in the table were re-calculated taking 350 and 75 as the assumed mean of x and y, then the total line at the bottom of the table would read as follows:

$\Sigma(x-\bar{x})$	$\Sigma(y-\bar{y})$	$\Sigma(x-\bar{x})^2$	$\Sigma(x-\bar{x})(y-\bar{y})$	$\Sigma(y-\bar{y})^2$
+260	—60	257,600	53,000	12,050

Substituting in the above equation for b, we get:

[1] See Chapter XI.

$$b = \frac{53,000 - \frac{(260)\,(-60)}{20}}{257,600 - \frac{(260)^2}{20}} = 0.2115$$

Since we are working from assumed means a further correction of the assumed mean is required to derive the regression equation. Thus:

$$\begin{aligned}
y - \bar{y} &= b(x - \bar{x}) \\
y - 72 &= 0.2115(x - 363) \\
y &= 72 + 0.2115x - 76.8 \\
y &= -4.8 + 0.2115x
\end{aligned}$$

As may be checked from the previous page, this is the same result as was derived by working from the true means.

The Coefficient of Correlation

As already explained, the coefficient of correlation is a measure of association. Sometimes, but not invariably, the relationship is causal, *e.g.* the age of a child and its weight; the number of hours of sunshine at a seaside resort and the receipts from the hiring of deck-chairs. The coefficient differs from the equation defining either of the lines of regression in so far as the latter define a unique relationship from which, given the change in (say) x, it is possible to compute the most probable change that will follow in y. The coefficient of correlation denoted by r indicates the closeness of the association without defining it. For example, the correlation coefficient of $+0.98$ given by the data relating to the 20 retail shops (the calculation of this statistic is given on p. 195) suggests that there is a close relationship between the turnover and profit. If the coefficient had been only $+0.3$ we would probably have deduced that the relationship was not sufficiently strong – at least from the data available – to justify any use of the relationship for analysis or prediction. Generally speaking, it is customary to compute the correlation coefficient and to ignore the lines of regression and the regression equations unless the relationship between the variables is such that it may reasonably be summarised in the form of a mathematical equation.

In the above illustration the relationship between x and y was such that the pairs of observed values increased together or declined together. In such a case the correlation is described as positive or *direct*. When an increase in one variable is accompanied by a fall in the other, for example, an increase in family incomes is accompanied by a fall in the consumption of cheaper foods such as bread and potatoes, then the correlation is known as *inverse* or negative. The distinction between the two types of relationship is always indicated by the sign, plus or minus, placed before the value of the coefficient or correlation. This coefficient is zero when there is no association between x and y, *i.e.* when the regression lines would be at right angles to each other (Graph D). When the regression lines coincide, however, *i.e.* perfect association, the coefficient has a value of unity. For example, in Graph C the relationship is very close and in consequence *r* is equal to +0·98, whereas in Graph D it is only +0·04.

The formula for determining the value of the coefficient is such that the latter will always lie between zero and unity, either positive or negative. It can never be greater than 1. Hence, if the student finds at the end of an exercise that his coefficient exceeds unity, then he will know he has made a mistake in the calculations.

The next few sections of this chapter are devoted to explaining methods of deriving the coefficient of correlation, *i.e.* *r*. In common with all statistics derived from sample data, the larger the sample the more reliable the statistic. In order, however, to simplify the exposition and keep the calculations to a minimum the illustrations are based on typical examination questions rather than realistic data.

Calculating the Coefficient

When the relationship between two variables is linear and the data have not been grouped, and only in such cases, the coefficient of correlation is calculated by means of the following formula:

$$r = \frac{\Sigma xy}{n \sigma_x \sigma_y}$$

This formula or method is sometimes referred to as the product-moment, or the Pearsonian coefficient; the first following the method of calculation and the second the name of its discoverer, Karl Pearson.

The symbols *x* and *y* in the numerator (*i.e.* the upper part of the fraction) represent not single values of *x* and *y*, but the deviations of all *x* and *y* values from their respective means, in the same way as we used the deviations from the mean when calculating standard deviations by the short method (see p. 145). To remind us of the meaning of the above formula for *r*, we can write the numerator as $\Sigma(x-\bar{x})$ $(y-\bar{y})$ where *x* is any single value of that variable and $\bar{x}$ is the mean of all the *x* values.[1] The same applies to *y*. Note that these 'deviations' will also be used for calculating the two standard deviations which the formula requires.

In the following illustration the data relate to the turnover and the profit margin of the sample of shops discussed earlier. It is required to calculate the coefficient of correlation between the size of the weekly turnover and profit margin. The data are given in columns 1, 2

The symbol Σ means the 'sum of' all these products.

and 3 and the calculations may best be followed if set out in stages. The true means of both distributions are easily found. In the case of the weekly turnover it is £363, and in the case of profit, £72. In columns 4 and 5 the deviations from the means of the values of each variable are set out. In columns 6 and 7 the deviations given in columns 4 and 5 have been squared and summed. The calculation so far is no more than would be required for deriving the standard deviations of any two distributions. Since the deviations of the individual

CALCULATION OF r BY PRODUCT-MOMENT METHOD

1 Re- tailer No.	2 Weekly Turn- over (x) £	3 Profit Margin (y) £	4 $(x-\bar{x})$	5 $(y-\bar{y})$	6 $(x-\bar{x})^2$	7 $(y-\bar{y})^2$	8 $(x-\bar{x})(y-\bar{y})$
1	150	30	− 213	− 42	45,369	1,764	+ 8,946
2	200	35	− 163	− 37	26,569	1,369	+ 6,031
3	210	40	− 153	− 32	23,409	1,024	+ 4,896
4	230	45	− 133	− 27	17,689	729	+ 3,591
5	260	50	− 103	− 22	10,609	484	+ 2,266
6	280	50	− 83	− 22	6,889	484	+ 1,826
7	300	60	− 63	− 12	3,969	144	+ 756
8	320	65	− 43	− 7	1,849	49	+ 301
9	350	70	− 13	− 2	169	4	+ 26
10	370	70	+ 7	− 2	49	4	− 14
11	380	80	+ 17	+ 8	289	64	+ 136
12	400	75	+ 37	+ 3	1,369	9	+ 111
13	410	85	+ 47	+ 13	2,209	169	+ 611
14	430	90	+ 67	+ 18	4,489	324	+ 1,206
15	460	100	+ 97	+ 28	9,409	784	+ 2,716
16	470	80	+ 107	+ 8	11,449	64	+ 856
17	480	90	+ 117	+ 18	13,689	324	+ 2,106
18	500	100	+ 137	+ 28	18,769	784	+ 3,836
19	520	110	+ 157	+ 38	24,649	1,444	+ 5,966
20	540	115	+ 177	+ 43	31,329	1,849	+ 7,611
	7,260	1,440	0	+0	254,220	11,870	+ 53,780

$$\bar{x} = \frac{7,260}{20} = 363. \quad \bar{y} = \frac{1,440}{20} = 72.$$

$$\sigma x = \sqrt{\frac{254,220}{20}} = 112\cdot7. \quad \sigma y = \sqrt{\frac{11,870}{20}} = 24\cdot4.$$

$$r = \frac{\Sigma(x-\bar{x})(y-\bar{y})}{n\sigma x\,\sigma y} = \frac{53,780}{20 \times 112\cdot7 \times 24\cdot4}$$

$$= \frac{53,780}{54,997\cdot6} = 0\cdot98.$$

values in both series have been measured from their means their sum is zero (see columns 4 and 5). Column 8 provides the sum of the cross products. The deviations in columns 4 and 5 are multiplied together and their products and their sum are in column 8. The mean of their sum, *i.e.* the total products divided by N, is often referred to as the *co-variance*. The next stage is to substitute these values in the appropriate formula. The numerator is given by the sum of the cross-products in column 8 and is divided by the number of pairs of items, *i.e.* 20, and the product of the two standard deviations. The two standard deviations are easily derived from the data given in columns 6 and 7. It will be noted that the working in this example is from the true means, hence no correction is necessary. Substituting the appropriate values in the formula for the correlation coefficient, the value of the coefficient is derived by simple arithmetic.

The numerator in the formula is based on the need to provide a meaning for 'high' and 'low' values of the coefficient. All the values of each variable must be related to a comparable value; in this case the means of the two distributions are the norm for each pair of values. Provided the pairs of x and y values follow some pattern in

			Ia			Ib	
x	$(x-\bar{x})$	y	$(y-\bar{y})$	$(x-\bar{x})(y-\bar{y})$	y	$(y-\bar{y})$	$(x-\bar{x})(y-\bar{y})$
3	− 6	7	−12	+ 72	28	+ 9	54
5	− 4	14	− 5	+ 20	24	+ 5	− 20
7	− 2	20	+ 1	− 2	21	+ 2	− 4
9	0	21	+ 2	0	20	+ 1	0
13	+ 4	24	+ 5	+ 20	14	− 5	− 20
17	+ 8	28	+ 9	+ 72	7	−12	− 96
6)54		6)114		+ 182	6)114		− 194
$\bar{x}=9$		$\bar{y}=19$			$\bar{y}=19$		

II.

x	$(x-\bar{x})$	y	$(y-\bar{y})$	$(x-\bar{x})(y-\bar{y})$
3	− 6	20	+ 1	− 6
5	− 4	14	− 5	+ 20
7	− 2	28	+ 9	− 18
9	0	21	+ 2	0
13	+ 4	7	−12	− 48
17	+ 8	24	+ 5	+ 40
6)54		6)144		− 12
$\bar{x}=9$		$\bar{y}=19$		

Note that the values of x are unchanged for all three sets of values of y. In Ia, the high values of y are related to high values of x; in Ib the reverse. In both cases the value Σxy is large in arithmetic or absolute terms. In case II there is no pattern about the values of y in relation to x and Σxy is a negligible quantity, therefore r would also be very small. The standard deviations of the three distributions of y given above will, of course, be the same in each case.

respect of their variation from their respective means – which will be the case if the two values are related – then positive deviations from the mean for the values of x associated with similar positive deviations of the other variable y means that r will also be positive. If, however, positive deviations of x are related to negative deviations of y, then r will be negative. It is clear from the example II above that if high and low values of x and y are indiscriminately associated (*i.e.* the paired variations from the respective means of both x and y values are not consistent in their signs) then the sum of the products of the deviations will be small. Therefore r, too, will tend to be small.

When there is any relationship between the variation in x and y values the sum of the cross-products will be large. And, the larger the absolute value of the deviations, the larger will be the sum of these cross-products. The case of the standard deviation may be recalled; this is expressed in the units of the distribution and if the values are large the σ is large, *e.g.* the σ of the weights of adult males in absolute terms is greater than the σ of the weights of adult females; but if related to their respective means, *e.g.* as with the coefficient of variation described on page 148, the dispersion of weight among females is greater. For similar reasons, in the product-moment formula the sum of the cross-products is related to the products of the standard deviations of the two distributions. In effect, the cross-products are 'standardised' so that the value of r is no longer influenced by the absolute value of the factors in the cross-products. In consequence the value of r is a coefficient that has no dimensions.

Students often complain that they cannot remember the formula for calculating the coefficient of correlation. This is understandable, but if they remember the basis of the statistic it should be possible to work it out. It has been explained that the value of r is dependent on the degree to which deviations of x and y move in sympathy. This means that the deviations of x and y from their respective means are consistent with regard to sign. Thus, either positive deviations in x are matched with similar or consistently negative changes in y. As was shown above, if the signs do not correspond, then the sum of the cross-products is small, if they do, then the sum of the cross-products tends to be high, particularly if there is any relationship between the variables.

On the other hand, the sum of the cross-products may be high because the actual values, and therefore the deviations, are large in absolute terms, *e.g.* they may be expressed in pounds instead of ounces. Secondly, their sum will tend to be greater, the larger the number of pairs of variables. Obviously a statistic which is affected both by the number of observations and the absolute size of the variates is unsatisfactory. This weakness is overcome by relating the sum of the cross-products of the x and y deviations to (a) the number of paired observations, i.e. N and (b) a measure of the actual deviations in both variables, i.e. the standard deviations of x and y. Since both the co-variance and the standard deviations are affected by the absolute size of the variates, by dividing one into the other this distorting factor is eliminated. If the student reader examines the formula for the coefficient in the light of the foregoing, he may not need to rely on his memory so much.

Calculating r using assumed means

In the second example given below the data are derived from a social survey in London. It is proposed to calculate the coefficient of correlation between poverty and overcrowding. For the purposes of

Calculation of co-efficient of correlation between Poverty (defined as living below given minimum standard) and Overcrowding (defined as more than two persons per room) in 12 London boroughs.

Borough	No. per 200 households in Poverty(x)	Over-crowded(y)	$(x-\bar{x})$	$(y-\bar{y})$	$(x-\bar{x})^2$	$(y-\bar{y})^2$	$(x-\bar{x})(y-\bar{y})$
A	17	36	+ 7	+14	49	196	+ 98
B	13	46	+ 3	+24	9	576	+ 72
C	15	35	+ 5	+13	25	169	+ 65
D	16	24	+ 6	+ 2	36	4	+ 12
E	6	12	— 4	—10	16	100	+ 40
F	11	18	+ 1	— 4	1	16	— 4
G	14	27	+ 4	+ 5	16	25	+ 20
H	9	22	— 1	0	1	0	0
I	7	2	— 3	—20	9	400	+ 60
J	2	8	— 8	—14	64	196	+112
K	10	17	0	— 5	0	25	0
L	5	10	— 5	—12	25	144	+ 60
12	125	257	+ 5	— 7	251	1851	+535

Actual means are 10·42 and 21·42 but to avoid calculations with such awkward figures, work from assumed means. Select 10 as the mean of x and 22 as the mean of y. The formula in this case is as follows:

$$r = \frac{\dfrac{\Sigma(x-\bar{x})(y-\bar{y})}{n} - \left(\dfrac{\Sigma(x-\bar{x})}{n} \times \dfrac{\Sigma(y-\bar{y})}{n}\right)}{\sigma_x\sigma_y}$$

$$\sigma_x = \sqrt{\frac{251}{12} - \left(\frac{5}{12}\right)^2} = 4\cdot5 \quad \sigma_y = \sqrt{\frac{1851}{12} - \left(\frac{-7}{12}\right)^2} = 12\cdot4$$

$$r = \frac{\dfrac{535}{12} - \left(\dfrac{5}{12}\right)\left(\dfrac{-7}{12}\right)}{4\cdot5 \times 12\cdot4}$$

$$= \frac{44\cdot83}{55\cdot8} = +0\cdot80$$

the survey poverty was defined as living below a prescribed minimum standard, and overcrowding was defined as living more than two persons per room. These definitions are unimportant for the purposes of the calculation. They are, of course, essential for purposes of interpreting the data. The figures for poverty and overcrowding, *i.e.* the variables x and y, are in the nature of percentages, although they are actually expressed per 200 households. For example, in borough A while 17 out of every 200 households were living in poverty, 36 were overcrowded.

The data are set out in the same way as in the earlier example, but the calculation is complicated by the fact that the standard deviations and the cross-products are worked not from the true means of the two variables but from assumed means. In other words, a correction must be introduced. The student will remember the correction required for purposes of calculating the standard deviation. It is shown in the example above. The correction for the sum of the cross-products measured from their true means is quite simple. The cross-products actually given in the final column of this table are based on the deviations measured from assumed means in each distribution. The error arising by using the assumed mean instead of the true mean for both x and y is given in the first two working columns. If the sum of the cross-products in the last column is divided by N, *i.e.* the number of pairs, we obtain the average product. From this we deduct the product of the two errors in the two averages or means divided by n^2. The result is then equal to the sum of the cross-products of the deviations just as if they had been measured from their true means. The subsequent arithmetic is as in the earlier example.

The student-reader will not have failed to note the considerable amount of arithmetic required in the first example on page 195. Quite apart from the fact that it contained twenty pairs of observed values, there was disproportionately more calculation than in the second example. As an exercise the student can apply the principles of the second illustration to the first set of data. Note, for example, that all the values of x are rounded to the nearest £10, similarly the y values are rounded to the nearest £5. Instead of taking the true means of x and y, use a multiple of 10 and 5 for the means of x and y respectively. Take, for example, £350 and £75 as the assumed means. All the deviations of x and y can then be given in multiples of 10 and 5. If, as in the illustration of calculating the standard deviation from an assumed mean in terms of class intervals given on page 146, you use deviations in terms of the class intervals, the calculations will be much easier. Note that the cross-products will then be in units of the product of the two class intervals, *i.e.* £10 × 5. If the actual value of the standard deviation for either variable were required, it would be necessary to convert the figure obtained, by multiplying it by the appropriate class interval. This correction is not required for calculating the coefficient of correlation since the sum of the cross-products making up the numerator in the formula, and the product of the two standard deviations, are both expressed in class-intervals. The answer derived from this calculation will be the same as for the more detailed method. By performing it, the student reader will ensure that he has followed the basis of the calculations.

Calculating r from grouped data

In the third example illustrating the calculation of the correlation coefficient the data are set out in what is known as a bivariate table. It will be noted that the pattern of the figures over the grids is somewhat similar in appearance to the scatter diagram discussed earlier. The data in this example relate to the monthly expenditure on accommodation and food of 33 individuals. All figures are given in pounds. Instead of the pairs of individual values of x and y in the two earlier examples, this illustration comprises two grouped frequency distributions, one of which is read horizontally, *i.e.* expenditure on food, and the other vertically, *i.e.* expenditure on accommodation. The layout of the calculation should be studied with especial care. The four vertical columns to the side of the table and the four horizontal columns below it are the same except that those to the right show the calculations for the y values and those below for x. The column headed f is nothing more than the frequencies derived by cross-adding the frequencies within each cell. Thus reading from the right-hand columns, there are 9 cases where the expenditure on accommodation is £50 per month. The second column in each case relates to the deviation from the assumed mean which is £45 for x and £55 for y. As before, these assumed means are represented by the symbols $\bar{x}$ and $\bar{y}$, and the third and fourth columns in each case are the sum of the frequencies and deviations and the deviations squared required to compute the difference between the assumed and true mean and the standard deviation. Note at the head of each column the reminder that the deviations are in class-interval units, hence we write $f(y-\bar{y})$ $\div c.i.$

The calculation of the cross-products is more complex, however. As in the two earlier examples, the related pairs of deviations must be multiplied together but, whereas in the earlier examples there was only one of each pair, in the present example there are more than one in several cases. For example, in the bottom left-hand corner of the grid it will be seen that there are four cases in which the expenditure on accommodation is £90 and over, while the expenditure on food is

Expenditure on Food (x)
(£)

Expenditure on Accom-modation y (£)	10—	20—	30—	40—	50—	60—	f	$\dfrac{y-\bar{y}}{c.i.}$	$\dfrac{f(y-\bar{y})}{c.i.}$	$\dfrac{f(y-\bar{y})^2}{c.i.}$
20—				1_{-3}			1	—3	—3	9
30—			1_2				1	—2	—2	4
40—		1_2		2_0	4_{-1}		7	—1	—7	7
50—		5_0		4_0			9	0	0	0
60—			1_{-1}	3_0	2_1	1_2	7	1	7	7
70—				2_0			2	2	4	8
80—								3		
90—	4_{-12}	2_{-8}					6	4	24	96
	4	8	2	11	7	1	33		23	131
$x-\bar{x} \div c.i.$	— 3	— 2	—1		1	2				
$f(x-\bar{x}) \div c.i.$	—12	—16	—2		7	2	—21			
$f(x-\bar{x})^2 \div c.i.$	36	32	2		7	4	81			

$$r = \dfrac{\dfrac{\Sigma f(x\text{-}\bar{x})(y\text{-}\bar{y})}{n} - \dfrac{\Sigma f(x\text{-}\bar{x}) \times \Sigma f(y\text{-}\bar{y})}{n^2}}{\sigma_x\,\sigma_y}$$

Sum of the cross products, *i.e.* $\Sigma f(x\text{-}\bar{x})(y\text{-}\bar{y})$: — 3 + 2 + 2 — 4 — 1 + 2 +2 — 48 — 16 = — 64.

$$\dfrac{\Sigma f(y\text{-}\bar{y})}{n} = \dfrac{23}{33}$$
$$= 0\cdot697$$

$$\dfrac{\Sigma f(x\text{-}\bar{x})}{n} = \dfrac{-21}{33}$$
$$= -0\cdot636$$

$$\sigma_y = \sqrt{\dfrac{131}{33} - \left(\dfrac{23}{33}\right)^2}$$
$$= \sqrt{3\cdot969 - 0\cdot485}$$
$$= 1\cdot87$$

$$\sigma_x = \sqrt{\dfrac{81}{33} - \left(\dfrac{-21}{33}\right)^2}$$
$$= \sqrt{2\cdot454 - 0\cdot405}$$
$$= 1\cdot43$$

by substitution we get $\dfrac{-64}{33} - (0\cdot697)(-0\cdot636) = -1\cdot94 + 0\cdot44 = -1\cdot5.$

$$r = \dfrac{-1\cdot5}{1\cdot43 \times 1\cdot87} = \dfrac{-1.5}{2\cdot67} = -0\cdot56$$

between £10 and £20. The deviations corresponding to this item are +4 and —3. These will be found in the second columns of the calculations beside and below the grid respectively. The product of the deviations —3 and 4, equals —12, and is inserted in the corner of the cell containing the four cases. In the adjacent cell, which shows that there are two cases where the expenditure on accommodation ranges from £90 while expenditure on food is £20 and over, the appropriate deviations are —2 and +4, so that —8, *i.e.* the product of these deviations, is inserted in the corner of the cell. This is done for each cell which contains a frequency. It will be noted, however, that all the cells opposite the classes containing the assumed means, 40– in the case of food and 50– for accommodation, have for obvious reasons a product equal to zero.

The next stage is then to multiply the cross-products of the deviations inserted in these cells by the frequency within that cell, due regard being paid to signs. This is done below the table, each product being set out individually, yielding in this case a net sum of —64. Very often the products of the cell frequency and the deviation product are inserted in the cell in the opposite corner to that containing the product of the deviations. This practice can be confusing for the student and entails a double lot of writing since the products have to be summed separately. The student should work these stages through by himself with the example, checking that he fully understands what has been done. The remainder of the calculation is then similar to that in our second example. A correction is required for the fact that the cross-products and standard deviations have both been measured from assumed means. As in the second example, the sum of the cross-products, *i.e.* —64, is averaged over the 33 pairs, and the product of the differences between the assumed and true means of x and y respectively deducted from the average cross-product. That value is then divided by the products of the two standard deviations.

The Significance of r

Correlation analysis has been applied to data from most scientific fields. It has been used to determine the relationship between crop yields and variations in the application of fertilisers; the level of fat-stock prices and its relation to the cost of feeding-stuffs. Engineers and chemists employ correlation to determine the extent to which properties of their products are affected by variations in the production processes. Its use has been extended to psychological tests designed to measure aptitude for particular types of work, *e.g.* accident proneness and temperament. It is largely for this reason, namely the widespread and frequent references to results derived from correlation analysis, that the topic is discussed in this elementary text.

In practice, the analysis is complicated by other than the purely statistical problems of technique.

In common with most statistical techniques, correlation analysis is usually employed on samples. Thus r, like other statistics derived from samples, must be examined to see how far the results may be generalised for the population from which the sample was drawn. Significance tests have also been evolved for the correlation co-efficient.[1] These lie beyond the scope of an elementary text, not because they are difficult to compute, but simply because, like correlation analysis itself, the technique has to be employed with great care and the interpretation of the data, as well as the results, demands a skill and knowledge of the field of enquiry only possessed by the expert. The value of correlation analysis is underlined by the variety of fields in which it finds application, but at all times it is essential to consider the data and ask 'what is the nature of the relationship measured by the coefficient?' Do not assume that the relationship is causal unless there is other evidence to support the assumption. Watch out for 'spurious' correlations; e.g. linking two related variables one of which is part of the other. For example, the number of households is obviously dependent on the size of the population and one would get a high value for r. But just what would it mean?

In the illustrative examples given above, the samples were extremely small, although in our final example, which contained 33 paired observations, it may be conceded in theory at least that this is a large sample. The most difficult problem is to interpret the value of the correlation coefficient. Thus the fact that in our final example the correlation coefficient was —0·5 might, since r falls considerably short of unity, lead the reader to assume that the correlation between the two types of outlay is negligible. Unfortunately it is not possible to interpret the coefficient correlation in this way. It is not possible, for example, to say that a value of r equal to 0·9 is very high and more significant than one equal to 0·8 since much will depend upon the size of the sample used. Nor should too much be read into the co-efficient. In the first example, which showed the relationship between the turnover and profit margin, it is apparent and reasonable to assume that these two variables are interrelated, and that the margin is dependent upon turnover, i.e. the relationship is causal. The coefficient of correlation tells us nothing about the nature of the relationship; it merely indicates its existence. It is for the statistician to interpret it and deduce its nature and significance. It is in this respect that regression is so useful, since it defines in exact terms the relationship between the two variables. In the second example, the correlation coefficient of +0·8 suggests a significant relationship

[1] Some of the simpler tests of significance are discussed in Chapter XIV.

between poverty and overcrowding which is probably causal too, *i.e.* people are overcrowded because they are poor. At all times, however, one must beware of drawing dogmatic conclusions from limited data.

One final use of correlation analysis may be mentioned. Generally speaking, the square of the value of r may be regarded as the percentage of the variation in y directly attributable to changes in x. Thus, as far as the first illustration is concerned, approximately 81 per cent of the variation in y is explained by variations in x. This figure is known as the 'explained variance', while the balance of 19 per cent is termed the 'unexplained variance'. This means that as far as the available data are concerned, no precise explanation of the cause of 19 per cent of the variation is given. It may be attributable to any or many of several causes.

Rank Correlation

The methods of correlation that have so far been demonstrated have ail been concerned with the measurement of the relationship between series of *numerical values*. It is possible, however, to measure the degree of correlation between two sets of observations or between paired values when only the *relative* order of magnitude is available for each series. For example, suppose a group of students sat two papers in an examination, and instead of the actual marks awarded on each paper, they were told only their ranking in order of merit. To establish whether the performances on the two papers were correlated or not, the method of *rank* correlation could be used.

The coefficient of rank correlation is given by Spearman's formula:

$$r_r = 1 - \left(\frac{6\Sigma d^2}{n(n^2-1)}\right)$$

where d is the numerical difference between corresponding pairs of ranks and n the number of pairs.

Student	Rank in French	Rank in Latin	d	d^2
A	1	3	2	4
B	2	2	0	0
C	3	1	2	4
D	4	6	2	4
E	5	5	0	0
F	6	8	2	4
G	7	4	3	9
H	8	10	2	4
I	9	7	2	4
J	10	9	1	1
				34

In the preceding example, ten students are ranked in order of merit on two examination papers in French and Latin.

Substituting the values derived from the above table in Spearman's formula

$$r_r = 1 - \left(\frac{6 \times 34}{10(10^2 - 1)}\right) = 1 - \left(\frac{204}{990}\right) = +0.79$$

which suggests quite a strong relationship between performance in the two papers. Here again, however, the sample is so very small that it would be unwise to infer from this evidence that students who are good at French are also good at Latin. This may be true and common-sense supports the thesis, but the *statistical* evidence here is too slight to confirm it without reservation.

As well as in the type of problem just illustrated the coefficient of rank correlation may be calculated for series of *qualitative* instead of *quantitative* data, *e.g.* colour of hair and intensity of emotion measured on a non-numerical scale, or any attribute which cannot be measured numerically. Similarly we could calculate the coefficient of rank correlation for any group of paired observations even if they were numerical values, *e.g.* marks instead of placings in an examination, and the normal coefficient of correlation could be calculated by the product moment formula shown earlier. Significance tests for rank correlation do exist, but they are not relevant in this elementary text.

As with all the techniques described so far, correlation analysis has no value for its own sake. It is useful solely because, if properly used, it permits theories and hypotheses to be verified or rejected on the basis of empirical evidence. At all times it must be remembered that such specialised tools may easily be misapplied and give misleading results.

Further Worked Examples

References to correlation and to regression are scattered throughout the literature of the social sciences; articles in the professional journals which include any statistical data will often be found which show the regression equation or the correlation coefficient of the relationships. For this reason it is important that the reader, who is probably interested in statistics not for their own sake but in their application, should comprehend what such statistics mean. For those readers who are preparing for an examination it is equally important that they understand not only why the regression equation or the correlation coefficient are calculated, but also how those calculations can be carried out. Almost all examination papers include questions on one or other of these statistics; quite often these days the candidate is given the choice of calculating one or the other of these statistics from the same data. For both these classes of reader two further illustrations are appended below. As with the worked examples which followed the chapter on dispersion, the reader is recommended to try to work through the question and then compare his workings with the answer given below.

Question 1. The following data relate to the number of accidents in the London area and the number of vehicle licences issued by the local authority over a ten-year period.

Number of vehicle licences issued (0,000s) (x)

| 52 | 55 | 60 | 68 | 77 | 84 | 92 | 96 | 103 | 113 |

Number of accidents (000s) (y)

| 34 | 34 | 36 | 39 | 46 | 45 | 45 | 53 | 58 | 60 |

From these data calculate (1) the regression equation of y upon x

(2) the coefficient of correlation.

Question 2. For a sample of ten towns the infant mortality rate (i.e. the number of live-born infants who die before reaching their first birthday expressed as a rate per thousand of all live-born infants) and the proportion of the population in the two lowest social classes IV and V were as follows:

Proportion of population (x)

| 26 | 35 | 27 | 26 | 25 | 37 | 31 | 19 | 23 | 26 |

Infant mortality rate (y)

| 22 | 31 | 28 | 20 | 29 | 43 | 21 | 19 | 20 | 26 |

As for the previous question calculate the regression equation of y upon x and the correlation coefficient.

With any statistical data, before carrying out calculations, it is essential to consider the data to ascertain what they reveal and to obtain some indication of what the further calculations will produce and what conclusions can be drawn from those results. This is especially the case with correlation and regression because it is possible to obtain what appear to be meaningful results in terms of, say, a high value of r, and draw from those results wholly unjustified conclusions.

In the first example common sense suggests that the density of traffic in a particular area is connected with the number of accidents which occur. An inspection of the two series shows quite clearly that with a continuous increase in the number of vehicles licensed there is a corresponding growth in the number of accidents. There is reason for believing that the two series are causally related although factors other than the mere number of vehicles can affect the number of accidents, *e.g.* speed limits, the weather conditions, etc. In other words, even if there appears at first sight to be a clear-cut causal connection between the series and this is supported by knowledge and common sense, don't immediately assume that nothing else matters.

With such basic impressions of the data in mind, it follows that we are likely to get a good fit with the regression line and that the value of the correlation coefficient should approach $+1 \cdot 0$. In stating what may appear to be obvious, the reader should be clear as to the further advantage such prior consideration of the data may provide. If it is possible, as it is with some forethought and, of course, experience, to make a good estimate of the probable results then, if a mistake is made in the calculation, the difference between the calculated result and what was expected may be such that one takes another look and checks the figures. Every examiner knows that, under the stress of examination conditions, candidates make arithmetic slips. These can be forgiven. What cannot be so easily condoned is the candidate who produces a ridiculous answer, such as a value for *r* of say 2.5 and leaves it without comment. In such circumstances it is better, if a quick review of the workings does not reveal the error, simply to point out to the examiner that such a result cannot be correct since *r* must lie between zero and unity and therefore some error has been made.

The old adage that 'any damned fool can calculate' has especial relevance in the field of statistics. Too many students believe that arithmetic accuracy is of overriding importance; it is not. It is far more important to understand and think about the data and what they mean than to be able to perform the most advanced calculations. In short, a very able mathematician might prove to be a poor statistician, whereas a relatively innumerate person could acquire a considerable competence in handling and interpreting statistical data.

Example 1

In the first example it is possible to work from the true means of each of the variables *x* and *y*. To derive the regression equation it is necessary first to calculate the value of *b* in the equation $y=a+bx$. That particular value gives the slope of the regression line, whereas the value of *a* indicates the point on the vertical axis of the scatter diagram where the regression line would meet the ordinate if the regression line were extended. In other words, it is the value of *y* when *x* equals zero. Given the value of *b*, in this case 0·44, by substitution in the equation $y=a+bx$ of the means of the *x* and *y* values, together with that for *b*, the value for *a* can be derived; in this case it is 10. The final regression equation of y upon x is then written $y=10 +0.44(x)$.

From the illustrations which the reader has already studied it will be apparent that the same figures are required for the calculation of the coefficient of correlation as for the regression equation. The only additional figure required for calculating r is the sum of the y deviations squared. These are needed to obtain the standard deviation of the y values. The corresponding figure for x is already calculated because it was needed for the calculation of b. Note that in calculating the two standard deviations, the values have been left rounded to the nearest whole number. The margin of error is negligible and if, as candidates sometimes do in their examinations, the square roots had been worked out to several places of decimals, not merely would it be a waste of time but also it would imply a degree of accuracy and precision which is quite unjustified. The value of r is, as was predictable from a preliminary examination of the data, very high; in this case $+0.98$.

x	y	$(x-\bar{x})$	$(y-\bar{y})$	$(x-\bar{x})(y-\bar{y})$	$(x-\bar{x})^2$	$(y-\bar{y})^2$
52	34	—28	—11	+308	784	121
55	34	—25	—11	+275	625	121
60	36	—20	— 9	+180	400	81
68	39	—12	— 6	+ 72	144	36
77	46	— 3	+ 1	— 3	9	1
84	45	+ 4	0	0	16	0
92	45	+12	0	0	144	0
96	53	+16	+ 8	+128	256	64
103	58	+23	+13	+299	529	169
113	60	+33	+15	+495	1,089	225
800	450			+1,754	3,996	818

$$\bar{x}=\frac{800}{10}=80 \qquad \bar{y}=\frac{450}{10}=45$$

(i) When $y=a+bx$, $\qquad\qquad b=\dfrac{\Sigma(x-\bar{x})(y-\bar{y})}{\Sigma(x-\bar{x})^2}$

$$b=\frac{1,755}{3,996}=0.44$$

In the special case $\bar{y}=a+b\bar{x}$
$$45=a+80(0.44)$$
$$45=a+35$$
$$\therefore a=45-35=10$$

(ii) Regression equation of y upon x reads $\qquad y=10+0.44(x)$

Coefficient of correlation $r=\dfrac{\Sigma(x-\bar{x})(y-\bar{y})}{n\sigma x\, \sigma y}$

$$\sigma x = \sqrt{\frac{3,996}{10}} \qquad \sigma y = \sqrt{\frac{818}{10}}$$

$$\sigma x = \sqrt{399 \cdot 6} \qquad \sigma y = \sqrt{81 \cdot 8}$$
$$= 20 \qquad\qquad = 9$$

$$r = \frac{+1,760}{10 \times 20 \times 9} = \frac{+1,760}{1,800} = +0 \cdot 98$$

Example 2

As with the first example, so the second illustration comprises two variables which are obviously related. The infant mortality rate (I.M.R.) has long been a most useful indicator of living standards and, in areas which contain a large proportion of poorer households, the I.M.R. tends to be high. The nature of the relationship between the two variables is more complex than the foregoing would suggest. While the I.M.R. and low living standards, including also poor educational attainment on the part of the parents, are closely correlated, the number of people in Social Classes IV and V is very large; well over a quarter of the population are so classified.[1] Inevitably, therefore, there will be a considerable difference in living standards, intelligence, housing, etc. between those whose occupations, which is the basis for this classification, bring them into a single heterogeneous category. For this reason one would not expect a relationship as close as that illustrated by the previous example. An examination of the data nevertheless suggests that while the two variables tend to move together, there is no obvious very close interdependence.

In the calculations on these data it is necessary to work from assumed means. This means that in the calculation of the regression line and the correlation coefficient some adjustment must be made for this fact. Thus, in the derivation of *b*, both the numerator and denominator are corrected; for the numerator the correction is the product of the net deviations for *x* and *y* respectively. The basic figures are given in the totals of the third and fourth columns of the worked example, *i.e.* +5 and —1, in each case divided by 10. Note how the minus sign in the formula for *b* overrides the fact that the product —0·05 of the average deviations. +0·5 and —0·1 is negative so that this 'error' or adjustment is actually added to the rest of the numerator, *i.e.* 274+0·05. The same applies to the denominator but, because the deviations are squared, the net figure is positive. This is then overridden by the minus sign and that figure +0·25 is subtracted from the rest of the denominator, *i.e.* 267—0.25=266.75.

[1] This classification is discussed in Chapter XVII in the section on social class.

x	y	$(x-x')$	$(y-y')$	$(x-x')(y-y')$	$(x-x')^2$	$(y-y')^2$
26	22	− 1	− 4	+ 4	1	16
35	31	+ 8	+ 5	+ 40	64	25
27	28	0	+ 2	0	0	4
26	20	− 1	− 6	+ 6	1	36
25	29	− 2	+ 3	− 6	4	9
37	43	+10	+17	+170	100	289
31	21	+ 4	− 5	−20	16	25
19	19	− 8	− 7	+ 56	64	49
23	20	− 4	− 6	+ 24	16	36
26	26	− 1	0	0	1	0
275	259	−17+22	−28+27	300 −26	267	489

$$\bar{x}=\frac{275}{10}=27 \cdot 5 \qquad \bar{y}=\frac{259}{10}=25 \cdot 9$$

(i) Use assumed means: $x'=27 \qquad y'=26$

$$b=\frac{\Sigma(x-x')(y-y') - \dfrac{\Sigma(x-x')}{n}\dfrac{\Sigma(y-y')}{n}}{\Sigma(x-x')^2 - \left(\dfrac{\Sigma(x-x')}{n}\right)^2}$$

$$=\frac{+274-\dfrac{(+5)(-1)}{10^2}}{267-\left(\dfrac{+5}{10}\right)^2}=\frac{+274+0 \cdot 05}{267-0 \cdot 25}$$

$$=\frac{+274 \cdot 05}{266 \cdot 75}=+1 \cdot 03$$

$$y'-\bar{y}=b(x'-\bar{x}) \qquad = \qquad y-25 \cdot 9=1 \cdot 04(x-27 \cdot 5)$$
$$y=25 \cdot 9+1 \cdot 03x-28 \cdot 3$$
$$y=1 \cdot 03x-2 \cdot 35$$

(ii) Coefficient of correlation $=\dfrac{\dfrac{\Sigma(x-\bar{x})(y-\bar{y})}{n}-\left(\dfrac{\Sigma(x-\bar{x})}{n}\right)\left(\dfrac{\Sigma(y-\bar{y})}{n}\right)}{\sigma x \ \sigma y}$

$$=\frac{\dfrac{+274}{10}-\left(\dfrac{5}{10}\right)\left(\dfrac{-1}{10}\right)}{\sigma x \ \sigma y}=+\frac{27 \cdot 4 +\dfrac{5}{100}}{\sigma x \ \sigma y}$$

$$\sigma x = \sqrt{\frac{\Sigma(x-\bar{x})^2}{n}-\left(\frac{\Sigma(x-\bar{x})}{n}\right)^2}$$

$$= \sqrt{\frac{267}{10}-\left(\frac{+5}{10}\right)^2}$$

$$= \sqrt{26 \cdot 7-0 \cdot 25} \doteqdot \sqrt{26 \cdot 45}$$

$$\sigma_y = \sqrt{\frac{\Sigma(y-\bar{y})^2}{n} - \left(\frac{\Sigma(x-\bar{x})}{n}\right)^2}$$

$$= \sqrt{\frac{489}{10} - \left(\frac{1}{10}\right)^2}$$

$$= \sqrt{48\cdot9 - \cdot01}$$

$$\sigma_x = 5\cdot1 \qquad \sigma_y = 7\cdot0$$

$$r = \frac{+27\cdot45}{7\cdot0 \times 5\cdot1} = \frac{27\cdot45}{35\cdot7}$$

$$= +0\cdot77$$

Note, too, that when the value of b has been derived the true means of x and y in the basic equation $y=a+bx$ must be substituted. In this case the mean values of x and y are subtracted from the assumed means. Thus, the left-hand side of the equation reads, $y'-\bar{y}$ and b is multiplied by $x'-\bar{x}$.

The calculation of the coefficient of correlation is also made rather more complex by the need to correct the numerator. However, the correction is the same as that used to adjust for the value of b needed for the regression equation. As far as the denominator is concerned any correction required is effected when the two standard deviations are worked out from the assumed means.

The advent of the pocket calculator, the use of which is now generally permitted in examinations, has made it possible to use alternative methods for calculating the coefficient of correlation and the constant b in the regression equation of the form $y=a+bx$. In all the previous examples in which the derivation of these two statistics has been illustrated, the calculations have been based upon the deviations from the means of x and y. This has made the arithmetic much easier but, with the pocket calculator, alternative formulae can be used.

Thus, for the calculation of the coefficient of correlation the relevant figures can all be derived directly from the data, using the following formula:

$$r = \frac{n\Sigma XY - \Sigma X\Sigma Y}{\sqrt{[n\Sigma X^2 - (\Sigma X)^2][n\Sigma Y^2 - (\Sigma Y)^2]}}$$

For the derivation of the constant b in the regression equation the formula is as follows:

$$b = \frac{n\Sigma XY - (\Sigma X)(\Sigma Y)}{n\Sigma X^2 - (\Sigma X)^2}$$

The application of these two formulae is illustrated hereunder using the data from the second worked example above. This enables the reader to check that whichever method may be used, the results are the same. Since increasingly it is the practice to provide the candidates with the basic formulae in an examination, it is not necessary to commit them to memory. It is obviously prudent, however, to learn one or other method so that reference to the textbook or examination formulae is not necessary except, perhaps, for checking.

To avoid questions which involve a lot of calculations, the candidate is sometimes given not just the basic data, *i.e.* the values for x and y, but the values for the above symbols and he is required merely to substitute them in the relevant formula. Thus, he might be given $\Sigma XY = 7,397$ $\Sigma X^2 = 7,827$ and $(\Sigma X)^2 = 75,625$ and asked to derive the regression equation. These values may be checked against the illustration which follows.

x	y	x^2	xy	y^2
26	22	676	572	484
35	31	1,225	1,085	961
27	28	729	756	784
26	20	676	520	400
25	29	625	725	841
37	43	1,369	1,591	1,849
31	21	961	651	441
19	19	361	361	361
23	20	529	460	400
26	26	676	676	676
275	259	7,827	7,397	7,197

(ii) $$b = \frac{n\Sigma xy - (\Sigma x)(\Sigma y)}{n\Sigma x^2 - (\Sigma x)^2} = \frac{10.7397 - 275.259}{10.7827 - 275^2}$$

$$= \frac{73,970 - 71,225}{78,270 - 75,625}$$

$$= \frac{2,745}{2,645}$$

$$b = 1.04$$

The rest of the equation follows the calculation earlier.

(i) $$r = \frac{n\Sigma xy - \Sigma x\Sigma y}{\sqrt{[n\Sigma xx^2 - (\Sigma x)^2][n\Sigma y^2 - (\Sigma y)^2]}}$$

$$= \frac{10.7397 - 275.259}{\sqrt{[10.7827 - (275)^2][10.\,7197 - (259)^2]}}$$

$$= \frac{73,970 - 71,225}{\sqrt{[78,270 - 75,625][71,970 - 67,081]}} \qquad = \frac{2,745}{\sqrt{2,645.\,4,889}}$$

$$= \frac{2,745}{\sqrt{12,931,000}} \qquad = \frac{2,745}{3,596} \qquad = +0.76$$

Increasingly nowadays examination candidates are required not merely to perform such calculations as these examples have illustrated, but also to interpret the results.[1] As emphasised earlier, this is really the important part of the question. Nevertheless, candidates often seem unable to answer this part, although they may have calculated either the regression equation or the correlation coefficient quite correctly. It is not necessary for the candidate to say a great deal on these points. The first relevant comment relates to the number of paired observations; in the two examples given there are only 10 apiece. This is a very small sample indeed and the examinee should remember that it is always dangerous to draw conclusions from limited evidence. At best, in both of these examples, it may be said that the results of the calculations support the earlier conclusions based upon observation and common sense. In the circumstances further statistical analysis on a considerably larger sample should be carried out.

Avoid assertions such as a value of r of say 0·98 is very high compared with another value equal to say 0·77. It is, of course, higher but it might not be what the statistician terms of greater 'statistical significance'.[2] The statistical significance of any sample statistic is largely dependent upon the number of observations upon which it is based.[3] Thus, if the value for r of 0·98 was derived from only 10 observations whereas the 0·77 was based upon say 50, there is little doubt that the second but smaller value is more meaningful or 'significant'.

Having made this point, the examinee can then consider the nature of the data and indicate why he considers it useful to calculate a value for r or the regression equation. This is because the two variables are apparently inter-related and the nature of the association or relationship can be explained as was the case with the data in the two previous examples. Sometimes the data may yield what appears to be a significant value of r or a good fitting regression line but the apparent relationship is spurious. For example, height and weight are probably closely related in young adolescents; intelligence and height or weight are not although a sample of such data might just reflect a close association. In other words, do not automatically assume because you are required to perform such calculations that the data themselves are appropriate or justify such analysis.

---

[1] In addition, if the regression equation has been asked for, the examiners will often ask the candidate to estimate the value of y for a given value of x, as discussed on p. 191.

[2] The meaning of statistical significance is discussed in Chapter XIV.

[3] This important topic is discussed in Chapter XIV.

Questions

REGRESSION AND CORRELATION

General

The subject of correlation and regression is very popular with examiners and a majority of examination papers on elementary statistical methods will include such a question. The candidate is not often required to calculate both the regression equation and the coefficient of correlation. He is usually given the choice and, in such cases, a further part of the question requires him to explain briefly the meaning and purpose of the other technique. Most candidates are usually quite well prepared for such questions and, as far as the computations are concerned, they gain quite high marks.

Increasingly in recent times, however, examiners have asked the candidate to comment on the result and to explain what it signifies. On this part of the question answers usually fall far short of what is desirable. It is a regrettable fact, based upon the reading of innumerable examination answers over the years, that the average candidate's capacity for reproducing correct calculations is considerably higher than his understanding of what it is all about! And a moment's reflection will reveal that it is understanding, rather than a facility at arithmetic skills, which the examiner really wants to see.

The answer to this part of the question need not fill more than half a dozen lines. To start with, it does not require the candidate, as he apparently sometimes believes, to write a long explanation of what correlation or regression is about. Basically, what he is being asked is, 'what does your result mean and what value can be attached to it?' This depends upon two considerations; the size of the sample and the derived value, for example, of the coefficient of correlation. But, even before that, one needs to consider the data themselves and ask oneself just what they signify. Is it sensible to correlate the two series? For example, over a period of many years the increase in imports of bananas into the United Kingdom matched the growth in the size of the Royal Navy and with appropriate data one could probably have got a coefficient of something like +0.9! But, what does it mean? Such a relationship is spurious in the sense that while the figures move 'in step', there is no real relationship of any significance between them.

In other words, there is no point in calculating the correlation coefficient or the regression equation unless there is, first, evidence of some association or inter-relationship between the variables and, second, if some explanation for that relationship can be provided. Thus, in the two previous worked examples, the link between infant mortality and poverty is well established; likewise, the probability that traffic density in terms of the number of licensed cars and the number of road deaths are directly associated. It is quite possible that a sample of young men would provide data which suggested that height and intelligence were correlated; there are, after all, many tall young men who are intelligent and such a sample is quite feasible. But, there are also many tall young men who are not very bright. In other words, because a particular result is obtained, do not assume that it means anything unless common-sense and your own observation support that conclusion.

Statements that a value of the coefficient is high, or low, should be avoided. For example, a coefficient of +0.98 is certainly higher than one of +0.65 but if the former is based upon a sample of 10 paired observations while the latter is obtained from say 100 such observations, there is no doubt which is the more significant statisitic. The point is that the reliability of any statistic derived from sample data is directly related to the size of the sample. (This subject is discussed in Chapters XIII and XIV.) Because of the computational work involved, most examination questions usually give the candidate no more than 10 or 12 pairs of observations. This is a very small sample indeed, and, even if the coefficient approaches unity, little reliance can be placed upon it. The same is true if the calculation gives a coefficient of little more than zero! In brief, a reference to the size of the sample, *i.e.* the number of paired observations is highly relevant.

At best the result derived from such small samples merely serves to remind the statistician that it would be better to collect more data.

In questions on regression, candidates are sometimes asked to derive a value from the regression equation. For example, take the first of the previous worked examples on the subject of car registrations and fatal road accidents. Given the regression equation it is possible to *interpolate* values within the range of the data. In other words, given the equation it would be a simple matter to estimate how many fatal accidents could be expected if exactly 100,000 licences were current. And, the resultant estimate might be reasonably correct. Often, however, the candidate is asked to *extrapolate* a value outside the range of the data. Thus, how many accidents could be expected if 200,000 licences were issued? There is no problem in substituting in the equation the figure of 200,000 for x and deriving a value for y. The question is, does it mean anything? The figure of 200,000 licences is so far outside the range of the data for the past decade that by the time, if ever, that number of licences has been issued traffic conditions, roads, etc. may be so different from present conditions that the relationship defined by the regression equation will no longer apply. The short answer to such a question is that such an exercise is unrealistic and that one could have no confidence whatsoever in the result. As a general rule, *extrapolation* from the regression equation is likely to give quite unreliable results unless other information is available to validate the estimate. The only possible exception to this statement is where the trend is very definite and the period which the extrapolation cover is short, *e.g.* one or two years. *Interpolation*, on the other hand, *i.e.* estimating a value within the range of the data, is quite permissible.

1. Calculate the coefficient of correlation between the consumption of spirits and beer over the period 1962-72.

	Spirits	Beer
1962	16	28
1963	17	29
1964	19	30
1965	18	30
1966	18	31
1967	18	32
1968	19	32
1969	18	33
1970	20	34
1971	22	36
1972	24	37

Answer to Question 1

	Spirit (x)	Beer (y)	d_x	d_y	$d_x{}^2$	$d_y{}^2$	d_{xy}
1962	16	28	−3	−4	9	16	+12
1963	17	29	−2	−3	4	9	+ 6
1964	19	30	=	−2	=	4	0
1965	18	30	−1	−2	1	4	+ 2
1966	18	31	−1	−1	1	1	+ 1
1967	18	32	−1	0	1	0	0
1968	19	32	0	0	0	0	0
1969	18	33	−1	+1	1	1	− 1
1970	20	34	+1	+2	1	4	+ 2
1971	22	36	+3	+4	9	16	+12
1972	24	37	+5	+5	25	25	+25
	209	352	0	0	52	80	+59

$\bar{x}=19$ $\bar{y}=32$

$$r = \frac{\Sigma xy}{n\sigma_x \, \sigma_y} = \frac{59}{11.\sigma_x \, \sigma_y}$$

σ_x $= \sqrt{\dfrac{52}{11}}$ $= \sigma_y = \sqrt{\dfrac{80}{11}}$

     $= \sqrt{4.73}$ $= \sqrt{7.27}$

     $= 2.2$ $= 2.7$

r $= \dfrac{+59}{11 \times 2.2 \times 2.7}$ $= \dfrac{+59}{65.3} = +0.9$

2. (a) Preferences of two groups of students for different examination subjects.

	Order of Preference among	
	Male students	Female students
Theories and methods of sociology ..	4	7
Statistical methods in social investigation..	6	8
Social institutions	7	4
Social philosophy	2	6
Social psychology	5	3
Social structure	1	2
Social history	8	5
Criminology	3	1
Principles of economics	9	10
Applied economics	10	9

By means of Spearman's rank correlation coefficient, examine these data for evidence of any similarity in the preferences of the male and female students. Comment on this method and discuss your findings.

(b) Explain briefly the computation and use of the ordinary (product moment) correlation coefficient. What are the main precautions to be taken in the interpretation of correlation coefficients generally?   B.A. (Soc.)

Answer to Question 2

Paper	Male	Female	d	d²
1	4	7	− 3	9
2	6	8	− 2	4
3	7	4	+ 3	9
4	2	6	− 4	16
5	5	3	+ 2	4
6	1	2	− 1	1
7	8	5	+ 3	9
8	3	1	+ 2	4
9	9	10	− 1	1
10	10	9	+ 1	1
			+11 −11	58

$$r = 1 - \left(\frac{6 \Sigma d^2}{n(n^2 - 1)} \right)$$

$$= 1 - \frac{6.58}{10(10^2 - 1)}$$

$$= 1 - \frac{348}{990}$$

$$= 1 - 0.35$$

$$= +0.65$$

3. The following are the gestation times and birth weights of 10 infants.

Gestation time (days)	Birth weight (lb.)
240	6·5
250	5·5
255	7·0
260	9·0
270	9·0
275	8·0
285	7·0
285	10·0
290	9·5
310	10·5

Calculate the correlation coefficient between gestation time and birth weight, and comment on your result. *Final D.M.A.*

Answer to Question 3

Gestation time (days) (x)	Birth weight (lb) (y)	d_x	d_y	$d_x{}^2$	$d_y{}^2$	d_{xy}
240	6.5	−32	−1.7	1,024	2.89	+544
250	5.5	−22	−2.7	484	7.29	+594
255	7.0	−17	−1.2	289	1.44	+204
260	9.0	−12	+0.8	144	2.64	− 96
270	9.0	− 2	+0.8	4	.64	− 16
275	8.0	+ 3	−0.2	9	.04	− 6
285	7.0	+13	−1.2	169	1.44	−156
285	10.0	+13	+1.8	169	3.24	+234
290	9.5	+18	+1.3	324	1.69	+234
310	10.5	+38	+2.3	1,444	5.29	+874
2,720	82.0	−85	−7.0	4,060	26.60	+2,410
		+85	+7.0			

$$\bar{x} = 272 \qquad \bar{y} = 8.2 \qquad N = 10$$

$$\sigma_x = \sqrt{\frac{4{,}060}{10}} = \sqrt{406} = 20.1$$

$$\sigma_y = \sqrt{\frac{2{,}660}{10}} = \sqrt{266} = 16.3$$

$$r = \frac{\Sigma(x-\bar{x})(y-\bar{y})}{N\,\sigma_x.\,\sigma_y}$$

$$= \frac{+2{,}410}{10 \times 20.1 \times 16.3} \qquad = \frac{+2{,}410}{3{,}156} \qquad r = +0.74$$

4. Using the data in Question 3, compute the regression line of weight on gestation time. The normal gestation time (believed to be most favourable to the survival of the baby) is 280 days. What, according to your equation, is the mean birth weight corresponding to this gestation time? What purpose would be served by computing the other regression line, of gestation time on weight? *B.Sc. (Sociology)*

Answer to Question 4

$$\bar{y} = a + b\bar{x}$$

$$b = \frac{\Sigma(x-\bar{x})(y-\bar{y})}{\Sigma(x-\bar{x})^2} = \frac{241}{4.060}$$

$$b = 0.06$$

By substitution, where $\bar{y}=8.2$ and $\bar{x}=272$

$$8.2 = a + .06(272)$$
$$8.2 = a + 16.3$$
$$8.2 - 16.3 = a$$
$$-8.1 = a$$

Regression equation of y upon x is:

$$y = .06b - 8.1$$

If mean gestation period were 280 days, expected birth weight would be:

$$y = 0.06 (280) - 8.1$$
$$= 16.8 - 8.1$$
$$= 8.7lb$$

5. The following data show for the ten standard regions in England and Wales, the Standardised Mortality Ratios (SMR) of deaths among males aged 15-64 from Bronchitis (y) and the pollution of air in the regions by smoke measured in micrograms per cubic metre (x).

	Pollution of air (x)	SMR's (y)
North	34	123
Yorkshire and Humberside	43	112
East Midlands	36	103
East Anglia	25	67
Greater London	34	108
Other South East	22	79
South West	21	70
North West	37	122
Wales	22	114
West Midlands	38	112

(a) Calculate the product moment correlation coefficient of deaths from bronchitis and smoke pollution.

(b) Calculate the regression equation of y upon x.

Answer to Question 5

x	y	x^2	y^2	xy
34	123	1,156	15,129	4,182
43	112	1,849	12,544	4,816
36	103	1,296	10,609	3,708
25	67	625	4,489	1,675
34	108	1,156	11,664	3,672
22	79	484	6,241	1,738
21	70	441	4,900	1,470
37	122	1,369	14,884	4,514
22	114	484	12,996	2,508
38	112	1,444	12,544	4,256
312	1,010	10,304	106,000	32,539

(a)

$$r = \frac{n \Sigma xy - \Sigma x \Sigma y}{\sqrt{[n \Sigma x^2 - (\Sigma x)^2] [n \Sigma y^2 - (\Sigma y)^2]}}$$

$$= \frac{10.\ 32,539 - 312.\ 1,010}{\sqrt{[10.\ 10,304 - 312^2]\ [10.\ 106,000 - 1,010^2]}}$$

$$= \frac{325,390 - 315,120}{\sqrt{5,696 \times 39,900}}$$

$$= \frac{10,270}{\sqrt{227,270,000}} = \frac{10,270}{15,075} = 0 \cdot 68$$

$$r = +0 \cdot 7$$

(b)
$$b = \frac{n \ \Sigma xy - \Sigma x \Sigma y}{n \ \Sigma x^2 - (\Sigma x)^2}$$

$$= \frac{10,270}{5,696} = 1 \cdot 80$$

$$\bar{y} = a + b\bar{x}$$
$$101 = a + 1 \cdot 80 \ (31 \cdot 2)$$
$$101 - 56 \cdot 2 = a$$
$$44 \cdot 8 = a$$
$$y = 44 \cdot 8 + 1 \cdot 80x$$

The following shows the same problem using the earlier formula to derive r and b

x	y	$d'x$		$d'y$	$d'x^2$	$d'y^2$	$d'xy$
34	123	+ 4		+23	16	529	92
43	112	+13		+12	169	144	156
36	103	+ 6		+ 3	36	9	18
25	67		− 5	−33	25	1,089	165
34	108	+ 4		+ 8	16	64	32
22	79		− 8	−21	64	441	168
21	70		− 9	−30	81	900	270
37	122	+ 7		+22	49	484	154
22	114		− 8	+14	64	196	−112
38	112	+ 8		+12	64	144	96
312	1,010	+42	−30	+94 −84	584	4,000	1,039

Assumed means $x^1 = 30 \ y = 100$

$$r = \frac{\dfrac{\Sigma \ (x - x') \ (y - y')}{n} - \left(\dfrac{\Sigma x - x'}{n}\right) \left(\dfrac{\Sigma y - y'}{n}\right)}{\sigma_x \ \sigma_y}$$

$$= \frac{\dfrac{1,039}{10} - \left(\dfrac{+12}{10}\right) \left(\dfrac{+10}{10}\right)}{\sigma_x \ \sigma_y}$$

$$\sigma_x = \sqrt{\frac{584}{10} - \left(\frac{12}{10}\right)^2} = \sqrt{58 \cdot 4 - 1 \cdot 44} = \sqrt{56 \cdot 96} = 7 \cdot 5$$

$$\sigma_y = \sqrt{\frac{4,000}{10} - \left(\frac{10}{10}\right)^2} = \sqrt{400 - 1} = \sqrt{399} = 20$$

$$r = \frac{103 \cdot 9 - 1 \cdot 2}{7 \cdot 5 \times 20} = \frac{102 \cdot 7}{150}$$

$$= +0 \cdot 68 = +0 \cdot 7$$

$$y = a + bx$$

$$b = \frac{\Sigma \ (x - x') \ (y - y') - \dfrac{\Sigma \ (x - x') \ \Sigma (y - y')}{n}}{\Sigma \ (x - x')^2 - \left(\dfrac{\Sigma (x - x')}{n}\right)^2}$$

$$b = \frac{1,039 - \dfrac{12 \times 10}{10}}{584 - \left(\dfrac{12}{10}\right)^2}$$

$$= \frac{1,039 - 12}{584 - 1 \cdot 44} = \frac{1,027}{582 \cdot 6}$$

$$b = \quad 1.80$$

6. The following table shows the number of hours worked each week (x) by 12 employees and the time taken on their journey to work (y).

x (hours)	5	10	10	15	17	20	20	25	30	35	40	45
y (minutes)	10	5	10	10	15	20	20	15	35	30	45	35

Calculate:
 (i) the regression equation of y upon x; and
(ii) the coefficient of correlation.

Answer to Question 6

Weekly hours of work x	Time of journey (minutes) y	d'_x	d_y	d'_{x^2}	d'_{y^2}	d_{xy}
5	10	−20	−10	400	100	+ 200
10	5	−15	−15	225	225	+ 225
10	10	−15	−10	225	100	+ 150
15	10	−10	−10	100	100	+ 100
17	15	− 8	− 5	64	25	+ 40
20	20	− 5	0	25	0	0
20	20	− 5	0	25	0	0
25	15	0	− 5	0	25	0
30	35	+ 5	+15	25	225	+ 75
35	30	+10	+10	100	100	+ 100
40	45	+15	+25	225	625	+ 375
45	35	+20	+15	400	225	+ 300
272	250	−78	−55	1,814	1,750	+1,565
		+50	+65			
		−28	+10			

Assumed means $x' = 25$ $y' = 20$

(i)

$$b = \frac{\Sigma (x - x')(y - y') - \dfrac{\Sigma(x - x')(\Sigma y - y')}{n}}{\Sigma (x - x')^2 - \dfrac{\Sigma (x - x')^2}{n}}$$

$$= \frac{1,565 - \left(\dfrac{-28 \cdot 10}{12}\right)}{1,814 - \dfrac{784}{12}} = \frac{1,565 + 23}{1,814 - 65}$$

$$= \frac{1,542}{1,749} = 0 \cdot 88$$

$$y' - \bar{y} = b\,(x' - \bar{x})$$
$$y - 22 \cdot 66 = 0 \cdot 88\,(x - 20 \cdot 8)$$
$$= 0 \cdot 88\,x - 18 \cdot 3$$
$$= 0 \cdot 88\,x - 18 \cdot 3 + 22 \cdot 66$$
$$y \quad = 0 \cdot 88\,x + 4 \cdot 36$$

If $x=25$ minutes then
$$y=0.88\,(25)+4.36$$
$$=22+4.36$$
$$=26.4 \text{ hours}$$

(ii)

$$r=\frac{\dfrac{\Sigma\,(x-x')\,(y-y')}{n}-\left(\dfrac{\Sigma x-x'}{n}\right)\left(\dfrac{\Sigma y-y'}{n}\right)}{\sigma_x\,\sigma_y}$$

$$=\frac{\dfrac{1{,}565}{12}-\left(\dfrac{-28}{12}\right)\left(\dfrac{10}{12}\right)}{\sigma_x\,\sigma_y}$$

$$\sigma_x=\sqrt{\frac{1{,}814}{12}-\left(\frac{-28}{12}\right)^2}=\sqrt{151.2-5.4}=\sqrt{145.8}=12.1$$

$$\sigma_y=\sqrt{\frac{1{,}750}{12}-\left(\frac{10}{12}\right)^2}=\sqrt{145.8-0.7}=\sqrt{145.1}=12.0$$

$$r=\frac{130.4-1.92}{12.1\times12.0}\;=\;\frac{128.58}{145.2}\;=+0.89\;=+0.9$$

CHAPTER X

INDEX NUMBERS

Ten years ago the word 'inflation' would not have conveyed very much to the ordinary man or woman in Britain. During the 1970s, however, the word has seldom been absent from the headlines. Inflation is synonymous with rising prices and the rate at which prices of consumer goods and services rise are measured by what is often referred to as a cost of living index. Well publicised changes in the government's *index of retail prices*, which is the nearest approach in the U.K. to a cost of living index, are often received with scepticism by the public. For example, during the period 1971-74 food prices rose much more than other prices and housewives were highly critical of an index which appeared to them to under-state the full extent of the price increases in the food shops. In contrast, the cost of products bought by their menfolk, such as tobacco, alcohol and travel to work did not rise very much during that period.

The simple fact is that prices do not all change either at the same time or at the same rate. For example, over the period 1971-74, according to the official index of retail prices, food prices rose 13·8 per cent, alcoholic drink by 3·1 per cent and tobacco by 0·9 per cent. Prices of durable household goods rose by 6·2 per cent while the cost of meals bought and consumed outside the home increased by 14·4 per cent. During the subsequent period 1974-77, however, food prices jumped 22.3 per cent and the price of tobacco by 24·5 per cent, meals bought outside the home by 19·9 per cent and durable household goods by 16·2 per cent. It is unlikely that any one who has just read these figures could estimate in his head the *average* increase in these prices during the two periods, which is what one really wants to know when the effect of inflation on living costs is discussed. In fact the average increase in all prices included in the official index of retail prices for the earlier period was 9·3 per cent and for the subsequent period 19·9 per cent.

Nevertheless that average increase in prices may be unsuitable as an indicator of the extent to which particular groups in the population have suffered from the inflation. The index cited above is the *general* index of retail prices and is suitable for households with a working head whose income did not exceed £160 per week in the first half of 1978 and excludes households with higher incomes as well as those households where the bulk of the income *i.e.* 75 per cent or more is derived from social security benefits. In view of the importance of keeping the State pension at least constant in real terms, *i.e.* in terms of its purchasing power, special indices are prepared for pensioner households. Since the pattern of expenditure of such households differs from that of younger working households in which there may also be children, the indices for pensioner households are based on their particular patterns of expenditure.

Two important points emerge from the above paragraphs. The first is that there is no such thing as the 'price level', although people often talk about the level of prices being higher this year than last. Admittedly, most prices tend to move more or less in the same direction, but not necessarily to the same degree. In constructing a price index it is therefore necessary to average the price increases in the various items included in that index. No index can include every price and, in any case, some prices, *e.g.* caviar, are quite irrelevant to the ordinary household's expenditure while others, such as meat, are very important. In other words, the prices included in a 'cost of living' index relate to those goods which are important items in the consumption pattern of the average household. Where the consumption pattern differs markedly from the average, *e.g.* as with households dependent upon social security benefit or wealthy households, then separate indices are needed. In short, an index number is always 'purpose built'.

For this reason there are quite a lot of index numbers and many of them relate to prices. Thus, in addition to the index of retail prices which started life before the first World War in 1914 as a cost of living index, a title which has since been abandoned, there is an index of wholesale prices, of Stock Exchange quotations, and of primary commodities internationally traded, among other price indices. Apart from price indices, index numbers are constructed for measuring changes in the volume of industrial output, of the value and volume of exports and imports, of sales of various goods from retail shops of all kinds, and even of food consumption! But, whether the problem is about constructing a price index or an index of the output of manufactured goods or of the earnings of manual workers, the basic problems are the same.

There are four main problems all of which will be discussed more fully later. The first is to define the purpose which the index is intended to serve for this will determine the prices, in the case of a price index, which are to be included. Second, since some price changes are more important than others within the index, it is necessary to ensure that the movements in those prices are fully reflected in the index. This involves the technique of *weighting* and, since each item in the index must have a weight the relative importance of each price has to be determined. Third, there is the question of the base or reference period. When an index is quoted, *e.g.* the general index for retail prices for 1977 was 185 with a base 100 on 15th January, 1974, how is the base date or period selected? If it is a time of, for example, high prices, then future increases will appear smaller than if the base date fell in a period when prices were low. As politicians know full well, by choosing the appropriate base date best suited to their argument it is possible to paint either a very rosy picture of subsequent improvement in the economy or a drab scenario of near-decline! Lastly, but not of such great importance for the average user of index numbers, there is the question of the type of index to be constructed. There is a considerable body of theory on the subject of index number construction, not that it is particularly helpful to the practitioner. Nevertheless some reference to it must be made.

Finally it is important to distinguish index numbers proper from what are really no more than proportions or relatives. For example, very often to facilitate comparison or the interpretation of a time series the values in the series are adjusted so that the first in the series (or one of the series) is re-calculated as 100 and the remainder are then calculated on that base 100. In the caption to such a table one reads, for example 1970 = 100, which is correct, and sometimes, 'index' for 1970 = 100, which is not. An index number is an *average* of a large number of such *relatives* as they are termed and it is important to keep the distinction clearly in mind.

Measuring Price Changes

The point has already been made that all prices do not change to the same extent within a given period of time; some rise more than others and some may even fall. The problem is how these changes can best be averaged to produce an index of those changes. As will emerge it is possible to get different answers to what appears to be the same question according to the method used to average the price changes. Suppose, for example, there are four price changes between the years 1970 and 1978. Commodity A now costs 50p compared with 15p in the earlier year; the corresponding figures for Commodity B are 75p and 25p; for Commodity C they are 150p and 60p while commodity D now costs 225p compared with 150p in 1970. If the prices of the four commodities in each of the two years are added together we get £2.50 for 1970 and £5 for 1978. It could then be said that prices in 1978 were exactly twice as high as in 1970; or one might say that the 1978 prices were 100 per cent higher. Alternatively, the change could be put in the form of an index of those four prices in which the 1970 prices = 100 and the index for 1978 was equal to 200. Such an index is known as a simple aggregative index.

Now, instead of adding together the actual prices in the two periods, work out the *percentage* increase in each price between the two years. Thus, A has gone up by 233 per cent derived by the following calculation: $\dfrac{50 - 15}{15} \times 100$. In the case of commodity B the increase is exactly 200 per cent, *i.e.* $\dfrac{75 - 25}{25} \times 100$. The percentage increases for C and D are 150 and 50 per cent respectively. If these percentage changes are aggregated, *i.e.* $233 + 200 + 150 + 50$ which equals 633 and that figure averaged over the four commodities, the result is an *average* increase of 158 per cent. Note that the increase shown by taking the actual prices in the two years and expressing them as a proportion one to the other with 1970 = 100, gave an increase of 100. Which figure is one to believe? The short answer is, neither! The trouble with this type of simple unweighted index or a simple aggregative index is that they can be distorted by large changes, either in absolute values or relative terms, in any one of the figures on which the index is based. Thus, in the first simple aggregative index when the prices were added together, the result is much influenced by the largest single change in C from 60p to £1·50. With the percentages, the largest single change is the first commodity A where the absolute change is the smallest of the four. To meet this particular problem it is necessary to take into account the importance of each price change, *i.e.* each change must be weighted by reference to some criteria which appear relevant.

Weighting

The term 'weighting' signifies that each price change which is included in the construction of a price index is adjusted to take account of its relative importance to other price changes within the index. Take, for example, the calculation set out in Table 29 below where in the central column of the table headed 'Quantity' the amount purchased, in pounds weight, of each of the four commodities is set down. It is assumed that the different weights, as these figures are termed, reflect the relative importance to the consumer of each of the commodities and hence the differing impact of the individual price changes. Under the column heading 'Prices' the four commodity prices for the two periods, 1970 and 1978, are set down. Each is then multiplied by the corresponding 'weight' and the products shown in the last two columns. The sum of the products in 1970 is divided into the equivalent figure for 1978, *i.e.* $\dfrac{1325}{540}$ which equals 245. What

TABLE 29
CALCULATION OF AGGREGATE TYPE INDEX

Commodity	Prices		Quantity	Prices × Quantity	
	1970 (p)	1978 (p)	lb (q)	1970	1978
A	15	50	4	60	200
B	25	75	6	150	450
C	60	150	3	180	450
D	150	225	1	150	225
	250	500	14	540	1325

does this mean? One way of looking at the result is simply to say that the basket of goods bought in 1970 would have cost £5.40 but, by 1978, that same basket of goods cost £13.25. Alternatively, one can use the indices and say that if the prices in 1970 are equated to 100, then the corresponding index for 1978 is 245. There has been, in other words, an increase of 145 per cent in the cost of that particular basket of goods.

The reader will have noted that this particular result differs from the two results derived from the simple aggregates of prices and percentage changes, both unweighted, which gave price rises of 100 and 158 respectively[1]. This latest figure is better than either of the preceding figures because, instead of assuming that each price change means the same to the buyer as any other, the latest index takes into account the fact that, because differing quantities of each commodity are purchased, price changes of those commodities which bulk largest in the basket ought to be given more weight in the index.

An alternative basis for weighting the individual price changes is illustrated in Table 30 below. Instead of using as weights the physical quantities purchased of each product, the expenditure on each product is used instead. The resultant figures are converted into weights in the column headed v (which is, of course, the same as $p_0 q_0$). The actual figures entered are the products of the two preceding columns, headed p_0 and q_0, i.e. 60, 150, 180 and 150. Note that the subscript $_0$ following the p and q in the heading of the columns is intended to denote that p_0 and q_0 represent the prices and quantities purchased in the base year, in this case 1970. The prices in the year 1978 are distinguished from the earlier prices by the subscript $_1$ as in p_1 and q_1 heading the columns relating to 1978. For the rest of the calculations described below these are the figures used for weighting the price relatives given in the central column. It would be easier from

_____
[1] Note that in the first case, if 1970 is equal to 100 an increase of 100 means that the index for 1978 is 200. Using the percentage rises as in the second example, if the average percentage increase is 158 and 1970=100, then the index for 1978 is 258.

TABLE 30

CALCULATION OF INDEX USING WEIGHTED PRICE RELATIVES

Com-modity	1970			1978		Price Relatives 1978 ÷ 1970 p_1/p_0 (1970 = 100)	P.R. × Value Weights		Prices & Quantities	
	p_0	q_0	$v(p_0q_0)$	p_1	q_1		1970	1978	1970	1978
A	15	4	60	50	3	333⅓	6,000	20,000	60	200
B	25	6	150	75	5	300	15,000	45,000	150	450
C	60	3	180	150	4	250	18,000	45,000	180	450
D	150	1	150	225	2	150	15,000	22,500	150	225
							54,000	132,500	540	1,325

Weighted Aggregative Index (1970 = 100)

(i) Using Prices × Quantities $= \dfrac{1325}{540} = 245$

(ii) Using Price Relatives and base year value weights $= \dfrac{132,500}{54,000} = 245$

the point of view of calculation to have used simpler numbers which reflected the relative size of these weights. For example, all those figures are divisible by 30 and the weights could then be adjusted to 2, 5, 6 and 5. The resultant index would be just the same. At least one could have left off the 0s for purposes of the remaining calculations but, to ensure the basic procedures are not complicated, the actual value weights have been used. Nevertheless, the student reader should bear in mind that it is not the absolute size of the weights which matters, but their relative size one to the other.

These *value* weights, as they are termed, are not multiplied with the prices of the individual commodities in the two years under review. First, the *ratio of the prices* in the two years is calculated to provide a *price relative*. Thus, commodity B cost 25p in 1970 and 75p in 1978; the ratio of the two prices is written $\dfrac{p_1}{p_0}$ which in this case gives $\dfrac{75}{25} = 3$.

Since the base year is always written as 100, then the price relative for 1978 in respect of commodity B is then 300. For each of the four commodities such relatives are calculated and are shown in the central column of Table 30. To derive the index these relatives are multiplied by the *value* weights for 1970. The products for 1970, where the price relative for each of the four commodities is 100, together with the products of the value weights and the price relative for 1978, are shown in the next two columns. They total 54,000 and 132,500 for 1970 and 1978 respectively.

Normally, when calculating these products one would drop the 000s or adjust the weights as described above. But, to make sure the reader can follow each stage they have been inserted. The resultant price index for 1978 where 1970 = 100, is then $\dfrac{132,500}{54,000}$ which equals

245. This result, it will be noted, is the same as was derived from the previous aggregative index in which actual quantities were used as the weights for each price. To save the reader referring back to Table 29, the calculation of that earlier index is set out in the two final columns of Table 30.

As before, although on that occasion the two methods produced *different* results, the reader will doubtless ask which of the two methods illustrated in Table 30, is preferable since both give the *same* result. In fact they are equally efficient as far as price indices are concerned; indeed the former aggregative type using quantities as weights is somewhat easier to calculate. But, in many indices such as those relating to manufacturing output, or volume of imports and exports where the items are not homogeneous like prices but hetero-geneous, *e.g.* bicycles and cars, in order to amalgamate all the changes in different products into a single index it is necessary to calculate for each product the proportionate change in output and this is done most easily by deriving the appropriate relatives.

Index Number Notation

As for other statistical methods so with index numbers there are a number of formulae using a conventional notation which needs to be understood if further reading is to be pursued. A price relative or, for that matter, an output relative is expressed, as noted above, as $\dfrac{p_1}{p_0}$ where $_1$ and $_0$ represent the periods to which the prices or output figures relate. Such relatives are always converted to base 100, *i.e.* the relative for the earlier year is given as 100 and that for the later year is a multiple thereof. Since any index comprises a number of such relatives the formula for an index number could be written as follows:

$$I = \frac{p_1^1 + p_1^2 + p_1^3 + p_1^4 \ldots \ldots \ldots + p_1^n}{p_0^1 + p_0^2 + p_0^3 + p_0^4 \ldots \ldots \ldots + p_0^n}$$

where the numbers $1,2,3,4 \ldots n$ over each p merely denote the different commodities or outputs. The above can be quite simply summarised as follows; thus $\dfrac{\Sigma p_1}{\Sigma p_0}$ which, it will probably be realised, is the formula for the simple aggregative index with which we started and then rejected. The introduction of weights into the formula for an index number is shown as follows:

$$I = \frac{(p_1 q_0) + (p_1 q_0) + (p_1 q_0) + (p_1 q_0)}{(p_0 q_0) + (p_0 q_0) + (p_0 q_0) + (p_0 q_0)} \quad \text{or} \quad \frac{\Sigma p_1 q_0}{\Sigma p_0 q_0}$$

This particular formula provides the aggregative index in Table 29 where *prices* were weighted by the *quantities* purchased in the base year. If, however, we want to represent the index which was derived by using the *price relatives* and the *values* for weights then we write for each relative $\frac{p_1}{p_0}$ ($p_0 q_0$). The reader will recognise that $p_0 q_0$ represents the expenditure on each commodity, i.e. price × quantity. This, multiplied by the price relative, gives the index in Table 30. Obviously the foregoing symbols merely represented one weighted price relative. For the index as a whole, which includes many such weighted relatives, the formula is written:

$$I = \frac{\Sigma\,(p_0 q_0)\,\dfrac{p_1}{p_0}}{\Sigma p_0 q_0}$$

Laspeyre or Paasche?

The reader will have noted that all the calculations of the indices so far, together with the formulae set out above, have used what is termed *base year* weighting. In other words, when quantities or values have been used to weight the prices or price relatives respectively, they have been based upon the prices and quantities in the base year. Hence, when the weighted relatives were set down as above, the symbol q for quantity or value weight was followed by the subscript 0. Suppose, however, the formula for a price index had been written $\frac{\Sigma p_1 q_1}{\Sigma p_0 q_1}$. This indicates that the weights were derived from the quantities or values in the current year, denoted by the subscript 1. Given, therefore, that there is a choice between what is termed *base* year or *current* year weighting, how are these represented in the conventional notation? A base year aggregative index is represented by the formula $I = \frac{\Sigma p_1 q_0}{\Sigma p_0 q_0}$ the current year weighted index is written $\frac{\Sigma p_1 q_1}{\Sigma p_0 q_1}$ The former index is often referred to as a *Laspeyre* index; the latter as a *Paasche* index after the people who developed them.

Table 31 below provides a simple illustration of the calculation of a base year weighted and current year weighted aggregative index. The method of calculation is the same for each index, the only difference being that for the former the weights are based upon the quantities purchased in the base or earlier year, while in the Paasche index the weights are determined by the quantities purchased in the current year, in this case 1978. It will already have been noted that the formulae are distinguishable in so far as the Laspeyre has the subscript 0 after the q, whereas the Paasche has the subscript 1 after the same symbol for weights.

TABLE 31
CALCULATION OF BASE YEAR AND CURRENT YEAR WEIGHTED INDICES

	1974		1978		Laspeyre		Paasche	
	Prices	Quantity	Prices	Quantity	1974	1978	1974	1978
	p_0	q_0	p_1	q_1	$p_0 q_0$	$p_1 q_0$	$p_0 q_1$	$p_1 q_1$
	(pence)	(000's)	(pence)	(000's)				
A	30	20	60	15	600	1200	450	900
B	120	6	250	10	720	1500	1200	2500
C	75	10	140	8	750	1400	600	1120
D	340	4	600	2	1360	2400	680	1200
		40			3430	6500	2930	5720

Laspeyre's Index $= \dfrac{\Sigma p_1 q_0}{\Sigma p_0 q_0} = \dfrac{6500}{3430} = 1.895$

$\therefore$ If 1974 index is 100, 1978 = 189

Paasche Index $= \dfrac{\Sigma p_1 q_1}{\Sigma p_0 q_1} = \dfrac{5720}{2930}$ yields 195 where 1974 = 100.

As is evident from the above example in Table 31 the two indices give different results. This is hardly a matter for surprise since the weights are different. But, once again the same question arises; *i.e.* which is the better index? The answer turns not on their theoretical merits but rather on the practical aspects of the calculation. The Laspeyre or base year weighted index has the great advantage that the weights are constant throughout the life of the index. On the other hand, this is also the source of its basic weakness since, over a long period of time, the quantities of the various commodities purchased will change and the base year weighting then becomes out of date. Against this weakness the Paasche index has the merit that it uses up-to-date weighting which takes account of the current expenditures of people on the commodities included in the index. Unfortunately, the Paasche index has the very considerable disadvantage that if a comparative series of indices is needed, then all the previous years have to be re-worked using the latest available weights.

In practice the Laspeyre index scores every time. The Paasche index also suffers from the fact that, while up-to-date information on prices may be available, similar data to determine the weights may not be. Hence, in the past only one official index, the average value index of imports (and exports), was prepared on the basis of the Paasche formula. To overcome the weakness of the Laspeyre type, *i.e.* weights which cease to have much relevance over time, the practice has evolved of frequently changing and up-dating the weights. Thus, since 1962 the weighting of the general index of retail prices has been revised in the January of each year in the light of the information on spending obtained from the latest Family Expenditure Survey.[1]

Selecting the Base Period

Whenever an index is constructed the question arises as to what date or period should be used for the base 100. It does not necessarily follow that the base will be the point of time at which the index is first constructed. When an index is introduced, it is customary to calculate for a few past periods the corresponding indices although the actual base will be later than those dates. For example, when the index of industrial production was revised on to 1970 as the base year, the index was worked back to 1968. The importance of selecting the best base period is that, since all future movements in the index will be measured from that bench-mark, if it is based in a period when, say, prices were low, then it will seem to reflect large increases in the future in relation to the base prices. If, on the other hand, prices at that date were at a peak and expected thenceafter to level out, then the index will give an impression of relative price stability in the future until the next major upsurge in prices. Also, it is desirable to avoid a period in which extraneous factors may seriously affect the index, such as a series of major strikes if one is calculating a new index of industrial production.

The problem can be overcome in much the same way as with weighting. The trouble with a base year index of the Laspeyre variety is that the more distant the base year becomes, the more likely it is that some of the constituents of the index are no longer as important in the household budget as they were and the index becomes out of date. To avoid this situation an index may be re-based with new items introduced at intervals. Thus, the *general* index of retail prices as it is now termed (before 1968 it was simply the index of retail prices but separate indices are now prepared for one and two person pensioner households) has been re-based on several occasions. The current base is 15th January, 1974 and before that it was based on prices on 16th January, 1962. Nevertheless, it is undesirable to change the base too often. The object of the index is to give a longer term perspective of movements in retail prices and, if the base and content are changed too frequently, then unless all the previous years' indices are adjusted on to the new base the longer term comparative picture is lost. When the base is changed, it is customary to 'link' the old and new series by calculating a few of the indices on the old base

[1] This is described in Chapter XVII

on to the new basis. Then, if a longer run is required it is possible to adjust the indices in the previous series on to the new base date.

Since by changing the base and the weighting of an index its usefulness for comparison over a long period is much reduced, an alternative method of keeping the index up to date may be used. This is known as a *chain-base* index. The principle in this case is that the index for each period is simply based upon the index of the immediately preceding period. The main advantage of this type of index is that it is easy to introduce new items into the index without the necessity of then re-calculating the indices for the previous periods. If this is done frequently, however, the index is really only suitable for the relatively short period since, in time, the composition of prices or outputs etc. will have changed. Thus, the index in later periods reflects price movements of products different from those when the index was first compiled.

Arithmetic or Geometric Mean?

The point was made earlier that an index is merely an average. The average most often used is the arithmetic mean but it is also possible to use the geometric mean. From Chapter VI it may be recalled that the geometric mean is the nth root of n values. Thus, if we have three numbers, then their geometric mean is the cube root of their product; for 10 values it is the 10th root of their product. In Table 32 the data relating to prices and weights are the same as in the example of the weighted arithmetic mean illustrated in Table 30. The use of logarithms greatly simplifies the calculation

TABLE 32
CALCULATION OF WEIGHTED GEOMETRIC MEAN

Com-mod-ity	Prices		Logarithms		Value Weights	Logs × Weights	
	1970	1978	1970	1978		1970	1978
A	15	50	1·1761	1·6981	6	7·0566	10·1886
B	25	75	1·3979	1·8751	15	20·9685	28·1265
C	60	150	1·7782	2·1761	18	32·0076	39·1698
D	150	225	2·1761	2·3522	15	32·6415	35·2830

54	92·6742 112·7679
Less	92·6742
54)	20·0937
	0·3721

Anti-log of 0·3721 = 2·35
∴ 1978 index with 1970 = 100 is 235.

of the roots. Note too that the difference between the logarithms for any two prices gives the logarithm of the *relative proportionate* change of the later value to the earlier value. In other words, to remind those readers who have forgotten their logarithms, the addition of two logarithms is effectively a simple way of multiplying together the original values, just as subtraction of the logarithms is equivalent to dividing one of the numbers by the other.

Since the difference between the logarithms of each price at the two dates gives the price relative, the appropriate weights in this case are the *value* weights and not the *quantity* weights. To simplify the arithmetic the original weights given in Table 30 have all been divided by 10. It will be recalled that this makes no difference to the weighting; it is the *relative* size of the weights one to the other that is important, not their absolute size. Note how the sum of the products for 1970 is subtracted from that for 1978 and the quotient divided by the sum of the weights, *i.e.* 54. The antilog of 0.3721 is then looked up in the tables of logarithms and the result is 2.35 which, when adjusted to 1970 = 100, gives an index for 1978 of 235. It will be noted that this index is smaller than the index value of 245 which was derived from the use of the arithmetic mean. This is a mathematical characteristic of the geometric mean which is always smaller than the arithmetic mean based upon the same data.

In view of the fact that there are other 'averages' such as the median and mode, it is theoretically possible to devise an index using these. In practice, however, their disadvantages are obvious and either the arithmetic or geometric mean is used. As between these two there is no strong reason for consistently preferring one to the other. Generally speaking, where the data have been converted into price relatives, then the geometric mean may be preferable not least since it does not tend to inflate the index if there are large individual changes. When using actual prices and not the price relatives for the construction of an aggregative type index, then the arithmetic mean is usually used. Nor should it be overlooked that the amount of calculation involved is much less for the arithmetic mean than for the geometric mean.

Which average to use poses much the same problems as choosing between a Laspeyre type index or the Paasche current period weighted index. In other words, it depends on what one wants of the index. As already noted, there is a substantial body of theory on the subject of index number construction which is well beyond the scope of this text. For the reader with some mathematical competence who wishes to acquaint himself with the subtleties of the subject there are several useful sources.[1]

[1] See appropriate chapters in *Applied General Statistics* by Croxton and Cowden, or *Applied Statistics for Economists* by Karmel, P. H and M. Polasek, or *Economic Arithmetic* by Marris, R.

As with the Arithmetic Mean, so with the Geometric Mean, the formula is often given in algebraic notation. Thus with the Geometric Mean described as the nth root of the product of n values the usual form is:

$$g = \sqrt[n]{x_1 \times x_2 \times x_3 \times \ldots \times x_n}$$

If weights are to be introduced as in the illustrative calculation above, then

$$g = \sqrt[w]{x_1^{w_1} \times x_2^{w_2} \times x_3^{w_3} \times \ldots \times x_n^{w_n}}$$

where w = the total of weights used and w_1, w_2, $\ldots$, w_n are individual weights.

Since the computation involves logarithms, the first form may be written:

$$\log g = \frac{\log x_1 + \log x_2 + \log x_3 \ldots + \log_n}{n}$$

$$= \frac{\Sigma \log x}{n} \text{ or } \frac{1}{n} \Sigma (\log x)$$

The weighted series is then written:

$$\log g = \frac{w_1 \log x_1 + w_2 \log x_2 + w_3 \log x_3 + \ldots w_n \log x_n}{\Sigma w}$$

$$= \frac{\Sigma w \log x}{\Sigma w}$$

where Σw represents the total weights.

The reader may care to transpose figures from the example in the preceding pages to test the above formula.

Conclusions

Whatever method of index number construction is employed and whatever its purpose, it is as well to remember that the resultant index is an arbitrary and imperfect measure of change. It is arbitrary since the choice of the prices or output values used to construct the index entails a selection from many such values. Ultimately, the choice of the sample of prices etc. to be used is subjective and arbitrary. The index is imperfect since the perfect or 'ideal' index does not exist because some indices tend to exaggerate the upward movement in prices while others to depress them.[1]

With the expansion of the government statistical service and the Central Statistical Office, which is also responsible for a considerable range of statistics other than those prepared by the depart-

[1] The term 'ideal' index was used by a leading statistician 'Irving Fisher' in his work on the subject of index number construction.

ments, the quality and quantity of statistical information have greatly increased since the war and, more especially, since the early 1960s. Official index numbers are no exception to this statement, with periodic revisions of all the main indices to improve their coverage and sensitivity to change. The following notes on two of the more important index numbers will serve to underline the points made regarding the construction of index numbers made in the preceding pages. Further references to various official indices are contained in Chapters XVII and XVIII.

Some Illustrations

Probably the most important of all the official index numbers compiled in the government statistical service is the index of retail prices which serves as a cost of living index for purposes of wage negotiations and the payment of welfare benefits. The index is of especial interest in view of the very wide range of prices included therein. The *general* index is compiled by the Department of Employment and details are first published in the Department of Employment's monthly *Gazette*. It measures the change from month to month in the *average* level of prices of goods and services purchased by the majority of households in the U.K.

The excluded households were cited on p. 222. Some 150,000 price quotations are obtained on the middle Tuesday of each month from a wide range of different types of retail shop. The data are collected by the Department's officers in some 200 local areas. The range of prices and the thoroughness with which the compilation of data is done are reflected in the fact that quotations for sugar alone may be derived from up to 800 shops. These individual prices are combined to produce an index for sugar prices and that index, together with all the other food indices, is then combined to produce the sub-groups for food items which in turn are combined to give the group index.

The need to collect prices over such a wide range of areas and shops – for most food items between 500 and 800 prices are collected – is due to the fact that the Department's research studies reveal that the form of organisation of retail outlets was the most important factor contributing to price differences for the same item and, in some cases, there are also significant differences between regions. To determine the price change in the item, *e.g.* bread, the Department estimates the percentage change in average prices between the two successive months.

The weighting of the individual group indices, of which there are 11 in the general index, is determined by the expenditure on the various items as revealed by the annual Family Expenditure Survey. Table 33 overleaf shows the 11 group indices (there are also 36 sub-groups among the 11 groups published each month) and the weights used to determine the annual averages of the monthly indices for 1974 and 1977. These indices are compiled and published in addition to the indices for the successive months. The current base year for the general index is January 1974; the previous base date was January 1962. As the index now approaches 200 there is some possibility that a new base date will be introduced. It will be appreciated that a five-point rise in the index, once the index reaches 200, is equivalent only to a 2½ per cent increase on an index with base 100. To that extent, some people could misinterpret the significance of the monthly change.

TABLE 33
INDICES OF RETAIL PRICES (Jan. 15, 1974 = 100)
(General and Two-Person Pensioner Households)

Commodity Group	General Index				Two-Person Pensioner Household	
	1977*		1974*		1977†	1974†
	Weight	Index	Weight	Index	Index	Index
Food ..	247	190·3	253	106·1	184·8	104·0
Alcoholic Drink ..	83	183·4	70	109·7	186·3	110·0
Tobacco	46	209·7	43	115·9	210·2	116·0
Housing	112	161·8	124	105·8	—	—
Fuel & Light ..	58	211·3	52	110·7	207·7	110·0
Durable Household Goods ..	63	166·8	64	107·9	170·3	108·2
Clothing & Footwear	82	158·3	91	109·4	158·5	109·7
Transport & Vehicles	139	190·3	135	111·0	194·9	111·0
Miscellaneous ..	71	188·3	63	111·2	197·4	113·3
Services	54	173·3	54	106·8	171·2	106·7
Meals bought out..	45	185·7	51	108·2	188·6	108·8
All items ..	1·000	182·0	1000	108·5	—	—
All items excluding Housing ..	—	184·9		108·9	186·7	

*Monthly Averages
†Annual Averages

The same table shows how the weights have changed over the period 1974–77 and this is because, since 1962, the weights have been revised annually. To this extent there is within the present index a strong element of the *chain-base* index discussed briefly on p. 232. In addition to the composition of the *general* index Table = also shows the group indices for two-person pensioner households. It will be noted that for this index the index for housing is omitted. This is because the rent element in the expenditure of pensioner households can vary widely from virtually nothing in the case of the owner-occupier to the relatively high rent of the person living in furnished accommodation. Rent is also treated separately for purposes of determining certain welfare payments due to low income households. Thus, it is felt that the index without housing provides a better indicator of relevant price changes for pensioner households. Note too that while the *general* index is published *monthly*, the *two* pensioner indices (for one and two-person households) are published *quarterly*. The quarterly figure is actually based upon the average of the three monthly figures for the quarter. These then form the basis for the annual average shown in the table. The importance of the two pensioner indices may be judged from the fact that about one third of all national insurance retirement pensioners live in households covered by these indices, *i.e.* about 3,000,000 persons.

The index of *industrial production* provides an interesting contrast with the index of retail prices in so far as the data available are more limited. The purpose of the index of industrial production is to provide a general measure of monthly changes in the volume of industrial output in the U.K. It covers all manufacturing industries, construction, gas, electricity and water, together with mining and quarrying. Agriculture, trade, transport and other public and private sector service industries are excluded. The current index is based on 1970 but the series was worked back to January 1968.

For weighting purposes the index relies upon the information collected from the 1970 census of production. The weight for each industry or group of industries making up one of the several group indices within the overall index is determined by the net output of the industry in 1970. But, this figure has to be adjusted to exclude the estimated amounts paid for services rendered to the industries by firms in sectors of the economy not included in the index, *e.g.* advertising and other services. Difficulties also arise with the measurement of monthly output from each industry in so far as such figures are not available from all industries. For rather less than half of the industries included in the current index data on actual physical output are available; for about the same proportion deliveries and sales data are used as indicators of the level of production. About 10 per cent of the data has to be derived from estimates based upon the deliveries of major raw materials used in the industry, while a much smaller proportion of the index depends on figures of persons employed. It will be appreciated that actual receipts, *i.e.* deliveries of raw materials, are not good indicators of the level of output in the shorter run, while the number of persons employed is a poor indicator of output in conditions when overtime is general or, conversely, holidays are being taken.

The index measures the change in output as a percentage of the level of industrial production in 1970 and, to ensure comparability between different months, adjustments need to be made for the variable number of working days in each month. Holidays are similarly allowed for. In sum, the monthly movements in the index are not to be taken too literally; as an indicator of longer term trends the index is more reliable. In other words, the index is an excellent example of a statistic which needs to be interpreted with very great care. The two indices quoted most frequently are those for *total industrial production* and for *total manufacturing industry*. The latter accounts for almost exactly 75 per cent of the weighting in the total index. Like the retail prices index, the index of industrial prodution is of the Laspeyre type, *i.e.*the base year weighted arithmetic mean of the output relatives. In publications where the full index is not reproduced, it is the *seasonally adjusted* index which is given. Recognition of the limitations of the index is provided in so far as recorded changes in successive months do not normally attract much attention or discussion. Instead the percentage change during the latest three months over the previous three months is given, as well as the corresponding quarter in the previous year. However, given the importance of this particular index for purposes of measuring the rate of economic growth within the national economy and as an indicator of industrial trends, it may be assumed that, as the volume of output information from industry increases, so the accuracy of the individual industry indicators will be improved.

Both the above index numbers are official indices and they represent, in the form of the final product, the two extremes of sophisticated index number construction. The coverage of the total index of industrial production is exceptionally wide and this fact undoubtedly contributes to its limitations. The point to bear in mind in reviewing these two indices, and there are others which can be studied in official publications such as *Economic Trends*, is that it is possible to construct an index for almost any purpose. Its accuracy, however, depends not on the nuances of index number theory or the type of index used, but on something much more basic, *i.e.* the availability of the data, its representativeness and the information available to determine a reasonably accurate weighting structure!

Questions

General

In recent years questions on index numbers have changed their form. They used to involve no more than routine calculations of indices from data of prices and quantities. Hence, any candidate who memorised the very simple techniques could obtain a pass mark quite easily. More recently, however, increasing attention has been paid by examiners to what, for want of a better term, may be referred to as the basic principles of index number construction. Thus, in addition to expecting the candidate to perform a few simple calculations for the compilation of an index, another part of the question requires him to explain such matters as the difference between Laspeyre and Paasche indices, or the problems in constructing an index number etc. Sometimes, in view of the increased number of official index numbers, the candidate may be asked to discuss a published index or illustrate his answer to a question on index number problems by reference to a published index number. It is sensible, therefore, for the candidate to learn something about a major index such as the index of retail prices or the index of industrial production. It is not necessary to learn a lot of detail. He should know what the index is designed to measure, the coverage of the index, the basis of the weighting and the base year; in other words, the main points which would be considered if one were contemplating the construction of a new index.

Generally speaking, particularly now that candidates may use hand calculators, such questions on index number construction should give few problems. There is little scope for variety at the elementary level and the following questions constitute a fair sample of the type of questions which may be expected.

1. The following table gives the prices per unit of three commodities in 1970 and 1972 and the value of purchases in those years. Calculate price indices for 1972 (1970 = 100) using (i) current (1972) year weights and (ii) base year (1970) weights.

Commodity	Unit	Prices (p)		Value of Purchases (£)	
		1970	1972	1970	1972
X	doz.	60	50	180	300
Y	box	80	100	80	200
Z	lb.	10	15	60	45

R.V.A.

2. Index of Retail Prices (August 1974)

Group		Weight	Price Relative (Jan. 1974 = 100)
I	Food	253	106·1
II	Alcoholic Drink	70	110·7
III	Tobacco	43	120·3
IV	Housing	124	105·1
V	Fuel and Light	52	115·7
VI	Durable Household Goods	64	109·5
VII	Clothing and Footwear	91	110·9
VIII	Transport and Vehicles	135	112·7
IX	Miscellaneous Goods	63	113·3
X	Services	54	109·3
XI	Meals consumed outside home	51	110·4

(i) Using the information above, calculate the General Index of Retail Prices for August 1974, with January 1974 = 100.
(ii) The previous base for this index was Jan. 1962 = 100. With Jan. 1962 as base, the index for Jan. 1974 was 191·8. Calculate the index for August 1974 with Jan. 1962 as base.

I.O.S.

3. The following table shows annual indices of (i) average earnings and (ii) retail prices for each year 1968–75.
(i) Calculate an annual index to show the change in *real*, as distinct from *money*, earnings over this period.

Year:	1968	1969	1970	1971	1972	1973	1974	1975
Average Earnings:	88·8	95·7	107·2	119·4	134·8	152·6	179·6	227·6
Retail Prices:	89·2	94·0	100·0	109·4	117·2	128·0	148·5	184·4

(ii) Explain the meaning of the index you have calculated and what it shows.

C.M.I.

4. Index of Industrial Production, G.B. (Average 1970 = 100)

Industry Group	Weights	Index (Dec. 1976)
Mining and Quarrying	37	95
Manufacturing:		
Food, Drink and Tobacco	84	110
Chemicals	65	127
Metals	57	78
Engineering	319	99
Textiles	76	105
Other Manufacturing	144	108
Construction	146	87
Gas, Electricity and Water	72	133

Calculate the Index for (i) All industries (ii) Manufacturing industries.

I.O.S.

5. The following table shows the price per unit of materials used in manufacturing a compound in 1974 and 1978. The quantities used in manufacturing the compound are given for the same two years.

Materials	1974		1978	
	Price	Quantity	Price	Quantity
A	15	1,200	32	1,610
B	22	20	50	25
C	39	980	55	1,310
D	20	100	30	125
E	50	90	72	130

From the above data calculate:
(i) an index of prices for 1978 with 1974 = 100.
(ii) an index of quantities used in 1978 with 1974 = 100.

Answers

1. This is a very easy question complicated slightly by the fact that one of the prices has fallen. Since, in each of the two years, this price has the largest of the weights, it exerts a marked effect on the resultant index and the overall or average increase in the index is quite small, despite the fact that the other two prices have risen by 25 and 50 per cent. Note too that, since the question refers to the expenditure on these three products, they are in effect value weights. These are multiplied, not with the prices in the two years, but by the price relatives. The latter are derived by expressing the price in the later year as a multiple of the price in the earlier year, which latter figure is taken as 100. The products of the price relatives and the relevant weights are given in the final two columns, the first with 1970 and the second with 1972 weights. The student may recall that it would be just as easy to derive the average percentage *increase* in the price level. In this case the figure shown under the heading 'price relatives' would merely show the percentage *change* in the three prices, *i.e.* $-16 \cdot 6$, $+25$ and $+50$. These, when multiplied by the appropriate weights, will give the same answers as were derived by using the relatives with 1970 price equal to 100. Note in this case that the first product is negative.

Prices		Value weights		Price Relatives	Products	
1970	1972	1970	1972	1972÷1970	$\left(\dfrac{P_1}{P_0} \times q_0\right)$	$\left(\dfrac{P_1}{P_0} \times q_1\right)$
(P_0)	(P_1)	(q_0)	(q_1)	100 P_1/P_0		
60	50	180	300	83·3	15,000	25,000
80	100	80	200	125	10,000	25,000
10	15	60	45	150	9,000	6,750
		320	545		34,000	56,750

Price indices 1970 = 100
1972 value weights, *i.e.* current year weighting

$$\frac{56,750}{545} = 104 \cdot 1$$

1970 value weights, base year weighting

$$\frac{34,000}{320} = 106 \cdot 2$$

2. This question provides a useful illustration of the compilation in the final stages of the general index of retail prices. Note that, for each of the main groups of expenditure in this index, a separate index is obtained. This group index is then weighted by reference to the relative importance of expenditure on that group of items to the total expenditure of the household covered by the index.

Group	Weight	Price Relative	Relative × Weight
I	253	106·1	26843·3
II	70	110·7	7749·0
III	43	120·3	5172·9
IV	124	105·1	13032·4
V	52	115·7	6016·4
VI	64	109·5	7008·0
VII	91	110·9	10091·9
VIII	135	112·7	15214·5
IX	63	113·3	7137·9
X	54	109·3	5902·2
XI	51	110·4	5630·4
	1,000		109798·9

(i) Index for August 1974 $\frac{109798}{1000} = 109 \cdot 8$

(ii) If index at Jan. 1974 = 191·8 (Jan. 1962 = 100)
then, on 1962 base, August 1974 = 191·8 × 109·8 = 210·6

The calculation is straightforward and, with a calculator, quite rapid and easy. The second part of the question often features in questions on index numbers. In this particular case, if we required a long run of the index from Jan. 1962, the fact of the revised base in Jan. 1974 would divide the series into two distinct parts. All that is needed is to multiply the post Jan. 1974 indices by the ratio of the original value (base 1962) to the revised value of 100, in this case 191·8. This will then provide a single continuous series on the same base.

3. This question is not so much concerned with the calculation of an index number, but with the application of index numbers to effect comparisons over time. In this case, we have two series of indices, one of average earnings and the other of retail prices. By dividing the index of retail prices into the corresponding index of earnings, a third index termed an index of *real* earnings is derived. The original series of average earnings indices over-stated the improvement in living standards which those earnings would provide, since no account was taken of rising prices. The change in prices over the period can be eliminated by dividing the earnings series by the index of retail prices. The resultant series, termed the 'real' earnings, shows the improvement in earnings which would have taken place if there had been no inflation.

The series of figures relating to earnings were in fact the index of average earnings, which is compiled by the Department of Employment. But, the calculation would have been much the same had the series consisted of the actual money earnings. By multiplying the cash figure for each year by 100 and then dividing the product by the index of retail prices, the earnings would have been 'deflated' to take account of the changing value of money.

(i)

Year	Average Earnings	Retail Prices	Index of Real Earnings
1968	88·8	89·2	99·6
1969	95·7	94·0	101·8
1970	107·2	100·0	107·2
1971	119·4	109·4	109·1
1972	134·8	117·2	115·0
1973	152·6	128·0	119·2
1974	179·6	148·5	120·9
1975	227·6	184·4	123·4

4. The particular merit of this question is that it provides an illustration of a major index, much the same as Q.2 which involved the retail price index. The calculation here is exactly the same. The indices for each industrial group are multiplied by the appropriate weight (which is determined by the output of that particular industry group relative to *total* industrial output), and the sum of the products divided by the sum of the weights. Note that the manufacturing industries as a whole account for virtually three-quarters (745:1,000) of the weighting. Just as this question requires the calculation of the two indices, *i.e.* one for All industries and the other for Manufacturing industries, so the two elements in this index which are published regularly are those two indices.

Group	Indices Dec. '76 (Average 1970 = 100)	Weights	Index × Weights
Mining and Quarrying	95	37	3,515
Manufacturing:			
Food, Drink and Tobacco	110	84	9240
Chemicals	127	65	8255
Metals	78	57	4446
Engineering	99	319	31581
Textiles	105	76	7980
Other Manufacturing	108	144	15552
			77,054
Construction	87	146	12,702
Gas, Electricity and Water	133	72	9,576
		1000	102,847

(i) All industries index for Dec. 1976 $= \dfrac{102\cdot847}{1000} = 102\cdot8$

(ii) Manufacturing industries index for Dec. 1976 $= \dfrac{77054}{745} = 103\cdot4$

5. In this case, since actual quantities of the materials are given, the index can be calculated without the derivation of the price relatives. All that is needed is to multiply the prices and corresponding quantities together and divide the sum of products of the former year into the sum of the products of the later year. This provides a simple weighted price index for 1978 with 1974 equal to 100.

For the quantity index, to show the change in quantities used between the two

years, instead of the conventional Laspeyre formula $\dfrac{\Sigma p_1 q_0}{\Sigma p_0 q_0}$, we use $\dfrac{\Sigma p_0 q_1}{\Sigma p_0 q_0}$ *i.e.*
Paasche. In other words, the quantities are changed while the prices are held constant.

Materials	1974 Price per unit p_0	Quantity q_0	1978 Price p_1	Quantity q_1	Products $(p_1 q_0)$	$(p_0 q_0)$	$(p_0 q_1)$
A	15	1,200	32	1,610	38,400	18,000	24,150
B	22	20	50	25	1,000	440	550
C	39	980	55	1,310	53,900	38,220	51,090
D	20	100	30	125	3,000	2,000	2,500
E	50	90	72	130	6,480	4,500	6,500
					102,780	63,160	84,790

(i) Index of 1978 prices $= \dfrac{102{\cdot}780}{63{\cdot}160} \times 100 = 162{\cdot}7 \ (1974 = 100)$

(ii) Index of 1978 quantities $= \dfrac{84{\cdot}790}{63{\cdot}160} \times 100 = 134{\cdot}2 \ (1974 = 100)$

CHAPTER XI

TIME SERIES

Numerical data, which have been recorded at intervals of time, form what is generally described as a time series. Thus the annual sales of a shop, the quarterly output of coal or the monthly totals of passengers carried by a bus company; all these are time series. Undoubtedly the most popular form of presenting such data is in the form of a graph as was shown in Chapter V. Graphs, however, have only a limited value in statistics. While they enable data to be presented in simple and easily intelligible form, they do not add anything to our knowledge of the data. They are of little value for analysis, although a graph does sometimes help to bring out the inter-relationship between two or more time series.

For the economist and business man a study of past events is an aid to making judgments concerning the future. Statistical techniques have been evolved which enable time series to be analysed in such a way that the influences which have determined the form of that series may be ascertained. If the regularity of occurrence of any feature over a sufficiently long period could be clearly established then, within limits, prediction of probable future variations would become possible. Thus a decline in capital investment is sometimes regarded as heralding the initial stages of a recession. If this assumption can be statistically tested and verified in the light of past experience, then the authorities responsible for economic policy possess a useful piece of knowledge to aid them in their contra-cyclical policy.

In practice, the economist and statistician are the first to admit that analysis of time series is extremely complicated since the economic life of a nation is subject to so many complex forces and influences, any one of which it is impossible to isolate. It cannot be too strongly emphasised, then, that the elementary techniques described in the following text appear deceptively simple. This field of study remains the undisputed preserve of the experts.

Types of Fluctuation

Most economic time series may be regarded as composed of four constituent elements:
(1) secular trend – or simply the 'trend';
(2) cyclical changes;
(3) seasonal variations;
(4) irregular or random fluctuations.

It should be noted that not all series combine all four elements, *e.g.* not all trades are seasonal although many are. Note too that not all time series consist of economic data. A college may maintain records of examination marks gained by students over their period of study; such a time series would hardly show the same type of fluctuation as that expected from a series based on the quarterly output of motor cars or monthly consumption of electricity. In other words, one applies the methods of time series analysis only to such data as justify their employment, *i.e.* where they help in understanding past events and where some useful lessons may be gained for the future.

The *secular trend* is the course which the data have followed over a considerable period. In other words, despite temporary deviations from the course, *i.e.* both large and small fluctuations, there is a clearly marked tendency in a given direction. For example, Table 34 (p. 247) shows a series of indices which measure the volume of sales of clothing and footwear from retail shops in each calendar quarter during the years 1966–76. Although quarterly fluctuations in the series are quite prominent, as can be seen in Figure 18, the *trend* of sales is continuously upward with the passage of time. If a trend can be determined, then the rate of change or progress can be ascertained, and tentative estimates concerning the future made accordingly. The period covered in this example is rather short to warrant the term 'trend' which, ideally, should be restricted to a definite continuous movement which has been observed over several decades. There is a tendency nowadays, however, to employ the term to indicate the main course followed by the series over a period of several years.

Cyclical fluctuations are far more complex, since their causation differs from period to period. In practice, they are the most difficult of all to anticipate for purposes of effective economic offsetting action. The term 'trade cycle' would imply a systematic regularity in its appearance, but economists have established a variety of 'cycles', with durations of 3, 5, 7, 9, or 11 years. It is only in recent years that economic opinion has crystallised on the *basic* features of the trade cycle – but despite almost monumental research, particularly in the United States, all that has been proven is that there is no such phenomenon as *the* trade cycle, every one is different. In practice, with most economic series one may at best hope to establish some approximation to a cyclical pattern, *e.g.* in the periodicity of the fluctuations, while the amplitude of the fluctuations will probably show even greater variation.

Seasonal variations, however, are somewhat simpler to deal with. It is common knowledge that many industries are more active at certain periods of the year than at others, *e.g.* the dress and fashion trade anticipates the Spring demand, the toy manufacturers the

Christmas season, the motor car industry the Easter and summer holidays, while the building and constructional trades are slack in the winter months. If a definite periodicity for any occurrence can be established and, more especially, the extent of the average fluctuation at that time can be determined, the change in conditions may be anticipated to some degree and provision made to offset any disturbance it might otherwise cause. For example, given the very obvious and regular fluctuation in the volume of retail sales evident in column 3 of Table 34, such shops should arrange for stock levels to be adjusted to meet prospective demand.

Irregular or random fluctuations: The economic life of society would be very much simpler if reliable forecasts concerning the future course of business activity were possible. Unfortunately, even with the most advanced existing techniques the forecasting of economic trends remains little more than intelligent estimating, since extraneous and unexpected factors continue to appear and upset the best-laid calculations. In the interpretation of any time series, apart from establishing the trend and the extent of the regular seasonal deviations from it, the economist or statistician tries to isolate not only the random but also the unusual fluctuations. For example, import statistics are made up from Customs records; in the event of a dock strike lasting many weeks, the goods would be landed late and the normal seasonal movement in import statistics would then be replaced by a single swollen figure for the month in which the strike ended. If the seasonal movement were to be computed for a long period, including that year, the distorted figure would have to be adjusted.

The foregoing classification of the elements which account for the fluctuations in most series of economic data over time is deceptively simple. To start with, not all series comprise all four of the above elements. There may be a cyclical element but no seasonal fluctuations. For example, a series relating to the output of electricity generating equipment is likely to show a marked cyclical pattern reflecting the periodicity of orders from a monopoly buyer and the state of the national economy. It is unlikely to reveal any seasonal movement whatsoever. Furthermore, although the classification above implies that time series analysis is concerned with breaking down the series into its parts, it should not be assumed that the techniques available actually enable such a complete breakdown to be achieved. In any case, the methods used are based upon the assumption that throughout the period covered by the series the underlying economic forces remain constant. Experience of the past may be the best available guide to the future in some areas of life but, in the field of economic forecasting, which is ultimately what time series analysis is about, the past can often be a highly misleading guide to the future. Whether elementary techniques are used to analyse a time series or more sophisticated techniques, it is the data which count. For example, how has the series been compiled? If it relates to industrial output or the movement of goods through ports, do the months all have the same number of working days; what adjustment needs to be made for seasonal influences such as holidays; can the series be 'smoothed' to eliminate the distortions caused by strikes etc? The analysis of time series is not so much a matter of statistical techniques as of judgment and experience with the data being used.

The Method of Moving Averages

The simplest and first approach to the analysis of any time series is to draw a graph. This has been done in Figure 18 on p. 249 for the

TABLE 34

Year (1)	Quarter (2)	Volume Indices (3)	Sums of 4s (4)	Sums of 8s (5)	Trend (6)	Fluctuations from Trend (7)	Seasonal Movement (8)	Residual Fluctuation (9)
1966	1	78						
	2	92	371					
	3	88	370	741	93	− 5	− 4	− 1
	4	113	367	737	92	+ 21	+ 23	− 2
1967	1	77	368	735	92	− 15	− 16	+ 1
	2	89	371	739	92	− 3	− 3	0
	3	89	375	746	93	− 4	− 4	0
	4	116	378	753	94	+ 22	+ 23	− 1
1968	1	81	380	758	95	− 14	− 16	+ 2
	2	92	382	762	95	− 3	− 3	0
	3	91	378	760	95	− 4	− 4	0
	4	118	381	759	95	+ 23	+ 23	0
1969	1	79	380	761	95	− 16	− 16	0
	2	95	383	763	95	0	− 3	+ 3
	3	92	384	767	96	− 4	− 4	0
	4	117	385	769	96	+ 21	+ 23	− 2
1970	1	80	387	772	97	− 17	− 16	− 1
	2	96	394	781	98	− 2	− 3	+ 1
	3	94	396	790	99	− 5	− 4	− 1
	4	124	399	795	99	+ 25	+ 23	+ 2
1971	1	82	400	799	100	− 18	− 16	− 2
	2	99	400	800	100	− 11	− 3	− 8
	3	95	402	802	100	− 5	− 4	− 1
	4	124	404	806	101	+ 23	+ 23	0
1972	1	84	411	815	102	− 18	− 16	− 2
	2	101	419	830	104	− 3	− 3	0
	3	102	432	851	106	− 4	− 4	0
	4	132	435	867	108	+ 24	+ 23	+ 1
1973	1	97	435	870	109	− 12	− 16	+ 14
	2	104	436	871	109	− 5	− 3	− 2
	3	102	428	864	108	− 6	− 4	− 2
	4	133	426	854	107	+ 26	+ 23	+ 3
1974	1	89	429	855	107	− 18	− 16	− 2
	2	102	428	857	107	− 5	− 3	− 2
	3	105	433	861	108	− 3	− 4	+ 1
	4	132	437	870	109	+ 23	+ 23	0
1975	1	94	435	872	109	− 15	− 16	+ 1
	2	106	433	868	108	− 2	− 3	+ 1
	3	103	428	861	108	− 5	− 4	− 1
	4	130	426	854	107	+ 23	+ 23	0
1976	1	89						
	2	104						

Source: Cols. 1-3 only Economic Trends

data in Table 34 which shows an extended series of quarterly indices for the period 1966 to mid-1976. The indices are based upon the retail sales of clothing and footwear; not by value of those sales, but by volume. The base period for the indices is 1971 and the reader may note that the four quarterly indices for that particular year sum to 400 which gives an annual average of 100 equal to the base year index. The quarterly totals given in Col. 3 are plotted on a linear scale graph in Fig. 18, on p. 249 which conveys almost immediately two clear impressions:

(1) The direction of the plotted series is gently upwards from left to right, *i.e.* throughout the period, apart from seasonal variations, the volume of sales has increased continuously until 1974-75.

(2) There appears to be a regular rise and fall in the volume of sales within the space of each year, and throughout the whole period these movements appear almost identical from one year to another.

At the outset it can be stated that the first observation concerns the *trend*; the second refers to the marked *seasonal* movement characterising this series. As a first approximation, the trend line may be drawn 'freehand', sketching through the middle of the fluctuations so that the seasonal fluctuations are ignored but indicating thereby the course of the data in the period. Unfortunately this method requires not merely a moderate degree of artistic skill, but a considerable knowledge of the data. In Fig. 18 the broken line which passes through the middle of the quarterly series has not been drawn freehand. It has been drawn so that the deviations of the original series from the dotted line, *i.e.* the approximate trend values, above and below that line cancel each other out. It will be recalled that the sum of the deviations of any series measured from the mean of the series is equal to zero; this was the basis of the short-cut method of deriving the arithmetic mean of a frequency distribution. The same principle has been applied to the quarterly series to locate the path of the so-called trend line. The technique of so determining the trend values is known as the method of moving averages.

The primary purpose of the moving average method is not, however, to determine the trend. The trend values are needed for the derivation of the seasonal movement which, as was remarked earlier, is very pronounced in this series. In any case, it will doubtless have occurred to the reader on studying Fig. 18 that the broken line marking the trend values did not suggest a smooth straight line. It is neither linear nor curvi-linear, *i.e.* neither straight nor curved. Instead it shows quite marked oscillations and, although the course of the line is reasonably consistent, in the last year it shows quite a distinct

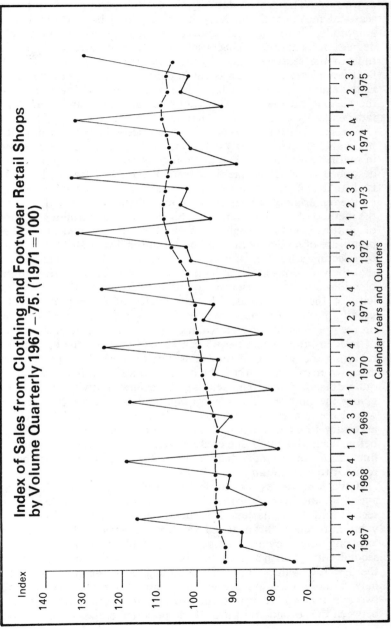

Figure 18

Index of Sales from Clothing and Footwear Retail Shops by Volume Quarterly 1967 – 75. (1971 = 100)

down-turn. The reason for this is that, superimposed upon the seasonal movement, which by itself may well be fairly regular in amplitude, there are the random fluctuations which, in varying degrees according to their causation, reduce or increase the amplitude of the seasonal fluctuations. Thus for a series in which the fluctuations are not as consistent in their periodicity or amplitude as in the example given, the trend line must inevitably be affected by the various fluctuations. It certainly cannot be drawn completely independently of the larger fluctuations in the series.

For such reasons, if trend values are needed for forcasting, it is preferable to have a clearly defined trend line which can be described in mathematical terms. The method of deriving such a trend line is described later. Given the data from Table 34 plotted in Fig. 18 it is clear that main interest in this particular series must concentrate on the remarkably regular seasonal movement. To derive this we use the method of moving averages. This involves ascertaining a number of plotting points through which the trend line should pass. These points are obtained by the method set out in Table 34, Cols. 4-6, *i.e.* by selecting a number of consecutive values and averaging them so that the variations in the individual values are reduced. The number of values utilised for determining the average depends on the periodicity of the fluctuations. The periodicity of these movements is usually measured by the time between the recurrent 'peaks' shown on the graph of the original values. In this example no real problem of selecting the correct period can be said to exist, the data clearly requiring the average of four consecutive values. In contrast, however, for many other series the determination of this figure may be quite difficult. Thus, data relating to business acitivity, *e.g.* a series giving the number of company liquidations over several decades, would cover a number of business 'cycles'. Probably it would be necessary to experiment with 5, 7, 8, or 9 years' moving averages before a suitable trend line could be clearly established, *i.e.* when the fluctuations of the individual values in the series from the trend are reduced to a minimum.

If the four values, *i.e.* those for the four quarters of 1966, are averaged, the average would be located between the values of the second and third quarters. It is then necessary to bring this average value into line with an actual value in the series. This is done by 'centring' the moving average, *i.e.* by finding the average of the second, third, fourth and fifth items, and adding this to the average of the first four values. Then if the aggregate of the two averages is halved, the moving average will be 'centred', *i.e.* the average of the two averages will lie against the third figure of the series, instead of between the second and third. If the period averaged covers an odd number of months or years (almost invariably the latter), the problem of centring does not arise. The average then lies against the middle item, *e.g.* a nine-yearly average would be placed against the fifth value. It should be noted that centring is only really necessary if the calculation of the extent of the seasonal or cyclical fluctuations is required; it is not absolutely necessary for the sole purpose of drawing the trend line, as plotting points can be derived from the 'mid-values' of successive averages.

A simpler way of working, used in Table 34, is to aggregate the first four values, then the second to fifth values inclusive, yielding successive totals of 371 and 370 (Col. 4). By adding them, as in Col. 5, and dividing by 8, the moving average is centred (Col. 6). By continuing this process throughout the series, the succession of averages referred to as trend values in Col. 6 is obtained.

The series of moving averages plotted on the graph (Fig. 18) are the trend values which yield the relatively smooth line passing through the graph of the original data. This line is described as the trend or line of trend. The subtraction of the trend values from the actual values of the series in Col. 3 gives the total fluctuations about the line of trend shown in Col. 7 of Table 34.

Derivation of Seasonal Movement

The quarterly figures in Table 35 below come from Col. 7 in Table 34; they are the recorded total fluctuations each quarter from the estimated trend. That is to say, they are an amalgam of the seasonal fluctuation and other random fluctuations which will vary from quarter to quarter in their impact, unlike the seasonal movement which is assumed to be regular in its impact upon sales. It is therefore necessary to split the total fluctuations from the trend into the seasonal element and the random fluctuations. To do this the total fluctuations are set out, quarter by quarter, as in Table 35. The reader will note that the figures for the last two quarters of 1966 have been omitted; this leaves exactly nine figures in each of the quarters for averaging. As a general rule one is reluctant not to use all the data that are available, assuming they are relevant but in this case it will simplify the arithmetic and the period covered is still long enough. The total fluctuations for the nine years are thus classified quarter by quarter and then aggregated.

Before the average seasonal fluctuation can be calculated and graphed, a further adjustment is usually necessary. It may be remembered that the sum of the individual deviations of a series of values from the mean of that series was equal to zero. Since the values on which the line of trend is based are also averages, the sum of the fluctuations from that line should equal zero. If they are totalled,

TABLE 35
CALCULATION OF MEAN SEASONAL MOVEMENT

	Quarters			
	March	June	September	December
1967	− 15	− 3	− 4	+ 22
1968	− 14	− 3	− 4	+ 23
1969	− 16	0	− 4	+ 21
1970	− 17	− 2	− 5	+ 25
1971	− 18	− 11	− 5	+ 23
1972	− 18	− 3	− 4	+ 24
1973	− 12	− 5	− 6	+ 26
1973	− 18	− 5	− 3	+ 23
1975	− 15	− 2	− 5	+ 23
Total	− 143	− 34	− 40	+ 210
Less Adjustment	− 2	− 2	− 2	− 2
Total Seasonal Move- ment ..	− 141 − 16	− 32 − 3	− 38 − 4	+ 212 + 23

as in Table 35 (−143 −34 −40 +210 = 210 −217 = −7) there is a difference of −7 between the sums of the positive and negative movements. Such a difference frequently arises since the effects of large but irregular seasonal fluctuations cannot be entirely eliminated by the moving average method. Since the source of the difference is unknown, it is eliminated by arbitrarily averaging it over the four quarters. In this case −7 is treated as −2 from each of the four quarters' total fluctuation, subtracting it from each quarter's total. The adjusted totals of each quarter's fluctuation from the trend line are then divided by the number of years covered. Here too the quotients are arbitrarily rounded to the nearest whole number. The quotients are the *average* or mean seasonal movement in the four quarters during the period covered by the data and are inserted in Col. 8 of Table 34. The *residual* movements (Col. 9, Table 34 are derived by subtracting the seasonal variation (Col. 8) from the total fluctuation from the trend, *i.e.* Col. 7.

The moving average method of deriving the trend of values and the seasonal fluctuations over a period is the main elementary method available for this work. It can be applied to series covering several decades provided the data can still be treated as a single series, the moving average in such a case being used to eliminate the so-called trade cycle. If the cycle were regular both in its periodicity and in the amplitude of fluctuations the moving average method would elimi- nate the fluctuations and yield a straight trend line. Such a cycle is the exception rather than the rule, hence, skill and knowledge in the selection of the period used for averaging are necessary where the cycle is not so clearly defined, *e.g.* is the cycle to which the data under scrutiny are subject one of 3, 5, 7, 9, or 11 years; how many cycles are superimposed on one another?

The moving average method, however, has certain disadvantages.

(i) The trend line cannot be derived for the period covering the whole series. The trend line falls 'short' at both ends, and if the cycle is one of, say, nine or eleven years, this may constitute a marked gap where the data cover only two or three cycles. It may be recalled that in the above illustration, so as to be able to use only those years with four quarters' figures, the first two figures of seasonal movement, *i.e.* 1966 3rd and 4th quarters, were omitted.

(ii) The difficulty already explained of establishing a definite periodicity in the fluctuations. Different views on this will result in differing trend lines. Unless, therefore, the seasonal or cyclical movement is definite and clear-cut, the moving average method of deriving the trend may yield only a rather unsatisfactory compromise line.

(iii) Since the trend values are arithmetic averages, any extreme individual variation affects them unduly. If the series varies considerably in extent from year to year, the trend may appear as a series of humps rather than a smooth line, as in Fig. 18. It is not possible to extrapolate, *i.e.* extend, such a line in order to estimate future values. Hence, if the primary purpose is to determine the trend for making such projections into the future, a different method of deriving the trend line is needed. This is explained in the next section.

Despite all the various warnings about the dangers of too ready an application of statistical techniques to time series, it is clear that the above series of volume indices relating to the retail side of the clothing and footwear industries lends itself to this type of analysis. It is abundantly clear from Figure 18 in which the indices and trend line are charted that there is a remarkably regular and consistent seasonal movement. For this reason the residual element made up of random fluctuations is, as may be seen in the final column, remarkably small. In other words, virtually the whole of the quarterly movement in the series from year to year has been consistent. While, given the sharp first quarter movement in the indices, the trend line is hardly straight, it is close enough if needed to warrant the derivation of a straight trend line such as is described in the next section.

While on the subject of seasonal movements the reader may like to know that the H.M.S.O. publication *Economic Trends* contains a large number of time series, some 'unadjusted' and others described as 'seasonally adjusted'. Both are given, for example, for unemployment statistics. The purpose here is to show, first the actual number of persons registered as unemployed and then the change in the monthly totals which arises from seasonal factors such as the entry into the labour market at the end of the summer term of the school leavers. Such a *seasonally adjusted* series can be derived by converting the actual seasonal movement into indices and then adjusting the original series by use of those indices. Such a process is often referred to as 'de-seasonalising' a series.

Fitting a Straight Line Trend

As was shown above, the seasonal movement in a time series can be obtained by averaging the differences between the actual values in the series and the estimated trend values. Quite apart from the obvious value of knowing the seasonal variations which may affect a business or trade, the trend too has its uses, particularly in forecasting future sales etc. Thus, if it can be reasonably assumed that the various factors which have determined the trend during the period covered by the time series are likely to continue to operate, then the trend can be projected to provide estimates of, for example, sales in future years. One way of doing this would be to extend the line of trend in Fig. 18 by freehand on the chart and then to read off the values for the years after 1975 from the graph. Since the line of trend in Fig. 18 is not straight an element of judgement would enter into any such projection and different people would probably arrive at somewhat different results.

Such projections or what are termed 'extrapolations' of the trend line are easiest when the trend approximates to a straight line. For example, Fig. 19 shows the movements in an index which measures output per employed person in the U.K. for each year between 1964 and 1975. The small dots which plot the series show a very close approximation to the path of a straight line. Such a line has, in fact, been superimposed upon the plots and it will be seen that the divergences of the individual plotted points from the line are quite small although they vary from year to year. In the language of the statistician, the 'fit' of the line is very good. Given this line and the equation which defines it, it becomes possible to calculate estimates of the prospective output per employee for several years ahead. More will be said about the justification for such estimates, not to mention their reliability, later. The next few sections of this chapter are devoted to an explanation of how such a straight line can be 'fitted' to data of this kind.

The method used is known as the *method of least squares*, which is

Figure 19

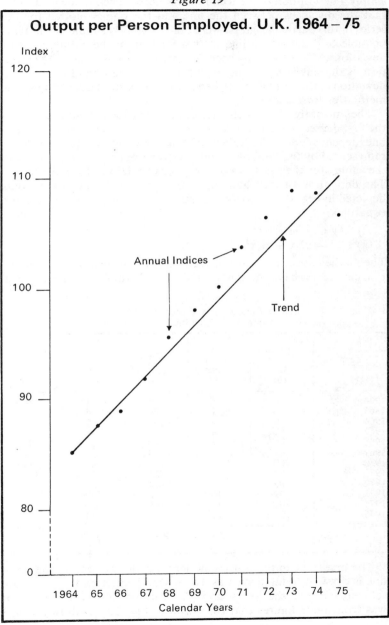

Output per Person Employed. U.K. 1964 – 75

simply a description of the technique. Reference was made to the fact that the distances between the line and the points plotted for the series in this particular graph were quite small. By simple algebra it is possible to draw such a line so that the sum of these differences or deviations, when each has been squared as with the standard deviation, is the smallest possible. In other words, the sum of the squared deviations is *at a minimum*; hence the name of the technique, the method of *least squares*.

The line of trend for such a series can be defined by an equation of the first degree, such as $y = a + bx$. The path of the particular trend line depends upon the values of what are termed the *constants*, represented by the symbols a and b. Given these values together with the value of x, the fourth value, *i.e.* y, can be derived from the others. The derivation of the equation of the line which best fits the data depicted in Fig. 19 involves an exercise in resolving two simultaneous equations:

(i) $\quad y = \quad na + bx$

(ii) $\Sigma xy = a\Sigma x + b\Sigma x^2$

The mathematical basis of this method is irrelevant; many examination candidates have enough trouble remembering the two equations!

TABLE 36
OUTPUT PER PERSON EMPLOYED: 1964–1975
(Seasonally adjusted indices 1970 – 100)

Year (1)	Output Index y (2)	Years in Sequence (x) (3)	Col. 2 × Col. 3 (xy) (4)	x^2 (5)	y_c (6)
1964 ..	86	1	86	1	86
1965 ..	88	2	176	4	88
1966 ..	89	3	267	9	91
1967 ..	92	4	368	16	93
1968 ..	96	5	480	25	95
1969 ..	98	6	588	36	97
1970 ..	100	7	700	49	99
1971 ..	103	8	824	64	102
1972 ..	106	9	954	81	104
1973 ..	109	10	1090	100	106
1974 ..	108	11	1188	121	108
1975 ..	106	12	1272	144	110
	1181	78	7993	650	

The first stage in the process of deriving the equation of the trend line is draw up a table such as Table 36. The first two columns are self-explanatory, the years and the corresponding index, and it was from these figures that the graph in Fig. 19 was drawn. Col. 3

merely ranks the series of years in the sequence of 1 to 12 inclusive. Col. 4 gives the products of Cols. 2 and 3, *i.e.* the rankings of the years are multiplied by the corresponding index. In Col. 5 the rankings of the years are squared. The final column may be ignored for the present. Each column, except the last, is totalled and it is these totals which provide the values which have to be substituted in the two equations above.

Thus, for the first equation $y = na + bx$
we get $1181 = 12a + 78b$

The basis of the substitution should be clearly understood; the symbols in the equations find their counterparts at the head of the columns with the sole exception of n which, it can be inferred, is the number of years in the series, *i.e.* 12.

The second equation was written $\Sigma xy = a\Sigma x + b\Sigma x^2$ and, by substitution, we get: $7993 = 78a + 650b$

To solve the simultaneous equations, either of the constants a or b must be found whereupon it becomes possible to derive the value of the other. If the first equation is multiplied by 6.5 throughout, the result is

$$7676 \cdot 5 = 78a + 507b$$

By doing this the coefficient of a is made the same as in the second equation *i.e.* 78 so that when this adjusted first equation is subtracted from the original second equation we get a relationship which enables the value of b to be determined.

Thus, the results are as follows.

Equation (ii)	7993	$= 78a + 650b$
Less ″ (i) $\times$ 6·5	$7676 \cdot 5$	$= 78a + 507b$

$$316 \cdot 5 = \qquad 143b$$
$$2 \cdot 21 = \qquad b$$

Having obtained a value for b this can be substituted in equation (i) in order to obtain a value for a. Thus: $1181 = 12a + 78b$ which by substitution gives: $1181 = 12a + 172$

from which we derive $12a = 1181 - 172 = 1009$

so that a has a value of $\dfrac{1009}{12} = 84.0$ to one decimal place.

The complete equation of the line of trend reads: $y = 84 + 2 \cdot 21x$

Given this equation just two values are needed to locate the trend line on the graph showing the annual plots. This is sufficient for the drawing of a straight line. Suppose we derive the trend values for 1968 and for 1974. Thus, for the year 1968 which is the 5th in the series:

$$y = 84 + 2 \cdot 21(5) = 84 + 11 \cdot 05 = 95$$
For 1974, the 11th year $y = 84 + 2 \cdot 21(11) = 84 + 24 \cdot 31 = 108$

By plotting these two values of 95 and 108 on the graph, then joining them with a straight line and extending it to cover the full 12-year period, the line of trend is obtained. Using the equation as for the calculation of the 1968 and 1974 values, it is possible also to calculate all the other trend values in the series. These have been inserted in the final column of the above table, headed y_c to distinguish those values from the original y values in Col. 2.

For future reference it will be sufficient to write: Trend of Index of Output per Person U.K. 1964-1975 (1970 = 100) $y = 84 + 2 \cdot 21x$ Origin 1963. Note the reference to 1963 as the year of origin which is a reminder that the plot on the graph for 1964 is not at the ordinate so that the line does not start from the ordinate at a value of 86. If the line is extended to cut the ordinate then the point of intersection is at 84 which is what the equation tells us. The constant a corresponds to the value of y when x = 0. This can easily be proved to the satisfaction of the reader by inserting 0 in place of b in the equation which then gives a value of 84. In other words, the value of a marks the point on the vertical axis of the graph where the trend line intercepts it. The other constant, b, provides the slope of the line. The value of $2 \cdot 21$ merely indicates that for each unit of x along the horizontal axis, the line will rise by $2 \cdot 21$ points. If the reader cares to look at the derived series headed y_c (calculated) he can hardly fail to note that the annual increase in the values is in most years two points but, in two years, is three to make up for the fraction which is lost in the rounding of the calculated values.

Conclusions

Time series analysis often requires more knowledge of the data and relevant information about their background than it does of statistical techniques. Whereas the data in some other fields may be controlled so as to increase their representativeness, economic data are so changeable in their nature that it is usually impossible to sort out the separate effects of the various influences. Attempts to isolate cyclical, seasonal and irregular, or random movements, are made primarily in the hope that some underlying pattern of change over time may be revealed. It is noteworthy that analysis of cycles up to

1914 does reveal what appear to be regular waves of alternating boom and slump. Some of the older trade cycle theories, such as the sun-spot and harvest variations, which are themselves natural phenomena, recognised that economic activity seems to follow a rhythmic pattern. But in present times, when economic forces are often repressed and government action is so widespread in its effect, the fluctuations of the economy become increasingly unpredictable.

The cyclical pattern of activity revealed over the major part of the last century, on which some of the above statistical ideas are based, gave an impetus to the use of statistical analysis for forecasting trends and cycles. Despite the use of both simple and complex techniques, ranging from the simple averaging of seasonal movements to multiple correlation of related series, *e.g.* coal output, rail transport and steel production, it remains a regrettable fact that 'scientific forecasting' has not added any laurels to statistical science. The ideal situation would be to have 'indicators' which could be used for forecasting the direction and amplitude of future changes. Both economists and statisticians, by examining and analysing business data over many decades have tried to determine which indicators are the most reliable and consistent. Whether the results justify the volume of work entailed remains to be seen.

In a subject as fraught with risks and problems as is time series analysis, it is appropriate that one should end on a note of caution. The interest in and the study of time series stems primarily from the need to be able to predict future fluctuations and movements either in the national economy, in a particular sector thereof, *e.g.* the car industry, or a firm making and selling just one product in a mass market. The logic of such analysis is the belief that if past movements and fluctuations can be analysed, then there exists the basis for estimating the amplitude and periodicity of such movements in the future.

The simplest method based upon this approach is the use of a trend line which is then projected to give estimates for future periods. As already noted, it can be done simply by sketching in freehand the continuation of the trend line on the graph or it can be done more objectively by using the equation of the line to derive values for later periods. It is a moot point whether the more 'scientific' method produces all that better results than the former when it is done with full regard for all the virtues and limitations of the series! This technique of *extrapolation* has serious limitations. As was pointed out earlier, the extension of the trend line along the path it has followed for say the last decade entails the assumption that conditions affecting the industry or market in the past decade will not change significantly. In any case, it should not be imagined that all lines of trend are as clear as that obtained in the example of the method of least squares or, for that matter, as clear-cut as the line used to estimate the seasonal movement in the first illustration. The degree to which a straight line or curve may fit the past data varies considerably and, whether or not it does fit, is no guarantee that it will continue to do so in the future. At best such an extrapolation should provide a starting point for discussion about future trends and little more.

There is, furthermore, the question as to how far it is legitimate to extrapolate the trend. For an annual series such as was used in the least squares method, the limit may be anything from 1 to 10 years. There is simply no way of forecasting the future. The point is that if such extrapolation techniques are to be used, then they should be used sensibly. Even if any violent external factor enough to upset the market or industry does not occur in the near future, even modest changes in the underlying economic and market forces can make a great deal of difference to the final outcome. Quite often in an examination question requiring the candidate to derive the trend, he is then required to make an estimate of the value in the series for, say, five or ten years ahead and to comment thereon. All that is required is to point out what has been said above and to suggest that even five years is a very long period to look ahead. As with the racing tipster who has a 'cert' for the 3.30 race, so with econometricians and statisticians. If they really could forecast the outcome or the future sales etc. they would not be wasting their time telling someone else about it! But, that does not mean that every method available should not be utilised to make the best possible appraisal of future trends.

Questions

General

Questions on the analysis of time series appear quite often in examination papers. Either the question is on moving averages, in which case the data usually comprise a quarterly series, or the question requires the candidate to derive the trend line by the method of least squares in which case the data are usually an annual series. There is not a great deal of scope for originality in this type of question; one question is much like any other although the amount of arithmetic may vary quite a lot. The main problem for the candidate, particularly where the calculation is of the moving average, is the risk of arithmetic mistakes. In aggregating the successive groups of values, *e.g.* the four quarterly figures, it is all too easy to make a mistake and this then tends to be carried on in a succession of aggregates and then averages. While this will not gain the student any marks, equally it should not involve the loss of many either. The object of the question, as of the examination paper as a whole, is to test understanding of the methods rather than arithmetic facility.

Nevertheless, to avoid overlooking the more obvious mistakes it is advisable to get into the habit of reviewing the columns of figures to see whether they look more or less right. For example, when groups of four quarters' values are being aggregated watch for a sudden and marked change in the figures in the 'sums of 4' or 'sums of 8' columns. Normally the effect of aggregating successive values is to reduce the amplitude of the fluctuations and, if a particular sum of 4 or 8 values shows a sharp change, it is well worth just checking to make sure that the component values show a similar movement and that the change is not due to an arithmetic slip.

When estimating the seasonal movement from the differences between the trend values and the observed or actual values do not worry too much about getting an exact value for the adjustment; provided it is very small relative to the actual size of the seasonal movement, don't hesitate to round off the adjustment to a convenient figure. The degree of approximation in most of these calculations is such that the use of rounding to simplify the arithmetic is common-sense. The same comment applies when working out the constants a and b for the trend line using the method of least squares. Reference to such practices is made in the solutions to the five questions below. There is no point in proliferating examples of this type of examination question; the technique is, as stated above, the same for virtually every question which could reasonably be asked in the examination.

1. Index of output of coal mining in the U.K. 1973–5 (1970=100)

Year	1	2	3	4
1973	99	92	84	73
1974	95	82	71	87
1975	91	82	67	87

Quarters

By means of a moving average, estimate the trend and seasonal movements.

2. The following table gives the quarterly sales of a manufacturer:

Year	1	2	3	4
1972	195	205	284	339
1973	193	236	274	324
1974	198	229	230	310

Quarters

(i) By means of a moving average find the trend and seasonal variation.
(ii) Estimate the quarterly sales for 1974 seasonally adjusted.

3. Live births in England and Wales 1974–76 (thousands)

Year	1	2	3	4
1974	162	163	164	150
1975	155	156	153	140
1976	151	150	147	137

Quarters

(i) By means of a moving average find the trend and the seasonal adjustments.
(ii) Forecast the number of live births in England and Wales for the first two quarters of 1977.
(iii) Discuss briefly the likely accuracy of your forecasts.

4. Total public sector expenditure in the U.K. Annual figures 1966–75

Year:	1966	1967	1968	1969	1970	1971	1972	1973	1974	1975
Expenditure £bn.	15	17	19	20	22	24	27	32	42	54

(i) Calculate by the method of least squares the trend of public expenditure over the period 1966–75;
(ii) Estimate the probable level of such expenditure by 1980. Comment upon your result.

5. Annual Consumer expenditure on gas U.K. 1965–75 at 1970 prices.

Year:	1965	1966	1967	1968	1969	1970	1971	1972	1973	1974	1975
£mn:	237	263	287	318	356	381	405	448	468	510	562

Estimate the probable consumption expenditure on gas by 1980 at 1970 prices using the method of least squares. Evaluate your result.

Answers

1. This is an easy question not least because the figures themselves are easy to calculate. The main point in aggregating the four quarters is to ensure that the average of the successive sums of four quarterly values lies opposite a central value of the series. It is customary for the first of the trend values to be centred against the third value of the series. A moment's thought will explain why this is the case. With successive additions of four values, the first total is usually put between the second and third value; the next sum of four values then lies between the third and fourth values in the series. When these two sums of 4 are aggregated their sum, which gives the trend value when that aggregate has been divided by 8, will lie between the two sums of four and opposite the third value in the series. Thus, the trend values are 'centred'. Finally, note that in the calculation of the seasonal movement the final figures have been rounded to the nearest unit, although the adjustment, which is negligible, has been subtracted from the seasonal averages.

Year	Qtr.	Index	Sum of 4s	Sum of 8s	Trend	Actual − Trend
1973	1	99				
	2	92	348			
	3	84	344	692	86.5	−2.5
	4	73	334	678	84.8	−11.8
1974	1	95	321	655	81.9	+13.1
	2	82	335	656	82.0	=
	3	71	331	666	83.2	−12.2
	4	87	331	662	82.8	+4.2
1975	1	91	327	658	82.2	+8.8
	2	82	327	654	81.8	+0.2
	3	67				
	4	87				

		Quarters		
	1	2	3	4
1973			−2.5	−11.8
1974	13.1	=	−12.2	4.2
1975	8.8	0.2		
Total	21.9	0.2	−14.7	−7.6
Average	10.95	0.1	−7.35	−3.8
Adjustment	−.025	−.025	−0.25	−.025
Seasonal Movement	11	0	−7	−4

2. This problem is similar to that in Q.1 and poses no real difficulties. The trend values have been given to one place of decimals with the possibility in mind that the adjustment would balance up the seasonal movements. In the event, after rounding, the negative movements (−65 and −23) just exceed the positive movements of 18 and 69 by one point. Since this is the result of a difference of only 0·6 in the averages of the differences between the trend values and actual observations, it is not worth wasting time making any further adjustment. That could only be done by expressing the seasonal movement in each quarter to one place of decimals which is pretentious rather than accurate.

Part (ii) of the question is unanswerable except on the basis of guesswork. In theory, all that is required is for the candidate to average the change between successive trend values over the years covered by the series. For example, suppose the change in the trend values between the 1st and 2nd quarters in three successive years had been 3, 5, and 4. The average movement is 4, so the change in the fourth year between the 1st and 2nd quarters could be taken as 4. The same

Year	Qtr.	Sales	Sum of 4s	Sum of 8s	Trend	Actual−Trend
1972	I	195				
	II	205	1023			
	III	284	1021	2044	255.5	+28.5
	IV	339	1052	2073	259.1	+79.9
1973	I	193	1042	2094	261.8	−68.8
	II	236	1027	2069	258.6	−22.6
	III	274	1032	2059	257.4	+16.6
	IV	324	1025	2057	257.1	+66.9
1974	I	198	981	2006	250.8	−52.8
	II	229	967	1948	243.5	−14.5
	III	230				
	IV	310				

	Quarters			
	I	II	III	IV
1972			28.5	79.9
1973	−68.8	−22.6	16.6	66.9
1974	−52.8	−14.5		
Total	−121.6	−37.1	45.1	146.8
Average	−60.8	−18.6	22.6	73.4
Less Adjustment	4.15	4.15	4.15	4.15
Seasonal movement	−65	−23	+18	+69

averaging would be done for each quarter and applied to the trend values in the 4th year. In this particular question, however, the series is not only too short; there are only two years of trend values. But, the early part of the trend is upward while, after the first quarter in 1973, the trend values start to decline. It seems reasonable to assume that sales will continue to decline in 1974 as is shown for the first two quarters. To calculate the probable fall between the 2nd and 3rd and the 3rd and 4th quarters we have only the experience of 1973 to guide us. The fall in sales between the 1st and 2nd quarters in 1973 is 3·2 and that between the 2nd and 3rd is 1·2. But, in 1974 the comparable fall in the first figure is 7·3, more than twice as much as in the previous year. Is it to be assumed that the decline between the 2nd and 3rd quarters will also be at least twice as large, if not larger, than the 1·2 in the previous year, with the drop in the sales between the 3rd and 4th quarters in 1974 rather larger than the 0·3 registered in the corresponding quarter of 1973? If such considerations are any guide then the values for the third and fourth quarters of 1974 might be written as 238·6 and 238·4, but it is idle to pretend that these values are any better than mere guesses.

3. As in the previous problem the rounding of the seasonal movement is arbitrary but, in this case, the quarterly figures balance. In relation to the actual values the seasonal movement is not particularly marked.

The feature of this question is the use of the trend line to derive an estimate of a future value, i.e. the births in the first and second quarters of 1977. This could be done just as easily if the series were plotted, the trend line sketched in and then extended for a couple of years. It is not likely to be any more or less accurate than the calculation shown. The trend values have been extended for another seven quarters which is the duration of the series shown. The decline in the trend values of the original series is assumed to continue until the first and second quarters of 1977, and, having derived them as shown in the answer below, they are adjusted for the seasonal movement. Although in this case the estimate for 1980 relates to a date relatively close to the end of the original series, which

Year	Qtr.	Births	Sum of 4s	Sum of 8s	Trend	Actual−Trend
1974	1	162				
	2	163	639			
	3	164	632	1271	158.9	5.1
	4	150	625	1257	157.1	−7.1
1975	1	155	614	1239	154.9	0.1
	2	156	604	1218	152.2	3.8
	3	153	600	1204	150.5	2.5
	4	140	594	1194	149.2	−9.2
1976	1	151	588	1182	147.8	3.2
	2	150	585	1173	146.6	3.4
	3	147				
	4	137				

	Quarters			
	1	2	3	4
1974			5.1	−7.1
1975	0.1	3.8	2.5	−9.2
1976	3.2	3.4		
Total	3.3	7.2	7.6	−16.3
Average	1.65	3.6	3.8	−8.15
Adjustment	0.25	0.25	0.25	0.25
Seasonal Movement	1.4	3.35	3.55	−8.4
Rounded	1	3	4	−8

Change per quarter in trend values between 1974(3) and 1976(2)=158.9 − 146.6÷ 7 which is approximately 1·8.

The quarter 1977(1) is also 3 quarters on from 1976(2) and, assuming continuation of trend as observed, the trend value for 1977(1) will be 146.6 − 5.1 or 141.5. The trend value for 1977(2) will be 141.5 − 1·7 = 139.8.

Adjusting the trend values for the seasonal movement to derive actual births, 1977(1) = 141.5 + 1 = 142.
1977(2) = 139.8 + 3 = 143.

would normally mean that such an extrapolation could be made with a reasonable degree of confidence, in the case of births we are dealing with a highly uncertain statistic. Attempts in the past to predict the future trend of fertility have not been noted for their accuracy. The rounding of the estimates to the nearest unit represents a measure of recognition of this fact.

4. The calculation of the trend values by the method of least squares is quite simple, provided that the candidate remembers the key equations for the derivation of the constants. Sometimes the examination paper will give these to aid the student but he cannot rely upon that. It may help memorise the two equations if the first is thought of as similar to the equation of a straight line, i.e. $y = a + bx$ modified to take account of the number of observations in the series in the case of the constant a and in the case of x and y bringing in the sum of the two variables. The second of the two equations is virtually the first equation multiplied throughout by x. Alternatively, it may be easier for the student to remember that only four columns of workings are required and, if these can be remembered, fitting their totals into the form of the equations is quite simple.

The calculation in this question calls for no comment but the projection made to estimate the expenditure in 1980 is unlikely to be correct. It will be observed from the series that from 1973 on the values rise quite sharply and, what up to that year had approximated fairly well to a straight line, now begins to take on the shape of a curve, somewhat similar to the curve of a sum increasing with compound interest. If this change in the trend from 1973 persists, then the estimate for 1980 will certainly be too low.

Year (x)	Expenditure (y)	x	xy	x²
1966	15	1	15	1
1967	17	2	34	4
1968	19	3	57	9
1969	20	4	80	16
1970	22	5	110	25
1971	24	6	144	36
1972	27	7	189	49
1973	32	8	256	64
1974	42	9	378	81
1975	54	10	540	100
	272	55	1803	385

(i)	Σy	$= na + b\Sigma x$
(ii)	Σxy	$= a\Sigma x + b\Sigma x^2$
(i)	272	$= 10a + 55b$
(ii)	1803	$= 55a + 385b$
(i) × 11	2992	$= 110a + 605b$
(ii) × 2	3606	$= 110a + 770b$
(ii) minus (i)	714	$= \quad .. \quad 165b$
	4.33	$= \qquad\qquad b$
	272	$= 10a + 55\,(4.33)$
	272	$= 10a + 238$
	272–238	$= 10a$
	34	$= 10a$
	3.4	$= \quad a$
	y	$= 3.4 + 4.33x$

Estimate for 1980 $y = 3.4 + 4.33(15)$
$= 3.4 + 65$
$y = £68.4$ bn.

5. The arithmetic is the biggest problem for the average candidate. The calculations are identical with those in Q.4 except that, whereas in that question to eliminate the constant *a* to derive *b*, the one equation was multiplied by 2 and the other by 11 (instead of multiplying the latter simply by 5·5), in this question it is merely necessary to multiply the one equation by 6. As in Q.4 the last two values for 1974 and 1975 show a marked increase and, if this trend persists, the estimate for 1980 given by the equation as £673 m will probably be too low.

Year (x)	Expenditure (y)	x	xy	x²
1965	237	1	237	1
1966	263	2	526	4
1967	287	3	861	9
1968	318	4	1272	16
1969	356	5	1780	25
1970	381	6	2286	36
1971	405	7	2835	49
1972	448	8	3584	64
1973	468	9	4212	81
1974	510	10	5100	100
1975	562	11	6182	121
	4235	66	28,875	506

(i)	= Σy	=na	+bΣx
(ii)	= Σxy	=aΣx	+bΣx²

(i)	= 4,235	= 11a	+ 66b
(ii)	= 28,875	= 66a	+ 506b

6×(i)	= 25,410	= 66a	+396b

(ii) − 6x(i)	= 3,465	= 110b	
	31·5	= b	
	4,235	= 11a	+66 (31·5)
	4,235	= 11a	+2079
	2,156	= 11a	
	196	= a	
	y	= 196	+ 31.5x

Estimate of consumption expenditure in 1980:

	y	= 196	+31.5
	y	= 196	+ 504

∴. Estimate for 1980 = £700 mn

ELEMENTARY SAMPLING:
THEORY AND PRACTICE

CHAPTER XII

CHANCE & PROBABILITY

In the earlier chapters illustrating the calculation of various statistics such as the arithmetic mean or the standard deviation, it has been assumed that the frequency distributions, from which they have been derived, constituted the entire relevant population. The term 'population', it may be remembered, is used in statistics to denote the aggregate of any group or collection of units with a particular characteristic in common. For example, all the private cars licensed in Great Britain until the end of December 1979 constitute a 'population'. Likewise, the total number of agricultural holdings under 100 acres in England and Wales; or the number of households in Greater London with a colour TV set; or the number of credit card holders who owe more than £100 on their accounts; these are all 'populations' for the statistician.

Some statistical populations are small, *e.g.* the number of millionaires in the U.K. Others are very large, *e.g.* the number of persons in receipt of the State pension; others are infinite and cannot be counted, *e.g.* the number of stars in the universe. In all cases where the population is of any size, when information concerning its members is required, it is usual to collect that information by means of a sample survey or enquiry. As was pointed out in Chapter III, such a sample must be chosen so that every member has an equal or calculable chance of inclusion; thus we refer to *random* selection. All samples should be random, otherwise they are of limited value to the statistician.

If it were not for the development of sampling techniques and the related theory in recent times, the science of statistics would be neither as effective nor as widespread in its application as it now is. This is not to assert that without sampling theory statistical work is impracticable. No one who has read the contributions of Dr. William Farr on the state of the population of England and Wales during the latter half of the 19th century would believe that. But, sampling has enabled the statistician to develop very powerful techniques for the analysis of data in virtually every field of human activity. The next three chapters are devoted to an exposition of the basis of modern sampling and the statistical tests which are used to interpret sample statistics.

This chapter is devoted to an explanation and illustration of elementary probability which is the basis of sampling theory. It is no good pretending that this theory is simple to understand. Years of reading examination scripts has demonstrated how often non-mathematical students have difficulty in either applying or understanding the concepts. It is hoped that the less numerate reader will be able to grasp the principles as set out in this chapter.

The sections which follow are no substitute for that part of even the Advanced level course in G.C.E. mathematics which deals with this topic. In short, any reader who needs these concepts for professional statistical work will need to read further.

Measuring Probability

The reader will be familiar with the concept of 'probability' as used in everyday speech. For example, how often do we hear, 'my wife will probably be late . . .', or 'it will probably rain as soon as we leave. . . .' In other words, we say something is probable if we believe that it will happen. However well understood the notion is by the ordinary man in the street, there is no agreement among scientists on a single definition of the term. The statistician, however, has his own interpretation of the term as evidenced by the concept of *relative frequency*. For example, if your train to work has, for some time, been late six days in ten then the probability of its coming in late today is 6/10 or 0·6.

The concept of relative frequency is more usually illustrated by reference to games of chance. For example, if a '6' is shown when a die is rolled and this is regarded as a success, then the probability of success is measured by the number of times a '6' appears divided by the number of times the die is rolled. With a fairly balanced die, any one of the six sides is as likely to appear as any other, hence the probability of rolling a '6' is given by the fraction 1/6 or 0·166. Similarly, the probability of a head on tossing a coin is 1/2; the probability of drawing an ace from a pack of 52 playing cards is 4/52. Such events are termed *independent;* in other words they are not affected by what has gone before. Thus, the mere fact that a coin has been tossed three times and on each occasion has fallen heads uppermost does not alter the simple fact that the probability of throwing another head with the fourth toss is still 1/2. There is no way, as gamblers in every generation have learned to their cost, of predicting which way a coin, a die or roulette wheel will show, always assuming of course that they are fair or properly balanced so that the outcome is truly random.

If the probability of success is represented by p then p is equal to the fraction S/N where S represents the number of successes and N the number of events, *e.g.* throws. The probability of failure is represented by the letter q. Thus, with a coin toss, if heads are counted as a success, then $p = 1/2$, as does q, for the chance of a tail is also $1/2$. It is certain that either of these outcomes will occur; in short $p + q = 1/2 + 1/2 = 1$. In the same way, each face of a die has an equal probability of appearing on any throw. Thus, if '3' is counted a success, the probability of a '3' is given by the fraction $1/6$; the probability that *any* one of the six faces will appear is obviously equal to unity. In other words, certainty is defined as unity and the sum $p + q$ equals 1. If either side cannot be thrown, *e.g.* a penny with two heads, then the probability of tails is clearly zero, *i.e.* $q = 0$ and the probability of a head is equal to 1, *i.e.* certainty. The values of p and q always add up to 1; each may take a value ranging from 0 to 1 but since $1 - p = q$, it follows that if p is, say $1/6$, then q is obviously $5/6$. Often the values of p and q are expressed in decimals, *e.g.* $1/6$ would be equal to $0·166$ or $1/2$ is represented by $0·5$; sometimes percentages are used, *e.g.* there is a $50·50$ chance of success or what the bookmakers refer to as an 'even money' bet.

The problem in determining the probability of certain events is to define correctly the probability or success earlier defined as S/N. It is clear that the chance of drawing a King card from a pack of playing cards is $4/52$ or $1/13$; the probability of drawing an Ace is the same. There are in each case 52 possible outcomes and only four chances of success: hence $S/N = 4/52$. What then are the chances of drawing *either* a King *or* an Ace? The answer must be $8/52$ since any of the four King cards and the four Aces count as a success. Alternatively, the same result can be obtained by adding together the probabilities of the events which will constitute a success. Thus, any one of the four Kings, $4/52$ plus any one of the four aces $4/52$; the two separate probabilities added together make $8/52$.

Exactly the same principle is followed if we are asked, what is the probability of throwing an even number with a die? There are three such numbers on a dice with six faces, '2', '4' and '6'. Any one of these constitutes a success. Thus, since the probability of any one side showing is $1/6$ and we have three sides to choose from, the answer is $1/6 + 1/6 + 1/6 = 1/2$. Now consider the probability of drawing *either* a black card *or* an Ace from a pack of 52 playing cards. There are four Aces in such a pack and 26 black cards (spades and clubs). Thus, at first sight, the probability of drawing *either* an Ace *or* a black card must be $4/52 + 26/52 = 30/52$. But this is wrong since *two* of the Aces are also black, either of which would twice count as a success. So the correct probability of drawing either an Ace or a black card is $4/52 + 26/52 - 2/52 = 28/52$. In other words there are 28 cards which count as successes, not 30.

To ensure the right values for S/N count all the values which count as successes (S) and all the possible outcomes (N). To illustrate: what is the probability of drawing a red card with an odd number of spots, *i.e.* the Ace (1), '3', '5', '7', '9' of either Hearts or Diamonds? In short, five cards in each suit which means that there are 10 cards among the 52 which constitute success. Thus, $S/N = 10/52$. Now try another example. What are the chances of drawing a card higher than '10', counting Ace as low? In other words, what are the chances of drawing a picture card (Jack, Queen or King) of the four suits which, together, make up 12 cards regarded as successes? The probability is thus 12/52. Had we counted Ace as high, *i.e.* higher than 10, then the probability would have been 16/52.

Where there are several possibilities of success, *e.g.* the four Aces, in drawing just one card no two successes can occur simultaneously; the one excludes the possibility of the other. For example, a coin when tossed will fall either heads or tails uppermost. It cannot show both sides; nor can one get both a '3' and a '6' with a single roll of a die. The outcomes defined as successes are in such cases *mutually exclusive*. Where they are mutually exclusive, the probability of success is given by adding together the probabilities of each outcome which counts as a success. Thus, the probability of drawing either a '7' or a '9' card from a pack of playing cards is $4/52+4/52 = 8/52$.

To sum up: Mutually exclusive events are defined as events which cannot both happen simultaneously; if we get a '6' with a die there can be no other number showing uppermost. The probability of one or other of two mutually exclusive events occurring is the sum of their separate probabilities. This is known as the *addition* rule.

To ensure that the basic points have been understood, here are two more simple examples: What is the probability of selecting either a card lower than '10' (counting Ace as low) or one which is black? Since there are nine cards in each of the four suits making up a pack of playing cards all lower than '10', the probability of drawing such a card is 36/52. The chances of drawing any black card from such a pack is 26/52 but the probability that it is also lower than 10 is 18/52. In short, half of the cards under '10' are black and to avoid double counting to arrive at the value for S, we add the probability that the card is black, *i.e.* 26/52, to the probability that it is lower than '10', *i.e.* 36/52. But, since half of those cards are black (and already included in the first probability) we subtract 18/52. Thus, $\dfrac{26 + 36 - 18}{52} = 44/52$ or 11/13. If the reader is still in doubt, let him count all the cards regarded as successes, *i.e.* 26 black cards plus 18 red cards lower than '10'. Alternatively, add up the number of cards not regarded as successes, *i.e.* the picture cards, J, Q, and K from the Hearts and Diamonds suits plus the '10' card from the same two suits. These total eight out of the 52, leaving the probability of success, $p=1-8/52=44/52$. The reader will probably recall that $p+q=1$, thus $p=1-q$, as just illustrated.

Now consider a slightly more difficult problem. A bag contains 30 coloured discs, ten each of red, blue and green. Each of the discs of each colour is numbered 1 to 10. What then is the probability of drawing either a blue disc or one which bears an odd number? The odds on drawing a blue disc are clearly 10/30, and since half of the numbers on the 30 discs are odd, then the chance of drawing a disc with an odd number is 15/30 or 1/2. But, one third of those discs are blue and, to avoid double counting in arriving at the value for S, we must exclude them. Of the ten blue discs, half, *i.e.* five, bear odd numbers, these have already been counted in the above probability of 15/30 of drawing an odd-numbered disc. They must be excluded, so the value of S is given by ten blue discs and ten odd-numbered green and red discs, which makes up 20 discs counting as successes. Thus the probability of drawing either a blue disc or an odd-numbered disc is $20/30 = 2/3$. The same result can be derived by adding the probability of a blue disc, 10/30, to the probability of an odd-numbered disc 15/30 less the chances of an odd-numbered blue disc

5/30. This gives $1/3 + 1/2 - 1/6 = \dfrac{3 + 2 - 1}{6} = 4/6 = 2/3$ as was

reached by simple counting.

Now it is necessary to consider how the probability is determined of random events which are inter-dependent or *multiple* events. For example, the probability of *either* '6' *or* '1' with a single roll of a die was given by adding the probabilities of each, *i.e.* $1/6 + 1/6 = 1/3$. But, what is the probability of rolling first '1' and then, with a second throw, '6'? The probability of a *multiple* event, such as a '1' and a '6' in two successive rolls of a die, is found by *multiplying* the separate probabilities of the two events which make up the experiment or trial. Thus, the chance that one will throw '1' and then a '6' in two throws is $1/6 \times 1/6 = 1/36$; the probability of throwing two successive '6's with a die is the same. For three successive '6's it is $1/6 \times 1/6 \times 1/6 = 1/216$.

The reader may verify the correctness of the foregoing by jotting down all the possible outcomes from rolling two dice. Whether this is done together or one after the other, the result is the same. With two dice, there are 36 possible outcomes and only one satisfies the requirement of showing the sides '1' and '6'. On the other hand, if the appearance of the '1' and '6' in reverse order is also counted a success, *i.e.* '6' with the first roll then '1', the probability of *either* '1' and '6' *or* '6' and '1' appearing on two successive rolls is the sum of their separate probabilities, *i.e.* $1/36 + 1/36 = 1/18$.

It is even easier to verify the correctness of the multiplication rule by experimenting with a coin. For example, what is the probability of getting two heads with two successive tosses of a coin or, the same thing, two coins tossed simultaneously and both showing heads? The answer is the product of the separate probabilities, *i.e.* $1/2 \times 1/2 = 1/4$. And, if the number of coins is increased to three, the answer is $1/2 \times 1/2 \times 1/2 = (\frac{1}{2})^3 = 1/8$. The answer can also be verified by writing down all the possible outcomes, *i.e.* HHH, HHT, HTT, TTT, TTH, THH, HTH and THT or eight possible outcomes of which only one constitutes a success, HHH. Now consider some examples from a pack of cards. What, for instance, is the probability of drawing two aces in two draws if the first card is replaced after the first draw? The probability of an Ace in the first draw is 4/52; it is the same in the second. Thus the probability of two successive Aces is $4/52 \times 4/52 = 1/13 \times 1/13 = 1/169$. What is the probability of drawing a picture card and an Ace in two draws, the first card having been replaced? Clearly, since there are 12 picture cards, the odds of such a card are 12/52 and for the Ace 4/52. The probability of the two successes is the product of the separate probabilities, *i.e.* $12/52 \times 4/52 = 3/169$. Note that, in each of the foregoing examples, the first card was replaced before making the second. If this had not been done, then the probability of success in the second draw would have been slightly different. For example, suppose we want the probability of drawing two Aces in succession without replacing the first card drawn. If the first card is an Ace, then this leaves not only three Aces in the pack but also only 51 cards. Thus, the probability of success in the second draw will be 3/51 or 1/17 and of the two independent events $1/13 \times 1/17 = 1/221$.

Before going any further it may be helpful to the reader to introduce the notation which is used in the calculations of probability. Then, if and when the reader picks up another book which uses the conventional notation, he will find it easier to understand. The letter p has already been defined as the probability of success in a particular event, just as the letter q represents failure. If S denotes the number of successes and N the total number of events, then clearly $p = S/N$. It will be recalled that p will always lie between 0 and 1; if an exercise produces a larger result than unity the reader will know that the values he has attached to S/N are wrong! Where we are dealing with separate events, such as, for example, a roll of a die and a toss of a coin and we ask what the probability is of a '6' with the former and heads with the latter, then the answer is $1/6 \times 1/2 = 1/12$. Since the number of possible outcomes is small, *i.e.* 12, the student may care to jot down all the possible pairs of outcomes to verify that there are only 12 possible outcomes of which only one is a success. In this case we can represent the problem in terms of the above notation. Thus, in the case of the die $p_1 = S_1/N_1 = 1/6$ and $p_2 = S_2/N_2 = 1/2$, therefore $p_1 \times p_2 = S_1/N_1 \times S_2/N_2 = 1/6 \times 1/2 = 1/12$. Note that there are altogether N_1 times N_2 possible outcomes in this experiment; *i.e.* six possible outcomes for the die and two for the coin thus $N = 6 \times 2 = 12$; likewise there are S_1 times S_2 possible successes, *i.e.* $1 \times 1 = 1$.

Some Problems

Now apply the rule to the following problem. Suppose we have a die, a pack of 52 playing cards and a coin. What is the probability of that we would roll a '6', draw an Ace and toss a head in succession? First, derive S/N for each trial. They are for the die 1/6, for the Ace 4/52 and for the coin 1/2; $p_1p_2p_3 = 1/156$. Bearing in mind the importance of defining S and N correctly, try to work out the next three problems. The answers are given immediately after.

  (i) What is the probability of selecting two red discs from a bag containing six blue, nine red and three yellow discs?

 (ii) What are the chances that two dice when thrown will both show (a) even numbers, (b) odd numbers and (c) one odd and one even?

(iii) A bag contains nine balls, three each of green, yellow and blue. What is the probability of (a) selecting two balls of the same colour in two draws; and (b) drawing three different colour balls in three draws.

In (i) there are 18 discs, so that $N = 18$. S is the drawing of two red discs so at first sight the answer would appear to be 2/18. But, this is wrong. Among the 18 discs only nine are red; the other nine do not satisfy that requirement. Thus, on the first draw the chances of getting a red disc are the number of red discs (S) over the number of all discs (N), *i.e.* 9/18 or 1/2. If a red disc is drawn first N is reduced to 17 and the number of red discs to only 8, so that in the second draw S/N is 8/17. Therefore, $p_1p_2 = S_1/N_1 \times S_2/N_2 = 9/18 \times 8/17, = 1/2 \times 8/17$ which equals 4/17.

In (ii) since there are three even and three odd numbers on a normal die, the chances of throwing an even number is 3/6 and on the second roll it is the same. Thus $p_1p_2 = 3/6 \times 3/6 = 9/36 = 1/4$. The answer is exactly the same for two odd numbers. But, in the case of (c) note that it does not matter whether an odd or even number appears on the first throw provided that the second throw produces the opposite result. Thus, the probability of S_1/N_1 is equal to 1 because *any* result will meet the requirements or constitute a success. With a second roll, if the first roll produced an even number, then, of course, an odd number is required with the next roll of the die. The chances of an odd number on the second roll are 3/6; thus $p_1p_2 = 1 \times 1/2 = 1/2$. The result would be the same if the first roll produced an odd number, requiring an even number on the second throw. This particular example will emphasise the crucial importance of getting S and N correct!

In (iii) the problem is not dissimilar to that posed in (i). Since it does not matter in (a) which colour is drawn, except that the two balls must be of the same colour, any of the nine balls will count as a success on the first draw, thus $p_1 = 1$. The second draw must produce a ball of the same colour as the first but there will now be only two such balls left in the bag; also the number of balls of all colours in the bag has been reduced by one. Thus, the probability *i.e.* p_2 of selecting a ball of the same colour as in the first draw is $2/8 = 1/4$. Thus, $p_1p_2 = 9/9 \times 1/4 = 1/4$. In the next part of the question, *i.e.* (b), we need three balls of different colours. Here too the main problem is to get S/N right for each draw. Once again, it does not matter which colour ball is drawn first so any of the nine in the bag will count as a success. Thus, $p_1 = 1$. In the second draw the number of balls left in the bag will be one less, *i.e.* eight but there will still be three each of two colours so that the chance of drawing a ball different from the first in colour is 6/8 or 3/4. It does not matter which of these two colours is drawn provided, of course, that it comes from the two colours of which there are still three apiece in the bag. For p_3 there are three balls of the remaining colour but the number of balls in the bag has now been reduced to 7; thus $p_3 = 3/7$. Thus, the probability of drawing three different coloured balls is equal to $1 \times 3/4 \times 3/7$; thus $p_1p_2p_3 = 9/28$. Just for practice the reader may now like to work out the probability of drawing from the same bag of nine balls three balls all of the same colour. The answer is given in the footnote below.[1]

Apart from providing the more numerate reader with some modest entertainment, the relevance of these rather elementary exercises to illustrate simple probability theory will not be immediately evident to the average reader. Yet it was the study of such problems with cards and dice which provided the basis for modern sampling theory. Much of the mathematical foundations of probability were produced by mathematicians in the 17th and 18th centuries in response to questions raised by the French nobility of the time who spent much of both their time and resources at the gaming

---

[1] As before, any one of the nine balls will constitute a success; thus $p_1 = 1$. For the next draw there are only two balls left of the same colour as the ball already drawn and the number of balls is one less, *i.e.* $p_2 = 2/8$; and p_3 must equal 1/7. Therefore the probability of drawing three balls of the same colour from this bag is the product of $p_1p_2p_3 = 1 \times 1/4 \times 1/7 = 1/28$.

tables. Consider the example of tossing a coin three times and determining the probability of getting three heads. It may be remembered the possible outcomes from such an experiment were set out on p. 274 There were, in fact, eight combinations of heads and tails of which only one comprised three heads so that the probability of three heads in three successive tosses is 1/8. Suppose the same question were asked about four tosses; here too we can set down all the alternative outcomes and we would arrive at 16 possible outcomes of which only one would give four heads. We could repeat the experiment with ten coins and since there are then 1,024 possible outcomes the reader will realise that tabulating all of those to determine the probability of say three, six or ten heads, would take quite a lot of time!

The Binomial Distribution

The solution to this computational problem is provided by what is known as the *binomial* distribution. The binomial distribution is the product of a series of identical but independent trials or experiments, *e.g.* a succession of coin tosses or rolls of a die where each trial is unaffected by the previous one and can produce only one of two outcomes. The alternative outcomes or results are usually referred to as success and failure; they are by convention represented by the symbols p and q respectively. Since there are only two possible outcomes, the sum of the probabilities of p and q is obviously unity. It will be recalled that the probability of throwing three heads in three successive tosses was given by the product of $1/2 \times 1/2 \times 1/2$ or, more simply $(\frac{1}{2})^3$. If p as in this case equals 1/2 or 0·5, then q also equals 0·5, *i.e.* $1 - p$. Suppose, instead of this procedure, which is simple only because we are dealing with very small numbers, we expand the expression $(p + q)^n$ where $p = q$ and $n = 3$. Then $(p + q)^3 = p^3 + 3p^2q + 3q^2p + q^3$. If the same is done for $(p + q)^4$; then we get $p^4 + 4p^3q + 6p^2q^2 + 4pq^3 + q^4$. The figures in front of the symbols p and q are known as the coefficients. Note in the case of $(p + q)^3$, the sum of the coefficients is 8, *i.e.* $1 + 3 + 3 + 1$. In the case of $(p + q)^4$ the sum of the coefficients is 16, *i.e.* $1 + 4 + 6 + 4 + 1$. It may be recalled from the earlier illustrations that if we tossed a coin three times, there were eight possible outcomes; if four times, then 16 outcomes.

Thus, by expanding the binomial for given values of p and q to the power of n which denotes the number of events *e.g.* tosses to be made, it is possible to derive the frequency of occurrence of all the *possible* outcomes. Hence, in the case of $(p + q)^3$, assuming that $p = q$ as is the case with a fair coin, we know already that we can get three heads once in eight times, or three tails equally often; we are likely to get two heads and one tail or two tails and one head three times respectively. In other words, the probability of getting two heads in three tosses of a coin is 3/8; the same is true of two tails in three tosses. With the expansion of $(p + q)^4$ the most likely outcome is two heads and two tails out of four tosses and the probability of that outcome is six out of 16 tosses. The probability of three heads is 4/16; of four heads only once in 16 times. In sum, if a series of trials is conducted where the probability of success remains constant, *e.g.* as with the appearance of a head with a coin toss, or drawing an Ace from a pack of playing cards, the successive terms of the binomial expansion of $(p + q)^n$ give the probabilities of all the possible outcomes of the series of trials.

Note the process carefully. The coefficients, *i.e.* the numbers in front of the p and q in each term of the expansion of $(p + q)^n$ indicate the frequency of occurrence of the powers of p and q, *e.g.* heads or tails. The sum of the coefficients is the total of all possible outcomes; the symbols p and q in each term, *e.g.* $6p^2q^2$, indicate the combination of heads and tails in six of the possible 16 outcomes, *i.e.* two heads and two tails. Likewise, p^4 represents four successive heads, an outcome which is likely – on average – to occur only once in 16 times.

This procedure is not restricted to simple coin tossing experiments; as stated above it can be used whenever there are two distinct outcomes. Thus, if we roll a die and '6' is regarded as a success and any other outcome a failure, then the chances of throwing two '6's in three rolls is also given by the expansion of $(p + q)^3$. But, in this case p and q are not equal; the probability of a '6' is 1/6 and the probability of a failure *i.e.* q is 5/6. However, we take the term which appears in the expansion of $(p + q)^3 = p^3 + 3p^2q + 3pq^2 + q^3$ which contains two '6's represented by the p^2 in the term $3p^2q$. This must be worked out for the appropriate values of p and q *i.e.* (1/6) and (5/6) and we get $3p^2q = 3 \times (1/6)^2 \times (5/6) = 5/72$. Now try to determine the probability of getting two '6's with four rolls of the die or by rolling four dice simultaneously. The answer is given below.[1]

That this method of determining the probability of particular events is not restricted to games of chance can be illustrated by the following example. An engineering works takes regular deliveries of castings which, experience has shown, contain 10 per cent defectives. The storekeeper takes a sample of five from the bag and checks them and, if three or more are defective, he rejects the bag. What is the probability of finding three out of the sample of five defective? The proportion of defectives is 0·1 (*i.e.* 10 per cent) so that $p = 0·9$ and $q = 0·1$ with n, in this case the size of the sample, equals 5. The

[1] The expansion of $(p + q)^4 = p^4 + 4p^3q + 6p^2q^2 + 4pq^3 + q^4$ shows that two '6s' reflected in the middle term $6p^2q^2$, have a probability of appearing in four rolls of a die equal to $6 \times (1/6)^2 \times (5/6)^2$. The probability is thus 25/216.

expansion of $(p + q)^5$ give the following expression: $p^5 + 5p^4q + 10p^3q^2 + 10p^2q^3 + 5pq^4 + q^5$. The relevant term here is $10p^2q^3$ which after substitution is 10. $(0·9)^2$. $(0·1)^3$ which equals 0·0081. Thus, the probability of selecting five castings from a bag and finding three of them defective is 0.8 per cent or less than one per cent. The chance of finding *three or more* from the sample of five is the sum of $P(3)$, $P(4)$ and $P(5)$ which is equal to 0.0085.

The result can be set out in the form of a table.

Terms in expansion of $(p + q)^5$	Number, r, of defectives in sample of 5	Probability $P(r)$
p^5	0	0·5905
$5 p^4q$	1	0·3281
$10 p^3q^2$	2	0·0729
$10 p^2q^3$	3	0·0081
$5 p q^4$	4	0·0004
q^5	5	0·0000
		1·0000

The above table demonstrates how the successive terms in the expansion of $(p + q)^n$ give the respective probabilities of 0,1,2,3 .....n successes in n events. Note how the sum of the probabilities of the separate outcomes is unity. This reflects the basic rule that if there are n mutually exclusive outcomes of an event, one of which must occur, then $P(0) + P(1) + P(2) ....P(n) = 1$. If the earlier notation is used in which S denoted a success and N was the total number of trials so that p was equal to $\frac{S}{N}$ then, if $S(r)$ represents the number of ways of obtaining r successes in n events and N is the total number of possible results from the n events, $\frac{S(r)}{N} = P(r)$. This merely signifies that the number of successes $S(r)$ is given by the probability $P(r)$ multiplied by the total number of results N.

It is also possible to derive a frequency distribution of the number of successes observed in a sequence of events and obtain the corresponding probability distribution by dividing each of the observed successes by N i.e. the total number of events. Suppose we start with a familiar example, *i.e.* what are the probabilities of obtaining nil, one, two, three and four heads from tossing four coins simultaneously? The expansion of $(p + q)^4$ is given in the first column; the second column indicates the particular outcome, *e.g.* one or two heads etc. the third column puts the probability of each outcome in terms of the ratio of S/N and the final column expresses the same probabilities in decimal terms.

Terms in expansion of $(p + q)^4$	Number of successes (heads) r	Relative frequencies	Probability of occurrence $P(r)$
p^4	4	1/16	0·0625
$4p^3q$	3	4/16	0·250
$6p^2q^2$	2	6/16	0·375
$4p\,q^3$	1	4/16	0·250
q^4	0	1/16	0·0625
		1	1·0000

The reader should at this stage note two points about the binomial expansion. When p and q are equal then the frequency distribution is symmetrical about the central value, in the above case 6. The reader may recall that in the discussion of frequency curves, which are a diagrammatic representation of frequency distributions, where the curve was symmetrical, the peak of the curve coincided with the mean, as well as with the median and mode. Where, however, p and q are *not* equal, as with rolling a die where $p = 1/6$ and $q = 5/6$, the resultant distribution is not symmetrical. Consider the following table based upon rolling four dice together. The expansion of $(p + q)^4$ is exactly the same as the above table in the first column so it is not repeated.

Number of '6's	Relative frequencies	Probability of occurrence $P.(r)$
0	625	0·482
1	500	0·386
2	150	0·116
3	20	0·015
4	1	0·001
	1296	1·000

The non-symmetry of the distribution is very clearly demonstrated in the second column showing the relative frequencies which range from all four dice showing '6's only once in 1,296 throws to 625 occasions out of the 1,296 rolls of the four dice when no '6' at all appears. The explanation for this degree of what, it may be recalled, is referred to as skewness, is that instead of p being equal to q as with the coin tossing experiments, in this case $p = 1/6$ and $q = 5/6$. Thus, when figures are substituted in the term $4pq^3 = 4.(1/6).(5/6)^3$, the result is the probability $P(1)$ corresponding to one '6' *i.e.* $500/1,296$ or 0.386. In other words, in 1,296 rolls of a set of four dice, one '6' will appear on average 500 times, or 38.6 per cent of the time – time being measured in rolls of the dice.

The second fact about the frequency distribution derived from depicting the expansion of the binomial in the form of a frequency curve is that such a diagram would not provide a smooth curve, but a histogram. This diagram, depicted on p. 94 was formed, it may be remembered, by drawing a series of contiguous columns, the width of which represented the class interval of the independent variable and the height of each column the frequency. If sometimes, *e.g.* at the beginning or end of the frequency distribution a wider class interval was used, the height of the corresponding columns was adjusted since it is the *area* and not the height of the $n+1$ columns which reflect the corresponding frequencies within the classes. It was pointed out (p. 94) that by joining the mid-points of the tops of each column it was possible to derive a frequency polygon which, in its turn, could be smoothed to yield a modified frequency curve which comprised the same area as the original histogram.

A feature of the binomial distribution is that for all values of n, and for virtually any values of p and q, the histogram approximates to a uni-modal *i.e.* single peaked, figure. As n increases, in order to get the histogram on to a page, the 'steps' or width of the $n+1$ columns must decrease while the total area of the histogram remains equal to unity. Then, because there are so many more 'steps' and the columns so thin, the former become so small that, for all practical purposes, the difference between the mid-points of each step and the tops of the columns in the histogram becomes negligible and there appears to be an almost smooth curve symmetrical in shape.

In Figure 20 the two upper histograms illustrate the binomial distribution when p and q are equal. But, whereas in the upper left-hand diagram n is equal to 4, in the right-hand diagram $n=12$. It is clear that both distributions are symmetrical. In the lower diagrams $p=1/4$ and $q=3/4$, but as in the upper diagrams n is equal to 4 and 12 in the left and right-hand histograms respectively. The point to note is that, although p and q are quite different and this is evident in the non-symmetry of the left-hand diagram, in the distribution where $n=12$ the approach to symmetry is very apparent. Note, however, the 'tail' to the right of the distribution which corresponds to the insignificant probabilities which are too small to show up in the diagram.

[1] It will be noted that each of the relative frequencies is obtained from the corresponding probability by multiplying by 1296, which is equal to 6^4, i.e. the denominator in any of the terms of the binomial.

Figure 20

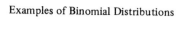

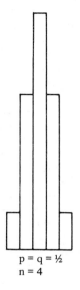

p = q = ½
n = 4

Examples of Binomial Distributions

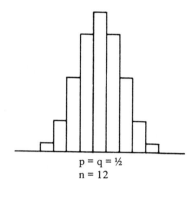

p = q = ½
n = 12

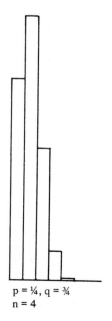

p = ¼, q = ¾
n = 4

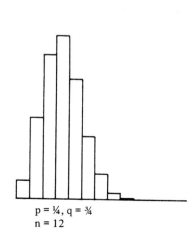

p = ¼, q = ¾
n = 12

Pascal's Triangle

This can be illustrated, not only by drawing the appropriate diagrams, but by demonstrating how rapidly the coefficients increase in the process of expanding the binomial[1]. The following tabulation shows the values of the coefficients derived by expanding the binomial for any values of p and q where n takes all values from 1 to 10. The tabulation is often referred to as Pascal's triangle, after the French mathematician of the 18th century.

Value of n						Coefficients					
1						1	1				
2					1	2	1				
3				1	3	3	1				
4			1	4	6	4	1				
5		1	5	10	10	5	1				
6	1	6	15	20	15	6	1				
7	1	7	21	35	35	21	7	1			
8	1	8	28	56	70	56	28	8	1		
9	1	9	36	84	126	126	84	36	9	1	
10	1	10	45	120	210	252	210	120	45	10	1

The basis of the above tabulation is quite simple. To start, remember that the first and second values in any line are 1 and the value of n respectively. Thus, in the table where $n=5$, the first two values are 1 and 5; in the case where $n = 10$, they are 1 and 10. It will be recalled that these values are the coefficients of the distribution derived from the expansion of $(p + q)^n$ where n is 5 and, in the second case, 10. In other words, $p^5 + 5p^4q$ and $p^{10} + 10p^9q$ respectively. But how are the rest of the terms of any distribution to be obtained other than by using a formula which is rather complex for the average reader? There are two ways in which they can be obtained.

The first and easiest is to work from Pascal's triangle. Suppose, for example, we remember that $(p + q)^4$ yields the coefficients of 1, 4, 6, 4 and 1. The coefficients where $n = 5$ are then quite simple to calculate. The first two values in the previous line 1 and 4 when added together give 5. This must be the second value in the expansion of $(p + q)^5$ since the coefficient of the second term, as was noted above, is always equal to n. The next value is derived by adding the second and third figures in the previous distribution, i.e. 4 and 6, which yields the third value where $n = 5$, i.e. 10. Then add the next two values, 6 and 4, so once again we get 10; then 4 and 1 which give 5 and the last term is always 1.

---

[1] The coefficients are the frequencies of each outcome and they determine the height of the columns which make up the histogram.

Now try with another line where $n=7$. The first two values are 1 and 7; the next value is the sum of 6 and 15 in the previous line, *i.e.* 21; the next is 35 derived by adding 15 and 20 from the line above; another 35 from the addition of 20 and 15 and so on. Once the left-hand side of the distribution has been obtained, the right-hand side requires no further calculation; just the values of the particular distribution in reverse. For practice, now use the line where $n = 9$ to obtain the values in the bottom line where $n = 10$.

The simple method has disadvantages. First, although a little unlikely, one may not remember the distribution of $(p + q)^n$ for whatever value of n! But, even if that difficulty is overcome, this is a very tedious process and this is especially true once we are dealing with values of n larger than 10. As will be seen below, if $n = 20$, then the central term in the distribution has a coefficient equal to 184,756. The alternative method may not appear quite so simple, but it merely requires a little practice to grasp the principle. Furthermore, it has the advantage that it can be used quite easily for values of n larger than 10 without working out all the earlier lines.

To illustrate the alternative method let n equal 10 then, as the coefficients of each term in the expansion of $(p + q)^{10}$ are derived, they can be checked against the bottom line of the Pascal triangle. As before, the first coefficient for p^{10} is 1; the second is the same as n, *i.e.* 10 since the full term reads $10p^9q$. For the third coefficient multiply the second by $\frac{n-1}{2}$, thus, $\frac{10-1}{2} \times 10 = 45$. The next coefficient is obtained by multiplying the previous one, *i.e.* 45 by $\frac{n - 2}{2 + 1}$ thus, $45 \times \frac{8}{3} = 120$. This coefficient is then multiplied for the next term by $\frac{n - 3}{3 + 1}$ which gives $\frac{7}{4} \times 120$ equal to 210. Following the pattern set so far it should be clear that the next fraction is $\frac{6}{5}$; in other words the numerator of the previous fraction is reduced by one and the denominator increased by one. The product of that fraction $\frac{6}{5} \times 210 = 252$.

If each result has been written down as calculated it will probably have been noted that the 252 is the sixth coefficient. Since the distribution from expanding $(p + q)^{10}$ contains one more term than the value of n, which makes 11, the sixth term is obviously the central value in that distribution. Since the distribution of the coefficients, whatever may be the values of p and q, is symmetrical, the remainder of the distribution has the same coefficients already obtained except that they are in the reverse order. This can be seen from the bottom line of the Pascal triangle. But, even if this were overlooked and the procedure set out above were continued for the seventh term, you would get 252 multiplied by $\frac{5}{6}$, which is equal to 210.

Just to make sure that the method is understood, derive the co-efficients for the terms in the expansion of $(p + q)^{14}$. As before, the first two coefficients are equal to 1 and the value of n, i.e. 14. Then multiply 14 by the fraction $\frac{n-1}{2}$ or $\frac{13}{2} \times 14$ which equals 91 and is the coefficient of the third term. Then multiply 91 by $\frac{12}{3}$ which gives 364. That value, in its turn, is multiplied by $\frac{11}{4}$ which yields 1,001. This latter value is then multiplied by $\frac{10}{5}$ which means the next value is 2,002; that in turn is multiplied by $\frac{9}{6}$ to give 3,003 which when multiplied by $\frac{8}{7}$ is increased to 3,432. This is the coefficient of the 8th term in a distribution which contains $n + 1 = 14 + 1$ or 15 terms, so it is obviously the central figure. For the values lying to the right of the central term merely reverse the sequence of the values derived for the left-hand side.

Suppose one required not merely the coefficients of the distribution derived from $(p + q)^{10}$ but also the powers of p and q for each term. Then it would be necessary to calculate the probability of particular outcomes as was shown in the table on p.279. This is just as simple. The expansion starts with p^{10}, i.e. the coefficient as may be seen from the figure is 1 and the power of p is equal to the value of n. The next term is $10p^9q$, then $45p^8q^2$, followed by $120p^7q^3 + 210p^6q^4 + 252p^5q^5$. This latter term is the central value and, since the distribution is symmetrical, the right-hand side of the distribution is the same with the coefficients in descending order of magnitude and the powers of p and q being reversed from the left-hand side. Thus, while we have $120p^7q^3$ on the left-hand side, on the right it will read $120p^3q^7$. Likewise, $45p^8q^2$ on the left-hand side will read $45p^2q^8$ on the right.

Note that the sum of the powers of p and q in each term always equals n, in this case 10. Note too that there is always one more term in the expansion than the value of n. This is why when we expand, for example, as above $(p + q)^5$ we get *six* terms representing $P(0)$ as well as $P(1)$, $P(2)$, $P(3)$, $P(4)$ and $P(5)$. Thus, to revert to the expansion of $(p + q)^{10}$, each term provides the probability of obtaining, as with a coin tossing experiment, nil to ten heads inclusive, providing each of 11 possible outcomes.

Obviously, the mathematicians have produced a formula for deriving such values for any value of p and q as for n. The formula is not for the relatively innumerate student; in any case it is easier to use special tables or the above method if the value of n is small. Just to drive home the point made earlier about the rate of growth in the coefficients which would represent the frequencies in such a frequency distribution, it will be recalled that the central value where n equalled 6 was 20 and, where n was 10, it was 252 and for $n = 14$ it was 3,433. And, when n equals 20 the central coefficient is 184,756!

The binomial theorem has its uses both in statistics and operational research and below are some simple illustrations of its applications. But, the main reason for spending so much time on it in this chapter is that, as was stated earlier, it is part of the foundation of sampling theory and it is to this we turn in the next chapter. Before that, however, the following illustrations and simple problems may help the prospective examinee.

(i) The proportion of students passing an examination in recent years has been 40 per cent. What is the probability that out of a group of six candidates this year two will pass? The probability $P(2)$ where $p = 0.40$, $q = 0.60$ and n is 6 is derived from the expansion of $(p + q)^6$. The term required is $15p^2q^4$ with $p = 0.40$ and $q = 0.60$. Then, given $(0.40)^2.(0.60)^4$ multiplied by the coefficient, *i.e.* 15, the result is 0.31104.

(ii) A period of observation reveals that any one of five telephone lines is engaged, on average, one minute in four. What is the probability that at some time all five lines are engaged? Since any one line is engaged only one minute in four, the probability that it is engaged is equal to 1/4 or 0.25. The probability that it is not engaged is $1 - p$, or $1 - 1/4 = 3/4$. To determine the probability that all five lines are engaged given this experience, we require $P(5)$ from the expansion of $(p + q)^n$ where $p = 0.25$, $q = 0.75$ and n is 5. This corresponds to the first term in the resultant distribution, *i.e.* p^5, which is equal to $(0.25)5$ or 0.001 approximately, *i.e.* less than a one in 1,000 chance. Such a result suggests that the firm has no real need for a fifth line. If only *four* lines were available, the probability that all four would be engaged at any time would still be only 0.004, *i.e.* $p^4 = 1/256$.

Probability Distributions

It would be just as effective to look at the problem the other way round. For example, what is the probability that less than two lines out of the five are engaged at any one time? This could be done by evaluating the sum of $P(0)$ and $P(1)$ which gives the probability that *no* lines or *only one* line are engaged at any time. The value of $P(0)$ is given by q^5 and $P(1)$ by the term $5q^4p$ which is equal to $(3/4)^5 + 5$ $(3/4)^4.(1/4)$. The result is $0.2373 + 0.3955 = 0.6328$. Since this means that the chances are almost two in three that at most only one line is engaged at any time, the firm can obviously afford to dispense with the existing fifth line without keeping a significant number of callers waiting.

Consider the following distribution which is the expansion of $(p + q)^{10}$, and, since $p = q = 0.5$, the distribution will be the same as that we would expect from tossing 10 coins 1,024 times and noting the frequency of occurrence of heads. In addition to the relative frequencies in the central column, the final column shows the probabilities associated with each value of n, *i.e.* from 0 to 10 heads. The probabilities are derived by dividing the successive frequencies by the total. Thus, for five heads, $p = \dfrac{252}{1,024} = 0.2461$ and so we have both a *frequency* distribution and a *probability* distribution.

Number of heads (r)	Frequencies (f)	Probabilities P (r)
0	1	0·0001
1	10	0·0097
2	45	0·0439
3	120	0·1172
4	210	0·2051
5	252	0·2461
6	210	0·2051
7	120	0·1172
8	45	0·0439
9	10	0·0097
10	1	0·0001
	1,024	1·000

Before performing any further calculations it may help the reader to draw attention to the salient features of this particular distribution. First, as is to be expected, since $p = q = 0.5$, the distribution is symmetrical. Commonsense suggests that there is no reason for getting more rather than less than five heads, *i.e.* the central value. After all, in such a random event as a toss of a fair coin, it is just as likely to show heads as tails. Hence the symmetry. Second, just as commonsense suggests that the distribution will be symmetrical about the central value, so our experience with coin tossing suggests that some outcomes are more likely than others. In theory, given a balanced coin, we should in the long run get as many heads as we get tails. If, therefore, we were having a bet on the outcome of tossing ten coins just once, even if one knows nothing about probability, commonsense and experience would suggest that as many heads as tails will appear and it follows that the most likely outcome is five heads. On the other hand, given our experience in such matters, it would not surprise any of us in the least if instead of five heads we got either four or six. This simple fact, based on observation and experience, is borne out by the probability distribution. The probability of five heads is 0·2461; that means, in the long run, 24·6 per cent of the time we would get five heads. The corresponding probability for four or six heads is not all that much less, *i.e.* 0·2051 or 20·5 per cent. This hardly warrants either surprise or comment. Likewise, if a companion observing the bet sought to persuade you to place your money on nine or ten heads, commonsense again would tell you that such an outcome would be a remarkable piece of luck for you! Just how remarkable is reflected in the probability of such an event. 0·0001 or 1 in a 10,000 chance. That too should evoke no surprise. In short, the important characteristic of such a probability distribution is that the chances of a particular outcome diminish as that outcome deviates further from the central value. The importance of this point for the practice of sampling will be developed later.

Now consider the derivation of the mean and standard deviation of the above distribution. It would be possible to calculate those two statistics in the way shown in Chapter VI, *i.e.* by multiplying the values of n in the first column by the frequencies in the second, and then to arrive at the sum of those products which in turn would be divided by n to give the mean of the frequency distribution. For the binomial distribution, however, there is a much simpler procedure. The mean of such a distribution is equal to $n\,p$, *i.e.* the product of the number of events and the probability of success. In the example above, the corresponding values for n and p are 10 and 0·5 respectively; the mean of the distribution $n\,p$ is therefore 5. For the calculation of the standard deviation the procedure is equally simple. The standard deviation is derived from $\sqrt{n\,p\,q}$, *i.e.* the square root of the products of n, p and q. In this case, $p = q = 0\cdot5$ while $n = 10$. Thus, the product of $n\,p\,q$ is 2·5 of which the square root is 1·6 to 1 place of decimals. To help understanding, use the example of the distribution derived from three tosses set out on p. = and derive the mean and standard deviation. In this case, the mean is $n\,p$ where $n = 3$ and p is again 0·5; thus the mean is 1·5. The standard deviation is the square root of the product of $n\,p\,q$ which equals $\sqrt{3.\frac{1}{2}.\frac{1}{2}}$ or $\sqrt{0\cdot75} =$

0·86. Thus, if three coins were tossed, say, 400 times, then we would expect 400 × 1·5 heads *i.e.* 600. This confirms the point made earlier that heads and tails are equally likely. 400 coins tossed three times equals 1,200 sides of which half, *i.e.* 600, are expected to show heads. Lastly, what is the mean and standard deviation of the coin tossing distribution based upon the expansion of $(p + q)^4$? The answer is given in the footnote below.[1]

Earlier in this chapter, on p. 280 the binomial distribution was used to determine the frequency with which nil, one, two, three and four '6's would appear when four dice were rolled. The main point made at the time was that, when the values of p and q were unequal, then the resultant distribution was not symmetrical. In fact the distribution obtained by expanding $(p + q)^4$, was markedly skewed. Later, the point was made that as n was increased, generally speaking, the frequency curve based upon the distribution increasingly approximated to a symmetrical uni-modal or 'hump-backed' distribution. Evidence for this can be seen in the following probability distribution which is based upon the expansion of $(p + q)^{10}$ where $p = 1/6$ and $q = 5/6$ when it is compared with a similar distribution (on p.280) where $n = 4$.

Number of '6's shown	Term in expansion of $(p + q)^{10}$	Probability distribution	Frequency distribution
0	q^{10}	0·1615	162
1	$10p\,q^9$	0·3230	323
2	$45p^2q^8$	0·2907	291
3	$120p^3q^7$	0·1550	155
4	$210p^4q^6$	0·0543	54
5	$252p^5q^5$	0·0130	13
6	$210p^6q^4$	0·0022	2
7	$120p^7q^3$	0·0002	0 ⎫
8	$45p^8q^2$	0·0000	0 ⎪ 1
9	$10p^9q$	0·0000	0 ⎪
10	p^{10}	0·0000	0 ⎭
		1·0000	1,000

The probabilities of $P(0)$ to $P(10)$ in the third column are derived by taking each of the successive terms of the expansion of $(p + q)^{10}$ and substituting the appropriate values for p and q, *i.e.* 1/6 and 5/6 respectively. Thus, the probability of getting three heads and seven tails on rolling ten dice is given by the term $120p^3q^7$ which, substituting for p and q, gives 120.(1/6)³(5/6)⁷ which equals 0·1550. Note that the sum

---

[1] Mean = 2·0 and the standard deviation 1·0.

of the probabilities of all the possible outcomes, *i.e.* any number of heads between nil to ten, is equal to unity. The probability of obtaining either eight, nine or ten heads is so low that even with four places of decimals (which signifies a probability of less than 1 in 10,000) it is still given as zero. In other words, the probability of these particular events, *i.e.* eight, nine or ten heads, is so remote that it can virtually be ignored. On the other hand, this does not mean that, if ten dice were rolled, eight, nine or ten heads might not appear. All that we can say with considerable confidence, in the light of the probability distribution, is that such an event is highly unlikely.

It was earlier stated that the mean of the binomial distribution was given by the product of n and p, *i.e.* $n.p$. In this particular example, this gives the result $10 \times 0.166 = 1.66$. (The reader is reminded that $1/6$ is equal to 0.166). This merely signifies that the mean proportion of '6's in the probability distribution is 16.6 per cent. Alternatively, for every 1,000 rolls of a die, 166 or 16.6 per cent should show a '6'. By converting the probability distribution into a *hypothetical* frequency distribution of the outcomes expected from rolling ten dice 1,000 times, we get the results in the final column. Thus, of the 1,000 throws of the ten dice on 162 occasions no '6' would be expected to appear and 323 rolls when only one of the faces of a die out of the ten would be expected to show a '6', etc.

As stated earlier, it is equally easy to derive the mean of the frequency distribution using the method explained in Chapter VI on averages, *i.e.* the sum of the products of the values of the independent variable and their respective frequencies, *e.g.* $(0 \times 162) + (1 \times 323) + (2 \times 290)$ etc. That sum is equal to 1,664, which divided by the sum of the frequencies *i.e.* 1,000 (which is the number of rolls used to convert the probability distribution into the hypothetical frequency distribution) gives the same answer as calculated from the binomial *i.e.* 1.66. This answer does *not* correspond to the frequency of any particular outcome in terms of the number of heads out of ten. It is totally different. What it does, in effect, is to add up all the times a '6' appeared in the course of rolling the ten dice 100 times, equal to 1,000 successive rolls of a single die. Since the mean is 1.66 out of ten rolls, then the expected average number of '6's in the long series of 1,000 rolls is 166 or 16.6 per cent.

A moment's reflection should confirm this result as correct for all that has been done is to estimate the number of times in every 1,000 throws that a '6' should appear. Given that the dice are fair, then there is as much chance of '6' appearing as any of the other sides showing '1' to '5'. Hence, the proportion of times a '6' will appear, at least in the very long run, is $100/6$ or 16.6 per cent. This fact, however, has no relevance to the probability distribution set out in the third column of the above illustration. That, it will be re-called, shows the relative frequency with which nil, one, two, three, four . . . ten '6's can be expected in such an experiment involving a long series of rolls of ten dice. Thus, on 162 occasions no '6' is likely to appear among the ten faces showing uppermost; a further 323 rolls will probably only produce one '6' among the ten faces and in another 290 one may expect only two '6's to appear.

It must be remembered that the probability distribution in the above illustration is a theoretical distribution. If such an experiment were actually to be carried out, the resultant distribution would almost certainly not coincide exactly with the distribution derived from the binomial. As was noted in the example on p.280, the fre-quency of appearance of each of the six possible sides did not equal $0\cdot166$ as would be expected from the theoretical distribution. On the other hand, with a fair die the approximation to the theoretical is fairly close and, as the number of trials is increased, so the resultant distribution would come ever closer to the theoretical although it might never actually coincide.

One final point about the binomial distribution. It has already been stated that if n is small then, only if p is equal to q will the dis-tribution by symmetrical. Hence the symmetry achieved with the distributions from the coin tossing experiments where $p = q = \frac{1}{2}$. But, even if p and q are not equal, as is the case, for example, with the dice rolling experiment, provided n is large the resultant distribution will approximate to symmetry. And, for this purpose n does not need to be all that large. Where n equals 100 then it would be easy to mistake the resultant graph of the frequency curve based upon the histogram as symmetrical. Even where n is as small as 30 the curve of the distribution displays a close approximation to symmetry. Thus, the distribution when $n=30$ given on p.00 demonstrates that for the lower values of $P(r)$, i.e. those up to $P(13)$ the familiar modal distribution is evident. The tail of the negligible probabilities in-creases with the size of n.

The calculations for $(p+q)^{30}$ could involve a great deal of arith-metic. Even with a hand calculator, if one sought to carry out the calculation along the lines that have been used in previous illustrations the results would only be very approximate in view of the very large numbers involved. Fortunately, we do not need to convert each term of the binomial as before, i.e. first derive the coefficient and the product of say $(0\cdot166)^{10}$ and $(0\cdot834)^{20}$ which is $p^{10}q^{20}$ and then multiply them all together. The short-cut method used to derive the following distribution is not dissimilar to the method described on pp.284-5 as an alternative to using the Pascal triangle for the derivation of the coefficients of the successive terms of the binomial.

As with the expansion of $(p + q)^{10}$ on p.289 we start with the value for $P(0)$ *i.e.* the probability of no '6's in 30 rolls of the die which, in the resultant distribution, would be represented by q^{30}. The probability represented by this term of the distribution is easy to derive on this occasion since from the previous example we already have the value of q^{10}. Since q^{30} is equal to $q^{10} \times q^{10} \times q^{10}$ all we need to do is to cube the value of q^{10}, 0·1617 which equals 0·0042. This signifies that in a long succession of experiments rolling 30 dice at a time no '6's would appear about four in every 1,000 times. We know that the coefficient for the next term is 30 since the first coefficient in the binomial distribution is always 1 and the coefficient of the second term is always equal to n. To derive the value of q^{29} from q^{30} it is merely necessary to divide the latter number by q and, for the rest of the term $q^{29}p$, we multiply the previous result by the value of p. But, since the value of q is five times larger than that of p (*i.e.* 5/6 to 1/6), p must be multiplied by 5. Thus, the probability of $P(1)$ is given by 0·0042 (the probability of q^{30}) multiplied by 30 (the appropriate coefficient) and multiplied by $\frac{p}{q}$ which is $\frac{1}{5}$. The answer for $P(1)$ is 0·0252.

For the next term $P(2)$ *i.e.* two '6's out of 30 rolls, we multiply the previous probability by 29/2 and again multiply by $\frac{p}{q} = \frac{1}{5}$. The reader may recognise the origin of the fraction 29/2, *i.e.* $\frac{n-1}{2}$ which gives the third term's coefficient when multiplied by the coefficient of the preceding term as was explained on p.284. Since it is not now necessary to derive the coefficient as such, but merely the product of the separate parts of the term with p^2q^{28} in it, we simply multiply through and get the answer 0·0736. (0·0252 × 29/2 ÷ 5).

For the next term giving $P(3)$ we need the product of 0·0736 × 28/3 divided by 5 which gives 0·1373. The fifth term is derived in the same way; the probability of the preceding outcome $P(3)$, which was 0·1373, multiplied by 27/4 divided by 5 which is equal to 0·1854. The process is repeated for each successive value of $P(0)$, (1), 2 . . . . 30 and the resultant distribution is given below.

There are several points about this probability distribution based upon the expansion of the binomial with $p = 0·166$; $q = 0·834$ and $n = 30$ which should be noted. First and most obvious is that after 13 '6's, the probabilities of getting more than that number of '6's are zero. Although the total in the column headed 'Probability distribution' is entered as 1·000 the sum of the individual probabilities relating to 0 to 13 is actually 1·0033. This is simply due to the effects of rounding the values from the first onwards; had the above probabilities been rounded to only three places of decimals with 0·0015 counting as 0·001, then the sum of the probabilities would have equalled 1·000. However, the error is so small that it can be ignored. The mean of this distribution is given by the product of np, *i.e.* $1/6 \times 30$

Number of '6's shown r	Probability distribution $P(r)$ ($p = 1/6\ q = 5/6$) $n = 30$
0	0·0042
1	0·0252
2	0·0736
3	0·1373
4	0·1854
5	0·1928
6	0·1607
7	0·1102
8	0·0633
9	0·0310
10	0·0130
11	0·0047
12	0·0015
13	0·0004

14⎤
15 ⎥ Note: The reliability of the fourth
16 ⎥ place of decimals will depend upon
16 ⎥ the accuracy of the calculator used.
17 ⎥
18 ⎥
19 ⎥
20 ⎥
21 ⎬ 0·0001
22 ⎥
23 ⎥
24 ⎥
25 ⎥
26 ⎥
27 ⎥
28 ⎥
29 ⎥
30 ⎦

1·0000

which equals 5. Not surprisingly, it is for this particular value of
r for which we get the largest probability, 0.1928. Lastly, the point
with which the example started! Apart from the long tail to the right
of the mean, due to the fact that all the probabilities from 14 to 30
heads are zero, the distribution is close to being symmetrical. The
reader may care to test this conclusion by drawing the histogram of
this distribution and then smoothing the outline by a curve. At the
same time he may care to compare the probability distribution on
p.280 based on the expansion of $(p + q)^4$ together with that on p.289
based on $(p + q)^{10}$ with the distribution just derived where, as in the
two preceding illustrations, $p = 1/6$ and $q = 5/6$ but n is raised to
30. Bearing in mind that in all these cases n is small albeit in the last
case where, at 30, it is on the fringes of what the statistician would
refer to as a large sample, the approximation towards symmetry is
noteworthy.

Conclusion

It will be recalled that the expansion of $(p+q)^n$ expressed as
$P(0) + P(1) + P(2)$ ....$P(n)$ is a convenient way of calculating the
probability of each number of successes from 0 to n in any experiment or set of trials consisting of n independent events, *e.g.* a series
of coin tosses, each event having a probability of success p *e.g.*
$S/N = 0.5$. The resultant expansion is a probability distribution, the
probability $P(r)$ being the expected proportion of experiments in
which r successes should occur. In other words, the probability distribution is a scaled-down frequency distribution derived by converting the expected number of successes into ratios of the total number
of events as in the examples on pp.287 and 289.

A probability distribution has the advantage of being independent
of the number of experiments and this is relevant for the graphical
representation of such a distribution. In any histogram depicting a
frequency distribution the area of the column over the class interval
represents the frequency with which the variate takes values within
that class. The *total* area of the columns of the histogram represents
the sum of all the frequencies. The *ratio* of the area of any column to
the total area of the histogram is the probability that the variate
takes values in that class. It will be recalled that the values of the
class are determined by reference to the class-interval. If, however,
instead of drawing the distribution of the actual frequencies we use
instead the probability distribution, then the total area represents the
sum of all the probabilities which is equal to unity. By using the
probability distribution instead of the frequencies, it becomes
possible to effect a comparison of two distributions based on different
total frequencies. For example, two experiments involving rolling

the same die, in the first case 1,000 times and in the second 400 times, produced the following distributions.

Score (x)	1	2	3	4	5	6	Total
Frequencies:							
Experiment 1	170	200	86	154	201	189	1,000
Experiment 2	68	80	35	61	80	76	400

It is difficult to judge from mere inspection of the two distributions whether they are in any respects similar and to what extent, if at all, they diverge. By converting them both into probability distributions, *i.e.* by dividing each score by the total number of throws, the following results are obtained.

Score (x)	1	2	3	4	5	6	Total
Frequencies:							
Experiment 1	0·17	0·20	0·09	0·15	0·20	0·19	1·00
Experiment 2	0·17	0·20	0·09	0·15	0·20	0·19	1·00

From a comparison of the two probability distributions it is quite obvious that the die has behaved consistently in the two experiments, although the distributions suggest that the die is by no means perfectly balanced. A perfectly balanced die would approximate much more closely to the theoretical distribution in which the probability of each side would be 0·166. This issue of the divergence between the actual distribution and the expected one based upon a mathematical model will be considered later.

The crucial point of all this discussion of probability distributions is that they illustrate the same principle as is involved in drawing a sample from a population. By ensuring, as far as is practicable, that the selection of the sample is random, the characteristics of the population should be reflected in that sample. For example, suppose we wish to know what proportion of the electorate intends to vote for the Liberal Party at the next election. In other words, what proportion of the electorate has the characteristic of this intention? The actual proportion is a parameter termed p and, provided the sample is selected by random methods, that parameter, *i.e.* the population proportion p, is in no way affected by the process of selection. Any sample of n electors may include any number, from 0 to n, *i.e.* from 0 to 100 per cent with the particular characteristic of intending to vote Liberal.

The problem is to determine the frequency with which each of the differing sample proportions occur. Thus, although the expected proportion of '6's thrown in 1,000 rolls of a die is 0·166, it is hardly a matter for surprise if the actual proportion is larger or smaller. Just as it is possible to estimate the probability of a particular outcome, *e.g.* the proportion of '6's in a very large number of throws, so it is possible to estimate the frequency with which a large number of samples could produce estimates of Liberal support ranging from 0 to 100 per cent. It is because probability distributions illustrate the behaviour of sample statistics that it is possible to determine how far a given sample statistic, which is an estimate of the corresponding population parameter, is likely to diverge from that parameter. Later, in Chapter XIII, we consider how the probability distribution derived from the binomial may be adapted to enable conclusions to be drawn about an unknown population from which a sample has been drawn.

Questions

1. If a blindfolded person selects three pieces of fruit from a bowl containing three apples, three pears and three oranges, what is the probability that he picks one of each kind?

2. What is the probability of a total of 7 followed by a total of 11 in two successive throws of a pair of dice?

3. What is the probability of selecting a white ball from one of two identical bags one of which contains three white and five black balls while the other contains one white and seven black balls?

4. Find the probability that a domino selected at random from a set of dominoes (which contains 28 pieces ranging from 0,0 to 6,6) will show a spot total of at most six.

5. Four card players are each dealt seven cards. The first player to play has six hearts and one spade. He lays down the spade and draws another card from the top of the pack. What is the probability that he will draw another heart card?

6. An urn contains a large number of marbles of which ten per cent are black. What is the probability if two marbles are selected at random that both are black? If four marbles are extracted from the urn, what is the probability that:
   (i) *exactly* two are black; and
   (ii) *at least* two are black?

7. Five out of six persons who usually work in an office prefer coffee in the mid-morning; the other always drinks tea. This morning of the usual six only three are in the office; what is the probability that one of them will drink tea?

8. A particular casting process averages 20 per cent defectives. If four such castings are taken at random, what is the probability that at most two of them are defective? What is the probability that, in a sample of eight, exactly four of the castings will be defective?

9. Ten per cent of the output of a manufacturing process is defective. The products are packed at random in boxes of six. What is the probability of selecting a box with :
   (i) *exactly* three defectives;
   (ii) *at least* three defectives; and
   (iii) *more* than three defectives?

10. What is the probability of throwing *either* a '5' or a '6' with a die four times running? What is the probability of getting *more* than two '6's in four throws?

Answers

1. This is the same problem as was illustrated on p.275. Since it does not matter which piece of fruit is selected first, the probability of a successful first choice is equal to unity, *i.e.* 9/9 = 1. For the second selection there are only eight pieces in

the bowl and of these only six (2×3) would be acceptable in combination with the fruit already selected, so the probability of success in this draw would be 6/8. For the last choice to be successful, the fruit chosen must be one of the only kind not yet chosen, of which there are three pieces, among the seven left in the bowl. Therefore the probability of selecting three different pieces is given by the product of the three probabilities, *i.e.* $1 \times 6/8 \times 3/7 = 9/28$.

2. The main point of this little problem is to test the derivation of S and N values. The total number of possible outcomes (N) is $6 \times 6 = 36$. To find S, *i.e.* the number of successes, the various outcomes which satisfy the requirement of totalling in the first instance 7 and then 11, must be enumerated. The outcomes which add up to seven and which constitute successes are as follows: 6,1 or 5,2 or 4,3. In the case of the total of 11, only one combination gives that total, *i.e.* 6,5.

Note, however, that in arriving at the total number of possible outcomes, *i.e.* 36, a '6' followed by '1' is different from '1' followed by '6', although they both meet the requirement of adding up to 7. Thus, the probability of throwing first, a total of 7 with the first pair of dice, is the three paired values given above multiplied by two, *i.e.* six possible outcomes which count as successes. The same point applies to the total of 11, 6,5 and 5,6 counting as two successes. Thus, the probability of the two successive rolls of a pair of dice giving totals of 7 and 11 is equal to $6/36 \times 2/36 = 1/108$.

The reader should note that the probability of success in throwing 11 in the second throw is not influenced by the result of the first throw. In the preceding question involving the selection of the pieces of fruit, we have to assume that the selection at each previous stage has been successful.

3. In selecting one white ball from either bag the probability is 4/16 since there are four white balls and 16 altogether in the two bags. The fact that the balls are split between the two bags is irrelevant. If the question had asked the probability of drawing a white ball from *each* of the two bags, then the probability would have been the product of the chances of selecting such a ball from each bag, *i.e.* $1/8 \times 3/8 = 3/64$.

4. This would be a difficult problem unless the reader is familiar with the game of dominoes, since it would not be possible to determine how many dominoes satisfy the requirement that the spots add, at most, up to 6. The distribution of a set of dominoes by reference to the number of spots on the two halves of each piece is as follows:

0,0	0,1	0,2	0,3	0,4	0,5	0,6
	1,1	1,2	1,3	1,4	1,5	1,6
		2,2	2,3	2,4	2,5	2,6
			3,3	3,4	3,5	3,6
				4,4	4,5	4,6
					5,5	5,6
						6,6

Of the 28 possible outcomes (there are 28 dominoes in the set) only those on which the spots add up to 6 or fewer are counted as successes. By inspection it is clear that all the first row (7), all but the last in the second row (5), the first three in the third row (3) and one in the fourth row, *i.e.* 3,3 satisfy the requirement of having at most six spots. In total they add up to $7 + 5 + 3 + 1 = 16$ so that the probability of selecting a domino with at most six spots is 16/28 or 4/7.

5. At first sight this may appear a confusing question but it is very simple. The first player has seven cards of which six are hearts. The other players have between them 3×7 or 21 cards and there will also be $24 = (52 - 28)$ cards in the pack on the table. The first player has no means of knowing what his opponents hold in the way of hearts or any other suit, any more than he knows what is left in the pack. All that he can be certain of is that since he already holds six hearts there are seven more somewhere else. Thus, when he exchanges his spade card for another, the probability of picking up another heart card is 7/45, *i.e.* the number of remaining hearts over the total of cards not held by the first player.

6. The probability of picking a black marble, when 10 per cent of the marbles in the urn are black, is clearly 1/10. Assuming that there is a large number of marbles in the urn, then the chances of picking a second black marble with the next selection is again 1/10. Thus, the probability of two successive black marbles is the product of the two probabilities, *i.e.* $1/10 \times 1/10 = 1/100$.

The second part of the question needs the use of the binomial distribution for its solution. If the probability of a successful (black) draw is $0.1 = p$, then $q = 0.9$ and $n = 4$. The probability of picking two black out of the four marbles is given by the relevant term in the expansion of $(p+q)^4 = p^4 + 4p^3q + 6p^2q^2 + 4pq^3 + q^4$, which is the central term $6p^2q^2$. By substitution we get $6.(0.1)^2(0.9)^2$ which equals $\frac{6 \times 81}{10,000}$ which is 0.0486 or 4.86 per cent.

The probability of getting *at least* two black marbles in four selections means that three and four black marbles also count as a success. Thus we require the sum of the separate probabilities of selecting two, three or four black marbles, *i.e.* $Pr(2) + Pr(3) + Pr(4)$. These are given by the following terms in the expansion of $(p+q)^4$ above, *i.e.* $p^4 + 4p^3q + 6p^2q^2$. By substitution we get $(0.1)^4 + 4(0.1)^3(0.9) + 6(0.1)^2(0.9)^2 = \frac{1 + 4(9) + 6(81)}{10,000} = 5.22$ per cent.

7. This is quite a difficult question unless the reader has learnt something about combinations and permutations. The problem is to determine S/N. This is done in two stages. First, we need to determine how often, when three persons are present, the tea drinker will be among them, given that there are five coffee drinkers. This is done by calculating the number of ways of choosing two coffee drinkers out of the five to join the tea drinker in the group of three. If the coffee drinkers are labelled A, B, C, D and E then we can write down how many different pairs of coffee drinkers might be with the tea drinker. Thus, AB, AC, AD, AE, BC, BD, BE, CD, CE, DE; in other words, ten groupings of three are possible which could include the tea drinker.

Now, it is also possible to have three people in the office other than the tea drinker. Once again it is necessary to determine how the five coffee drinkers can be grouped in three's. The answer is ten, as follows: ABC, ABD, ABE, ACE, BCD, BCE, BDE, CDE, CDA, DEA. To derive S/N, it is clear that S must be the groupings which contain the tea drinker, that is ten. But, from the tea drinker and the five coffee drinkers the 'tea lady' could find any one of 20 groupings of three, *i.e.* the ten which include the tea drinker and the ten which do not. In other words, only ten out of the possible 20 groups of three would have the tea drinker, so the probability that the tea lady will find that person in the group of three that morning is $10/20 = 1/2$.

8. Using the binomial distribution where $p = 1/5$, $q = 4/5$ and $n = 4$, we need the *sum* of the separate probabilities of getting 0,1 or 2 defectives, *i.e.* at most two implies any number up to two. The relevant terms of the binomial distribution with $p = 1/5$, $q = 4/5$ and $n = 4$ are $p^4 + 4p^3q + 6p^2q^2$ which by substitution gives $0.0016 + 0.0256 + 0.1536 = 0.1808$.

To determine the probability that exactly four defectives will be found in the sample of 8, the terms of the expansion of $(p+q)^8$ up to the central term are $p^8 + 8p^7q + 28p^6q^2 + 56p^5q^3 + 70p^4q^4$ and it is the central term $70p^4q^4$ which is the one needed. By substitution we get $70.(0.2)^4(0.8)^4 = 70.(.0016)(.4096) = 0.0459$.

9. This question is similar to the previous question with $p = 0.1$ or $1/10$; $q = 9/10$ and $n = 6$. We need to determine $Pr(3)$ and *at least three* which means the sum of $Pr(4)$, $Pr(5)$ and $Pr(6)$, as well as *less than three* defectives, *i.e.* $Pr(0) + Pr(1) + Pr(2)$. The binomial distribution for $(p+q)^6$ reads as follows: $p^6 + 6p^5q + 15p^4q^2 + 20p^3q^3 + 15p^2q^4 + 6pq^5 + q^6$ which, by substitution, gives $(0.1)^6 + 6(0.1)^5(0.9) + 15(0.1)^4(0.9)^2 + 20(0.1)^3(0.9)^3 + 15(0.1)^2(0.9)^4 + 6(0.1)(0.9)^5 + (0.9)^6$. Reading from left to right the first three terms of the binomial distribution give the probability that there are *more* than three defectives in a box of six, *i.e.* $Pr(6) + Pr(5) + Pr(4)$ which equals 0.0027.

The middle term $20(0.1)^3(0.9)^3$ gives $Pr(3)$, *i.e. exactly* three defectives $= 0.01458$. The last three terms summed give $Pr(2) + Pr(1) + Pr(0)$, *i.e.* the probability of *less* than three defectives in a box and this equals 0.098415.

The reader should note that since the probabilities of all the possible outcomes have been evaluated, their sum should equal unity. Thus, $0.98415 + 0.01458 + 0.00127 = 1.0000$.

10. Since a '5' or '6' counts as success, then the probability of success in a single throw of the dice is $2/6$ or $1/3$. Thus, $p = 1/3$ and $q = 2/3$. The probability of four successes (either '5' or '6') in four successive throws is given by the term p^4 in the expansion of $(p+q)^4$ and this equals $(1/3)^4$ which equals $1/81$.

The probability of getting *more* than two '6's in four throws is the sum of $Pr(3)$ and $Pr(4)$, *i.e.* the sum of the terms p^4 and $4p^3q$. This gives the following result $1/1296 + 4.5/1296 = 21/1296$ or $7/432$, *i.e.* 0.01620 using $p = 1/6$ and $q = 5/6$.

CHAPTER XIII

THE NORMAL DISTRIBUTION

It will have been noted already that the binomial distribution can be most easily used when n is small. Given the rate at which the coefficients of the terms of the expansion of the binomial increase then, as was shown in Fig. 20, the histogram based upon a binomial distribution becomes increasingly difficult to fit on a single page, and to do that the scales must be so reduced that before long the step-like outline of the histogram takes on the appearance of a smooth curve. For example, the expansion of $(p + q)^{20}$ where $p=0.3$ and $q = 0.7$ would produce a histogram of 21 columns. But, 14 of these would represent probabilities so low that their numerical value requires three places of decimals. The area in the histogram which they represent would be minuscule. Because p and q in that case are not equal the distribution would not be symmetrical; it would be asymmetrical or skewed. But, as n increases then, for almost any values of p and q, so the asymmetry or skewness would disappear and the distribution would begin to take on the shape of a symmetrical bell-shaped curve.

This particular curve is referred to as the Normal curve. Note that the binomial distribution is not the same as the Normal distribution; both are theoretical distributions but the binomial is merely an approximation to the Normal distribution. The larger the value of n the closer the similarity of appearance; i.e. a bell-shaped symmetrical distribution. Unlike the binomial, which is a distribution in which the variable is discrete, the Normal curve represents a continuous distribution. The reader will recall that a discrete variable is one which can take only certain specific values within the range of the variable, e.g. the number of rooms in a house or members of a household. In contrast, a continuous variable can take any value within the range of the variable. Because a temperature reading is given to the nearest point, e.g. 20°C, does not alter the fact that the actual temperature when that reading was taken could have been any value between 19.5° and 20.5°. When measurements of a continuous variable are taken, however carefully and accurately this may be done, the effect is to replace a genuinely continuous distribution by one which is discrete. By grouping the values recorded in the form of a grouped frequency distribution, this is partially compensated for because the readings within each class interval reflect the

300

fact that they may lie anywhere within the limits of the class interval.

The Normal curve is defined by a rather complex formula which need not concern the reader; it is not necessary for routine statistical work. The most important feature of the Normal curve is that its shape is determined by the mean and the standard deviation of the distribution which it depicts. The characteristic bell-shape is shown in Figure 21.

Figure 21

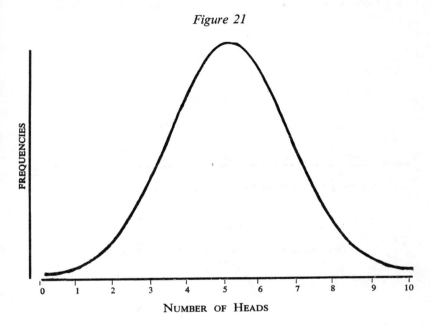

FREQUENCIES

NUMBER OF HEADS

In Figure 22 two curves have been superimposed; one tall and narrow and the other flatter and broader. In this case the means are the same; the central point or apex of each curve is over the same point on the X axis. The difference between the curves in this case is due solely to the differences between their respective standard deviations. This statistic, it will be recalled, measures the dispersion of the variable and it is obvious that curve A, which is narrow at the base, has a smaller dispersion and thus a smaller standard deviation than the broader flatter curve.

If the Normal distribution can apparently take a variety of similar shapes how, it may well be asked, can one know which particular Normal distribution to use to interpret sample statistics? Equally,

Figure 22

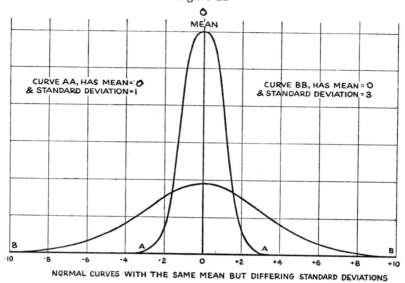

NORMAL CURVES WITH THE SAME MEAN BUT DIFFERING STANDARD DEVIATIONS

Figure 23

DISTRIBUTION OF AREA UNDER NORMAL CURVE

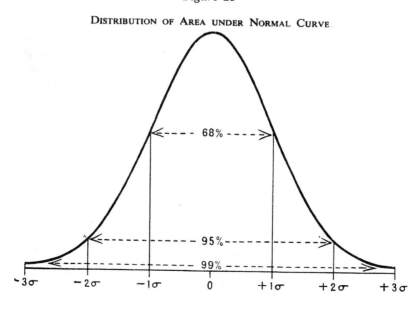

it may be observed, how can one refer to *the* Normal distribution or curve if there is apparently some variation between them? The answer is quite simple. There is a Normal distribution which is sometimes referred to as the *standard* Normal distribution. Because it is this particular standard distribution which is invariably used, no one bothers to refer to it as the 'standard'; one refers only to the Normal distribution. What then is this standard? It is the curve which would be obtained if the Normal distribution had a mean of zero and where the variable is measured in units of the standard deviation. The area under the curve, as with any other probability distribution, is equal to 1.

The importance of this 'standard' distribution is that, if it is stated that a variable is 'normally distributed about a mean – with a standard deviation s.d.' then all the information is available which will enable a specific value of the particular variable to be located by reference to the mean. The point is that (in this standard Normal distribution) the probability of any particular value of a normally distributed variable depends upon the distance – measured in terms of the standard deviation – it lies from the mean. In Figure 23 the axis has been marked off in terms of the standard deviation of the distribution. There are three points located on either side of the mean marked, 1 s.d.; 2 s.d. and 3 s.d. Those under the left-hand half of the curve are prefaced by a minus sign and those in the right by a plus sign. The signs indicate their values relative to the value of the mean. In other words, those particular values of the variable to the left of the mean are smaller and those to the right larger than the mean of the distribution. At each of these six points a vertical line, termed an ordinate, has been drawn from the base to meet the curve. The effect is to divide the area under the Normal curve into several sections. The largest section in the middle of the curve is enclosed by the ordinates at 1 s.d. distance from the mean. The proportion of the area under the curve enclosed by these two ordinates is 0·683 or 68·3 per cent of the area under the curve. Similarly, the ordinates drawn at 2 s.d. distance both sides of the mean enclose 0·954 or 95·4 per cent of the area under the Normal curve while the corresponding proportion between 3 s.d. on each side of the mean is 0·997 or 99·7 per cent. Rounded figures of 68 per cent, 95 per cent and 99 per cent are inserted in Figure 23 to simplify the picture.

Just as it is possible to calculate the proportion of the area under the standard Normal curve between ordinates drawn at the above intervals, so it is possible to derive the proportion of the area between the mean ordinate and any other. Fortunately it is not necessary to calculate such values. They are available in specially prepared tables and an example of one such table is reproduced on

p.318 which is headed 'Areas of the Standard Normal Distribution'. The figures in the table show the proportion of the area under
the curve between the mean ordinate and any other ordinate drawn
on one side only of the mean ordinate up to a distance equal to 3·09
standard deviations. To use this table look down the first column
headed z and, for this first example, look for the value 1·0. The figure
in the adjacent column to its right is 0·3413. This states, in effect,
that the proportion of the total area under the Normal curve between
the mean ordinate and an ordinate drawn 1 s.d. to the right is 34·13
per cent. If the corresponding ordinate at 1 s.d. to the left were
drawn, then the proportion enclosed would be the same since the
Normal curve is symmetrical. Thus, between these two ordinates the
area enclosed equals 2 × 0·3413 = 0·6826, i.e. approximately 68 per
cent of the total area under the curve as was indicated on Figure 23.
For practice, look down the z column to 2·0; the adjacent figure is
0·4772 which, when doubled, yields 0·9544 equal to 95·4 per cent,
denoted on the diagram in Figure 23 as 95 per cent. Now check the
corresponding entries in the table for 3 s.d. That value has been
rounded to 99 per cent on Figure 23.

Just to make quite sure the reader can find his way around this
table, find the proportions which correspond to the z values of 1·96
and 2·58. For reasons to be explained later, these are very important
in statistical work. Start by looking down the column of z values and
find 1·9 which is the nearest to the value required, i.e. 1·96. Now look
along the row with 1·9 in the z column to the column headed 0·06.
The required value is 0·4750. Now repeat the procedure for a z
value of 2·58. Look first for 2·50 in the z values and then along the
row to the column headed 0·08 where the required value is given as
0·4951. The proportions 0·4750 and 0·4951 relate to one side of the
curve only. By doubling the proportions and expressing them in
percentage terms we get the percentage of the total area under the
Normal curve enclosed by ordinates drawn at 1·96 and 2·58 s.d. on
both sides of the mean. The resultant percentages are 95 and 99. As
stated above, the significance of these figures will be explained in
the next chapter. For the moment they have served to explain how
to use the table of areas under the Normal curve.

It is important to be quite clear what the figures in that table
mean. The figures given to four places of decimals in the body of the
table represent the proportion of the area under the standard Normal
curve between the mean ordinate and another ordinate on only one
side of the mean. Because the curve is symmetrical to determine the
area under the curve with given ordinates, e.g. at 2.33 s.d. on both
sides of the mean, it is only necessary to double the value given in
the table, i.e. 2 × 0.4901 = 0·9802 or 98 per cent. But, more important

for statistical purposes, it also measures the probability of a given value of the variables *i.e.* a variate, lying between the mean and a specific value of z. The z value is the difference between the mean and the value in which we are interested, measured as a multiple of the standard deviation of the standard Normal distribution. The basic point can be expressed in simple numerical terms. If $\bar{x}$ is the mean of the distribution and x is the value of the required variate, then z is equal to $\dfrac{\bar{x} - x}{\text{s.d.}}$. A few simple illustrations should make the subject clearer.

Given a normally distributed population of males with a mean weight of 70 kg and a standard deviation of 8 kg, what proportion of that population will weigh between 70 and 74 kg? The z value is the difference between the mean and the required value, 70 and 74 kg respectively, divided by the standard deviation. Thus, $\dfrac{74-70}{8} = 0.5$.

Reference to the table on page 318 shows the proportion of the area under the normal curve between the mean and a z value of 0·5 is 0·1915. In other words, just over 19 per cent of this population will weigh between 70 and 74 kg. What is the corresponding proportion of the same population which weighs between 74 and 78 kg? To find the z value for 78 kg take the mean (70 kg) from that value which gives 8. Divide that by the standard deviation also 8 and the z value required is 1·0. The entry in the table corresponding to a z value of 1·0 is 0·3413. Hence 34 per cent of this population weighs between 70 and 78 kg. Since about 19 per cent of the population were between 70 and 74 kg, it follows that the percentage between 74 and 78 kg is 0·3413–0·1915 = 0·1498 which is virtually 15 per cent.

Given the same population, what is the proportion of males weighing more than 90 kg? The difference between $\bar{x}$ and x is 90–70 = 20 which, divided by the s.d. = 8 gives a result of 2·5. The figure in the table corresponding to a z value of 2·5 is 0·4938. This is the proportion of area under the curve *between* ordinates drawn at the mean and a value of 90 kg. Since the question concerns the proportion of males *over* 90 kg only the tail end of the right-hand side of the area under the curve is relevant, *i.e.* the difference between 0·5000 and 0·4938 which is 0·0062. Remember that the Normal curve is symmetrical about the mean hence each side of the curve contains exactly half, 0·5000, of the total area under the curve. The result 0·0062 signifies that just over 6 per cent of the males in this population weigh more than 90 kg. Although the upper limit of the Normal distribution is set, in the table, by a z value of 3·09 per cent the Normal curve has no upper limit as such since the Normal curve is asymptotic to the horizontal axis. That means that the curve, although it continuously approaches the axis, never actually touches it. Nevertheless, for most practical purposes, the proportion of the Normal distribution which lies outside the limits of 3·09 standard deviations about the mean is so small that it can be ignored. For example, in the table on page 318 the largest z value is 3·09 which encloses a proportion of the area under the Normal curve on *both* sides of the mean equal to 0·9980 or 99·8 per cent of the total area. This means, in effect, that the probability of a value of the variate lying outside those limits is equal to 2 in 1,000 or 1 in 500. Such an event is, to put it no stronger, rather unlikely and can for most practical purposes be ignored.

A few more simple applications of the use of the table of area under the Normal curve will help the reader to familiarise himself with the application of the table. Assume that the time required by the local fire tender to reach a fire after receiving an alarm call is normally distributed with a mean of 8 minutes and standard deviation 2 minutes. In what proportion of calls will the tender reach the fire in less than 11 minutes? The method here is to determine the proportion of calls where the tender takes between 8 and 11 minutes. The z value is derived by dividing the difference between these two times by the standard deviation. Thus, $\dfrac{11-8}{2} = 1·5$.

The z value of 1·5 denotes a probability of 0·4332 which means that in 0·5000 + 0·4332 or 93 per cent of all calls the tender takes less than 11 minutes to reach the fire. On all other occasions, *i.e.* 7 per cent (or 0·5000 less 0·4332) the time taken is 11 minutes or more. Using the same distribution, what proportion of calls will be answered within 1 minute either side of the mean time for answering, *i.e.* between 7 and 9 minutes? The z value is given by $\dfrac{8-7}{2} = 0·5$ which gives a probability of 0·1915 but this is for the time *below* the mean. We also need the corresponding value when the time required is between 8 and 9 minutes, *i.e.* *above* the mean. In this case the z value is the same, so the total probability is 0·1915 × 2 or 0·3830 signifying that, in about 38 per cent of all calls, the tender will arrive within 7 to 9 minutes.

Suppose the weekly earnings of lorry drivers are normally distributed about a mean of £90 with a standard deviation of £8. What proportion of drivers will earn between £90 and £100? The z value is given by the fraction $\dfrac{100-90}{8} = 1·25$ and the proportion given in the table is 0·3944 or just over 39 per cent. Now consider the following question. What range of earnings will cover 95 per cent of all drivers? In this case it is necessary to work back from the table of z values. Bearing in mind that the 95 per cent figure means 47·5 per cent on each side of the mean, the value in the table required is 0·4750. This corresponds to a z value of 1·96 and, since we know that the range of 1·96 s.d. about the mean encloses 95 per cent of the area under the Normal curve, then the values corresponding to ordinates at $+$ 1·96 s.d. and $-$ 1·96 s.d. about the mean will be £90$\pm$ 1·96(£8). Alternatively we might say that a z value of 1·96 corresponds to an income differing from the mean by 1·96 (£8) or £15·68. This means that the range of earnings for 95 per cent of drivers is £74·32 to £105·68.

At the beginning of this chapter the statement was made that the binomial distribution was an approximation to the Normal distribution. Because the arithmetic is increasingly complicated for the binomial distribution once n is no longer small, it is much easier to derive estimates by use of the Normal distribution. Now that both of these distributions have been described, it is possible to demonstrate the truth of that earlier statement. The simple examples which follow illustrate the use of the Normal distribution to estimate values in the corresponding binomial distribution.

Start with the question, what is the probability of obtaining 6 heads from 14 tosses of a coin? Since we are concerned with a discrete variable this question requires the application of the binomial distribution. Given the expansion of $(p+q)^{14}$ where $p=q=0·5$, the required term in the resultant distribution, i.e. $P(6)$, is given by $\binom{14}{6}$ $(0·5)^6$ $(0·5)^8$. Before performing the necessary calculations an explanation of the figures $\binom{14}{6}$ is necessary. These two figures in brackets denote what is called the binomial coefficient. In the preceding chapter two methods of deriving these coefficients were explained, but when we have only one or two to calculate there is a more practical method than either the method using Pascal's triangle or the method of calculating each term from the preceding term as explained on pp.283-5. Since this method is also used in the textbooks expounding probability the reader may as well familiarise himself with the conventional notation, etc., to assist him in reading more widely on this topic.

The figures $\binom{14}{6}$ are used nowadays instead of $^{14}C_6$ to denote the formula $\dfrac{n!}{(n-r)!r!}$ which shows how to calculate the number of times *r* successes will occur in *n* trials. The exclamation mark after the letter *n* is read *n factorial* and, when the relevant values are transposed into the formula, we get $\frac{14!}{6!\,8!}$. The numerator 14 factorial is an instruction to multiply the sequence of numbers from 14 down to 1, *i.e.* $14 \times 13 \times 12 \ldots \times 1$; likewise 6 factorial requires the product of $6 \times 5 \times 4 \ldots \times 1$ and so on. Fortunately, it is not necessary to write out all these numbers because in this case 14! overlaps 8! so that we can cancel these out leaving then only the first 6 values which are $14 \times 13 \times 12 \times 11 \times 10 \times 9$. These are to be divided by 6 factorial, *i.e.* $6 \times 5 \times 4 \times 3 \times 2 \times 1$ and the possibilities of further cancellations of the values in the numerator and denominator are obvious. The final result of this calculation, which merely requires the processes of multiplication and division, is that $\binom{14}{6}$ is equal to 3,003. That is the coefficient for the term in the binomial distribution in which we have $p^6 q^8$. It will be recalled that p^6 gives the probability for 6 heads and q^8 that for 8 tails. Since $p=q=0.5$ the rest of the calculation for obtaining the probability of 6 heads is straightforward. Thus, we have $3,003 \times (0.5)^6 \times (0.5)^8$ which equals 0.18328. In other words, the probability of 6 heads from 14 tosses of the coin is 0.18 or we would expect 6 heads to appear about 18 per cent of the time.

Now let us use the Normal distribution to approximate the answer to this same question. Since the Normal distribution is determined by its mean and standard deviation, the closest approximation to this particular binomial distribution will be obtained by using the same mean and standard deviation, *i.e.* as for the binomial distribution. It will be recalled that the mean of that distribution is equal to *np* which, in this case, is $14 \times 0.5 = 7$. The standard deviation of the same distribution is derived from $\sqrt{npq}$ which equals $\sqrt{14 \times 0.5 \times 0.5}$ or $\sqrt{3.50}$, *i.e.* 1.87. Just in passing, since $p=q$ the distribution must be symmetrical about its mean, which is the central value. This, in a distribution of 15 values is the middle value which is 7 with seven values on either side (remember that we have, in addition to the 14 values ranging from $P(1)$ to $P(14)$, also $P(0)$ as well).

It is important to remember that the binomial distribution is *discrete*, *i.e.* it comprises a series of separate integers, *e.g.* 0, 1, 2, 3, 4 etc. whereas the Normal distribution is *continuous*. This means that in the discrete binomial distribution the value 6 corresponds to the interval 5.5—6.5 in the continuous Normal distribution. The question to be answered now is, what proportion of the area under this particular Normal curve lies within the interval set by the limits 5.5—6.5?

Since the mean of the distribution is 7 the area under the curve enclosed by ordinates drawn at the values of 5·5 and 6·5 encloses an area to the left of the mean, *i.e.* the value on the base directly under the apex of the Normal curve. (It may help the reader if he draws such a curve with mean 7 and marked off to the left 6, 5, 4, etc. and then draws the ordinates at 5·5 and 6·5 just as they were drawn in Figure 23 on p.303).

The area under the curve between those limits must be found in two stages. First, we derive the z value for the lower value of 5·5. To do this we take the difference between the mean of the distribution and the appropriate value and then divide the difference by the standard deviation. In this case, the relevant figures are $\frac{7-5·5}{1·87}$ which gives a z value of 0·806. Reference to the table of areas under the Normal curve (see p.318) shows that this corresponds to an area equal to 0·2881 of the entire area under the Normal curve.

Next we derive the z value appropriate to the higher limit of 6·5 and this is given by $z=\frac{7-6·5}{1·87}$ which is 0·269 and, as may be seen from the table of areas under the Normal curve, this is equivalent to 0·1064 of the entire area. Since both of these area figures (*i.e.* based on the two z values) have been measured from the mean, there is obviously overlap. If the reader has drawn the diagram suggested he will realise that the larger area lies between the mean and an ordinate drawn at 5·5 which also includes the area under the curve enclosed between the mean and the ordinate at 6·5. So, to derive the area under the Normal curve contained *between* these two ordinates we have to eliminate the area between the mean and the ordinate at the higher limit of the interval equal to the binomial discrete value 6. So, we subtract the smaller from the larger, *i.e.* 0·2881−0·1064= 0·1817 to give the proportion of the area below the Normal curve which actually lies within the prescribed limits. The reader will appreciate that the areas equivalent to the two z values are only subtracted when both lie on the same side of the mean, whether above the mean, *i.e.* to its right or, as in this case below the mean. If the interval contains the mean, *e.g.* suppose we were interested in the area under the curve within the limits 6·5 and 7·5, then the two areas − one to the left and the other to the right − would be added together. (Questions 2 and 3 in the Question and Answer section at the end of this chapter will illustrate this point.)

If the proportion of the area under the Normal curve within the limits defined as corresponding to a value of 6 in the binomial is 0·1817, then the probability of getting 6 heads with 14 tosses is equal to 0·18 or 18 times in every 100. This result, it should be noted, corresponds closely to the result given by the binomial distribution.

When p and q are not equal but, more especially, when n is small the correspondence between the results derived from the two methods is not always as pronounced. Take, for example, the question, what is the probability of getting 3 6s in 10 rolls of a die? From $(p+q)^{10}$, where $p=\frac{1}{6}$ and $q=\frac{5}{6}$ we get $\binom{10}{6}\left(\frac{1}{6}\right)^3\left(\frac{5}{6}\right)^7$ for the required term in the expansion. Start by calculating the coefficient of this particular term. This is given by 10 factorial divided by 3 factorial and this gives a result of 120. Note that we use only the first 3 terms in the product described as 10 factorial, $i.e.$ $10 \times 9 \times 8$ which corresponds to the number of values in 3 factorial, $i.e.$ $3 \times 2 \times 1$. Had we had, for example, 15! and 8!, then the result would have been the product of the first 7 values in 15 factorial. The product of p^3q^7 or $\left(\frac{1}{6}\right)^3\left(\frac{5}{6}\right)^7$ is equal to (0·0046) (0·2791), $i.e.$ 0·00128 which, when multiplied by the coefficient of 120, gives a result of 0·1541, equal to about 15 times in every 100 rolls of the 10 die when we might expect 3 6s.

In this example the appropriate Normal distribution will have a mean $np=10\times\frac{1}{6}=1·66$ and a standard deviation of 1·18 derived from $\sqrt{npq}=\sqrt{10\times\frac{1}{6}\times\frac{5}{6}}=1·18$. Within that distribution we are concerned with the area under the Normal curve corresponding to 3 6s which is, in such a continuous distribution, $2\frac{1}{2}$-$3\frac{1}{2}$. The relevant z scores are given by the difference between the mean of the distribution less the upper (and lower) limit divided by the standard deviation. In the case of the lower limit $z=\frac{2·5-1·66}{1·18}$ and, for the upper limit, $z=\frac{3·5-1·66}{1·18}$ the results of which are 0·712 and 1·559. These z values correspond with the proportions of the area under the Normal curve of 0·2617 and 0·4405 respectively.

Since both of the values are to the right of the mean of the Normal distribution, it is necessary to subtract the 2 area figures derived from the z values to avoid overlap. The result of the subtraction is 0·1788 which is the probability of getting 3 6s in 10 throws of a die or about 18 in every 100 throws. This figure, it will be noted, is rather higher than that obtained by using the binomial, $i.e.$ 15. This is not unexpected both because n is quite small and because p and q differ considerably. It will be recalled that the asymmetry in the distribution arising from the disparity on the values of p and q

is rapidly offset as *n* is increased.

Some further illustrations are given in the Question and Answer section following this chapter but, since the purpose of introducing these two distributions is to learn their relevance to statistical sampling, it is to this topic that we must now turn our attention.

Evaluating Sample Statistics

The dependence of the statistician upon sample data has already been emphasised; the bulk of the data used in statistical work is derived from samples. A complete enumeration of the population which is defined for statistical purposes as the totality of the units or observations which the statistician is studying, is usually impracticable. The population is usually too large to be enumerated in a reasonable space of time and such an enumeration would also be extremely expensive. It should not be assumed that sample data are invariably inferior to that derived from a census, *i.e.* a complete enumeration. If the population is very large, there are likely to be mistakes in the data collected. In any case, with large populations 100 per cent enumerations are virtually impossible since one cannot hope to trace all the units making up the population. With the more limited numbers in a sample it is possible, particularly when the units are members of the human population, to collect more accurate and wide-ranging information than is the case in a census.

The important question which the layman will ask is, how can the statistician rely upon the sample data being truly representative of the population from which they are drawn? The short answer is that he cannot know with certainty. At best the sample, if large enough and properly drawn, will reflect accurately the characteristics of the population. At worst, the sample may be biased – although if it has been drawn by random methods this should not be the case – but the sample may nevertheless evince characteristics which are not representative of the population. For example, visualise a large bag containing 500 blue and 500 red marbles which have been thoroughly mixed. The lesson of the past two chapters is that the most likely outcome, if a sample of 20 marbles is drawn, is equal numbers of red and blue marbles. On the other hand, it was conceded that some samples would show different proportions of red and blue marbles. It was even possible that a sample might contain all red or blue marbles, even though that particular outcome was highly improbable.

Since the statistician is not interested in the sample for its own sake but only for what it can tell him about the population from which it was drawn, some theory or technique is needed to enable him to decide to what extent he can accept the evidence of the sample data as an accurate reflection of the population. There are two types of problem which have to be resolved. The first is to determine from the sample statistic the corresponding value for the population which is termed the population parameter. The main reason for calculating a sample statistic is to derive an estimate of the corresponding parameter. These are known as *estimation* problems. The second category – to be discussed in the next chapter – are referred to as *testing hypotheses*. For example, a new drug has been tried upon a sample of patients and it is found that the rate of cure is say 50 per cent. The drug used in the past had a success rate of 40 per cent. The problem for the statistician is to decide whether the 10-point difference between the percentage success rates reflects a genuine superiority of the new drug or whether it is attributable to what are referred to as sampling errors or variation.

Earlier in this chapter it was noted that by using the table of areas under the Normal curve, it was possible to find the probability of a value in the distribution lying between the mean and any value of z. How can this characteristic of the Normal distribution help in statistical sampling? Suppose a series of samples of equal size, *e.g.* each with n units of the population, were drawn and for each sample a particular statistic, *e.g.* the mean, was calculated. The individual sample means could then be tabulated in the form of a frequency distribution and, provided the samples were random and numerous enough, that frequency distribution when plotted as a frequency curve would approximate to or resemble the shape of the Normal curve. This distribution is referred to as a *sampling distribution;* in this particular case it would be a distribution of sample means. The mean of this particular sampling distribution as well as the standard deviation can be worked out and, provided there is a very large number of sample means, the mean of that sampling distribution will correspond to the mean of the population.

The standard deviation of the sampling distribution is known as the *standard error* (s.e.) and it is used in much the same way as the standard deviation. In other words, it measures the dispersion of the values in the distribution, in this case the individual sample means, about the mean of that distribution which, as noted above, corresponds to the mean of the population. The standard error is used in the same way as was the standard deviation to determine the z value. From that we derive the probability that a particular value in the sampling distribution diverges from the mean of the distribution to a given extent or that it will lie within limits about the mean set by the standard errors. For example, one might say the specified value lies within the limits of the mean plus or minus 1 s.e.

The term *error* in this context has nothing to do with arithmetic slips etc. It is a technical term used in sampling to describe the variation between sample statistics where the samples have been drawn from the same population. It is this variation between such sample statistics, *e.g.* the mean or proportion which gives rise to the sampling distributions which were referred to at the end of the last chapter; hence the use of the term *standard error* instead of standard deviation to describe the dispersion of the sample statistics. These errors are random. Only if the sample is biased because it has not been selected in accordance with statistical principles, will the sampling errors not be random. Such random errors arise by chance and are just as likely to be above as they are to be below the value of the population parameter; hence the symmetry of the Normal distribution. But, as will be seen, they must always be taken into account in problems of estimation to which we now turn.

However, before illustrating the use to which the standard error of the mean is put, it may be helpful to explain the basis of this particular statistic in order to appreciate its function. It is self-evident that the value of the standard deviation of any population depends on the dispersion of the variable or attribute within the population. Assume, for example, two populations made up from the marks awarded the candidates sitting the Mathematics and English papers in a public examination. Assume, too, that the mean mark in the two papers was the same but the range of marks in Mathematics is from 0 to 90 while for English the range is from 25 to 70. If the standard deviation of each distribution of marks were to be calculated, then that for the Mathematics paper would be larger than that in English. If, for example, an experiment were conducted in which a large number of samples of, say, 50 papers were drawn from each examination, then the resultant sampling distribution of the means for Mathematics would be more dispersed than that for the English paper. In consequence, the standard error, which measures the dispersion of such a sampling distribution in the same way as the standard deviation measures the dispersion of a sample or population, would also be larger for the Mathematics distribution than for the English.

We also know, if only from experience and commonsense, that a large sample is more likely to reflect accurately the distribution of a characteristic in a population than will a small sample. For this reason, the sampling distribution of means based upon a considerable number of large samples will be less dispersed about their mean than will a corresponding distribution of smaller samples. This is because the derivation of the mean from a sample involves averaging the individual values making up the sample. In a small sample, if a few extreme values are drawn then they will affect the mean much more than if those same values had been drawn in a much larger sample where the other values would swamp their distorting effect.

It is these considerations which determine the formula for the standard error of the mean which is written, $\dfrac{s.d.}{\sqrt{n}}$. Just looking at the formula it is clear that the larger the standard deviation, given the size of the sample, the larger will be the standard error, Similarly, the larger the sample given the standard deviation, the smaller will be the standard error. These points will be developed more fully below but with these basic aspects of the standard error formula in mind, its use can now be illustrated in the following example.

According to a sample survey of 400 households in Greater London the mean weekly expenditure of households on alcohol and tobacco was £7·50 with a standard deviation of £1·00. What estimate can be made of the corresponding average expenditure for all households in the Greater London area? We know that the distribution of sample means is normal and, since the standard error of the sample mean is given by the formula $\dfrac{s.d.}{\sqrt{n}}$ it is possible to estimate the way in which such sample statistics are distributed about the mean of that particular sampling distribution. Substituting in the formula the sample values, s.d.=£1 and n=400 the standard error (s.e.) is given by $\dfrac{100}{\sqrt{400}} = \dfrac{100}{20} = 5p$. It will be recalled that 95 per cent of the area under the Normal curve lay between ordinates drawn at 1·96 s.e. on both sides of the mean. Combining this with the calculated standard error, it follows that in such a distribution of sample means where n = 400 and the mean was £7·50, in the long run 95 per cent of the means would lie within the interval of £7·50 ± 1·96 (5p), *i.e.* between approximately £7·40 and £7·60. Alternatively, it can be stated that there is a 95 per cent probability that this particular mean will lie within the limits of 1·96 s.e. about the population mean, since the mean of the sampling distribution is the same as the mean of the population from which the sample was drawn. In short, the statistician can be 95 per cent confident that the calculated interval of 1·96 (5p) about the sample mean of £7·50 does contain the population parameter.

The interval calculated above is referred to as a *confidence interval* and the values at the two extremes *i.e.* £7·40 and £7·60 are referred to as the *confidence limits*. It is not possible, when sampling from a population, to derive an exact value for a particular parameter such as the population mean. The sample mean is simply the best estimate available of the population mean. Just how good that estimate is considered to be by the statistician is indicated by two factors; the size of the confidence interval and the degree of confidence expressed in the estimate. Suppose in the above survey of household expenditure the sample size was only 100. Substituting 100 for 400 in the formula for the standard error of the mean yields a result of 10p. If this value of the standard error had been used instead of the figure above, 5p, then the confidence interval would have been £7·50±1·96×(10p) and the confidence limits £7·30 and £7·70 approximately. Obviously, smaller confidence limits at a given level of confidence are always preferable since the sample estimate of the parameter is so much more precise.

It may occur to the reader to ask why the estimate of the population mean is not simply written as £7·50. Were this to be done, then it would be referred to as a *point estimate*. It would be quite logical to do this for, has it not been stated above, the sample statistics is the best available estimate of the population parameter? Nevertheless, giving the sample statistic with the corresponding confidence limits, in which form it is referred to as an *interval estimate*, has important advantages. Because of sampling errors the particular sample statistic may be a good or poor estimate of the corresponding parameter. Thus, if it were the mean of the sampling distribution it would also equal the mean of the population from which the sample was taken. It could also deviate quite substantially from that mean. But, there is no way of knowing the *exact* location of that statistic in relation to the parameter. The merit of using the interval estimate is that it indicates the precision of the estimate, given by the size of the confidence interval. The smaller the interval, the greater the precision of the estimate.

From this it follows that it is possible to obtain a greater degree of precision in the estimate of the parameter by increasing the size of the sample. Referring back to the above illustration, the standard error for the distribution of sample means with n = 100 was 10p; when the sample size was increased to 400 the standard error was reduced by half, *i.e.* to 5p. Suppose we wanted to reduce the standard error to $2\frac{1}{2}$p; what size sample should be taken? Using the formula for the standard error of the mean, *i.e.* s.e. $= \dfrac{\text{s.d.}}{\sqrt{n}}$ then by substi-

tution $2·5 = \dfrac{100}{\sqrt{x}}$·It follows that $\sqrt{x} = \dfrac{100}{2.5} = 40$. Thus, the sample size required to reduce the standard error to 2·5 is $40^2 = 1,600$.

Note the sample sizes derived for successive reductions in the standard error. To halve the error from 10 to 5 the sample was quadrupled from 100 to 400; to do the same from 5 to $2\frac{1}{2}$ required a similar proportionate increase to 1,600. The main point to note here is not the arithmetic. It is that a more precise estimate of the parameter provided by the sample statistic can be obtained by increasing the sample size and thereby reducing the confidence interval. But the gain in precision does *not* correspond to the increase in sample size. Thus, to *halve* the standard error of the sample mean we had to *quadruple* the sample size. This illustrates an important point about sampling. The larger the sample, the better from the point of view of precision in the results, but the costs of gaining that extra measure of precision are often considerable. Also one can now give an answer to the question so often asked by laymen, *i.e.* 'how big a sample should one take?' Clearly, the answer is that it depends upon the degree of precision required in the result; in terms both of the size of the confidence interval and the level of confidence used. In other words, there is no standard size of sample for particular enquiries.

Now consider the meaning of the statement that the statistician is '99 per cent certain that the confidence limits will include the population mean'. The point has already been made several times that in the field of statistical inference there is no such thing as 100 per cent certainty. The value of the mean of a population about which we have very little information is unknown; the mean of a sample taken from that population will give only an estimate of the population mean. Nor is it known for certain whether the estimate is good or bad. By using the confidence interval, however, it is possible to give a more-or-less precise estimate in the form of a probability statement as above. The degree of certainty, *i.e.* confidence expressed in that *interval estimate* as it is termed, is important. Clearly, if the statistician expressed only 50 per cent confidence in the estimate then it is an admission that half the time the estimate would be wrong. By using the figure of 95 per cent, the statistician is asserting that his estimate is likely to be wrong only 5 per cent of the time and 95 per cent of the time it will be correct. The obvious question which springs to mind is, what determines the level of confidence to be used when a sample statistic is calculated to estimate the corresponding population parameter? Since there is no possibility of 100 per cent certainty, the actual level of confidence used is a matter for the statistician, given the nature of his data and the implication of his results. For example, if he is testing the breaking point of a sample of towing wires to be used in mines where a breakage could cause death or serious injury, then he will want to ensure with maximum possible confidence that his estimate of the breaking point is as reliable as he can make it. In such cases, he will use the 99 per cent or higher limits. The figure used earlier was 95 per cent when it was noted that the z values of 1·96 and 2·58 were of especial importance. These correspond to the 95 and 99 per cent confidence levels. In effect, the statistician using these levels is indicating that his estimate or statement could be wrong either 1 in 20 or 1 in 100 times respectively.

Why these particular odds? After all, it would be possible to use a 50 per cent level, or 75 or 90. If the first of these were used then, as already stated, the chance of accepting a wrong statement (and in consequence taking a wrong decision) would be too high; a 50 : 50 chance. Even with a 75 per cent level of confidence the estimate is likely to be wrong 1 in 4 times. At 90 per cent the chance of acting on an incorrect estimate is still 1 in 10, but occasionally, this level may be used. By convention and for reasons which should be fairly clear, it is customary for statisticians working on economic and social data to use either the 95 or 99 per cent confidence level. When working with certain industrial data or in medical research then the statistician will often use higher levels of confidence, e.g. 99·5 or 99·9 per cent.

The reader may have noticed already that there is a fairly obvious relationship between the confidence interval and the level of confidence. Using the earlier example, where the standard error of the mean was 5p (where n = 400) confidence limits of £7·40 and £7·60 were given at the 95 per cent level of confidence. The interval had been derived by the adding and subtracting from the mean the product of 1·96 (5p), i.e. 1·96 times the standard error. Instead of using 1·96, however, it would be equally easy to use 2·58, the z value which coincides with the 99 per cent confidence level. Had this been done, the interval would have been increased to 2·58 (5p) = 12·90 (say 13p) and the confidence limits would have been rather wider at £7·37 to £7·63. The reader may well ask which of the two alternatives is the better; in other words, how does one decide in practice which confidence level to use? Ultimately, this is a matter for judgement. (In examinations the candidate is often told which figure to use!) But, generally speaking, it is better to have a smaller interval, i.e. a more precise estimate of the parameter, at a given level of confidence such as the 95 per cent level, than a large interval at a higher level of confidence. In practice, the 95 per cent level is extensively used rather than the 99 per cent. The main concern of the statistician is to ensure that he has reliable data in the largest sample that can be afforded. (In Chapter XIV methods of improving the precision of a statistic from a given-sized sample are discussed.)

The mean is obviously an extremely important statistic particularly when one is concerned with frequency distributions. But, on many occasions and not least in the statistics derived from sample surveys of the human population the figure required is not the arithmetic mean but a proportion. For example, in a hypothetical public opinion poll, it emerges that 65 per cent of the 800 respondents declared a preference for a particular cause, *e.g.* an English Assembly. The obvious question is, how reliable an estimate is this particular sample proportion of the proportion in some 36,000,000 people on the English electoral register who could vote for such an Assembly? Just as the standard deviation of the sampling distribution of means was defined as the standard error and derived by use of the formula $\dfrac{\text{s.d.}}{\sqrt{n}}$ so the standard deviation of a distribution of sample proportions is defined by its own standard error which, in this particular case, is given by $\sqrt{\dfrac{pq}{n}}$. The symbols p and q are familiar enough; p represents the proportion with the characteristic of voting in favour and q the balance of the respondents, *i.e.* $p = 0.65$, $q = 0.35$ while $n = 800$. Some readers may find it easier to work in the original percentages, since it is easy to put the decimal point in the wrong place when deriving the square root. Thus, we get

$$\sqrt{\frac{65 \times 35}{800}} = \sqrt{\frac{2,275}{800}} = \sqrt{2.844} = 1.7 \text{ per cent approx. As}$$

with the sample mean when it is used as an estimate of the population mean, so with the sample proportion it is necessary to derive the confidence interval. Using the 99 per cent confidence limits, the interval estimate from these data of the proportion of the English electorate which would support an English Assembly is 65 ± 2.58 (1.7) per cent. This gives confidence limits of $65 \pm 4.4 = 60.6$ to 69.4 per cent.

Most readers will have come across press reports of similar findings from pre-election polls. When the newspaper reports the survey results, it is usually given in the form of a single figure, rather like the point estimate and usually without any reference either to the standard error or the level of confidence. This is understandable. The present reader will be able better than most to appreciate the problems of explaining such concepts to the man in the street! It should be remembered that most people believe figures are exact; to try to tell the average newspaper reader that the figure of 65 per cent might be as high as 69 or as low as 61 will lead many of them to reject the finding altogether since, for many readers, figures are either right or wrong! The best way to overcome this problem is at least to draw attention to the fact that a sample can only provide an estimate of the population figure. The sample statistic is at best an estimate of a value which in this population may be as high as 69 or as low as 61. Most laymen will tend naturally to suspect a sample, particularly if ever they learn just how small it is in relation to the population and they may therefore accept a 'margin of error' in the result.

A major problem with assessing the validity of pre-election polls lies in the fact that, of the electorate as a whole, about a quarter do not cast their votes on polling day. When the weather has been bad on voting day, it used to be claimed that this affected the Labour Party more than the Conservatives, just as the latter party has hitherto been more successful in getting in its postal vote from absent members on the electoral roll. In addition, some people change their minds during the run-up to voting day. The various organisations which carry out such polls have naturally sought to devise means of overcoming these problems. For example, by polling up to the last day practicable before the actual voting starts helps to reduce the risk that voters may change their minds. Questions are also asked to try to assess the likelihood that the respondent is sufficiently committed to his Party preference to take the trouble to vote. On balance, the record of election prediction by the polling organisations has been surprisingly good. The point of drawing the reader's attention to such considerations is to remind him that before any statistics are taken at their face value, their limitations, actual and possible, need to be taken into account.

The content of this chapter can be summarised quite briefly. The Normal distribution is a theoretical distribution of great importance in the evaluation of sample statistics. Mathematical theory demonstrates that the mean of a distribution of sample means is equal to the mean of the population from which the samples were drawn. Because of sampling errors, the sample means tend to distribute themselves about their mean in a particular pattern which approximates to the Normal distribution. This enables an estimate to be made as to the probability that any sample mean will deviate by a given amount from the mean of the sampling distribution. Because that mean corresponds to the population mean it is possible to infer just how good an estimate of the population parameter the sample statistic provides. In the next chapter further aspects of statistical inference, as the interpretation of sample statistics is known, are discussed, in particular the branch of the subject known as the testing of hypotheses.

AREAS OF THE STANDARD NORMAL DISTRIBUTION

z	·00	·01	·02	·03	·04	·05	·06	·07	·08	·09
0·0	·0000	·0040	·0080	·0120	·0160	·0199	·0239	·0279	·0319	·0359
0·1	·0398	·0438	·0478	·0517	·0557	·0596	·0636	·0675	·0714	·0753
0·2	·0793	·0832	·0871	·0910	·0948	·0987	·1026	·1064	·1103	·1141
0·3	·1179	·1217	·1255	·1293	·1331	·1368	·1406	·1443	·1480	·1517
0·4	·1554	·1591	·1628	·1664	·1700	·1736	·1772	·1808	·1844	·1879
0·5	·1915	·1950	·1985	·2019	·2054	·2088	·2123	·2152	·2190	·2224
0·6	·2257	·2291	·2324	·2357	·2389	·2422	·2454	·2486	·2517	·2549
0·7	·2580	·2611	·2642	·2673	·2703	·2734	·2764	·2794	·2838	·2852
0·8	·2881	·2910	·2939	·2967	·2995	·3023	·3051	·3078	·3106	·3133
0·9	·3159	·3186	·3212	·3238	·3264	·3289	·3315	·3340	·3365	·3389
1·0	·3413	·3438	·3461	·3485	·3508	·3531	·3554	·3577	·3599	·3621
1·1	·3643	·3665	·3686	·3708	·3729	·3749	·3770	·3790	·3810	·3830
1·2	·3849	·3869	·3888	·3907	·3925	·3944	·3962	·3980	·3997	·4015
1·3	·4032	·4049	·4066	·4082	·4099	·4115	·4131	·4147	·4162	·4177
1·4	·4192	·4207	·4222	·4236	·4251	·4265	·4279	·4292	·4306	·4319
1·5	·4332	·4345	·4357	·4370	·4382	·4394	·4406	·4418	·4429	·4441
1·6	·4452	·4463	·4474	·4484	·4495	·4505	·4515	·4525	·4535	·4545
1·7	·4554	·4564	·4573	·4582	·4591	·4599	·4608	·4616	·4625	·4633
1·8	·4641	·4649	·4656	·4664	·4671	·4678	·4686	·4693	·4699	·4706
1·9	·4713	·4719	·4727	·4732	·4738	·4744	·4750	·4755	·4761	·4767
2·0	·4772	·4778	·4783	·4788	·4793	·4798	·4803	·4808	·4812	·4817
2·1	·4821	·4826	·4830	·4834	·4838	·4842	·4846	·4850	·4854	·4857
2·2	·4861	·4864	·4868	·4871	·4875	·4878	·4881	·4884	·4887	·4890
2·3	·4893	·4896	·4898	·4901	·4904	·4906	·4909	·4911	·4913	·4916
2·4	·4918	·4920	·4922	·4925	·4927	·4929	·4931	·4932	·4934	·4936
2·5	·4938	·4940	·4941	·4943	·4945	·4946	·4948	·4949	·4951	·4952
2·6	·4953	·4955	·4956	·4957	·4959	·4960	·4961	·4962	·4963	·4964
2·7	·4965	·4966	·4967	·4968	·4969	·4970	·4971	·4972	·4973	·4974
2·8	·4974	·4975	·4976	·4977	·4977	·4979	·4949	·4979	·4980	·4981
2·9	·4981	·4982	·4982	·4983	·4984	·4984	·4985	·4985	·4986	·4986
3·0	·4987	·4987	·4987	·4988	·4988	·4989	·4989	·4989	·4990	·4990

Questions

General

Problems involving the use of the binomial and Normal distributions are becoming increasingly popular in elementary statistics examinations. The following selection of questions (Nos 1 to 6) illustrates the range of difficulty of these questions which may be encountered in the average examination in elementary statistics.

The remaining questions are concerned with the use of sample statistics to estimate the corresponding population parameters. These are popular questions and often form part of a larger question in which the candidate is required, first, to calculate the mean and standard deviation of a frequency distribution and, second, derive a confidence interval for the mean or test whether the sample came from a population with a specified mean. Often an important element in this type of question is the addition of a subsidiary part of the question requiring an explanation of the meaning of the term 'confidence limits' or 'interval' and how they are interpreted. This part of the question usually carries just as many marks as the part requiring the calculation and candidates should be able to explain the basic principles involved.

Q.1. The heights of a particular group of males are known to be normally distributed with mean of 1·73 metres and a standard deviation of 10cms. If one man is picked at random what is the probability that he will be between 1·78 and 1·83 metres tall?

Q.2. A card is selected from a pack of 52 playing cards and is then replaced and a further card selected which is also replaced. If this process is repeated for 48 selections how often would you expect a hearts card to be drawn? Assuming that the binomial distribution can be approximated by the Normal distribution, determine the probability that the number of hearts drawn lies between 9 and 15.

Q.3. The marks in a mathematics examination are normally distributed with a mean of 60 and S.D. of 8. Out of the total candidates 24 were awarded marks in the range 50 to 60 inclusive. How many candidates sat the examination?

Q.4. If a coin is tossed 10 times what is the probability of obtaining 5 heads? Use the binomial distribution to arrive at your answer and then derive an approximation to that result using the Normal distribution.

Q.5. A pea is placed under one of three pots by one player while his opponent tries to guess where the pea is hidden. If he chooses at random between the three pots in a sequence of 18 games use the binomial distribution to calculate:
(i) his chances of guessing correctly more often than not, i.e. at least 10 times; and
(ii) his chances of guessing correctly exactly 9 times.
How would these answers compare with estimates obtained by using the Normal distribution instead of the binomial distribution?

Q.6. A manufacturer makes T shirts in three sizes, small, medium and large. The sizing is to be arranged so that if equal numbers are made in each size none of the three sizes will be more likely than another to be sold. Assuming that the measurements of potential buyers are distributed normally with mean 90cms and S.D. 5cms determine the measurements which must be included in each fitting so that 95 per cent of the customers could purchase a T shirt to fit.

Q.7. The mean monthly earnings of a sample of 256 executives in manufacturing ndustry are estimated at £650 with a standard deviation of £50. Estimate the mean monthly earnings of the population of such executives at the 95 per cent confidence level.

Q.8. Out of a random sample of 1,000 married women 450 claimed to be gainfully occupied. Give an estimate of the proportion of married women in the population which is gainfully occupied. Calculate the 95 and 99 per cent confidence intervals.

Q.9. In a random sample of 200 shoppers 40 claimed to have purchased a particular product during the past week. Estimate at the 95 per cent confidence level, the proportion of shoppers in the population which may have purchased this product during the same period. What size of sample would be required to reduce the confidence interval to 2 per cent?

Q.10. A sample survey among 900 married women showed that on average the weekly expenditure on clothing and footwear in their households was £4 with a standard deviation of £1. What size of sample would be required to estimate the mean expenditure at the 95 per cent level of confidence to ± 4 pence?

Answers

Answer to Question 1

To calculate the probability that the selected male will be between 1·78 and 1·83 metres derive the z scores for those two values.

Thus, when x=1·78 metres $z = \dfrac{1·78 - 1·73}{10} = \dfrac{5}{10} \text{cms} = \tfrac{1}{2}$

when x=1·83 metres $z = \dfrac{1·83 - 1·73}{10} = \dfrac{10}{10} \text{cms} = 1$

The z values of $\tfrac{1}{2}$ and 1 correspond to the following proportions of the total area under the Normal curve, 0·1915 and 0·3413 respectively. Since both the measurements are larger than the mean, both values of x are on the same side of the Normal curve, *i.e.* to the right of the mean. Hence, to determine the probability that the selected male has a height between the two values of x it is necessary to take the difference between the two areas, *i.e.* 0·3413 − 0·1915 = 0·1498. This signifies that there is a probability of 0·15 approximately that the male selected will be between those two heights.

Answer to Question 2

From the information given relating to the binomial distribution, *i.e.* n=48, p=14 and q=34 it follows that the mean of the distribution is equal to np = 48 × 14 which equals 12 while the standard deviation $\sqrt{npq}$ is $\sqrt{48 \times 14 \times 34} = \sqrt{9} = 3$.

The range of the number of hearts 9 to 15 will, in the case of a *continuous* distribution, *i.e.* the Normal distribution, be equal to $8\tfrac{1}{2}$ to $15\tfrac{1}{2}$. We need the z scores for those values of the variable. Thus, $z = \dfrac{12 - 8\tfrac{1}{2}}{3} = 1·17$; the z score for the value of x of $15\tfrac{1}{2}$ is exactly the same, 1·17. This z value corresponds to 0·3790 of the area under the Normal curve so that the two added together give 0·7580. Note that since the interval $8\tfrac{1}{2} - 15\tfrac{1}{2}$ includes the mean, the areas either side are added. In other words, the probability that the number of hearts drawn in the 48 selections will be between 9 and 15 is just over 0·75.

Answer to Question 3

The area under the Normal curve corresponding to a range of values, *i.e.* marks of 50 to 60 inclusive, is contained within the interval $49\tfrac{1}{2} - 60\tfrac{1}{2}$. With a mean of 60, the first z value $= \dfrac{60 - 49\tfrac{1}{2}}{8} = \dfrac{10·5}{8} = 1·312$; the second value is given by $\dfrac{60\tfrac{1}{2} - 60}{8} = \dfrac{0·5}{8}$ which equals 0·0625. Reference to the table of areas under the Normal curve shows that the area corresponding to the first z value is 0·4053; in the second case it is 0·0240. (The reader will note that this latter value is read off the top line of the table (0.0) and small adjustments made for the final 0·0025. Since these two areas are on either side of the mean, they are as in Q.2 added to give a result of 0·4293 or 43 per cent of the area under the curve. Since this accounted for 24 candidates, the total number of candidates sitting the examination is equal to $24 \times \dfrac{100}{42} = 57$.

Answer to Question 4

This is a straightforward example of the use of the binomial as explained in the previous chapter. The probability of 5 heads from 10 tosses of a coin is given by the term $\binom{10}{5} (0·5)^5 (0·5)^5$ since p=q=0·5 and n=10. The calculations are straightforward. The coefficient is given by $\dfrac{10!}{5!}$ which is $\dfrac{10\times9\times8\times7\times6}{5\times4\times3\times2\times1}=252.$

The reader should note that the denominator, *i.e.* 5 factorial determines the number of values in the numerator, *i.e.* the first five values in 10 factorial.

The rest of the term requires the calculation of $(0.5)^5$ $(0.5)^5$ which is equal to (0.03125) (0.03125) or 0.0009765. When multiplied by the coefficient, we get 0.2461 which is the value of P(5), *i.e.* the probability of 5 heads.

Using the Normal curve approximation where the mean equals $np=10(0.5)=5$ and the standard deviation is $\sqrt{npq}=\sqrt{10\cdot(0.5)\,(0.5)}=1.58$. The range corresponding to 5 in the continuous distribution is 4·5 to 5·5. Since the mean of the distribution is 5, this means that the two areas under the Normal curve will lie on each side of the mean.

The first area to the right of the mean corresponds to $z=\dfrac{5\cdot5-5}{1\cdot58}$, the second to the left of the mean by $\dfrac{5-4\cdot5}{1\cdot58}$. In both cases *z* equals 0.3165 so the corresponding area under the Normal curve is equal to $0.1241+0.1241=0.2482$. Thus, using the Normal curve approximation to the binomial distribution the probability of 5 heads out of 10 tosses is equal to 0.25, the same as was derived from the binomial. Note that in this case, unlike the two illustrations in the chapter, the areas given by the *z* values lie on each side of the mean, therefore they are added. When they are on the same side, either to the left or right of the mean, then take the difference.

Answer to Question 5

This is a rather more difficult question, not least because it entails quite a lot of arithmetic in deriving the probabilities from the expansion of $(p+q)^{18}$ where $n=18$, $p=13$ and $q=23$. The values for *p* and *q* should be obvious; there are three pots and only one of them counts as a success. The probability distribution is as follows; note that the 9 terms which have been evaluated in the table below account for over 95 per cent of the total probabilities. In other words, the chances of guessing correctly more than half the time are remote indeed, *i.e.* 1 less the sum of P(0)+P(1)+P(2)+P(3). . .P(9)=0·9566 which leaves the probability of guessing correctly *at least* 10 times at only 0·0434 or just 4 per cent of the time.

The probability of guessing correctly half of the time, *i.e.* exactly 9 times out of 18 games, is not much higher, *i.e.* 0·0643 or 6 per cent. This probability, it will be seen from the table below, corresponds to P(9), *i.e.* the probability of guessing correctly 9 times out of 18. In the above probability, *i.e.* at least 10 times, we add together all the probabilities for each number *below* 10.

P(0)=0·00067   P(5)=0·1812
P(1)=0·0061   P(6)=0·1963
P(2)=0·0259   P(7)=0·1682
P(3)=0·0690   P(8)=0·1157
P(4)=0·1294   P(9)=0·0643

0·9566

Using the Normal distribution, for which the mean is 6, *i.e.* $np=18\times13$ and the standard deviation $\sqrt{npq}=\sqrt{18\times13\times23}=2$, we need the area corresponding to the interval under the curve between $9\frac{1}{2}$ and the mean, *i.e.* 6 divided by the standard deviation. Thus, $\dfrac{9\frac{1}{2}-6}{2}=1.75$ which *z* value in the table reads 0·4599. In other words, the chance of exceeding 9 correct guesses is given by $0.5-0.4599=0.0401$ or 4 per cent which is the same as the answer derived by using the binomial. Note that all the correct guesses between 6 and 9 are on the right of the mean and account for most of the area on that side of the distribution, *i.e.* 0·4599 out of 0·5 (remember that the table gives only one half of the symmetrical distribution). What is left of that half represents the probability of guessing correctly more than 9 times out of 18. That is very small.

The probability of guessing correctly *exactly* 9 times is given by the area corresponding to the range $8\frac{1}{2}$-$9\frac{1}{2}$ for which the z values are 1·25 and 1·75. The area is $0·4599 - 0·3944 = 0·0655$.

Answer to Question 6

This is an interesting little question which needs to be read with care if it is to be answered correctly. First, note that it involves only the use of the Normal distribution; the binomial does not enter into this problem. The mean of the distribution is given as 90cms and the standard deviation as 5cms. The next point to note is that we need to ensure that 95 per cent of the customers can be fitted. In other words, the sizes must cover the range of 1·96 S.D. under the curve about the mean, *i.e.* 9·8cms.

The point to note is that we are here concerned with the area not the interval between successive values of x. Thus, one third of the area is allocated to cover the medium-sized customers' needs, and similar areas for those requiring large and small sizes. Thus, one third of 95 per cent is equal to approximately 32 per cent which is the same as 16 per cent of the area on either side of the mean. Reference to the table of areas shows that an area of 16 per cent corresponds to a z value of about 0·412. Thus, the range of the medium size includes measurements differing from the mean, *i.e.* $0·412(5)$cms $= 2·06$cms.

The medium size of T shirt must then be equal to 90 plus/minus 2.06 which gives an interval of 87·94 to 92·06cms. The total interval covered by 1·96 S.D. is 1·96 (5cms) i.e. 9·8cms so that the minimum and maximum sizes range down to $90 - 9·8 = 80·2$ and up to $90 + 9·8 = 99·8$cms.

Thus, the small size of T shirt will be 80·2 to 87·94cms, the medium size will be 87·94 to 92·06cms and the large size 92·06 to 99·8cms. Thus, when ordering his supplies the vendor could order the same number of large, small and medium in say 92-100, 80-88 and 88-92 with every confidence that 95 per cent of the customers will find a shirt to fit and that, in the longer run, he will not be saddled with unsold stock in one size any more than in the others.

Answer to Question 7

Assuming that the sample was random then the standard error of the statistic in question, *i.e.* the sample mean, is given by the formula s.e. $= \dfrac{\text{S.D.}}{\sqrt{n}}$. In this example the corresponding figures are s.e. $= \dfrac{£50}{\sqrt{256}} = 3·125$ and it may be concluded at the 95 per cent level of confidence, that the interval of $£650 \pm 1·96 (3·125) = £650 \pm 6·13$ includes the population mean of this particular population.

Answer to Question 8

This requires the standard error of a proportion, in this case the proportion of women with jobs, *i.e.* $450/1,000 = 45$ per cent. The formula for the standard error of a proportion (or percentage) is written s.e. $= \sqrt{\dfrac{pq}{n}}$. Substituting the appropriate figures we get s.e. $= \sqrt{\dfrac{45 \times 55}{1,000}} = 1·57$. The confidence interval corresponding to the 95 per cent level is given by $45 \pm 1·96 (1·57)$; for the 99 per cent level the figure of 1·96 before the bracket containing the standard error is replaced by 2·58; in this case the confidence interval will be 41-49 per cent approximately.

Answer to Question 9

As in the previous question calculate the standard error of the percentage of shoppers buying the product, *i.e.* $40/200$ which is 20 per cent. The standard error of that proportion is given by calculating $\sqrt{\dfrac{20 \times 80}{200}} = 2·82$. If the foregoing fraction gives a result of 2·82 which, at the 95 per cent level would give an interval of 1·96 (2·82) which is 5·53 to two places of decimals, what size of sample will give an interval of 2 points at the same level of confidence? By substitution, in the formula for the standard error $\sqrt{\dfrac{20 \times 80}{n}} = 1$ we get an answer of 1,600. This answer is an approximation where, instead of calculating the interval by 1·96 × s.e., we merely multiply the standard error by 2. Generally speaking, for the 95 per cent level it is easier to use 2 rather than 1·96 s.e. and the difference in the result is negligible. In fact, the only reason for writing down 1.96 in the examination room is to show the examiner that you know the correct figure to use! However, if we need the exact answer it is given by $\dfrac{1,600}{x} = 1·0204$. The product of the last part of this equation, *i.e.* 1·96 (1·0204) is equal to 2, the interval required.

The rest is simple arithmetic. Thus, if $\sqrt{\dfrac{1,600}{x}} = 1·0204$, then squaring both sides to remove the root sign on the left gives $\dfrac{1,600}{x} = 1·0412$ from which we get $x = \dfrac{1,600}{1·0412}$ which equals 1,537, *i.e.* the size of the required sample if the confidence interval at the 95 per cent level is to be equal to 20 ± 2 per cent.

Answer to Question 10

This follows the same pattern as the previous question. The standard error of the mean when $n = 900$ and the standard deviation is £1 is equal to $\dfrac{£1}{\sqrt{900}}$ or $\dfrac{100}{30}$ pence. At the 95 per cent level the interval would be £4 ± 1·96 (3·3)p. Thus, it follows that, if a sample of 900 yields a standard error of 3·3, the size of the sample where the standard error will be $\dfrac{4}{1·96}$ is equal to $\dfrac{100}{\sqrt{x}}$. Thus, we get $\sqrt{x} = 49$ so that the sample required is 49^2 or 2,401. To check the correctness of the sample size, the reader can work out the standard error using this sample and multiplying the s.e. by 1·96 which should give the answer 4 (1·96 × 2·04).

Finally, it will have been noted that none of the last four questions above required anything more than routine calculations. But, as was noted in the introduction to the Question and Answer section, examiners are increasingly requiring candidates to explain the basis of their calculations or the theory underlying them. This is especially the case with standard error calculations and confidence limits. In short, read carefully the relevant sections in the chapter to ensure that you understand the principles involved. It is not enough merely to be able to reproduce the calculations.

CHAPTER XIV

TESTS OF SIGNIFICANCE

In the previous chapter reference was made to a second group of problems which arise in the interpretation of sample statistics. The first, which was discussed in the last chapter, were termed estimation problems. The second group are known as tests of hypotheses or significance tests. The latter expression is derived from the full title, *i.e.* tests of *statistical* significance. Such tests have no significance outside the realm of sample statistics! The term tests of hypotheses is derived from the basis of the significance test. The simplest illustration is to adapt one of the examples given in the last chapter involving the estimation of a population proportion from the sample proportion.

Suppose the leaders of a particular political party are considering their prospects in a forthcoming general election. As is usual in such discussion opinion tends to outweigh the few facts available but, in the opinion of a majority of those involved their party has a good chance of winning at least 50 per cent of the votes. If this belief can be supported by any evidence, then there is every reason to welcome a general election. A public opinion poll for private use is commissioned; it will be carefully designed to ensure that particular emphasis is attached to key constituencies which are marginal and the sample will probably be rather larger than usual. Let it be assumed that the result from a sample of 1,000 respondents is a percentage vote of 55. The reader will by now, it is hoped, appreciate that this figure is one of many which might have been derived from such a sample from the particular population under investigation. Had, for example, two similar samples been commissioned for the same day it is quite possible that the results would have differed, *e.g.* the other poll might have yielded a percentage of 53. Ignore for the moment the hypothetical second sample. In practice there is only one sample and in this case it indicates 55 per cent of the votes would go to one particular party. How reliable is this estimate as an indicator of how the electorate as a whole would vote?

Testing an Hypothesis

The statistician, who would be consulted, would approach the problem along the following lines. Information on the state of public opinion available to the leaders of the party before the poll was commissioned led them to the conclusion that they had 50 per cent of the electorate behind them. The question the statistician would ask is, 'from a population with a proportion p of 0·50 what is the probability of drawing a sample of 1,000 which has a p value of 0·55?' For working purposes one starts by setting up the hypothesis or proposition that the difference between the two proportions can reasonably be attributed to sampling errors and that, in consequence, it does not reflect a significant change in the degree of support for the party. Alternatively, we are testing the proposition that a sample value of $p = 0.55$ is entirely consistent with a value of $p = 0.50$ in the population from which the sample was drawn. Because the basis of the significance test to be used is that the difference between the population and sample proportion can reasonably be attributed to sampling errors we refer to the *null hypothesis*.

The next stage is to determine, by means of a test of significance, whether or not the null hypothesis should be accepted or rejected. Note that the significance test *does not prove* the null hypothesis wrong any more than it can prove it to be correct. What the test of significance does, is to determine the probability that the difference between the two observed percentages as in the above illustration is due to chance, *i.e.* random sampling errors. Whether or not the probability is such as would lead to the rejection of the null hypothesis depends on the level of significance adopted by the statistician. At best, the test will either strengthen or weaken the belief in the correctness of the null hypothesis. A simple example of the appropriate test of significance will probably make the above points clear.

The standard error of a proportion is given by the formula $\sqrt{\dfrac{pq}{n}}$ where p is the proportion possessing the attribute and q is the balance, *i.e.* $1 - p$; n denotes the sample size. Substituting in the formula we get $\sqrt{\dfrac{55 \times 45}{1,000}} = \sqrt{2.47} = 1.6$ per cent. The observed difference between two proportions of 5 points is $\dfrac{5}{1.6} = 3.18$ times as large as the standard error. This signifies that the probability of drawing a sample of 1,000 with p at least equal to 0·55 from a population with p equal to 0·50 is less than 2 in 1,000. This figure is derived by looking up the area under the Normal curve table to ascertain the proportion of the total area which corresponds to a z value of 3·18. The proportion is 0·4984 which means that only 0·5000−0·4999, or 0·0001, of all such samples drawn from a population in which $p = 0.50$ are likely to have a p value of 0·55 or higher.

The next question is, 'at what point does the statistician decide to reject rather than accept the null hypothesis?' Suppose the result of the test had been such that there was a 1 in 10 chance of getting the above sample of 1,000, with p at least 0.55, from the population under review? Would the null hypothesis have then been rejected or accepted? The decision depends entirely upon the level of significance adopted by the statistician in advance of the test. It has already been stated that the 95 and 99 per cent levels of confidence were key values in the interpretation of sample statistics. The same values are commonly used for levels of significance. In other words, if there is a better than 1 in 20 chance e.g. 1 in 10, that the sample could have come from the population concerned, then the null hypothesis would be accepted if the criterion for acceptance was the 5 per cent level. If in a similar example the observed difference was more than 1·96 times as large as the standard error, then the null hypothesis would be rejected, again assuming the criterion chosen was the 5 per cent level of significance. It would, however, be accepted if one were using the 1 per cent level and the z value was between 1·96 and 2·58.

Thus, in the example used above to illustrate the significance test as applied to a sample proportion, if the probability of about 1 in 500 or under 2 in 1,000 means anything at all, then there is no reasonable doubt that the null hypothesis should be rejected. Strictly speaking, one cannot say 'there is *no* doubt about rejecting the null hypothesis' even in this particular case. Or in any other, for that matter. It must not be forgotten that there is no such thing as certainty in sampling. Whatever the value of p in the population, a sample may, in theory, yield any value between 0 and 1. There is always the possibility, even if the probability of that particular outcome is indicated by the test in odds of 10,000 to 1, that a freak outcome has occurred. The statistician usually uses as criteria for rejecting the null hypothesis one of the two levels of significance already quoted, i.e. the 5 and 1 per cent levels. These correspond to probabilities of 0·95 and 0·99 and they serve as the boundaries between rejection and acceptance of the null hypothesis. Using the 5 per cent level it would mean that if the significance test indicates a difference between, say, sample means, it could have arisen as the result of sampling variation more than 5 in 100, i.e. 1 in 20 times, then the null hypothesis would be accepted. If, however, the difference is unlikely to have arisen from such causes as often as 5 in 100 samples, then the hypothesis would be rejected and the differences attributed to other factors, i.e. the differences would be regarded as significant.

These levels of significance indicate that in the first case there is a

5 per cent probability that such a conclusion is wrong; with the 1 per cent level of significance the risks of such a mistake are reduced to 1 per cent. In short, there is no guarantee that the conclusion based upon a test of significance is correct. Even when the null hypothesis is accepted, this is not to be interpreted that the hypothesis is true. All that is certain is that the evidence available from the test result was insufficient to justify its rejection! Note, too, that the level of significance to be used when testing an hypothesis should always be determined in advance. One should consider the data and the implications of the test and decide before the test is carried out whether it is more appropriate to use a higher rather than a lower level of significance.

Statisticians distinguish between two types of error which may arise with the testing of hypotheses. They are classified as Type I and Type II errors and the basis of the classification is as follows. Having set up an hypothesis and then tested it, there are two possible ways in which the test can give rise to the wrong conclusion. First, although the hypothesis is true the result of the test leads to its rejection. Second, the hypothesis is false but the test leads to its acceptance. The first case of a true hypothesis being rejected on the basis of the test is known as Type I error. The second, in which a false hypothesis is accepted on the evidence of the test, is a Type II error.

What needs to be kept clearly in mind is not so much the particular type of error but rather the fact that some incorrect decisions are, in the long run, inevitable. Consider for a moment the consequences of using the 5 per cent level of significance as the criterion for acceptance or rejection. Given the nature of random processes, using the 5 per cent level means that, in the long run, 5 per cent of hypotheses which are true will be rejected. The reason for this is that although 95 per cent of samples will fall within the 95 per cent confidence limits, because of the operation of random errors, 5 per cent of the samples will fall outside those limits. And, of course, there is no means of knowing when this happens. Likewise, in the case of Type II errors where a false hypothesis is accepted then, at the 95 per cent level, there is the risk that 5 per cent of the time incorrect decisions on the basis of that result will be taken.

What can be done to avoid mistakes of this kind? The answer is, very little. In the case of Type I errors, the chances or probability of taking a wrong decision are the same as the level of significance used to test the hypothesis, i.e. 5 per cent. Clearly then, it is possible to reduce the risk of Type I errors by using a higher level of significance, i.e. the 1 per cent, thus reducing the probability of such an error from 5 to 1 per cent. Unfortunately, in doing this the probability of committing a Type II error is correspondingly increased. With a given size of sample, increasing the level of signifi-cance means that the interval about the sample statistic is widened with a corresponding loss of precision. The problem of the interval could be met by increasing the size of the sample, but it is too late to do that once the results have been compiled. The only rational policy is to consider the sample at the outset of the survey or experiment (a topic discussed in Chapter XVI) and ensure that, for a given cost, the maximum possible precision is obtained.

The reader need not concern himself greatly with this particular topic; it is essentially a problem for specialists. But, even in fairly elementary statistics examination papers candidates are sometimes asked to indicate, albeit briefly, what is meant by the two types of error. Hence this reference to a complex topic!

S.E. of Difference between Means

We can now consider a further example of the application of tests of significance. Records were kept to determine the mean life of two types of transistor radio batteries. Brand A batteries, of which 120 were tested, had a mean life of 75 hours with standard deviation ten hours. In the case of Brand B the sample tested totalled 100; these gave a mean life of 78 hours with standard deviation nine hours. Which battery, if either, is the better buy? The basis of the method used to answer this question is similar to the previous signi-ficance test. The relevant question is whether the difference between the two means of 78 and 75 hours is statistically significant or whether it can reasonably be explained by sampling variations. As before, the test requires the setting up of the null hypothesis, *i.e.* there is no real difference since it is assumed that the observed difference between the means can be attributed quite reasonably to the fact that, the tests having been based upon two samples, the means were affected by the consequent sampling variation. Following the conventional procedure, the hypothesis will be tested at the 5 per cent level of significance.

The significance test in this case requires the determination of the *standard error of the difference between means*. The formula for this particular standard error is given hereunder. It is based on the theory that, if the samples are large then the means of those samples will be normally distributed and, likewise, the differences between those means. The standard error in this case is given by the formula

$$\sqrt{\frac{\text{s.d.}_1^2}{n_1} + \frac{\text{s.d.}_2^2}{n_2}}$$

The   subscripts   1   and   2   merely   denote   the   particular samples. By substitution, s.e. $= \sqrt{\dfrac{10^2}{120} + \dfrac{9^2}{100}}$ which equals

$\sqrt{\cdot83 + \cdot81}$, the square root of which is 1·28 approx. The next step is to divide the difference between the means by the standard error. Thus, $\dfrac{78-75}{1\cdot28} = \dfrac{3}{1\cdot28} = 2\cdot3$. Such a difference between sample means, based upon samples of the above size drawn from the same population, is likely to occur about once in 50 such experiments. This is well beyond the 1 in 20 probability set by the 5 per cent level of significance.*

In short, the difference between the means is statistically significant and it can be concluded that Brand A battery with the life of 78 hours really is a better buy. Note the reference in the previous paragraph to the samples having been 'drawn from the same population'. What does this mean? It is merely another way of saying that if the two samples of batteries had come from the same population their means were only likely to differ, if at all, because of sampling errors. And, it is this hypothesis or assumption which the significance test is designed to test. Note that, initially, we start by assuming that the null hypothesis is justified. Only if the result of the significance test does not support this belief at the pre-determined level of significance is the hypothesis rejected.

The point has already been made that the larger the sample, the more reliable are the sample statistics likely to be. In the above example of a standard error of a difference between two means the samples were, by statistical standards, large samples. Strictly speaking, a large sample is one in which n is greater than 30. For reasons which should be obvious by now, small samples pose considerable problems for statisticians; there is, in fact, an important body of theory about their interpretation. The above test of significance is only appropriate when the samples are large. If they are small, then a different test is used known as the 't' test. But in view of the special problems which arise with small samples there is no point in discussing this particular test in an elementary text such as this. At this point, therefore, a brief recapitulation of the main points may be helpful.

When a sample statistic has been derived for purposes of estimating the corresponding population parameter, a confidence interval is calculated and the degree of belief that this interval includes the parameter is given by the level of confidence. Thus, one might be '95 per cent confident that the confidence limits of $\bar{x} \pm 1\cdot96$ s.e. say, 63–68 inches, include the population mean'. With tests of

* The 1 in 50 probability is derived by using the z value for 2·3 which shows that almost 98 per cent of the area of the normal curve would lie within the limits of the mean difference $\pm$ 2·3 s.e.

significance, however, the term 'confidence level' is replaced by the concept of a level of significance. This has the result that, instead of referring to the 95 per cent confidence level or the 99 per cent level, one talks about the 5 and 1 per cent levels of significance. As with most practices there is a reason for this.

In an estimation problem, the question is whether the sample statistic which serves as the basis for the estimate of the population parameter lies *within* a given proximity of the mean of the sampling distribution. It will be remembered that if a large number of equal-sized samples were drawn from the same population, their means (or any other statistic) would distribute themselves normally and the mean of such a sampling distribution would correspond to the population mean. Since the bulk, *i.e.* 95 per cent, of all such sample means in the distribution would lie within the interval of 1·96 standard errors about the mean of the distribution, the probability that any one sample selected at random would have a mean within the foregoing interval is 0·95 or 95 per cent. And, since the mean of the sampling distribution coincides with the population mean the interval of 1·96 s.e. about the sample mean will also include the population mean. That statement is made at the 95 per cent level of confidence, *i.e.* there is only a 5 per cent chance of it being wrong, but 95/100 chance of it being right.

In the case of a test of significance, the null hypothesis is rejected only if the statistic lies *outside* the limits set by the 95 or 99 per cent probability levels. If, for example, the sample statistic diverges from the corresponding population parameter by as much as 1·96 s.e., then that particular statistic will be found in one of the tail areas of the Normal distribution, *i.e.* in the area beyond the ordinate representing 5 per cent of the area under the Normal curve. In consequence, it is stated that the null hypothesis is rejected at either the 5 or 1 per cent level of significance. The basic principle underlying both estimation and tests of significance is, however, the same. Thus, the 95 per cent level of confidence and the 5 per cent level of significance denote the same probabilities, just as do the 99 per cent confidence level and the 1 per cent level of significance. Now, having been reminded of *these* basic points, we can turn to another test of significance.

S.E. of Difference between Proportions

Just as it is possible to test the difference between sample means, so it is equally practicable to test the difference between two proportions. The basis of this particular significance test is similar to that used for means and the following example of its application should emphasise the previous point. Assume that a sample of 800 was used in a public opinion poll to test the popularity of a particular political party. The proportion of the 800 respondents which approved its policies was 48 per cent. A similar poll involving 720 respondents had been carried out six months previously and, on that occasion, the proportion of respondents expressing approval of the same party's policies was 45 per cent. This particular problem involves the testing of a hypothesis that the two samples were drawn from a population in which the proportion p has not changed and the difference of 3 points is therefore attributable to random sampling errors.

The test requires the calculation of the standard error of the difference between proportions which is given by the formula $\sqrt{\dfrac{p_1 q_1}{n_1} + \dfrac{p_2 q_2}{n_2}}$. Substituting the values we get

$$\sqrt{\frac{48 \times 52}{800} + \frac{45 \times 55}{720}} = 2\cdot56.$$

The standard error is then divided into the observed difference between the sample proportions; $\dfrac{3}{2\cdot56} = 1\cdot17$. This result is considerably less than $1\cdot96$, the z value which would indicate that the difference of three points in the two proportions would just be significant at the 5 per cent level. That figure of $1\cdot96$ would mean the chances of such a difference arising between the proportions from two samples drawn from the same population would be 5 in 100. The actual result, i.e. $1\cdot17$ suggests that the three-point difference could arise by chance about one in every four samples. In the circumstances, there is insufficient reason for rejecting the null hypothesis; in other words, there has been no real change in public support for the particular political party.

To ensure that the mechanical operations involved in the last two tests have been understood, here are two further problems which the reader may care to resolve and then compare his result with the workings which follow.

(i) A group of 80 students sit an examination in mathematics. The mean mark achieved is 45 with standard deviation 10. After a month's revision course the same students are re-tested. The mean mark achieved is 50 with standard deviation 9. Is it reasonable to assume that the performance of the candidates in the second examination is significantly better than in the first?

(ii) Two groups of patients suffering from the same disease are treated with two different drugs. The first group comprising 90 patients is given drug A and, after two weeks, there is a marked improvement in the condition of 36 of the patients. The second group of 80 patients is given drug B and after two weeks a marked improvement is noted in the condition of 40. Do these results support the conclusion that drug B is more effective in the treatment of the particular disease?

Note that in both of the foregoing questions, we start by setting up the null hypothesis that any difference between the results in each sample can be attributed to chance factors. Then, in each case, it is necessary to calculate the standard error of the difference between the sample results, in the first case between the means and, in the second, between the proportions. Having derived the standard error it is then compared with, i.e. divided into the observed difference between the sample means or proportions. If the resultant z value is less than 1·96 then there is a greater than 1 in 20 probability that the difference has arisen by chance and therefore the null hypothesis is accepted. If the z value is greater than 1·96 but less than 2·58 it can be inferred that the chances that the difference arose by chance are less than 1 in 20 but not as low as 1 in 100. As such they must be regarded as statistically significant and the null hypothesis rejected. If the z value is 2·58 or more then one may reject the null hypothesis with even greater confidence since this z value implies that the chances of the means of two such samples from the same population differing so much are 1 in 100 or less. If the lower z score is used as the criterion for rejection of the null hypothesis, then one is testing the hypothesis at the 5 per cent level of significance; if the higher z score, i.e. 2·58 is chosen, then the hypothesis is tested at the 1 per cent level.

The workings of the above problems are as follows. The standard error of the difference between sample means is given by $\sqrt{\dfrac{s.d._1^2}{n_1} + \dfrac{s.d._2^2}{n_2}}$

which, after substituting the actual values, gives $\sqrt{\dfrac{10^2}{80} + \dfrac{9^2}{80}}$

$= \sqrt{1·25 + 1} = \sqrt{2·25} = 1·5$. (Note the approximation of the second fraction to 1; the error involved is negligible and clearly makes the working simpler.) The observed difference between the mean marks in the two tests is 45–40 = 5. The resultant z score of $\dfrac{5}{1·5}$ is 3·3 which is well above the 5 per cent and even the 1 per cent significance levels for rejection. A z score of 3·3 signifies that the probability of two such sample means arising by chance is 5 in 1,000. The null hypothesis is therefore rejected because the probability that the difference between the sample means can be accounted for by random sampling errors is well below the 5 or

1 per cent levels, according to which particular level one may have chosen to use. It may be inferred with fair confidence that the revision period has contributed to the improved performance of the candidates.

In the second problem the standard error of the difference between proportions is given by the formula $\sqrt{\dfrac{p_1 q_1}{n_1} + \dfrac{p_2 q_2}{n_2}}$. Note that the symbols p and q in this formula represent the *proportion* in the samples which either do or do not possess the particular attribute. They do not represent the actual figures from the experiment. Thus, the cure rate of 36 out of 90 patients becomes 40 per cent and in the second sample 40 out of 80 patients is clearly 50 per cent. In each case q is equal to $1 - p$, or in percentage terms $100 - p$. Note, however, that the symbol n is replaced by the actual sample size.

Substituting the values we get $\sqrt{\dfrac{40 \times 60}{90} + \dfrac{50 \times 50}{80}}$ which equals $\sqrt{58}$, *i.e.* 7·6 per cent approx. Dividing this standard error into the difference between the actual proportions, $50-40 = 10$ (note that here too it is the difference between the *proportions* in the samples and not the actual number of patients whose condition improved) the z score is 1·3 approx. This is far below the z value of 1·96 which would signify that the difference between the two sample proportions was significant at the 5 per cent level. Thus it must be concluded, in the absence of any other evidence, that the new drug is not better than the first.

The reader may have noted that sometimes in the calculations the answer has been approximated. As was noted in the earlier chapter on Accuracy and Approximation statisticians do not always give figures as exact values as is the case, for example, in accountancy. The limitations of the data, and their inaccuracies, not to mention the sampling errors, are probably quite as important a factor in affecting the result as is any approximation. In any case, where it is obvious that the result will either be well under or in excess, for example, of the 1·96 or 2·58 z values which are so widely used, there is little point in adding to the number of decimal places in the answer! A good rule for examination candidates to follow is that where the answer will be given to one place of decimals one should work to two places of decimals in the intermediate stages of the calculation. Then, in the final stage, unless it is fairly clear that the result will be close to the value and the exact answer is needed, there is no harm in approximating. Nor is there any virtue, even with calculators, in working to several places of decimals when it is clear from the data that the values are probably correct only to the nearest unit, if that! The examiner may even conclude that, if the data are expressed to, say, the nearest £100 and an answer of, say, £1,345 as a mean is given to four places of decimals, that the candidate does not really understand what he is about! For all the emphasis that has been placed in this and other chapters on calculation, it should never be forgotten that the data with which one is working are more important. However sophisticated the statistical test and however exact the answer may appear, unless the data are reliable the rest of the work is a waste of time. It may appear at times to the reader that statistics is all about calculations and formulae. So it is, up to a point. But what distinguishes the well- from the poorly-trained statistician is not their relative facilities for applying the formula, but in assessing just what degree of analysis the data will stand in order to produce reliable results from which reasonable conclusions may be drawn.

Chi-squared test

In Chapter XII two distributions of the results from rolling a die 400 and 1,000 times were given on p. 295 and then converted into probability distributions to compare them. The actual results in the frequency distribution so converted suggested that the die had behaved consistently because the probability distributions were identical. The comment was made, however, that the die was probably not properly balanced otherwise the distributions would have approximated more closely to the theoretical distribution which would show the same number of appearances for each side. Thus, in 1,000 rolls of the die each side would be expected to appear about one-sixth of each series of throws, e.g. in every 1,000 the frequency for each side would be 166. It is possible, using a particular significance test, to determine whether or not the die was biased. The appropriate test is known as chi-squared pronounced 'ki' after the Greek letter χ. The formula is written as follows:

$$\chi^2 = \Sigma \frac{(O-E)^2}{E}$$

The test is used to determine whether a particular distribution differs significantly (in the statistical sense of the term) from another distribution which, it could reasonably be expected, should be the same. The easiest way to explain the test is to illustrate its application by some examples. Like any other mathematical formula, that for χ^2 merely summarises the operations which have to be carried out with the data. Thus, the letter O refers to the frequencies which have been observed, sometimes termed the actual frequencies, while E refers to the expected frequencies. The formula instructs us to obtain the difference between the two, i.e. (O–E) and then square the differences. The squared values are then to be divided by the corresponding E values. The summation sign in front of the formula indicates that all these results are then added together to give a value for χ^2. Now carry through these operations using the data on p. 295, but first adjusting the figures for 600 rolls of the die. The reason for this is that the expected frequencies will then be 100 for each side and this makes the calculation easier. The actual frequencies are the result of applying the outcomes for each of the six

Number of spots shown	1	2	3	4	5	6
Actual frequencies (O)	102	120	54	90	120	114
Expected frequencies (E)	100	100	100	100	100	100
(O–E)	+2	+20	−46	−10	+20	+14
(O–E)^2	4	400	2,116	100	400	196
(O–E)$^2 \div$ E	0·04	4	21·16	1	4	1·96

$$\chi^2 = 32\cdot16$$

sides of the die shown on p. 295 to a series of 600 throws. Thus, given the probability of 0·17 for the side showing one spot, out of 600 throws of the die one would expect 600 (0·17) or 102; in the case of the side showing five spots, the actual frequency is 600 (0·20) or 120. Assuming that the die is balanced then the *expected* distribution should reflect the fact that no side should occur more frequently than any other. In short, the frequencies for each side should be the same, 600/6=100 each. The rest of the table is self-explanatory.

How then do we interpret the calculated value of χ^2 of 32·16? On the next page there is part of a larger table entitled the Distribution of Chi-Squared. The first column is headed d.f. which stands for *degrees of freedom*. For the moment this does not concern us since the tabulated values in which we are interested are those along the row opposite the figure 5 in the column headed d.f. Along the top of the table, at the head of each of the three columns of the table of χ^2 values, are what are known as probability or P levels. These are simply the significance levels such as were used in interpreting the z values. The three columns shown in the table are headed 0·05, 0·02 and 0·01 which will be recognised as the 5, 2 and 1 per cent levels of significance. In other words, the tabulated values of chi-squared show, for any given degree of freedom, the level of probability at which the differences between the expected and observed values can be attributed to chance. The *smaller* the value of P, the *lower* is the probability that the differences (between the O and E values) are due to chance. We shall have more to say about

DISTRIBUTION OF CHI-SQUARED[1]
Level of Significance (P)

d.f.	0·05	0·02	0.01
1	3·84	5·41	6·64
2	5·99	7·82	9·21
3	7·82	9·84	11·34
4	9·49	11·67	13·28
5	11·07	13·39	15·09
6	12·59	15·03	16·81
7	14·07	16·62	18·47
8	15·51	18·17	20·09
9	16·92	19·68	21·67
10	18·31	21·16	23·21

[1] This table is adapted from Table III of R. A. Fisher: *Statistical Methods for Research Workers*, published by Oliver and Boyd Ltd, Edinburgh, by permission of the author and publishers.
The reader should note that in the full table values for the d.f. up to 30 are shown as well as giving values of χ^2 correspondingly to many more levels of significance.

this table later; for the moment we need only the line of χ^2 values corresponding to 5 degrees of freedom.

The calculated value of χ^2 in the example above was 32.16 which is far in excess of any of the values in the table for 5 d.f. This signifies that the differences between the observed and expected frequencies are statistically significant. Had the calculated value of χ^2 been 11·07 then the result would just have been significant at the 5 per cent level. In other words, we would have concluded that the differences between the observed and expected frequencies could have occurred as the result of sampling errors only 1 in 20 times. Had the value of the calculated χ^2 been 15·09 the result would have been significant at the 1 per cent level. In the event the value of 32·16 is far in excess of the χ^2 value appropriate to a 1 in 100 probability that the differences between the observed and unexpected frequencies were due to sampling errors. In short, the comment made on p.295 that the die was not properly balanced was correct!

Now let us consider another application of the same test.

A great deal of data are given in the form of frequency distributions, especially when the independent variable x is expressed in numerical form. For example, a distribution showing the number of persons earning salaries within a given range which is subdivided into classes. If in any doubt as to what this means, the reader may refresh his memory by looking back at the frequency distribution on p.48. But, as was explained in the chapter on tabulation, the characteristic in the sample with which the statistician is concerned is not always a *variable*, i.e. one which can be expressed in numerical terms, e.g. an income of £5,000 p.a. but sometimes it is an *attribute*, i.e. a quality which cannot be expressed in figures. For example, the population of people who own colour TV sets, or who use a car for travelling to work, or those who both smoke and drink, can all be counted and we thereby obtain a count of persons possessing a particular attribute. Consider the following data given below. A sample of 1,000 women is classified by reference to two attributes; their educational background and the radio programmes to which they listen regularly.

	Educational Background		
	Primary & Secondary	Grammar and further	Total
Radio 1 and 2	520	180	700
Radio 3 and 4	230	70	300
Total	750	250	1000

Studying these data it would appear that there are two groups with differing educational backgrounds, *i.e.* 750 who attended primary and secondary school and 250 who enjoyed the benefit of grammar school and in some cases further education. In both groups some listen to Radio 1 and 2 and some to Radio 3 and 4. If the two attributes were not associated, in other words, the type of education one had experienced had no influence upon one's tastes in radio programmes, then it would be reasonable to expect the two 'educational' groups of 750 and 250 women to contain the same proportions of listeners to either pair of programmes. Thus, in the group with 750 the proportion who listen to Radio 3 and 4 is 230/750 which is equal to about 31 per cent. In the other group of 250, there are 70 who listen to the same programmes and these represent 70/250 or 28 per cent. Clearly, the corresponding proportions in the two groups listening to Radio 1 and 2 must then be 69 and 72 per cent.

Since the data are derived from a sample, random errors have to be taken into account which means that the percentage figures derived above may or may not correspond to the percentages in the population. Thus, the difference between 31 and 28 per cent and the corresponding difference between 72 and 69 per cent may be due to such sampling errors. If that is the case then it follows that there is no association between educational background and listening tastes. The reader will probably appreciate that it would be more correct to say that the evidence of these particular data may not support such a hypothesis. Nevertheless, the latter does not appear inconsistent with one's observations of the listening public. It could also be that the educational backgrounds should be more precisely defined, since both these samples will contain highly heterogeneous groups of the listening public. Such considerations apart, however, how can one use the χ^2 test to determine whether the difference between the two groups is statistically significant?

The basic procedure is much the same as in the earlier example when the fairness of the die was tested. The only new element in this particular example is the derivation of the expected values. In the previous example, the expected theoretical values were easy to derive; six sides of the die all with equal probabilities of showing on any throw, hence the 600 throws were apportioned equally between the six sides. In the present example, it is slightly more complicated. Reference back to the data reveals that there are just four basic figures or frequencies; *i.e.* 520, 230, 180 and 70 with which we are concerned; they are in what are termed four 'cells'. Note that, for the moment, the total column and row are ignored. The relevant frequencies are the *actual* or *observed* values in each of the four cells. The *expected* values are those which would be expected in those cells, given the initial assumption that there is no association between the attributes, if the sample were free from sampling errors. How are the expected values derived?

As with the other tests of significance a working hypothesis is assumed, usually the null hypothesis. In this example the null hypothesis states that any differences between the listening figures for the two educational groups between the actual and expected values are due to sampling errors. The two attributes are not associated.

If, therefore, there are no real differences between the two groups, there is no reason why the two groups should not be regarded as part of a larger sample made up in the total column, *i.e.* 1,000, distributed between the different radio programmes as to 700:300. For, if the null hypothesis were valid and sampling errors did not exist, the two educational groups could be expected to distribute themselves between the radio programmes in the same way as the total sample, *i.e.* 300:700. On that assumption we calculate the expected distribution between the radio programmes for each of the two educational groups. Thus, since 700/1,000 of the total listen to Radio 1 and 2, then the same proportion of the first educational group of 750, *i.e.* primary and secondary, should be similarly divided. Then, 700/1,000 of 750 yields 525 and, for the grammar school group, 700/1,000 of 250 in that group gives 175. For the bottom row of figures in the two cells of the table relating to Radio 3 and 4, the expected frequencies are derived by multiplying the group totals of 750 and 250 by 300/1,000 which gives the expected values of 225 and 75 respectively.

The observed and expected values can now be set down as follows: first for the Primary and secondary group.

	Observed	Expected	O – E	$(O-E)^2$	$\dfrac{(O-E)^2}{E}$
Radio 1 & 2	520	525	−5	25	25/525=0.05
Radio 3 & 4	230	225	+5	25	25/225=0.11
	750	750	0	50	

and next for the Grammar School group. Thus,

	Observed	Expected	O – E	$(O-E)^2$	$\dfrac{(O-E)^2}{E}$
Radio 1 & 2	180	175	−5	25	25/175=0.14
Radio 3 & 4	70	75	+5	25	25/75=0.33
	250	250	0	50	

Note that the differences defined as O – E are either positive or negative depending on whether the expected figure is smaller or larger than the actual values. The sign ceases to have any significance when the differences are squared; it may be recalled that, when the deviations from the mean were derived for purposes of calculating the standard deviation, they were squared to eliminate the negative deviations. The result of squaring the (O – E) differences is to convert all the differences into positive values since the test is designed to take the total differences, whatever their direction, into account.

The next stage is to divide the $(O-E)^2$ values by the corresponding expected values in each cell. Thus we get 25/525; 25/225; 25/175 and 25/75, and the sum of the successive quotients is (approximately to two decimal places) $0.05 + 0.11 + 0.14 + 0.33 = 0.63$. What exactly does this value signify apart from the fact that 0·63 is the required value of chi-squared? This question can only be answered by reference to the table giving the distribution of χ^2 values. First, we need the number of degrees of freedom. In this particular example, the number of d.f is only 1. (The reader is asked to accept this for the present; an explanation of the concept and method of calculating the number of d.f. to be used is given on p. 344.) The smallest value of χ^2 corresponding to 1 d.f. shown in the table on p. 338 is 3·84. The derived value in the above example is 0·63 so there is no hesitation in accepting the null hypothesis and concluding that there is no significant difference in the listening tastes of the two educational groups.

It may already have occurred to some readers that a similar conclusion from the data in the foregoing example of a simple chi-
squared test might have been derived by using the significance test
for the difference between proportions. The reader may care later to
convert the actual figures in the four cells into the appropriate
percentage values and use the standard error of the difference
between proportions to test the null hypothesis. The result should be
the same as with the chi-squared test.[1]

However, the data to which the chi-squared test is applied are not
always contained in simple two-by-two tables as above. Depending
upon the number of variables involved, the table may have many
more rows and columns e.g. $5 \times 4 = 20$ cells, but the principle set
out above is precisely the same.

To ensure that the principles have been grasped by the reader here
is an interesting 3×2 tabulation on a matter of public concern.
These data relate to cigarette smoking and cancer of the lung. The
obvious question is, do these data support the view that the two are
related, i.e. if a person smokes heavily is he more likely to contract
lung cancer than if he either does not smoke or smokes but little?

Number of Patients smoking daily

	1+ Cig.	5+ Cigs	15+ Cigs	Total
Lung-carcinoma patients	7	19	15	41
Control patients with diseases other than cancer	12	10	6	28
	19	29	21	69

Source: Smoking and Carcinoma of the Lung. B.M.J. 1950 ii 739

A study of the data suggests that the number of lung cancer
patients tends to increase with a higher intake of tobacco, whereas in
the control group the trend is the other way. Here the majority are
in the lowest consumption group of $1 +$ cigarettes daily. As before,
by setting up the hypothesis that there is no association between the
incidence of lung carcinoma and smoking habits we then test the
hypothesis with the chi-squared test. The expected distribution in the

[1] Note that when the chi-squared test was used to determine whether radio listening and educational background were associated, it was the frequencies in each group which were used. If the
same hypothesis is tested by means of the significance test relating to the difference between means,
it is the percentages which are used. For the chi-squared test never use percentages; only the actual
figures of the distribution. The reason for converting the frequencies into percentages in the educational / radio listening example in the preliminary discussion was to determine the relative
differences between the two groups. Given the different sizes of the groups, comparison of the actual
frequencies did not help.

columns relating to each level of smoking is derived by re-distributing the three column totals in accordance with the distribution of 41:28 in the total column. Thus, $41/69 \times 19 = 11\cdot3$; $41/69 \times 29 = 17\cdot2$; $41/69 \times 21 = 12\cdot5$. Similarly for the lower row, but use the fraction $28/69$. The results are given hereunder.

Observed frequencies	Expected frequencies	$O-E$	$(O-E)^2$	$\dfrac{(O-E)^2}{E}$
7	11·3	−4·3	18·49	1·6
19	17·2	+1·8	3·24	0·2
15	12·5	+2·5	6·25	0·5
12	7·8	+4·2	18·40	2·4
10	11·8	−1·8	3·24	0·3
6	8·5	−2·5	6·25	0·7

$$\chi^2 = 5\cdot7$$

Reference to the table of the chi-square distribution reveals that with two degrees of freedom given by the formula $n = (c-1)(r-1) = (3-1)(2-1) = 2 \times 1$ the calculated value of 5·7 falls marginally short of the P value corresponding to the 5 per cent level of significance, which is 5·99. Since the criterion for rejection has been set at the 5 per cent level, then the result means that the null hypothesis should be accepted. In short, on the evidence of the test smoking and lung cancer are not associated. However, before rejecting completely the possibility of some association, other considerations should be taken into account. First, the sample is rather small, more especially some of the cell totals, hence the sampling errors could be rather large and distort the result. Also it is evident from the top row of the data that, as the cigarette consumption rises, so does the proportion of lung cancer patients in each of the three 'smoking' groups. Thus, while the evidence of the statistical test may not be conclusive, an examination of the data does suggest some association between lung cancer and smoking. At best one could bring in the verdict used in Scottish courts, *i.e.* not proven! The data are clearly such that there is every reason for seeking to continue the research with new and preferably larger samples. It should be observed in passing, that this is the sort of result which does occasionally arise. It is then left to the judgement of the statistician which decision he should take. It also serves as a reminder that statistical significance testing is not a set of 'cook-book' rules to be followed uncritically at all times!

In each of three examples of the application of the chi-squared test, reference has been made to the *degrees of freedom* or d.f. as the appropriate column in the table of the distribution of that statistic is headed. Its calculation, as may have been guessed from the last example, is quite simple. The number of degrees of freedom is given by the formula $n = (c - 1)(r - 1)$, where c and r represent the number of columns and rows in the table respectively. Thus, in the last example there were three columns classifying the patients according to their smoking habits and two rows which classified the same patients according to whether they had either cancer of the lung or some other illness. Thus, $(3 - 1)(2 - 1) = 2 \times 1 = 2$. For the two-by-two classification in the previous example there were two columns classifying the sample units by educational background and two rows showing their listening preferences. Thus, the number of degrees of freedom was 1 *i.e.* $(2 - 1)(2 - 1)$ as stated on p.341. In the first example using the chi-squared test a *single* distribution was being tested and here the degrees of freedom numbered 5, *i.e.* one less than the number of classes.

But, what does the term mean? Before considering the concept, let it be said that it is not necessary even to grasp the simplified explanation which follows in order to use the chi-squared test, provided one remembers how to calculate the number of d.f. This concept in particular but more especially the basis of the chi-squared distribution is extremely complex. Here is the framework of a 4×2 table in which entries have been made in only three of the eight cells, *i.e.* 400, 140 and 50. All of the totals both for rows and columns have been given. The number of degrees of freedom is the smallest number of cell entries required to enable the table to be completed. In this table three entries are sufficient to enable the gaps to be filled.

					Total
	400 **	** 140	** 50	** **	700 400
Total	600	300	100	100	1,000

Thus, the missing figure in the first column is 200 given by 600 less 400; $300 \text{ less } 140 = 160$ which is the missing figure at the top of the second column. The figure at the top of the third column is $100 - 50 = 50$. The entry in the top row of the final column is 700 less the sum of $(400 + 160 + 50) = 90$. There remains only the figure in the final column in the bottom row which is 100 less the 90 in the upper row which means that it is 10. The reader should insert the additional figures and check that they add up along the rows and vertically.

For a 4×2 tabulation there are three degrees of freedom; thus, $n = (c - 1) (r - 1) = (4 - 1) (2 - 1) = 3$. And, as was stated above, this corresponds to the smallest number of cell entries required to complete the table provided that the totals of rows and columns are known. The reader will appreciate that the three cell figures actually given must be placed in positions within the table that enable one to complete the calculations. The relationship between the number of cells and the value of chi-squared should also be apparent. To the extent that the differences are squared so that they are all positive, it follows that the larger the number of cells in the table, the larger will be the resultant χ^2 value. A glance at the table of the distribution of that statistic reveals how at any level of probability the tabulated value of chi-squared increases with every increase in the number of degrees of freedom.

The chi-squared test is extensively used in the field of social statistics where data are so often classified by reference to possession of attributes. The problem is usually to determine the probability that there is an association within a sample between two attributes, such as smoking and lung cancer or between social class and sickness rates or the infant mortality rate. As was noted in the chapter on correlation, the fact that a coefficient of correlation indicates a close relationship between two variables is not at the same time any explanation of that relationship. In the same way, a set of data may yield a value of chi-squared which is significant at a high level of significance, but this provides no evidence of the nature of the association. The calculation of statistics such as the coefficient of correlation or chi-squared should only be undertaken when the data have been carefully studied and grounds for believing some relationship or association have been established. As has been observed on many occasions, any damned fool can calculate; to interpret the results correctly is another matter altogether!

Conclusions

It is not suggested that, equipped with this limited survey of significance testing, the reader is now equipped to venture forth and assess the validity of any sample data which may come his way! The reason for devoting so much space to this topic is first, that it is a reflection of the outstanding importance of this topic in statistical work. Second, it provides a reminder of the emphasis that must be placed upon the quality of the data derived from sample enquiries. Occasionally sample data are biased and the results of the significance test may conflict with both knowledge of the population and common sense.

In that case it is better to reject the entire data rather than the null hypothesis! The prospective examination candidate need not concern himself with the reliability of the data. Usually the examination question is concerned primarily with testing the candidate's ability to apply the test. Sometimes, however, he will also be asked to comment upon his results. He is not likely to lose marks if he draws attention to the fact first, that the sample is either rather small as for example in the previous illustration, or adequate as in the preceding illustration, and second to emphasize the importance of supporting the results of the test with other evidence if available. Remember that there is always a small probability of what was termed a Type 1 error. It is also helpful, since sometimes it is asked by the examiner, if the candidate can explain in simple terms the basis of the test. At the end of this chapter a number of past examination questions have been selected and suggestions offered for their solution. They should be studied.

Before commencing to work out the various examination questions on significance testing which follow, a brief recapitulation of the salient points of this chapter may help the reader put his thoughts on the subject into some sort of order. The first point to remember is that *no* sample can provide a perfect replica of the population from which it has been drawn. As a general rule, provided the sample is random, then the bigger the sample the greater the confidence one may have in the results. This is true whether the sample statistic is being used as an estimate of the parameter of the population from which the sample was drawn, or for the purpose of testing an hypothesis based upon sample data. For estimation purposes one derives an interval estimate at a given level of confidence. In the case of testing an hypothesis, one starts with the null hypothesis and then decides whether or not the evidence of the result of the significance test strengthens your belief in it enough to accept the null hypothesis or so weakens it as to persuade you to reject it. The criterion for acceptance and rejection is provided by the level of significance used and this, let it be remembered, should always be decided at the start of the experiment or survey. Lastly, remember that no matter how improbable a result may be derived from applying the significance test, there is no certainty that it is wrong. In sample statistics anything is possible in the way of a result. Some outcomes are very much less probable than others but, occasionally, they occur and may lead to a Type II error. What the statistician has to do is to decide, to the best of his knowledge of the data and the evidence of his statistical analysis, what decision he should take on the basis of his findings given the degree of uncertainty that exists. In the matter of statistical inference, as the interpretation of sample statistics is termed, there is in the last resort always an element of judgement.

General

The interpretation of sample statistics is the most important branch of statistical method. For this reason, only the most elementary examination papers will not include questions on estimation and/or significance tests. The following selection of questions illustrates the main type of question set. First, there is the basic question on estimation in which the candidate is usually required to calculate the confidence interval or limits for a sample statistic such as a mean or proportion at a specified level of confidence. Increasingly nowadays a further part of the question asks for an explanation of such a confidence interval; Question 1 is typical in this respect. Alternatively, as in Question 2, the candidate is required first to calculate the sample statistic from a distribution and then the standard error before deriving the confidence interval. Another variant on this type of question is to ask, as in Question 7, to test whether the sample could have come from a population with a specified mean or proportion. This is another way of asking for the derivation of the confidence interval but also enables the examiner to judge whether the candidate understands the technique.

A second type of question involves the use of significance tests such as the difference between two sample means or percentages. Question 3 is an example of the simpler form of this question and, with this type of question too, examiners tend to ask for an explanation of the basis of the significance test. Question 6, although slightly wrapped up in a prose passage so that the relevant figures have first to be derived, is another question of the same kind. Here too an explanation is asked for. Question 9 is similar to Question 5, in which the candidate first calculates the sample statistic and is then required to determine whether the sample from which it was derived could have been drawn from a specified population with a given parameter. This is quite a popular type of question since it enables the examiner to test also the candidate's understanding and ability to calculate the mean and standard deviation at the same time.

The third type of question involves the use of the chi-squared distribution. Whether the data consist of a simple 2×2 table (often referred to as a contingency table) or a more detailed tabulation, *e.g.* 4×3, the principles are the same. The main need is for the candidate to remember how to calculate the expected value for each cell of the table. With this type of question too, candidates are often asked for some explanation. Since the mathematical basis of chi-squared is extremely complex, all that is required is a statement of the underlying principle, *i.e.* that we test the hypothesis that the variations between the actual, *i.e.* observed values and the corresponding expected values can be attributed to random sampling variation. Our decision is based upon whether the calculated value of chi-squared either exceeds or is less than the values of chi-squared at a predetermined level of significance, *e.g.* 5 per cent, given in the tables. If larger, then the differences are regarded as statistically significant; if not, then the differences can reasonably be attributed to chance or sampling variations.

In sum, the prospective examinee must not content himself with learning just what calculations to perform; he must also ensure that he understands why and what he is doing. There is no need to write pages in the examination on this point. It will help to learn and to remember if the student drafts for himself a short paragraph appropriate to each type of problem, before the examination!

Questions

1. Over the past eight years the proportion of students in a very large firm passing their final examination at first attempt has averaged 40 per cent. This year, for the first time, all candidates were sent to special pre-examination courses and the proportion of candidates who were successful was 50 per cent out of the 70 who sat. The senior partner is impressed with the result and is now urging that in future all finalists should attend similar courses.

Indicate, in the form of a report, to what extent the statistics support the senior partner's argument. In drafting the report you should bear in mind that it will be read by some partners who have had no statistical training.

2. Age Distribution of Employed Women.

Age	Percentage
16–24	17·4
25–34	20·2
35–44	22·9
45–54	21·2
55–64	18·3
Sample size 7,391	100·0

(a) Calculate the arithmetic mean and the standard deviation of the above data.

(b) Calculate the 95 per cent confidence interval for the mean age of all employed women.

(c) Discuss the theoretical basis of the establishment of confidence intervals.

3. Your company employs 2,500 men and 1,750 women. A random sample survey of one in five of the employees was carried out to test opinion about the adoption of a new incentive payments scheme. Of those interviewed 320 men and 245 women were in favour. You are required to:

(a) test the hypothesis that there is a statistically significant difference between the reactions of the two sexes to the proposed scheme;

(b) explain the basis of the statistical test of significance employed in part (a).

4. The following data relate to the number of years a school has been established and the number of pupils in the upper sixth studying 'A' level subjects:

	Arts	Science	Social Studies
Schools established within last six years	13	48	26
Schools established over 100 years ago	23	37	20

Assuming the data are obtained from a random sample examine whether there is any relationship between the period of establishment of the school and the distribution of pupils studying Arts, Science and Social Studies. Discuss your results. Explain the reasoning underlying the test you have employed.

5. Age Distribution of Elderly People.

Age	Percentage
65–69	34·6
70–74	29·4
75–79	20·0
80–84	11·0
85 and over	5·0
	100·0

(a) Calculate the arithmetic mean and the standard deviation for the above distribution.

(b) Assuming the data to be based upon a randomly drawn sample, test whether the mean age differs significantly from a population mean age of people over 65 of 73·8 years.

(c) Explain the reasoning underlying the test.

6. At a treatment centre for addicts of dangerous drugs two treatments, A and B, are administered. Out of 80 addicts given treatment A, 43 had not reverted to drug-taking within one year of leaving the treatment centre. For addicts given treatment B, 55 out of 120 were still free of drug-taking one year after leaving the centre. Carry out an appropriate test to examine whether the difference between the percentages of the two groups who had not reverted to drugs within one year is statistically significant.

7.

Age		Percentage of households
	Under 30	12
30 and ,, 40		18
40 ,, ,, 50		20
50 ,, ,, 60		18
60 ,, ,, 65		10
65 ,, ,, 70		9
70 ,, ,, 75		6
75 or more		7
		100 (n = 7,009)

(a) Calculate the mean and standard deviation of this distribution.

(b) In 1966 the average age of the head of the household was 51·5 years. Is there any evidence that the average age of the head of household has changed between 1966 and 1969 when the above sample data were collected?

(c) Discuss the theoretical reasoning behind the test which seeks to examine whether a mean calculated from a simple random sample differs from a specified value.

8.

Desired social position	Type of school attended			
	Grammar	Comprehensive	Sec. Modern	Total
Middle class	20	59	9	88
Upwardly mobile within working class	8	41	29	78
Stable or downwardly mobile	1	21	14	36
Totals	29	121	52	202

Using the table above, calculate whether there is a significant relationship at the 99 per cent level of confidence between type of school attended and desired future social position.

9. (a) Explain the reasoning underlying a confidence interval.

(b) In the Family Expenditure Survey 1969 it was found that of 426 households in the East Midlands Region 243 owned a refrigerator. Assuming this information was obtained from a random sample calculate a 95 per cent confidence interval for the percentage of households in the East Midlands owning a refrigerator.

(c) The percentage of households in the rest of the United Kingdom with a refrigerator was 61·5. Is there any statistically significant evidence that a lower proportion of households in the East Midlands own a refrigerator?

10. A study of undergraduates in higher education showed that they had come from the following social classes:

Parental Occupation	Type of Institution		
	Oxbridge	Other University	Polytechnic
Professional	56	46	48
Managerial	27	19	29
Manual	17	15	43

(a) Examine the proposition that the differences in the class composition of undergraduates at these various types of institution are statistically significant.

(b) Interpret your results and explain the reasoning behind the test you chose.

Answers

Answer to Question 1

The essence of this particular question is whether it is reasonable to assume that a sample with $p = 50$ per cent could be drawn at random from a population (based upon the last eight years' results) with $p = 40$ per cent. To answer this question calculate the standard error of the sample percentage from the formula $\sqrt{\frac{pq}{n}}$.

Thus $\sqrt{\frac{50 \times 50}{70}} = \sqrt{35 \cdot 7} = 5 \cdot 97$ and the confidence limits at the 95 per cent level are given by $50 \pm 1 \cdot 96 (5 \cdot 97) = 50 \pm 11 \cdot 7$ or $38 \cdot 3$ to $61 \cdot 7$ which limits include the population p of 40 per cent. It must be concluded therefore that this year's pass rate of 50 per cent could have occurred by chance and, as far as the evidence of the significance test is concerned, it cannot be assumed that the pre-examination course was responsible for the higher pass rate. It would be sensible in the examination to point out that judgement should be suspended pending another year or two in which candidates continued to attend such courses to learn whether the pass rate remained consistently higher than that recorded in the previous eight years.

As far as the report is concerned two points should be made. The first is as above, *i.e.* the result and the interpretation of the result. The other part of the report should explain the reasoning behind the test, *i.e.* is the difference between the two percentages so large that it is unlikely to have arisen by chance? Emphasise that there can be no 100 per cent certainty; only a judgement based upon the result of the test at the pre-determined probability level which in this case, signifies that the conclusion from the test could be wrong although the probability of this wrong conclusion is less than 1 in 20.

Answer to Question 2

First calculate the mean and standard deviation. In the workings below note that the class interval 16–24 is one year less than for all the other classes. In the calculation it has been treated as the same, *i.e.* 10 years, since the consequent error will be very small. But, if you do this in the examination, point it out to the examiner otherwise you may lose marks because he believes you have not noticed the difference!

Age (x)	f	d=10	fd	fd²
16–24	174	−2	−348	696
25–34	202	−1	−202	202
35–44	229	=	=	=
45–54	212	+1	+212	212
55–64	183	+2	+366	732
	1,000		+ 28	1,842

$$\bar{x} = x' + \frac{\Sigma fd}{\Sigma f} \times \text{c.i.} = 40 + \frac{28}{1,000} \times 10 = 40.28 \text{ years}$$

$$\sigma^2 = \frac{1,842}{1,000} - \left(\frac{28}{1,000}\right)^2 = 1.842 - (.028)^2$$

$$\sigma = \sqrt{1.841} \times \text{c.i.} = 1.35 \times 10 = 13.5 \text{ years}$$

$$\text{s.e.} = \frac{\sigma}{\sqrt{n}} = \frac{13.5}{\sqrt{1,000}} = \frac{13.5}{31.6} = 0.43$$

$$
\begin{aligned}
95 \text{ per cent confidence interval} &= 40.28 \pm 1.96 \ (0.43) \\
&= 40.28 \pm \ .84 \\
&= 39.44 - 41.12
\end{aligned}
$$

Note that having calculated the mean and the standard deviation, the next stage is to calculate the standard error of the mean from the formula $\frac{\text{s.d.}}{\sqrt{n}}$ Then, given that the 95 per cent level of confidence is required, the interval is given by 1·96 (s.e.).

As for part (c) it will be sufficient to point out that a succession of sample means will tend to distribute themselves normally about their own mean which is equal to the mean of the population from which the samples are drawn. Note that the population itself need *not* be normally distributed as so many candidates seem to believe! From our knowledge of the sampling distribution we can estimate the probability that the mean of any one sample will deviate more than a given extent from the population mean. The confidence interval indicates, at a given level of probability, the likelihood that it will contain the population mean and, in this way, the population parameter, in this case the mean can be estimated from the sample statistic, *i.e.* sample mean.

Answer to Question 3
This is a simple question involving the calculation of the standard error of the difference between two percentages. The latter are the proportions of men and women respectively who vote for the proposed scheme.

These percentages are derived by expressing the two figures of support, *i.e.* 320 men and 245 women as percentages of the number in each sample, *i.e.* 20 per cent of 2,500 men and of 1,750 women. In other words, 320/500 men and 245/350 women which equal 64 and 70 per cent respectively.

The s.e. of the difference between means is given by the formula

$$\sqrt{\frac{pq}{n} + \frac{pq}{n}} = \sqrt{\frac{64 \times 36}{500} + \frac{70 \times 30}{350}} = \sqrt{\frac{2,304}{500} + \frac{2,100}{350}}$$

$$\text{S.e.} = \sqrt{4.608 + 6.0} = \sqrt{10.608} = 3.256$$

The observed difference of $70 - 64$ is divided by the standard error which gives a result of 1·84. This is less than 1·96 which would indicate that the observed difference could be expected to arise as a result of sampling variation about 5 in 100 times. If this is to be the criterion (strictly speaking, this should be decided before carrying out the test) then it must be concluded that the difference in the proportion of men and women supporting the scheme can quite reasonably be attributed to sampling variation and is therefore not statistically significant.

Answer to Question 4

This 3×2 table requires the application of the chi-squared test. Set out the complete table as follows:

	Arts	Sciences	Social Studies	Total
Schools established in last six years	13	48	26	87
Schools over 100 years old	23	37	20	80
Totals	36	85	46	167

The reasoning underlying the chi-squared test rests on the assumption that any differences between the three columns in respect of their composition regarding the type of school can be explained by random sampling variation, *i.e.* we set up the null hypothesis. If such random variation did not arise then the composition of each column as between the two types of school would be the same as in the total column, *i.e.* in the ratio of 87:80. Such variation does, however, arise and the problem is to determine whether its extent is greater than can reasonably be attributed to random variation. This is done by calculating a value for the statistic chi-squared, which is done by calculating and then aggregating the differences between the actual cell values in the table and the expected values. If the calculated value of chi-squared is greater than the value which would arise at a given level of probability from random variation, then we conclude that the differences are statistically significant.

To arrive at the expected values in the top row, apply the fraction from the total column, *i.e.* 87/167 to the column totals, *i.e.* 36, 85 and 46. If this is done then the expected values for those three cells are 19, 44 and 24. It would be sufficient to subtract these figures from the column totals to obtain the expected values for the second row, *i.e.* in place of 23, 37 and 20 we would have, 17, 41 and 22. In practice, because there is always the chance of making an arithmetic slip in the first set of calculations, it is worth while calculating the second row by using the fraction 80/167 in the total column on all the column totals. The sum of the expected values must, of course, equal the sum of the rows and columns in the original table with the observed values.

Having obtained these expected values it is easiest to use a simple columnar arrangement as below for the rest of the calculations. It is remarkable how often one sees examination scripts in which the candidate has scrawled figures all over the paper, without any prior arrangement, so that it is hardly surprising when mistakes occur. Keep the workings neat and tidy; it promotes accuracy and, if a mistake has arisen, it is easier to find.

O	E	$O-E$	$(O-E)^2$	$(O-E)^2 \div E$
13	19	-6	36	1·89
23	17	6	36	2·12
48	44	4	16	0·36
37	41	-4	16	0·39
26	24	2	4	0·17
20	22	-2	4	0·18
			$\chi^2 =$	5·11

The calculated value of chi-squared is well within the limit of 6·00 which is the value of chi-squared appropriate to 2 degrees of freedom where $P = 0.05$. In other words, the differences between the observed and expected values in the cells of the table could quite easily have arisen as the result of sampling variation. Hence the difference between schools is not significant.

Answer to Question 5

The calculation of the mean and standard deviation for this distribution is straightforward since it may reasonably be assumed that using the same class interval for the last class of '85 and over' will not markedly affect the mean or standard deviation. The mean of the distribution is 73·1 years and the standard deviation 3·72.

The standard error of the mean is given by $\frac{3·72}{\sqrt{100}} = 0·372$ and the 95 per cent confidence interval is therefore $73·1 \pm 1·96 (·372) = 73·1 \pm 0·73$ which is 72·37 to 73·81.

The essence of part (*b*) is whether the above sample, with a mean of 73·1 years, could have come from a population with a mean of 73·8 years. From the confidence interval it is clear that at the 95 per cent level the interval would just include the parameter of 73·8. In short, the difference is not statistically significant.

Answer to Question 6

This is much the same as Question 3 where the figures need first to be converted into percentages and then the standard error of the difference between the two percentages has to be obtained. Thus, with Treatment A, $n=80$ and p (successes) $=43$ so that the proportion p is $43/80=53·7$. For Treatment B $n=120$ and the number of successes $p=55$. The proportion p in this case is $55/120=45·8$.

The s.e. of the difference between the two proportions is:

$$\sqrt{\frac{53·7 \times 46·3}{80} + \frac{45·8 \times 54·2}{120}} = \sqrt{\frac{2,486}{80} + \frac{2,482}{120}}$$

$$=\sqrt{31·10+20·69}=\sqrt{51·79}=7·2 \text{ to one place of decimals.}$$

The observed difference between the proportions in the two samples A and B is $53·7-45·8=7·9$ which is only marginally larger than the standard error of 7·2. It must be concluded, therefore, that the difference between the two treatments is not statistically significant. For that to be the case at the 5 per cent level of significance, the observed difference would need to be at least twice as large, *i.e.* 1·96 times the standard error.

Answer to Question 7

The calculation of the mean and s.d. is straightforward except for one point. While the first four classes have an interval of 10 years – the lower limit of the first open-ended class under 30 is assumed to be 20 – the last four classes have an interval of 5 years. To make it possible to use an arbitrary origin and units based upon the class interval, let each deviation equal 2·5. The result in terms of the deviation is evident from the workings hereunder.

Age	f	$d'=2·5$	fd'	fd^2
Under 30	12	−12	−144	1,728
30–40	18	−8	−144	1,152
40–50	20	−4	−80	320
50–60	18	=	=	
60–65	10	+3	30	90
65–70	9	+5	45	225
70–75	6	+7	42	294
75 or more	7	+9	63	567
	100		−188	4,376

$$\bar{x}=55+\left(\frac{-188}{100}\right)2·5=55-4·7=50·3 \text{ years}$$

$$\frac{\sigma}{2·5}=\sqrt{\frac{4,376}{100}-\left(\frac{-188}{100}\right)^2}=\sqrt{43·76-3·53}$$

$$= \sqrt{40 \cdot 23} = 6 \cdot 34$$

$$\sigma = 6 \cdot 34 \times 2 \cdot 5 = 15 \cdot 85 \text{ years}$$

$$\text{s.e.} = \frac{\sigma}{\sqrt{n}} = \frac{15 \cdot 85}{\sqrt{7,009}} = \cdot 0023$$

Having calculated the standard error of the mean using the actual sample size of 7,009 and not 100 it is simple to calculate the confidence interval which is given at the 95 per cent level. The interval is very small indeed given the exceptionally large sample size (7009), *i.e.* it is only ·002 years either side of the sample mean. When this is related to the difference between the sample mean of 50·3 (from the sample taken in 1969) and the population mean in 1966 of 51·5, it is clear that the probability that the sample with a mean of 50·3 came from a population with a mean age of 51·5 is extremely remote. Thus, in answer to the question, has the average age of the population changed in the three years between the census and sample, we can say 'yes' with every confidence.

As far as part (iii) is concerned, all that need be said is that it is highly improbable that the sampling distribution of sample means where the sample is taken from a population with a mean age of 51·5 would contain a sample with a mean of 50·3 years. This cannot be stated with 100 per cent certainty, but the odds on that event are so remote that they can be ignored.

Answer to Question 8

This question involving a chi-squared test is much the same as Question 4 above, the only difference being that there the table was 3×2 and in this case it is 3×3. As in the previous example, it is assumed that the distribution within the columns should correspond to that in the total column, the differences arising, it is assumed for purposes of the null hypothesis, from sampling variation. First obtain the expected values from the following table:

Desired social position	Type of school attended						Total
	Grammar		Comprehensive		Sec. Modern		
	O	E	O	E	O	E	
Middle class	20	13	59	53	9	23	88
Upwardly mobile within middle class	8	11	41	47	29	20	78
Stable or downwardly mobile	1	5	21	21	14	9	36
	29		121		52		202

As before, the expected values in each column are derived by apportioning the total of each column by reference to the total column distribution. Thus, the three figures in the first column will be obtained by $\frac{88}{202} \times 29$, $\frac{78}{202} \times 29$ and $\frac{36}{202} \times 29$.

The same procedure is followed for the expected values in the columns headed Comprehensive and Sec. Modern, but, in place of the multiplier 29, we use there 121 and 52. The results if set out as in Q.4 yield a value of chi-squared of 24·59. The number of degrees of freedom is 4, *i.e.* (c-1) (r-1) and reference to the table of chi-squared values shows that for 4 d.f. a value of 13·277 would indicate that the probability of such differences between the observed and expected values arising by chance is 1 in 100. The calculated value of 24·59 is far in excess of that value, which represents the 99 per cent level, and it must be concluded that the type of school attended and the pupil's social ambitions are strongly associated. In other words, the null hypothesis is rejected.

Answer to Question 9

This question is similar to the first question in which a sample percentage is compared with a population percentage and the question asked whether the sample came from that particular population. If 243 out of 426 households in the East Midlands sample own a refrigerator, then the proportion with such a consumer durable is given by $\frac{243}{426} \times 100 = 57 \cdot 0$ per cent. The standard error of that percentage is given by the formula $\sqrt{\frac{pq}{n}}$ which, by substitution, reads $\sqrt{\frac{57 \times 43}{426}} = 5 \cdot 75$. The 95 per cent confidence interval for the sample proportion is given by $57 \pm 1 \cdot 96 \, (5 \cdot 75) = 57 \pm 11 \cdot 27 = 45 \cdot 73$ to $68 \cdot 27$.

The proportion of households in the rest of the United Kingdom owning such a durable is $61 \cdot 5$ which falls within the confidence interval. It can therefore be concluded that there is no difference between the East Midlands and the rest of the United Kingdom in respect of ownership of this particular consumer durable.

Answer to Question 10

This is a straightforward question on chi-squared; the arithmetic involved in deriving the expected values is very easy; the student should note that the distribution in the total column requires half and then quarter and another quarter of the three column totals.

	Oxbridge	Other Universities	Polytechnics	Total
Professional	56	46	48	150
Managerial	27	19	29	75
Manual	17	15	43	75
Totals	100	80	120	300

As noted above, the expected values are easy to obtain: the fractions 150/300 × 100 in the first column for Professional, 75/300 × 100 for managerial and the same for manual. The same fractions apply to the other two columns with the results given hereunder.

O	E	(O-E)	(O-E)²	$\frac{(O-E)^2}{E}$	degrees of freedom
56	50	6	36	0·72	(c-1) (r-1)
27	25	2	4	0·16	(3-1) (3-1)=4
17	25	− 8	64	2·56	
46	40	6	36	0·90	
19	20	− 1	1	·05	
15	20	− 5	25	1·25	
48	60	−12	144	2·40	
29	30	− 1	1	·03	
43	30	13	169	5·63	
				13·70	

With 4 degrees of freedom a value of chi-squared of 13·70 is in excess of the value which could be expected to arise by chance 1 in 100 times. The class composition of undergraduates at these institutions is obviously associated with the type of institution. The differences are statistically significant. The comments on (ii) should follow the remarks made in Question 4 and Question 8.

CHAPTER XV

SAMPLE DESIGN

In statistical work the purpose of sampling is to gain information about the nature and characteristics of the population from which the sample is drawn. In the two preceding chapters we have seen that a sample statistic is no more than an estimate of the corresponding population parameter. The extent to which the sample statistic may differ from the parameter based on a complete count or census is measured by the sampling error. The statistician is concerned with the *precision* of the sample statistic and modern sampling theory enables him to measure the precision or reliability of the statistic.

The statistic derived from a sample is also affected by the process of selection from a population. If the final sample is not the result of a strictly random selection, but is affected by practical difficulties in the selection procedure which change the probabilities of selecting individuals, then the resulting estimate will not tend to the value in the population being sought but to some other value, relating to another population. The difference between these values is a measure of *sampling bias* and suggests that the process of selection is inadequate. Thus, as well as a concern with the *precision* of a sample statistic, the statistician is, in most cases, interested in producing *unbiased* estimates.

Considering first, ways of improving the precision of sample estimates, we know from our sampling theory that by increasing the sample size it is possible to increase the precision of the result. The majority of sample surveys are, however, quite expensive undertakings. To increase the sample size to the extent required to achieve any substantial gain in precision would entail heavy additional expenditure. Furthermore, it would mean more interviews, more schedules to edit, more data to process. Thus the interval of time between the survey and the production of its results would be increased. Since one of the objects of sampling is to save time and money, merely increasing the sample size would be self-defeating policy. For such reasons statisticians in recent times have devoted much effort to devising methods whereby the precision of sample results may be improved. This can be done by using specially constructed samples, but underlying all these sample designs, as they are known, is the basic principle of random sampling. However complex the sample design may be, the selection of the sample units must ultimately be made in accordance with some random process.[1] The designing of samples is a highly specialised branch of statistics; the design appropriate to one survey may be quite unsuited to another. The purpose of this chapter is to outline in simple terms the basic notions underlying the choice of sample used in various types of sample enquiry.

Random Sampling

Stress has been laid on the need to ensure that all samples should be random. What is meant by 'random' in this context? It will be recalled that the term does not possess the usual meaning, *i.e.* haphazard, when applied to sampling. For the statistician a sample is random only when every unit in the population from which the sample was selected and which it is intended to represent, had a calculable and 'non-zero' chance of selection. Even the reader with little understanding of mathematics will appreciate that it is important to introduce the term 'non-zero' into this definition. If the chances of inclusion of any units are 'zero', then this means that the sample cannot possibly represent the entire population which is the object of the exercise. The simplest method of sampling is that in which every population unit has the same chance of inclusion in the sample. But, as will be seen later, many samples are designed in such a way as to ensure that some types of units in the population will be chosen more often than certain other groups of units. But, however small the chances of selection for any unit may be, they must always be 'non-zero'.

To ensure random selection, various methods of selection of units from the population have been devised. The simplest is to number all the population units and then to draw, in lottery fashion, counters bearing the corresponding numbers of the selected numbers determining the choice of sampling units. This method is known as simple random sampling, in which every unit in the population has an equal chance of selection. This method is suitable where the population is relatively small and where the sampling frame is complete. As a matter of interest, it should be noted that even such an apparently foolproof method may give biased results. Professor Kendall has instanced the case where a particular colour of counter proved to be more slippery than those made from other colours, with the result that biased results were obtained. Instead of using the lottery method of selecting numbers from a hat, an alternative method is to use a table of random sampling numbers. Such tables have been specially prepared and comprise a series of digits drawn up in such

---

[1] Strictly speaking this statement does not apply to quota samples which are discussed on p. 372. All other samples must be random. See below.

a way that all the numbers are produced with equal frequency. An illustration of part of such a table is given in Yule and Kendall's book[1] on page 379. The electronic machine known as ERNIE, used for selecting Premium Bond Winners, is really no more than a machine which produces random numbers in such a way that every valid bond held by a member of the public at the time of the 'draw' has the same chance as any other.

Systematic Sampling

In practice, simple random sampling is not practicable unless there is a sampling frame and the population is fairly small, e.g. in experimental work, when a sample of a group of results is to be chosen. For most practical work it is easier to select every nth item in a list of the population, the first of the sample units being selected by some random process. This method is termed systematic, or quasi-random sampling. Thus, if the lists comprise a population of, say, 25,000 and the sample required is 500, then the selection of every fiftieth item will yield the required sample. The starting point is determined by selecting at random a number between 1 and 50. Thus, if 37 turns up, the thirty-seventh item in the list is the first, the eighty-seventh and one-hundred-and-thirty-seventh, the second and third in the sample, and so on. Thus, when the Government Social Survey carried out its enquiry among ex-miners suffering from pneumoconiosis, the first name was selected by picking a number between 1 and 7 and thenceafter every seventh card was selected from the files of the pension authority. If the 'list' is in the form of a card index, there is no need to count the intervening cards if the interval is large. By setting a ruler across the file, the card coinciding with a predetermined interval, e.g. every $3\frac{1}{2}$ inches, can be selected.

An illustration of the official use of systematic sampling was provided in 1960 by the Government Social Survey in an investigation into housing.[2] The sample for the Greater London area – a single-stage systematic sample – was used again in 1963 in an enquiry into privately rented accommodation for the Milner-Holland Committee.[3] A selection of domestic rateable units was made from the valuation lists maintained by the Inland Revenue with every eight hundredth rateable unit throughout the Greater London conurbation being selected after a random start. This resulted in a sample of 2,999 rateable units all of which were included in the 1960 investigation. In 1963, the concern was with privately rented accommodation

[1] *Introduction to the Theory of Statistics.* 14th edition. pp. 376–9.
[2] *The Housing Situation in 1960.* By P. G. Gray and R. Russell. 'The Social Survey'.
[3] Report of The Committee on Housing in Greater London. Cmnd. 2605. Appendix V.

and initially 1,201 rateable units were included; those which in the 1960 survey were said to contain one or more households privately renting its accommodation.

Strictly speaking, systematic or quasi-random sampling is not truly random. This is because once the initial starting point has been determined, it follows that the remainder of the items selected for the sample are predetermined by the constant interval. Thus, if we are selecting every twentieth address from a street list, the first is admittedly chosen by random methods, but the remainder are thence-after pre-selected. For this method of sampling too, a complete sampling frame is necessary. Nevertheless, because the first unit is chosen at random and thus all other units, this form of sampling approximates sufficiently closely to pure random sampling to justify its widespread employment. The list or sampling frame should be checked to see whether it has been previously arranged in such a way that a particular type of unit may occur at the appropriate interval and therefore be over-represented in the sample. Generally speaking, street-lists and alphabetical lists of names are free from such bias, *i.e.* non-randomness in the arrangement of the charac-teristic.

Stratified Sampling

So far it has been assumed that the population to be sampled consists of a single homogeneous group, *e.g.* ex-miners disabled by pneumoconiosis. In many surveys the population is far from homo-geneous, but markedly heterogeneous. This applies to the adult population of a country which comprises both men and women in different social circumstances and indeed to the population of rate-able units, *e.g.* houses in Greater London. Because it can be reason-ably assumed that the quality of housing measured in terms of age of the unit and the amenities found in it is likely to vary from inner to outer London and from borough to borough, a more accurate reflection of the overall housing situation in Greater London would be achieved by making sure that rateable units in all the London boroughs are included in the sample, in the proportion in which they are found in the population.

If the population of rateable units can be classified by borough, both in the aggregate so that we know the proportions of units in each borough and we can also identify for each rateable unit the borough to which it belongs, then the sample of rateable units can be stratified by borough. The result will be that each borough will be represented in the correct proportion within the sample. Such a sample is known as a *proportionate stratified* sample and the individual boroughs or groups of similar boroughs are known as stratum.[1]

Stratified samples can be drawn without first stratifying the population list and selecting from each stratum. Provided the relative sizes of the strata one to another are known, the sample members can be divided among the strata as they are drawn. As soon as the quota for any stratum is complete, any further items of that type are rejected and sampling continues until each stratum has its quota. This method will probably entail sampling a larger number than would be necessary if the population had been classified into its various strata at the outset. If the population can be so classified, then a stratified sample, *i.e.* one made of random samples from each of the 'stratum' is likely to be more representative of the population than any other sample of that size. The greater the degree of homogeneity of each stratum, the better and the smaller the overall sample can be. However, even if the population is not stratified, a random sample may nevertheless reproduce the distribution of the characteristic within the population. In short, stratification of the sample *may* be derived automatically.

A little thought will reveal why a sample drawn from a previously stratified population is more likely to be 'representative' than a similar-sized random sample drawn without prior stratification of the population. When the population is stratified the statistician is in effect drawing a random sample from each stratum or homogeneous sub-population. Within each stratum random sampling errors must be taken into account. But the composition of the total sample, as far as its distribution *between* the various strata is concerned, corresponds with that of the population – because the statistician has arranged it so. In the case of a simple random sample, *i.e.* one without stratification, from that population two sets of sampling errors must be taken into account. The first are those *within* each stratum – as in the case of the sub-populations or strata within a stratified sample. Further sampling errors, however, arise in the simple random sample because the distribution of units as *between* the various strata in that sample may not correspond with that of the population. It is this risk which prior stratification eliminates. The simple random sample *may* yield the correct composition of units from the various strata; but we cannot be certain. Therefore, when the sampling error for a simple random sample is computed, it is always greater than in the case of an *equal-sized* stratified sample.

A stratified sample can only be drawn if the statistician is in possession of information relating to the distribution in the population of the variable used for stratification *and* if he can identify for

---

[1] This point is discussed more fully on pp. 362-3.

each sampling unit the stratum from which it comes. For example, if a survey of farms in England and Wales is to be undertaken, then it is clearly relevant to ensure that all sizes are properly represented in the sample. This is possible because the Ministry of Agriculture has a complete list of farms together with their sizes. Thus, the number of farms of different sizes in the population can be determined and, hence the proportion of each size to be included in the sample. Moreover, on selection, each farm can be allocated to its appropriate stratum. On the other hand, stratification of the adult population of England and Wales is much more difficult. Although information from the decennial Census of Population provides the basis for dividing the population into strata according to sex, age and socio-economic group, the most commonly used list for the selection of the sample – the Electoral Register – does not identify individuals by these characteristics and, therefore, a sample of the general adult population cannot be stratified by these variables at the time of selection.

The Social Survey developed two indices which were employed for the purposes of stratifying areas and, hence, of the populations living within them. The first of these – the 'J' Index is no longer used because changes in the qualifications for jury service has eliminated the value of the index as a measure of the socio-economic status of an area. Originally, the 'J' or Juror Index was based on the proportion of the population which possessed a jury qualification. An examination of the Electoral Register for each polling district reveals that certain names are preceded by the letter 'J', which implies that those individuals are liable for jury service. This qualification was previously dependent upon ownership or occupation of property above a certain rateable value. In other words, the larger the proportion of 'J' names in an electoral district, the higher is the number of occupiers and owners of property of a rateable value over certain limits. Since ownership or occupation is correlated with income and social status, a high value for the 'J' Index in any area reflected a corresponding social class.[1]

The second is the Industrial index, which serves much the same purpose. In this case the rateable value of an area attributable to industrial hereditaments and transport undertakings is expressed as a proportion of the total rateable value of that area. The Social Survey has ascertained that in the provinces there is a significant degree of correlation between the degree of 'industrialisation' and the proportion of the population in the highest income group. This index, however, is not suitable for the London area and an amended

[1] The Social Survey report on this index is contained in a paper by Gray, Corbett and Jones entitled 'The Proportion of Jurors as an Index of the Economic Status of a District', published by the Central Office of Information.

form of the index is therefore employed. Here the rating areas are classified according to the rateable value per head of the inhabitants within each area. The higher the per capita rateable value, the wealthier is the district. These latter indices, but not the Juror index, of stratification are nowadays regularly employed by the Government Social Survey and other organisations in the preparation of their samples.

The difficulty with stratified sampling is that it is not usual for the population lists to be stratified. In every survey, therefore, the sampling units may have to be stratified in accordance with that particular factor which is relevant to that survey. Stratification of areas may be based on rateable value per head, on the population per square mile in some sparsely populated areas, or by reference to size, *e.g.* population of urban districts. The stratification factor will depend on what type of stratification will be most useful for the particular survey. For example, before 1969 the sample of Parliamentary constituencies used in the National Readership Survey carried out for the Institute of Practitioners in Advertising was stratified by reference to the ratio of non-Labour to Labour votes cast in the Parliamentary election. The higher the proportion of the Labour vote, the lower the social class of that constituency. Little purpose, however, is served by stratifying a sample by reference to a characteristic or factor which is irrelevant to the survey. For example, a survey among school children to ascertain their TV viewing habits would hardly be improved by stratifying the juvenile population by reference to the political affiliations of the areas in which the children interviewed resided. Stratification by reference to whether they lived in urban or rural communities, and the type of school they attended would be significant for such a purpose.

When describing '*simple*' random sampling the point was made that this method ensured that every unit of the population had an equal chance of selection. When 'random' sampling was first defined, it was stated that this meant that each unit had a calculable non-zero chance of selection. This merely means that all the units have a chance of selection which can be estimated, but it does not signify that all units have equal chances. This is often the case with stratified samples where a larger proportion, or what the statistician terms *sampling fraction*, is taken from one stratum than from another. For example, in the Oxford Institute of Statistic's Savings survey proportionately more rateable units, *i.e.* households, were drawn from the highest income stratum than from the lower rated units. This was done because there are relatively few of the former compared to the others and it was essential to ensure adequate representation of this group in the final sample. When the final results are prepared, adjustments for the difference in the representation of the two strata can be made. This type of sampling is known as sampling with a *variable sampling fraction*, or disproportionate sampling. In the case of a stratified sample, which reflects in the sample the strata as they exist in the population, the fraction will be equal or, to use the statistical terms, *uniform* or *proportionate* for all the strata.

The basic principle of sampling with variable fractions from the different strata of a population is illustrated in Table 34 below. It can be assumed that the survey of household expenditure requires a sample of about 1,000 from an area comprising a population of

TABLE 34

RANDOM AND STRATIFIED SAMPLES WITH VARIABLE SAMPLING FRACTIONS

Social Class	Total Population	Sampling Fraction	Stratified Sample with v.s.f.	Random Sample 1/100
I	4,000	1/25	160	40
II	10,000	1/50	200	100
III	50,000	1/200	250	500
IV	18,000	1/75	240	180
V	12,000	1/75	160	120
	94,000		970	940

94,000. The population can be sub-divided between five strata – each of which it can be assumed is highly homogeneous – but the strata, as can be seen from the illustration are of widely differing sizes. To ensure adequate representation in the sample of each stratum, but more especially of Class I which is important in any survey concerned with household finance, the proportion sampled from each stratum is different. Thus, the sampling fractions range from 1 in 25 in the first stratum to 1 in 200 in the large class III. Thus, in the final sample of 970 households each group is adequately represented so as to enable reliable estimates for each group to be derived. The advantages of this type of sampling with variable sampling fraction are readily apparent by comparing the final column of Table 34 with that showing the stratified sample. A simple random sample, even if all the *between* strata variation was eliminated (see p. 360) would produce a sample in which the most important class was inadequately represented with only 40 households. Given the likely variability within this class, such a small sample might well produce a distorted or biased result. On the other hand, since it has been assumed that each class is reasonably homogeneous, the sub-sample of 500 from Class III is certainly more than enough and would involve unnecessary interviewing to collect more data than were required from that group.

Cluster Sampling

In simple random sampling what is termed the *sampling unit* is the individual unit to which the measurements apply, *e.g.* an adult or a household. The larger the number of sampling units, the greater will be the cost of the survey. Sometimes the cost factor may necessitate a different form of sampling whereby interviewers concentrate all their interviews in a relatively small number of areas or groups. Suppose that a survey is being carried out over a large area in which the population is extremely dispersed. A simple random sample would be quite impracticable. Alternatively, the survey may be concerned with measuring the number of homes with refrigerators in a large area for which there exists no list of these homes, *i.e.* there is no sampling frame. To carry out a census to derive a sampling frame would be very expensive indeed. This was in fact done in the United Kingdom in 1950 as a preliminary to the Census of Distribution which was later to provide a sampling frame for future periodic sample surveys. But usually, where no list or frame exists, systematic random sampling is impossible. Furthermore, where the sampling units are widely scattered, the costs of a simple random sample could be considerable. Suppose, however, in an urban area a few blocks of dwelling houses or localities were selected at random and every individual in each block interviewed. Then, if the blocks when put together form a sample which constitutes a 'representative' group of the population, the statistician will have achieved his objective, *i.e.* a random sample of the entire population.

To meet the problem of costs or inadequate sampling frames in the United States this method of *cluster* sampling, sometimes known as *area* sampling, has been devised. By the use of map references, the entire area to be surveyed is broken down into smaller areas and a number of these areas are selected by random methods. The primary sampling unit is then no longer the individual; it is a group of individuals or households to be found within the selected area. Such groups are termed 'clusters'. Within each area selected every unit, *e.g.* household, may be interviewed. Sometimes only a proportion, say, one in four households, will be interviewed and then it becomes a two-stage sample (see below). Nothing need be known in advance about the area, the number or type of sampling units in it, but by following these procedures the chances of inclusion in the sample can be made the same for all individual units to be found within the area.

The basic problem with this type of sampling method is whether or not the units within the clusters are homogeneous. The danger undoubtedly exists that clusters often tend to comprise people with similar characteristics and, since the statistician is picking out only a few clusters, there are likely to be large fluctuations from sample to sample depending on the degree of homogeneity of the clusters selected. Thus the estimate from a single cluster sample may be less precise than if a simple random sample had been selected. If, however, the individual clusters are heterogeneous, *i.e.* made up of all types of individual, then the final collection of 'clusters' may well constitute a simple random sample. If the clusters are highly homogeneous in their composition, then the reverse is true.

In other words, whereas the statistician who wants to be able to stratify his sample is concerned to ensure that each stratum in the population is homogeneous, the same statistician using cluster sampling would prefer the areas, *i.e.* clusters from which he is sampling, to be heterogeneous. In practice, the statistician using cluster sampling is well advised to take a sample consisting of a large number of small clusters rather than a similar-sized sample containing only a few large clusters.

Cluster sampling has been developed in the United States because it permits surveys to be undertaken with low costs. For example, cluster sampling may be used in the second stage (see below) where, instead of sampling at random from a group of towns, all the interviews are concentrated in one or two, in order to save time and money. This technique is also useful where adequate sampling frames for the relevant populations are not available, *e.g.* in the underdeveloped countries. In this country we are not confronted with the problems of widely dispersed populations, although area sampling was used in the United Kingdom for the Census of Woodlands in 1942 for which it was eminently suited.

Multi-stage Sampling

For most practical purposes, an elaboration of cluster sampling, known as *multi-stage* sampling is used to select from a widely dispersed population. Where the population is dispersed throughout the country, simple random or systematic sampling would prove to be extremely time-consuming and expensive. For example, a sample of 3,000 adults would require using systematic sampling to tick off every 10,000th name in the Electrocal Register! Furthermore, a sample of the electorate drawn by either of these methods would be distributed throughout the length and breadth of the kingdom in such a way that interviewers would spend very much more time travelling from one place to another than in actually interviewing, since they would be required to contact widely scattered respondents.

Clearly it would be advantageous if the interviewing could be so arranged that groups or clusters of respondents were interviewed in certain areas. For example, instead of, say, sixty interviews being dispersed all over Yorkshire, as might well be the case if simple random sampling had been used, could not these same interviews be concentrated in two towns in that area, *e.g.* Darlington and Halifax, or in any other two towns selected *at random* from the towns in the region?

This concentration of interviewing is the primary objective of what is known as multi-stage sampling which, as the name suggests, is no more than a series of samples taken at successive stages, the selection at each stage being made randomly from the cluster at the previous stage. Thus, in the case of a national sample of adults for the purposes of, say a national pre-election opinion poll the adults would need to be considered in clusters which cover the whole country, *e.g.* local authority areas or constituencies. The first stage would be to select, randomly, a number of these clusters and at the second stage, adults would be selected, again randomly, from the clusters selected at the first stage.

Intermediate stages could be introduced which would further concentrate the interviewing by selecting wards or polling districts randomly from the first stage units selected before drawing the sample of adults from the selected wards or polling districts. This would be a three stage sample. At any or all of the stages, the clusters could be stratified, depending on the availability of information for doing so, to increase the precision of the sample estimate. For example, before selecting the first stage local authority areas, they could be stratified by Standard Region[1] and by type of area, *e.g.* urban or rural, for example, to eliminate the possibility of selecting a sample which is concentrated in one part of the country or in one type of area.

It will be seen that the essence of this type of sampling is that a sub-sample is taken, at random, of what is in effect successive groups of clusters. To ensure that ultimately, each individual has an equal chance of selection, it is usual in practice to select the clusters in all but the last stage with a probability *proportionate to their size*. Assume that we have five towns in the region to be sampled, one of which contains 1 million inhabitants, and the others 50,000 apiece. If a simple random sample of those five towns were taken, the chances of the large city being selected would be no better than those of any one of the smaller towns. This means that the individual inhabitants of the city would have a very much smaller chance of selection than the individual people living in the smaller towns. To

[1] Great Britain is currently divided into 8 Standard Regions for England, 2 for Wales and 4 for Scotland.

avoid this situation, the selection of towns, at the first stage, is made with a probability proportionate to their size. This method ensures that the inhabitants of any town, whatever its size, have equal chances of inclusion. The method, in principle, is somewhat similar to numbering of the inhabitants of all towns and then drawing a sample using a table of random numbers. The effect of this procedure is to ensure that all inhabitants, regardless of the size of the community in which they live, have equal chances of being selected.

The sample introduced in 1967 for the annual Family Expenditure Survey is a three-stage stratified design in which the first stage or primary sampling units (psu's) are local authority administrative areas in Great Britain. In each period 168 primary sampling units are used, selected randomly from all the administrative areas in Great Britain, with a probability proportionate to the size of the population in the administrative areas. Before selection, the administrative areas are stratified by a regional factor, by area type and by an economic indicator based on rateable value.

The object of this procedure is to ensure that the final sample of 168 p.s.u's is representative of the whole of Great Britain. The 'regional factor' in this case is the means of ensuring that each region or area of G.B. will be represented. To this end, the country is divided into 14 major strata each comprising a standard region, *e.g.* two parts of Wales, 8 standard regions of England and four parts of Scotland. The second stratification factor, *i.e.* 'area type', breaks down each of the individual regions into four component parts. These are the major provincial conurbations, *i.e.* excluding Greater London (this is incorporated as a region in the first stage), then the urban areas which are outside the conurbations, *e.g.* smaller towns, as well as the grouping of semi-rural areas above a minimum population density measured by persons per acre, and finally all other rural districts. The third 'economic factor' is based on various measures of rateable value within four areas, two in England and Wales and two in Scotland. In the former, the London boroughs are classified by reference to the proportion of domestic property with a rateable value over £200, elsewhere in England and Wales the same proportion is calculated but with a lower limit of £100, In Scotland to classify the local areas the industrialisation index is used, *i.e.* ratio of total rateable value accounted for by industrial property within each urban authority.[1] In the Scottish rural districts, there is a classification by population density. It will be evident from the above outline that the sample of 168 p.s.u's drawn should reflect the characteristics of the whole country in respect of regional differences, urban and rural ways of life and, for all practical purposes, the

[1] As explained on p. 361.

various socio-economic groups within the community since the rateable value of an individual's home is a good indicator of his income.[1]

From each of the 168 selected p.s.u's, *i.e.* local areas, a single second stage unit is randomly chosen so that the fieldwork can be confined to an area capable of being handled by a single interviewer. In urban areas, the second stage units are wards and in rural districts, groups of parishes. The third and final stage consists of the selection of addresses within the chosen wards or parishes, from the Electoral Register. Sixteen addresses are drawn from each.

The sample used in the current National Readership Survey provides a further illustration of the above principles. A two stage sample design is used, involving the selection of 1,200 polling districts as the primary sampling units and, at the second stage, persons aged 16 and over. Before selection, all polling districts are stratified by local authority area, by region, by three area types – conurbation, urban, rural, and for the particular purposes of this survey, by evening newspaper coverage. A socio-economic stratification factor is also used. This factor is the percentage of economically active and retired males in the Registrar-General's socio-economic groups who are described as being in 'professional and managerial' occupations. From these sub-cells, a total of 1,200 sampling points are selected with a probability of selection proportionate to the adult population. A systematic selection is made; that is a fixed sampling interval is used after a random start. At the second stage, a selection of 30 electors is made from the Electoral Register for each of the polling districts selected at the first stage. From the households containing these electors, a further random selection was made of non-electors so that the sample would consist of all persons aged 16 and over.

Sampling Bias

So far, we have been concerned with designing samples in order to produce as precise estimates as the available resources allow. Usually, the introduction of stratification increases the precision of estimates derived from samples compared with simple random sampling, while cluster and, to a lesser extent multi-stage sampling, decreases the precision for a given sample size. On the other hand their cost advantages usually means that a larger sample can be investigated.

What we need to consider now is how far a random sample can be achieved in practice; that is, what processes are likely to alter the probability of selecting individual units so that some units have an

---

[1] The reader will find a readable summary of the sample design in *Statistical News No. 1*. See W. F. Kemsley on 'Re-designing the Family Expenditure Survey'.

unknown and, in some cases, zero chance of being included in a random sample. Sample estimates derived from such samples are said to be biased.

Bias in samples can arise from two factors. The first is inherent in the sample itself. Thus, if the sampling frame used for a particular survey is out-dated, deficient in coverage, units duplicated or omitted, etc., or the drawing of the sample has not followed the rules of random sampling procedures, the sample will be biased. The second factor which introduces bias stems from the fact that the interviewers seldom if ever find it possible to interview all the members in their sample. This arises because either they are unable to make contact with the person listed in the sample of names and addresses or, having established contact the person is unwilling to be interviewed. It is customary to refer both to non-contacts and non-respondents as comprising the problem of 'non-response'. This is discussed below in more detail. For present purposes, however, it is the extent of non-contact, due to the fact that the person to be interviewed may have moved, may have died, or be too ill to be interviewed, that may bias the sample. Usually this group of non-contacts represents a much smaller group than the non-respondents.[1] The immediately relevant point is that, to the extent that the 'effective' sample of respondents is smaller than the original sample, there is the risk of bias.

The Sampling Frame

Before the sample can be drawn, the units of the population under review must be defined. For example, the Electoral Register contains the names of all those entitled to vote in the United Kingdom; each local authority has a rating roll on which all rateable units in its area, *i.e.* houses, flats, shops, etc., are listed; every school will have registers containing the names of all the children enrolled for attendance. Such lists, card indexes, etc., form what is known as the sampling frame. It is imperative that, before drawing a sample, the statistician examines his sampling frame to ascertain to what extent it is adequate for his purpose. Since a random sample has been defined as one in which every unit in the population has a calculable chance of being included, if the sampling frame is deficient in respect of a number of units, then those units cannot possibly have any chance of inclusion and any sample drawn will be biased. That there are mistakes in a sampling frame of any size is inevitable. For example, with lists relating to a human population, *e.g.* the Electroal Register, some of the people listed thereon appear more than once. According to Dr Yates, 'all frames are likely to suffer to a greater or

[1] See p. 388 for illustration.

less extent from various defects, *i.e.* inaccuracy, incompleteness, duplication and being out of date![1]

Thus, the first stage in any enquiry is to define the sampling unit and then to ascertain whether an appropriate sampling frame is available. In a study concerned, in part, with the income and resources of the elderly,[2] the unit of measurement was to be the 'income unit' – a single person or couple who could be expected to pool their resources. No sampling frame for such units exists. Hence sampling units, defined as addresses, were drawn from the Electoral Register and all 'income units' within those addresses were included for investigation. This process would theoretically produce a random sample of 'income units' although the unit of selection was the 'address'. Care has to be taken in using the Electoral Register as a frame for addresses that the probability of selecting addresses is unaffected by the varying number of individuals to be found at the addresses. This problem does not enter into the selection of adult individuals from the Electoral Register.

When, however, the then Ministry of Pensions and National Insurance carried out a large scale sample enquiry into the financial circumstances of pensioners, it had available as a sampling frame its own lists of those individuals entitled to a State pension. On the other hand, an element of bias was present if the results had purported to relate to the circumstances of the aged generally. This was because a significant minority of persons over 75 years of age were ineligible for the State pension and there was evidence to indicate that some of these were in very real poverty. The Ministry's report stressed that the survey was concerned with pensioners and not the aged.

In contrast, when the Government Social Survey prepared the sample for an enquiry into prospective family size, it had no sampling frame of married women under 45 years of age which was the population at risk. In this case, the Electoral Register was used to select addresses and all women within the defined population living at those addresses were included in the sample. Such a procedure would produce an element of bias into the final results since, in a small minority of addresses, more than one eligible woman would be found and the resulting 'cluster' would probably be homogeneous.

In the 1953/54 Household Expenditure Enquiry too, households formed the unit of measurement and since no list of households was available, the Technical Committee had earlier[3] recommended the sample of rateable units be drawn from local rating lists, rather than

---

[1] *Op. cit.*

[2] *The Aged in the Welfare State.* 1965. By P. Townsend and D. Weddeburn.

[3] Interim Report of Cost of Living Advisory Committee Aug. 1951. Cmnd. 8238.

from either the Electoral Registers or the then available National Register.

For sampling the human population of this country there used to be three lists, *i.e.* sampling frames: the National Register, the local authority rating lists, and the Electoral Register. The first was the only complete list, but the second is especially useful for sampling rateable units. The Government Social Survey was for many years favoured by enjoying access to the National Register; other survey organisations used the Register of Electors. When, however, the National Register was discontinued in 1952, the Government Social Survey was also compelled to adopt the Register of Electors as its sampling frame but it continued to use the Local Authority rating lists for such surveys as required them. Prior to this, and since, the Social Survey has undertaken an enquiry into the value of the Register of Electors as a sampling frame.[1]

The Electoral Register was estimated to include some 96 per cent of the resident civilian population of England and Wales aged twenty-one years and over. Since the 1969-70 Register came into effect, however, it covers all persons who are British subjects aged 18 and over in October of each year, plus those who will be 18 on or before October of the following year. There is evidence to suggest that a considerable proportion of the 18–21-year-olds and particularly of the $17\frac{1}{2}$-year-olds failed to register in 1969–70 and for this group the frame remains deficient for sampling purposes. Since the Register is used in both parliamentary and local government elections it is possible for sampling purposes to distinguish between parliamentary constituencies and local government wards. The former are broken down into polling districts which constitute the smallest sampling unit from this frame. Although the Register is revised each year so that it is reasonably up-to-date, any given Register is already four months old by the time it is published. It appears in February, the lists being based upon the electors' residence in the preceding October. It is effectively sixteen months old, of course, by the time the new edition appears. In other words, the Register is not continuously revised, but merely at yearly intervals, *i.e.* the October census of electors. Herein lies its main defect.

Its other defect lies in the fact that a proportion of the population entitled to inclusion in the Register has not in fact been enumerated. A Social Survey Report, however, contains an account of an investigation into this problem.[2] It appears that about 4 per cent of

---

[1] *The Register of Electors as a Sampling Frame.* By P. G. Gray, T. Corlett, and Pamela Frankland, C.O.I., November 1950; *Electoral Registration for Parliamentary Election.* By P. G. Gray and Frances A. Gee. 1967. 55-391; *The Electoral Register.* Practical information for use when drawing samples for interview and postal surveys. By Sheila Gray. 1971.

[2] See P. G. Gray and Frances A. Gee, *op. cit.*

the loss is due to non-registration, while there is a further loss of $\frac{1}{2}$ per cent monthly arising from removal. Thus, whereas at the date of publication, 94 per cent of the eligible population are included, 12 months after, *i.e.* immediately before the new Register is due to appear, only 88 per cent of the eligible population is correctly registered. If this short-fall in numbers were evenly distributed throughout the population by reference to sex, class and income, the sampling frame would not be seriously biased. The authors of this report estimate that the 4 per cent initial loss, *i.e.* due to non-registration is small in relation to the whole. Young voters and those who were not members of the same 'family' as the head of the household were most likely to be omitted from registration. The $\frac{1}{2}$ per cent monthly loss by removal is more serious, since it appears that a high proportion of the removals are accounted for by the under-thirties, so that the age distribution of the population remaining within the sampling frame is slightly distorted. The Social Survey report concluded that the current Register of Electors 'can be used with confidence as a sampling frame if some procedure to deal with "moves" can be evolved'.

The other main sampling frame available for selecting samples of the population of England and Wales is the Valuation Lists. These are lists of 'hereditaments' held by the local valuation offices of the Inland Revenue for rating purposes. For practical purposes, only the list of domestic hereditaments is required for sampling purposes; this is the list specifying mainly dwelling property, in terms of rateable units. In most cases, this unit is the same as the accommodation occupied by one household, but, in a minority of cases, more than one household may be living in one rateable unit and in a very small number of cases, one household may occupy more than one rateable unit. The list is continuously up-dated, but if new housing is subject to rating appeals, it may be some time before it appears on the valuation lists. Thus, if used as a sampling frame for *new* housing or if the subject of study is related to whether or not an individual is in a *new* house, the resulting sample is likely to be biased.

Quota Sampling

The particular feature, indeed the main virtue, of *random* sampling lies in the fact that the interviewer plays no part in the selection of her respondents. Where the survey is based on a random sample of householders or addresses, the interviewer is provided with a list of names and addresses and there must be no variation from that list, *e.g.* calling next door when no one is at home at the given address. Admittedly, the interviewer may have to spend time on 'recalls' if she finds the named person away from home. In practice such recalls are limited to two, following the first unsuccessful call. Even if she finally makes contact with the particular person she may find she has wasted her time because that person is unwilling to give an interview. Such refusals are a feature of any survey.[1] In such cases the interviewer notes the fact of no-contact or a refusal and, where possible, she should note any characteristics, *e.g.* middle-aged, living alone, which will help the survey organisers determine whether or not the non-respondents constitute a particular group rather than a cross-section of the original sample. As was explained earlier such information, although incomplete, may enable the organisers to assess the extent of any bias in the sample.

Important and indeed essential as such call-backs by the interviewer may be, the fact remains that they are expensive both of time and of money. To economise in time and cost, a method of sampling known as *quota* sampling is extensively employed by many commercial survey organisations. The essence of quota sampling is that the final choice of the respondent lies with the interviewer, although in making her selection she must ensure that the respondent satisfies certain criteria which are laid down by the survey organisation, Thus, instead of obtaining from head office a list of names and addresses, as is the case with random samples, the interviewer is instructed to carry out a number of interviews with individuals who conform to certain requirements. For example, she may be asked to interview ten men and ten women, two of them upper middle class, five from the lower middle class, and thirteen from the working class. Furthermore, some of them should be between 16 and 24 years of age, others between 25 and 44, and the balance over 45. In other words, the interviewer's choice of respondent is partly dictated by these 'controls'.

The basic controls used by the survey organisations which employ quota sampling are three in number: age, sex, and social class. The first two are obviously straight-forward. The determination of social class is somewhat more difficult. Additional controls may be introduced by the survey organisation in order to ensure that the interviewers carry out their interviewing with the appropriate respondents. For example, further controls such as married or single and, in the case of women, housewife or gainfully occupied may be employed. At the foot of the schedule reproduced on page 414 there are several such classificatory questions. A difficulty arises with the multiplication of such controls since it becomes increasingly difficult for the interviewer to ensure that her respondents satisfy the various criteria laid down by the controls. Since the object of quota sampling is to

---

[1] See p. 388.

simplify the interviewer's task and to save the survey organisations money, it is customary to restrict the controls to the three main characteristics cited above.

Quota sampling has in the past been severely criticised by professional statisticians because it does not satisfy the fundamental requirement of a sample, *i.e.* that it should be random. Consequently there is no justification for calculating the standard error of statistics based on quota samples. In other words, it is not possible to determine the precision of the results on any valid basis. While this is the main defect, there are other criticisms. For example, the social classification of the population used to identify respondents is based on somewhat shaky statistical foundations. The Registrar General's decennial Census of Population provides a break-down of the population both by social class, *i.e.* five groups, and since 1951 a socioeconomic classification comprising thirteen groups. In 1961 this was modified to number 17 groups.[1] The classification used by survey organisations in compiling their quotas, however, is very much simpler than this. Three or four main groups are usually employed. For example, the Gallup Poll uses four groups, the upper group comprising 5 per cent of the population; the upper middle class estimated to contain 21 per cent of the population; while the lower and middle working class has 59 per cent; and the very poor 15 per cent. Other organisations employ a somewhat similar breakdown. The interviewer is given instructions as to the characteristics which are relevant to each social class. The best guide is the nature of the respondent's employment or occupation, but the interviewer may pay due regard to the appearance, accent, and other visible attributes of the respondent, *e.g.* he lives in an expensive house with large car, in order to classify him.

In the 1963 National Readership Survey the interviewers were required to classify their respondents, who were selected by random sampling methods and not by quota, by reference to their social class. To ensure a standardised and uniform classification by all the interviewers, the following classification was prepared for their guidance. They were also told that the respondent's social class was primarily determined by his occupation, or if retired, by his former occupation. Where there was no occupation, or information about it was unobtainable, then other characteristics had to be taken into account, *e.g.* the type of dwelling, the amenities in the home or the presence of domestic help. In particular, interviewers were reminded that the above income classification was only an indication and did not determine the social grade of the respondent.

In an attempt to ascertain the extent to which quota samples were

[1] These are discussed in Chapter XVI.

CLASSIFICATION OF RESPONDENTS BY SOCIAL GRADE

Social Grade	Social Status	Head of Households	
		Occupation	Income likely to be
A	Upper middle class	Higher managerial administrative or professional	£1,750 or over per annum
B	Middle class	Intermediate managerial, administrative or professional	£950 – £1,750
C1	Lower middle class	Supervisory or clerical, and junior managerial administrative or professional	Under £950 per annum
C2	Skilled working class	Skilled manual workers	Between £12 and £20 per week
D	Working class	Semi and unskilled manual workers	£6 10s. – £12 per week
E	Those at lowest levels of subsistence	State pensioners or widows (no other earner), casual or lowest-grade workers	Under £6 10s. per week

Source: I.P.A. National Readership Survey 1963.

truly representative of the population, Professors Moser and Stuart carried out certain tests on a number of experimental quota samples interviewed by various survey organisations.[1] They found that interviewers tended to complete their quotas with too many better educated members of the various social groups, and furthermore that certain industrial groups, particularly in the lower and less well paid occupations, tended to be under-represented given their relative importance in the overall population. The authors recommended that a form of 'industrial' control should be introduced, *i.e.* instructing interviewers to select respondents who followed particular occupations. The introduction of further controls, however, as is pointed out above, complicates the interviewer's task. This criticism has been met by most of the organisations by giving their interviewers instructions as to how they can contact suitable respondents, for example, in shops, office workers, housewives at home, etc. Nevertheless, the fact has to be faced that the statistical foundations for this type of social classification of respondents are still rather limited.

Another weakness of quota sampling stems from the fact that a great deal of interviewing is often carried out on the streets. While this facilitates making contact with respondents, it means that people

[1] An experimental Study of Quota Sampling, *J.R.S.S.*, Part 4, 1953.

who are out and about are more likely to be represented in the sample than those whose work tends to keep them at home, for example housewives with children. In some cases, where the interviewer may start work a little later in the morning, she will tend to get a disproportionate number of office workers, rather than factory workers who leave home earlier. Here again, the survey organisations have sought to remedy this potential defect by instructions to interviewers as to where they should try and select their respondents.

As against these various shortcomings of quota sampling, there are a number of advantages. The first is obviously cheapness. Each interview tends to cost about half that of an interview in a random sample. Second, of course, there is speed. There is no need for call-backs on absent householders. An important point made in the defence of quota sampling is that the more serious defects and mistakes in any survey tend to be made at the interviewing stage and in the processing of the schedules. There may, of course, also be defects in the schedule itself. The sample itself is probably a smaller source of error than are these factors. Consequently it can be argued that a survey based on quota sampling, when the overall results are assessed, may yield just as reliable information as one using a random sample.

Another argument in favour of quota sampling is that the problem of non-response does not invalidate or affect the representativeness of the sample. This is incorrect. Obviously there is non-response in so far as some people, when approached by an interviewer, will refuse to be interviewed. But since the interviewer can then approach someone else who fits her control and get an interview, unless she records the fact of the refusal it will be unknown. Interviewers using quota sampling are generally required to keep a note of such refusals, but Moser[1] has pointed out that these records are of limited value in so far as nothing is then known of the characteristics of people who refuse to be interviewed.

Statisticians generally and, of course, the commercial survey organisations, recognise that quota sampling cannot in a purely statistical sense be regarded as a substitute for random sampling. The Government Social Survey in its early days used quota samples occasionally but has for many years used only random samples. More recently, a leading commercial survey organisation announced that its public opinion polls would be based only on random samples. Certainly the worst features of quota sampling which characterised the early American experience with it, for example, interviewers sitting at home and completing schedules based on imagined interviews, have been overcome. To avoid this particular problem, all the survey organisations carry out checks on interviewers' work, usually by

[1] Quota Sampling, *J.R.S.S.*, Part 3, 1952.

contacting respondents[1] or re-interviewing them. These checks are effective, no doubt, primarily in so far as the knowledge of their existence may deter an interviewer from trying to cheat the employing organisation. Survey organisations are well aware of the potential defects and in most cases take great pains to train and instruct their interviewers, on whom in the last resort the validity of the results must depend. After an extensive analysis of the results of quota sampling, Professors Moser and Stuart concluded that in practised hands this method gave fairly accurate results. Certainly the past record of the pre-election opinion polls lends weight to this conclusion and it seems as though it will be many years before this speedy and economical method of carrying out surveys is replaced entirely by random sampling.

The Sample Size

The point has already been made that the costs of a sample survey are directly related to the size of the sample used. The object of sample design, as it is called, is to maximise the degree of accuracy or precision in the sample results for any given outlay. We have seen that a stratified sample will give a greater degree of precision than a simple random sample; while both multi-stage and, to an even greater extent, cluster sampling represent compromises between statistical and economic considerations. Whichever type of sample design is used in a survey, the inevitable question arises as to the size of sample to be taken. If one asks the simple question, 'what is the appropriate sized sample for a particular survey', the answer is invariably, 'the largest practicable' since every increase in the sample size brings with it some increase in the precision of the sample estimate. The point has also been made, but it bears repetition since it often puzzles the layman, that the size of the population from which the sample is to be drawn is quite irrelevant.

The key to the question as to the appropriate size of a sample is determined by the results required. Let us assume that the leaders of a political party want to know the proportion of the electorate which approves their particular policy. The statistician may inform them after an opinion poll has been taken, that he is 95 per cent certain that between 40 and 50 per cent of the electorate support the party. This is clearly of little value; 50 per cent means victory at the polls, the figure of 40 means defeat. In the example quoted, it is quite clear that the standard error of the percentage is $2\frac{1}{2}$ per cent since the 95 per cent level of confidence sets limits of twice that error about the sample statistic of 45 per cent. To give more precise results at the

---

[1] At the end of the interview the respondent is asked for his name and address.

same level of confidence, the statistician must take a larger sample and his clients must therefore pay more for his work. Suppose the clients will be satisfied to know with 95 per cent confidence within one per cent either way the proportion of the electorate supporting them. In other words, the sample must yield a standard error of 0·5 per cent. From the formula for the standard error of a percentage, *s.e.* $\% = \sqrt{\frac{\overline{pq}}{n}}$ we can by substitution arrive at the required sample size. Thus:

$$0\cdot5 \ = \ \sqrt{\frac{45 \times 55}{x}}$$

$$0\cdot25 \ = \ \frac{45 \times 55}{x}$$

$$0\cdot25x \ = \ 2{,}475$$

$$\therefore \ x \ = \ 9{,}900$$

Strictly speaking, the above formula applies only to a simple random sample. As has been explained, the gains in precision from prior stratification of the population or the sample are considerable. But the formula for deriving the standard error of a stratified sample is much more complex. It consists largely of summing the standard errors within each of the strata making up the sample. Similarly, the calculation of the standard error of a multistage sample is complicated by the fact that at each stage a random sample is taken of the relevant sampling units and these standard errors accumulate. Generally speaking, however, the above simple formula based upon the standard error of a proportion gives a useful and easily calculated guide to the maximum sample required in a survey which is concerned to ascertain the extent to which the population possesses a particular attribute, *e.g.* watches I.T.V. or votes Liberal, etc. When the statistician is dealing with variables, *e.g.* the average income of members of a given population, then a different formula is required.

The main object of the foregoing section is to impress upon the reader that the size of the population has nothing to do with sample size and that, in a sense, the statistician works backwards from his probable results to decide upon the required sample size. The important consideration is the degree of precision required in the results. The importance of costs has been much stressed, but no statistician will subordinate statistical considerations to considerations of finance. His function is to advise his clients as to the best and cheapest way of obtaining the information they require. If they are not prepared to meet the cost of what the statistician considers to be the minimum sample required to yield the information they have asked for, then he will advise them that to undertake the enquiry will merely waste their money.

Conclusions

In this chapter an attempt has been made to describe in simple terms the main types of sample which are currently employed in survey work. Reference has also been made to the considerations which may determine the sample design employed by the statistician. Great emphasis has been placed upon the need for random selection of the sampling units because only if this rule is observed can the precision of sample statistics be measured by calculating their standard error. Considerations of economy and time have led to the widespread adoption by many commercial market research agencies of quota sampling. From the statistical point of view this method is inferior to random sampling; but random sampling is itself subject to other weaknesses.[1] Provided the data are available to enable quota samples to be stratified in some detail, the results are undoubtedly adequate for the purposes for which quota samples are generally used.

[1] These are discussed in Chapter XVI.

SAMPLE SURVEYS

Development of Surveys

The enumeration of populations by means of a census is centuries old; the Egyptians and Romans both carried out censuses for fiscal and military purposes. The sample survey, however, is of quite recent origin. It is, nevertheless, customary to start any history thereof with the great social enquiry of Charles Booth entitled 'Labour and Life of the People of London' which filled seventeen volumes and took more than a decade to complete.[1] A few years after Booth had published his main findings, Seebohm Rowntree carried out his enquiry into poverty among the working classes of York. This was published in 1901 under the title 'Poverty: A Study in Town Life'.[2] Neither of these pioneer enquiries could be described as sample surveys. They were virtual censuses of the relevant populations. In Booth's case the population was the working class families in London with children of school age. For Rowntree it was all working class families, the latter being defined as households where no resident domestic help was kept!

The first survey based upon a random sample of the population was carried out in 1912 in Reading by the late Professor Bowley. Like his great predecessors, he was concerned to measure the incidence of poverty among the working classes. He incorporated Rowntree's device of measuring the incidence of poverty by reference to a minimum living standard, but in place of a census used a one in twenty sample of addresses taken systematically from a street directory. With the growth of unemployment after the war, surveys into poverty were undertaken in many cities. The best known are those in London by Professor Bowley and his assistants from the London School of Economics and that on Merseyside prepared by Caradog Jones of the University of Liverpool. It was not until the later 1930's that the public became at all aware of the growing use of sample surveys. Their attention to this subject was attracted by the well-publicised public opinion polls which had established a considerable reputation in the United States. One or two commercial agencies were also beginning to adapt the technique for market and consumer research

---

[1] There is an excellent summary of this classic study in the Penguin Classics entitled *Charles Booth's London*, edited by A. Fried and R. Elman.

[2] A most readable book which describes vividly what life was like for the working class at the turn of the century.

purposes. On the outbreak of the war, the Central Office of Information created the Wartime Social Survey.

The Government Social Survey, as it is now called, is a division of the new Office of Population Censuses and Surveys and has contributed much to the development of the techniques used in sample survey work. Originally it was employed by various government departments on *ad hoc* surveys to learn what the public felt about certain issues, *e.g.* clothes and fuel rationing. After the war, it carried out surveys into labour problems, *e.g.* why recruitment to the nursing profession was so poor and why miners were leaving the mines. In later years the Social Survey has become increasingly involved in the work of improving the quality of economic statistics necessary to the formulation of a coherent economic policy, in particular, consumer expenditure surveys and consumer outlays on durable consumer goods. The annual National Food Survey enabled the Ministry of Food and Agriculture to adjust its policy in the light of changes in nutritional standards and dietary habits of households. The Family Expenditure Surveys undertaken for the Department of Employment form the basis of the index of retail prices. Other surveys have been used to determine the use made of scientific and technically trained manpower, as well as to measure the degree of mobility of labour between jobs and between occupations. Increasing emphasis is nowadays placed on surveys concerned with social issues. Recent Social Survey work ranges from studies of the handicapped to local government organisation and to smoking habits among schoolboys. On the other hand it is a matter for regret that the post-war Survey of Sickness was abandoned, because it provided the first comprehensive data on the nation's state of health. A similar survey among users of the National Insurance hearing aid resulted in some improvements in design, as well as the organisation of repair facilities. The Social Survey assisted in a study of Borstal inmates and the problem of recidivism; the same organisation played a major role in the statistical surveys which formed the basis of the recommendations of the Robbins Report on Higher Education. In short, the Social Survey has become an integral part of the machinery available to the government for briefing itself on any public issue. The sample survey has become both an efficient and recognised tool for the administrator.[1]

Definition

To the layman a sample survey may appear to be an inferior substitute for a census. Reasons for not taking a census may be that the

[1] For an interesting exposition of this point read 'The Government Social Survey: An Aid to Policy Formation' by L, Moss, a lecture to the Royal Institute of Public Administration published in the Journal of the Institute 1960.

population in question is too large and the census would take too long and would be too expensive. In many cases, however, the sample survey may be preferable to a census, not merely on account of the lower cost and greater speed with which results are made available, but because it is superior to the census for the particular enquiry. The outstanding advantage of such a survey over the census lies in the fact that it is practicable to collect much more detailed information from a relatively small number of people than from a large number. The former method permits the use of trained interviewers who can elicit a great deal of detailed information not merely of a factual nature, but also opinions. The census is only satisfactory for collecting factual data and even then some of the information received must be regarded as distinctly doubtful in terms of its accuracy.

However representative the sample may be, it is still inferior to the 100 per cent enumeration of all the population units which is implied in the term 'census'. In practice, however, no census covering a population of any size is 100 per cent complete. For example, the Register of Electors in this country based on a census of householders appears to have a deficiency of 4 per cent due to non-registration alone.[1] The U.S. Bureau of the Census carried out a series of investigations to test the reliability of data assembled from its 1950 population census which revealed quite substantial 'under-counts' and deficiencies for certain groups within the population. Clearly this type of problem is much more serious in a country so great in area and so diversified in race, education and language as the United States. But in varying degrees the problem is present in any census. In contrast, the survey has the merit that the information is collected under what have been called 'controlled' conditions. It is difficult to exercise close control at the critical point, the point when the informant's information is put down on the questionnaire or schedule Even when the census authorities use enumerators as with the population census in Britain (few of whom can be really well trained in the work) to collect the forms and where necessary help the respondent to complete them, this weakness is very serious in any large census. With a sample survey covering at most a few thousand informants it becomes possible to employ trained interviewers. They can explain the purposes of the survey to the respondent and try to ensure that each question is correctly put and understood.

It is for such reasons that the sample survey has come into prominence for its own merits rather than as an inferior substitute for the infrequent and cumbersome census. As a Director of the Social Survey has pointed out, 'experience seems to show that it is wrong to assume that a census must automatically be more correct than a

[1] See pp. 371-2 for details of its deficiencies.

sample'. Indeed, American experience and more recently the 1966 Census in England and Wales[1] suggest that the only method for testing the reliability of census data is a properly designed sample survey!

Some survey organisations are much better known to the public than the Social Survey, for example, the survey bodies responsible for the pre-election polls which are published at regular intervals in the daily press. Among these, the Gallup Poll and the National Opinion Poll are probably the best known. The B.B.C. Audience Research Department uses part-time interviewers to learn the views of radio and television audiences. Each day 3,000 adults in the seven B.B.C. regions are interviewed as well as a further 1,000 children under sixteen years of age. The purpose of these daily surveys is to ascertain the audience size for each programme broadcast. Audience reaction to the programmes is learned from the returns made by volunteer panels of listeners and viewers. An important and well-organised survey is that sponsored by the Institute of Practitioners in Advertising. This is concerned with media research, in particular the readership of papers and journals so that advertising agencies may be better able to advise their clients on their advertising policies. For this survey a very large sample of nearly 36,000 names and addresses is drawn, the reason for the large number being the need to ensure that minority interests are adequately represented and that analyses are made available for different times throughout the year. Illustrations and references to the work of all these bodies are made in the rest of this chapter.

Stages in the Survey

Without some understanding of the principles and problems of survey work an adequate assessment of survey data and results is hardly possible. Most surveys are designed to assess individual views on current political, economic and social issues; they have in common a carefully designed – what is termed 'structured' – schedule of questions and intensive interviewing. Different types of schedule will be employed for various types of enquiry, just as the sample may differ. The basic pattern, however, of all surveys may be described quite briefly. As a start it is sufficient merely to detail the successive stages in such a survey.

1. The first stage may be described as providing an answer to the question 'what is the problem under review and in what way can the survey help?' This cannot be answered without a detailed study of all the facts. The organiser may have to spend a long

[1] A Quality Check on the 1966 Ten Per Cent Sample Census of England and Wales. P. Gray and F. A. Gee. H.M.S.O.

period immersing himself in the subject and learning just what his client's needs really are. Published material must be examined to see how far it is of any use and whether it will simplify the survey or even make it unnecessary. The maximum information must be derived from the survey for a given cost. Not merely must the information be relevant to the enquiry but it is important to avoid the situation which can so easily arise at the end of a survey, when it becomes clear that it would have been helpful if only some additional data had been collected on a particular point. Too much time cannot be spent on these initial stages if time and money are to be spent to the best advantage. Such observations may appear somewhat trite and obvious; it is nevertheless surprising how often it is the obvious which is overlooked!

2. How is the information to be obtained? The two main methods are the postal enquiry and the survey employing interviewers. The merits of each are discussed below.

3. The preparation of the schedule of questions and instructions for their completion. A badly designed questionnaire may ruin an otherwise well conducted survey. When, as is usually the case, machine tabulation is employed, the answers to the individual questions in the schedules will have to be coded. It may seem premature to discuss tabulation at this stage, but the main tabulations, particularly those which are to bring out the inter-relationships between different characteristics of the sample units, should be carefully prepared at the outset. This minimises the danger of omitting to ask for information which will be needed. Information is sometimes required from a particular section or sections of the sample which may contain relatively few units. With too small a sub-sample it would be impossible to obtain the necessary degree of precision in the results. The size of the sample will have to be increased or special steps taken to increase the number of units in the particular sub-sample.[1] Such a point could easily be overlooked in the initial stages of the survey unless all the analyses of the final data are considered in advance.

4. The sample selected must be of such size and composition that it will yield the most reliable results for a given expenditure. If interviewers are to be employed, where the sampling is random or systematic, 'substitutes' may sometimes be drawn in the same way. There is the danger, however, that in using substitutes the interviewers will be less effective and persistent in seeking interviews with 'difficult' persons on the original list. As already

---

[1] As was illustrated in the discussion of sampling with variable fractions for different strata. See p. 363.

stated, the Social Survey no longer uses substitutes; all the emphasis in training interviewers is on achieving a satisfactory interview. This is undoubtedly a sound principle to follow. If quota sampling is to be used, suitable quota sheets and instructions for classifying respondents are necessary.

5. The preparations having proceeded so far it is advisable to pre-test the schedule of questions, by a *pilot* survey, which is a survey in miniature. The number interviewed is unimportant, but the respondents are selected at random. Usually the more experienced interviewers are engaged on this pilot survey, since they are capable of assessing the weaknesses of the approach or any questions on the schedule. The results are not so important in themselves as are the lessons learned. It is essential to carry out a pilot survey, although financial considerations or the need for speed may sometimes be pressed as grounds for dispensing with it. It is a safe generalisation that to omit testing the schedule by means of a pilot survey is to risk ruining the entire survey. It is a false economy in terms both of time and money. On the other hand, if the organisation has had a wide experience of similar surveys, *e.g.* the same survey was carried out, say, eighteen months ago, then clearly the pilot survey may be dispensed with.

6. Before the field work starts a briefing conference for the inter-viewers is normally held. Any difficulties met and the lessons learned in the pilot survey are examined and a course of action laid down for specified circumstances. The interviewers will have been issued with their instructions and care should be taken to ensure that they fully understand them.

7. Soon after the field work begins, completed schedules will begin to pour into the office. The schedules should be edited for omissions and any obvious mistakes such as inconsistencies in the replies entered. When necessary, the area organisers may check back on the respondent.

8. If the information is transferred to punched cards, the tabulation may be rapidly completed by machine. The questions should have been coded in advance for this purpose. The classification of those answers which are not of the simple 'Yes/No' or 'once a week/more often' variety, but may be expressions of opinion which cannot be easily coded in advance, will require careful con-sideration and supervision. The data once assembled, the report on the survey may be prepared. Usually several people will dis-cuss the results together to ensure that all aspects of the informa-tion are brought out and correctly interpreted.

These, then, are the main stages of any survey. Because each stage has been dealt with separately, it should not be imagined that each is independent of the others. Each survey must be considered in its entirety. At every stage, what has gone before, or what is to be done later, must influence the design of the survey. For example, the type of information sought will largely decide whether the postal or personal enquiry method is used, while the type of respondent will influence the design of the questionnaire.

Problems can arise all along the line, but if a survey is well planned many difficulties may be anticipated and provision made accordingly. For example, interviewers may be required to classify their respondents by social class. Unless a method of classification suitable for the survey is determined in advance and the interviewers instructed in its application, part of the data may be valueless. Different interviewers will assess individual respondents by different standards, with obvious results. It was precisely this type of problem which has led to the loss of much useful information from the National Farm Survey carried out in 1942. Part of the schedule required an evaluation of the quality of the farm holding by layout, type of farming and condition of buildings. Unfortunately, the interviewers available were inexperienced in survey work. They were normally employed by the County War Agricultural Committees and were usually local men. Consequently, they assessed the holdings for the purposes of these questions in the light of their local knowledge. The result has been that the data are most unreliable for inter-county comparisons, although they are probably satisfactory for providing a local view of farming in the individual counties.

In brief, the quality of the data derived from any survey rests largely on the efficiency of the work at three stages. The first is the selection of the *sample*. If this is unsatisfactory, then clearly no reliable conclusions may be drawn about the population from which the sample was taken even if the data are in themselves accurate. Unless the sample is random, then the results cannot be generalised for the population. And that, after all, is the object of any sample survey! Secondly, the design of *the schedule* of questions requires careful thought. Since few respondents appreciate the full implications of any lengthy question, the questions must be such that only one interpretation is possible. Finally, the all-important task of *interviewing*. As will be seen, more mistakes may creep into the results at this stage than any other. The remainder of this chapter will be devoted to these three basic stages in survey work.

The Sample

Generally speaking, the object of a sample survey is to learn something about the population. If the sample is truly random, then as has been pointed out earlier, certain conclusions regarding the population may be inferred from the evidence of the sample statistics. If the sample is, for whatever reason, a biased sample of the population from which it was drawn, then the sample results cannot be generalised with any confidence to the population. If in the process of selecting the random sample of individuals certain groups are inadvertently omitted or if in effect, the sample is self-selected because only certain individuals agree to take part, then this will detract from the randomness of the sample. Two illustrations will demonstrate the significance of ensuring that the sample is capable of representing all groups. In 1946 a government committee studying the problem of shop closing hours requested a sample survey to assess public opinion on the matter. Evidence already submitted by interested parties had suggested that a certain change would affect only a minority of the public. The survey revealed that this was true, but it also revealed that this minority comprised mainly working housewives who at the time constituted an important part of the labour force. Without the survey this highly important piece of information would never have come to the notice of the committee.

The second case concerned Dr Kinsey's studies in the United States of the sexual behaviour of human beings, in particular the report on the female. As Dr Kinsey himself has emphasised, the sample of informants was for obvious reasons largely self-selected, *i.e.* volunteers only. When the composition of the sample is compared with the entire American female population over fourteen years of age, it emerges that Dr Kinsey's sample is seriously overweighted with the, younger married woman who had had the benefits of a college education. In other words, the report may be a fair summary of the behaviour of this particular group of American women, but no inferences regarding the female population at large can safely be drawn from it. As is so often the case when a sample survey attracts publicity, the warnings of the organisers tend to be overlooked.

When sampling from a human population or even when carrying out a complete enumeration there are two major sources of selection or sampling bias. The first derives from faults in the sampling frame or list covering the defined population. This was considered in the earlier chapter on sampling.[1] The second is the consequence of not being able to contact individuals selected for the sample or, if contacted, an unwillingness on the part of the individual selected to answer the questions put to him. In contrast, in the National Readership Surveys just over three-quarters of the original sample are interviewed, the bulk of the non-response arising from the inability of interviewers to contact the prospective respondent; only a

[1] Pp. 369-70.

relatively small proportion of those contacted refuse to be interviewed.

The Social Survey experience is that for general individual or household surveys, only a very small minority of individuals selected cannot be contacted, particularly if the sampling unit is the address listed in the Electoral Register or the Valuation Lists. But, the problem of persuading people to co-operate once contacted is greater and, of course, the extent of the problem varies with the population being studied and the nature of the investigation. The experience with the Family Intentions survey carried out by the Social Survey illustrates this point.[1] The sampling procedure was complicated by the lack of a sampling frame and, in the event, a random sample of 20,800 addresses was drawn and of which 15,550 contained married women. These addresses contained 16,239 married women because some addresses were in multiple occupation. Of that number 7,171 were under 45 years of age and of them only 87 could not be contacted for purposes of the interview, i.e. a mere 1·2 per cent. There were, however, 781 refusals, equal to 10·9 per cent of the effective sample. The experience of the Family Expenditure Survey suggests that where respondents are called upon to keep detailed records and, in addition, all members of a household are required to participate, then proportionately fewer of the contacted households will agree to co-operate; in this case, about 27 per cent of the selected households refused to take part while only 2 per cent could not be contacted.

Similarly, if the population to be investigated consists of groups who are always busy or who cannot be persuaded that the subject of investigation has any relevance for them, then fewer will participate. The bias which originates from an inability to contact individuals is most commonly limited to special populations. Thus, teenagers are frequently cited as a population most difficult to contact by means of the usual sampling frames because, even if addresses are selected as the sampling unit, young people are often out of the house. Nevertheless, most general studies nowadays can expect response rates of the order of 85 per cent, 10 per cent being lost by refusals and 5 per cent due to non-contact or other losses. This problem of 'non-response' is handled in quota sampling by the simple expedient of seeking out additional suitable respondents, i.e. those who correspond to the interviewer's list or quota of respondents, until such time as the interviewer's quota is complete. This policy does not really solve the question of 'non-response'; it merely ensures that the same number of interviews are made as were intended when the sample was designed. The 'non-co-operating' members of the

[1] Family Intentions, by Myra Woolf. S.S. 408. 1971.

public whom the interviewer sought to interview may, however, form a particular group which will, as a result of non-response, be under-represented in the sample. If this is the case, then the sample is biased or incomplete and to that extent the results of the survey cannot reflect the true position.

The problem of non-response with random samples in which the interviewer is given a list of names and addresses is at all times serious. The experience of the Social Survey is that in a survey of adults the chances that an interviewer will find the respondent at home on her first call are about one in three. If the respondent is not available, then a further visit is necessary. Experience shows that a maximum of three calls is the economic limit. Admittedly, continuous attempts to establish contact will produce a larger proportion of effective interviews out of the sample, but the improved results are of disproportionate value to the efforts involved. Hence, the Social Survey instruct their interviewers to make a maximum of three calls at any one address to contact the prospective respondent.

The emphasis is placed on the need to obtain a satisfactory interview with the selected individual. No substitutes are provided, but the interviewer is required to make a note of all failures and unsatisfactory interviews so that these 'non-respondents' can to some extent be classified. As a result of this policy the Director of the Social Survey reports that once contact has been made, interviewers have an average response rate of between 80 and 90 per cent. The object of noting the characteristics of non-respondents is to endeavour to determine whether they are merely a representative sub-sample of the main sample, in which case the only drawback is that the statistician will have a smaller sample than he had hoped for, and his results will be to that extent less precise. The real danger is that the non-respondents will form a particular group which, in consequence of the non-response, will be under-represented in the sample. If some means of classifying these non-respondents can be found, then this risk can be reduced. For example, suppose a sample of households has been interviewed and it appears that 40 per cent of the households have no children in them. According to the 1966 census data that 52 per cent of households have no children under sixteen, hence this sample is probably biased. In consequence the views of households without children will not be given their due weight in the final analysis. The probable explanation of this deficiency is that in childless households all the adults go out to work and when the interviewers called they received no reply. They may have been slack about call-backs and in consequence an insufficient number of such households have been interviewed. It is for such reasons that classificatory questions are introduced into the schedule; for example, the number of children, size of income, occupation, daily newspaper read, among others.[1] The distribution of the population, in respect of certain such characteristics is known and the sample should correspond with the population.

The value of such classificatory questions is largely attributable to the wealth of information collected in the decennial census of population. These data can be supplemented and in some cases kept up to date by reference to the annual reviews of the Registrar General. Thus, the conventional classificatory questions relate to age, sex and region, the replies to which can then be compared with the official data for the population as a whole. An example of this practice is provided in the appendix to the Government Social Survey's report on women's employment.[2] The survey was restricted to women aged 16–64 for which no sampling frame existed. Hence the sample was drawn from a random selection of 10,000 addresses in Great Britain and interviews attempted with all eligible women in these households. The final, i.e. effective, sample of respondents was then matched with the population of such women in respect of several characteristics. These were the age composition of the sample and population; the information for the population being derived from the 1966 Census; the same source was used to match the sample in respect of marital status but a further check was provided by the findings of a mid-1965 Ministry of Labour sample survey of insurance records; the same data were used to compare the industrial classification of the sample, i.e. the distribution according to the industry employing the women. Finally, the effective sample was matched against the estimates by the Registrar-General of the regional distribution of the population in 1965.

It needs to be borne in mind, however, that the census data relate to a different period of time from the sample to investigation and, in any case, the census information itself suffers from inaccuracies. Nevertheless, comparability of data adds to the confidence of its accuracy.[3] Other questions in the schedule, which are of interest in themselves can also be used to test whether or not the sample was biased. Thus, replies to a question asking at what age the respondent's full-time education ceased may be compared with the information derived from a similar question in the most recent census of population. Additional questions relating to the ownership of a car, a TV set, telephone and refrigerator also provide further checks

[1] See the classification schedule on pp. 414-5.
[2] A Survey of Women's Employment by Audrey Hunt. Vol. 1. p. 199 S.S.379. H.M.S.O. 1968.
[3] On this point see remarks made in above-mentioned appendix in Women's Employment Survey. pp. 199-201.

upon the sample. Car ownership admitted or claimed can be checked against the national figures prepared by the Department of Environment; while cinema attendances are compared with the data published each quarter by the Board of Trade. The check data in respect of TV ownership are provided by the results of an earlier enquiry carried out by the B.B.C. Audience Research department and that relating to the ownership of refrigerator by similar national surveys. Obviously, there is a limit to the number of classificatory questions that can be inserted in a schedule but the more 'control' questions there are the better, assuming always that there are no major deficiencies in the data used for checking. American research has shown that apparently satisfactory results sometimes emerge when a sample is compared with one type of control, but when other control data are used, the sample is deficient. In other words, the more cross-checks on the sample composition the better. It is, however, desirable that the checks themselves should be independent of one another.

The results of two important surveys in respect of the proportion of the sample successfully interviewed illustrate the type of problem that the organisers have to deal with. In the 1963 National Readership Survey sponsored by the Institute of Practitioners in Advertising, which was based upon a random sample of individuals whose names and addresses were taken from the Electoral Register, the proportion of successful interviews was 76·9 per cent of the original sample drawn. This consisted of 19,200 names but of this number 2,655 had either died, moved away, or the premises at the address were empty or demolished. Effectively the interviews had to contend with 16,545 available respondents and of this number another 4,013 proved to be failures. Almost one-third of them refused to be interviewed, nearly one-fifth of them were out on each of three or more calls and about one-tenth of their number were either sick, senile or otherwise un-interviewable. The effective sample of 76·9 per cent was analysed by regions and by age, the results being weighted to adjust for any under-representation.[1] The other survey was the Household Expenditure Enquiry of 1953–54. The information required of all members of households was a detailed analysis of their expenditure over a three-week period. From experience with the annual National Food Surveys it was anticipated that the refusal rate in the sample would be high; a rate of 60 per cent was considered likely. For purposes of the Expenditure survey it was considered that a sample of 8,000 effective interviews and completed budgets would suffice and, on the basis of an expected 40 per cent

[1] The 1963 edition of the I.P.A. National Readership Survey contains extremely clear and detailed explanatory memoranda which set out the sample, schedule of questions and interviewer instructions.

response, some 20,000 households were selected as the sample. In the event, about 65 per cent, *i.e.* some 13,000 households co-operated.

The important point to note is that the organisers of the survey would have to check the composition of their effective sample of replies very carefully against the known make-up of the population to ensure that it was fully representative. Furthermore, those households which co-operated may have rather different[1] expenditure and consumption habits from those which refused to co-operate. In the event, the Cost of Living Advisory Committee which was responsible for the survey declared that the sample of some 12,900 returns, which they had used for constructing the new Index of Retail Prices, could be regarded as fully representative of households in this country. Since then, the Household Expenditure Enquiry has undergone two major changes in 1957 and again in 1967 as well as acquiring a new name – the Family Expenditure Survey. The information is collected partly by interview and partly by diaries of expenditure kept for a period of 14 days by members of the sample. Altogether about 10,000 addresses are selected in a twelve month period, that is about 2,500 addresses are selected for each three month interview period. In 1967, the effective sample was 10,210 resulting in 7,201 (71 per cent) budgets from co-operating households and in 1972 the proportion was raised to 74 per cent. Information about the remaining households was limited. Data on household size and composition were available for those who initially promised to keep records but failed to do so (3 per cent) while for the remainder, the available information was confined to that used for sampling – the region and type of area in which the units fell. This indicated that the non-response is highest in the Greater London Council area and in provincial conurbations and lowest in rural areas.[2]

An early but nevertheless interesting illustration of the importance of assessing the extent of non-response and making allowance for it is provided by the 1946 Family Census. This enquiry covered a very large sample of over 1·7 million married women. When the returns were checked there was a deficiency of some 17 per cent and it was suspected that among this group, childless women were in the majority. This was an especially important group in what was really a study of human fertility. Follow-up letters asking the 'non-respondents' to co-operate produced only a proportion of replies but from these it was clear that the suspicion was fully justified. In the final results, the figures for childless married women were adjusted in the light of this knowledge.

[1] As described on p. 387.
[2] Family Expenditure Survey. Handbook on the Sample, Fieldwork and Coding Procedures, by W. F. F. Kemsley. M. 146. H.M.S.O.

Another way of estimating the possible effects of the non-response is to assume that the non-respondents take up one or other extreme position in the continuum of replies. This was done in the Family Intentions Survey.[1] One object of the study was to assess the family size expected by married women. The response rate was of the order of 80 per cent and the non-respondents consisted of disproportionately more women in two particular groups, i.e. those aged 40–44 years and those under 20 years. There was some evidence to suggest that they tended to be those who married young and had no or few children. For the respondents in the sample, expected family size declined with decreasing age. It was assumed for the purposes of estimating the effect of the non-response that the omitted, i.e. non-respondent, married women under the age of 20 years expected a family of mean size comparable to that of the responding married women aged 40 and 44 years and vice versa. Recalculating the estimate for the total population on this basis resulted in an estimate very little different from that of the responding sample. This suggested that the estimates for the total population were unlikely to be affected even if the non-respondents were very different from the respondents in their own age groups.

A further illustration of this technique of matching the sample and non-respondents is provided by the report Women in Medicine published by the Office of Health Economics. The survey was conducted by the Medical Practitioners' Union in 1962–63 based on the distribution of 11,594 postal questionnaires to women doctors. The final sample was based on the replies by 8,209 doctors resident in the U.K. and the characteristics of the respondents were compared with material available from the Medical Directory and the Ministry of Health files. The report concluded that the non-respondents were generally older women who had qualified earlier and were less likely to be working. Thus, the report shows that 19·4 per cent of non-respondents were born in 1904 or earlier compared with only 13·8 per cent of the respondents. Whereas 7 per cent of respondents qualified in 1924 or earlier, the figure for non-respondents was 12·3 per cent; of the respondents 28·9 per cent were in general practice compared with only 7·7 per cent among the non-respondents.

The control and measurement of non-response remains among the more intractable problems of survey organisers. The solution is to be found partly in first-class interviewing with well-designed schedules of reasonable length and partly in checking, as above, on the non-respondents so that allowance for their omission from the sample can be made. This should not be read as implying that the organisers guess the facts about them.

[1] Family Intentions, by Myra Woolf. H.M.S.O. 1971.

It means that the answers given by respondents who appear to be similar – as far as they can be compared by reference to certain classificatory data – can be proportionately weighted in the final analysis. Because of the danger that non-response may introduce bias into the sample, it is far better to use a smaller sample in which interviewers are expert and can therefore ensure accurate replies as well as a very high response rate, rather than a much larger sample with poorer interviewing and low response rate. Even if the latter sample yields a larger number of interviews, the bias may lead to erroneous conclusions.

Given the importance of keeping non-response to a minimum it may be worth considering for some enquiries the use of an introductory letter as is used with any postal questionnaire.[1] Thus, when the Ministry of Pensions and National Insurance carried out factual surveys into the financial circumstances of retirement pensioners and of large families, in each case, shortly before the interviewers called a letter signed by the Minister was sent to the selected respondents. This emphasised the value placed by the Ministry in getting information from the respondent and, by implication, the likelihood that such information would form the basis of future policy. The letters proved extremely helpful in facilitating a very high response rate.[2]

The Social Survey does not use this technique, although it would probably save their interviewers quite a lot of re-calls. It is not used in most surveys of opinion because it is desirable for the respondent to answer the questions without previous reflection on how – possibly by trying to anticipate the questions on the given subject – he would answer them. There is the further possibility that other members of the household may discourage the prospective respondent from giving an interview, or influencing the answers he might otherwise give. Thus, for the Social Survey interview the first contact with the named person in her list, is 'face to face' and it is up to her, from that point on, to ensure an effective interview.

The conclusion to be drawn from the foregoing review of sampling problems is that there is often a sizeable difference between the number in the original sample and the number of respondents in what is often termed the 'effective' sample. The difference is accounted for by non-contacts and by non-response; with well organised surveys the former is rather less important than the latter. Because of the bias such a shortfall in the effective sample can produce, it is essential that interviewers keep records of all such cases. That information can be used when the sample is matched with the

---

[1] See example on p. 417.
[2] See, for example, Circumstances of Families at p. 74. Ministry of Social Security. H.M.S.O. 1967.

population in respect of the distribution of certain known characteristics, *e.g.* age, sex, owner-occupier or council tenant. The last assumption that should be made is that such non-response merely has the effect of reducing the effective sample.

Designing the Questionnaire

The old dictum about asking silly questions and getting silly answers in return provides a useful warning to anyone engaged in survey work. The simple fact of the matter is that the questionnaire (as it is usually called in a postal enquiry) or the schedule of questions completed by an interviewer is the keystone of any sample survey. The construction of the schedule for any survey involves two problems; first, what information is required and second, how should the questions be framed in order to get that information. Reference has already been made (p. 385) to the importance of the pilot survey in which the schedule can be pre-tested. This requirement alone should emphasise the simple truth that it is almost impossible to get a schedule correct at first attempt. What may appear to the survey people drafting the schedule to be perfectly simple questions may create quite unsuspected problems and difficulties for the respondents. The pre-test should bring any such weaknesses to light.

The schedule may take a relatively *unstructured* form or it may be completely *structured*. The first term signifies that the schedule provides merely a guide to the interviewer to the sequence of subjects that are to be touched upon in the interview. In such cases the interviewer may vary the order of topics or questions, and phrase the questions as she thinks best. This type of unstructured interview was widely used when surveys were in their infancy, not least because it was felt that such an informal approach ensured a better measure of co-operation and rapport between interviewer and the respondent. This was the basis of the interviews used by Dr Kinsey and his colleagues in their studies of sexual behaviour and it is rather similar to the technique known as the 'case study' in which each interview and respondent is treated as a separate and individual case.

While the unstructured interview still has a place among the research worker's tool kit, in virtually every major survey – not least those conducted by the Social Survey – it is the structured schedule and interview which is used. The reason for this is fairly obvious. Quite apart from any biases which interviewers following their own particular incliniations may be introduced into the results, there is the even more serious problem of ensuring that respondents all answer the same questions, otherwise it will be impossible to decide what their answers signify. As two members of the Social Survey Division have put it, 'the problem is . . . to design questions that mean the same thing, a single thing, a defined thing and the intended thing, to everyone'.[1]

As a general rule questions should be short, if only because lengthy questions tend to confuse the respondent. Furthermore, the language used in the questions should be as simple as is consonant with conveying the intended meaning. Questions may be classified into two main groups; those which seek to elicit a factual answer, *e.g.* how many persons are there living in this house? and opinion questions, *e.g.* Do you think workers on strike should receive social security benefits for their wives and children? It is also pertinent to remind the reader that there is no point in asking people questions to which they predictably do not know the answer or have not the knowledge or experience to answer the question. Some years ago householders in an urban area scheduled for re-development were asked which form of heating they would prefer, the choices ranging from paraffin stoves and coal fires to central heating. At that time very few households had any experience with central heating, the choice offered in the question was beyond the comprehension of most respondents. In another survey in which housewives were asked about their husband's work, a significant minority professed ignorance. And, as the statisticians in the Office for Population Censuses well know, it is not just ignorance of a deceased husband's occupation which creates problems, but also the natural inclination to overstate it, *e.g.* engineer rather than a mechanic or fitter.

A particular problem in many surveys arises from the respondents' memories. Generally speaking, the less reliance that the survey organiser needs to place on questions dependent for their answers on memory, the better. In commercial surveys as in market research respondents are usually asked whether they have a particular product in their homes rather than 'when they last bought it'. Questions relating to the newspapers and periodicals which the respondent reads can lead both to some being overlooked and others included even if not read. In such enquiries the interviewer will show the respondent a list of the main journals and ask him to indicate which he sees regularly or occasionally. Even this poses its own particular problem, since respondents tend to pick out the names in the upper part of the list rather than those at the bottom. To meet this human weakness, the lists are regularly, sometimes daily, rotated to give each paper a chance of 'early' selection. A similar list of radio or TV programmes is shown by the B.B.C. Audience Research interviewers to remind respondents what programmes were available. A study of the incidence of sickness among civil servants required a

---

[1] Fothergill and Willcock: 'Interviewers and Interviewing' in Modern Sample Survey Methods published by the Institute of Statisticians, but now out of print.

group of respondents to recall what sick leave they had taken and when. Replies suggested that the main error lay in forgetting *when* the leave was taken rather than forgetting it completely.[1]

The use of aids to memory recall or even questions in which a range of possible answers is set out, from which the respondent selects his answer, will produce answers different from those which would have been given in the absence of any such aid. Research is still being done on the question as to which method gives the more valid answers. All that is certain at present is that when such prompts are used in a survey, they should be standardised and as far as possible neutral so that they do not inadvertently suggest answers to the respondent.

Any question in a schedule must be so phrased that the respondent can understand what is meant. This also signifies that the respondent has the knowledge and intelligence to grasp the point of the question. It is doubtful whether some of the questions asked in recent opinion polls on the subject of Britain's entry into the European Economic Community meant very much to the respondent. In fairness to the polls, when they asked the average member of the public whether he thought that it would be to Britain's advantage to join the E.E.C., the mere fact that he answered 'yes' or 'no' at least indicated that he held an opinion on the issue. The basis for that opinion and whether or not he had any inkling of what was involved are matters for conjecture. In short, such surveys may produce a valid answer but its meaning remains unclear. In such opinion polls it is essential to avoid words with any emotional overtones such as 'Tory' or 'Socialist'; better to refer to the main parties by their proper names, *i.e.* Conservative and Labour. A good illustration of this point was provided in the American public opinion polls before the U.S.A. became involved in the last war. Many more Americans were 'anti-Nazi' before December 1941 than were 'anti-German'; the juxtaposition of German and Nazi could completely change the results of any survey of this kind.

Apart from basic principles to be observed in the construction of schedules and questionnaires touched upon above, there is also the need to facilitate the work of the interviewer. Considerable study has been given to the best lay-out of the schedule, not least because it may have to be completed on the doorstep or in the street rather than inside the respondent's home on a table. Thus, instructions to the interviewer should always be set in bold type; *e.g.* 'If respondent answers "No" to this question, omit the next section'. It is both impracticable and undesirable that the interviewer should have to

---

[1] The Memory Factor in Social Surveys, P. G. Gray, *Journal of the American Statistical Association.* June 1955.

write down the respondent's answers to each question. The interview is more likely to proceed satisfactorily if the interviewer can face the respondent as he speaks, rather than be seen, head bowed over her schedule noting down the answers. Such an aspect is likely to have a somewhat intimidating effect on the respondent, not to mention what it does to the 'spontaneity' of the question and answer process. This problem is solved partly by the interviewer familiarising herself with the content of the schedule and the wording of the questions so that a cursory glance to refresh her memory is enough. To avoid too much writing many questions will have pre-coded answers. For many questions in a survey, the pilot survey will indicate that many answers can be anticipated, *e.g.* Yes/No/D.K., *i.e.* respondent doesn't know. Similarly, where the question concerns the frequency of an event, *e.g.* visits to the cinema, the answer can be pre-coded, *e.g.* once/twice/more often/seldom/never.

The technique of pre-coding raises its own difficulties in so far as it forces the interviewer to classify the respondent's answer on the spot, although the precise interpretation to be placed upon it may be somewhat vague. For example, a survey on television viewing contained the following pre-coded answer: more interesting/better without/no difference/don't know, to classify answers to the question 'Would you say that television has made your home life more interesting and happier, or do you think your family life would be better without it'. How do you code the following answer? 'Well, it keeps the kids quiet and gives the wife a chance to put her feet up while they are viewing; but they don't want to go to bed at night and the older one rushes his homework; but it saves me having to take the wife to the local cinema because she is content to sit at home in the evening with me watching the telly.'

Some questions are known as 'open' questions, e.g. do you think the government should do more to protect the environment? These are distinct from the foregoing type of 'closed' questions; sometimes they are referred to as 'free-answer' questions. While such open questions can be extremely useful in offering the respondent the opportunity to express his own views freely, they create some difficulty for the interviewer who is required to record the respondent's reply as fully as is possible. Such questions also have the disadvantage that the answers are not easy to classify for purposes of tabulation in the preparation of the survey report.

Some of the most interesting problems of schedule design arise in assessing the strength with which the respondent may hold a particular opinion on a controversial subject. It is of course possible to use open questions for this purpose, *e.g.* 'It is suggested that the government re-introduce flogging as a punishment for crimes of violence.' What do you think? A good interviewer should be able to indicate the strength of the respondent's feelings but, unless some standard measure is used, differences between interviewers' assessments will be inevitable. For this situation, what are known as *scaling* questions are introduced. Thus, the interviewer will read out a statement such as 'People are saying that robbers who shoot policemen should be hanged'. What do you think? Then, the interviewer marks off the appropriate answer on a scale such as Agree strongly/Agree mildly/Neither agree nor disagree/Disagree mildly/ Disagree strongly. Usually the respondent is given a card with these alternative responses and the interviewer will usually ask him to state which of the several opinions listed comes nearest to his own. It should be noted that, with such questions as with pre-coded questions, if the respondent's answer does not fit any of the alternatives, then the interviewer must record the fact.

For all that non-response is a considerable problem with most surveys, it remains one of the minor curiosities of human nature just how ready a majority of the populace is to give such interviews when asked. Even lengthy interviews of up to an hour are practicable, provided the respondent has been warned in advance. There is, after all, such a thing as 'respondent fatigue', reflected in a growing indifference and even impatience as the successive questions are put! The next few pages provide an excerpt from a survey of parents with children in primary schools which was carried out for the Plowden Committee.[1] The entire schedule comprising 61 questions and a classification section, is too long to reproduce in its entirety, but the section given on pp. 400–5 is sufficient to indicate not only the type and range of questions, but also to give some idea of the interviewer's work. Most major surveys use extended schedules of this kind and the interview can easily last between 40 and 60 minutes.

[1]'Children and their Primary Schools. Vol. I Report'. 'Vol. II Research and Surveys'. H.M.S.O. 1967.

TO ALL
7. How long has .... been at (PRESENT SCHOOL)?

One term or less	1
Over 1 term, up to and exactly 1 school year	2
Over 1 school year, up to and exactly 2 school years..............................	3
Over 2 school years, up to and exactly 3 school years	4
Over 3 school years	5
D.K.	6

---

8. Have any other members of your family been to (PRESENT SCHOOL)?   RING ALL
                                                                             THAT APPLY

	No, not as far as parent knows	1
PROMPT	Yes, brothers, sisters of selected child (include step, etc.)	2
AS NEC.:	Yes, father, mother	3
	Yes, other relatives, e.g. uncle, aunts, cousins	4

---

9. 'X' IN THIS QUESTION AND Q.10 REFERS TO SELECTED CHILD OR TO
   HIS/HER ELDER BROTHER OR SISTER, WHICHEVER STARTED FIRST IN
   PRESENT SCHOOL.
   Before X started at (PRESENT SCHOOL) did you know anything about what the
   school was like (now)?

CODE AS 2 IF KNOWLEDGE	Knew something about what school was like......	1
OF SCHOOL IS ONLY OF	Did not know what school was like	2
WHAT IT WAS LIKE IN	New school, child started on first term	
PARENT'S TIME	opened	3

---

10. Were you (or your husband) able to make any inquiries about the school, or to visit it,
    before deciding to send X there?

IF PARENTS' GENERATION THERE,	Yes, made enquiries, or visited school.........	1 ask (a)
WERE ANY INQUIRIES OR VISITS	No inquiries or visit made........................	2
MADE TO FIND OUT WHAT	No inquiries needed, worked there	3
SCHOOL IS LIKE NOW?		

   (a) If Yes (1): Who did you talk to about the school?

	Head, or other teacher from the school......	1
	Education Office official............................	2
	Friends, relatives, neighbours with	
	children in school, or previously	3
	Friends, relatives, neighbours *without*	
Other (specify)	children in school, or previously	4

---

11. Was there any other school near here that .... could have gone to if you had
    wanted him/her to?

CODE 1 IF THERE IS A POSSIBLE SCHOOL	Yes	1 ask (a)
ALTHOUGH RELIGION OF PARENT OR SCHOOL WOULD	No	2
DETER PARENT FROM SENDING CHILD TO IT	D.K.	3

   (a) If Yes (1): What were your reasons for choosing this particular school?

No particular reasons/D.K...	1
Nearest, most convenient, safest, no main roads to cross	2
Religious reasons (Catholic, other church school)	3
Nice buildings, new buildings, modern, beautiful grounds	4
Other children, relatives, friends, parents there, or had been	5
Had heard good reports about it, told it was a good school.....................	6

---

12. IF HUSBAND AND WIFE IN HOUSEHOLD
    Was your husband able to take much interest in which school .... went to or did
    he leave that to you?

D.N.A. No husband/wife	3
Husband took an interest	1
Left to mother	2

13. We have been talking about when .... started at (PRESENT SCHOOL)
Could you tell me now whether you have at any time asked the Education Office or
anyone else in authority for permission for .... to go to a different school from
the one he/she was to have gone to?

(IF NO, CHECK PROBE: Have you ever asked the Education Office, or anyone else
in authority, to allow you to send .... to a particular school, or to allow ....
to change schools?

Yes, asked Ed. Office or other authority for permission for child to go to a different   ask (a) (i)
school, to change schools, or go to a particular school... 1   & (ii)

No, never asked for permission for child to go to different school, D.K......................... 2
Other (specify)

(a) If Yes (1): (i) At what stage in ....'s schooling was this?

       RECORD EACH OCCASION IN SEPARATE COL., EARLIEST IN COL. (1)
       PROMPT PRECODES AS NEC: (1)   (2)   (3)

     When child first started in infants school .... 1 ...... 1 1
     When wanting child to transfer between infants schools/depts .... 2 ...... 2 2
     When child was transferring from infants to juniors............................ 3 ...... 3 3
     When wanting child to transfer between junior schools/depts................ 4 ...... 4 4
     When child was transferring from junior to secondary school .... 5 ...... 5 5

ASK FOR EACH OCCASION & RECORD IN APPROP. COL.

(ii) Did you get permission to send .... to the school you
      wanted?   Yes .... 1 ...... 1 1
                              No .... 2 ...... 2 2
     Not heard yet; no decision made, parent moved........................... 3 ...... 3 3

14. Can we talk now about the contacts parents have with the teachers at ....'s
present school? Did you have a talk with the head when .... first went to
(PRESENT SCHOOL)?

     CODE 1 IF TALKED TO HEAD JUST ————   Yes .... 1 ask (a)
     BEFORE CHILD STARTED, IF   No 2
     TALKED TO DEPUTY OR ASSISTANT   D.K. can't
     HEAD, OR IF PARENT KNEW HEAD   remember 3
     PERSONALLY AT THAT TIME

(a) If Yes (1): Apart perhaps from .... being there, did the head talk to you on
your own or with other parents?

      Talked to mother and/or father on own (or knows head personally) 1
      Talked to mother/father with other parents... 2
      D.K. Can't remember 3

15. Have you had a talk with any of ....'s class teachers since he/she has been at
(PRESENT SCHOOL?)

                     Yes 1
                     No 2
                     D.K. Can't remember 3

16. About how often have you had a talk about .... with the head, or with ....'s class teacher since he/she started there?

No talk with head or teacher 6

INCLUDE ANY TALK WHEN CHILD STARTED. IF TALKED TO HEAD AND CLASS TEACHER ON SAME VISIT, COUNT AS ONE TALK.

One talk with head or teacher 1
Two talks with head or teacher .... 2 ⎫ ask (a)
Three talks with head or teacher .... 3 ⎬ and (b)
Four to six talks with head or teacher 4
More than six talks with head or teacher............ 5 ⎭

(a) If had a talk with head or class teacher (1 to 5): Have you ever been to see the head without him/her asking you to go?

Yes 1
No 2
D.K. Can't remember 3

(b) We would like to know what sort of things parents want to be able to see the teachers about. Would you mind telling me what sort of things you have been to see the head or ....'s teacher about?   RING ALL THAT APPLY

INCLUDE ALL VISITS, WHETHER INITIATED BY THE HEAD OR PARENT

Child's progress educationally, teaching methods used 1
To notify school of illness, holiday, other absence from school 2
Bullying behaviour of other children............................. 3
Behavioural problems of informant's child, e.g. nervousness, worry, bad behaviour 4
To dicuss or look for lost items of clothing and other property 5
Other (specify)

17. INTERVIEWER CODE:—
Informant has made a complaint to head or class teacher 1
Informant has not complained to or has not talked to head or class teacher 2
D.K. Can't say 3

18. I am going to read out a list of things which some schools provide for parents.
(a) I would like you to tell me whether (PRESENT SCHOOL) has had any of these since .... started there: PROMPT LIST BELOW AND RECORD IN (a).
(b) FOR EACH ITEM CODED 1 IN (a) ASK: Have you (or your husband) been able to go to any of these? RECORD IN (b).

| PROMPT LIST | (a) Whether school has this:— | | | (b) Whether attended:— | |
	Yes	No	D.K.	Mother and/or Father attended	Neither attended or D.K.
(i) Open days (include open evenings)	1	2	3	1	2 .... (i)
(ii) Prize days	1	2	3	1	2 .... (ii)
(iii) Sports days, swimming galas	1	2	3	1	2 .... (iii)
(iv) School plays, shows, concerts, school carol and other services	1	2	3	1	2 .... (iv)
(v) Parent/teacher association meetings or other activities	1	2	3	1	2 .... (v)
(vi) School outings	1	2	3	1	2 .... (vi)
(vii) Jumble sales, bazaars, social evenings to raise money for school	1	2	3	1	2 .... (vii)
(viii) Medical or dental examination	1	2	3	1	2 ....(viii)

OFF: USE

a   b   c   d   e

19. Are there any (other) things which you have been to at (PRESENT SCHOOL) which
I haven't mentioned?
INTERVIEWER SEE INSTRUCTIONS AND BACK CODE INTO Q.18 IF
APPROPRIATE, DELETING FROM THIS QUESTION

20. IF HUSBAND AND WIFE IN HOUSEHOLD
Has your husband been able to go to ....'s school at all?

D.N.A. No husband/wife 3
Yes .... 1 ask (a)
No, D.K. Can't remember 2

(a) If Yes (1): Has he talked with the head at all? Yes 1
No 2
D.K. 3

21. What do you think of the arrangements at (PRESENT SCHOOL) for seeing the head
or class teacher? Are you quite happy with the present arrangements or not?

Completely happy with present arrangements, no reservations.............. 1
Not completely happy with present arrangements .... 2 ask (a)
D.K. Can't say 3

(a) If not completely happy (2): Could you tell me what sort of arrangements you would
prefer?

Should be able to/easier to see class teacher 1
Should be able to see head, class teacher in private 2
Sould be a parent/teacher association 3
Other (specify)

22. INTERVIEWER CODE: (SEE Q.7 PAGE 000)
—CHILD STARTED IN INFANTS THIS TERM (I.E. IN
RECEPTION CLASS) .... 1 ask (a)
and (b)
CHILD NOT IN RECEPTION CLASS .... 2 go to Q.23
—(a) This is/was ....'s first term in the infant school then. Have you been quite
happy with the way the teachers have helped him/her to settle in or not?

Parent quite happy with settling in 1
Parent has some worries, complaints, criticisms .... 2 ask (i)
D.K. Can't say 3

(i) If has any worries, criticisms (2): What is it that has worried you

—(b) Has .... been quite happy in infants school this term or has he/she been
worried or disturbed by it all?

Child has been quite happy............. 1
Child worried or disturbed .... 2 ask (i)
D.K. Can't say 3

(i) If child worried or disturbed (2): In what way has he/she been worried or
disturbed?

23. **TO ALL.**
I am going to read out some things that parents have said about going to their children's schools. I would
like you to tell me whether you feel the same way or not about (PRESENT SCHOOL).

	Feels the Same. Agrees	Does not feel this, disagrees	D.K. Neither agrees nor disagrees. No personal experience. Can't answer	
(i) It's very easy to see the teachers whenever you want to	1	3	2	(i)
(ii) I would feel that I was interfering if I went to the school ininvited	1	3	2	(ii)
(iii) If you go up to the school they only tell you what you know already	1	3	2	(iii)
(iv) The teachers seem very pleased when parents go along to see them	1	3	2	(iv)
(v) I feel that teachers have enough to do already without having to talk to parents	1	3	2	(v)
(vi) The teachers have favourites among the parents	1	3	2	(vi)
(vii) The teachers definitely seem interested in what you think about your child's education	1	3	2	(vii)
(viii) I feel that the teachers would like to keep parents out of the school	1	3	2	(viii)

24. Can we talk now about the methods of teaching which they use at (PRESENT
SCHOOL)?

Has the head, or have any of the other teachers talked to you about the methods they
use at (PRESENT SCHOOL)?

(e.g. about the way they
teach different subjects,
or what they are trying
to do in the school).

Yes, parent had a talk alone, or in a group of
parents 1
Parent has received leaflet, but not had a
talk 2
No, no leaflet or talk 3
D.K. Can't remember 4

25. Does .... talk to you much about the work he/she does in school, or show you
the sort of things he/she does?

IF NOT GIVEN SPONTANEOUSLY,
PROMPT WHETHER THIS HAPPENS
OFTEN OR OCCASIONALLY.

Yes, often 1
No, only occasionally, or hardly ever 2

26. Do you feel quite happy about the methods of teaching used at (PRESENT SCHOOL) and the way .... is getting on in his/her work, or is there anything which worries you at all?

    Quite happy with methods and with child's progress 1

    Worried about methods and/or child's progress, including worried because does not know how child is getting on .... 2 ask (a)

RING ALL
THAT APPLY

(a) **If worried (2)**: What is it that worries you?

    Feels that child is not up to standard for his/her age, not being brought on fast enough 1

    Not enough individual attention given, particularly to backward, slow pupils, classes too large, teacher not interested in child's progress................................... 2

    Too much time spent on play or other subjects which parent feels are not useful for child's progress 3

    Criticisms of or anxiety about new methods of teaching 4
    e.g. of reading, spelling, arithmetic

    Does not know how child is getting on. Would like to be told more about, to have reports on, child's progress.. 5

    Fault in child, untidy, won't pay attention, lazy, too talkative........................... 6

    Other (specify)

---

27. Do you know how the children of ....'s age are put into classes at (PRESENT SCHOOL)?

Are they put into classes by age or do they put the quicker ones into one class and the slower into another?

IF GROUPED BY ABILITY WITHIN A CLASS, CODE as 1. IF CLASSED BY AGE EXCEPT FOR OCCASIONAL BRIGHT OR SLOW CHILD. CODE AS 1.	In classes by age .... 1 In classes by ability/streamed .... 2 D.K., Can't say................................ 3 Other (specify)

The selection of questions contained in the reproduction illustrates most of the points made earlier. Thus, most of the questions have pre-coded answers and the interviewer is required to ring the number corresponding to the answer in the final column. This practice facilitates the transfer of the answers on to punched cards which are similarly printed with successive columns on the card relating to the sequence of questions. In most of the questions the interviewer is given instructions in capital letters so that she will not overlook them, *e.g.* Q.9 and 11 are two of several such cases. Question 18 is a good example of a prompt list but which, in this case, is not handed to the respondent, each item being read out by the interviewer. The same method is used in Q.23 to elicit the parent's reaction to contacts with the teaching staff. Note that in this question using scaling techniques there is no graduation of the questions to reflect intensity of feelings. However, the various statements reflect contrary views, *e.g.* compare iv and viii, iii and vii. In this case, there is no point in the interviewer reading out these eight statements one after the other; they would merely confuse the intelligent respondent and the less intelligent would be. hopelessly muddled. Each of these statement should be preceded by some form of words to the effect that parents have said such things and what does the respondent think about the statement.

In the instructions for the interviewer in Q.8 and 25 the word 'prompt' appears. This is a method of eliciting a response when the respondent seems to be vague about the meaning of the question, or is struggling to recall some piece of information. It is a technique to be used with caution. In fact, interviewers working with the Social Survey are instructed not to prompt unless the question on the schedule contains specific instructions to do so. The reason for this is self-evident; it is imperative with this type of standardised or structured schedule that each question is put to every respondent in the same way. Also, variation between interviewers must be avoided; the matter of what is known as interviewer bias is discussed below. It will be appreciated that if one interviewer prompts and another does not, the former's respondents may have more and possibly different things to say than those questioned by an interviewer who does not prompt. A more obvious danger from prompting stems from the risk that the interviewers will 'put words into people's mouths'. Most people suffer from the weakness that, if they cannot think of the right answer to the question, will grasp at any hint of what it might be given by the questioner.

Not all interviews are quite so intensive or as long as in many of the Social Survey enquiries; this is especially true of those used in market research or commercial surveys. These bodies are not in the same position as the Government Social Survey to exploit the public's patience although, clearly, no one is compelled to give an interview. The following reproduction is a good example of a straight-forward fact-finding schedule which has been used by the Gallup Poll organisation for pre-testing potential interviewers. None of the questions is difficult to answer and the interviewer's work is facilitated by the pre-coded answers, also numbered for the punch-card operators. Note the instruction to the interviewer at the foot of the second page below Q.12; first, that she may not prompt and second, that she must record exactly what the respondent said in reply to the question. Note too the classification section which follows the final Q.13; these enable the organisation to compare its effective sample of respondents with the population in respect of various characteristics such as age, sex, occupation, etc.

One last point is worth mentioning in connection with the schedule, if only because the layman so often asks about it. Do people tell the truth when they are interviewed? People undoubtedly vary in this respect and some schedules contain questions which some respondents may answer less than truthfully or in some cases lead them to exaggerate. For example, in a survey of young mothers who were asked, among other matters, whether they smacked their children, a surprising proportion of the respondents contended they never did anything so old-fashioned or, at most, only in exceptional circumstances! Some respondents were more honest in their implied comment that it was no business of the interviewer to ask such questions, but clearly they were aware of modern attitudes which influenced their reaction to the question.

The same consideration is reflected in the experience of the Social Survey with the Family Expenditure Surveys which year after year reveal that household expenditure on tobacco and alcoholic drink is understated by half.[1] The extent of the collective understatement can be assessed by reference to the receipts of duty by the Customs and Excise but, as far as individual households are concerned, the problem of adjusting the householder's figures is more difficult. There is, of course, the further possibility that keeping a record of expendi-

THE GALLUP POLL

When the answer is coded please ring number like this (2)
For other answers write in contact's own words

1. What is your favourite radio programme?

    ....

2. (a) About how often do you go to the cinema?

More than twice a week	..	1	Once a month	5
Twice a week	.. ..	2	Less than once a month ..	6
Once a week ..	.. ..	3	Never go	7
Once a fortnight ..	..	4	(If 'never go' skip to Q. 3)	

   (b) When did you last go to the cinema?

   .... **ago**

(c) Can you remember one film you saw? (*Write in name*)

....

Ask All

3.　What is your favourite form of entertainment?

Theatre..	..	..	1	Ballet ..	..	4
Cinema	..	..	2	Musical Hall	..	5
Concert	..	..	3			

Other (*Write in*)..

4. (a) Do you ever go to watch a football match or any other form of sport?

Yes, regularly	..	..	6	No ..	..	8
Yes, occasionally..		..	7	(*If 'No' skip to Q. 5*)		

(b) If YES:

What is your favourite sport to watch?

Rugger ..	..	..	1	Tennis ..	..	4
Soccer ..	..	..	2	Hockey..	..	5
Cricket ..	..	..	3			

Other (*Write in*)..

Ask All

5. (a) Have you had a holiday away from home during the past twelve months?

Yes	..	..	6	No ..	..	7
				(*If 'No' skip to Q. 6*)		

(b) If YES:

What sort of accommodation did you stay in?

Hotel ..	..	..	1	Holiday Camp ..	..	4
Boarding House ..		..	2	Stayed with relatives/friends		5
Private Lodgings..		..	3	Other ..	..	6

6.　What do you consider the ideal way of spending a summer holiday?

....

7. (a) Have you ever stayed in a Holiday Camp?

Yes	..	..	1	No ..	..	2
				(*Skip to Q. 7(e)*)		

(b) If YES: Which one?

....

(c) What did you like most about it?

....

(d) What did you like least about it?

....

(e) **Ask all those replying 'No' to Q. 7(a)**
Do you think that you would enjoy staying at a holiday camp?
Yes 9   No x

(f) If No: Why not?

....

Ask All
8. (a) Do you happen to be reading a novel or other book at the moment?
Yes 1   No 2
                                                (*Skip to Q. 9*)
(b) If YES: What is it?

....

Ask All
9.   What is the most urgent problem facing you and your family at the present time?

....

10.   Compared with six months ago are you finding it harder, easier or about the same to make both ends meet?
Harder 3   The same 5
Easier 4   Don't know 6

11.   Will you please tell me about how much you/your husband earns each week? (*Show card A and ring appropriate number*)
1   2   3   4

12. (a) Do you have a TV set at home?
If YES: Can it receive ITV commercial programmes or only BBC?
No TV Set 1   Set receiving ITV and BBC 2
BBC only 3

(b) Do you happen to have seen any TV advertisements during the past week?
Yes 4   No (*skip to keys*) .. 5

(c) Ask all replying 'Yes' to Q. 12 (b)
Which ones can you recall? (*Write in*)

....

....

Ask about the first advertisement mentioned in Q. 12 (c). Encourage the contact to answer as fully as possible, but do not prompt. Write down exactly what (s)he says very carefully.

13.   I would like you to describe the .... advertisement to me.
    (a) Who or what was in it?

    ....

    (b) What happened in the advertisement?

    ....

    (c) What did the advertisement say?

    ....

Man   .. 1   Woman.. 2   Married   3   Single   .. 4

Date of birth..

Date of interview:..

Home:
Owner-occupier   5   Tenant   .. 6   Other..   .. 7
Age:
21 – 29 ..   8   30 – 49 ..   9   50 – 64 ..   X   65 and over   V

Contact's Name and Address (Please PRINT)

Mr./Mrs./Miss   ....

Address:..

Town:...

No. of children and adults in household:
Children 0 – 4 years ..   ..
Children 5 – 15 years   ..   ..
Adults (16 and over including contact)..   ..   ..

                                                                    Total

---

Present/former occupation: (Husband's if housewife not working):

....

....

Manual:		Non-manual:	
Factory; mine; transport; bldg.	1	Professional	4
Farmworker	2	Director; propr; mngr. ..	5
Other manual	3	Shop; personal service etc.	6
		Office and others ..	7

I hereby certify that these interviews have been conducted in accordance with your directions, with persons who were previously unknown to me.

Signature: ....

ture as is required from the respondent, may affect his consumption and expenditure habits during that period.

Similar human weaknesses have been revealed in various readership surveys where respondents often claim to read daily the 'heavies' and similar journals at the weekend. To meet this problem the respondent could be asked when he last looked at a copy of a particular publication. This gives the respondent a loophole without admitting that he never reads that particular paper. If, however, he claimed to have read the paper recently, then he would be asked further questions. Likewise, it would be more sensible to ask respondents if they had *yet* acquired a colour T.V. set; without that keyword there is little doubt that the professed ownership of colour sets would greatly exceed the actual number in use.

The last few pages should have destroyed any illusions the reader may once have had, that asking questions is a relatively easy task. In a sense that is true; what makes the process difficult in survey work is that we need to know that all the interviewers are asking the same questions in the same way of all respondents. Hence, before the field work starts, it is essential to ensure that the questions are clear and, through the medium of the pre-test in the pilot survey, designed to produce the information required. It is hardly surprising, in view of the importance of the schedule, that any serious survey report should include a copy of the schedule used. The reader may thereby judge for himself the source and validity of the final data. Nevertheless, even the best designed schedule is only as effective as the efficiency of the interviewers permits. This aspect of the survey therefore deserves just as much attention as do the sample design and the schedule and this is considered below.

The Problems of Interviewing

It has been stated that the 'representativeness of a sample depends on the ability of field workers to trace their subjects and persuade them to co-operate in the completion of a questionnaire; and the accuracy of the results depends on that of the information recorded. Much hinges on the address, skill and tact of the interviewer, who thus becomes a possible source of serious bias in the enquiry'.[2]

[1] For details of this and other problems of expenditure surveys, see W. F. F. Kemsley: 'Family Expenditure Survey', Social Survey Report M. 146. 1969.

[2] J. Durbin and A. Stuart 'Difference in Responses Rate of Experienced and Inexperienced Interviewers'. *J.R.S.S.* 1951, Part II.

The majority of sample surveys are conducted by interviewers. A good interviewer can persuade his subject to reply to almost any question and it is fortunate, if somewhat surprising, that there appears to be no limit to the variety of questions which the average person is prepared to answer. Such willing co-operation can only be attributed to a general human weakness of being flattered by others seeking one's views. Occasionally, the respondent may be interested in the subject of the survey and be especially willing to participate, particularly if he feels that his opinions may influence the attitude of others. The non-response will, of course, vary from enquiry to enquiry, depending on what is expected of the respondent, but it is seldom large. One exception is the high refusal rate – approx. 60 per cent of the respondents contacted – in the National Food Survey. The reason for this lies in the fact that the housewife is expected to keep a detailed account of food purchases for a week and allow the interviewer to check the contents of her larder.

The ability to express thoughts and ideas varies widely from one individual to another. Thus, even the simplest of opinion questions in a schedule may evoke from the respondent either a vague imprecise answer or, just as bad, a long incoherent reply in which he contradicts himself. The interviewer has then to decide just what the respondent meant, whether his response fits in with any of her pre-coded answers or how she could write down the reply to a free-answer or open-ended question. Not unnaturally, her first reaction will be either to try and clarify the answer or try to find out, by further enquiry, just what the respondent has in mind. This is known as *probing* and the interviewer's ability to probe effectively can make a considerable difference to the quality of the information collected. Thus, the respondent who stops, almost in full spate, can be asked if he has anything else to say on the point. But to stress overmuch this question is possibly to force him to put forward some further thoughts, not because he necessarily had them in his mind when the question was asked, but merely because he feels that the interviewer is expecting him to add something.

This is a very real danger when a respondent is asked for an opinion on an issue about which he has no views and as little knowledge. Unless he has the courage to say frankly he does not know the answer, when the interviewer would merely ring the D.K. coded answer, there is a danger that persistent probing will force him to say something which, quite fortuitously, will fit in with one of the pre-coded answers. On the other hand, the 'don't know' answer from the respondent may just be a means of dodging the question and a little encouragement from the interviewer may produce a different answer. Clearly, this is a matter in which the experienced interviewer has a considerable advantage, As already noted the interviewer needs to be particularly careful in probing on questions which depend on the respondent's memory. It is usually fatal to hint at a date or period when probing since the respondent will grasp at the answer, right or wrong. In such cases it is best to try and work backwards over time, endeavouring to link the particular event with some other event which will fix it in time, *e.g.* before or after a recent Bank Holiday or his birthday.

The manner in which the interviewer probes is all-important.[1] Thus, to say sharply to the respondent, 'can't you remember' a particular event or payment can imply either a measure of criticism, which is likely to be resented, or suggest to the respondent that it is not unreasonable for him to have forgotten and thus to give up the effort to recall the required information. Likewise, leading questions should be avoided since they may put ideas to the respondent which he will then use to provide some sort of answer to satisfy the interviewer. For example, the question, 'you do consider that the present government is handling the economic situation well don't you?' will bring forth quite different answers from the question, 'in your opinion, is the government's handling of the economic situation good or bad?' It is in such matters that a good basic training and a thorough briefing before the fieldwork commences can make all the difference in a survey.

Just how significant training of interviewers may be in affecting the response of informants and the quality of that response, is difficult to judge. The results of a detailed investigation to test the relative efficiencies of two groups of professional investigators from the Social Survey and the British Institute of Public Opinion on the one hand and a group of University students on the other suggest at first sight that training may not be all that important.[2] It appeared from this enquiry that while the professionals enjoyed a higher success rate in establishing contact with the respondents than the students, the relative differences between the three groups of interviewers with regard to the quality of response in terms of completed and accurate schedules were not such as to warrant the inference that the students were much inferior to the professionals. There was some evidence, however, to suggest that on the more difficult questions the students were not as effective as the professionals. In view of the present trend towards longer schedules and intensive interviewing of the respondent, *i.e.* 'depth' interviewing to seek out causes and reasons for attitudes, the importance of training becomes more evident. In the early stages of survey work, the main quality required of an inter-

[1] The same is true of 'prompting' as was noted on pp. 405-6.
[2] Durbin and Stuart, *op. cit.*

viewer was 'personality' in the sense that she could easily establish 'rapport' with her informant and persuade him or her to talk freely on the survey topic. Nowadays much more attention is being paid to sequence of questions, the form in which they are posed, accurate recording, hence more skill and concentration is required of the interviewer.[1]

Apart from the difficulties already discussed in connection with the schedule, the actual interview is attended by even greater problems. The simplest is the risk that the interviewer may misunderstand a reply, or merely mark off the wrong code number for any pre-coded answer. The risk of misinterpretation is greater with opinion questions, irrespective whether the main replies have been classified in advance on the schedule or not, than with questions of fact. More important, however, is the actual conduct of the interview itself. There is always the danger of prompting the hesitant respondent or even putting the answer to him. To avoid this risk according to the official B.B.C. handbook the B.B.C. interviewer is instructed to help the respondent recall his listening or viewing the day before by getting him to recall when 'he first put the wireless on'; what did you do when you came in after work, etc. In other words, she uses a technique based upon 'association of ideas'. If this method fails, and many respondents are extraordinarily hazy on such matters, she may show the respondent the 'log' or programme list to remind him what was on.

A particular cause of concern is the extent of what is termed 'interview bias'. This can affect the data in two ways: First, it can increase the variability of the data because individual interviewers make random errors in recording the answers or each individually may affect the answers given to her. For example, the studies by Hyman,[2] suggest that the expectations interviewers have about each respondent may affect the interviewer's interpretation of ambiguous answers. If these errors are not systematic for all interviewers, they may cancel out over all provided a large enough group of interviews is used or the effect of such errors can be estimated by the use of interpenetrating samples. An example of a simple interpenetrating design to estimate the effects of the variability that interviwers introduce would be to randomly divide a sample in two sub-groups. Each would then be a random sample of the population. If each is then allocated to a different set of interviewers, then an estimate of the effect of the interviewers would be obtained by considering the variability, *i.e.* differences of the estimates between the two sub-

---

[1] Fothergill and Willcock, *op. cit.*

[2] H. Hyman, 'Interviewing in Social Research'.

samples. In practice, the use of interpenetrating samples incorporated into the design of a survey, adds to the fieldwork costs.

More important, because its effects on the data are usually unknown, is the faulty training or the use of faulty techniques of measurement that affects all interviewers in the same way. If all interviewers have been trained to over-probe on open-ended questions to the extent that respondents feel they must give exaggerated answers, then the resulting survey data will be biased. The effect will be the same if the standardised measuring technique is inappropriate. Asking direct questions to gauge the extent of expenditure on tobacco or drink seems to result always in an underestimate, for whatever reason. Such errors are impossible to detect within the context of any one survey and can only be assessed with data from other sources. In most instances, such data does not exist.

The Princeton Office of Opinion Research has carried out many tests on the extent of such bias and has revealed that even with professional interviewers some bias is unavoidable. In one American pre-election poll the interviewers were divided into groups of opposite political faiths. Their returns revealed quite clearly the effects of their subconscious sympathies on their respondents. Nor is this a new problem; it has been known to exist from the earliest days of sample surveys. For example, as long ago as 1914 an American sociologist found that the replies of 2,000 destitute men explaining their distress were markedly influenced by the interviewers' sympathies and views. Thus a Prohibitionist interviewer's results revealed a strong tendency among his respondents to attribute their destitution to drink; an interviewer with Socialist leanings recorded many who ascribed their position to industrial causes. According to the author, 'quantitative measures of interviewer bias in this particular survey turned out to be amazingly large. The men may have been glad to please anyone that showed an interest in them'.[1] The same authority comments that interviewers will influence their respondents' replies by the mood into which the latter are put. For example, 'the interviewer may make the respondent gay or despairing, garrulous or clammish. Some interviewers unconsciously cause respondents to take sides with them, some against them'. As Dr Deming points out, training can do much to overcome the more obvious causes of interviewer bias, but even with a well trained corps of interviewers it may arise, even quite unconsciously. The experience of the Social Survey in the course of collecting data on the probable response of ex-Service men to the offer of 1939-45 Campaign Stars is noteworthy in this respect. It was found that the age of the female interviewer had a definite influence on the attitude of the male respondent. The younger the interviewer,

[1] 'On Errors in Surveys', W. E. Deming in *American Sociological Review*, August 1944.

the more likely was the man to disavow any intention of applying for the awards. A recent survey among adolescents on the subject of juvenile delinquency revealed that respondents were markedly influenced in their answers where male interviewers had the physical characteristics of policemen, *i.e.* tall, etc.

Despite the intensive training given to interviewers, the holding of briefing conferences and the issue of detailed instructions with the schedule setting out the considerations which have prompted the various questions and the best way of putting them to the respondent, mistakes are inevitable. It is not the obvious mistakes and glaring inconsistencies between answers that are troublesome. These can usually be detected in the editing of the schedule. When all the problems involved in the organisation and conduct of a survey are taken into account, the errors occurring at the interview remain the most serious. In the words of two members of the Social Survey, 'sampling errors are the least serious, it is the human errors such as errors in classification and memory errors on the part of the respondent . . . that are less easily detected'.[1] A more recent enquiry into the problem carried out by the Social Survey revealed that over three-quarters of the mistakes made by investigators during the course of the interviews (and noted by observers present at the interview) could not have been detected from a scrutiny of their schedules when returned to head office.[2]

Some idea of the task imposed upon the investigator is given by the form below headed 'Classification'. This is actually a supplementary questionnaire to the main questionnaires which were concerned with surveys of the public's knowledge of and attitude towards tuberculosis, on reading habits and on savings. The purpose of this supplementary list of questions was to provide information concerning the informant's living conditions, social class, household composition, etc., independently of the three main surveys. The questions are quite clear and it will be noted how the investigator seeks to ascertain the respondent's income group. The respondent is not actually asked what he earns, but is asked to indicate to which particular income group, as given in Question VIII, he belongs. The letters S.W.E. stand for senior wage earner, usually the male head of the household. Since it may not be possible to interview him if the investigator calls during working hours, the 'subject', usually his wife, will provide the information. The interviewer will need briefing on the appropriate method of answering Question X; assessments by the individual directly concerned of his success or otherwise are not usually very satisfactory for comparative purposes, *e.g.* comparing the perform-

[1] Gray and Corlett, *Sampling for the Social Survey*, J.R.S.S., 1948, Part II.
[2] Fothergill and Willcock, *op. cit.*

ance of interviewers. The question does give some indication of the tenor of the interview and indicates the degree of co-operation which the investigator received from the informant.

In the National Readership Survey 1963, interviewers were required to classify their respondents, who were a random sample of names and addresses, by social grade. To ensure that all interviewers used the same standards, the survey organisers drew up a six-fold classification of the respondents.[1] The highest social group was defined as 'upper middle class', the occupation of the head of the household in this group being described as higher managerial, administrative or professional with an income of £1,750 or more. Another group was referred to as the 'skilled working class', comprising skilled manual workers with an income of between £12 and £20 per week. The lowest

CLASSIFICATION † *

(i)   Interviewer's name ....
      Interviewer's number........./........./......

(ii) **RING DATE OF INTERVIEW.**

	Sun.	Mon.	Tues.	Wed.	Thur.	Fri.	Sat.
April	16	17	18	19	20	21	22
	23	24	25	26	27	28	29
	30	—	—	—	—	—	—
May	1	2	3	4	5	6	7

(iii) Subject. Where living.
       At home .... Y
       In institution, hotel X
       As a boarder............................0
       In rooms 1
       As resident servant 2

(iv)   Type of dwelling.
       Detached house 3
       Semi-detached house 4
       Terraced house 5
       Self-contained flat 6
       Part of house 7
       (Other (specify) 8
       ....

(v) **HOUSEHOLD COMPOSITION**

Relationship to Subject	Age	Sex M F	Status M S W	Working F P N
A. Subject		1 2	3 4 5	6 7 8
B.		1 2	3 4 5	6 7 8
C.		1 2	3 4 5	6 7 8
D.		1 2	3 4 5	6 7 8
E.		1 2	3 4 5	6 7 8
F.		1 2	3 4 5	6 7 8
G.		1 2	3 4 5	6 7 8
H.		1 2	3 4 5	6 7 8
I.		1 2	3 4 5	6 7 8
J.		1 2	3 4 5	6 7 8
K.		1 2	3 4 5	6 7 8

Total 0—4 ....

Total 5—15 ....

Total 16 and over...............

Total in household............

Housewife is
(give letter) ....

S.W.E. is
(give letter) ....

[1] Reproduced on p. 375.

(vi) Number of rooms ....

(vii) Subject occupation (full description)

....

....

Subject industry, trade or profession......

....

Self employed 1
Employee 2

S.W.E. occupation (full description)

....

....

S.W.E. industry, trade or profession......

....

Self employed 1
Employee 2

viii) Income per week less deductions plus bonuses.

	Sjt.	S.W.E.
Nil.............................0		0
Up£ to 3.......................1		1
Over £3 to £5 2		2
Over £5 to £7 10s. 3		4
SHOW Over £7 10s. to £10 4		4
CARD Over £10 to £20 5		5
Over £20 6		6
Don't know 7		7
Refusal, not asked 8		8

If SJT. D.K., REFUSAL, NOT ASKED
Why? ....

If S.W.E. D.K., REFUSAL, NOT ASKED
Why? ....

....

(ix) Interview situation.
CODE   Informant alone..........................
ALL   Spouse present..........................1
THAT   Other adult(s) present................2
APPLY   Children present 3

(x) Interviewer's assessment of success of interview.
Above average (give reason)........4
Average 5
Below average (give reason) 6
Very poor (give reason) 7

....

(xi) Serial number on record sheet..............

(xii) Subject education.
Age left school ....
Type of last school:
Elementary ....Y
Central, Technical, Commercial...X
Secondary, Public 0
University...............................1

† Reproduced by permission of Director of Research Techniques, London School of Economics and the Editor of the *Journal of the Royal Statistical Society.*

* *Source:* Durbin and Stuart, *op. cit.* This particular paper contains three schedules of questions which will repay study by the student. The discussion following the paper is also useful.

group were defined as those living at the lowest levels of subsistence, with an income of under £6 10s. per week. This group comprised State pensioners or widows, casual and lowest grade workers. The interviewers were instructed that such a classification was at best a general guide; the income figures were to be regarded as at best approximate. Where no information concerning the occupation of the respondent was available, the interviewer was to base her assessment 'on environmental factors such as the type of dwelling, the amenities in the home, the presence of domestic help, and so on'.

Obviously, the consistency with which individual interviewers would follow such a classification would vary with their experience. There would also be some variability between interviewers. The solution is clearly to give the interviewers as detailed instructions as is possible for each survey as well as adequate training. Furthermore, it is always worthwhile checking for any overall bias by comparing the survey data with external information.[1]

[1] As described on pp. 389-90.

Postal Enquiries

Quite apart from the problems and weaknesses of personal interviewing as a survey method, an important consideration is cost. A cheaper method is to use a postal questionnaire. At first sight the postal questionnaire has several advantages. It can be sent to a very large number of people at low cost, so that the sample size may be increased considerably, relatively to the survey sample for the same cost. Further, the risk of bias or mistakes on the part of the interviewer is absent. All these apparent advantages, however, prove on examination to be fictitious. The fundamental weakness of the postal method is the low proportion of returns. It may be argued that if 100,000 schedules can be sent out for the same cost as interviewing 5,000 people, and the final sample still contains 20,000, it is therefore preferable. Unfortunately, there is no means of ascertaining whether or not the 20 per cent return constitutes a representative sample of those people to whom the schedule was sent. It almost certainly does not. It is probably true to say that the cost per completed schedule by interviewing is ultimately little above that for the postal enquiry. There is, too, the greater reliability of the former, since despite the risk of interviewer bias and mistakes, the respondents will themselves make mistakes in completing the forms.

The experience of the Social Survey with postal schedules is worthy of note. Some years ago 16,000 members of a profession were circularised and 38 per cent returned the forms immediately. A further 32 per cent replied, after a reminder had been sent. Ultimately, the response was just over 80 per cent. Such an experience was at that time quite exceptional for the following reasons. The subject of the enquiry was connected with the future of the profession, a matter of considerable interest to the members. They would in any case return a higher proportion than would be received in an enquiry on any subject covering the general population for, as professional people, their reaction to forms would not be that of the average member of the public. Finally, a pilot survey had provided many useful lessons and the schedule of questions was devised with very great care. The last points should not be exceptional, but the fact that the organisers of the survey comment on them suggests that they are not always accorded the same degree of attention.

More recently the Social Survey has been experimenting with further postal enquiries. In a paper read to the Royal Statistical Society Mr Christopher Scott argued, on the evidence of several highly successful postal surveys, that response rates of 80 per cent and more could be achieved, provided certain obvious conditions were observed.[1] It is perhaps worth stressing again that no survey, whether

---

[1] Research on Mail Surveys. *J.R.S.S.* 1961. Part II.

it be carried out by interviewer or by post, will achieve 100 per cent response. One would be as suspicious of the results of such a survey as we tend to be of elections in 'people's democracies' where 99·9 per cent of the voters vote for the ruling party. One of the postal surveys discussed by Mr Scott in his paper concerned road safety, and the schedule used is illustrated on pages 418–9. Two points emerge very clearly from a scrutiny of that schedule. The first are the brief and simple questions, with underlining, italicised print, and large capitals to get the point of the questions across to the respondent. Secondly, the letter itself, Note the stress on confidentiality, the statement that a wide response is needed. The enclosure of an envelope and stamped label is in itself important and helps the response. In this survey the response rate was equal to 84·4 per cent of the original sample and, when account was taken of those in the sample who no longer possessed a motor cycle, the effective response was equal to 91·4 per cent.

With a postal survey, it is obviously essential not merely to invoke the prospective respondents' co-operation, but where possible to convey the idea that the results of the survey are likely to be useful and beneficial to him. This approach is very obvious in the Spring 1964 enquiry carried out by the Southern Region of British Railways among its suburban passengers. The forms in this case were issued to passengers on a particular day at the various stations and to encourage their completion, the front page of the schedule contained a note which, after explaining that the enquiry was concerned to build a new pattern of services in the area, stated that the object was 'to do the best we can for you in the years ahead', and later again, 'in order to ensure that your own travel needs are taken into account, please complete this enquiry, etc.' While it is arguable that not every respondent passenger was entirely convinced by such assurances, the effect of this approach was surely to increase the response.

For all the undoubted success that has accompanied some of the Social Survey postal enquiries, generally speaking, most organisations find that the response to such forms is insufficient to justify generalising the results for the population as a whole. The plain truth of the matter is that it is, generally speaking, a self-selecting class which returns the schedules, usually because they have a particular interest therein and as such are not representative of the entire population. However, a sequence of follow-up letters and questionnaires and even calls from interviewers will do much to improve the response rate.

The obvious method of overcoming non-response with such enquiries is to make the return of the questionnaire compulsory. In practice the only body with statutory powers to compel a return is the government. For this reason they are the main users of this method

Central Office of Information,
Social Survey Division,
Montagu Mansions,
Baker Street,
LONDON, W.1.

Dear Sir or Madam,

Road Safety

I am writing to ask for your help in an enquiry we are making for the Government Road Research Laboratory.

In carrying out its work on road safety, the Laboratory needs to know who are the chief road users, how much they use their vehicles, and how much experience they have with different kinds of vehicles. At present we are asking only about motor-cyclists, including drivers of motor scooters and mopeds.

We can only get this information by writing to motor-cycle owners. To save expense we are not writing to all, but only to a small number, chosen at random from the registration records. In order to be sure that all points of view are taken into account we are anxious to get a reply from every person we write to.

The questions are on the back of this letter. Would you please fill in the answers and post the sheet back to us, using the enclosed label and envelope. There is no need for a stamp.

Please note that it is *your* reply we want, even if you do not at present ride any machine. Do not ask any one else to fill in the form instead of you, or we will not have a true cross-section of owners.

Your reply will be kept strictly confidential, and will *only* be used for counting how many people give each different answer. We shall pass these total figures to the road safety authorities, but we shall not mention any names.

I would be most grateful for your help.

Yours faithfully,

C. SCOTT.

PLEASE TURN OVER

Vehicle registration No........................

————————

————————

1. Is the above machine   a motor-cycle with side-car?   ————

a motor-cycle without sidecar?   ————   **WRITE YES**
AGAINST
a motor scooter? ....   ————   **ONE OF**
THESE
or a moped or auto-cycle? ......   ————   ————————
(A moped or auto-cycle means anything
which has a motor and pedals.)

2. Are you yourself still the owner of the above machine?............
(If your answer is NO, please state when you sold it, then answer
questions 3 and 4 for the period before you sold it.)
                                                   1958
                                                    date when sold by you

3. Have you yourself driven the above machine during the
last 4 weeks? If so, roughly how far?

(If you did not drive it, write 0)   ....miles   Give rough mileage for
                                              in last 4 weeks   the last 4 weeks. You
                                                                  may explain below if
Please note that the figure you write above should be the   that period was **very**
mileage you yourself have done, as driver, on the above   different from your
machine.   normal.

4. When did you first take out a PROVISIONAL LICENCE to drive any vehicle?

Month.................... Year: 19............

5. Since that time, how much driving experience have you had?
Please answer below for each type of vehicle.

Motor-cycle   *When did you first drive a motor-cycle?*............19......   WRITE NEVER if
                                                    month   year   never driven.
              Have you driven more than 1,000 miles
              on a motor-cycle? (Write YES or NO)............

Motor scooter   *When did you first drive a motor scooter?*.........19......   WRITE NEVER if
                                                    month   year   never driven.
                Have you driven more than 500 miles on
                a motor scooter? (Write YES or NO)............

Moped or   *When did you first drive a moped or*
auto-cycle   *cycle?*
(with motor   ....19......   WRITE NEVER if
and pedals)   month   year   never driven.
              Have you driven more than 250 miles
              on these?   (*Write YES or NO*)............

PLEASE DO NOT LEAVE BLANKS. If not sure of the month, give the year only.

6. What is your date of birth?   Yes: 19......   Month:............   Day:............

PLEASE RETURN THIS FORM AS SOON AS POSSIBLE USING THE ENVELOPE AND LABEL
PROVIDED. PLEASE DO NOT DELAY EVEN IF YOU CANNOT ANSWER ALL THE QUESTIONS

WE WILL BE VERY GRATEFUL FOR YOUR CO-OPERATION

and employ it for both samples and censuses. Nevertheless, it would be idle to pretend that because the respondent is compelled to return the schedule, it is necessarily completed accurately. One of the features of recent censuses, particularly the Censuses of Production and of Distribution, has been the reduction in the size and coverage of the questionnaires sent to shops and industrial undertakings listed in the Board of Trade sampling frames for the purposes of these Censuses. When these Censuses were first introduced after 1947, the schedules were sent to most firms and were in many cases small volumes of closely printed notes and questions. Inevitably the refusal rate was high, and although statutory powers are available to compel the return, once the number of non-respondents becomes at all large this threat ceases to be effective. In consequence, the statisticians responsible for the Censuses of Production and of Distribution have gradually reduced the size of their forms for smaller firms and simplified them in the case of the larger firms. In the case of the Census of Production, whereas originally all firms with under eleven employees were approached, more recently the practice is to approach firms with 25 or more workpeople. In other words, the majority of industrial undertakings may not be approached at all, particularly in the case of the sample surveys between the main Censuses.[1] The contribution to the national output of these small firms is estimated on the basis of other data.

Lastly, it should be borne in mind that postal surveys are suitable only for the collection of limited factual data; in other words, only questions which require a simple yes/no answer, or a figure or a date, are really suited to this method of enquiry. Once the survey concerns itself with attitudes and opinions, it becomes necessary to use interviewers. One qualification of this last statement is perhaps necessary. There is nothing to prevent long questionnaires being sent out with questions on attitudes, opinions, etc., incorporated in them. For example, the basis of one well-known sociological study[2] is the collection of schedules returned by readers of a Sunday newspaper. These schedules were four foolscap pages in size, with detailed questions on all aspects of the respondent's life, ranging from his material possessions to his views on sex, marriage, etc. It could, of course, be argued that a greater degree of frankness in the answers would be achieved by this method. This may well be true, but the basic defect remains that only a limited number of people, *i.e.* a non-random sample, would take the trouble to complete the questionnaire. However interesting their collective responses might be, and

[1] See Chapter XVIII for details.

[2] Geoffrey Gorer, *Exploring the English Character*. The structure of the sample and its method of compilation are clearly described.

the above study does make interesting reading, the fact is that there would be no statistical justification for describing the attitudes reflected in the completed schedules as fully representative of the British way of life, although it may reflect, as the author suggests, the views of the readers of this particular Sunday newspaper.

Longitudinal Studies

The type of survey discussed so far involves the collection of information from a sample of respondents at a particular point of time. Generally speaking, the information relates to that point of time since, given the fallibility of the human memory and the effect of the passage of time upon the recollection of particular events by individuals, retrospective studies are fraught with difficulties. One way of meeting this difficulty is to repeat a particular survey after an interval of time to detect such changes as may have taken place. Where, however, the research is concerned with measuring change over time, the conventional survey is inadequate. Such surveys are often termed *cross-sectional* studies to distinguish them from surveys which are concerned with assessing and measuring changes in the members of the sample over time. These are known as *longitudinal* studies and these comprise a series of repeated measurements of the characteristics of the same individuals over an extended period.

Longitudinal studies were first developed on any scale in the U.S.A. during the 1920s and 1930s and were concentrated in the social, biological and medical sciences. The surveys were in general designed to measure over a period of years the physical and emotional development of a sample of young children as they grew to adolescence and in some cases to adulthood. In particular, they were concerned to establish the existence of cause and effect relationships which affected the development of the child. It is from such studies that we now know that the first four years of a child's life are critical in determining its ultimate physical and intellectual development.

Such studies may be concentrated upon a relatively small sample of individuals so that, in effect, what is obtained is a series of individual case studies. But, there are also surveys based upon large samples which are needed for the analysis of the extremely complex set of influences which determine people's development. Not surprisingly, longitudinal studies have attracted criticism, not least because it was argued many such studies were no more than extended case studies of individuals and not longitudinal studies.

Furthermore, while the results of such studies into the physical development of children were generally accepted, there were critics who pointed out that, while it was possible to measure with some precision a range of physical characteristics, similar techniques were not available for the measurement of emotional and behavioural development where the nature and extent of any causality between the variables is very much more complex. Some of the samples were criticised because inclusion in the sample was not so much a matter of random selection as the willingness of the individual to co-operate in the enquiry. This would, of course, introduce its own biases into the results.

Nevertheless, the value of longitudinal studies has now been recognised and several international congresses have discussed the problems and techniques to overcome those problems. It is note-worthy that, while most of the work to date has been on the develop-ment of individuals in the early part of their lives, attention is now being directed at the nature of the ageing process. As the authors of *Longitudinal Studies and the Social Sciences*[1], Dr W. D. Wall and Mr H. L. Williams point out, much of the criticism of earlier studies begun 30 or 40 years ago is justified – but mainly by hindsight. Many of the defects attributed to them can, assert the authors, 'now be avoided by more carefully thought-out sampling and experi-mental design, by allowing for more rapid data analysis and feed-back, and by advances in measurement techniques.'

Before a longitudinal study is undertaken a number of points need to be clarified. First, the subject matter of the study must be measurable over time. Second, some causal relationships between the characteristics to be studied must be hypothesised, probably upon the basis of earlier researches and existing knowledge. Finally, the results of the survey should be capable of generalisation from the sample to the population at large. Particular attention needs to be paid to the sample. The problem is not so much the obvious question of random selection but to ensure that when losses occur, and these are inevitable when the enquiry continues over a period of years, that the drop-outs are properly matched by the replacements. It is, however, argued that this problem can be exaggerated since, pro-vided the interest of the sample members is kept alive, experience has shown that up to 90 per cent of the sample can be kept intact over the duration of the enquiry.

One of the best known of all such studies in the U.K. was the survey sponsored by the Population Investigation Committee (PIC) into the development of a sample of children born in 1946. The actual sample comprised all children born in a particular week in March of that year. The survey has followed through the development of the sample units in respect of their health, physical development, school progress and occupation on leaving school.

[1] Published by Heinemann for the Social Science Research Council, 1970.

A particular problem of any major longitudinal survey is cost and the time involved of the persons conducting the research, although there are many leading exponents of this technique who seem fully prepared to devote many years of their working lives to a particular study. Whatever the problems and weaknesses of longitudinal surveys, in the words of Dr Wall and Mr Williams, 'they have been productive of new insights and new and more powerful theories which could not have been gained by other means – even if we now know that they might have been obtained somewhat more economically and less equivocally'.

Observation

All research depends upon observation, whether it be in the laboratory or about the behaviour of human beings. As the Webbs observed in their *Methods of Social Study* 'an indispensable part of the study of any social institution . . . is deliberate and sustained personal observation'. The advantages of personal observation are self-evident. It is direct and does not come second-hand through the notes or reports of others such as interviewers. Unfortunately, the observer cannot be completely objective about what he has observed. He will have his own theories on the subject, his own prejudices and degree of involvement. Several observers of any scene may give, especially if they are trained, similar accounts of what they have witnessed. But, when it comes to interpreting those incidents or behaviour, that is a different matter.

A particular advantage of observation is that the subjects of the investigation are assessed in their natural environment. Nor is it too difficult to observe events and behaviour and record what is seen, at least in some cases, e.g. the number of hours children in a household watch TV in a day, or the diets of elderly people living alone. But the observer cannot spend 24 hours a day with his subjects; he only observes in the periods he is with the subjects and it need hardly be stressed that, when he is present, the subjects may well behave differently.

The difficulty and limits of observation have been well put by M. D. Shipman in *Limitations of Social Research*.[1] An observational study, he writes, 'would be fully controlled to ensure reliability. It would be fully participant to ensure maximum insight. It would be carried out and reported with scientific rigour. It would be done, from planning to publication, with the full knowledge of the observed'. But, as the author notes, 'full control and full participation are usually incompatible; scientific rigour will usually disturb the

[1] Longmans, 1972.

rapport of observed and observer and is a difficult role to maintain while participating'.

The main type of observational technique is known as *participant* observation. In this case the observer involves himself in the activities of the group he is studying, although they may not always be aware of his true role. To avoid the risk of involvement and consequent loss of objectivity, an alternative technique is used known as *non-participant* observation. In this case the observer is separated from the group and works in what are almost laboratory conditions, e.g. he may observe children at play from behind a one-way glass partition. Such a method may ensure a lesser degree of involvement with his subjects, but it suffers from the disadvantage that the interpretation of what he observes is much more difficult than if the observer were in contact with his subjects. It is not surprising that it has been asserted that non-participant observation produces data which is largely unintelligible, since the observer has no means of ascertaining the reasons for the behaviour he has observed, while participant observation tends to be too subjective to produce data usable for scientific generalisation!

The above point is well made in W. F. Whyte's *Street Corner Society* which reports the author's experiences of observing over several years the activities of a street corner teenage gang. The latter had accepted the author as a person writing a book and he was able to observe what they did. But, as the author notes, the leader of the gang concedes at one point, 'now when I do something I have to think what Bill Whyte will want to know about it and how I can explain it. Before, I used to do things by instinct'.

There is also the problem of what may be termed the ethics of the technique. Have the observers the right to 'pry' into the affairs of others and subject them to publicity in their writings? But even in the writing up of the study, the author may be less than entirely objective in his analysis. As Dr Shipman observed of Whyte's study of the street corner gang, the author was probably affected in his judgements not only because of his respect for the members who had befriended him, but also by the fear that excessive disclosure might lead to the author being 'carved up'!

The main advantage of participant observation is that it gives insights into human behaviour unobtainable in any other way. But, however scientific the observer may try to be in his approach, there is the ever-present danger that he will impose upon his findings the interpretations of his own background and training.

Conclusions

The opening chapters of this book stressed the need to verify the source and quality of any published statistical data. This warning applies with especial force to economic and social investigations where the existence of a few figures sometimes tempts the user to make statements the validity of which rests entirely on some highly dubious and often scanty data. If such data are to be used, their source should be checked. Any good survey report will contain a copy of the schedule used, a summary of the sample design and sometimes the instruction to interviewers on matters such as classification, non-contacts, etc. In other words, all the main points made in the foregoing chapter should find some mention.

For the student reader interested in this branch of statistics, an ounce of practice is infinitely more instructive than a ton of theory. Participation in a survey teaches quite a lot, even if the participation is restricted to acting as an interviewer. The student who would like to try his hand at such work can sometimes find occasional work with survey organisations. These often advertise in the press for temporary staff; while a letter of enquiry to commercial organisations may sometimes produce a response. Failing such opportunities for practice, the student should get hold of as many reports as possible and study them in the light of the above comments. The list below offers some suggestions for further reading in this field.

Selected Survey Reports

General Household Survey 1979.

Family Expenditure Survey (Annual).

National Dwelling and Housing Survey 1979.

Report of Royal Commission on Civil Liability and Compensation for Personal Injury. Cmnd 7054 Vol. II.

Royal Commission on the Distribution of Income and Wealth. Background Paper No. 5 on *Causes of Poverty*.

Report of Committee on the Working of the Abortion Acts. Cmnd 5579 Vol. III A Survey of Abortion Patients.

The Elderly at Home, Audrey Hunt, Social Survey, *Attitudes to Letting*, Social Survey Division of OPCAS.

All the above are published by H.M. Stationery Office.

CHAPTER XVII

SOCIAL STATISTICS

Introduction

Any Government needs to control those functions of society for which it accepts responsibility. In the earliest days the responsibility was limited to making war or keeping the peace. Even at this level for the Government to be able to prosecute its policies most effectively, it needed to know what resources it could draw upon, in particular of men and money. Because of this we find that virtually every civilisation has some records of population counts. The Babylonians (4000 B.C.), the Chinese (3000 B.C.), the Egyptians (2000 B.C.), the Greeks (1000 B.C.) and the Romans (100 B.C.–A.D. 100) all had some form of population count that was often the first stage of more sophisticated Government action. Thus the Greeks went on to prepare electoral rolls and the Romans to organize a system of conscription.

As the need to raise money for state enterprise grew so were more extensive schemes of taxation developed. Initially, these schemes were particularly concerned with ownership of land and overseas trade. It is therefore not surprising that these two areas were the first to be developed statistically. As governments accepted further responsibilities e.g. public health, so more statistical data were collected to enable the state to know the extent of particular problems. A Census of Population in England and Wales was first taken in 1801 and the General Register Office for registering births and deaths was established in 1837. As the state began to discharge responsibilities – both in the social and economic spheres – that it had undertaken there developed an increasing volume of published statistics recording the activities of the state. Statistics of overseas trade, of crime and unemployment are early examples of these activities.

During the nineteenth century the attitude of the state was generally to let economic and social forces function freely regardless of the effects the operation of such forces might have upon society, a policy referred to as *laissez-faire*. Gradually governments began to realise that if they did not intervene to ameliorate the worst effects of economic forces then the overall prosperity of the nation and the living standards of the people would suffer. Thus, with the development in the late 1880s of overseas industries that were in sharp competition with domestic industries, the Government intervened to protect British industries with import duties. Two World Wars followed by the great economic depression in the 1920s and early 30s intensified the need for Government intervention. Thus, the Government was drawn into a partial management of the economy with all this entailed in terms of the collection of data. In his 1956 Budget address Mr Harold Macmillan, then Chancellor of the Exchequer, commented that using the available economic statistics as a basis for stabilising the economy was like looking up this week's trains in last year's Bradshaw. From that time on the output of economic statistics was greatly enlarged and their quality improved. Similarly, the comments of the Committee on the Working of the Monetary System in 1959 led to a significant improvement in the availability and range of financial statistics.

Government intervention was not restricted to management of the economy. In the late 1940s the emergence of the welfare state led to Government intervention in all the main areas of social activity; social security, health, housing and education in particular. The inevitable consequence was the increase in the late 1960s of social statistics to match the expansion of economic statistics which had occurred during the previous decade. In the social sphere, however, definition of variables, the measurement and collection of data are much more difficult and less developed than in the longer established economic areas. Such difficulties have stimulated development of such concepts as social indicators (index numbers of social variables) and means of measuring the 'quality of life'.

It may be seen, therefore, that *official* statistics, *i.e.* those compiled and published by the government, arise from two main sources. The major source of official statistics is that which records the ever-expanding administrative activities of the government. These data are sometimes published in specialist volumes, *e.g.* Criminal Statistics, Statistics of Education, or sometimes as part of the annual report of the government department or body responsible for the particular area. Identifying the source of the data is important because of the variable levels of accuracy and precision that apply to such data. In general, data arising from specific surveys (discussed below) tends to be better defined, more accurate and more comprehensive than administrative data. Furthermore, the statistics generated by administrative action are confined strictly to the action itself rather than covering the whole area of which the administration is but a part. For example, the statistics of unemployment refer only to those registered as unemployed. As the advantage of registration is that those entitled to unemployment benefit must register to be able to draw the benefit, those not entitled to benefit *e.g.* many married women, tend not to register and therefore not to be included in the official estimates of the number of unemployed.

Despite the continuous and rapid expansion of both economic and social statistics produced by the various government departments and, not least, by the Central Statistical Office which had the task of co-ordinating the output and coverage of official statistics, many gaps remained. It was noticeable that a succession of official enquiries during the 1950s and early 1960s found it necessary to supplement the available official statistics with special *ad hoc* surveys. In 1966–67 the House of Commons Estimates Committee took evidence on the subject of the government statistical services and made a number of far-reaching recommendations for their development. A particular and indeed major development in the collection of statistics by the government has been the use of sample surveys. Such surveys, usually *ad hoc*, now constitute a major source of statistical data. As a result of the Estimates Committee recommendations, the then General Register Office and the Government Social Survey were merged into the Office for Population Censuses and Surveys. This body is responsible not only for the population census and the collection and analysis of vital statistics, *i.e.* births, deaths and marriages, but also for carrying out frequent and specialised surveys on subjects and in areas about which the government departments need further information.

These areas may be very wide, such as that nowadays covered by the General Household and Family Expenditure Surveys. In contrast, some topics covered may be very specialised, as may be judged from an extract from just one recent list of new *ad hoc* surveys in 1978 below.

In this chapter and Chapter XVIII key areas of economic and social statistics are reviewed in some detail. There are, however, a few general publications that will provide some indication of the very wide range both of economic and social statistics published by the government. These constitute major source books for official data and the reader should take the earliest opportunity to browse through them in his local reference library. All are published by H.M. Stationery Office.

(i) *Guide to Official Statistics No. 2 – 1978*

The latest edition contains nearly 500 pages of crossed reference description of all the regular publications in the main areas of society and the economy together with special reports and articles with significant statistical content. An extensive and most useful bibliography is included.

(ii) *Annual Abstract of Statistics*

An annual publication which contains about 400 tables giving annual figures usually over a ten-year period from the year before publication. There are also some explanatory notes.

(iii) *Monthly Digest of Statistics*

Each month's issue includes some 175 tables covering the main statistical series relating to the economy and industry for which monthly or quarterly figures are available. The tables of monthly data give at least a year's run of figures and the quarterly series cover at least two years. An *annual* supplement of definitions and explanatory notes published each January is extremely useful.

(iv) *Statistical News*

A quarterly publication of articles and notes of changes and developments in all the main statistical areas. A two-year cumulative index facilitates the tracing of articles in past issues.

(v) *Regional Statistics*

An annual publication of 80 or so tables of mainly economic and industrial data relating to U.K. or Great Britain analysed by the Standard Regions. Time series are usually annual. Appendices give sources of data and define the regions.

(vi) Supplementing the overall perspective provided by the previous publication, there are the following specialist source books:

Scottish Abstract of Statistics
Digest of Welsh Statistics
Digest of Statistics, Northern Ireland
Annual Abstract of Greater London Statistics*.

These are all annual volumes except that for Northern Ireland which is published every six months.

(vii) *Abstract of British Historical Statistics. Second Abstract of British Historical Statistics*

These two specialist publications for economic historians provide major time series for the United Kingdom most of which start in the nineteenth century. The series extends up to 1938 in the first volume and from 1938 to 1965 in the second. The series are mainly of economic data but population and some vital statistics are included. Each section is preceded by descriptive and interpretative notes, and is followed by a bibliography.

* Published by the Greater London Council.

TABLE 35

EXTRACT OF NEW SURVEYS ASSESSED BY THE SURVEY CONTROL UNIT

Title	Sponsor	Those approached	Approximate number approached	Location	Frequency
Pesticide usage in beef and dairy cattle and pig enterprises	DAFS	Farmers	5,850	S	AH
Behavioural responses to new productivity-based incentives	DEM	Managers	100	GB	AH
Developments in industrial democracy in Scotland	DEM	Managers	100	S	AH
Evaluation of the Temporary Employment Subsidy Scheme	DEM	Companies	500	GB	AH
Employers' opinions of proposed short-time working scheme	DEM	Employers	250	GB	AH
Employment opportunities in the inner city	DOE	Employers	850	GB	AH
Commercial application of Queen's Award winning innovations	DOE	Manufacturers	450	GB	AH
Study of land for housebuilding in Greater Manchester	DT	Construction companies	300	NW	AH
Evaluation of European Components Service	MAFF	Engineering companies	582	UK	AH
Duplicate diet study and blood lead survey in Glasgow	MAFF	Mothers	1,000	S	AH
Initial training courses in agriculture 1978 – employees	MSC	Trainees	150	EW	AH
Special measures evaluation – 2nd survey of schoolleavers	MSC	Schoolleavers	1,000	S	AH
Attitudes of the disabled towards employment quota and registration	OME	Adults	NK	GB	AH
Medical assistants' pattern of work and responsibilities in the NHS	OPCS	Doctors/Dentists	702	GB	AH
Debt recovery in Scotland		Debtors	2,500	S	AH
Above tolerable standard housing repairs – social survey	SDD	Households	1,770	S	AH

Abbreviations used

Sponsors
DAFS – Department of Agriculture and Fisheries for Scotland
DEM – Department of Employment
DOE – Department of the Environment
DT – Department of Trade
MAFF – Ministry of Agriculture, Fisheries and Food
MSC – Manpower Services Commission
OME – Office of Manpower Economics
OPCS – Office of Population Censuses and Surveys
SDD – Scottish Development Department

Location
EW – England and Wales
GB – Great Britain
NW – North West England
S – Scotland
UK – United Kingdom

Frequency
AH – Ad Hoc or single time

(*Source: Statistical News No. 43 H.M.S.O.*)

Development of Social Statistics

The growth in the volume of published social statistics is of relatively recent origin, although statistics relating to the population have been collected since the beginning of the 19th century. As noted earlier, the impetus to collection of such data came with the acceptance by the government of its responsibilities for the welfare of the population, starting with the Factory Acts, old age pensions, and unemployment benefit. Nevertheless, the bulk of the data was collected by government departments more as the by-product of their administrative activities than as a conscious part of policy formulation. Furthermore, with the large-scale unemployment of the pre-war period emphasis tended to be placed upon the collection of economic rather than social data.

The bulk of social data, like economic data, was collected by the various departments but, whereas in the case of the economic data the Treasury had an overview of all economic affairs there was no comparable review of the collection of social statistics. This led to a number of deficiencies in various areas of the government statistical service which, in turn, prompted the Estimates Committee of the House of Commons to investigate the situation in the Parliamentary Session 1966-67. The Report on the Government Statistical Services[1] made many detailed observations but, in particular, they noted the lack of development of statistics on social matters when compared with economic statistics. The Committee stressed the need for a much stronger central co-ordinating role for the Central Statistical Office as well as the need for better dissemination of statistics.

A number of important developments in social data occurred shortly after the publication of the report as follows:

(i) Early in 1970 the General Register Office for England and Wales was merged with the Government Social Survey to form the Office of Population Censuses and Surveys controlled by a policy committee chaired by the Director of the Central Statistical Office. Thus the C.S.O. was given much wider powers of control and co-ordination.

(ii) The then Director of the Central Statistical Office, Sir Claus Moser, outlined the policy of his office as developing a system of social statistics, the aim of which 'is to construct a system in which many statistics bearing on social conditions social resources and the flows of people through various activities and institutions are brought together coherently and meaningfully'[2]. The Director also declared the intention of the C.S.O. to

[1]Fourth Report from the Estimates Committee, Session 1966-67, published December, 1966.

[2]Social Trends No. 1.

develop various kinds of social 'indicators' to summarise the
'quality of life'. For example, to derive some quantities to
'measure' job satisfaction.*

(iii) Dissemination of statistics was improved by the publication of a
new annual volume in 1970 entitled *Social Trends*. This brought
together many statistical series covering 15 or so of the main
areas of social activity including population, health, education,
housing, personal expenditure and public order. *Social Trends*
also includes in each edition two or three major articles on
developments in social statistics as well as extensive notes of
explanation and commentary.

Statistical News started publication on a quarterly basis in
1968 and, as mentioned earlier, contains articles and notes on
developments in all areas of statistics.

Such improvements have created a great advance in social statistics
in the 1970's. It must be remembered, however, that the advance is
measured from a very small beginning and that there is still a considerable way to go before we can approach anything like a statistical
model of even one area of social activity. The rate of advance
slowed considerably towards the end of the 1970's because of the
restrictions on public expenditure to fund research and provide
additional statistical services. It is of interest that the United States
of America has experienced a similar cycle of events. In 1970 the
U.S. Federal Bureau of Health published a document entitled *Toward
a Social Report*. This outlined in some detail the way in which there
should be a social statistical coverage of the country at least equivalent to that provided in economic statistics, so that the President's
annual address to the nation could cover both social and economic
developments.

One further fundamental development must be mentioned. This
arises from the work of Professor Richard Stone using the idea of
flow in social statistics. He started in the education sphere by
demonstrating that flow is the concept of following the individual
through the stages of pre-school, nursery, primary, secondary and
then possibly into further or higher education and training. It is only
by showing this flow from one stage to another that the operation
of the whole system can be studied. The Perks Report on *Criminal
Statistics* (see p.505) advocated the replacement of a number of
separate series of administrative statistics by a system charting the
course of an accused person through the stages of trial and punishment. While the principle was accepted its application is still awaited.
The whole idea of 'flow' breaks down the isolated 'snapshots' of

*This topic is discussed later on pp.521.

administrative action and is a positive step towards a social model.

The student with any interest in social statistics should obtain a copy of *Social Trends* for the latest available year and familiarise himself with the range and coverage of the current output of published social data. In the sections which follow, particular areas of social data are described and discussed.

Population Statistics

The most important single source of statistical information relating to the social scene is the Census of Population. The Census consists of a complete enumeration of persons in the country on a given night. In addition to counting the number of people, information relating to their sex, age, civil status, *i.e.* married, single, etc., their occupations, and the industry in which they work, together with further information on housing conditions, educational attainment, etc. are usually collected. The first Census in Great Britain was taken in 1801 and there has been one at ten-yearly intervals ever since, apart from 1941. It is customary to use the national registration figures prepared in September 1939 as the best measure of the population between the 1931 and 1951 Censuses. The Census data for England and Wales are published separately from those for Scotland and Northern Ireland. Although the Census is taken at decennial intervals, since the passage of the Census Act 1920 power has existed to hold a Census at five-yearly intervals. These powers were exercised for the first time ever in 1966. It was the intention of the government to hold *sample* censuses between the decennial full censuses. However, having undertaken much of the preparatory work for a sample census in 1976 it was cancelled at short notice to economise in public expenditure. The importance of the Census cannot be over-estimated. Quite apart from providing information relating to the population, its age, sex, geographical and occupation distribution, all of which analyses are relevant to the effective administration of the country, the Census provides a great deal of information relating to social conditions, particularly in respect of housing, occupational mortality, and fertility. Questions on the educational attainment of citizens and the number of persons with scientific qualifications are relevant to the formulation of educational policies and manpower distribution in industry. In 1966 information was collected relating to the mobility of the population, *i.e.* the movement of persons and households from one part of the country to another, and also some information relating to private cars, garage facilities and the journey to work.

The average Census contains about two dozen questions most of which remain unchanged from Census to Census, *i.e.* those relating to the age and sex composition of households, etc., and the occupations of their members.* However, the Census is also used to collect information relating to special problems of the time. For example, the 1911 Census is often referred to as the Fertility Census, since this was the first occasion on which questions relating to fertility were asked. The 1921 Census is known as the Dependency Census because special questions were asked relating to widows and orphans in view of the manpower losses sustained during World War I.

The 1931 Census was of interest in that it collected data, in the usual way, of all the people actually in the household at the appointed time of the Census (the *de facto* basis) but also asked all respondents their usual place of residence (the *de jure* basis). The inclusion of the normal residence question enabled a check to be made on differences in the population count that arose between the *de facto* and the *de jure* basis of enumeration. The response to these questions in the Census revealed that, provided the day of the Census was chosen to minimise the numbers of people absent from their own homes, the *de facto* basis had no major inaccuracies. It was also much easier to administer since the *de jure* basis frequently posed problems for the enumerator who is required, on collecting the schedule, to check the entries on the Census form as completed by the householder. In the 1951 Census new questions were asked relating to fertility, and also some new questions relating to housing conditions. A feature of the 1961 Census was the introduction for the first time of multi-phase sampling, whereby 10 per cent of the population were asked to complete an additional schedule, which asked questions relating to their qualifications in science or technology. In 1971 questions on accommodation and amenities were asked. The questions on technical qualification asked for the first time in 1961 were repeated in 1971.

The accuracy and reliability of the information collected in a Census depend on a number of factors. The first and most important is the enumerators themselves. These are part-time workers whose task is to distribute the Census schedules to every household within their allotted enumeration district, of which there are 71,400 in England and Wales alone. In other words, the completeness of the coverage depends on the knowledge possessed by the enumerator of his enumeration district. To the extent that he misses any households, there is under-counting. Having distributed the schedules, he must ensure that immediately after the Census night he collects the completed schedules and checks that there are no omissions or obvious mistakes. This is by no means a simple task. In 1951, for example, the weather on the day after the Census was very bad, and the scrutiny of the schedules undoubtedly suffered, since in most cases the schedules

*Guides to Official Sources, No. 2, Census of population 1801-1951, provides comparative tabulations of all the questions asked at each Census since 1801, as well as providing detailed information about each Census.

were merely handed back over the doorstep. The choice of date needs perhaps some explanation. The Census in England and Wales normally takes place on a Sunday in April. In 1951 it was April 8, in 1961 April 23 and in 1971 it was April 25. The choice is dictated partly by weather conditions, which affect the enumerators, but above all by the need to avoid periods in which there is extensive population movement; the Easter or August Bank Holidays would obviously be unsatisfactory in so far as the population of the seaside resorts would be grossly inflated at the expense of that of the inland industrial and urban centres.

Further sources of inaccuracy and error arise in the completion of the schedule itself. This is performed by the head of the household, and since the standard of education and literacy varies widely among the 18 million or so heads of households in this country, mistakes are likely to be made. Many of these can be picked out in the editing, which is carried on during the tabulation process at the Census Offices. Here, too, of course, is a potentially fruitful source of error. Classification of occupations, for example, is extremely complex.

The Department of Employment in 1972 produced a *Classification of Occupations* and *Directory of Occupational Titles* containing some 3,500 separately identified and defined occupations. From these a list of 400 key occupations has been prepared that will be used for, amongst other purposes, collecting similar data in the 1981 Census. Errors may arise here, just as errors are possible in transferring information from the schedules on to the punched cards. In due course the information on the punched cards is transferred to magnetic tape. Since 1961, an electronic computer has been used in the preparation of the published data.

The use of computers is being further extended to enable the data to be edited in certain respects automatically. Such editing has two components. One is a batch quality control scheme for each enumeration district where the data for each district are compared automatically in the computer with a set of previously inserted tolerance limits which determine the permitted margin of error. Only if the errors in the batch of data exceed those limits is it necessary for a clerical examination to be made. The other component of the automatic editing system is an imputation system. This automatically supplies missing data items from a previously compiled data bank. It is hoped to use these processes of automatic editing on the data from the 1981 Census.

In view of what has been said about the likelihood of error in the Census, it is hardly surprising to learn that the Census Office undertakes what are known as small-scale post enumeration surveys. The object of these enquiries is to see how well the questions and instructions have been understood, and how accurate are the replies to the questions. In addition, of course, they also provide some indication as to the completeness of the count, *i.e.* the degree of under-counting or omission. In the 1951 Census, post-enumeration surveys were made into the information relating to household arrangements, *i.e.* the number of households sharing or without certain domestic facilities such as piped water, w.c.'s, bath, etc. These surveys revealed substantial errors in the information provided. This was also true of the questions relating to education in the same Census, as described later. Misstatements of age and occupation were detected by comparing the information relating to a sample of persons who had died within a few weeks of the Census with that contained on their death certificates. Nevertheless, despite such mistakes, and it would be foolish to pretend that in a survey of some 18 million households containing nearly 50 million persons some mistakes are not inevitable, the Census authorities believe, and it seems with ample justification, that a high degree of accuracy can be claimed for most of the information provided by the Census. Furthermore, in the case of age, special techniques for adjusting misstatements and errors in age are available to the statisticians.* In 1961 the post-enumeration survey was published in Part II of the *General Report*. This showed that improvements were needed in the data processing system, in the sampling techniques and the pre-testing of enumeration procedures. The results at the post-enumeration survey of the 1971 Census have yet (March 1979) to be published.

The mass of information produced by the Census of Population takes several years to process and publish. The pattern of publications is more or less as follows. The first report, appearing within a few months of the Census itself, is the *Preliminary Report*, which states the populations of the administrative areas of England and Wales at the last two Census dates, with the absolute and proportionate change therein. This is then followed by a series of *County Reports*, although in 1951 two invaluable volumes entitled *One Per Cent Sample Tables* were produced within less than two years of the Census being held. This experiment was unfortunately not repeated in 1961, since it was hoped that the use of an electronic computer would expedite publication of the main data. For various reasons this was not practicable. However the computer problems were largely resolved by the time of the 1971 Census and *One Per Cent Sample Tables* were published in 1972. The *County Reports* appear in rapid succession, and these contain comprehensive data based on the entire schedule of questions for the population resident in the county at the time of the Census. They are especially useful for information relating to housing conditions

*See General Report 1951, p.35.

and household composition. Then follow the major special 'subject' volumes on occupation, housing, industry and, in 1951 the Fertility Report; and then the *General Report*. For most purposes the reader can obtain all the information he requires as far as his own administrative areas is concerned from the *County Report* and the *General Report*. The latter is especially valuable in drawing attention to any defects in the data that the Census authorities have come across in the processing thereof. Details of the census publications are normally provided in any of the individual publications. Accompanying the Census volumes are the so-called *Decennial Supplements*, which in 1951 comprised a two-volume study of occupational mortality, a separate study of area mortality, and the official English Life Table No. 11.

A similar pattern of publication of Census material was followed in 1961. Thus:

1. *Preliminary Report* giving the population by sex of the administrative areas with comparable figures for earlier Censuses.

2. *County Reports* separate volumes for counties and groups of counties containing detailed figures classified by age and sex as well as information on dwellings and housing conditions.

3. (*a*) National Subject Volumes based on the *full* enumeration of age, marital condition, usual residence, birthplace, nationality, housing household composition and fertility.

   (*b*) National Subject Volumes, based on the 10% sample, covering scientific and technological qualifications, occupation, industry, workplace, education and migration.

4. *General Report* – Part I of which dealt with the historical background, organisation, enumeration, processing and publication procedures. Part II dealt with the sampling procedures, postenumeration survey, the quality of the data and comparison of 1951 and 1961 Censuses. Part III dealt with the special points of procedure and publications dealing with Scotland.

The *Ten Per Cent Sample Census* was taken on Sunday 24th April, 1966.

This Census was primarily intended to give detailed information for the country as a whole and the larger towns and administrative areas in particular. It did not, however, provide the detail for the smaller areas that a full Census enumeration would provide. The sampling frame was made up from the 1961 Census records of dwellings supplemented by Inland Revenue valuation records of accommodation brought into rating since the beginning of April 1961. Systematic interval sampling with a random start was used to select respondents.

The questions asked were similar to those used in the 10% sample enquiry on technical qualifications in the 1961 census, with certain additions. The latter included questions on:

1. usual place of residence five years ago, together with information on place of birth, the purpose of these questions being to give more information on internal migration;

2. car ownership and garaging, and means of transport to work. This information was needed to help urban planners;

3. information on educational qualifications obtained since the age of 18 and of people having more than one job.

As the volume of data from the Sample Census was considerably less than in a full Census and sole use of a computer was obtained (in 1961 the General Register Office had to share the War Office computer) all reports relating to the 10% sample were published by the middle of 1969. The reports were extended and reorganised and published as follows:

(a) Great Britain – overall summary, technical qualifications, immigration, qualified manpower and economic activity tables.

(b) *County Reports* for the administrative areas of England and Wales.

(c) National Volumes on workplace, transport, education, household composition, housing, usual residence, and migration by region.

The 1971 Census of Population was held on 25th April, 1971. A few changes from the 1966 schedule of questions were made. These included:

(i) addition of the country of birth of each person's father and mother to examine more closely the number and distribution of second generation immigrants;

(ii) additional questions on all live births to help ascertain trends in family size and spacing;

(iii) more detail on scientific and technical qualifications for the educational and manpower planners;

(iv) a new way of categorising buildings to determine what was defined in the Census as a 'structurally separate dwelling';

(v) a description of work done to help in the coding of occupations.

The published analyses of the 1971 Census were more than twice as large as those of 1961 – some 26,000 tables compared with 12,000 tables. In addition, there is a large number of unpublished tables available for the specialist user. More staff were employed to speed up publication and some of the topics were analysed and published on the basis of a 10% sample of the data.

The *Preliminary Report* of the Census giving provisional population counts by sex in local authority areas was published in August 1971. Two other early publications were made;

(*a*) an *Advance Analysis* of a few topics, *e.g.* sex, age, marital status and country of birth were published on a county basis during 1972. The interesting aspect of this publication was that it was based on the use of direct-machine-readable returns made by the enumerators.

(*b*) (One per cent sample) *Summary Tables* of the main topics of the Census were published in 1973.

The bulk of the remaining reports were published in the years 1973 to 1975 and included:

> Housing (4 volumes)
> Persons of Pensionable Age
> Car Ownership
> Economic Activity
> Demography
> Fertility (6 volumes)
> Country of Birth
> Qualified Manpower
> Usual Residence
> County Reports (3 volumes per county)
> Non-Private Households
> Migration (25 volumes)
> Occupation Industry and Socio-Economic Class (3 volumes)
> Workplace and Transport
> Household Composition (3 volumes)

Table 36 shows the growth in the population of England and Wales between 1841 and 1971. The figure shown for each year is the Census count, with the exception of 1941 when the mid-year estimate, *i.e.* as at 30th June, is used. The two adjacent columns illustrate an exercise in very simple statistical analysis, a comparison of the absolute increase in population numbers with the proportionate or percentage increase. Thus it will be seen that although the absolute increase between 1841 and 1851 was almost the same as that between 1941 and 1951, the relative rate of increase in the earlier decade was two-and-a-half times as high.

TABLE 36'
POPULATION CENSUS OF ENGLAND AND WALES 1841-1971

Census Year	Population 000's	Absolute Increase 000's	Decennial Percentage Increase %
1841	15,914	—	—
1851	17,928	2,014	12·7
1861	20,066	2,138	11·9
1871	22,712	2,646	13·2
1881	25,974	3,262	14·4
1891	29,003	3,029	11·7
1901	32,528	3,525	12·2
1911	36,070	3,542	10·9
1921	37,887	1,817	5·0
1931	39,952	2,065	5·5
1941*	41,748	1,796	4·5
1951	43,758	2,010	4·8
1961	46,072	2,314	5·1
1971	48,900	2,828	6·1

Sources: Reg. Gen. Statistical Review 1962, Part II. Table A.1. and Social Trends No. 8.
*Mid-year estimate; no Census held in this year.

Registration Data

The Census of Population as a decennial snapshot of the population at a specific point in time provides a detailed analysis of many aspects of the population. However, a method for estimating changes that occur between the Censuses is needed. Such a method is found in the system of registering such vital events as births, deaths and marriages as they occur. The General Register Office in this country was established in 1837. Two years later Dr William Farr became 'Compiler of Abstracts' in that office, and, according to a biographer, 'the next forty years of his life were almost exclusively devoted to the, to him, congenial task of creating and developing a national system of vital statistics, which has not only popularised sanitary questions in England in such a manner as to render health progress an accomplished fact but which has, practically, been adopted in all the civilised countries of the world'.* Apart from underlining the tremendous work carried out by Farr in the analysis of vital statistics during the 19th century, this quotation also reflects the change in emphasis which has taken place in vital statistics since the days of Farr. In the past, the analysis of vital statistics was predominantly a concern with public health, hence the stress on birth and death registration. More recently, however, more importance has been attached to marriage registration statistics, as well as those relating to divorce, adoption, legitimation and separation, etc. According to a United Nations study, 'the vital statistics system includes the local registra-

*N. A. Humphreys, quoted in the *Handbook of Vital Statistics Methods*, U.N. 1955.

tion, the statistical recording and reporting of the occurrence of, and the collection, compilation, presentation, analysis, and distribution of statistics pertaining to vital events, *i.e.* live births, deaths, foetal deaths, marriages, divorces, adoptions, legitimations, recognitions, annulments, and legal separations'.[1]

It should be noted that the mere setting up of a registration system does not by itself automatically ensure the notification to the authority of vital events. For example, in some countries, the birth of female babies is frequently unnotified, but this deficiency can be picked up by comparing the ratio of registered male to female births. Since this ratio is more or less constant, any variation is immediately evident. Likewise, under-notification of deaths can also be deduced by comparing the death rates derived from the available data with those of other countries where living conditions are almost comparable and where the registration system is better developed.

The practice of registering vital events is well established in this country, and it is unlikely that the figures are subject to any significant degree of inaccuracy.[2] There are both legal and other kinds of pressures to ensure registration. For example, a corpse cannot be buried until the Registrar's certificate of registration has been produced. The birth of infants is notified by the hospital authorities and medical practitioner to ensure that the parents of the child ultimately register all the requisite details. A marriage is automatically registered whether it takes place in church or register office. On the occasion of registration, a good deal more information is required than the mere fact of the vital events. In particular, the Population (Statistics) Acts of 1938 and 1960 require the informant to give not only the obvious facts concerning the vital event, *e.g.* birth of a child, but also information relating to the duration of marriage, age of parents, occupation of father, etc. The later Act also collects further information about still-births, on the basis of which the statistician can carry out detailed analyses which may ultimately form the basis for future health policies. In brief, then, it can be said that the system of vital registration in Britain is efficient and the data collected thereby highly reliable. Once this has been proved to the statistician's satisfaction, it then remains to consider to what purposes these statistics are put.

The detailed analysis of the data arising from the registration system will be considered later. Here the use of the data in estimating the population between Censuses and of projecting population trends into the future will be examined.

Up to 1975 the Registrar General published a three-part *Statistical*

[1]U.N., *op. cit.*

[2]See General Report, 1951 Census for a discussion of such inaccuracies.

Review of England and Wales* which contained mid-year population estimates and a commentary on trends in vital events (the 1975 publication contained the figures for 1973 while the last *Commentary* volume appeared in the 1967 volume). The *Statistical Review* has now been replaced by a wide range of specialist publications from the Office of Population Censuses and Surveys (OPCS). The three series relevant to this section are:

PP1 Population Estimates

PP2 Population Projections – national figures

PP3 Population Projections – sub-national figures, *i.e.* regions and conurbations

There is also a quarterly journal entitled *Population Trends*, 16 issues of which had appeared by mid-1979 which contains articles on population and medical topics as well as statistical tables.

Until 1975 the Registrar General also published *Weekly* and *Quarterly Returns* which were then replaced by a series of OPCS *Monitors* dealing with individual topics, *e.g.* abortion, deaths, births, adoption, migration, together with a *Weekly Return* of vital events similar to that previously published by the Registrar General.

The process of estimating mid-year population size involves:

(*a*) defining the population of the Census year;

(*b*) adding to the Census population the net natural change in population (*i.e.* the difference between the numbers of births and deaths) from the date of the Census to the middle of the year for which the size of the population is required;

(*c*) applying to the Census population the net effect of migration over the same period as in (*b*), *i.e.* the difference between emigration and immigration).

The matter of definition of the population is important in this as in all statistical work. There are *three* definitions of population. The first is the *home* population, which is the number of people of all types actually in England and Wales on the night of the Census. This is sometimes referred to as the *de facto* population. The second definition, *i.e. total*, is the home population plus members of H.M. Forces belonging to England and Wales but serving overseas, minus the Forces of other countries temporarily in England and Wales. The final definition, *civilian*, is the total population minus members of H.M. Forces belonging to England and Wales at home or overseas. It will come as no surprise to the reader to learn that pre-war population estimates were defined on a slightly different basis, and that the *home* population is the present figure most nearly comparable with pre-war totals.

* (i) Medical (ii) Civil, and (iii) Commentary volumes

The actual count from the registration of live births and deaths is relatively accurate because of the safeguards built into the registration system mentioned earlier. The migration figures, however, are subject to substantial error, largely because of the difficulty of applying the definition of an immigrant. The definition of an *immigrant* is a person who having resided elsewhere for at least the previous year states on entry to this country that he intends to stay here for one year or longer. An *emigrant* is a person who has been a resident of this country for at least the past year who states on his departure that he intends to stay abroad for at least one year. As people can be admitted as visitors and then be granted residence, while people can emigrate and then change their minds quite quickly and return to this country, it is hardly surprising that the resultant figures are unreliable.

The basis for adjusting the Census population to obtain the mid-year estimate is illustrated in the following table from *Social Trends No. 8*.

TABLE 37

POPULATION CHANGES – UNITED KINGDOM

	Census enumerated			Mid-year estimates				
	1901 –11	1911 –31	1931 –51	1951 –61	1961 –66	1966 –71	1971 –76	1976 –77[1]
Home population (millions) at start of period	38·2	42·1	46·0	50·3	52·8	54·5	55·6	55·9
Average annual change (thousands):								
Live births	1,091	899	785	839	988	937	766	..
Deaths	624	622[2]	598[2]	593	633	644	670	..
Net natural change	467	277	188	246	355	293	96	..
Net civilian migration	−82	−79	+22	− 7	− 8	−56	−45	..
Other net changes				+13	− 8[3]	−16[3]	13[3]	..
Overall annual change	385	198	213	252	339	222	64	..

[1]Provisional.
[2]Including deaths of non-civilians and merchant seamen who died outside the country.
[3]The England and Wales component includes changes in armed forces and in visitor balance and balancing adjustments to reconcile population increase with estimates of natural increase and the civilian migration.

Sources: Census of Population Reports; Office of Population Censuses and Surveys

One of the most interesting features disclosed by successive Censuses is the changing pattern in the age distribution that has emerged over the past century. Even in the past fifty years there have been marked changes. Whereas at the 1911 Census children under 15 constituted 30·6 per cent of the entire population and only 5·2 per cent were over 65, in mid-1961, the proportion of under-15s had fallen to 22·9 per cent, while those who had passed their 65th birthday comprised 11·9 per cent of the population. Fifteen years later in 1976, although the proportion of under-15s remained at 22·9 per cent, the number of those who were 65 years or older had increased still further to form 16·3 per cent of the population. The Registrar General devotes considerable space to analyses of the changing age structure. The population is classified by reference to age usually by single years up to age 20, although there are sub-groupings for each quinquennial age group, and thenceafter, *i.e.* from 20 onwards, quinquennial age groups, *e.g.* 20-24, 25-29, etc., are used. This is done for both sexes and for each of the three definitions of population to which attention was drawn earlier. The age structure of the population is important, not merely in terms of knowing how many young working and old people there are, but also for purposes of making population projections. Since the Royal Commission on Population reported at the end of the last war, the Registrar General has prepared a number of population projections which appeared in the *Annual Review* and the fourth quarter's issue of the *Quarterly Return*. Table 38 overleaf illustrates the form in which such data are published.

A highly practical method of bringing home the effects of the changing age structure is illustrated in Figure 24. Basically the diagram is akin to the bar diagram illustrated in Figure 25, the bars to the left of the central ordinate measuring off the number of males at each age (this is usually done in quinquennial age groups), while those to the right measure the number of females. The age structure

Figure 24

POPULATION PYRAMIDS

1891

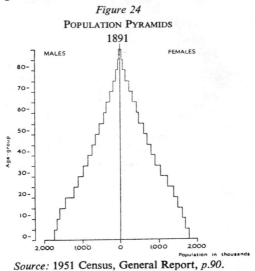

Source: 1951 Census, General Report, *p.90.*

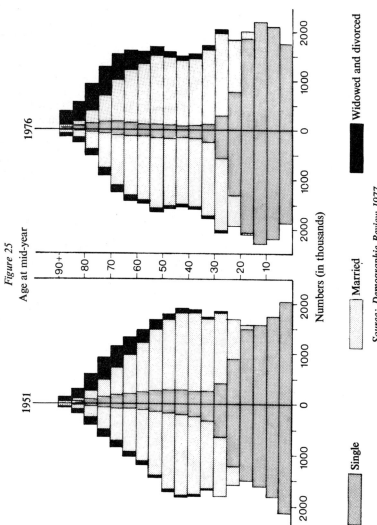

Figure 25
Age at mid-year

Numbers (in thousands)

Source: Demographic Review 1977.

Single

Married

Widowed and divorced

TABLE 38

SEX AND AGE STRUCTURE OF THE POPULATION[1]

Great Britain

	Census enumerated				Mid-year estimates					Projections[2,3]		
	1901	1911	1921	1931	1941	1951	1961	1971	1977	1981	1991	2001
By sex and age group (millions):												
Males:												
Under 16[4]	6·2	6·5	6·2	5·6	5·1	5·8	6·7	7·3	6·9	6·3	6·3	6·9
16–29	5·2	5·4	5·3	5·8	5·8	5·3	4·9	5·6	5·8	6·1	6·2	5·1
30–44	3·6	4·3	4·3	4·5	5·5	5·5	5·3	4·9	5·2	5·5	6·0	6·6
45–64	2·7	3·2	4·1	4·6	5·0	5·6	6·4	6·5	6·2	6·1	6·0	6·5
65–74	0·6	0·7	0·9	1·1	1·4	1·6	1·6	1·6	2·2	2·2	2·1	2·0
75–84	0·2	0·3	0·3	0·4	0·5	0·7	0·7	0·7	0·8	0·9	1·0	1·0
85 and over							0·1	0·1	0·1	0·1	0·2	0·2
All ages	18·5	20·4	21·0	22·1	23·3	24·4	25·7	27·1	27·2	27·2	27·8	28·3
Females:												
Under 16[4]	6·2	6·5	6·1	5·5	5·0	5·6	6·4	6·9	6·5	6·0	5·9	6·5
16–29	5·6	5·8	5·9	6·0	5·8	5·2	4·8	5·4	5·6	5·8	5·9	4·8
30–44	3·9	4·6	5·0	5·2	5·8	5·7	5·5	4·8	5·1	5·4	5·9	6·3
45–59	2·4	2·9	3·6	4·2	4·6	5·1	5·5	5·2	5·0	4·8	4·6	5·3
60–74	1·3	1·5	1·9	2·4	3·0	3·5	3·9	4·5	4·5	4·5	4·2	3·9
75–84	0·3	0·4	0·5	0·6	0·8	1·1	1·2	1·4	1·6	1·7	1·8	1·8
85 and over							0·2	0·4	0·4	0·4	0·6	0·6
All ages	19·7	21·7	23·0	24·0	24·9	26·1	27·3	28·6	28·7	28·5	28·9	29·2
Sex ratio (males per 100 females):												
Under 16[4]	99·8	100·4	101·4	102·0	102·8	104·3	104·5	105·5	105·6	105·9	106·2	106·2
16–44	92·4	92·8	87·9	91·4	97·4	98·7	101·1	102·7	103·4	103·5	103·9	104·8
45 and over	86·6	86·9	87·7	85·2	81·9	80·8	81·1	81·0	81·3	81·5	82·5	84·1
All ages	93·7	93·7	91·5	92·0	93·3	93·4	94·1	94·7	95·0	95·2	96·0	96·9
By country (millions):												
England	30·5	33·6	35·2	37·4	41·7	41·4	43·7	46·2	46·4	46·2	47·1	47·8
Wales	2·0	2·4	2·7	2·6		2·6	2·6	2·7	2·8	2·8	2·9	2·9
Scotland	4·5	4·8	4·9	4·8	5·2	5·2	5·2	5·2	5·2	5·2	5·2	5·2
Northern Ireland	1·2	1·2	1·3	1·2	1·3	1·4	1·4	1·5	1·5	1·5	1·6	1·6
United Kingdom	38·2	42·1	44·0	46·0	48·2	50·6	53·0	55·7	55·9	55·7	56·7	57·5

Note: See also Table 1.7. (International comparisons).

[1] See Appendix B, Chapter 1: Population.

[2] Figures in italics are based partly on assumptions made about future fertility rates.

[3] 1977-based.

[4] 15 for 1901–1951.

Source: Census of Population Reports: Population Projections 1977–2017, *Office of Population Censuses and Surveys*

of the population in 1891 with its predominantly young population and very small proportion aged over 60 is in marked contrast to that of 1951, which shows in every sense of the term a middle-aged spread. The diagram for 1976 shows the 'middle-age spread' of the 1950s has moved into the retirement groups, while the birth bulge just beginning to show in 1951, has developed into an adolescent spread. The population pyramids below come from the General Report of the 1951 census and the 1977 *Demographic Review.**

Infant Mortality

In the discussion of standardisation reference has been made to the death rates of specific ages. The deaths at the beginning of life are a matter of particular concern and a number of specialised death rates are calculated. Most of these are defined below for information but, in terms of calculation and interpretation, they are viewed in the same way as other age specific rates.

Stillbirth Rate:

A stillbirth is a child born dead and over 28 weeks gestation and the ratio is given by:

$$\frac{\text{Number of stillbirths}}{\text{Stillbirths} + \text{live births}} \times \frac{1,000}{1}$$

Early neo-natal Rate:

$$\frac{\text{Number of deaths in first week of life}}{\text{Number of live births}} \times \frac{1,000}{1}$$

Peri-natal mortality Rate:

$$\frac{\text{Stillbirths} + \text{early neo-natal deaths}}{\text{Stillbirths} + \text{live births}} \times \frac{1,000}{1}$$

Neo-natal Rate:

$$\frac{\text{Number of deaths in first four weeks of life}}{\text{Number of live births}} \times \frac{1,000}{1}$$

Infant mortality Rate:

$$\frac{\text{Number of deaths under one year of age}}{\text{Number of live births}} \times \frac{1,000}{1}$$

Maternal mortality Rate:

$$\frac{\text{Number of maternal deaths}}{\text{Stillbirths} + \text{live births}} \times \frac{1,000}{1}$$

As a further variant the above rates can be calculated separately for legitimate and illegitimate births.

*This was a separate special publication reviewing the state of the population and post-war demographic changes published by H.M. Stationery Office in late 1978.

Internal Migration

The distribution of population throughout the country is continually changing. Most of these changes reflect the impact of changes in the national economy.

Most of the data on internal migration comes from the Census of Population. Since 1851 there has been a question included on place of birth and, from this, a crude indication can be obtained of the scale of movement. However it is only since 1961 that specific questions were included to measure internal migration. Some studies of internal migration had been made earlier using data other than the Census. Thus Newton and Jeffery (1951)[1] and Rowntree (1957)[2] used the National Register Data for 1948-50 while Hollingsworth (1968)[3] used the Central Register of the National Health Service for Scotland. A particularly interesting study of population movements in England and Wales 1851-1951, was made by Friedlander and Roshier (1966)[4]. This study showed that in the period 1851-1901 there was quite heavy migration from Central, West and South-West England to Glamorgan and Monmouthshire and from the Eastern and Southern Counties to London, Surrey and Middlesex. The pattern changed in the period 1901-1951 so that there was a movement of people away from London to the surrounding counties, e.g. from South Wales to North Wales, the Home Counties and the Midlands; and generally from the Northern Counties to Eastern and Southern Counties.

Since 1951 the rate of internal migration has tended to increase. Thus, in 1961 in Great Britain 5·1 million people had changed their address during the previous year. By 1971 the number had increased to 5·9 million and even allowing for the increase in total population this represented a rise from 9.9 per cent in 1961 to 10·9 per cent in 1971. The current trends in overall terms of migration flows are from the South-East and the North to East Anglia, East Midlands and the South-West. Between 1966 and 1971 there were very few movements between conurbations (the very large city areas such as London, Manchester and Glasgow) only 200,000. However, there were large movements of population (2·3 million) from the conurbations to other parts of the country.

[1]Newton, M. P. and Jeffery, J. R. 'Internal Migration: Some aspects of population movements within England and Wales.' General Register Office Studies on Medical and Population Subjects No. 5. H.M.S.O.

[2]Rowntree, J. A. 'Internal Migration: A Study of the frequency of movement of migrants.' General Register Office Studies on Medical and Population Subjects No. 11, H.M.S.O.

[3]Hollingsworth, J. H. 'Internal Migration Statistics from the Central Register for Scotland of the National Health Service. JRSS Series A 131, 3pp. 340-383.

[4]Friedlander, R. and Roshier, R. J. 'Internal Migration in England and Wales 1851-1951. Population Studies No. 19, H.M.S.O.

Other Vital Rates

The second element in the projection of population by the component method is that of estimating the addition to the population by births. As mentioned earlier, the trend of births can and does change much more frequently and sharply than the trend in deaths. It is for this reason that a number of variables are measured to give indications of possible changes in current birth trends. Such variables include legitimacy, marriage, divorce, abortions, reproduction and fertility. The actual process of counting the number of events occurring as a proportion of the number of the population (defined perhaps in various ways) and then multiplied by, say, 1,000 gives a rate.

For example, the *crude marriage rate* is the result of expressing the number of men and women marrying in that year per thousand of the population of all ages. Over long periods of time, this may prove to be an unsatisfactory measure for comparative purposes, since not everyone in the population is eligible to marry, *i.e.* what proportion of the population is already married, what proportion of the population is too young? Thus, also calculated are marriage rates per thousand of unmarried men of 15 years and over, a similar rate for women aged 15 and over. In addition to these there is a further rate for unmarried men aged 20-44, and one for unmarried women aged 15-39. The choice of the last two age groups is reasonably self-evident. These are the age limits between which most people marry.*

The *crude birth rate*, like the marriage rate, is a simple measure derived by expressing the number of births in each year as a rate per 1,000 of the mid-year population of that year – in England and Wales the population as estimated on the 30th June. The reader should note the important statistical point that the date of registration is seldom the date of the vital event. This means that children born at Christmas may not be registered until the New Year, and thus might be counted in to the births of the following year for purposes of calculating these birth rates. At present it is customary to take the date of occurrence into account, not dates of registration.[1] But this was not always the practice. The crude birth rate as a measure of fertility suffers from the defect that a large section of the total population has nothing to do with child-bearing, *i.e.* the very young or aged, and the majority of unmarried people. A better measure of changes in fertility is provided by the *legitimate fertility rate*, which expresses the number of children born to married women as a rate per thousand of married women who are aged between 15 and 44. The illegitimate rate is merely a form of percentage of all births. Thus, in 1977 the

---

*Given the age groupings used it is convenient to use the number of unmarried women aged 15-39 as the denominator although the minimum legal age for marriage is 16.

rate of 98 per thousand merely indicates that approximately 10 per cent of all live births were illegitimate.[2] The *infant mortality rate*, to which reference was made above is interesting not least because of the tremendously rapid fall that has taken place within this century. It is derived by expressing the number of deaths in the year among babies under one year of age per thousand of all live births recorded in that year. Note that, strictly speaking, the sum of the deaths of such infants occurring in the year may, in fact, relate to children born in the previous year, but no adjustment is normally made for this fact.

An alternative, as was explained earlier, is the so-called *fertility rate*, whereby the number of births are related to the number of women of child-bearing age, normally taken as between 15 and 44. This is not completely satisfactory, for while about 90 per cent of births take place within wedlock, a small proportion do not, and therefore if the proportions of women in the population who are married changes significantly, the fertility rate may be affected, merely by the greater frequency of marriage in the population.

Net Reproduction Rate

An improved measure of fertility may be derived by using the female *age specific* fertility rates, *i.e.* we compare the fertility rates of each age group of women of reproductive age, *i.e.* 15-19, 20-24, etc. This comparison can be simplified by aggregating the age specific fertility rates as in cols. 2-4 in Table 39 below. This provides a hypothetical total of babies who would be born to a group of women who commenced their child-bearing period together, and neither die nor migrate until they have reached the end of that period. Such a rate is known as the *gross reproduction rate* (G.R.R.) and this has a value of unity where the number of female children born corresponds with the number of women in this hypothetical group. The G.R.R. suffers from the defect that a number of women will die during their child-bearing period, and thus the G.R.R. gives an upper limit to the number of babies that may be born given the age specific fertility rates. To take account of mortality, there is calculated a so-called *net reproduction rate* (N.R.R.). This estimates the average number of daughters that would be produced by women throughout their lifetime if they were exposed at each age to the fertility and mortality rates on which the calculation is based. As with the G.R.R., so an N.R.R. of unity represents replacement of the female generation. Table 39 below illustrates the calculation of both reproduction rates. The age specific fertility rates are based on both male and female

[1]The registration of a birth may be made any time up to 6 weeks after the event.

[2]An illegitimate fertility rate can be calculated by expressing the number of such births as a rate per 1,000 unmarried, divorced and widowed women aged 15-44.

births to the women in the various age groups. Column 5, headed lx, shows the number of female survivors in the successive age groups, while Column 6 shows the number of total years of life lived within each five-year period by the survivors in each age group.[1]

The reader should note that the only difference between the gross and net rates in the above calculation is that while for purposes of calculating the female G.R.R. it is assumed that the original cohort of 1,000 women remains alive throughout the reproductive period 15-49, in the case of the female N.R.R. allowance is made for some of them dying.[2] No significance attaches to the fact that in the G.R.R. the cohort of women is 1,000 and for the N.R.R. it is 10,000. In the first case this follows because all the fertility rates are already expressed per 1,000 women; in the second an adjustment from the rate per 10,000 to the rate per 1,000 is needed since the values in col. 5 are based upon a cohort of 10,000. In both cases the rates measure the average number of daughters that would be produced per woman if, in the case of the G.R.R. the women were subject to the fertility rates used in the calculation, and in the N.R.R. subject not only to the G.R.R. assumption re fertility, but also if the cohort of women were subject to the mortality experience summarised in the life table from which cols. 5 and 6 are derived.

G.R.R. = 540·9 infants in one year but, since each age group covers

[1] The basis of this column is explained in the appendix to this chapter dealing with the construction of life tables. For the moment the reader is asked to accept the statement.

[2] It is possible to calculate both a male and all persons N.R.R. but the female rate is the best measure and most generally used.

TABLE 39

CALCULATION OF GROSS AND NET REPRODUCTION RATES

(1)	(2)	(3)	(4)	(5)	(6)	(7)
Age x	Total number of women '000's	Total number of births M & F	Live births per 1,000 women or Age-specific F/R per 1,000 (fx)	lx	$5Lx$	All babies born to generation of 10,000 $5Lx \times fx$
15–19	1,424	27,639	19·41	9,645	48,130	934
20–24	1,531	226,817	148·20	9,607	47,900	7,099
25–29	1,653	280,506	169·70	9,554	47,610	8,079
30–34	1,658	194,526	117·30	9,489	47,265	5,544
35–39	1,741	113,966	65·48	9,416	46,850	3,068
40–44	1,669	32,363	19·39	9,324	46,315	898
45–	1,561	2,215	1·42	9,201	45,515	65
				9,005		
		878,021	540·90			25,687

five years, the correct figure is $540.9 \times 5 = 2,704$ infants per 1,000 women. These infants are both male and female and the proportion of female births in that year was 0·485. Hence the number of female births to 1,000 women is $2,705 \times 0.485 = 1,312$ signifying a G.R.R. of 1·31. N.R.R. is given by adjusting the total number of births in col. 7, *i.e.* 25,687 to female births only; *i.e.* multiply by 0·485,[1] which yields a total of female births of 12,458. This relates to 10,000 women, *i.e.* the original hypothetical cohort which was reduced by mortality to 9,645 by the time it entered into the reproductive period (see col. 5). Thus the N.R.R. is equal to 1·25, *i.e.* 12,485 divided by 10,000. (Note that whereas with the G.R.R. the total of births in col. 4 had to be multiplied by 5, this has already been done in the N.R.R. calculation when the figures in col. 5 are converted into those in col. 6.)

When first developed by Dr Kuczyncski during the early 1930s, it was assumed the net reproduction rate provided the basis for reliable population projections. It was widely adopted, and even now when its defects are generally recognised, the United Nations demographic publications and the Office of Population Censuses and Surveys all give the latest indices, both gross and net, for the various populations. The basic defects of the N.R.R. are that it is determined by the rates of fertility and mortality that are adopted for purposes of its calculation. Thus in so far as the rates for any selected year are employed, the N.R.R. merely indicates what will happen on the basis of these rates. But since it is common knowledge that mortality and, more especially, fertility may change rapidly within the space of a few years, the N.R.R. as a basis for projecting population trends is quite unsatisfactory.

For purposes of evaluating trends in birth rates a number of factors have to be taken into account. Quite apart from the number of women in the population, there is the question of how many of them are already married and for what period, how many have just married, to what extent they are having small or large families, and the extent to which their family-building is being compressed into a short period or extended over most of their married lives. Since the publication of the Family Census in 1954, undertaken by Professors Glass and Grebenik on behalf of the Royal Commission on Population,[2] what is known as *cohort fertility* is used to study the trend of births. Instead of making projections on the basis of the fertility experience of any single year, cohort fertility necessitates following through the family-building history of a cohort of married women. The cohort may be of women born in a particular year or, more usually, of

[1] The ratio of male to female births is 0·485 : 0·515
[2] Vol. VI of the Papers of the Royal Commission on Population entitled *The Trend and Pattern of Fertility in Great Britain*, H.M.S.O. 1954.

TABLE 40
BIRTH RATES: GREAT BRITAIN

Rates and percentages

	1951	1961	1966	1971	1973	1974	1975	1976	1977
Birth rates									
Live births per 1,000:									
Crude birth rates (persons all ages)	15·7	17·8	17·8	16·1	13·8	13·0	12·3	11·9	11·6
Age specific birth rates[1]:									
Mothers aged 15–19	21	37	48	51	44	41	37	33	30
20–24	126	173	177	155	132	124	116	111	105
25–29	135	178	175	155	136	130	124	120	119
30–34	91	104	98	78	64	60	59	58	59
35–39	47	49	46	33	25	22	20	19	18
40–44	14	14	12	8	6	5	5	4	4
All ages (15–44)	72·5	90·0	91·1	84·2	71·8	67·6	63·6	61·0	58·8
Live births									
Illegitimate as percentage of all live births	4·9	5·8	7·7	8·4	8·6	8·9	9·1	9·2	9·7
Legitimate live births to women married once only occurring within eight months of marriage[2] as a percentage of all legitimate live births:									
Mother aged under 20	55·1	56·5	54·9	56·8	54·5	53·2	51·5	50·6	N/A
20–24	12·4	10·5	10·7	10·3	9·2	8·6	8·2	7·6	N/A
Extra-maritally conceived live births[3] as a percentage of all live births:									
Great Britain	11·5	13·0	16·1	17·0	16·5	16·2	16·0	15·5	15·8
England and Wales	11·5	13·3	16·3	17·0	16·3	16·0	15·8	15·3	N/A

[1] Births to mothers aged under 15 are included with the group 15–19; the group 15–44 contains all births.
[2] The England and Wales component for 1951 relates to maternities in present marriage, Scottish data relate to first live births to women in their first marriage.
[3] Includes illegitimate and premaritally conceived births.

Source: Office of Population Censuses and Surveys

TABLE 41

SELECTED VITAL STATISTICS: ENGLAND AND WALES

Year and quarter	Live births	Illegitimate live births	Marriages	Deaths	Infant mortality (under 1 year)	Neonatal mortality (under 4 weeks)	Stillbirths	Perinatal mortality (stillbirths and deaths under 1 week)
Number (thousands)								
1961	811·3	48·5	346·7	551·8	17·4	12·4	15·7	26·5
1966	849·8	67·1	384·5	563·6	16·1	10·9	13·20	22·7
1971	783·2	65·7	404·7	567·3	13·7	9·11	9·90	17·6
1973	676·0	58·1	400·4	587·5	11·4	7·53	7·94	14·4
1974	639·9	56·5	384·4	585·3	10·5	7·07	7·18	13·2
1975	603·4	54·9	380·6	582·8	9·49	6·47	6·30	11·8
1976	584·3	53·8	358·6	598·5	8·33	5·66	5·71	10·5
1977	569·3	55·4	357·0	575·9	7·84	5·28	5·40	9·76
Rates*								
1961	17·6	60	15·0	11·9	21·4	15·3	19·0	32·0
1966	17·8	79	16·1	11·8	19·2	12·9	15·3	26·3
1971	16·0	84	16·6	11·6	17·5	11·6	12·5	22·3
1973	13·8	86	16·3	12·0	16·9	11·1	11·6	21·0
1974	13·0	88	15·6	11·9	16·3	11·0	11·1	20·4
1975	12·3	91	15·5	11·9	15·7	10·7	10·3	19·3
1976	11·9	92	14·6	12·2	14·3	9·7	9·7	17·7
1977	11·6	97	14·5	11·7	13·8	9·3	9·4	17·0
1978 March	11·7	100	11·7	14·1	14·6	8·6	8·8	15·9
June	12·2		14·5	12	13			16
September				10	11			15

*Live births, deaths, persons marrying per 1,000 population of all ages. Illegitimate live births, infant mortality, neonatal mortality per 1,000 live births. Stillbirths perinatal mortality per 1,000 live and stillbirths.

Source: Population Trends No. 14

women married in a particular year. The former are known as *birth cohorts*, the latter as *marriage cohorts*. By studying the trend in the cumulative numbers of children born to married women at successive points of time up to the end of their child-bearing period, the limitations of annual rates such as fertility rates or N.R.R., are avoided. Thus, if at the end of the child-bearing period each member of a marriage cohort has produced on average 2·2 children as compared with a completed family of 5·8 children of an earlier generation (*i.e.* marriage cohort), then it is clear that fertility has fallen.* The main limitation of cohort analysis is that definite conclusions regarding the fertility of a particular marriage cohort can be drawn only when that cohort has reached the end of its reproductive period. Since at any time a large proportion of married women are under 45 years of age, it is arguable that their future child-bearing activities may markedly affect the resultant figures. A partial solution to this problem was seen in the fact that two of the characteristics of family building in the 1950s and 1960s were:

(i) a fall in the age of marriage; and

(ii) a reduction in the completed size of families.

However, by the 1970s:

(i) the fall in the age of marriage has stopped; and

(ii) the rapid increase in knowledge of contraceptives and their use has reduced the numbers of births. The birth rate and completed family size are thus increasingly affected by social and economic factors rather than biological inevitability.

These circumstances make forecasting the number of births an even more difficult task than in former times.

The way in which some of these vital rates are published is shown in tables 40 and 41 from *Social Trends* and *Population Trends*.

The official population projections for this country are made by the Government Actuary's Department and are published annually by the Office of Population Censuses and Surveys in Series PPI. A brief outline of the application of the component method they employ is as follows:

1. the total population is sub-divided into groups according to sex, marital status and then into single year age groups;

2. from each sub-group is subtracted the number of deaths expected to occur over the next twelve months to give the numbers surviving to the next year;

---

*These are the actual numbers of children in completed familites for women who married during 1870-79 and 1925 respectively. See Glass and Grebenik report *op. cit.* Table 1.

TABLE 42

POPULATION PROJECTIONS, 1976 BASED: SHORT TERM FERTILITY VARIANTS

Great Britain

Millions

	1976 (base)	1977	1981	1991	2001
High short-term fertility:					
Persons aged:					
0–15	13·3	13·0	12·0	12·3	13·0
16–64/59[1]	31·8	32·0	32·7	33·7	34·3
65/60 and over[2]	9·4	9·4	9·6	9·8	9·3
All ages	54·5	54·4	54·4	55·8	56·6
Principal projection:					
Persons aged:					
0–15	13·3	13·0	11·8	11·7	12·9
16–64/59[1]	31·8	32·0	32·7	33·7	33·7
65/60 and over[2]	9·4	9·4	9·6	9·8	9·3
All ages	54·5	54·4	54·2	55·1	55·9
Low short-term fertility:					
Persons aged:					
0–15	13·3	13·0	11·7	10·7	12·5
16–64/59f	31·8	32·0	32·7	33·7	33·1
65/60 and overf	9·4	9·4	9·6	9·8	9·3
All ages	54·4	54·4	54·0	54·1	54·9

[1] 16-64 for males; 16–59 for females.
[2] 65 and over for males; 60 and over for females.

Source: Office of Population Censuses and Surveys

TABLE 43

POPULATION CHANGES AND PROJECTIONS[1]

United Kingdom

Millions and thousands

	Population at start of period (millions)	Average annual change (thousands)				
		Live births	Deaths	Net natural change	Net civilian migration[5]	Overall annual change
Census enumerated[2]						
1901–11	38·2	1,091	624	467	−82	385
1911–21	42·1	975	689[4]	286	−92	194
1921–31	44·0	824	555[4]	268	−67	201
1931–51	46·0	785	598[4]	188	+22	213
Mid-year estimates						
1951–61	50·3	839	593	246	− 7	239
1961–66	52·8	988	633	355	− 8	347
1966–71	54·4	937	644	293	−56	237
1971–74	55·6	807	666	142	−42	100
1974–75	55·9	721	671	50	−72	−22
1975–76	55·9	789	681	7	−29	−22
1976–77	55·9	655	660	− 5	−35	−40
1977–78	55·9	664	665	− 1	∶	∶
Projections[3]						
1977–81	55·9	671	689	−18	−32	−50
1981–91	55·7	854	715	139	−40	99
1991–2001	56·7	840	717	123	−40	87

[1]See Appendix B, Chapter 1.
[2]There was no census in 1941.
[3]Projections based on the mid-1977 estimate of total population.
[4]Including deaths of non-civilians and merchant seamen who died outside the country.
[5]Plus other adjustments.

Source: Census of Population Reports: Population Projections 1977–2017, *Office of Population Censuses and Surveys*

3. the relevant fertility rates are applied to each sub-group of women to give the number of births expected in the next twelve months;

4. an allowance is made for net migration;

5. the results of the calculations in 1-4 above are added to give the projected population in twelve months' time for each sub-group. Then the sub-groups are totalled to give an overall projection of population size for twelve months;

6. the process is repeated year by year according to how far ahead the projection is required (N.B. The farther ahead the projection the greater the likelihood that the fertility and mortality rates would have to be adjusted in some arbitrary way dependent upon subjective estimates of future changes in the rates as shown in Tables 41 and 42.

These provide some tabulated results of current (1979) projections, which are self-explanatory.

Standardised Rates

The actual numbers of vital events, *e.g.* deaths, births, and marriages, are not of themselves of much importance. Thus, the fact that more people die each year in London than in Brighton could be initially the result of there being more people living in London than in Brighton! Therefore the first step is to express the deaths in the form of rates; that is how many deaths or births or marriages, etc. have occurred for each 1,000 people in the population. The population in Greater London in 1977 was approximately 6·956 million people and, in that year, 79,300 people died. Therefore, the crude death rate for Greater London in 1977 was $\frac{79 \cdot 3}{6,956} \times \frac{1,000}{1} = 11 \cdot 4$ deaths per 1,000 of the population. A similar process can be performed for Brighton and the two crude death rates then compared. While the effect of the variation in *total size* of the two populations has been removed, no allowance has been made for the possible variation due to differences in the composition of the populations. Thus because of the more pleasant climate people tend to move to the South Coast towns when they retire. These towns tend to have a far higher proportion of old people than other towns in Great Britain. It is to make an adjustment for these differences that the process of standardisation was developed. There are various methods of standardising, but the two most generally employed methods are known as the *direct* and *indirect* methods.

The *direct* method consists of calculating the total number of deaths which the actual death rates for a particular population would have produced in a standard population. As may be seen from the following table, towns A and B have somewhat similar crude death rates of 14·5 and 13·7 per 1,000 respectively. The crude

TABLE 43

CALCULATION OF STANDARDISED DEATH RATES (DIRECT METHOD)

Age Group	Town A			Town B			1977 England and Wales Standard Population millions	No. of thousands of expected deaths in standard population if subject to mortality of	
	Population 000's	No. of Deaths	Crude Death Rate per 1,000	Population 000's	No. of Deaths	Crude Death Rate per 1,000		A	B
(1)	(2)	(3)	(4)	(5)	(6)	(7)	(8)	(9)	(10)
0—	5	40	8	7	70	10	3	24	30
5—	15	15	1	10	20	2	8	8	16
15—	15	15	1	15	60	4	7	7	28
25—	15	30	2	19	114	6	12	24	72
45—	25	375	15	25	500	20	11	165	220
65—	5	400	80	3·5	210	60	7	560	420
85—	1	300	300	0·5	125	250	1	300	250
	81	1,175	14·5	80	1,099	13·7	49	1,088	1,036

death rate is simply the weighted arithmetic mean of the *age specific death rates*. An age specific death rate is merely the death rate of a particular age group arrived at by dividing, for example, the number of deaths of males aged 5–14 by the total number of such males in the population. By applying the age specific death rates of each town to a standard population, as is done in columns 8–10 inclusive, we can calculate the number of deaths that would have arisen from the mortality rates of towns A and B if their populations had been identical with the standard population. The result in this case is, whereas the crude rates per 1,000 are 14.5 and 13.7, the standardised

rates for the two towns are 22·2 and 21·1 respectively (*i.e.* $\dfrac{1,088}{49} = 22·2$

and $\dfrac{1,036}{49} = 21·1$).

The alternative *indirect* method is slightly more complicated, and is normally used where the age specific death rates of the local populations are not available. In this case, instead of using a standard population a set of standard age specific death rates are applied to the two populations to be compared. The standard death rates are the national age specific death rate of England and Wales in 1977. The basis of the calculation is demonstrated in Table 44. In this case, we derive the number of deaths which would have occurred in the two areas had their individual populations experienced a common mortality, *i.e.* the same or standard age specific mortality rates. Expressing the total of these deaths per thousand of the actual populations, we derive what are termed *index* death rates. The index death rate must not be confused with the crude rate. The index

TABLE 44

CALCULATION OF INDIRECT STANDARDISATION

Age Group	Town A Population 000's	Town B Population 000's	1977 Standard death rate per 000's	Expected Deaths on basis of 1977 death rates A	B
0—	5	7	3·2	16	22
5—	15	10	0·25	4	3
15—	15	15	0·7	11	11
25—	15	19	1·6	24	30
45—	25	25	9·7	243	243
65—	5	3·5	60·0	300	330
85—	1	0·5	206·0	206	103
Total	81	80	11·7	804	742

	Town A	Town B
Index death rate per 1,000	$\frac{804}{81} = 9 \cdot 93$	$\frac{742}{80} = 9 \cdot 28$
$\frac{\text{Standard death rate}}{\text{Local index death rate}} = \text{ACF}$	$\frac{11 \cdot 7}{9 \cdot 93} = 1 \cdot 18$	$\frac{11 \cdot 7}{9 \cdot 28} = 1 \cdot 26$
Local crude death rate × ACF = local adjusted death rate	$14 \cdot 5 \times 1 \cdot 18 = 17 \cdot 1$	$13 \cdot 7 \times 1 \cdot 26 = 17 \cdot 3$
Ratio of local adjusted death rate to standard rate	$\frac{17 \cdot 1}{11 \cdot 7} = 1 \cdot 46$	$\frac{17 \cdot 3}{11 \cdot 7} = 1 \cdot 48$

death rate will tend to be lower than the actual national crude death rate if the local population is abnormally young. Correspondingly it will tend to be higher than the national crude death rate if the population is older than the population of the country as a whole. By dividing the index death rate into the standard or national death rate we derive what is known as the Area Comparability Factor. The A.C.F. is then multiplied by the local crude death rate and the product, termed the local adjusted death rate is then comparable both with the national death rate and any other local death rate calculated on the same basis. Thus in Table 00 above, in place of the crude death rates of 14·5 for Town A and 13·7 for Town B, the indirectly standardised or adjusted death rates are equal to 17·1 for Town A and 17·3 for Town B.

It is worthwhile examining why the three rates, crude, directly standardised and indirectly standardised, are different. With the crude rates no account is taken of the different age composition in the two towns. However, when the national population structure is applied not only is the resulting standardised rate comparable one with the other but also with any other rate calculated on the same basis. The fact that the rates have leaped from 14·5 to 22·2 for Town A and from 13·7 to 21·1 for Town B demonstrates that both towns have a younger than national average population distribution, as Table 45 below illustrates.

TABLE 45

COMPARISON OF POPULATION DISTRIBUTIONS

Age Group	Town A Nos. (000's)	%	Town B Nos. (000's)	%	1977 Population in England and Wales Nos. (m)	%
0—	5	6	7	9	3	6
5—	15	19	10	13	8	16
15—	15	19	15	19	7	14
25—	15	19	19	24	12	25
45—	25	31	25	31	11	23
65—	5	6	3·5	4	7	14
85—	1	0	0·5	0	1	2
Total	81	100	80	100	49	100

Thus, it will be seen that in the 65+ age groups, where the numbers of deaths and the death rates are naturally high, Town A has less than half the proportion of the national population and Town B has just over one-quarter of the national figure.

When the local crude age specific death rates are replaced by the national rates in the *indirect* method the standardised rates for Towns A and B are lower than by the *direct* method. This suggests that the national mortality experience is better than that of either of Town A or Town B. Again this can be demonstrated by a comparison of the three sets of age specific death rates.

TABLE 46

COMPARISON OF AGE SPECIFIC DEATH RATES

Age Group	Crude death rates		
	Town A per 1,000	Town B per 1,000	1977 England and Wales per 1,000
0—	8	10	3·2
5—	1	2	0·3
15—	1	4	0·7
25—	2	6	1·6
45—	15	20	9·7
65—	80	60	60·0
85—	300	250	206·0

Thus it can be seen that for all but one of the age groups (which is equal) the local death rates are higher than the national average. In brief, Towns A and B have younger but apparently unhealthier populations than the nation generally. This example demonstrates that the *direct* method of standardisation is more accurate and therefore is preferred to the indirect method provided the necessary data (the age specific death rates) are available.

As has been shown above the indirect method of standardisation produces an *Area Comparability Factor* (A.C.F.) that can be used to form a basis of comparison between local areas and between local and national figures. The A.C.F. has now been replaced for official purposes by an alternative index known as the *Standard Mortality Ratio* (S.M.R.). This ratio is that of the actual deaths that have occurred, to those which would have occurred in that population if the *national* death rates had applied. (If you look back to Table 44, showing the method of indirect standardisation, you will see the bottom line shows the 'ratio of local adjusted death rate to standard rate, 17·1 to 11·7 is 1·46'. This ratio of 1·46 multiplied by 100 is, in fact, the standard mortality ratio of Town A. There is, however, a much quicker method of calculating the S.M.R. as is shown below in Table 47.

TABLE 47

CALCULATION OF STANDARD MORTALITY RATIO FOR TOWN B

Age group	Population 000's	Death rates for England and Wales 1977	Expected number of deaths if national rates applied	Actual deaths occurring Nos.
0—	5	3·2	16·0	40
5—	15	0·3	4·5	15
15—	15	0·7	10·5	15
25—	15	1·6	24·0	30
45—	25	9·7	242·5	375
65—	5	60·0	300·0	400
85—	1	206·0	206·0	300
Totals	81		803·5	1,175

$$\text{Standard Mortality Ratio} = \frac{\text{Actual Deaths}}{\text{Expected Deaths}} \times 100$$

$$\therefore \text{S.M.R.} = \frac{1,175}{803·5} \times \frac{100}{1} = 1·44 \times 100 = 146$$

To verify this point now calculate by the same method the S.M.R. for Town B to demonstrate that it is 148.

The standard mortality ratio can be used for comparison between *areas* and also *over time*. It is also calculated for males and females,

TABLE 48

DEATHS BY MAJOR CAUSES, SEX, AND SOCIAL CLASS, 1970-72[1]
England and Wales

SMRs[2] (ages 15-64)

| | Social class | | | | | | | | | | | |
| Major causes of deaths of persons aged 15 to 64 (SMRs): | Professional and similar | | Intermediate | | Skilled non-manual | | Skilled manual | | Partly skilled | | Unskilled | |
	Males	Married females	Males	Married females	Males	Married females	Males	Married females	Males	Married females	Males	Married females
Cancer:												
Trachea, bronchus and lung	53	73	68	82	84	89	118	118	123	125	143	134
Cervix, uteri		—		66		69		120		140		161
Breast[3]	—	117	—	112	—	110	—	109	—	103	—	92
Prostate	91		89		99		115		106		115	
Ischaemic heart disease	88	58	91	77	114	81	107	125	108	123	111	146
Other forms of heart disease[4]	69	45	75	75	94	83	100	114	121	137	157	173
Cerebrovascular disease	80	76	86	84	98	93	106	116	111	124	136	139
Pneumonia	41	63	53	66	78	80	92	120	115	129	195	171
Bronchitis, emphysema and asthma	36	41	51	60	82	74	113	125	128	130	188	189
Motor vehicle accidents	77	118	83	102	89	91	105	82	120	96	174	126
All other accidents	58	105	64	93	53	87	97	88	128	100	225	156
Suicide	110	124	89	110	113	118	77	83	117	87	184	94
All causes	77	82	81	87	99	92	106	115	114	119	137	135

[1] For the definition of social class see note in Appendix B. Married females are classified according to their husbands' occupation.

[2] See note in Appendix B. SMRs based on < 20 deaths shown as —.

[3] Death through breast cancer for men is small, the SMRs are therefore not shown.

[4] Excludes chronic rheumatic heart disease and hypertension.

Sources: *Office of Population Censuses and Surveys*

(N.B. For an explanation of social class see p. 248)

for different occupations, for different diseases, and generally where data are available to allow for standardisation. Examples of its use are shown in Table 48 on the opposite page.

Since 1958, the S.M.R. has been used for showing the trend of mortality over many decades. In this case the S.M.R. shows the number of deaths registered in the year as a percentage of those which would have been expected in that year had the sex and age mortality of the standard period operated on the sex and age population of the year of experience. Until 1958, the *Statistical Review* Part I published by the Registrar General showed not the S.M.R., but an index known as the C.M.I. (Comparative Mortality Index). This was derived by the method of direct standardisation, *i.e.* by using a standard population as in Table 00. The standard population was the mean of the population of 1938 and the year under review. In other words, instead of taking as the standard a population of any single year, an 'average' population was used which, in the opinion of the Registrar General, was more representative and provided a better base for long period calculations.[1] By dividing the standardised death rate for the 1938 mean population into the standardised death rate for the other year, a ratio known as the C.M.I. was derived. The base year was 1938, in which year the C.M.I. had a value of unity. This method, as already stated, has now been discontinued.[2]

It should be noted in passing that, although the illustrations of standardisation given above relate to mortality rates, precisely the same techniques are employed in connection with birth rates. For the reader who wishes to consult the method of presentation of these data the following publications can be consulted. The latest editions of:

(*a*) the quarterly publication *Population Trends*, H.M.S.O.;

(*b*) the occasional publication *Demographic Review*, H.M.S.O. (The latest edition in Spring 1979 is Series DR No.1 entitled '1977' and was published in 1978;

(*c*) the annual publication *Social Trends*.

Population Projections

There are three methods used to forecast the size and composition of the population in the future. They are known as the economic, the mathematical and the component methods of projection.

The first and crudest form of projection is that used in areas where

[1] The C.M.I. was worked back to 1841.
[2] Method of calculation is given in the *Review* for 1940-45, Vol. I, pp.6-11.

no data exist and it is not practicable to obtain a representative sample. The economic method involves assessing the population in terms of the country's resources of food, raw materials and energy sources that could support estimated numbers of population at various times. The United Nations have used this method in respect of under-developed countries to obtain quickly some projection of population movements.

The mathematical method of population projection has been used in circumstances where there have been successive Censuses but no registration system of births and deaths. These projections are simple to understand but cannot be analysed beyond the nature of the projection. Thus, if *total* population size is projected, it is not possible to deduce an age distribution from it.

The technique of mathematical projection involves fitting a curve to existing data and then projecting the line of the curve forward. Yule, a British statistician, plotted the population of England and Wales from 1801 to 1911, drew a line through the points, expressed the line in the form of an equation and then estimated the future population from the equation. The problem with this process is that there is obviously an upper limit to the numbers that can live in a given space and there cannot be a negative population, therefore this must be represented by a limiting factor in the equation. The resulting curve is shaped like a capital letter 'S' and is known as a 'logistic' curve.

The third and most widely used method of population projection is the component method. This method was first used by an economist, Edwin Canaan, in 1895, when the Metropolitan Water Board needed an estimate of the population in 1931 so that they could plan their future services. The general framework of the component method consists of two parts:

(i) estimating the number of people surviving in the future; and

(ii) estimating the number of births in any period.

(External migration, being a social phenomenon largely influenced by political decisions, is added to the result of the estimates in (i) and (ii) above.) It will be appreciated that, the shorter the period over which the population is to be projected, the greater the importance becomes of the estimation of survival rates of people already born. As death rates change much more slowly than birth rates the short-term projections are more reliable than would be the case in the longer period. The further ahead one projects the population the more one has to rely upon the very much less predictable birth rate. While, in general terms, the component method consists of forecasting the two elements of births and deaths there are many variations within these two elements. Further, the forecasting of birth and death rates are themselves relatively complex procedures which are broken down into a number of separate techniques. One of the commonest of the techniques used is that of *standardisation*.

Morbidity

One of the more difficult social variables to measure is morbidity (sickness). First, there is the problem of defining sickness. If a person attends a general practitioner, is certified as being sick and, on the basis of the certificate claims national sickness benefit then the event will be entered into the national statistics of the Department of Health and Social Security, and published in their Annual Report or the annual Digest of Health and Personal Social Services. However, if a person is not eligible for sickness benefit and therefore does not claim it (and this includes children under 16, many housewives, people receiving retirement pensions) no record, beyond the doctors' personal notes, is made of medically certified sickness. Further, persons may treat themselves for many minor bouts of sickness (*e.g.* common colds, influenza, rheumatism) and no record is made at all of the event. Many people, particularly the elderly, put up with sickness because they think, often mistakenly, that it is inevitable and nothing can be done for it. People suffering from the milder kinds of mental illness are often treated without being recorded as sick. A sample of general practitioner records showed that one in five patients was being treated for mental symptoms. The General Household Survey in the 1975 and 1976 Reports asked questions as to those members of the household who were suffering from chronic or acute sickness; defining sickness as that condition which limited activities of the individual. Table 49 shows the results.

The second problem relating to morbidity is the collection of the data. Only those people who are admitted to hospital or who claim national sickness benefit enter into national sickness statistics. This would suggest that the absolute measurement of sickness is highly deficient. One could, however, use changes in the levels of the statistics that are collected as indicators of change in the general level of sickness.

An examination of the problems involved in the construction of indicators of the level of health and some suggested solutions is to be found in article 'Health Indicators' by Culyer Lavers and Williams.*

Within the limitations of the definitions given overleaf the Hospital In-Patient Enquiry set up in 1949 is a reasonably accurate analysis of the services provided by the hospitals and the people for whom

Social Indicators and Social Policy edited by Shonfield and Shaw

TABLE 49

ACUTE SICKNESS: BY SOCIO-ECONOMIC GROUP, AGE, AND SEX, 1975 AND 1976

Great Britain

Numbers

	Males aged:					Females aged:				
	0–14	15–44	45–64	65 or over	All ages	0–14	15–44	45–64	65 or over	All ages
Average number of restricted activity days per person per year:										
Professional	15	10	11	23	12	9	17	21	39	16
Employers and managers	14	9	13	20	13	8	15	16	20	14
Intermediate and junior non-manual	11	12	22	20	15	12	17	18	26	18
Skilled manual and own account non-professional	12	14	22	25	16	11	16	19	29	16
Semi-skilled manual and personal service	12	13	20	26	16	10	17	24	35	21
Unskilled manual	8	15	31	23	19	12	18	24	25	21
All persons	12	12	20	23	15	10	16	19	29	17

Source: General Household Survey, 1975 and 1976.

the services are provided. The enquiry is based on an annual 10% sample of all discharges and deaths. There is a similar enquiry for psychiatric hospitals and units entitled *Mental Health Enquiry* (England and Wales). This is also published annually, but is based upon a full set of data as opposed to the 10% sample of the non-psychiatric enquiry. A summary of the hospital statistics obtained is given opposite.

TABLE 50,
HOSPITAL SUMMARY: ALL SPECIALITIES
United Kingdom

	1961	1966	1971	1974	1975	1976	1977[4]
All in-patients[1]:							
Waiting lists – surgical (thousands)	—	557	554	593	657	685	676
– other	—	47	42	36	47	37	39
Total waiting lists	—	604	596	629	704	722	715
Discharges and deaths	5,007	5,736	6,437	6,447	6,214	6,525	6,622
Average number of beds occupied daily:							
Maternities	18	20	19	17	16	16	16
Other patients	454	441	417	390	380	378	372
Total – Average number of beds occupied daily	472	461	436	407	396	394	388
Average length of stay (days):							
Psychiatric	—	—	—	—	—	249	243
Geriatric and units for young disabled	—	—	—	—	—	93	91
Other patients	14	12	10	10	10	10	10
Private in-patients[2] (thousands):							
Discharges and deaths	84	102	115	114	98	94	94
Average number of beds occupied daily	3	3	3	2	2	2	2
New out-patients							
Accidents and emergency (thousands)	—	7,909	9,358	9,870	9.989	10,463	10,658
Other out-patients[3]	—	8,935	9,572	9,509	9,714	9,170	10,546
Average attendances per new patient:							
Accidents and emergency (numbers)	—	1·9	1·6	1·6	1·5	1·6	1·5
Other out-patients[3]	—	4·1	4·2	4·2	4·2	4·0	4·0
Patients as a percentage of population:							
In-patients:							
Discharges and deaths	*9·4*	*10·5*	*11·6*	*11·5*	*11·1*	*11·7*	—
Waiting lists	—	*1·1*	*1·1*	*1·1*	*1·3*	*1·3*	—
New out-patients[3]:							
Accidents and emergency	*10·5*	*14·4*	*16·8*	*17·6*	*17·9*	*18·7*	—
Other out-patients	*16·3*	*16·4*	*17·2*	*17·0*	*17·3*	*16·4*	—

[1] All maternity cases are included.
[2] Figures relate to England and Wales only.
[3] Figures for out-patients in Scotland include ancillary departments.
[4] Provisional.
Source: Department of Health and Social Security; Welsh Office; Scottish Health Service, Common Services Agency; Department of Health and Social Services, Northern Ireland.

The hospital service appears to be increasingly under pressure with discharges and deaths rising from 5,736,000 in 1966 to 6,622,000 in 1977. Similarly new out-patients have risen from 16,844,000 to 21,194,000 over the same period. This pressure must be seen against a fall in the number of occupied beds from 461,000 in 1966 to 388,000 in 1977. The increases in the number of patients is not simply a function of the large total population, for if the numbers of patients are expressed as a percentage of the total population the following increases are shown overleaf in Table 51.

TABLE 51
PATIENTS AS A PERCENTAGE OF POPULATION

	1961	1966	1971	1976
In-patient discharges and deaths	9·4	10·5	11·6	11·7
Accidents and emergencies	10·5	14·4	16·8	18·7
Other out-patients	16·3	16·4	17·2	16·4

Source: Social Trends, No. 9

The number of home nursing cases attended has increased from 991,000 in 1966 to 3,132,000 in 1976 and to 3,314,000 in 1977.

Similarly, the number of employees in the health and personal social services has shown increases in virtually every classification rising from about 1,000,000 in 1971 to 1,172,000 in 1976.

Against a background of increasing numbers of patients and more staff, it is to be expected that current expenditure would rise, as it has. However, capital expenditure is substantially reduced.

TABLE 52
PUBLIC EXPENDITURE ON HEALTH AND PERSONAL SOCIAL SERVICES
INDICES 1976–77 = 100 AT CONSTANT PRICES

		1972–73	1975–76	1977–78
Hospitals	Current Expenditure	91	99	104
	Capital Expenditure	127	106	78
Family Practitioner	Current Expenditure	86	95	102
	Capital Expenditure	130	104	115
Personal Social Services	Current Expenditure	78	97	110
	Capital Expenditure	72	106	94

Source: Social Trends, No. 9

The Department of Health and Social Security are active producers of special studies. Some of these are published in a special series known as the Statistical and Research Series. Thus, as an example, in 1978, the Department of Health and Social Security issued Number 20 in their Statistical and Research Series entitled *In-Patient statistics from the Mental Health Enquiry for England 1975*. It contains numerous statistical tables, together with a special paper on the probability of admission which shows that one in ten of the population can expect to be admitted to a mental illness hospital at some time in their lives. Number 19 in the same series deals with many other aspects of the mental health of the country.

In addition the Department publishes three other series:

(*a*) Statistical Report Series;

(*b*) Reports on Public Health and Medical Subjects;

(*c*) Reports on Health and Social Subjects.

Mortality

The inevitability of death has not in any way reduced the interest in the analysis of causes of death. The object of such analysis is, of course, concerned primarily with postponing death and the allocation of resources to this end. A secondary consideration is the prediction of the span of life and the social effects of variation in the length of this span. In the section on population projections (pp.457-9) the use of mortality prediction was discussed but, in this section, a closer look will be taken at the trends of mortality as revealed by the analysis of registered deaths.

In Great Britain it is a legal requirement for all deaths to be registered and, because the failure to register a death incurs direct penalties, e.g. fines and indirect penalties e.g. no funeral, no legal acquisition of the dead person's property, very few deaths indeed go unregistered. The coverage of mortality analyses is therefore practically complete. Further, with the improvement of medical science the registered causes of death are usually quite accurate. The trends in mortality by age and cause are therefore of a reasonable degree of validity and reliability. The interpretation of these trends in terms of causality is far more controversial as will be shown below.

The trends by age and cause over the last 30 years can be summarised as follows:

From birth to one year: The death rate for the first day of life has not fallen very sharply, only from 8·1 per 1,000 live births to 5·6. This is now very largely a matter of congenital malformations. The death rate in the first four weeks of life has roughly halved, while in the period from four weeks to one year the rate has been reduced to one-third of its previous level. The cause of the reduction has been the ability to combat infective and parasitic diseases. Over two-thirds of all infant deaths are now due to congenital malformations or birth injuries. Nevertheless there are large Social Class differences, with infant mortality in Classes IV and V exceeding Classes I and II by over 70 per cent.

One year to four years: The death rates for both males and females have reduced by nearly two-thirds and now stand at the very low levels of 0·8 and 0·6 deaths per 1,000 respectively. The cause of the reduction is the 90 per cent drop in deaths from infection and parasites. Over one-quarter of the deaths are now due to accidents.

Five to fourteen years: Death rates have fallen by 55 per cent for males and 61 per cent for females. The most frequent cause of death is accidents for boys (they are three times as likely as girls to be killed in an accident – mainly by motor vehicles) and cancer for girls where the death rate has remained virtually unchanged over recent decades. The main reduction has again been in infective and parasitic diseases.

TABLE 53
Deaths by Selected Causes[1]: Standardised Mortality Ratios
Great Britain

SMRs base year 1968 = 10

	Males SMRs			Number of deaths in 1975	Females SMRs			Number of deaths in 1975	All persons: percentage of total deaths 1975
	1961	1971	1975		1961	1971	1975		
Tuberculosis, all forms	174	68	56	1,001	162	71	64	465	0·23
Cancer:									
Digestive system	102	100	98	22,498	105	96	94	21,586	6·82
Lung, bronchus, trachea	88	102	102	29,019	72	111	131	7,517	5·66
Breast	105	99	100	88	97	107	110	12,735	1·99
Cervix uteri				—	105	93	87	2,387	0·37
Prostate	101	98	101	4,803				—	0·74
Leukaemia	93	98	101	1,917	91	92	94	1,581	0·54
Diabetes	82	100	107	2,277	98	102	95	3,495	0·89
Chronic rheumatic heart disease	139	94	79	2,380	134	94	80	4,111	1·00
Hypertensive disease	156	83	69	3,895	170	78	63	4,837	1·35
Ischaemic heart disease	90	101	103	99,119	97	97	100	73,544	26·73
Other forms of heart disease	—	86	77	11,384	—	83	75	18,048	4·56
Cerebrovascular disease	105	95	86	33,531	105	95	87	53,445	13·46
Influenza	190	17	30	669	141	12	29	993	0·26
Pneumonia	84	92	106	22,124	76	92	107	28,971	7·91
Bronchitis, emphysema, and asthma	101	85	73	20,893	108	81	72	7,490	4·39
Peptic ulcer	118	81	82	2,654	106	97	108	2,005	0·72
Congenital anomalies	123	100	87	2,194	128	99	92	2,027	0·65
Motor vehicle accidents	114	108	91	4,638	99	110	86	2,013	1·03
All other accidents	126	98	91	5,169	115	94	88	5,884	1·71
Suicide	117	85	81	2,410	115	89	82	1,710	0·64
All other causes	—	—	—	53,679	—	—	—	64,780	18·34
All causes	103	95	94	326,342	106	94	93	319,624	100·00

Sources: General Register Office for Scotland; Office of Population Censuses and Surveys

Fifteen to twenty-four years: A marked difference in the rate of improvement in mortality in females (down 71 per cent) and males (down 41 per cent). The reductions have been achieved again by controlling infective and parasitic diseases, and especially in this age group, tuberculosis. Death rates from cancer have remained virtually constant. Violent and accidental deaths account for two-thirds of all male deaths and nearly half of all female deaths.

Twenty-five to thirty-four years: Mortality in this age group has halved for both sexes, again largely due to the control of infective and parasitic diseases more especially tuberculosis. The most important cause of death for men is accidents and, for women, cancer.

Thirty-five to forty-four years: While death rates have fallen in the last 30 years by some 30 to 40 per cent for both men and women, cancer and circulatory failure are becoming increasingly significant causes. Coronary disease has more than doubled for both men and women.

Forty-five to fifty-four years: Death rates have fallen by 16 per cent for men and 21 per cent for women, but coronary heart disease for both sexes, and lung and breast cancer for women, have markedly increased as causes of death.

Fifty-five to sixty-five years: The 20 per cent reduction in mortality of women was double that of men, but the trends of increasing death rates from coronary heart disease and lung cancer were more marked than in the previous age group.

Sixty-five years and over: Death rate for men has only fallen very slightly while the rate for women has dropped by 20 per cent. The distribution of causes of death has remained very stable over the past 30 years with circulatory diseases accounting for half the deaths and cancer for about one-quarter.

General: The *expected* length of life at the younger ages has much increased since fewer deaths occur among these age groups since the turn of the century. The control of infective and parasitic diseases has meant that many more people are living to their expected full life span. Further the removal of these diseases has disclosed the effect of accidents in youth, particularly amongst the males, and of heart disease in middle age. More recent figures supplementing the trends outlined above are illustrated in Table 53 opposite:

Suicide

As a postscript to this section on mortality and, in view of the importance of suicide in the debate on the interpretation of official statistics, a brief comment should be made on suicide as a cause of death. Where an individual is suffering from a pathological condition capable of identification, either before or after death, there would seem to be little argument about the actual cause of death. Accidents, homicide, suicide, etc. are not, however, pathological causes of death – they are situations which give rise to causes of death. Thus, it is normally pathologically straightforward to diagnose that a man has died of gunshot wounds. But, it is very often much more difficult to be assured that the man intended to shoot himself, shot himself accidentally or was shot by someone else either deliberately or accidentally. It is therefore essential that, although accident and suicide are listed among the 'causes' of death, in official statistics these diagnoses are on a very much less reliable plane than, say, the incidence of death from tuberculosis.

Emile Durkheim in 1897 published a study of the causes of suicide entitled *Suicide: A Study in Sociology* (Routledge and Kegan Paul) using official published statistics. In post-war years there has been a strong attack against the statistical basis of Durkheim's work and those who have subsequently used official statistics in a similar way. Without entering into the detail of the argument it has highlighted the necessity of examining closely the method that has given rise to each piece of data and to take into the interpretation of the data the limitations imposed by the methodology. Uncritical acceptance of official statistics, even those published in the same official table, is as reprehensible as that view which equally uncritically rejects all official statistics as worthless.

Accidents

Accidents to people often result in a period of incapacity or death. However, statistics of accidents are normally separated from data on morbidity and mortality on the grounds that there is a much better chance of preventing accidents than of the incidence of most illnesses.

From the viewpoint of the community the importance of accident statistics arises from the fact that each accident results in economic waste. Whether the accident results in damage, personal injury or death it causes the expenditure of material, time or life for no return whatsoever. Consequently close watch is kept upon statistics of accidents as a measure of the success or otherwise of any move to prevent accidents. The interest is hardly surprising when it is estimated that in 1977 in Great Britain road accidents alone cost £750m.

The basis of classification of accidents is, at present, by the place of occurrence of the accident as distinct from classification by the type of accident. The reason for this is that there is no single authority responsible for collecting and analysing statistics of all types of accident. Accident statistics can therefore be divided into the particular spheres of influence of the interested bodies:

(i) industrial statistics are covered mainly by the various inspector-ates of the Department of Employment, and the Department of Health and Social Security;

(ii) transport accidents are covered by the Department of Transport;

(iii) accidents in the home are only imperfectly covered by several different sources such as the Hospital In-patient Enquiry, the Office of Population Censuses and Surveys and the Royal Society for the Prevention of Accidents.

In dealing with accidents it must be remembered that as all deaths must be reported, the analysis of accidental deaths is far more re-liable than that for any other accident statistics. Only in some situa-tions do accidents resulting in personal injury have to be reported, e.g. on the roads and in the factories. However, while in 1976 there were some 17,000 accidental deaths (about 3 % of total deaths) there were some 3m. cases of accidental injury of which 200,000 were classified as serious. The important point is that the proportion of deaths to injuries is by no means constant. Thus, on the road at least one death is recorded for every 50 injuries while in the coal mines the proportion falls to one death for every 650 injuries. This does not mean that the mines are safer than the roads (the proportions of injured to those exposed to injury is totally different). It does mean that where only the number of accidents resulting in death are known (e.g. in the home) it is very difficult to estimate from experience in other spheres the number of accidents resulting in non-fatal injuries.

A further difficulty arises in attempting to estimate the seriousness of injury arising from accidents. The only reasonably uniform basis of classifying injury is that provided by the Department of Health and Social Security, where an accident results in a claim for benefit under the National Insurance Acts. In these cases the number of days absent from work can be used as a measure of seriousness of the injury arising from the accident. While this is hardly a perfect basis of assessing the injury, it does at least provide the basis for a uniform classification.

Where an accident does not involve personal injury such statistics as are produced, and there is no regular series available, are reduced to the level of intelligent guesses. The reason for this is the lack of necessity to report such accidents. In some spheres, e.g. industrial accidents and collisions between cars that result in a claim for damage under insurances, there is some factual guidance but the supporting evidence, even here, is incomplete.

As stated above the sphere of accident statistics can be divided roughly into three main groups discussed individually below.

Industrial Accidents

The two main agents in the collection of statistics in this field are the Department of Employment and the Department of Health and Social Security. The former operates under the Health and Safety at Work Act as well as various Factory Acts and is interested in the incidence of accidents primarily from the point of view of accident prevention. While various specialised inspectorates exist within the Department of Employment they have been grouped together to form what is now known as the Health and Safety Executive. This grouping arose following the introduction of the Health and Safety at Work Act of 1974 which increased the powers of the various inspectors. Not only were their powers increased, but a further seven to eight million people were brought under the protection of the legislation. The scope of the 1974 legislation can be demonstrated by the fact that of the 231 deaths in factories in 1975 nearly two-thirds of them resulted from breaches of the 1974 Act.

The Department of Health and Social Security records applications for benefit under the National Insurance Acts for industrial injuries (short term), industrial disablement (long term) and industrial deaths. Statistics relating to these applications are published in the Annual Report of the Department. However, the main source of statistics relating to illness and injuries at work is the annual publication of the Health and Safety Executive entitled *Health and Safety Statistics.* The first volume relating to 1975 was published in September 1977.

The Royal Commission on Civil Liberty (the Pearson Commission) published its report (Cmnd 7054) in March 1978. As with so many other Royal Commissions it felt obliged to put together an appreciable amount of statistical data and is therefore a useful source of data on accidents, and related matters. Thus, the Pearson Report shows that for people in the labour force the risk of an accident of any type is about 40 per 1,000 for women and over 80 per 1,000 for men. For women, less than one quarter of the risk arises from accidents at work, while for men, the proportion is about one-half, *i.e.* 40 per 1,000. The general tendency is for the incidence of industrial accidents, both fatal and serious, to decline although as can be seen from the table opposite some industries have not achieved this objective.

Transport Accidents

The most important source of transport accident statistics is provided by the authority of the Road Traffic Acts. These provide that any road accident resulting in personal injury must be reported to the police. The resulting information is published, primarily by the Department of Transport at monthly intervals, and then annually in

TABLE 54
INDUSTRIAL ACCIDENTS – GREAT BRITAIN
Incidence per 100,000 employees

	Fatal			Serious (Group I)[3]		
	1971	1975	1976	1971	1975	1976
Manufacturing industries:						
Food, drink and tobacco	4·5	1·7	3·1	770	660	690
Coal and petroleum products	—[1]	22·4	19·2	600	960	—[4]
Chemicals and allied industries	8·4	6·7	7·0	520	650	620
Metal manufacture	13·7	10·0	9·4	1,150	970	920
Mechanical engineering	3·5	3·4	3·9	780	650	680
Instrument engineering	—[1]	—[1]	—[1]	240	280	—[4]
Electrical engineering	1·4	1·8	1·4	360	290	310
Shipbuilding and marine engineering	12·4	14·0	13·3	840	820	570
Vehicles	2·3	1·9	0·9	520	420	350
Metal goods not elsewhere specified	3·6	2·9	2·5	680	740	660
Textiles	4·1	1·7	0·8	540	460	500
Leather, leather goods and fur	—[1]	—[1]	—[1]	380	410	—[4]
Clothing and footwear	—[1]	—[1]	—[1]	140	130	210
Bricks, pottery, glass, cement, etc.	7·6	7·2	7·9	900	690	900
Timber, furniture, etc.	4·3	5·5	3·5	890	660	880
Paper, printing, and publishing	2·4	2·9	1·9	480	340	530
Other manufacturing industries	2·4	2·5	—[1]	600	360	490
All manufacturing industries	4·3	3·7	3·4	630	540	560
Agriculture	—[2]	11·7	14·1	—[2]	—[2]	—[2]
Construction	19·6	17·7	15·3	770	740	650
Coalmining	24·2	24·7	19·6	—[2]	—[2]	—[2]
Railways	24·1	18·7	18·8	—[2]	—[2]	—[2]

[1]Number of fatal accidents less than 5.
[2]Comparable data not available.
[3]Those which are both severe and unambiguously the direct and undoubted result of an accident at work. Based on 5 per cent sample.
[4]Sample size too small.

Source: Health and Safety Executive.

greater detail in *Road Accidents in Great Britain* (H.M.S.O.). A basic table from this publication is shown overleaf.

The statistics collected by the Department of Transport are supplemented and analysed further in a monthly publication of the Royal Society for the Prevention of Accidents entitled *Road Accident Statistical Review*. An interesting feature of the Review is the definitions of terms used in the booklet listed on the inside front cover. In addition, insurance companies publish figures from time to time of claims for damage to cars caused by accidents.

Railway accidents are analysed in detail in an annual report entitled *Railway Accidents in Great Britain* by the Department of Transport. In general the classification is into:

(*a*) Train Accidents;

(*b*) Movement Accidents;

(*c*) Non-Movement Accidents.

And into:

(i) Passengers;

(ii) Servants;

(iii) Others.

TABLE 55
ROAD ACCIDENTS: CASUALTIES – GREAT BRITAIN

	1961	1966	1971	1974	1975	1976	1977
Road motor vehicles with licences current (thousands)[1]	9,966	13,286	15,478	17,252	17,501	17,832	—
Index of motor vehicle kilometres (1966=100)	69	100	127	136	138	144	147
Casualties from road accidents (thousands):							
Killed	6·9	8·0	7·7	6·9	6·4	6·6	6·6
Seriously injured	85	100	91	82	77	80	82
Slightly injured	258	285	253	236	241	254	260
Total	350	392	352	325	325	340	348
Persons killed or seriously injured By class of road user (thousands) Pedestrians:							
Under 15	8·3	10·6	11·1	9·3	8·2	7·9	8·3
15–59	7·0	9·3	8·4	7·9	6·9	7·0	7·3
60 and over	7·1	7·9	7·1	6·4	5·8	5·6	5·7
Pedal cyclists							
Under 15	2·9	2·5	2·5	1·9	2·1	2·1	2·1
15 and over	6·9	4·6	3·1	2·6	2·5	2·8	2·9
Two-wheeled motor vehicle riders							
Under 17	1·6	2·8	2·4	1·4	1·7	2·2	2·2
17–19	6·2	7·5	4·7	5·9	6·6	7·9	8·6
20 and over	14·6	8·8	6·3	6·2	6·8	7·8	8·5
Two-wheeled motor vehicle passengers	4·5	3·2	2·1	1·3	1·6	1·9	2·2
Drivers of other vehicles							
Under 25	3·5	7·8	8·5	7·8	7·1	6·9	6·7
25 and over	10·2	15·9	17·8	17·2	15·2	15·2	15·4
Passengers of other vehicles	17·3	25·2	24·5	21·1	19·2	18·4	18·0
Total all known ages[2]	90·2	106·0	98·5	88·9	83·5	85·6	87·8
By class of road user per 100 million vehicle kilometres:							
Pedal cyclists[3]	91	102	122	116	107	112	116[4]
Riders of two wheeled motor vehicles[3]	237	303	333	319	294	293	291
Drivers of other motor vehciles[3]							
Cars and taxis	14	15	13	11	10	9	9[4]
Goods vehicles	9	11	9	7	7	6	6[4]
Public service vehicles	3	3	3	4	3	3	3[4]

[1] Includes all vehicles requiring a licence.
[2] Includes unknown class of road user.
[3] Includes unknown age.
[4] Provisional

Source: Road Accidents, Department of Transport.

A number of accident categories attributable to certain particular circumstances, *e.g.* at level-crossings, are subject to a more detailed analysis.

The numbers of aircraft accidents are comparatively low giving rise to less than 1 % of all deaths from accidents in Great Britain but because of the seriousness of any one accident the statistical analysis of accidents is important. Statistics are primarily used to search for preventive measures or to assess the effectiveness of such measures as have been taken. However, statistics are also used to measure the liabilities of airline operators, in insurance studies, in planning rescue services and in designing accident investigations themselves. The two basic units of measurement in this field are fatalities per aircraft kilometres flown and fatalities per hundred million passenger kilometres. Some care in the interpretation of these statistics is needed. A comparison between two airlines, one of which has long routes and the other short-distance routes, is difficult. The latter may well appear to have a higher accident rate per hundred million passenger kilometres, but since a high proportion of aircraft accidents occur either on take-off or on landing, the aggregate distances flown may be misleading if used as the sole guide. The central body for the collection and publication of these statistics is the International Civil Aviation Organisation. Their statistical digests are published through the H.M.S.O. and are summarised in the United Nations' statistical publications, *i.e. Monthly & Annual Digest of Statistics*. The title of the annual publication of the Civil Aviation Organisation is *Accidents to Aircraft on the British Register*.

Accidents in the Home

Nearly one half of all accidents that enter into statistics occur within the home. The field is obviously important but it is badly documented. The only accurate but limited measure of home accidents is the analyses of the causes of death. Some estimates are made of injuries arising from home accidents by sampling hospital admission lists, but the results cannot be considered as more than rough indications of the order of magnitude. The most important source of statistics in this field is the Royal Society for the Prevention of Acci-

TABLE 56

DEATHS FROM ACCIDENTS* IN THE HOME AND IN RESIDENTIAL ACCOMMODATION
Great Britain   Numbers

	1951	1961	1966	1971	1974	1975	1976
Male deaths:							
Poisoning:							
by solid/liquid substances	90	188	339	225	245	255	268
by gases and vapours	270	518	440	137	95	83	92
Falls	1,122	1,373	1,370	1,181	1,204	1,172	1,154
Fires and flames	192	244	347	319	373	337	342
Other	740	659	768	649	572	564	581
Total	2,414	2,982	3,264	2,511	2,489	2,411	2,437
Female deaths:							
Poisoning:							
by solid/liquid substances	113	217	428	326	313	344	290
by gases and vapours	362	678	512	136	55	54	60
Falls	2,584	3,363	3,290	3,131	2,898	2,846	2,742
Fires and flames	499	429	530	419	473	453	423
Other	550	475	559	522	489	488	455
Total	4,108	5,162	5,319	4,534	4,228	4,185	3,970

*There are some differences in classification between 1951–1966, and 1971, and later years. Comparability between the years may therefore be approximate in some cases.
Source: Mortality statistics: accidents and violence, *Series DH4, Office of Population Censuses and Surveys, General Register Office for Scotland.*

dents. Their annual report is a valuable source of information in which they collate and analyse all available published data. To give an idea of the importance of accidents in the home a table analysing deaths arising from this area published in *Social Trends No. 9* is reproduced on the previous page. It should be noted that some two-thirds of the deaths arising from accidents in the home are of people over the age of 65.

The study of accident statistics is most important if the waste resulting from accidents is to be eliminated. While some fields are quite well documented there are serious gaps and some whole areas that are barely touched upon. Currently the only attempts at comprehensive statistical coverage of accidents are made by the Royal Society for the Prevention of Accidents which is largely dependent for its statistical material upon outside sources.

Social Class

The English, it has been observed, are extremely class conscious. Certainly most people are ready to classify others by reference to their social class, such as working, middle or upper class. There is, nevertheless, no single measure of 'class'; for example, different people might well classify a particular individual either as working or 'lower' middle class. The conventional basis for social classification is well understood, but it is not sufficiently precise for statistical purposes. In any case many people dislike 'class consciousness' as such, and would reasonably ask why it interests the social statistician. There are, however, a number of reasons why the subject is important. First of all, it is common knowledge that fertility among labourers is higher than among the professional community; just as is infant mortality. It is not sufficient merely to believe that a difference exists between the two extreme groups. We want more precise information as to its extent. For example, before the war, in certain districts of England and Wales the infant mortality was almost four times as high as in the wealthy areas of the South East.[1] This is criminal waste and once we have the information as to the extent thereof, social policy can be adapted to cure such blots on the community. It is a commonplace to talk of the opportunity open to the poor boy to get 'to the top'. But how many get there? The extent to which the academic achievement of grammar school boys is related to the home background, the latter being defined by the father's occupation, has been measured in a Ministry of Education report which is of particular sociological interest.[2] To what extent is there what the sociologist calls 'social mobility', *i.e.* do sons and daughters generally move into a higher or

[1]See *Population and Poverty*, R. Titmuss, for a study of pre-war society based entirely on such data. Even now there are large differences, see for example Table 62 p.488.
[2]*Early Leaving*, H.M.S.O., 1954.

lower social class than their parents?[1] Before such enquiries are practicable, there must be a generally accepted classification of social status.

There are, of course, a number of criteria which are employed to classify people. Accent is often a good guide; but statistically it is useless. Education is a useful indicator but is not enough. Income is a better guide and lends itself to statistical treatment; but there are many people with a great deal of money these days whom no one would place in the 'upper class', just as few people would classify a parson in a poor living as 'working class'. The most generally acceptable basis for classifying people is their occupation. Furthermore, surveys have shown a high degree of unanimity among all classes as to the relative status of given trades, occupations and professions.[2] The Registrar General introduced in the 1911 Census of Population a five-fold classification in order to emphasise the great variation in death rates between occupational groups as follows: the figures in brackets giving the proportionate distribution of the population between the classes as disclosed by the 1951 Census. The obvious defect in this classification is that over half the population are in one class, *i.e.* III.

I. Professional, etc., occupations, *e.g.* doctor, lawyer. (3).

II. Intermediate occupations, *e.g.* business executive, manager of large store. (15).

III. Skilled occupations, *e.g.* draughtsman and policeman. (53).

IV. Partly skilled occupations, *e.g.* ticket collector and plumber's labourer. (16).

V. Unskilled occupations, *e.g.* dock labourer, watchman. (12).[3]

Such a classification is a good deal better than the rough and ready three-fold classification, working, middle and upper! It is precise, but for that reason it is arbitrary. For most people the members of classes II and III inevitably merge one into the other, and in fact the latter is so large that it is not really homogeneous, *i.e.* it is too mixed. In an attempt to reduce this effect Social Class III was sub-divided in the 1971 Census into Non-manual (N) including typists, clerical workers, sales representatives, and shop assistants while Manual (M) included cooks, plasterers, railway guards, and foremen. Before the 1961 Census a major revision was undertaken in both the classification of occupations and the social class allocation of occupations. The whole classification gives most weight to skilled occupations and the length of time spent in formal education, with pre-eminence of

[1] Social Mobility in Britain. ed. D. V. Glass.
[2] Glass. Op. cit.
[3] *Note:* Due to rounding percentages do not total 100.

the professions. The classification does not take income into account as such.

A number of points arise concerning the operation of social classi-fication. Thus, in allocating an individual to a particular class the method used is either on the basis of their present employment, or on some previous employment, or upon the employment of another member of their household or family. Table 57 opposite shows the differences that result by varying the bases of allocation. These variations in base particularly affect the retired, household and family classification, the unemployed and married women. The last group, married women, are particularly complicated if the woman goes out to work as well as the man.

Social classification, like all aspects of society, is continually changing. For example, J. W. B. Douglas in his eleven-year longi-tudinal survey of education[1] found that, over the period of his sur-vey, 43 per cent of the families had moved out of their original occupational groups. Inter-generational social mobility (*i.e.* the children being in a different social class from their parents) is in-creasingly the case, largely as a result of improved educational facilities.

TABLE 58

MARRIED COUPLES BOTH ECONOMICALLY ACTIVE, 1971

Great Britain   Percentages

Social Class of wife:	Social Class of husband							Total (thousands)
	I	II	III N	III M	IV	V	NC	
I	6	2	–	–	–	–	1	44
II	31	34	15	9	8	5	12	806
III N	46	40	51	32	25	19	29	1,868
III M	3	4	7	12	11	10	7	502
IV	9	13	19	32	36	37	26	1,443
V	2	2	5	11	14	22	10	518
Not classified	4	4	3	4	4	6	16	232
Total (=100%) (thousands)	242	1,031	647	2,111	955	339	92	5,414

Source: Census of Population, 1971.   *Classification: Own Social Class.*

It was recognised that the social classification did not produce groups homogeneous enough for some analyses. Hence, in 1951, the Registrar General introduced the concept of *socio-economic groupings* (S.E.G.). Whereas social class was an attempt to rank occupations in terms of skill and to some extent also in terms of standing in the community, S.E.G.s are simply groups of unranked occupations. The concept of S.E.G.s was modified as a result of the Conference of European Statisticians in 1959. The revised groupings were intro-duced in the 1961 Census of Population and their sizes shown in

[1]*The Home and the School, 1964.*

TABLE 57

SOCIAL CLASS COMPOSITION OF PEOPLE AGED 15 AND OVER, 1971 FOR VARIOUS GROUPS

Great Britain

Percentages and thousands

	Men only			Women only			Men and women aged 15 and over		
				Married		Single, widowed and divorced				
	Economically active	Retired	Economically active and retired	Own[1] class	Husband's[2] class	Own[3] class	Own occupation of economically active and retired	Head of family	Chief economic supporter
	(1)	(2)	(3)	(4)	(5)	(6)	(7)	(8)	(9)
Percentage in each Social Class:									
I	5·2	3·0	5·0	0·9	5·3	1·2	3·6	5·1	4·9
II	17·8	19·1	18·0	16·2	19·8	19·2	17·8	20·0	19·8
III N	11·9	12·1	11·9	35·4	11·3	41·2	21·1	11·9	14·2
III M	39·0	34·2	38·5	10·0	39·0	10·8	28·4	37·9	34·8
IV	17·8	20·3	18·1	28·2	17·5	22·7	20·9	18·0	18·6
V	8·3	11·2	8·6	9·4	7·1	4·9	8·2	7·3	7·7
Total classified (=100%)	15,368	1,911	17,279	5,697	12,365	3,834	26,809	13,150	15,907
Total[4] unclassified	516	323	909	1,101	471	1,549	3,488	694	1,374
Total in Great Britain	15,884	2,304	18,188	6,797	12,835	5,383	30,367	13,844	17,281

[1] Economically active and retired married women by own social class.
[2] Married women enumerated with their husband by the social class of husband including both the economically active and retired, and those economically active single, widowed, and divorced women.
[3] Economically active and retired single, widowed, and divorced women.
[4] Unclassified persons: those for whom no occupation or inadequate information was reported in the Census. A large proportion of this group were out of work retired, or inactive at Census date.

Source: *Census of Population, 1971, Economic Activity Tables*

TABLE 59
Socio-Economic Groups of Males, 1961 and 1971
Great Britain   Thousands

	1961	1971
Employers and managers (large establishments)	640	642
Employers and managers (small establishments)	1,051	1,444
Professional – self-employed	144	155
Professional – employees	500	703
Intermediate non-manual	685	965
Junior non-manual	2,252	2,158
Personal service	162	174
Foremen – manual	595	647
Skilled manual	5,549	5,286
Semi-skilled manual	2,657	2,299
Unskilled manual	1,568	1,432
Own account (non-professional)	621	773
Farmers – employers	195	156
Farmers – own account	191	157
Agricultural	444	286
Armed Forces	336	254
Inadequately described	489	654
Total	18,080	18,187

Source: Censuses of Population.   Classification: own occupation of economically active and retired

Table 59 which gives the numbers of males in each group in the Censuses of Population of 1961 and 1971.

The General Household Survey (G.H.S.) which was started in October 1970 (see p.490) produced what are called General Household Survey Socio-Economic Groupings. Here an attempt has been made to collapse the basic S.E.G.s into a social class classification for the purposes of analysing the data from the Household Survey. The way in which the S.E.G.s have been re-grouped in the G.H.S. is as follows:

General Household Survey Socio-Economic Groupings		*Corresponding Socio-Economic Groups*
No.	*Name*	*Nos.*
1	Professional	3, 4
2	Employers and managers	1, 2, 13
3	Intermediate and Junior non-manual	5, 6
4	Skilled manual	8, 9, 12, 14
5	Semi-skilled and personal service	7, 10, 15
6	Unskilled manual	11

The Family Expenditure Survey which started in 1957 (see p.512) uses a further modification of the social class classification as follows:

Class	*Name*
1	Professional and technical workers
2	Administrative and managerial workers

3	Teachers
4	Clerical workers
5	Shop assistants
6	Manual workers
7	Member of H.M. Forces.

It will be seen that all these classifications and groupings depend upon the individual's occupation. It is not surprising therefore that the Census authorities pay great attention to the need for accurate recording of the individual respondent's occupation. The census form itself gives detailed instructions and before the 1961 and 1971 Censuses factories and offices were circularised with notices explaining to the employers how they should answer this particular question. The object was to ensure uniformity and accuracy, for it is well known from previous Censuses that the replies to the questions on occupation and the employer's business or trade have frequently been inaccurate. It will be readily understood that while for the larger occupational groupings such inaccuracies may not be serious, for the smaller groupings widespread errors could invalidate some of the comparisons which are made using these data, for example, in respect of occupational mortality and industrial morbidity, *i.e.* industrial disease, etc. The census workers are given extremely detailed instructions and voluminous lists of the various occupations so that they may adopt a uniform tabulation. Any reader who is sceptical as to the problems involved is advised to examine the Census volume entitled 'Classification of Occupations'. He will be astounded at the number and variety of occupations.

The fact that variations in social class are associated with variations in many other social variables is commonly accepted. However, the extent of these variations and its widespread presence throughout our society is well demonstrated in an article on social class produced by the Central Statistical Office and appearing in *Social Trends* No.6 (1975) (pp.10-32). Three of the tables in that article illustrating the relevance of social class are reproduced overleaf and their content requires no comment here.

A word of caution is necessary in the interpretation of such tables. The concept of social class is not a simple one. Although occupation is used as an indicator of class, there are undoubtedly other elements in class itself, *e.g.* education, income, behaviour patterns, etc. It is very difficult to attempt to allocate cause to apparent associations. Thus, infant mortality decreases as social class moves to the first category, but why? Is it because of better food or better housing or better health care or less ignorance of pre-natal care or, some or all of these factors or many others? It is in trying to unravel the complex patterns of causality that lie under the apparent simple blanket of

TABLE 60
LIVE BIRTHS TO MARRIED COUPLES: BY SOCIAL CLASS OF HUSBAND
AND AGE OF MOTHER AT BIRTH OF CHILD, 1970-1972
Great Britain   Percentages

Social Class of husband:	Age of mother at birth of child						Estimated annual no. of births (=100%) (thousands)
	Under 20	20–24	25–29	30–34	35–39	40–44	
I	1	21	48	21	6	1	51
II	3	26	42	19	8	2	116
III N	5	34	40	15	5	1	82
III M	9	39	30	13	6	2	322
IV	12	40	27	12	6	2	130
V	17	40	22	12	6	2	48
Not classified	12	46	29	9	3	–	27
All classes	9	36	33	15	6	2	776

Source: Office of Population Censuses and Surveys.   *Classification: Social Class of husband*

TABLE 61
MALE STANDARDISED MORTALITY RATES: BY SOCIAL CLASS
England Wales

Social Class:	1921–23 (age 20–64)	1930–32 (age 20–64)	1949–53 (age 20–64)	1959–63 (age 15–64)	1970–72[1] (age 15–64)
I	82	90	86	76	77
II	94	94	92	81	81
III	95	97	101	100	104
IV	101	102	104	103	113
V	125	111	118	143	137

[1]Provisional data.
Note: For detailed discussion of the changes in classification and problems of interpretation, see the sources to this table. Trends from one decade to the next should be interpreted with care. For example, between 1949–53 and 1959–63, a major reclassification of occupations by Social Class took place, which affects the interpretation of changes in Social Class mortality differentials between the two periods.
Sources: 1921–63, Registrar General's Decennial Supplements. Occupational mortality, 1951 and 1961. 1970–72, Office of Population Censuses and Surveys.
Classification: Last full-time occupation.

TABLE 62
STILLBIRTHS AND INFANT DEATHS TO MOTHERS AGED UNDER 25, 1959–63
England and Wales   Rates

	Mother's Parity (No. of previous live and stillbirths)		
	0	1 or 2	3 and over
Stillbirth rates per 1,000 total births			
Social Class I and II	10·5	8·6	5·1
Social Class III	14·6	9·8	11·4
Social Class IV and V	15·6	10·4	13·2
Neonatal deaths (at ages under 4 weeks) per 1,000 live births			
Social Class I and II	9·6	8·8	12·8
Social Class III	12·2	11·1	16·5
Social Class IV and V	13·3	12·1	16·3
Post-neonatal deaths (at ages 4 weeks to 1 year) per 1,000 live births			
Social Class I and II	3·9	4·3	10·3
Social Class III	4·4	9·2	17·3
Social Class IV and V	6·1	10·2	15·4

Source: Regional and Social Factors in Infant Mortality, Spicer and Lipworth, H.M.S.O. 1966.
Classification: Social Class of father.

social class that the social researcher hopes to find clues to the improvement of society.

Households and Families

While the overall view of the population requires the counting of individual heads, much of the social significance of population depends on how the individuals are combined into households and families. For statistical purposes a *household* is a group of people who live and eat together, while *families* consist of a married couple with or without children or a single parent with children. Very often a household and family coincide but, when for example a household contains a married daughter with her husband, there exists in the household an additional *nuclear* family. This represents a potential demand for additional housing and a potential centre for population growth; two very important elements in terms of social planning.

The two principal sources of data relating to households are the Census of Population and the General Household Survey (GHS). The GHS is an annual sample survey which started in October 1970. A sample of about 12,000 households is drawn on a geographical cluster basis to cover the whole of Great Britain. As the survey takes place annually it is particularly useful in obtaining data during the period *between* two Censuses. It is also used to investigate specific topics of current concern and the designers of the survey are now moving towards a third idea where specific topics are investigated regularly but not annually, *e.g.* once every three or five years.

To achieve the inter-Census data mentioned above the GHS must contain certain questions which are asked every year. Such 'core' information comes in two main areas:

(i) Household Schedule which includes:
   Age, sex, colour, marital status.
   Number of years at present address.
   Number of moves in last five years.
   Age and tenure of home.
   Size of home and facilities.

(ii) Individual Schedule which includes:
   Employment status.
   Type of job, conditions of work and income.
   Education and qualifications.
   Ethnic origins.

The introductory report of the GHS was published in 1973 and is entitled *The General Household Survey: Introductory Report*. The first two chapters of this report gave a description of the methodology of the survey and an account of some similar surveys carried out in other countries. It should be noted that subsequent to the publication of the *Introductory Report* there have been some changes in the sample design. These changes are detailed in the first chapter of the 1975 *Report*. To date (March 1979) five reports of the GHS have been published for the years 1972-76 inclusive, the last report being published in 1978.

Some of the trends in the size and composition of families and households revealed by a combination of the Censuses of Population and the General Household Survey are given in the two tables below and opposite, i.e. Table 63 and 64.

Of particular note is the fall between 1971-76 of average household size from 2.91 to 2.76 persons. This was largely due to the increase in the number of single-person households, especially in the 70+ age group. The results suggest that there is a growing tendency for recently

TABLE 63

HOUSEHOLDS[1]: BY SIZE AND YPE

Great Britain   Percentages and thousands

	Percentages				Thousands		
	1961	1966	1971	1976	1961	1966	1971
Households by size:							
1 person	*12*	*15*	*18*	*21*	1,919	2,572	3,320
2 people	*30*	*30*	*32*	*32*	4,820	5,158	5,771
3 people	*23*	*21*	*19*	*17*	3,780	3,592	3,458
4 people	*19*	*18*	*17*	*17*	3,100	3,042	3,148
5 people	*9*	*9*	*8*	*8*	1,489	1,480	1,515
6 or more people	*7*	*6*	*6*	*5*	1,080	1,093	1,106
Total households	*100*	*100*	*100*	*100*	16,189	16,937	18,317
Average household size (number of people)	3·01	2·99	2·88	2·76			
Households by type:							
No family[1]:							
one person							
– under retirement age[2]	*4*	*5*	*6*	*6*	726	890	1,122
– over retirement age[2]	*7*	*10*	*12*	*15*	1,193	1,682	2,198
two or more people							
– one or more over retirement age[2]	*3*	*3*	*2*	*2*	536	463	444
– all under retirement age[2]	*2*	*2*	*2*	*1*	268	251	304
One family:							
married couple only	*26*	*26*	*27*	*27*	4,147	4,377	4,890
married couple with at least one dependent child[1]	*38*	*36*	*34*	*34*	6,117	6,054	6,304
married couple with independent child(ren) only[1]	*10*	*10*	*8*	*7*	1,673	1,746	1,565
lone parent with at least one dependent child[1]	*2*		*3*	*4*	367	400	515
lone parent with independent child(ren) only[1]	*4*	*4*	*4*	*4*	721	755	712
Two or more families	*3*	*2*	*1*	*1*	440	317	263
Total households	*100*	*100*	*100*	*100*	16,189	16,937	18,317

[1]The data for 1961, 1966, and 1971 are taken from the population Censuses of those years; the 1976 data are from the General Household Survey.
[2]60 and over for women, 65 and over for men.

Source: Office of Population Censuses and Surveys

Percentages

TABLE 64
FAMILIES: BY SIZE AND AGE OF HEAD, 1971 AND 1976
Great Britain

| | 1971 (Census) | | | | | | 1976 (General Household Survey) | | | | | |
| | Age of family head | | | | All families | | Age of family head | | | | All families | |
	Under 30	30–44	45–64	65 and over	Per-centages	Millions	Under 30	30–44	45–64	65 and over	Per-centages	Sample size (numbers)
Married couples with dependent children:												
1 child	31	21	18	2	19	2·44	30	20	19	1	18	1,508
2 children	23	36	9	—	18	2·40	26	41	10	—	20	1,683
3 children	6	18	3	—	8	1·03	5	19	3	0	8	668
4 or more	2	11	2	—	4	0·57	2	8	2	0	4	297
Total	*63*	*86*	*33*	*2*	*49*	*6·44*	*62*	*89*	*35*	*1*	*50*	*4,156*
Married couples without dependent children	37	14	67	98	51	6·70	38	11	65	99	50	4,161
All married couples (percentages)	*100*	*100*	*100*	*100*	*100*	*13·14*	*100*	*100*	*100*	*100*	*100*	*—*
(millions)	*2·00*	*3·96*	*5·27*	*1·91*			*—*	*—*	*—*	*—*		*—*
Lone parents with dependent children												
Men	*8*	*17*	*11*	*1*	*8*	*0·11*	*4*	*16*	*6*	*—*	*7*	*72*
Women	*92*	*74*	*31*	*3*	*37*	*0·51*	*96*	*80*	*35*	*0*	*48*	*489*
Total	*100*	*90*	*42*	*4*	*45*	*0·63*	*100*	*95*	*41*	*—*	*55*	*561*
Lone parents without dependent children	—	10	58	96	55	0·75	0	5	59	100	45	464
All lone parents (percentages)	*100*	*100*	*100*	*100*	*100*	*1·37*	*100*	*100*	*100*	*100*	*100*	*—*
(millions)	*0·15*	*0·30*	*0·42*	*0·49*			*—*	*—*	*—*	*—*		*—*

Source: Population Census 1971; General Household Survey, 1976.

married couples to delay having a family; a marked increase in married women with young children going out to work and an improvement in living standards including the beginning of a levelling-out process of the differences between white and coloured populations.

Movements within family groups are reflected by a large number of social activities that give rise to statistical series. These are used, first, to chart and then to forecast changes in family size and composition. Some of these series have already been mentioned in the section on population projections but a summary of the main series are given below.

Marriage

The average age at first marriage fell from 26·8 years for men and 24·6 years for women in 1951 to 24·6 years for men and 22·6 years for women in 1971. Since 1971 the average ages at first marriage has tended to rise slightly for both men and women. The percentage of re-marriages to *all* marriages has increased from 18 per cent in 1951 to 20 per cent in 1971 and to 31 per cent in 1976. The increase is mainly amongst divorced persons and, as they tend to remarry while they are still in their 30's such marriages could affect the birth rate.

Divorce

The rate of divorce in the United Kingdom per thousand of the married population rose from 3 per 1,000 in 1951 to 6 per 1,000 in 1971, and then remained fairly constant at 10 per 1,000 over the years 1972 to 1976. The number of divorces rose from 31,000 in 1951 to 80,000 in 1971 and 136,000 in 1976.

Births

The number of legitimate births fell from 765,000 in 1951 to 698,000 in 1971, 504,000 in 1976 and 485,000 in 1977. The number of illegitimate births rose from 40,200 in 1951 to 65,700 in 1971 but were 53,800 in 1976. The *Family Formation Survey* carried out for the Office of Population Censuses and Surveys and published in 1976 showed that only 17 per cent of women used no form of contraception and that, if the women of 40 and over were not considered, the percentage of non-users dropped to 12·3 per cent. The total number of abortions were 102,000 in 1971 and 109,000 in 1976. There does not appear to be any marked trend up or down in these figures.

While households and families form the broadest statistical groupings within society, considerable interest is being generated by other social groups that can be identified by a common characteristic. Thus, the elderly (people over 60 years old) the young (those under 20), ethnic minorities and the handicapped are considered as separate groups in *Social Trends No. 9*. Once the government accepts responsibility for treating a social group in some special way then the group will be identified statistically. In other words, to pursue the declared policy effectively, the government will have to collect information about the group to determine, first, the nature and extent of the particular need and, second, progress achieved in meeting that need once legislation has been passed. Sometimes the data are already available and only requires analysis but, undoubtedly, the General Household Survey will be a major source of additional data for such purposes.

Housing

Of the three basic necessities of life – food, clothing, and shelter, it is the last that is the most difficult to regulate in any form of planned society. It is possible to regard housing as a product or service subject to the forces of supply and demand which are equated by price. While this basic market structure exists, its workings are considerably affected by government intervention at both national and local levels. The consequential statistical picture is similarly complicated by the government's efforts to assess demand, regulate supply and control price, either directly or indirectly, and in part or in whole. However, to clarify the picture the divisions of demand, supply and price will be retained.

Demand: The commonest measure of demand is the number, size and characteristics of households on which the main source of data is the Census of Population. In the 1971 Census the household was defined as 'either one person living alone, or a group of persons (who may or may not be related) living at the same address with common housekeeping'. In turn 'common housekeeping' means having at least one meal a day with the household. The information on households is analysed by size and type and then the data are broken down into the social context of the family unit as in Table 65.

The analysis overleaf forms the basis of any forecast of demand for housing. A more detailed description of how this demographic material is used in forecasting the demand for housing can be found in *Social Trends No. 1* in an article by A. E. Holmans.

The size of households in England and Wales has fallen from an average of 3·19 in 1951 to about 2·75 in 1976, a fall of some 14 per cent. This change is accounted for partly by the falling birth rate and partly by the increased survival rate amongst the elderly. In other words, more and more people are living to a greater age than in the past. The result of this demographic change is to reduce the demand for larger housing units and increase the demand for the

TABLE 65

HOUSEHOLDS: BY TYPE; AND PERSONS: BY HOUSEHOLD TYPE

Great Britain   Percentages and thousands

	Percentages			Thousands		
	1961*	1966	1971	1961*	1966	1971
Households by type:						
No family:						
one person	11·9	15·2	18·1	1,919	2,572	3,320
two or more persons	5·0	4·2	4·1	804	714	749
One family:						
married couple only	25·6	25·8	26·7	4,147	4,377	4,890
married couple with at least one dependent child	37·8	35·7	34·4	6,117	6,054	6,304
married couple with child(ren), none dependent	10·3	10·3	8·5	1,673	1,746	1,565
lone parent with at least one dependent child	2·3	2·4	2·8	367	400	515
lone parent with child(ren), none dependent	4·5	4·5	3·9	721	755	712
Two families	2·7	1·8	1·4	431	312	258
Three or more families	0·1	0·0	0·0	9	5	5
Total households	100·0	100·0	100·0	16,189	16,937	18,317
Persons by household type:						
No family:						
one person	3·8	5·1	6·3	1,919	2,572	3,320
two or more persons	3·6	3·2	3·2	1,821	1,600	1,675
One family:						
married couple only	17·7	18·2	19·3	8,874	9,224	10,187
married couple with child(ren)	63·7	63·7	61·8	31,860	32,218	32,663
lone parent with child(ren)	6·2	6·4	6·6	3,119	3,238	3,514
Two families	4·7	3·4	2·7	2,345	1,698	1,438
Three or more families	0·1	0·1	0·1	72	43	50
Total persons in households	100·0	100·0	100·0	50,011	50,594	52,848

*Due to slight classification differences these figures are not exactly comparable with the others.
Note: Figures for 1951 are not available on a similar basis.

Source: Office of Population Censuses and Surveys

smaller, *i.e.* smaller houses and flats. To these changes must be added a rising standard of living that generates a demand for better quality housing. This development is reinforced by the legal imposition of higher minimum standards both in terms of density of population per housing unit and the provision of certain facilities, *e.g.* inside water-closet and water supply. Additional information on the changing structure of the household and the changing nature of housing demand is obtained from the Family Expenditure Survey and the General Household Survey.

Supply: The basic unit of the supply of housing is the dwelling. This was redefined in the 1961 Census of Population in terms of the concept of a 'household space' in order to help the enumerator to identify separate dwellings. The decennial Census provides a detailed survey of the number of dwellings and, from its inception in 1801, has always included questions on housing. These have often been concerned with the quality of the housing in terms both of overcrowding and the provision of facilities. However, the main source of statistics on supply of housing is now the publication by the Department of the Environment's *Housing and Construction Statis-*

tics. This is a quarterly publication started in 1972 and covers, in considerable detail, the physical provision of housing accommodation.

TABLE 66

STOCK OF DWELLINGS: CHANGE OF TENURE

United Kingdom   Thousands

	1951–60	1961–70	1971–73	1974	1975	1976	1977
Stock of dwellings at end of period* (thousands):							
Owner-occupied	6,967	9,567	10,377	10,567	10,760	10,957	11,155
Rented from local authorities or new town corporations	4,400	5,848	6,089	6,227	6,401	6,557	6,700
Rented from private owners	4,306 } 927 }	3,768	3,416	3,303	3,186	3,093	3,010
Total	16,600	19,183	19,882	20,097	20,347	20,607	20,865
Annual net gain (+) or loss (−) (annual averages) (thousands):							
Public sector							
New construction							
local authorities	+ 169	+ 152	+ 115	+ 109	+ 135	+ 136	+ 127
new town corporations	+ 9	+ 9	+ 11	+ 12	+ 16	+ 16	+ 16
housing associations	+ 4	+ 4	+ 9	+ 10	+ 15	+ 16	+ 25
government departments	+ 7	+ 5	+ 2	+ 3	+ 2	+ 2	+ 2
Total	+ 189	+ 170	+ 137	+ 134	+ 167	+ 169	+ 170
Other changes	− 2	− 26	− 57	+ 4	+ 7	− 13	—
Net gain	187	144	80	138	174	156	170
Private sector							
New construction	+ 104	+ 198	+ 196	+ 145	+ 155	+ 155	+ 143
Other changes	− 57	− 83	− 54	− 68	− 79	− 51	− 55
Net gain	47	115	142	77	76	104	88
Total net gain	+ 234	+ 258	+ 222	+ 215	+ 250	+ 260	+ 258

*Estimates based upon Census data, see Appendix B, Chapter 9: Dwellings.

Source: Housing and Construction Statistics, *Department of the Environment*

Table 66 shows that about one-third of all housing is supplied by the public sector – very largely local authorities. In addition, the public sector is providing some two-thirds of the new dwellings becoming available each year. However, this table refers to the *numbers* of dwellings only and not to the *size* of the dwellings.

Since 1891 the Census of Population has included information (published in the *Housing Volumes*) on the density of population, *i.e.* the number of rooms in a household divided into the number of persons in the household up to 1966. The definition of room excluded the bathroom as well as the kitchen 'if meals are not eaten there regularly'. In 1966 kitchens were included whether or not meals were eaten there but, in 1971, if a kitchen was less than six feet wide it was totally excluded. If these variations are added to all those decisions that have to be made concerning landings and passageways used for living accommodation, not to overlook the problems of modern 'open-plan' housing in terms of the equivalent number of rooms, one can see the problem of relying on detailed movements in the measurement of population density in housing. It is interesting to note that the official standards of overcrowding laid down in the Housing Act of 1957 are not used in the general run of housing statistics. In fact, the latest information on 'over-crowding' is that collected by the General Household Survey. Thus:

TABLE 67
PERSONS PER ROOM[1]: BY TENURE AND AREA, 1977
Great Britain   Percentages

	Persons per room						Total sample size (numbers of households)
	Over 1	1 exactly	⅔ but under 1	½ but under ⅔	Under ½	All	
Tenure (percentage of households):							
Owned outright	1·2	2·1	9·9	20·0	66·8	100	2,725
Owned with mortgage	2·1	6·7	35·1	28·7	27·4	100	3,379
Total owner occupiers	1·7	4·7	23·9	24·8	45·0	100	6,104
Rented from local authority or new town	5·8	9·1	25·2	26·1	33·8	100	3,960
Rented from private owners, furnished and unfurnished	2·4	9·5	17·8	25·4	44·9	100	1,447
Rented with job or business	3·6	9·5	31·3	24·0	31·6	100	358
All tenures 1977	3·2	6·9	23·8	25·3	40·8	100	11,869
1971	4·8	8·9	24·4	25·3	36·6	100	11,990
By area (percentage of households):							
Greater London	3·1	7·3	26·3	24·1	39·2	100	1,484
Rest of England and Wales	2·8	6·3	23·2	25·3	42·4	100	9,225
Scotland[2]	6·4	12·5	24·5	25·3	31·3	100	2,323

[1]Including kitchens; excluding bathrooms, water closets, garages, and rooms used entirely for business.
[2]Double sample.   *Source:* General Household Survey, 1977

Generally speaking, housing statistics have been inadequate for meeting the increasing government intervention in this field. A major impetus was given to the development of the statistical coverage by the Governmental Green Paper published in 1977 – *Housing Policy, A Consultative Document (Cmnd 6851)*. The most important statistical development was the establishment of the National Dwelling and Housing Survey and three follow-up surveys consisting of:

(*a*) a longitudinal survey of some 5,000 accommodation units in the private rented sector collecting data on the characteristics of tenants, rents paid and household incomes. The first rounds of interviews were held in the Spring of 1978 and of 1979.

(*b*) A survey of all of those who have moved house recently; their characteristics; where they came from and why. This was a follow-up of similar surveys held in 1972 and 1974.

(*c*) A national survey of voluntary and involuntary sharing of households in an attempt to confirm the extent of 'potential households'. As noted earlier, this is an important concept in forecasting demand.

These three follow-up surveys all use the National Dwelling and Housing Survey as the basis for their sampling frames. The survey itself collected information on the nature of the dwelling in terms of size and amenities, including parking facilities as well as on the characteristics of the occupants. A sample of 433,000 household units was drawn from the valuation lists of the Inland Revenue. Full results of the survey are awaited.

In addition to the above, the following surveys have also taken place:

(i) a review of the Rent Acts and the attitudes of landlords, tenants and owner-occupiers to the letting of accommodation. Some 1,300 tenants and 1,000 landlords were involved;

(ii) a survey undertaken in Autumn of 1976 of some 8,600 dwellings drawn at random from the valuation lists to up-date information collected in 1967 and 1971 on the physical condition of permanent housing;

(iii) a survey of vacant properties;

(iv) a feasibility study to see if a longitudinal survey could be made of the housing experiences of the 1958 birth cohort of 16,000 used in The National Child Development Study.

New legislation, e.g. Rent (Agriculture) Act 1976 and Housing (Homeless Persons) Act 1977 have also generated new statistical series so that the operation of the Acts may be monitored.

Some 15 to 20 years ago the statistics of housing were woefully deficient but rapid strides have been made recently to improve the position. Improvements there have undoubtedly been but there is still a long way to go before full statistical coverage of this basic social need can be claimed.

Education

The importance of education and the role of the educational system in our society is underlined first, by the fact that it is the single most expensive social service that the government has to provide and second, by the continuing controversy over the effectiveness of present-day educational methods in terms of the end-product with which, it seems at times, neither parents nor employers are satisfied!

More than many, educational statistics suffer from the defect inherent in many government statistics, i.e. the bulk of the data are the by-product of the administration of the educational system. As such their usefulness in answering many of the questions asked about education and its products is limited In any case, the gaps in our knowledge – despite the vast volume of data produced over quite a long period – is underlined by the statistical enquiries undertaken by a series of public enquiries on various aspects of education. Thus, the Robbins Committee on Higher Education, the Central Advisory Council for Education under the late Lord Crowther, the Newsom and the Plowden reports dealing with the 13-16- year-olds and the under-11's respectively, have each generated a wealth of statistical data much of them from specially commissioned surveys. The latter, in particular, were undertaken largely to repair the gaps in the official statistics.

Under the continuing pressure of public debate and official enquiry, the volume of education statistics has grown very rapidly. Thus, the annual *Statistics of Education* produced by the Department of Education and Science now comprises six volumes. The first five relate to England and Wales, only the last covers the United Kingdom as a whole. But, to try to condense this mass of data and to provide a national coverage for the United Kingdom, the Department publishes a summary volume under the title *Education Statistics for the U.K.*

Each volume of the DES annual statistical report covers a particular topic or group of related topics. Thus, Volume 1 classifies schools by type and size as well as providing a regional analysis of the number of pupils per teacher. Volume 2 reviews the school leavers, classifying them by age, by their academic attainment and school attended, as well as their destination on leaving school, *i.e.* employment or further education. Volume 3 is devoted to further education and reviews the students at Polytechnics, evening institutes, adult education courses and at any other establishment providing opportunities of studying for national qualifications. Volume 4 looks at the teachers, in particular their training and distribution between the different types of educational establishment, as well as giving information on their age distribution and academic qualifications. Volume 5 is devoted to finance, analysing the expenditure of the central and local government on education as well as their outlay on student awards. The last volume, No. 6, covers the universities for the United Kingdom as a whole, analysing staff and students by subjects studied, degrees and diplomas awarded, as well as providing an analysis of the income and expenditure of each university.

Given the mounting costs of the educational provision in the United Kingdom and the recurrent criticisms of particular aspects of the educational system, there is continuing pressure upon the DES and the local authorities to produce information which will enable the government and critics to appraise the developments within the system. This has produced since the later 1960s occasional reports published by H.M. Stationery Office on particular topics ranging from the curriculum and deployment of teachers in the secondary system, a survey of in-service training for teachers and two recent studies on school buildings.

Both on educational and on economic grounds, in view of the large number of married women who are gainfully occupied, there is growing demand for nursery education. This topic was discussed at length in the Plowden report entitled *Children and their Primary Schools* (1967) and in 1972 the government's White Paper *Education: A framework for expansion* (*Cmnd 5174*) – based largely upon the recommendations of the Plowden Committee – stated that the government had decided to launch a new policy for the education of the under-fives. Volume II of the Plowden report is especially interesting given its ten survey reports on different aspects of young children's education. The survey on the relationship between the social environment of the child and its educational progress is of special interest.

The second volume of the Crowther report '*15 to 18*' contained a number of surveys of which the most important is that dealing with the educational attainment of some 7,000 entrants into H.M. Forces in 1957-58. The Newsom report entitled *Half our Future* contained in Part III the findings of a survey of secondary modern and comprehensive schools with reference to teaching methods, social background, as well as the educational and social activities of the older pupils.

While there may be legitimate debate over the precise aims of the present educational system, it is not unreasonable – however unfashionable it may be in some quarters – to take account of educational attainment in terms of success in examinations. The table overleaf taken from Volume 2 of the DES *Statistics of Education* gives some interesting information of the grades attained in the Certificate of Secondary Education and the General Certificate of Education at both Ordinary and Advanced levels.

At a time when unemployment faces many boys and girls leaving school it is important to know what happens to school-leavers. The table on page 501, which also comes from the second volume of the DES *Statistics of Education*, provides a detailed analysis of the destinations of school-leavers. Of interest is the different experience of girls from boys.

Another matter of contemporary interest is the problem of adjustment within the educational system to the reduction in the number of children coming into the various grades of school. This informa-

TABLE 68

THE ACADEMIC ATTAINMENT OF SCHOOL LEAVERS

England and Wales

Percentages

	Boys					Girls				
	1960-61[1]	1965-66	1970-71	1975-76	1976-77[3]	1960-61[1]	1965-66	1970-71	1975-76	1976-77[3]
No GCE or CSE qualifications	—	51·0[2]	44·1	18·0	16·4	—	51·0	44·9	16·1	14·6
1 or more other grades GCE or CSE	—	11·0[2]	13·2	33·7	33·9	—	11·5	11·0	31·8	32·1
Total No. and 1 or more other grades GCE or CSE	71·9	62·0	57·3	51·7	50·3	73·4	62·5	55·9	47·9	46·7
1-4 higher grades GCE or CSE	11·6	15·2	18·1	24·1	24·9	11·5	16·4	19·3	27·5	28·5
5 or more gigher grade 'O' level GCE or CSE	6·7	7·1	6·8	7·3	8·1	8·5	9·6	9·3	9·9	10·3
1 'A' level pass	1·7	2·8	3·5	2·9	3·1	1·8	2·8	3·6	3·3	3·3
2 'A' level passes	2·5	4·0	4·7	4·1	4·0	2·0	3·8	4·9	4·5	4·1
3 or more 'A' level passes	5·6	8·9	9·6	9·9	9·5	2·8	4·8	7·0	7·0	7·1
All leavers (percentages)	100	100	100	100	100	100	100	100	100	100
(thousands)	312	321	315	364	384	300	302	298	344	367

[1]Not strictly comparable with later years as Certificate of Secondary Education began in 1965.
[2]Estimates.
[3]Provisional figures.

Source: Statistics of Education Volume 2, School leavers CSE and GCE, *Department of Education and Science*

TABLE 69

DESTINATION OF SCHOOL LEAVERS: BY TYPE OF SCHOOL, AND SEX, 1975-76

England and Wales

Percentages

	Degree courses at		Other establishments	Teacher training courses	Other full-time further education	Employment*	Total sample size	
	Universities	Polytechnics					(percentages)	(thousands)
Boys								
Grammar	26·2	4·5	0·2	1·4	14·7	53·0	100	23·8
Comprehensive	4·7	0·9	0·1	0·5	8·0	85·7	100	254·6
Secondary modern	0·2	0·0	0·0	0·1	10·1	89·6	100	55·2
Other maintained secondary	4·9	1·2	0·2	0·3	8·5	84·8	100	6·7
Direct grant	41·4	3·6	0·2	0·9	17·1	36·8	100	8·0
Independent recognised	32·7	2·7	0·3	0·5	22·7	41·1	100	15·5
Total boys (thousands)	27·1	4·3	0·4	1·9	35·0	295·1		363·9
Girls								
Grammar	16·9	1·8	0·6	7·7	26·7	46·3	100	24·4
Comprehensive	2·9	0·5	0·1	1·9	15·3	79·2	100	241·7
Secondary modern	0·1	0·0	0·0	0·2	19·4	80·3	100	52·2
Other maintained secondary	3·7	0·3	0·2	1·2	14·9	79·7	100	5·9
Direct grant	30·1	2·4	0·6	8·1	24·5	34·4	100	7·6
Independent recognised	15·5	1·4	0·8	2·6	42·6	37·0	100	11·
Total girls (thousands)	15·6	2·1	0·7	7·5	61·3	256·4		343·6

*Includes those entering temporary employment, pending entry into full-time further education, and those who left for other reasons and whose destinations were not known.

Source: Statistics of Education, Volume 2, School Leavers, CSE and GCE, *Department of Education and Science*

TABLE 70
PUPILS[1]: PROJECTIONS AND AGE DISTRIBUTION
United Kingdom

Thousands and percentages

	Actual							Projections		
	1961	1966	1971	1974	1975[3]	1976[3]	1977[3]	1981[3]	1986[2]	1991[3]
All schools: Thousands of boys and girls in January each year aged:										
2–4	255	288	384	509	532	576	569	613	—	—
5–10	4,550	4,991	5,544	5,614	5,549	5,453	5,374	4,657	3,825	4,372
11–14[3,4]	3,484	3,044	3,286	4,391	4,493	4,609	4,681	4,568	3,948	3,175
15	282	475	534							
16	172	226	273	400	429	432	455	502	464	382
17	87	128	157	163	167	175	181	206	208	180
18 and over	29	49	53	54	53	56	60	67	69	60
	8,859	9,102	10,230	11 130	11 222	11,301	11,321	10,613	—	—

[1] Part-time pupils counted as 1.

[2] Figures for the Scotland component are at previous September.

[3] In Scotland 11-year-olds are customarily in primary schools. The numbers of Scottish 11-year-olds included above were 95·6 thousand in 1976 and are expected to decrease to 65·9 thousand in 1986.

[4] The statutory leaving age was raised by one year to 16 in the educational year 1972-73. January 1974 (January 1973 for Scotland) figures are the first to reflect this change and hence age group 11-15 is taken from 1974 onwards.

Source: Education Statistics for the United Kingdom, *Department of Education and Science*

tion is given in the table on the previous page which comes from summary the volume of education statistics for the United Kingdom published by the DES.

Crime and Justice

An increasing wave of public concern over the steep rise in the number of offences of a more serious nature (indictable offences) known to the police has directed both attention and criticism to the statistics of crime and their weaknesses in providing evidence of cause. The overall increase in known indictable offences from 1·3m. in 1967 to 2·5m. in 1977 is striking enough but, particularly impressive to the general public, is the increase of crimes of violence against the person from 30,000 in 1967 to 82,000 in 1977, while cases of criminal damage (which includes vandalism) have risen from about 12,000 in 1967 to 124,000 in 1977. Even when allowance is made for the increase in population over the period the number of indictable offences recorded by the police per 100,000 population has increased from 2,717 in 1967 to 5,014 in 1977.

The source of the above information and indeed the main source of all statistics of crime are the annual H.M.S.O. publication *Criminal Statistics: England and Wales* and its companion volumes *Criminal Statistics: Scotland*, and *Report on the Administration of Home Office Services (Northern Ireland)*. These publications present, in a rather prosaic form, the annual statistics relating to Crime and Criminal Proceedings. In the England and Wales volume for 1977 there were nine chapters of comment with illustrative tables followed by some 280 pages of statistical tables giving detailed information. The nine chapter headings are illustrative of the contents and are as follows:

Chapter 1 Introduction and Summary
    „   2 Indictable offences recorded by the police and cleared up
    „   3 Indictable offences in which firearms were reported to have been involved
    „   4 Court proceedings
    „   5 Offenders found guilty or cautioned
    „   6 Sentencing
    „   7 Legal aid
    „   8 Use of remand
    „   9 Homicide

As may be deduced from the above list the statistics can be considered in two categories; that which refers to the number of crimes known to the police and that which gives details of the operation of the judicial system. The defect of this form of categorisation is that, as the two categories contain statistics from two different sources, the various police forces and the courts, they are subject to different kinds of error.

The major error associated with police statistics is that they refer only to crimes reported to the police. A study carried out in Brixton, Hackney and Kensington in 1972 and 1973 suggested that only about one in ten of all crimes committed in these areas was actually included in statistics of recorded crime (*Surveying Victims: A Study of Criminal Victimisation* by Sparks, Genn and Dodd 1977). This estimate is undoubtedly subject to considerable error. For example, Sparks estimates that only about one-quarter of burglaries in private houses were recorded by the police but, when the General Household Survey examined the same point, the proportion was estimated as one-half of all burglaries in private houses recorded by the police. It can be assumed with reasonable confidence that a significant proportion of all crimes goes unrecorded. Unfortunately, the proportion of unrecorded crimes is not the same for each type of crime nor does it remain stable over time. This proportion of unrecorded crime is sometimes referred to as 'the dark figure'.

A further source of error in police statistics is the non-recording or mis-recording of crimes by the police. Neville Amson, in his contribution entitled 'Criminal Statistics as social indicators'* showed that something of the order of 60 per cent of attempted housebreaking, in the area of his observation, was recorded as malicious damage. When motor vehicles which had been stolen were recovered intact in the same police area within three days no crime was recorded at all.

A serious analytical problem arises from the rather broad categorisation of crime that stems partly from legal definitions and partly from the fact that police statistics are based upon the area covered by the particular police force. This is often very large; for example, the Metropolitan Police Force area covers some 8m. people (some 17 per cent of the total population in England and Wales) and within that area about 20 per cent of the total reported crimes in England and Wales take place. Any analysis of trends in crime depends on the ability to analyse down to homogeneous groups, both in terms of the type of crime and the people who commit them. Thus, under the 'List of indictable offences showing classification numbers' which is the basis of the classification of crimes used in *Criminal Statistics*, number 28 is Burglary in a dwelling, and number 40 is Theft in a dwelling. The distinction between burglary and theft can well be a matter of legal opinion, while the concept of a dwelling is a particularly broad one. Further, the analysis in the statistics has only one category of age above 21 years which is sub-divided into male and female. There is no sub-division at all on the basis of other

Social Indicators and Social Policy, edited by Shonfield and Shaw, 1972.

variables in society which may have a relevant effect on the incidence of crime.

The *judicial* statistics are also liable to error arising from the basis of recording that refers to persons who commit offences. Thus, a count of ten 'persons' who were found to be drunk in one year could refer to ten people who were drunk once in the year or one individual who was drunk on ten separate occasions. Furthermore, if an individual commits more than one offence, in most of the statistical analyses that are published, only the main offence is recorded.

Many of the drawbacks in the statistical recording of crime were examined by the Departmental Committee on Criminal Statistics chaired by Mr Wilfred Perks. The report of this committee was published in December 1967 (*Cmnd. 3448*, H.M.S.O.) and recommended that more information about the offences, the circumstances in which they occur, the offenders and their treatment should be recorded, together with a great deal more analysis and interpretation. The Perks Committee also recommended that there should be a single computer organisation for all police and judicial statistics with provision for the linkage of all stages of police and judicial activity so that complete criminal histories would be available. The Home Office's reponse to the report was that implementation would require a considerable amount of pilot investigation, additional manpower and improved computer facilities. Progress would 'depend upon the availability of staff.' Progress is undoubtedly being made, but not nearly so fast as users of criminal statistics would like.

The analysis and interpretation of criminal statistics depends upon the establishment of trends and patterns .A major disturbance of analysis are changes in legislation which affect criminal statistics by changing the range of offences, modes of trial and penalties. *Criminal Statistics: England and Wales 1977* lists 17 major changes in legislation in the years 1957-1977 which could have affected the statistics. Examples of these changes are:

(i) *Theft Act 1968* which made major changes in the categorisation of burglary, robbery theft, handling stolen goods, fraud and forgery.

(ii) *Criminal Justice Act 1972*, which introduced day training centres and suspended sentences.

(iii) Children and Young Persons Act 1969 which introduced supervision and care orders for persons under 17.

(iv) *Murder (Abolition of the Death Penalty) Act 1965* whose title is self explanatory.

These and other changes make the interpretation of trends and changes in criminal statistics even more difficult than they would normally be.

Two excellent articles on the measurement of crime appeared in *Social Trends No. 7* (1976 H.M.S.O.). The first on Crime in England and Wales is by Charles Glennie and the second on Crime in Scotland is by David Bruce.

TABLE 71

TYPES OF OFFENCE, ENGLAND AND WALES　　　　　　　Thousands

	1951	1961	1966	1971	1974	1975	1976	1977
Indictable offences recorded as known to the police:								
Violence against the person	7	18	27	47	64	71	78	82
Sexual offences	15	20	21	24	25	24	22	21
Burglary	⎫			⎧ 452	484	522	515	604
Robbery	⎪			⎪ 7	9	11	12	14
Theft and handling stolen goods	⎬ 497	820	1,247	⎨				
Fraud and forgery	⎪			1,004	1,190	1,268	1,286	1,488
	⎭			100	117	123	120	121
Criminal damage	5	6	10	27	67	79	93	124
Other offences	6	4	2	6	8	8	10	10
Total indictable offences	529	868	1,307	1,666	1,963	2,106	2,136	2,464
Indictable offences cleared up (percentages)	*47*	*44*	*39*	*45*	*44*	*44*	*43*	*41*
Persons found guilty: Indictable offences	133	182	233	322	375	402	415	429
Non-indictable offences:								
Assault	12	12	11	12	12	12	12	13
Drunkenness	51	72	67	83	98	100	103	103
Motoring offences	291	655	898	988	1,173	1,181	1,225	1,130
Malicious damage	9	15	17	20	—	—	—	—
Motor vehicle licences	6	21	40	85	85	94	102	86
Wireless and Telegraphy Acts	3	10	21	27	34	33	35	45
Other offences	213	187	159	152	157	167	179	173
Total non-indictable offences	584	970	1,213	1,366	1,559	1,587	1,656	1,550

Source: Home Office

Dr. Glennie in the first of the articles recognises that changes in the amount of measured crime may be due to:

(1) an actual increase in criminal activities;

(2) a change in the perception or recording of criminal activity;

(3) a change in the definition of a criminal.

These changes disturb comparisons not only over time but also between areas.

With all the limitations so far set out the patterns of crime reported to the police between 1951-76 revealed in Table 00 show that 'theft and handling stolen goods' is still by far (60 per cent of the total) the most common serious crime. In contrast, despite the attention they receive in the media, sexual offences have shown no increase despite the rise in population. The less serious crimes show signs of levelling out in the 1970s. Among the non-indictable offences, the most striking feature is the absolute rise in motoring offences although, in relative terms the increase in Motor Vehicle Licences is even more striking.

TABLE 72

PERSONS FOUND GUILTY PER 1,000 OF THE POPULATION: BY AGE AND SEX

Great Britain   Numbers per 1,000 population

	1971†	1972	1973	1974	1975	1976
England and Wales (indictable offences)						
Males aged: 10 and under 14	11·8	12·3	12·5	14·1	12·9	12·1
14 ,, ,, 17	41·8	46·0	47·4	54·2	52·3	51·4
17 ,, ,, 21	52·3	54·8	55·2	59·5	64·3	63·4
21 ,, ,, 30	23·7	24·3	23·5	25·1	27·1	27·8
30 and over	5·5	5·7	5·4	5·9	6·4	6·9
All ages (10 years and over)	14·1	14·8	14·6	16·0	16·9	17·3
Females aged: 10 and under 14	1·2	1·2	1·3	1·5	1·5	1·5
14 ,, ,, 17	5·1	4·9	5·1	6·3	6·6	6·6
17 ,, ,, 21	6·2	6·4	6·6	7·5	8·3	8·4
21 ,, ,, 30	3·5	3·7	3·6	4·0	4·6	5·0
30 and over	1·3	1·4	1·3	1·5	1·7	1·9
All ages (10 years and over)	2·1	2·2	2·1	2·5	2·8	3·0

Source: Home Office

TABLE 73

SENTENCES[1] FOR INDICTABLE OFFENCES: BY AGE AND SEX OF OFFENDER, 1976

England and Wales   Percentages and thousands

	Under 17		17 and under 21		21 and over		All ages	
	Males	Females	Males	Females	Males	Females	Males	Females
Sentences[2] (percentages):								
Absolute discharge	1	1	1	1	1	1	1	1
Conditional discharge	22	31	7	19	9	20	11	21
Probation order	—	—	8	20	5	12	5	12
Fine	34	33	57	51	53	57	50	52
Community service order	—	—	4	1	2	1	2	1
Attendance centre order	11	—	0	—	—	—	3	—
Detention centre order	6	—	6	—	—	—	3	—
Borstal	2	1	7	2	—	—	2	1
Suspended sentence	—	—	4	3	13	5	7	4
Immediate imprisonment	—	—	5	2	16	3	10	2
Other	24	34	1	1	1	1	6	6
Total (=100%) (thousands)	80·4	9·8	91·5	11·6	177·8	43·7	350·3	65·2

[1]Sentences are shown on a principal offence/sentence basis.
[2]The numbers sentenced to 'Hospital order' were too small to show in this table.

Source: Home Office

If, however, the variations in the size of population are taken into account one sees (Table 72 on the previous page) that there are marked differences in the incidence of crime between males and females and that most crime is committed between the ages of 14 and 30. During the 1970s the greatest increases have occurred in the age groups 14 to 21 years.

The pattern of sentences shown in Table 73 on the previous page shows the very small proportion of serious crime that is punished by imprisonment – 10 per cent of male offenders and 2 per cent of female offenders. Even when detention centres and Borstal sentences are added the percentages increase to only 15 per cent of male offenders and 3 per cent of females found guilty.

The less serious (non-indictable) offences consist mainly (nearly

TABLE 74

CIVIL PROCEEDINGS: BY TYPE OF PLAINT AND MEANS OF SETTLEMENT

Great Britain   Thousands

	1951	1961	1971	1974	1975	1976
County Courts – England and Wales						
Proceedings started:						
Plaints for:						
Goods sold etc.	—	—	—	1,160	1,183	1,095
Hire purchase etc.	18	60	57	152	180	154
Bank etc. loans	—	—	—	137	96	79
Other debt	—	—	—	137	181	162
Damages for personal injury	—	—	—	51	22	15
Recovery of land	31	26	56	90	109	122
Other claims, Rent Act etc.	—	—	—	14	14	17
Other proceedings (excluding divorce)	7	6	8	10	31	15
Total proceedings started	535	1,683	1,539	1,752	1,815	1,659
Proceedings disposed of:						
Settled in default, on admission						
or by consent	303	1,162	999	1,006	904	826
Settled after trial, or arbitration	29	33	41	130	146	146
Total proceedings disposed of						
(excluding paid, struck out, etc.)	332	1,195	1,040	1,137	1,050	972

Table specifically excludes divorce proceedings which are dealt with seperately in the same publication.

Source: Judicial Statistics. *Lord Chancellor's Office (H.M.S.O.).*

three-quarters) of motoring offences and in recent years show signs of levelling out at about 1·5m.

Apart from the main block of information as illustrated above there are other forms of analysis available. For example, it can be shown that in Crown Courts 63 per cent of those charged plead guilty. Of those who plead 'not guilty' just over half are convicted.

Data on civil proceedings come in an annual publication entitled *Civil Judicial Statistics*, from the Lord Chancellor's Office. As Table 74 above shows, the majority of cases arise from sales of goods while disputes etc. over loans, hire purchase and recovery of land each account for some 15 to 20 per cent of the total cases. The total number of proceedings started in the County Courts appears to be fairly stable in recent years between 1·7 and 1·8m.

The final main area of statistics of crime are those which relate to the resources combating crime. The data on manpower given in Table 75 show a 75 per cent increase over the last 25 years, with a 14 per cent increase in the last six years, in the strengths of police forces on ordinary duty. Over the last six years government expenditure on law and order in general has increased by about 5 per cent.

TABLE 75

POLICE FORCES: MANPOWER

United Kingdom   Thousands

	1951	1961	1966	1971	1974	1975	1976	1977
Police forces: strength for ordinary duty:								
England & Wales								
Men	60·5	72·7	82·5	91·8	96·1	99·9	101·0	100·3
Women	1·4	2·3	3·2	3·8	4·7	5·8	7·0	7·9
Scotland								
Men	7·1	8·8	9·7	10·4	11·2	11·7	11·6	11·3
Women	0·1	0·3	0·4	0·4	0·5	0·7	0·7	0·8
Northern Ireland								
Royal Ulster Constabulary								
Men	2·7	2·9	2·9	4·0	4·3	4·5	4·8	5·1
Women	—	0·1	0·1	0·1	0·3	0·4	0·4	0·5
U.K. total	71·8	87·1	98·8	110·5	117·1	123·0	125·5	125·9

Source: Home Office

While the foregoing comments refer mainly to the general nature of criminal and civil judicial statistics and the two most important publications from the Home Office and the Lord Chancellor's Office, it should be remembered that there are well over 100 police forces under the jurisdiction of their own local authorities and Chief Constables. Additional information relating to crime is given in the annual reports of the Chief Constables to their local Watch Committees or Joint Standing Committees, in the case of counties. In the case of the Metropolitan Police Area, the annual report of the Commissioner of Police is a substantial document which is published by the Stationery Office. In addition to this source material, there are the annual reports of the Prison Commissioners, which provide information relating not so much to crime as to the state and condition of H.M. Prisons, and those inside them.

For the reader who is interested to learn what information can be derived from statistics on crime, as well as studying the employment of statistical methods, the publications of the Home Office research unit published by H.M. Stationery Office deserve close study.

Personal Income, Expenditure and Wealth
Income

It is difficult to distinguish clearly between income and wealth. It could be said that income represents a flow of cash while wealth represents the value of assets. But, from a statistical point of view, it is more than ever essential to study the definitions to be sure what is, or is not, included under such headings. Thus, some statistics relate to one source, *e.g.* earnings, while others refer to multiple sources for one person, *e.g.* taxable income. Still others refer to multiple recipients, such as with family income and expenditure. In short, as the Royal Commission on the Distribution of Income and Wealth observed (Initial Report *Cmnd. 6171*), 'important sources' of data on the distribution of income from all sources are, for the most part, by-products of the administrative processes of government departments; as such they may be deficient in many respects for our purposes.

Much data relating to income and expenditure, etc. are brought together in the annual National Income and Expenditure (the Blue Book). More detailed reference is made to the Blue Book on pp.563 as it is a publication more concerned with the overall economic situation than with the individual. The data for personal incomes rely mainly on two sources; the *Survey of Personal Incomes* and the *New Earnings Survey**.

The *Survey of Personal Incomes* was designed to help the Commissioners of Inland Revenue in assessing the probable yield of direct taxes and the effect of any system of taxation upon individual groups in society. The first survey was carried out in 1937, then in 1949, 1954, 1959 and annually from 1962. There are really two series, a large quinquennial sample, starting in 1949, of about one million individual tax units (*i.e.* either a single person or a married couple taxed jointly) and, in the intervening years, a smaller annual sample of about 125,000. A full description of the methodology of the survey can be found in the *Notes* to the 1969 Survey Report and in *Statistical News No. 17*. Briefly, the samples are of a stratified random nature with different sampling fractions in the various strata. These fractions vary from 1 in 1 in the higher surtax brackets to 1 in 60 in the lower Schedule E income levels.

There are three main criticisms to be made of the Survey of Personal Incomes.

(*a*) Only income liable to taxation is included, *e.g.* income below the taxable limit and undistributed profits are excluded.

(*b*) The income unit for tax purposes can be subject to sharp fluctu-

*Additional and corroborative data are also derived from the Family Expenditure Survey discussed below.

ations, *e.g.* two single people with low incomes marry and then become one tax unit with a fairly high income.

(c) Prior to 1969 taxpayers were classified by place of work and not by their residence. While the anomaly has now been rectified, the rectification has caused a break in the continuity of regional analysis.

TABLE 76

DISTRIBUTION OF PERSONAL INCOMES BEFORE AND AFTER TAX, 1975-76

United Kingdom £s, £ million, and percentages

Quartile groups*:	Income before tax		Average income before tax	Income after tax		Average income after tax
	£ million	*Percentages*	£	£ million	*Percentages*	£
Top 1%	4,637	*5·7*	16,361	2,553	*3·9*	9,006
2– 5%	8,662	*10·7*	7,641	6,318	*9·7*	5,573
6–10%	8,011	*9·8*	5,653	6,199	*9·5*	4,375
Top 10%	21,310	*26·2*	7,519	15,070	*23·1*	5,317
11–20%	13,095	*16·1*	4,621	10,352	*15·8*	3,653
21–30%	10,726	*13·2*	3,785	8,832	*13·5*	3,116
31–40%	9,294	*11·5*	3,280	7,402	*11·4*	2,612
41–50%	7,494	*9·2*	2,644	6,240	*9·5*	2,202
51–60%	6,101	*7·5*	2,153	5,037	*7·7*	1,777
61–70%	4,711	*5·8*	1,662	4,139	*6·3*	1,460
71–80%	3,673	*4·5*	1,296	3,441	*5·3*	1,214
81–90%	2,854	*3·5*	1,007	2,776	*4·2*	979
Bottom 10%	2,045	*2·5*	722	2,027	*3·2*	715

*Based on tax units. The total number of tax units is 28,341 thousand.

Source: Central Statistical Office

As the above table shows a major basis of analysis is the distribution of personal incomes before and after tax.

Since about three-quarters of personal income comes from employment, such earnings form the basis of a sample survey carried out by the Department of Employment known as the *New Earnings Survey*. This was first carried out in September 1968 and subsequently each April from 1970 onwards. A sample of some 170,000 employees is taken, about three-quarters of whom were taken in the immediately preceding sample – an example of matched sample design. The earnings consist of all payments received in the particular period. They include bonuses, etc. but exclude all deductions. The data are analysed to identify overtime incentive payments, premium payments, etc. Income from basic hours worked and from overtime are separated.

In addition to the *New Earnings Survey* the Department of Employment hold an annual enquiry among some 35,000 establishments covering some 5m. manual workers. The results are published in the Department's *Gazette* for the following March.

TABLE 77

GROSS WEEKLY EARNINGS[1] IN APRIL 1977 AND INCREASES SINCE APRIL 1976: BY AGE

Great Britain   £s and percentages

	Average gross weekly earnings, April 1977 (£)				Percentage increases[2] in average gross weekly earnings, April 1976-April 1977			
	Men		Women		Men		Women	
	Manual	Non-manual	Manual	Non-manual	Manual	Non-manual	Manual	Non-manual
Age[3]:								
Under 18	32·3	29·7	29·7	28·8	39·7	34·6	32·1	32·3
18–20	49·9	43·4	38·9	39·0	24·5	24·3	16·9	20·2
21–24	65·4	60·5	43·5	48·9	13·1	16·5	12·5	14·2
25–29	71·9	77·9	45·7	57·4	11·8	13·5	12·0	12·6
30–39	75·8	93·5	45·1	58·7	10·3	10·1	12·1	10·9
40–49	74·5	99·4	44·7	58·8	9·5	8·3	11·1	10·2
50–59	70·1	95·3	44·0	57·9	8·9	8·0	10·0	9·2
60–64	64·1	81·6	1·2	—	7·6	7·1	8·1	—
65 and over	52·7	—	—	—	4·3	—	—	—
All ages 18 and over	70·0	86·9	43·7	53·8	10·5	10·2	11·4	12·1
All ages 21 and over	71·5	88·9	44·2	56·2	9·9	9·9	10·9	11·2
All ages	68·8	86·2	42·8	52·6	10·9	10·3	12·0	12·6

[1]Of full-time employees whose pay for the survey period was not affected by absence.
[2]These figures relate to those in each age group at January 1st, 1976, for whom returns were received in both the 1976 and 1977 surveys. Increases are expressed as a percentage of the average in April 1976.
[3]Age is measured in completed years on 1st January, 1977.

Source: New Earnings Survey, *Department of Employment*

Personal Expenditure

The *Family Expenditure Survey* is a continuous enquiry into the income and expenditure of private households in Great Britain that was started in January 1957. For the first decade the annual sample consisted of about 5,000 households but, in 1962, when the value of the information was fully recognised, the sample size was increased to 11,000 addresses of which there are some 10,400 effective households. These yield about 7,500 units of data, *i.e.* a response rate of over 70 per cent. The household is defined, as in the Census of Population, as all those who live at the same address having meals prepared together and with common housekeeping. Income collected is the gross income, *i.e.* before tax and other stoppages are deducted. The sample is in the form of a three-stage, stratified, rotating design with a uniform sampling fraction. The administrative areas of Great Britain are used as the primary sampling units; 168 are used each quarter and after four samples have been drawn, *i.e.* one year's use, the area is replaced by another. This continuing replacement of areas is what is meant by rotation. Each household which co-operates, about 70 per cent of those selected complete a diary of two weeks' expenditure plus questionnaires of expenditure which occurs less frequently, *e.g.* on furniture, annual holidays, etc. A handbook on the methodology of the survey was produced by W. F. F. Kemsley in 1969*. The annual publication of the Department of Employment on the *Family Expenditure Survey* is the main source of current data. The original use of the survey, and a continuing important use, is the provision of weights for the Index of Retail Prices. The importance of the Index of Retail Prices is its use in attempting to measure changes in the standard of living.

Wealth

It has been said that more concern and interest have been displayed in public discussion about the *distribution* of wealth than on the need to *increase* the national wealth. Nevertheless, is is generally accepted that large concentrations of wealth in private hands tend to perpetuate the inequalities of income distribution. How far, for example, inflation has made the rich richer as asset values have appreciated or redistributive taxation has reduced those inequalities of income and wealth are matters of public debate. It was the interest in such matters which has led to a considerable increase in the volume of statistical information relating to personal wealth.

For almost a decade the annual report on *Inland Revenue Statistics* has included estimates, not only of the aggregate wealth in individual hands but also its distribution according to the type of asset, *e.g.* land or government bonds, etc. Before then there were only private estimates, although there was a fair degree of unanimity in the overall results. Nevertheless, there was a very large element of estimation or what some people would call guesswork, in these estimates.

The method used to arrive at the total of wealth and its distribution was quite simple. It was based upon the fact that the only information ever available on the size of a person's estate, *i.e.* his assets, was that compiled upon his death so that the liability to estate duty, as it then was, and the capital transfer tax as it is now, could be calculated. Thus, by assuming in effect that those who died in any year were a random sample of the population, their assets could be multiplied by the appropriate mortality rate to arrive at an estimate of the total wealth of those still alive. The dangers of such an assumption are obvious. For example, if in any year only two or three persons in, say, the age group 25-34 die (probably as the result of an accident), this is a very slender basis for estimating the total wealth of the remaining or living members of that age group. There is also the problem that the mortality rate for particular age groups or sections of the community will differ from year to year. Nor should one overlook the fact that the assets included for purposes of taxing the

Family Expenditure Survey. Handbook on the Sample, Fieldwork and Coding Procedures. Government Social Survey. 1969.

deceased's estate are not always complete nor accurately valued. Not surprisingly, in the absence of reliable data, the protagonists of a greater measure of equalisation of wealth and those who claimed that such a redistribution of wealth was not in the interests of the national economy expressed strikingly divergent viewpoints unmarred by reliable statistics.

A major contribution to the debate and, not least, to the output of statistics on wealth was made by the Royal Commission on the Distribution of Income and Wealth which was set up in 1974. The Commission has published a series of reports indicating the changing pattern of wealth distribution and, in its first report[1] outlined the statistical problems in making estimates of aggregate personal wealth and its distribution. The opinion of the Royal Commission was that while 'such estimates are subject to a number of well-known deficiencies . . . we believe that, subject to careful interpretation and adjustment, the official estimates provide a reasonable basis for studying some aspects of the distribution of wealth in Great Britain'. One may read into that conclusion what one will; hence it is difficult either to reject or accept it. An alternative viewpoint was put forward in a study from the Institute of Economic Affairs in which, apart from stressing the problems of estimation and what should be included in such estimates, the two authors not unreasonably observed that the statistics were in conflict with the evidence of the state of present-day society[2].

In the meantime the Inland Revenue continue to publish their estimates and Table 78 provides an overall picture of the probable distribution of wealth in this country as between the sexes, by reference to the size of the holding and such changes as have been estimated over the period 1961 to 1976.

Living Standards

Politicians are fond of demanding a 'decent' standard of living for all sections of the community, but seldom trouble to define just what they understand by 'decent'. For most people, living standards are measured largely in terms of their consumption levels and ownership of consumer durables such as washing machines and cars. While it is generally agreed that as the national product rises so living standards improve, there is no such unanimity as to how living standards may best be measured, or what constitutes a minimum standard below which no section of the community, *e.g.* old age pensioners dependent entirely on State benefit, should fall.

The classical approach to this problem was provided by Seebohm Rowntree's famous study of poverty in York at the turn of the

[1]*Initial Report on the Standing Reference (Cmnd 6171).*
[2]*How Much Inequality:* G. Polyani & J. B. Wood.

TABLE 78

DISTRIBUTION OF WEALTH AMONG IDENTIFIED WEALTH OWNERS

Percentages

	Great Britain				United Kingdom			
	1961	1966	1971	1974	1975	1976	1976 Men*	1976 Women*
Distribution of wealth among identified wealth owners:								
Percentage of wealth owned by:								
Most wealthy 1 per cent of owners	28	23	20	18	17	17	17	17
" " 2 " " " "	37	31	28	25	24	23	23	23
" " 5 " " " "	51	44	40	37	35	35	34	35
" " 10 " " " "	63	56	52	49	47	47	46	47
" " 25 " " " "	80	75	72	71	70	68	67	70
" " 50 " " " "	93	91	90	90	90	88	88	89
Total wealth (£ thousand million)	55	77	113	157	190	204	121	83
Distribution of owners by individual net wealth:								
Percentage of owners with assets covered by estate duty statistics valued:								
Over — Not over (£)								
— 1,000	49	35	23	18	16	12	12	11
1,000 — 3,000	33	31	30	25	23	20	18	22
3,000 — 5,000	8	15	16	12	12	12	12	12
5,000 — 10,000	6	11	20	22	22	24	25	23
10,000 — 25,000	3	5	9	18	21	25	26	22
25,000 — 100,000	1	2	3	5	5	7	7	8
100,000 —	—	—	—	—	—	1	1	1
Total owners of wealth covered (millions)	18·3	17·9	18·6	18·8	21·0	18·1	10·8	7·3
as percentage of home population aged 15 and over	46	44	46	45	49	42	52	32

*In interpreting the greater inequity of distribution of wealth for women than for men it should be remembered that the distributions are affected by the fact that for married couples a large proportion of the property is owned by the husband although it may be used by both partners.

Source: *Inland Revenue Statistics*

century.[1] He prepared, in consultation with the leading authorities of his time, a diet which would provide each man, woman and child with sufficient calories to maintain physical efficiency. He then converted the calories into the cheapest possible foods; it was in fact predominantly starch with some carbohydrate. The diet was even more uninteresting than the workhouse diets of the time. He allowed a minimum of clothing, a basic rent appropriate to working class accommodation in York, plus fuel and light. There were no extras for tobacco, alcohol, newspapers, fares, etc. The cost of this minimum needs or bare subsistence standard was then compared with the average level of wages. Those whose earnings fell short of that sum were deemed to be in primary poverty. In his famous Five Towns survey of 1912 and repeated in 1923-24 the late Professor Sir Arthur Bowley estimated a similar needs standard, but on a slightly more generous scale, by introducing meat into the weekly diet.[2]

The difficulty with this method of defining living standards is to obtain agreement on what should be included once the level is raised above the bare subsistence level. Some years ago an Oxford research worker was ridiculed by one of the popular newspapers for an article in which she employed the Rowntree technique of a minimum subsistence lowest cost diet which any old age pensioner could have afforded. Nowadays, a 'modest' consumption of alcohol, tobacco and certainly the weekly rental of a TV set, seems to be automatically included in any 'reasonable' standard and those in the community unable to afford these things are usually regarded as 'deprived'. Discussions as to the adequacy of the State welfare benefits in unemployment and old age are clearly influenced by the standards it is felt the community should provide for these sections of the community. Nevertheless, unless the standards are clearly defined, any such discussion is a complete waste of time except to illustrate the classic dictum of the Red Queen in *Alice in Wonderland* who always used words to mean what she meant them to mean.

The most suitable method of measuring changes in living standards at the present time is to use a cost of living index. In Britain the index is termed the Index of Retail Prices and was introduced in 1947, since when it has been subject to several revisions. It replaced the old Cost of Living index introduced in 1914, which for all its limitations, reflected quite fairly the fluctuations in living costs up to the second World War. Table 79 shows the main classes of expenditure incorporated in the 1914 cost of living index as it was known until its abandonment in 1947, together with those used in the *interim* index of retail prices introduced in that year and amended in 1952. The

[1] Poverty: A Study of Town Life.

[2] *Livelihood and Poverty*. A L. Bowley and A. R. Burnett Hurst. The later study was entitled *Has Poverty Diminished*, Bowley and Hogg.

weights shown reflect the distribution of the weekly household income among the constituent groups of related goods. What is obvious from the table is the decline in the proportion of income spent on food as living standards have risen between the pre- and post-war period. Note that the 1947 weighting for food is distorted due to the effects of food subsidies. This was one of the major reasons for the 1952 revision.

TABLE 79

COMPARISON OF WEIGHTING IN SUCCESSIVE RETAIL PRICE INDICES

	Cost of Living Index 1914	Interim Index of Retail Prices 1947	Interim Index of Retail Prices 1952	Index of Retail Prices 1977
i. Food	60	348	399	247
ii. Rent and Rates	16	88	72	112
iii. Clothing	12	97	98	82
iv. Fuel and Light	8	65	66	58
v. Household Durable Goods	}	71	62	63
vi. Miscellaneous Goods		35	44	255*
vii. Services	} 4	79	91	54
viii. Alcoholic Drink		101 } 217	78	83
ix. Tobacco		116 }	90	46
	100	1,000	1,000	1,000

*Includes Transport and Vehicles at 139.

It is important for the reader to realise that such an index is an average which measures the change, month by month, in the retail cost of a particular or standard collection of goods and services. In this case it is the goods and services normally bought by the average household. Since this index is used as the basis for wage and salary negotiations it must be acceptable to all parties to such negotiations. The present index of retail prices originated in the 1953-54 Household Expenditure Enquiry undertaken jointly by the Ministry of Labour and the Social Survey. This produced a three-weekly account of expenditure, household and personal, from each member over 16 years of age in nearly 13,000 households. Because the expenditure patterns of households subsisting in the main on State pensions and those where the head of the household earned more than £20 per week differed markedly from the bulk of households, the sample of usable returns was cut down to some 11,600 household budgets. The Cost of Living Advisory Committee, which had been formed in August 1946 to advise the government on the desirability and form of a new post-war index, were of the opinion that this sample of budgets gave an adequate reflection of spending habits of over 90 per cent of the households in Britain.* It recommended the introduction of a new Index (note the word 'interim' was then dropped since wartime

*This Committee first reported in March 1947 (*Cmnd. 7077*) recommending a new index based on the 1937-8 enquiry into working-class expenditure. This formed the basis of the 1947 'interim' index of retail prices which was used with some modifications in 1952 until 1956 when the results of the 1953-4 survey became available.

conditions had passed) of Retail Prices with a base 100 as at mid-January 1956.

In March 1962 the Advisory Committee presented a report entitled the 'Revision of the Index of Retail Prices' (*Cn.nd. 1657*). The proposals for revision were based not upon a further major sample enquiry on the lines of the Household Expenditure Enquiry, which had sampled 20,000 households and got a 65 per cent response, but on the Family Expenditure Survey as described above. In their report the Advisory Committee recommended that revised weightings should be introduced based upon the average of the three preceding years' expenditure patterns as disclosed by the surveys. It is not practicable to use the results of a single year's survey for the construction of a new index, since there is a substantial sampling error in

TABLE 80
INDEX OF RETAIL PRICES
United Kingdom   Index numbers and weights

	January 1974 = 100							
	12-month averages					Quarterly average		
	1961	1966	1970	1975	1976	1st Qtr 1977	2nd Qtr 1977	Weights 1977
General								
All items	50·8	60·7	73·1	134·8	157·1	174·1	181·9	1,000
Food	45·5	53·3	64·7	133·3	159·9	184·7	191·1	247
Alcoholic drink	57·1	73·3	86·7	135·2	159·3	176·5	183·0	83
Tobacco	67·0	85·0	95·9	147·7	171·3	193·7	209·7	46
Housing	43·5	57·1	70·2	125·5	143·2	154·8	165·0	112
Fuel and light	50·6	64·1	77·3	147·4	182·4	198·5	209·3	58
Durable household goods	62·1	67·7	79·6	131·2	144·2	159·7	165·0	63
Clothing and footwear	59·5	66·0	74·3	125·7	139·4	151·0	154·7	82
Transport and vehicles	55·5	62·8	75·5	143·9	166·0	180·9	191·5	139
Miscellaneous goods	53·2	61·7	78·4	138·6	161·3	178·5	187·0	71
Services	45·6	56·6	72·3	135·5	159·5	167·5	171·7	54
Meals bought and consumed outside home[1]	—	—	63·4	132·4	157·3	174·2	181·6	45
Pensioner[2] households								
All items excluding housing:								
One-person households	—	59·0	71·1	135·0	160·8	179·0	186·9	
Two-person households	—	59·0	71·1	134·6	159·9	178·9	186·3	
Internal purchasing power of the £ (1974 = 100p)	196·0	178·5	148·5	80·5	69·0	64·0	59·6	

[1]Not separately identified until 1968.
[2]Pensioner households are those in which at least three-quarters of the total income was derived from pensions and supplements thereof.

Sources: Department of Employment Gazette; *Central Statistical Office*

respect of certain large items in household expenditure, *e.g.* furniture, motor cars, etc., which are purchased only at intervals. Thus the weighting used for the index during 1977 was based upon the results of the three years' surveys to June 1976. In other respects the current index is similar to that first introduced in January 1956.

It will be self-evident that the surveys indicate the goods and services to be included in the index and also provide the basis for the individual weights. The index is constructed each month and published in some detail, *e.g.* group indices, in the Department of Employment *Gazette* each month. These data provide the figures in Table 80 on the previous page.

The compilation of the index to ensure its representativeness is interesting. Information on individual prices is collected by visiting several shops selling the same kind of goods, such shops being those which normally handle the bulk of ordinary households' spending. There is also a classification of areas in which the shops are located, ranging from Greater London to small townships with less than 5,000 inhabitants. This ensures both adequate geographical representation and type of retail outlet in the prices collected. The prices are collected on the Tuesday nearest the 15th of the month. The official account explains the construction of the index as follows:

1. The price relative for each item in each town is calculated and the resulting figures combined as an unweighted average for all the towns in *each* population group.

2. The separate indices for the various population groups are averaged to give indices for *each item* for the country as a whole.

3. The national indices of the items, *e.g.* bread, are next combined to arrive at indices for each group, *e.g.* food. In the construction of the group index, the percentage increase in each item in the group is weighted by reference to its proportionate share in the aggregate outlay on all items in that group. Thus the group index is the weighted arithmetic mean of the percentage changes in its constituent prices.

4. The indices for the various sections are then combined, being weighted as in the last column of Table 80. This gives the index for each of the main expenditure groups, and the final all-items figure. It will be noted from Table 80 that all indices for sections are given to one place of decimals. This has the advantage that quite minor changes in prices will be reflected in the index.

It may reasonably be concluded that the present index is an adequate method of measuring changes in the cost of living as far as the average household is concerned. It had been suggested that a separate index should be prepared for the professional and middle classes, whose expenditure probably differs in some major respects from that of the 'average' household, *e.g.* heavy outlays on private education, less on entertainment, etc. Since the latter in recent years have demonstrated their capacity for maintaining their real income despite the inflation, this particular proposal seems to have been dropped. There is, however, a very good case for preparing a similar index for old age pensioner households, where at least half or even more of the total income comes from a State pension and national assistance.

This case was recognised in the *Report of the Cost of Living Advisory Committee* dated May 1968 (*Cmnd. 3677*) when two new series of special indices of retail prices for one-person and two-person pensioner households were recommended. These recommendations were implemented in June 1969. For those indices pensioner households are defined as those in which at least three-quarters of the total household income is derived from national insurance retirement pensions or similar pensions or payments. The households are those specifically excluded from the main Index of Retail Prices. These special indices are, however, constructed in the same way as the Main Index.

Quite apart from the index of retail prices and the Family Expenditure Surveys upon which the latest indices are based, the annual Blue Book on the National Income and Expenditure contains some additional data relating to spending habits of the public. The analysis of consumer expenditure is given both in terms of actual prices for each year and the expenditure adjusted to a common basis, *i.e.* in terms of 1975 prices. These data are used by the Central Statistical Office for the compilation of an index of consumer prices. This index differs quite substantially from the index of retail prices. First, there is the coverage of the two indices. The Blue Book index covers all sections of the community and their expenditure on all goods and services. The retail prices index covers only some 90 per cent of households and only selected goods and services. The method of construction also differs slightly since while the retail price index is base 'year' weighted, the Blue Book index uses current year weights. The different type of weighting used will affect the relative movements of the two indices.

From the purely statistical point of view both indices have their limitations. The breakdown of consumer expenditure given in the Blue Book is at best based upon estimates which in some cases, *e.g.* private motoring, travel, are rather tentative, to put it no more strongly. Where the goods are subject to tax, *e.g.* tobacco, or purchase tax, some effective check is provided on the estimates. In the case of the retail price index the validity of the weighting and the choice of items depends on the accuracy and truthfulness of the respondent household's replies. There is certainly considerable understatement of expenditure on alcohol and tobacco, also on sweetstuffs including ice cream, and in respect of meals eaten outside the home. Some of the figures can be estimated with a fair degree of reliability from other sources, e.g. tobacco duty receipts, but even so there remains the problem of apportioning the duty in terms of consumption between the households at different income levels.

While there is a good deal of published information available on both the retail price index and the Blue Book index of consumer prices, it should never be forgotten that statisticians, any more than other people, cannot make silk purses out of sows' ears. The data are probably uneven in quality and reliability and whenever such information is used, it is essential that the usual caution be exercised in drawing conclusions from small changes in the published data.

Social Indicators

The development of social indicators can be traced from two sources. The first of these was the growth of the scientific investigation of society. The desire of sociologists to analyse social relationships, measure social variables, and synthesise social models created considerable pressure upon the statistician to produce techniques to help satisfy such desires. The second source is the increasing awareness by central government that it should accept responsibility for social as well as economic affairs and intervene in the social life of the country. To intervene effectively the government must first measure the trends in various areas of society to determine if intervention is necessary. Then it has to check the effectiveness of any intervention by detecting changes in trends. The two sources can be said to represent the desire and the need to create some technique that social administrators could use and understand, and that would detect changes in broad areas of society.

It was immediately obvious that many of the variables that were concerned in social life were not immediately measurable. For example, what made the environment more or less congenial; what made a job more or less satisfying; what balance of restriction and liberty was most acceptable in society? However, even if it was not possible to measure directly the congeniality of environment or the satisfaction of a job there were a number of statistical series in each of these areas which pointed in various ways to how the central variable was moving. For example, in the industrial world, the number of trade disputes, the rate of labour turnover, the rate of absenteeism, the general level of wages, the level of productivity, etc., could all be measured with some degree of accuracy and all contributed –

to some extent – to measuring what was happening to the general level of job satisfaction.

The problem was, and still is, to bring together the various statistical series into one figure which would measure movement in the whole area. Social indicators, therefore, can be considered as extentions of the concept of index numbers. They have the same problems of representation, sensitivity and weighting as do index numbers (see Chapter X) but of a much higher order of magnitude. Further, the definition and measurement of variables and the complexity of the area covered ensure that, at least at present, the aim of social indicators is only to indicate movements in trends. Such indicators have no immediate pretensions of actually measuring – in the conventional sense – the health or happiness or satisfactions of society.

Social indicators are a relatively recent development. Many countries after the Second World War accepted a continuing intervention in the fabric of society which the waging of war had made necessary. However, one specific point of origin was the development of the American space programme. The American agencies needed to measure the effects of massive expenditure and technological advance upon American society. This initiative was taken up politically and developed more widely as the American government recognised the need to be able to measure the progress of their society in the social as well as the economic sphere. This led to the publication in 1969 by the U.S. Department of Health, Education and Welfare of a report *Toward a Social Report*. This study advocated a system of social indicators to cover such areas as health, social mobility, environment, income, public order, education and participation in society.

In the United Kingdom the 'social indicator movement' can be said to have taken off officially with the appointment of Professor (now Sir) Claus Moser as Director of the Central Statistical Office. Work on social indicators in various fields had been going on for some time. Professor Moser, however, established at national level the objective of devising a system of statistics and indicators that would show changes in the 'quality of life'. His article in *Social Trends No. 1* (H.M.S.O. 1970) entitled *Some general developments in social statistics* outlined his ideas. These ideas are in line with those being pursued by the United Nations Statistical Commission and the Conference of European Statisticians. This was further underlined in a report prepared by Harvey Brooks for the Organisation for Economic Co-operation and Development (Paris 1971). He stated that 'major efforts should be stimulated to devise social indicators that will permit social components to be fully taken into account when evaluating cost and benefit in technological innovation'. Later in the same year

(1971) a group of social scientists and government administrators were brought together by the Social Science Research Councils (S.S.R.C.) of the U.K. and U.S.A. at Ditchley in the U.K. The papers presented at that conference form the basis of the book *Social Indicators and Social Policy* edited by Shonfield and Shaw[1] and give an excellent introduction to the study of social indicators with a more detailed study of the areas of crime, education and health.

The progress that has been made in developing social indicators as subjective measures of life quality in 1971 to 1975 is reviewed in an article in *Social Trends No. 7*, p.47. The conclusion that the author, John Hall, has reached is that research on a very limited budget has yielded promising results in such measures as a Housing Insurance Index and a Health Symptom Index. Progress in this country is, however, very severely restricted by a lack of research funds.

The interest in the development of social indicators is world-wide and the first international seminar was held in April 1976 by the United Nations under the aegis of the European Social Development programme. The aim of the seminar was to contribute to the study of the role of social reporting and social indicators in policy making. In the event although much information was produced agremeent was limited. It was, however, concluded that a social report should:

(i) deploy data to build as comprehensive and balanced a picture as possible of the state of society;

(ii) aim to uncover the interaction between various facets and elements of social reality;

(iii) aim at elucidating the general directions in which society is evolving and the perceivable changes in the relationships between its components;

(iv) be produced at regular intervals. An example of social indicators is described in an article in *Statistical News No. 32* on Indicators of Local Prosperity.

The study of social indicators will undoubtedly remain a major topic of interest and activity for many years to come, although the pace of development may vary.

Conclusion

It is sometimes claimed that 'you can prove anything with statistics'. It would be more accurate to say that by a careful but biased selection from the published data it is often possible to make out a good, if not convincing, case in support of a particular policy. This is certainly true where the mass of published statistics lends itself to such practices. Perhaps. however, this is preferable to those who

[1]Heinemann for the S.S.R.C.

would argue without any knowledge of 'damned statistics'! In the field of social statistics, however, it is as well to remember that the statistics tell only part of the story.

LIFE TABLES

Earlier, in the section discussing various vital statistics, reference was made to the life table and the fact that an official life table, known as the English Life Table, is compiled after every census by the Government Actuary. In recent times, however, life tables have been compiled for inter-census years on the basis of the estimated mid-year populations. In addition to publishing such tables for the population of England & Wales, they are also prepared for Scotland and N. Ireland and now for the population of the U.K. The *Annual Abstract of Statistics*, which is probably the most widely available source book of official statistics, contains examples of such tables.

Quite apart from the value of such tables in making estimates of future population growth and size, the life table is useful as an indicator of the mortality prevailing during a particular period. In particular, the columns l_x and e_x are especially useful. These particular values are calculated to show the number of survivors from a hypothetical cohort of births at successive ages together with the expectation of life, *i.e.* the average number of years into the future which a person of a given age could expect to live.

The basis of any life table must be the age-specific death rates; these alone determine the rate at which the initial cohort of new-born males or females diminishes with the passage of time and, from these latter figures which make up the l_x column, the expectation of life figures corresponding to each age are then derived. In view of the crucial importance of the death rates for these calculations it is customary in the preparation of a life table not to use the age specific death rates of a single year. Thus, when the Government Actuary is preparing the 13th English Life Table, which will be based upon the 1971 population as enumerated in the census, the death rates will be the average of 1970, 1971 and 1972. This avoids the danger of using the death rates of a year when, for some reason, *e.g.* an influenza epidemic or a particularly severe winter which took a heavy toll of elderly lives, such rates would distort the life table values.

In the case of the official English Life Table the table shows the number of survivors (l_x) and the expectation of life (e_x) for *every* year of life, *i.e.* year by year from birth through to 105 when the last member of the original cohort of births has died. That, at least is the age limit for males. In the case of the life table for female lives, the oldest can go up to 109! Separate tables are prepared for the two sexes since, at all ages, female mortality is lower than for males. The result is that women tend, on average, to live longer by about 5 years, than men. For example, on the basis of the mortality of 1973–75 the number of survivors (1_x) among males who reach age 40 is equal to 95 per cent of the original cohort of births; for females the corresponding percentage is 97. By age 60, the life table figures diverge more markedly; 83 per cent of the female cohort is still alive but only 71 per cent of the males and, at age 80, there are almost twice as many female survivors as male, *i.e.* 47 to 25.

Before 1973 the life tables prepared for the intercensus years were 'abridged'. In other words, instead of using age specific death rates to calculate the number of survivors at *every* age, the average for 5-year age groups and, in some cases, 10-year age groups, were used. The resultant life table then gave the survivors and expectation of life figures at 5- and 10-year intervals. Since then, however, the Office of Population Censuses and Surveys (OPCAS) and the Government Actuary's department prepare even the inter-censal life tables on an annual basis. This gives a higher degree of accuracy in the resultant 1_x and e_x figures and the technique is possible given accurate data for annual mortality rates. Nevertheless, the intercensus life tables are still published in abridged form. For purposes of illustrating the basis of life table calculation there is no advantage in working on an annual basis. The worked example on p.536 is an example of an 'abridged' life table.

Before embarking upon the actual calculations involved in the abridged life table, using the estimate of the population of the U.K. in mid-1975 and the death rates of 1974–76, the principles underlying the calculations can best be introduced by means of a highly simplified example set out in Table 81 opposite. The first column shows the age in single years from birth to 7 and the second column gives the probability of surviving one year from exact age x. This is represented by the symbol p_x and the p value corresponding to 0 is 0·9. This simply means that 90 per cent of the birth cohort will survive until their first birthday; the corresponding value of p for age 1 is only 0·7 and this, in turn, signifies that 70 per cent of those who have survived until their first birthday will survive to their second. The adjacent column headed q_x denotes the probability of dying during the interval between one birthday and the next. Since a person can either live or die, but not both, it follows that $p_x + q_x = 1$ and it will be seen from the table that the corresponding values of p and q for any age add up to unity. Column 4 is important since it shows the number who survive to exact age x. Given that

TABLE 81
SIMPLIFIED LIFE TABLE CALCULATIONS

(1)	(2)	(3)	(4)	(5)	(6)	(7)	(8)
Age	Probability of surviving one year from x	Probability of dying within one year of x	Number of survivors at x	Number dying within year of x	Years lived between x and $x+1$	Years lived after x	Mean expectation of life at x
x	p_x	q_x	l_x	d_x	L_x	T_x	e_x
0	·9	·1	100	10	95	290	2·90
1	·7	·3	90	27	76·5	195	2·17
2	·6	·4	63	25	50·5	118·5	1·88
3	·7	·3	38	11	32·5	68	1·79
4	·6	·4	27	11	21·5	35·5	1·31
5	·4	·6	16	10	11	14	·88
6	·0	1·0	6	6	3	3	·50
7			0				

there are 100 births and 0·9 of these survive to the first birthday, it follows that the number of survivors to exact age 1 is 90. The number surviving to exact age 2 is given by the product of 90 and the probability of survival from age 1 to exact age 2, *i.e.* 0·7 which leaves 63 reaching exact age 3. The differences between the successive l_x values are given in column 5 which is headed by the symbol d_x. This denotes the number of deaths occurring during the interval between age x and $x + 1$. The same results could have been obtained by multiplying the l_x values by the corresponding q_x values, *i.e.* the number of survivors at age x times the probability of dying between age x and $x + 1$. The rest of the calculations in the first four columns follow the pattern just described and from them is derived (in col. 4) the number of survivors at each age. These l_x values are useful for comparative purposes. One may compare the l_x columns in two life tables relating to different populations and gain an impression of their mortality experience. For example, the English Life Table No. 1, based upon the mortality experience of 1841, shows the number of males surviving to age 5 as 7,420 out of 10,000. Compare the corresponding l_x value for the life table for males in England and Wales in 1973-75 of 9,790. The two figures provide an eloquent comment on living conditions then and now.

Just as the l_x values provide a summary picture of the general level of living conditions for the population, so the e_x values, *i.e.* the expectation of life, is a most useful indicator of comparative mortality. Thus, the expectation of life of a male child at birth in 1841 was 40 years; by 1974 it was almost 70 years. Such figures tell their own story.

The next stage is, therefore, to obtain the e_x values. Column 6 of

Table 81 is headed 'Years lived between x and $x + 1$' and denoted by the symbol L_x. This particular figure is merely the total number of years lived collectively by the persons alive during that year. For example, 90 out of the original cohort survived the first year of life so that together in that year they 'lived' 90 years. The actual figure in the L_x column is not, however, 90 but 95. This arises because of the 10 deaths in the first year. It is assumed that they lived on average six months so that those 10 between them lived five years, which has to be added to the 90 years lived by the survivors. If all the years lived as shown in the L_x column are aggregated, their sum comes to 290. That, it will be noted, is the first figure in the next column headed 'Years lived after age x' and denoted by the symbol T_x. In other words, between them the 100 persons born and none of whom survived beyond their sixth birthday (at least according to this particular life table!) collectively experienced 290 years of life. Thus, the average number of years lived by the original 100 persons was 290/100 which equals 2·90 years. That is the first figure in the final column headed e_x and is described as the mean expectation of life. The expectation of life for a 2-year-old was, according to this table, 1·88 years which is derived by dividing the corresponding T_x value by the corresponding figure in the I_x column, i.e. 118·5 divided by 63. Note that the key column of the life table is the second, i.e. the p_x values. Given those values the derivation of the I_x values is merely a matter of arithmetic, i.e. the product of corresponding p_x and I_x give the value denoted I_{x+1}, i.e. $0.7 \times 90 = 63$. Columns 6 and 7 are necessary only for the derivation of the e_x values.

Table 81 merely served to illustrate the arithmetic processes, given the p_x values, needed to determine the I_x and e_x values. Nevertheless, the same principles underlie the construction of the life table set out in Table 82 below despite the fact it may well appear much more complex. The first factor contributing to the much more extended life table is that this particular population, i.e. males in the U.K. in 1975, does not die off in 6 years. The range of ages denoted by x is from 0 denoting birth to 85. As noted earlier, the official English Life Table for males would cover ages from 0 to 105 but the number of lives at risk after 85 is not large. The annual abridged life tables now prepared by OPCAS do not extend beyond the age of 85. Also, the official life table uses a birth cohort of 100,000 for greater accuracy. For an abridged life table the cohort is 10,000.

The second important difference between Table 81 and this extended life table in Table 82 is that, whereas in the former the p_x values were assumed, in this case they are calculated for each age group in the particular population. This is a crucial part of the life table since inaccurate data relating either to the population count within each age group or deficiencies in the recording of the number of deaths at each age in the relevant years will, of course, affect the life table results. Note, too, that this life table does not give the x values, *i.e.* ages from 0 to 85 in single years. Only the first year is given at an interval of one year and the next age 5 gives a four-year interval. From 5 to 20 the age interval is five years and from 25 up to 85 a 10-year interval is used. Obviously, this is why the table is called an 'abridged' life table. Such a degree of approximation as this procedure involves does not greatly affect the final results. As will be shown later, the e_x values are only slightly different from those which would have been derived if the full life table had been calculated on an annual basis for every year of life. The justification for this use of age intervals of five and 10 years after the first five years of life is that the mortality rates do not vary sufficiently within the age interval to debar the use of what is, in effect, an average mortality rate for the particular 5 or 10 year age groups. Obviously, there is a margin of error but, as noted above, it is not important enough to prevent the use of abridged life tables for most purposes. In other words, the average death rate for the quinquennial or decennial group provides a good approximation to the number of deaths which would be obtained if the death rates for each single year within the age interval were used as in a full life table.

It is now possible to consider the abridged life table set out in Table 82 in some detail. The first four columns are required to calculate the p_x values. The method is as follows: For each age given in the life table, the second column shows the number of males (in thousands) of that age in the U.K. population at mid-1975. The next column headed 'Annual deaths 1974–76' is the *average* number of deaths each year in that three-year period. It is obtained by aggregating the number of deaths in each age group registered in those three years and dividing their sum by 3. For example, in the 20–24-age group the number of deaths in each of the three years was 1,968, 2,018 and 1,993. If the deaths for 1975 alone had been used for this life table, then the specific death rate for the age group 20–24 would have been higher than if the number of deaths in the years on either side of 1975 had been used. By averaging the three years' deaths such variations are largely eliminated and the resultant figures in the life table less distorted than they would otherwise be. The age specific death rate is derived by dividing the average number of deaths by the corresponding population. This is usually expressed as a rate per 1,000 lives. Thus, the death rate for 20–24 year-old males was 1·0 per 1,000 from dividing 1,993 by 1,951,000 and expressing the result as a rate per thousand.

It is worth looking down the age-specific death rates and noting how, after the first year of life, they decline to very low levels. It is not until the age group 55–64 that the rate is once again in double figures. The result of these very low rates is that, even by age 50, 90 per cent of the original birth cohort is still alive. If one looks up the corresponding life table for females in the U.K. at age 50 over 94 per cent of the original cohort of births is still alive. Equally noteworthy is the fact that in the same life tables, whereas at age 75 nearly 6,300 females are still alive, of the men just over 4,200 have survived to that age.

Returning to the abridged life table, the next stage is to convert the age specific death rates into p_x rates which measure the *probability of survival* from age x to $x + n$, where the symbol n may represent either 1, 4, 5 or 10 years as in this table. The annual rates are termed *central* death rates since they are based upon the estimated mid-year population of the corresponding age group. What the p_x rate measures is the probability of surviving the interval between one birthday and the next, or if a five-year interval is used, surviving from age x to $x + 5$. It is necessary, therefore, to determine first, the number of lives at risk at exact age x and the number of deaths that occur between that birthday and the next. An estimate of that probability can be provided by calculating the death rate for the population in each age group at *the beginning of the year* instead of the *mid-year*.

If the *mid-year* population is denoted by P, then the age-specific or central death rate, represented by the symbol m_x, is D/P where D is the number of deaths which occur during the year. If it is assumed that the deaths are spread evenly throughout the year, then the population, *i.e.* number of males in the age group, which was alive at the *beginning* of the year is equal to the *mid-year population plus half the deaths* which occurred in that year. Thus, the population at the beginning of the year can be written $P + \frac{1}{2}D$. The probability of *dying* in that year is given by the fraction $\dfrac{D}{P + \frac{1}{2}D}$ which is represented by the symbol q_x.

If, as stated above, $m_x = \dfrac{D}{P}$ then, by multiplying both sides by P we get $Pm_x = D$. Since it has been established that $q_x = \dfrac{D}{P + \frac{1}{2}D}$, by substituting in that fraction for D the symbol Pm_x (since they are the same) we arrive at the following fraction: $q_x = \dfrac{Pm_x}{P + \frac{1}{2}Pm_x}$ from which the Ps can be eliminated in the numerator and denominator to yield $q_x = \dfrac{m_x}{1 + \frac{1}{2}m_x}$. By multiplying both the numerator and denominator of that fraction by 2 we get $q_x = \dfrac{2m_x}{2 + m_x}$. That is the formula from which it would be possible to derive the probability of dying (q_x) at age x from the central death rates for that age which were calculated from the mid-year population and the number of deaths in each age group. It is, however, more practical to calculate the p_x values for use in the life table, *i.e.* the probability of surviving from exact age x to exact age $x + n$. This is easily done since $p_x + q_x = 1$. As q_x is equal to $\dfrac{2m_x}{2 + m_x}$ then it follows, since

$$1 - q_x = p_x, \text{ that } p_x = 1 - \frac{2m_x}{2 + m_x} = \frac{2 + m_x}{2 + m_x} - \frac{2m_x}{2 + m_x}$$

which equals $\dfrac{2 - m_x}{2 + m_x}$.

Thus, to convert the central death rates in the column headed m_x into p_x values, it is necessary only to substitute in the foregoing fraction the value for m_x for the corresponding age. Thus, at age 0 the m_x value is 0·01760. The reader will appreciate that this is exactly the same as the 17·6 in the previous column, except that this latter figure is expressed as a rate per 1,000 population whereas the m_x rate is converted into decimals. In the next column headed by the fraction $\dfrac{2 - m_x}{2 + m_x}$, the values corresponding to the numerator and denominator of that fraction are given. Thus, for the numerator 2 − 0·0176 we get 1·9824 and, for the denominator, 2 + 0·0176 which gives 2·0176. The denominator is then divided into the upper figure and the result is shown in the next column headed p_x. For age 0 the p_x value is 0·9825.

At the next age 1 this procedure needs to be modified slightly. Since the next age (*i.e.* x value) in the first column after 1 is 5 the p_x value must be that which measures the probability of surviving from exact age 1 to exact age 5, *i.e.* an interval of four years. The m_x values, it may be recalled, are *single* year values and therefore an adjustment has to be made. Clearly, if the interval is four years instead of one year, then the probability of dying in that interval is higher than it would be if the interval were only one year. The adjustment necessary is quite simple. Instead of calculating $2 - m_x$, we now calculate $2 - 4m_x$ and similarly for the denominator which now becomes $2 + 4m_x$. The calculation is then as follows. The m_x rate corresponding to age *1* is 0·00070 and, working now to four figures instead of five, that figure multiplied by 4 becomes 0·0028.

The upper figure in column 5 is therefore $2 - 0.0028 = 1.9972$ and the lower figure is 2.0028. The latter divided into the former gives the p_x value, i.e. the probability of surviving the four years after the first birthday, as 0.9972.

For the next three x values, i.e. ages 5, 10, 15 and 20 we are using five-year age intervals. Thus the above formula for p_x, which now gives the probability of surviving five years after the 5th, 10th, 15th and 20th birthday, is written $\dfrac{2 - 5m_x}{2 + 5m_x}$. The rest of the calculations are as before and can be checked against the table. At age 25 the interval is again changed, this time to 10 years and this interval is used for the rest of the ages given, with the exception of 85. (The method for estimating p_x where $x = 85$ is explained later.) If we start with age 25, the m_x value is 0.0010 (to four places of decimals) and substituted in the fraction $\dfrac{2 - 10m_x}{2 + 10m_x}$ we get the values 1.9900 and 2.0100. The lower divided into the upper figure gives p_{25} as 0.9900. The remainder of the p_x values up to, but not including, 85 are derived in the same way.

At this point it may be helpful to introduce the reader to some of the conventional notation of life tables. So far reference has always been made to the p_x value where x is, say, 85. It is clearly much easier simply to write p_{85} as denoting the probability of surviving from exact age 85 to the next birthday. If, however, the interval is more than one year, then the p is prefaced by either 5 or 10, assuming the interval is five or 10 years. Thus, the probability of a man of 25 surviving from his 25th birthday to his 35th is written $_{10}p_{25}$. Or, for a 10-year-old to survive the next five years, we write $_5p_{10}$. For the probability of dying, i.e. q, the same notation applies.

As explained earlier when discussing Table 81. the key to the derivation of the two main columns in a life table, i.e. l_x and e_x are the p_x rates. These have now been derived and are shown in column 7 of the life table. Starting with the hypothetical 10,000 live births represented by the symbol l_o we have to calculate how many will survive from birth to their first birthday. The probability of survival is p_o which equals 0.9825 so that, if we have initially 10,000 male births, by the first birthday there will only be 9,825 alive. This, it will be noted, is the second figure down the l_x column. From this it is clear that $l_0 \times p_0 = l_1$. To determine the number who survive to their fifth birthday out of the 9,825 who reached their first birthday, multiply that figure by $_4p_1$. This is the symbol representing the probability of surviving from exact age 1 to exact age 5, i.e. an interval of four years. Alternatively, the symbol may be read as the probability of surviving four years from,exact age 1. Using symbols, we get $l_1 \times {}_4p_1 = l_5 = 9{,}825 \times 0{\cdot}9972 = 9{,}797$. The same procedure is used to derive all the figures in the l_x column up to and including l_{75}. From these it is then possible to calculate the expectation of life at each age, *i.e.* the e_x values.

Since the mortality among the males of 85 and over is so high, almost 245 per thousand which signifies that one in four dies each year, an alternative method of calculating e_{85} has to be used. This is largely because, with this very high mortality the assumption that the deaths are spread evenly over the 10-year interval is no longer justified. When the full English Life Table is being prepared the Government Actuary uses single-year death rates. But, because the number of persons in this age group and beyond is relatively small, in an abridged life table age 85 is usually the upper limit. A fair approximation to the expectation of life, based upon a full life table, which is the main figure of interest at this stage of the life table, can be derived from the fraction $1/m_{85}$. In this case, the resultant fraction is 1 divided by $0{\cdot}2249$ which gives a result of $4{\cdot}1$. This particular figure is an estimate of the number of years which a male of 85 will – given the 1974–76 mortality – on average survive after attaining his 85th birthday. This figure is inserted into the final column headed e_x. We will be returning to it a little later.

The first part of the abridged life table is now complete since the important l_x column, which shows the number of survivors to each age, has been derived. The rest of the table and calculations are needed solely to estimate the expectation of life. From these figures, assuming that only the l_x values were available, it would be possible to calculate both p_x and q_x for any age. Also, it is only a matter of subtracting one l_x value from another to arrive at the number of deaths at that age which is represented by the symbol d_x. Thus, the number of deaths among males between their 5th and 10th birthdays was 9,797 less 9,780 which equals 17 from the original cohort of 10,000. Put in terms of the conventional notation, $l_5 - l_{10} = {}_5d_5$. While on the subject of notation, it may have occurred to the reader that the derivation of the p_x rates from the l_x values is merely a matter of division. Thus, ${}_5p_{10}$ is obtained by dividing l_{15} by l_{10}, *i.e.* $\dfrac{9762}{9780} = 0{\cdot}9982$.

The column after the l_x column is headed L_x. This figure, it may be recalled from the description of Table 81, was the sum of the years lived by the persons who survived the interval between two specified birthdays. The easiest way of understanding this concept is to work through to one of the L_x values. The l_{10} value is 9,780 and the l_{15} figure is 9,762. Just how many years did this group live during the interval between their 10th and 15th birthdays? Clearly those who survived throughout the five years each contributed five years to the sum of all years lived by the cohort of 10,000 between birth and death of that cohort. Thus, the l_{15} group, *i.e.* the survivors, contributed $5 \times 9,762$ years. But, 9,780 men entered upon the period of five years. Hence, it follows that 9,780 less 9,762, *i.e.* 18 died before completing the five years. Some probably died early in the quinquennium, others may have died later. We can assume that the deaths were spread out over the quinquennium between the 10th and 15th birthdays, so that *on average* each man who died lived for half that period. Thus, they contributed $2\frac{1}{2}$ years apiece so that the 18 men, who died, collectively lived 45 years. If this is added to the product of $5 \times 9,762 = 48,810$ we arrive at a total of 48·855 years. Reference to Table 82 in column 9 will show that the value for $_5L_{10}$ is 48,855. The calculation of the l_x values is much easier by adding together successive pairs of l_x values, then dividing them by 2 and multiplying the result either by 5 or 10 according to the size of the interval. Thus, if we take l_{55} and l_{65} and sum them we get $8,699 + 7,103 = 15,802$. That multiplied by 10 and divided by 2 gives the result 79,010, which corresponds to the value of L_{55} in column 9.

But, not all the L_x values can be derived in this way. To obtain L_4 we still sum the values for l_1 and l_5, *i.e.* 9,825 and 9,797 = 19,622. In this case, however, we have a 4- and not a 5-year interval so that, instead of as before, dividing the sum of the two l_x values and then multiplying by 5, in this case we multiply by 4. However, it is easier simply to multiply the *sum* of l_1 and l_5 by 2 with the same result, *i.e.* 39,244. The problem with L_0 is somewhat different. To start with, the interval between the successive l_x values is only one year, *i.e.* $l_0 + l_1 = 10,000 + 9,825$ and then divide by 2. The result of doing this, 9,912 does not correspond to the value for L_0 in the life table which is 9,877. Why not? The reason is that the latter figure was not obtained by taking the mean of the two successive l_x values, but by multiplying l_0 by 0·3 and l_1 by 0·7 which gives $3,000 + 6,877 = 9,877$. Why is this age group treated differently? The answer lies in the fact that the earlier assumption, that deaths are spread evenly throughout the interval between the birthdays, does not apply to the first year of life. Many babies die within the first 24 hours. In fact, as is explained on page 450, a special mortality rate for babies in the first month of life is calculated, known as the neo-natal rate. Obviously, using this rate (which can be further broken down into deaths in the first week of life and those in the rest of the month), it would be possible to make exact calculations of the number of months of life experienced by the infants who died in the first year. This is unnecessary in an abridged life table and a good estimate can be provided by 'averaging' the l_0 and l_1 values as described. Finally, we need to know the value of l_{85}. That is the number of years of life contributed by those who have completed the first 85 years of life, *after attaining that age*, to the total number of years lived by the entire cohort of 10,000. Since the values of e_{85} and l_{85} are known and, because e_x is equal to T_x divided by l_x, T_{85} must be the product of e_{85} and l_{85}. Hence $4 \cdot 1 \times 1,113$ gives the value of T_{85}, *i.e.* 4,545 and, since for the last figure in the L_x column, $T_x = L_x$ the entire table is now completed.

The T_x column is the sum of all the years lived after a given age by the number of survivors to that age. For example, the 9,718 males who reach their 20th birthday together live another 496,302 years between them before they all die. As for the original cohort of 10,000 males they live collectively 691,920 years which, it will be noted, is the value of T_0. As explained, the T_0 value of 691,920 is the sum of the entire column of L_x values. To derive T_1 substract L_0 from T_0 *i.e.* 691,920 less 9,877 which gives 682,043. To obtain T_5 follow the same procedure but this time deduct L_1 from T_1; thus 682,043 less 39,244 = 642,799.[1]

The expectation of life represented by the symbol e_x can be derived for any age given in the life table by dividing the appropriate T_x value by the corresponding l_x value. Thus, e_{10} is equal to T_{10} divided by l_{10},

i.e. $\dfrac{593,857}{9,780}$ which equals $60 \cdot 7$ years. In other words, the average

number of years lived by males subject to the mortality of this life table after reaching their 20th birthday is $60 \cdot 7$ years. The expectation of life at birth is $69 \cdot 2$ years, yet the corresponding figure at age 1 is $69 \cdot 4$. How is this possible? The answer lies in the very nature of the e_x value which, as was emphasised earlier, is simply an average. Like all averages it may be distorted by extreme values and the e_0 value includes a substantial number of infant deaths. These very short lives contribute little in relation to the *total* years lived by the cohort, *i.e.* T_0. In contrast, the l_1 value excludes all these very short lives and thenceforward, as may be seen from the death rates, the loss of life is very small and consequently the number of years of life contributed to T_1 is substantial.[2]

The abridged life table overleaf has been designed to give an indication of the basic method of its construction. In some abridged life tables, the first 5 years of life are given in single years and this increases slightly the accuracy of the table, in particular the l_x and

---

[1] With a hand calculator the addition of all the L_x values to obtain the T_x values can best be done by starting from the *bottom* and adding in successive L_x values, noting the sum after each addition in the T_x column. Thus, $4,545 + 26,570 = 31,115 + 56,520 = 87,635$ and so on.

[2] This is similar to the cricketer whose average innings in the season is, say, 40 runs. If, however, all his innings in which he scored a 'duck' were eliminated, then his average score would be higher.

TABLE 82
ABRIDGED LIFE TABLE – MALES
U.K. 1975

Age (1)	Population 1975 000's (2)	Annual Deaths 1974–76 (3)	Age Specific D/R per 1000 (4)	m_x (5)	$\dfrac{2-m_x}{2+m_x'}$ (a) (6)	p_x (7)	l_x (8)	L_x (9)	T_x (10)	$\overset{\circ}{e}_x$ (11)
0	365	6,424	17·6	·01760	1·9824 / 2·0176	·9825	10,000	9,877	691,920	69·2
1	1,668	1,161	0·7	·00070	1·9972 / 2·0028	·9972	9,825	39,244	682,043	69·4
5	2,309	828	0·4	·00036	1·9982 / 2·0018	·9982	9,797	48,942	642,799	65·6
10	2,372	794	0·3	·00035	1·9982 / 2·0018	·9982	9,780	48,855	593,857	60·7
15	2,108	1,914	0·9	·00091	1·9955 / 2·0045	·9955	9,762	48,700	545,002	55·8
20	1,951	1,993	1·0	·00102	1·9949 / 2·0051	·9949	9,718	48,467	496,302	51·0
25	3,854	3,845	1·0	·00100	1·9900 / 2·0100	·9900	9,669	96,205	447,835	46·3
35	3,231	7,142	2·2	·00221	1·9779 / 2·0231	·9781	9,572	94,675	351,630	36·7
45	3,364	24,716	7·3	·00735	1·9265 / 2·0735	·9291	9,363	90,310	256,955	27·4
55	2,939	59,330	20·1	·02019	1·7981 / 2·2019	·8166	8,699	79,010	166,645	19·1
65	2,162	111,026	51·0	·05135	1·4865 / 2·5135	·5914	7,103	56,520	87,635	12·4
75	746	87,288	117·0	·11701	0·8299 / 3·1701	·2618	4,201	26,570	31,115	7·4
85	129	31,595	244·9	·24492	–0·449 / 4·449		1,113	4,545	4,545	4·1

(a) $\dfrac{2-4m_x}{2+4m_x}$ at age 1, $\dfrac{2-5m_x}{2+5m_x}$ at ages 5 to 20, $\dfrac{2-10m_x}{2+10m_x}$ at age 25 on.

m_x = central death rate of age group x to $x+1$.
l_x = number of a generation surviving to age x
p_x = proportion of the generation surviving to age $x+1$ having reached age x.
T_x = total years of life lived by the generation between ages x

T_x = total years of life lived by entire generation to age x.
$\overset{\circ}{e}_x$ = average length of life of those surviving to age x.

[1]Since $l_x \times \overset{\circ}{e}_x = T_x$ then $l_{85-} \times \overset{\circ}{e}_{85} = 1113 \times 4{\cdot}1 = T_{85-} = 4545$.

e_x values. Similarly, when l_{85} is very small then the approximation procedure used to obtain T_{85} would not make much difference to the T_x values and the successive values of e_x. The reader will appreciate that, if a mistake in, or under-statement of, a l_x value or any other figure in the L_x and the T_x column is made, it will affect all the following figures. Thus, if e_{85} from which we derived L_{85} is too low—and at 4·1 years is rather low in relation to the full life table value of 4·5 then all the T_x values will be reduced by that deficiency.

In the event, despite the considerable measure of approximation used in this illustrative table, the results are close to the values from a full life table calculated on the basis of annual ages. Thus, the e_0 figure of 69·2 compares with 69·4 in the full life table; at 25 the official expectation of life is 46·6 years compared with the above value of 46·3; at 65 the corresponding figures are 12·4 and 12·3 years but, at 85, the official figure is 4·5 compared with the above figure of 4·1.

The accuracy of the life table depends not on the arithmetic but on the quality, *i.e.* accuracy, of the basic data. That means an accurate enumeration or estimate of the age distribution of the population of males or females, depending for which sex the life table is being compiled, and accurate registration of deaths. The latter has been in the past and still is, but nowadays to a much lesser extent, a source of error. As people die later in life there is often confusion over the age at death and the wrong age is sometimes recorded. Obviously, if this were a frequent event, then the death rates would be inaccurate and the resultant life table would be unreliable. Not all countries have such sophisticated registration systems for births and deaths as in the U.K., nor are their census figures always reliable. In such cases, therefore, it is better to compile an abridged life table in which, one hopes, some of the registration and enumeration errors may actually cancel each other out!

Quite apart from the value of the life table in providing very useful summary indices of the nation's mortality experience, it provides a picture of the age distribution of the population which will ultimately emerge if the mortality upon which the table is based remains unchanged and if the birth rate is just sufficient to replace the deaths. The population remains constant in size and is therefore referred to as a 'stationary population'. Remember that the life table is a hypothetical model of a population in which it is assumed that mortality remains unchanged and births are equal to deaths. The numbers at each age or in each age group in the population would correspond with the values in the L_x column and the total population would be equal to T_0. Given this information it is possible to calculate the crude birth rate and the crude death rate by dividing l_0 by T_0 which, in this particular case, equals 14·4 per 1,000.

Since the L_x column also gives the age distribution of this life table population, one can follow through the diminishing survivors through the successive age groups. For example, according to the L_x column there are 48,942 males aged between 5 and 9. Ten years later when those males would be between 15 and 19, according to the L_x column there will be 9,762 left alive. In another five years' time, when they will have reached the ages 20–24, there will be 48,855 alive. Suppose that there are currently 3, 4 million males in the U.K. aged between 45–54. How many of these will be alive 10 years hence, assuming that they experience the mortality of the above life table ? According to the life table L_{45} is 90,310 and L_{55} 79,010. If the current population of 45–54-year-old males has the same mortality, then out of the existing 3,4 million there will be alive in 10 years' time, $\dfrac{79,010}{90,310} \times 3{\cdot}4$ mn which equals 2,975,000. It is important not to take such estimates too literally. Over the next decade it is always possible that changes in mortality will take place although, in the U.K. with the current very low death rates, it is difficult to visualise any significant changes in the near future. Such calculations are useful, however, when the data relating to the population and its age distribution are of uncertain reliability and, by experimenting with such calculations, it is possible to judge whether the available figures make sense.

Quite apart from the relevance of the life table to assessing the effects of mortality upon the population of either sex, the technique has wider applications. For demographers there is what is termed a nuptiality table which shows the rate at which a hypothetical cohort of spinsters will be married. This is useful when estimates are being made of future fertility, since about 90 per cent of all births occur to married women. Obviously, the life table's main function is to guide insurance companies in the determination of the premium rates for life assurance at various ages. The reader can easily appreciate why premiums appear so low when the male life is young; these days 95 per cent of males survive until 45 and over 56 per cent to 65. The same technique can be used for pension schemes to estimate the future demand on their funds of present and future pensioners. It can be used for estimating, using the experience of the past or some assessment of the future rate of labour turnover, the rate at which employees in a large organisation will leave for various reasons. The life table has even found application in industry to estimate the life of bus or aircraft engines where there are large numbers of them to be maintained and replaced at intervals.

The main point to remember in connection with such estimates as are derived from life tables, in whatever field of application they may be employed, is that the results are no better than the data upon which the life table is compiled. The past, as was noted in the description of time series analysis, is not always a good guide to the future. Also, the best of estimates, as the Scots bard 'Bobby' Burns observed, 'gang aft agley'. It could equally well be said that one man's guesses are often another man's statistics.

CHAPTER XVIII

ECONOMIC STATISTICS

Introduction

Despite the relatively long history of economic statistics in the United Kingdom the growth in the coverage and volume of economic data collected by the government departments was, until the last war, fairly slow and was marked by an absence of co-ordination between the various departments which concentrated on collecting such data as their own administrative requirements dictated. Thus, three departments not only collected incomplete data upon the labour force, but there was no comparability between their figures.

With the acceptance by post-war governments of responsibility for the maintenance of economic stability and full employment, the scope of the data collected increased and the creation of the Central Statistical Office ensured a greater degree of co-ordination between departments. After 1957 when Mr Macmillan, as Chancellor of the Exchequer, commented critically upon the shortcomings of the available statistics for economic planning[1] there was a major expansion and improvement in the coverage and quality of such data. These efforts were supplemented by the reaction to the criticisms of the Radcliffe Committee on the Working of the Monetary System which produced a significant improvement in the range and quality of financial statistics.

Thus, by 1973 when Sir Claus Moser, then Director of the C.S.O., delivered the Mercantile Credit lecture at the University of Reading, he could with considerable justice comment that 'the relationship between statistics and economic policy is ever changing. It is very different now from, say, 25 years ago . . . then the statistical system was rudimentary by today's standards . . . Our statistical operations are now unrecognisably more extensive and sophisticated than two decades ago. We have figures about almost every aspect of the economy, we produce them more quickly and we are constantly out to improve their accuracy'.[2] Although now somewhat dated this is a most valuable and readable summary of the subject and the work of the government statistical service.

The qualities sought after in the production of economic statistics were, according to Sir Claus, first, relevance; second, they should be

[1] Quoted on page 12
[2] Published by the University of Reading under the title *Statistics and Economic Policy.*

as up to date as possible; third, they should be reliable enough for their purpose, and, fourthly, the statistics should be presented clearly, honestly and helpfully. In the sections on selected areas of current economic statistics which follow, the reader may judge for himself – as far as any outline permits – the extent to which Sir Claus's objectives have been attained. But, it must be emphasised there is no substitute for actually consulting the various statistical publications to which reference is made. It is not suggested that the student reader should study all such publications; this would be an impossible labour. But, some reading is essential of the major annual publications such as the *Annual Abstract of Statistics*, which is more general in its coverage, and of the monthly publications such as *Economic Trends* and, to a lesser extent, the *Monthly Digest of Statistics*. It will also be helpful to gain some insight into the sheer volume of data currently produced on the economy if some issues of the monthly publication, the Department of Employment's *Gazette* and the weekly Department of Trade's *Trade and Industry* were examined.

Manpower

Between mid-1951 and mid-1976 the total working population in Great Britain increased by over 10 per cent to over 26 million. Of this total two-thirds were men and one-third women. The importance for the economy of an adequate supply of labour hardly needs stressing, and in recent years there has been a tremendous improvement both in the quantity and quality of statistics relating to the working population. One of the results of these recent changes in labour statistics is that comparisons with earlier years, *i.e.* pre-war and post-war, are rendered difficult and, in some cases, impossible.

The change in the nature of the statistics reflects the change in the attitude towards manpower problems that has taken place in the post-war era. Before the war the then Ministry of Labour, which is the primary producer of labour statistics, published reliable data relating to the registered unemployed, but in respect of the working population estimates only could be made. Up to that time estimates of the working population could be derived partly from the Census of Production, from the Census of Population, and the Ministry of Labour annual estimates. These various figures were neither reliable nor comparable. The first steps to improvement were taken during the war as a result of the direction of labour policy and the necessity to conserve labour supplies. After the war, with the establishment of full employment, *i.e.* a very low level of unemployment, it became equally necessary to know more about the quantity and distribution of the labour force. Hence, during the war and more especially since 1945 there were a succession of changes, amendments, revisions of classification, etc., in labour statistics, the most important of which arose from the introduction in July 1948 of the National Insurance Act. This provided that every gainfully occupied individual was legally bound to register. Unfortunately there are a number of omissions due to failure on the part of some members of the community to register, *e.g.* some married women and self-employed persons. In 1948 a Standard Industrial Classification was introduced whereby all industrial statistics were classified by industry on a common basis, and this classification was amended in 1958 and again in 1968 with inevitable results for the comparability of certain series.

Prior to 1971 the basic method of estimating the working population was to use the quarterly exchange of insurance cards, since each quarterly group constituted a random selection of insured persons. The industrial classification and analysis which was carried out once yearly was based upon the June quarter figures, which were supplemented by the annual June returns from employers with five or more workpeople. This particular enquiry covered more than three-quarters of the employed population. However, the use of insurance cards was phased out in April 1975 and a new method of estimating the working population was needed. In 1971 a Census of Employment was introduced. This census counts every employee on the payroll for whom the employer is responsible for deducting income tax. All individual tax deduction points are approached every third year but, in the intervening two years, estimates are made of the numbers working for the small employers. To the figures of the Census of Employment must be added both employers and the self-employed. These totals are obtained from the decennial Census of Population and up-dated as appropriate. The aggregate of the employed, employers and self-employed give the total *employed* labour force. To obtain an estimate of the total *working* population, figures of the unemployed and members of H.M. Forces must be added to the total employed labour force.

The number of unemployed is based upon the number registered for employment at local employment or career offices. Adult students registered for vacation work only are deliberately excluded. Severely disabled people are also omitted and, implicitly excluded are those who would work if they could find suitable employment but are not registered. This figure includes a substantial proportion of married women together with some self-employed. (A fuller discussion can be found in the White Paper entitled *Unemployment Statistics* published in 1972 (*Cmnd. 5157*).)

To give a more up-to-date figure of trends in the number of employed people a monthly count (called the L returns) is made of a sample of firms in the production industries only.

While the above data give a reasonable estimate of how many people are employed or available for employment, account must be taken of the number of hours that they actually work. This information is provided in the annual *New Earnings Survey* which is based on a 1·0-per-cent sample of employees. The annual figure is subsequently up-dated by taking into account monthly variations in sickness, overtime, short-time and changes in normal hours worked.

All the data are published initially in summary form in the monthly Department of Employment *Gazette* and then in the monthly publication *Economic Trends*. More detail with analysis by sex, industry and region can be found in the *British Labour Statistics Year Book* published by the Department of Employment. This Year Book is the major long-term source of labour statistics. Some detail additional to that published in the monthly journals can be found in the Annual Supplement to *Economic Trends*. As an example of the scope and the complexity of interpretation of labour data consider the footnotes in Table 83 overleaf which is taken from *Economic Trends No. 305* (March 1979) which illustrates – in part only – the key series.

The overall figures of employment and hours worked are only part of a mass of data produced from the study of manpower. For example, the importance of juvenile workers for the economy is reflected in a special classification published in the August issue of the *Gazette* each year, which shows the number of young persons under 18 years of age taking up employment for the first time during that year. The new entrants are classified by the industry, their age, and the type of employment taken up.

The *Gazette* also regularly publishes data on the following:

(1) labour turnover for employees of both sexes in each manufacturing industry in selected months;

(2) the number of operatives working short- or over-time in each industry, together with percentages and averages designed to indicate the extent of the abnormal working in various industries;

(3) the number and percentage of administrative, technical, and clerical workers in manufacturing industries is published each year, just as is

(4) the number of women in part-time employment in manufacturing industry; the information relating to this is in fact collected quarterly;

(5) the numbers employed by local authorities and in the police force analysed by age and sex is published annually; while

TABLE 83

NATIONAL EMPLOYMENT AND UNEMPLOYMENT[1]

| | Seasonally adjusted | | | | | | Great Britain Manufacturing industry | | Unadjusted |
| | United Kingdom (Thousands) | | | Unemployed excluding school leavers | | Thousands | 1975=100 | 1975=100 | United Kingdom (Thousands) |
	Working population[2]	Employed labour force[2]	Employees in employment[2,3]	Thousands	Percentage of employees[4]	Vacancies notified to employment offices	Employees in employment[2,3]	Average hours worked per operative	Total unemployed including school leavers
1967	25,532	24,985	22,806	547.2	2.3	175.1	111.0	104.7	556.7
1968	25,417	24,830	22,644	574.4	2.4	189.5	110.0	105.5	583.3
1969	25,409	24,844	22,611	566.3	2.4	202.0	111.5	105.6	576.2
1970	25,344	24,739	22,465	602.0	2.6	188.3	111.3	104.5	612.2
1971	25,166	24,390	22,113	775.8	3.4	130.9	107.5	102.6	792.1
1972	25,244	24,386	22,116	854.9	3.7	147.3	103.8	102.1	875.6
1973	25,601	24,971	22,663	611.0	2.6	307.0	104.5	103.9	618.8
1974	25,654	25,060	22,790	599.7[5]	2.6[5]	301.6[5]	105.0	101.1	614.9[5]
1975	25,847	24,934	22,712	929.1	3.9	148.1[5]	100.0	100.0	977.6
1976	26,136	24,764	22,542	1,269.9[5]	5.3[5]	120.0[6]	96.7	100.3	1,358.8[6]
1977	26,356	24,869	22,656	1,378.1	5.8	155.6[6]	98.1	101.3	1,483.6
1978	26,394	24,914	22,710	1,375.6	5.8	210.3	97.5	101.1	1,475.0
1978 1	26,378	24,891	22,684	1,409.4	5.9	187.7	97.7	101.3	1,506.1
2	26,394	24,914	22,710	1,372.7	5.7	210.3	97.5	101.1	1,428.2
3	26,380	24,941	22,735	1,380.6	5.8	213.0	97.2	100.9	1,570.6
4	—	—	—	1,339.7	5.6	230.3	96.8	100.8	1,395.3
1979 J	—	—	—	1,339.1	5.6	235.9	96.7	100.3	1,455.3
F	—	—	—	1,362.5	5.7	230.9			1,451.9
M	—	—	—						

Source: Economic Trends No.305

[1] Unemployment figures do not include adult students registered for temporary employment during a current vacation.

[2] The working population consists of the employed labour force and the unemployed (including school-leavers); the employed labour force includes employers, self-employed and H.M. Forces as well as employees in employment.

[3] From 1971, the employees in employment estimates are based on annual census of employment. For the years before 1971 estimates are taken from the continuous employment series published in the October 1975 issue of the Department of Employment Gazette. Annual estimates relate to mid-year. From June 1976 the employees in employment figures for the U.K. are provisional until the publication of the results of the Census of Employment for June 1977. A constant component for Northern Ireland is included from December 1977.

[4] The base used in calculating the percentage rate of unemployment is the appropriate mid-year estimate of total employees (employed and unemployed); the latest figure available is that for mid-1976.

[5] The figures shown are averages of eleven months' figures.

[6] The figures shown are averages of ten months' figures.

(6) monthly statistics on stoppages of work due to disputes over pay and conditions of employment are analysed by industry, cause, duration and number of days lost.

An interesting development in the field of manpower statistics was the publication of forecasts of the future working population for the United Kingdom and Great Britain. These were first made in 1962 and have been subsequently up-dated so that currently they are projected annually up to 1991. As with the previous data the information is published in the Department of Employment *Gazette* – the latest figures in the April 1978 issue. The basis of these forecasts is the Government Actuary's forecasts of total population, and the statisticians then apply to each age and sex group the ratio between the working and total populations to estimate the working population in the years ahead. The relationship or ratio, between the working and total population in each age/sex group, is termed 'activity rate'. They are no more than estimates for among the factors influencing the activity rates are the rates of retirement, disablement, migration, school leaving, etc. Closely related to these data are the periodic studies of regional employment and unemployment, with special reference to the degree of labour migration between the regions.

It is evident from the foregoing outline of the main manpower statistics that this field is now well documented. The primary source of information is the Department of Employment *Gazette* and the student reader is urged to consult a few copies of the *Gazette* to see the type of information published.

Production

The importance for the national economy of knowing the level of production and its composition needs no emphasis at the present time. Many industries publish data relating to their activities, *e.g.* the Department of Energy publishes quarterly statements on the coal mining industry, as well as an annual digest of statistics on all forms of fuel production and consumption. *Lloyd's Register of Shipping* provides an annual return of all ships over 100 tons gross under construction in the United Kingdom. The iron and steel industry publishes a monthly bulletin of statistics containing figures relating to the level of employment, output of various products, prices, international trade, and foreign production. Invaluable as these published data undoubtedly are, they relate only to segments of the national economy. The only way to find out the total value of all production in the country is to carry out a Census of Production.

The Census of Production is the most valuable source of information available to the Central Statistical Office for computing the national product. It is particularly important in view of the information it gives relating to changes in stocks of both finished products and work in progress, as well as of materials and fuel expenditure on plant, machinery and vehicles as well as new building work.

For statistical purposes the term 'production' requires careful definition. Thus, from the economic point of view, any goods or services produced and exchanged for value constitute 'production'. The Census, however, is restricted to the extractive and manufacturing industries in both private and public ownership. The first category includes mining and quarrying, but not agriculture, the second group includes firms which are engaged in repair work for the trade, *e.g.* a ship repairer. Despite the use of the term 'Census', the enumeration of firms is far from complete. In Great Britain only those firms employing 25 or more workers return the full schedule. For smaller firms, *i.e.* those with fewer than 25 workers, a return giving the nature of the trade carried on and the number of employees only is required. In a few cases where firms employing between 11 and 25 are responsible for an important part of the industry's output they are asked to complete a Census form. It should be noted that the data derived from the Northern Ireland Censuses does not include any information relating to small firms.

Despite such limitations a Census provides much information on other points. It reveals the division of the national industrial product between the various industries. The changes in these data over time bring out the trend and relative importance of the individual industries. Without such information, central economic planning in respect of the distribution of labour and new capital construction is virtually impossible. Estimates can also be made of labour productivity and the ratio of supervisory staff to operatives in the different industries although such figures are of limited accuracy and value. Without all these data, the index of industrial production would be unreliable and estimates of the national product subject to wide margins of error.

The table opposite is an extract from the Summary Table of the Census of Production data giving some indication of the type of data collected for *all* industries covered by the Census of Production. Note, as is indicated in the footnotes, how changes in the Standard Industrial Classification have affected the comparability of the series over the years.

The first Census of Production in the United Kingdom was taken in 1907, and was followed by others in 1912, 1924 and 1930. The last pre-war Census, known as the fifth Census, was held in 1935. Since the end of the war, following upon the *Statistics of Trade Act, 1947,* a partial Census has been taken in respect of industry in 1946, while

TABLE 84

CENSUS OF PRODUCTION: SUMMARY TABLE

	Standard Industrial Classification 1968 order numbers	Gross output (production) (1) (2)	Net output (3)	Stocks and work in progress (4) — At end of year	Stocks and work in progress (4) — Change during year	Capital expenditure less disposals (5)	Wages and salaries	Average number of persons employed (6)	Net output per person employed
		£ million	£ million	£ million	£ million	£ million	£ million	Thousands	£
All Census industries									
1951	II–XXI	18,733	6,838	—	—	768	3,960	10,669	641
1954		21,897	8,435	—	—	984	4,951	10,894	774
1954		20,709	8,180	—	—	990	4,748	10,450	743
1958		26,980	10,438	—	—	1,402	6,145	10,570	988
1963		34,467	14,423	6,189	+ 176	1,884	7,799	10,705	1,347
1963		34,456	14,406	6,276	+ 169	1,886	7,793	10,684	1,348
1968		43,216	20,284	9,085	+ 594	2,662	10,316	10,263	1,976
1968		51,402	20,998	10,543	+1,009	3,081	10,651	8,801	2,386
1970(7)(8)		51,402	21,817	10,543	+1,009	3,081	10,651	8,801	2,479
1971(7)(8)		54,721	23,375	10,892	+ 493	3,125	11,580	8,576	2,725
1972(7)(8)		58,771	25,988	11,688	+ 729	2,944	12,481	8,236	3,155
1973(8)		68,509	29,584	13,800	+2,452	3,467	14,142	8,311	3,560
1974		103,037	42,740	20,246	+6,017	4,684	20,931	9,956	4,293
1975		116,734	48,795	21,515	+2,231	5,664	25,101	9,623	5,071
1976		143,239	58,561	—		6,340	28,620	9,461	6,190

Note: The figures for each year are for industries included in the Census of Production for the year. The figures for 1951 and 1954 are classified according to the 1948 edition of the Standard Industrial Classification (SIC). Those for 1954 below the line have been reclassified according to the 1958 edition of the SIC. The figures for 1958 and 1963 (above the line) are also based on the 1958 SIC. The reclassified figures for 1963 (below the line) and the figures for 1968, and from 1970 onwards are based on the 1968 edition of the SIC. The figures for 1976 are provisional estimates only. All figures include estimates for establishments not making satisfactory returns, and for establishments exempted because of their size.

Source: *Business Statistics Office*

a full Census was held in 1949 relating to industry in 1948. A Census was taken for the years 1949 and 1950, but the information then required was rather less than was required in the full Census covering the year 1948. The 1948 Census was restricted to Great Britain, *i.e.* no Census was taken in Northern Ireland, but with the passage there of an Act similar to the 1947 Act in this country, Censuses were taken in Northern Ireland for the years 1949-51 inclusive and the results incorporated with those for Great Britain in the appropriate Board of Trade Census reports for those years. It was intended to hold an annual Census of Production as from 1948 onwards. In the event, a complete Census like that of 1948, in which a great deal of detailed information was required from firms, is to be carried out now only once every five years. The years to which full Censuses refer are, since the War, 1948, 1951, 1954, 1958, 1963 and 1968. In the intervening years the Board of Trade has conducted either a restricted or limited *Census* which covers a wide range of industry with a few questions or a *sample survey*, which selects fewer industrial units, but asks the full Census range of questions. Thus a limited Census was taken for 1959 while sample surveys were taken for the years 1960-62, 1964-67 and 1969.

For purposes of the sample surveys, separate samples were drawn each year from base year size tabulations, the sampling unit being normally the larger firm or business unit. Normally one in every ten of the firms was included in the sample. The sample Census held in 1960 had a fairly broad industrial stratification consisting of 31 headings. The sampling within each stratum was random and all the units in the same stratum had an equal chance of being selected, except that, where possible, the smaller units selected in one year were excluded in the following year. The estimates of the larger establishments were obtained by multiplying the total figures for each item returned by the selected units in each sampled stratum of each industry by a 'grossing-up' factor and then adding together the results for all the strata of each industry. The grossing-up factor was the denominator of the fraction used in selecting the sample. Thus, if one firm was selected in every ten, the grossing-up factor was 10. Beginning with 1953 the figures obtained for each sampling stratum were adjusted by multiplying the results by a correction factor consisting of the ratio of total employment in the sampling field as recorded in the Census for the base year, and the estimate of employment in the base year obtained by grossing-up the base year figures for those units which were excluded from the sample. It is estimated that the sampling errors in total manufacturing industries in 1957 ranged from 0·1 per cent for employment to 1·0 per cent for capital expenditure.

Some changes were introduced in the full detailed Census for 1958. Some of these were due to the revised Standard Industrial Classification which replaced in 1958 the original version published in 1948. Apart from the changes arising from the S.I.C., an important variation was to exempt firms employing less than 25 persons as opposed to the previous practice where the exemption limit was under 11 persons. There were also some changes in the instruction governing the making of returns for two or more establishments operated by the same firm, as well as in the question on sales where increased statistics were being collected at more frequent intervals.

The full Census for 1963 included detailed questions about the different classes of goods bought and sold, and also questions about certain business expenses. Full particulars were required only from larger firms employing 25 or more persons. Information copies of the forms to be completed by larger firms were issued in 1962 to give firms the opportunity of adapting their records where necessary so that the figures required by the Census authorities could be extracted more easily.

The above outline of the history of the statistics of production has been included to show the complexity of problems that face not only the collectors of economic data but the interpreters and users of that data. The outline is historic for, in 1970, an annual Census of Production was introduced as part of a new integrated system of business statistics. However, the importance of the pre-1970 data has been recognised in the publication of the *Historical Record of the Census of Production 1907 to 1970* (H.M.S.O. 1978). In this record an attempt has been made to re-classify all the data so that it is in line with the 1968 revision of the Standard Industrial Classification and long-term comparisons are now possible.

The scope of the annual Censuses commenced in 1970 is similar to that covered by the previous Census. Questions include: (1) working proprietors; (2) employment; (3) wages and salaries; (4) stocks; (5) capital expenditure; (6) work done by other firms, transport costs and certain other expenses; (7) materials, goods and fuel purchases and sales work done are only collected in very broad outline compared with 1968.

In the purchase section (7), firms were asked for details of the items purchased as well as their total costs; but the number of items for which particulars of the quantity purchased were required as well as the value was kept to a minimum. Questions were included about the number of persons engaged on transport work, and about the costs of operating road goods vehicles. Other business costs on which questions were asked include employers' National Insurance contributions and payments to superannuation and other pension funds;

payments for rates, postage, telephone, etc.; and the cost of plant and machinery hired.

The data collected in the Census of Production do not always relate to the calendar year, although we write about the '1970' Census. To facilitate the completion of the schedules, the 'establishment' or firm may give figures relating to its *financial* year and not the calendar year. The effect of this concession is that '1970' for example, can mean any 12-month period ending between 6th April 1970 and 5th April 1971. According to Mr H. Leak, a former director of the Census, the mean year-end of the reporting firms is mid-December.

The Department of Trade publishes reports on each industry covered in the Census. In addition, for each Census at the commencement of the publication of these industry reports, a document entitled 'Introductory Notes' is produced. This contains a detailed account of the scope and scale of the Census together with the definitions employed as well as an explanation of the tables published in the individual industry reports. Whenever data are to be extracted from the industry reports, although the latter contain notes relating to the tables, it is advisable to turn to the fuller 'Introductory Notes' to avoid errors in extraction.

For each industry the following data are given:

   1 Number of enterprises, *i.e.* groups of firms commonly owned;
   2 Number of establishments, *i.e.* number of premises;
   3 Sales of goods produced and work done;
   4 Sales of goods bought (including canteen takings);
   5 Purchases of materials and fuel;
 6-7 Products on hand for sale;
 8-9 Work in progress;
10-11 Stocks of materials and fuel;
  12 Payments for work done;
  13 Payments for transport;
14-15 Customs and Excise duties;
16-17 Net output;
18-19 Average number employed;
20-21 Total wages and salaries;
      Capital expenditure is separately classified
  22 New building work;
23-24 Plant and equipment: acquisitions and disposals;
25-26 Vehicles: acquisitions and disposals.

The Census of Production, however, suffers from the inevitable disadvantage of any attempt to provide comprehensive and accurate data. It is comparatively expensive to collect and takes some little time to process and publish. To fill the need for up-to-date indications of trends between Censuses the Department of Trade publish in *Trade and Industry* series of sample statistics relating to various aspects of industry. These statistics include information on:

(i) capital expenditure by types of industry;

(ii) industrial building;

(iii) orders, deliveries, production and exports in mechanical and electrical engineering;

(iv) production of man-made fibres;

(v) changes in the volume of industry's stocks at 1970 prices, seasonally adjusted;

(vi) textiles including indices of production of made up clothing and orders and deliveries of textiles, and volume of production of cotton and wool;

(vii) deliveries of scientific and industrial instruments and apparatus;

(viii) sales and stocks of plastic material;

(ix) production and exports of cars and commercial vehicles; and

(x) registrations of business names.

This list is not exhaustive, but it gives an indication of the steps that have been taken to provide comprehensive and up-to-date information on various sectors of the national economy.

The statistics are usually published quarterly but there are some variations, *e.g.* car production is reported monthly. In addition some annual reviews are carried out covering particular industries.

It is essential that the difference in nature between the Census figures and these supplementary sample statistics is clearly understood. The former are complete enumerations; the latter are more in the nature of estimates and are more significant in the changes they show from period to period than in their absolute totals.

For the benefit of businessmen the Department of Trade also provide a statistical survey for individual industries on a subscription basis, known as the Business Monitor series. (See pp. 597-8).

Index of Industrial Production

The purpose of the Index of Industrial Production is to provide a general measure of monthly changes in the level of industrial production in the United Kingdom. The index is prepared by the Central Statistical Office in collaboration with the various statistical divisions of certain Ministries, in particular the Department of Trade. The index is published monthly in the *Monthly Digest of Statistics* and *Trade and Industry.* An official account of the construction of the index is published by H.M.S.O. in Studies in Official Statistics No. 25. *The Measurement of Changes in Production.*

The index of industrial production covers mining and quarrying, manufacturing, building and the public utilities, gas, electricity and water, but excludes trade, agriculture, transport and all other public and private transport. The precise coverage of the index is brought out in the following table.

PERCENTAGE CONTRIBUTIONS TO GROSS DOMESTIC PRODUCT, 1975
Industries included in the index of industrial production:

	%
Manufacturing	28·2
Mining and quarrying	1·7
Construction	7·5
Gas, electricity and water	3·3
Total	40·7

Industries excluded from the index:

Agriculture, forestry and fishing	2·8
Distributive trades	10·1
Transport and communication	8·8
Other services	37·6
Total G.D.P. at factor cost	100·0

While the index is designed to reflect changes in the level of industrial production from month to month, the individual series or indicators used in the construction of the index are often weekly or quarterly, and sometimes annual, rates of production. In fact, about half the series upon which the various indicators are based are for calendar months; the remainder are for weekly or quarterly periods. Since it is the purpose of the index to compare the level of production in different months, corrections have to be made for the fact that calendar months do not all contain the same number of working days. Furthermore, some contain four and others five Saturdays, a day upon which production is likely to be considerably lower than on other days of the week. Such vagaries of the calendar have as far as possible to be eliminated.

The index has been calculated with the average monthly production for 1975 as the base period, for each month from January 1975. There have been previous bases of this index and on the occasion of each change of base the Central Statistical Office has calculated a number of back years on the new base to provide a sufficient overlap on the old and new bases to effect some continuity. This is reasonably effective for the 'all manufacturing industries' index, but much care is needed in attempting long-term comparisons of movements in the indices of individual industries.

The index is a weighted arithmetic mean combining individual production series weighted in proportion to the net output of each industry covered by the index. The latter figures are derived from the

Census of Production and are adjusted by deducting the estimated amounts paid for services rendered to the industries by firms outside the field covered by the index, *e.g.* insurance and advertising. Nearly all production series are incorporated in the index, most of which represent physical quantities produced. Where output figures are not available alternatives such as the consumption of raw materials, or the numbers of persons employed, have been used. For some industries, however, value series are used, adjusted to eliminate changes in price by using the index of Wholesale Prices. If the individual product of an industry takes a long time to produce, as in shipbuilding and construction of buildings, the amount of work in progress is taken into account. Large engineering contracts are treated in the same way.

Not all the series on which the indicators are based are available when the index for each month is first prepared, since a large number of sources are used and some of them are available only quarterly. Thus the advantage of an up-to-date index of production has to be weighed against the dangers of early estimates based on insufficient data, which may prove wrong. At present the index is published six to seven weeks after the end of the month to which it relates. By then about 40 per cent of the data used are in final form and there are provisional figures for another 40 per cent of the indicators.

A complete list of the series and weights used in the index on the 1975 base awaits publication. The indices are published in two series; the second of which is merely the first adjusted for holidays and other seasonal causes of variation in production. The second series is designed to eliminate normal month-to-month fluctuations and thus to show the trend more clearly. Nevertheless, the seasonally corrected series should not be regarded as in any way more reliable than the uncorrected series, nor are they intended to replace them.

The correction for seasonal variation is based on the assumption that the seasonal pattern for recent years will recur in the current year. Nevertheless, the seasonal pattern may be changing and hence it must be kept constantly under review and reassessed each year.

The adjustments for seasonal variation are made in two stages. The first step is to adjust the indices for those movements which arise from regular public holidays and annual holidays. When the effect of holidays has been removed the annual average is adjusted so that it equals the average of the unadjusted indices. The second step is to calculate a seasonal adjustment factor for each month using the moving average method (see Chapter XI). The vast amount of calculation involved in the second step has been greatly facilitated by performing the work on an electronic computer.

While the substantial improvement in this index since its introduction is freely acknowledged, it would be a mistake to place too much emphasis on month-to-month changes. For both the ordinary monthly, as well as the 'seasonally adjusted', indices it is the general persistent movement in one direction or another which is the most satisfactory and reliable guide to production levels. Thus, an official comment on the index advises that a better indication of the underlying trend of industrial production is probably obtained by comparing a run of months, taking say the average of the last three or four.

Table 85 entitled Index of Industrial Production is reproduced (in part only) from *Economic Trends No. 305*, and shows the major industrial groupings for which monthly, quarterly and annual indices are produced and published.

Distribution

Almost a century and a half elapsed after Napoleon described this country as a 'nation of shopkeepers' before official action was taken to ascertain the truth of this comment! In 1977 over 10 per cent of the working population was engaged in the distributive trades, a total of 2·7 million persons. A further 5·6 million workers were engaged in service trades and occupations, an increase of 1·2 million, or over 25 per cent, within a decade. With rising living standards and new technological processes in production, the proportion of the working population engaged in distribution and services will continue to increase. The term 'distribution' covers all the various channels through which goods pass from the manufacturer or grower (in the case of food) to the final consumer, *i.e.* all wholesalers and retailers. Included with these for the purpose of the Census are the service trades such as hairdressing, shoe repairing and garages. The first Census of distribution ever was taken in Great Britain by the then Board of Trade in 1951. Before this, information on the extent of the distributive trades, the number of shops, scale of their activities as reflected in the number of employees, their wage bill and annual turnover were unknown. Even the number of distribution outlets could only be estimated at something over three-quarters of a million as compared with an actual figure in 1951 of about 583,000.

A government committee set up in June 1945 recommended the taking of a Census and the government acquired powers to conduct such an enquiry under the 1947 Act. The Census was conducted by post during 1951 and the respondents were asked to provide information relating to their activities in 1950. The same concession regarding use of the firm's financial year in place of the calendar year was made as is given in the Census of Production. Traders were given three months to complete the forms but it may be noted in passing

TABLE 85

INDEX OF INDUSTRIAL PRODUCTION

Seasonally adjusted 1975=100

	By industry					By market sector*		
	All industries covered	Mining and quarrying	Manufacturing	Construction	Gas, electricity and water	Consumer goods industries	Investment goods industries	Intermediate goods industries
1975 weights	*1,000*	*41*	*697*	*182*	*80*	*243*	*218*	*349*
1968	97·0	132·4	94·1	114·4	77·0	86·9	90·6	100·7
1969	99·6	123·9	97·6	113·5	80·9	89·4	95·7	102·9
1970	99·7	119·1	98·0	111·4	84·1	91·0	95·6	103·0
1971	99·8	119·1	97·4	113·3	87·3	93·3	93·7	102·1
1972	102·0	100·2	100·0	115·4	93·6	99·9	91·2	104·1
1973	109·5	110·2	108·3	118·2	99·3	108·0	99·0	112·6
1974	105·1	90·0	106·5	105·8	99·2	106·1	102·1	106·1
1975	100·0	100·0	100·0	100·0	100·0	100·0	100·0	100·0
1976	102·0	125·7	101·4	98·6	102·9	101·9	96·1	107·5
1977	105·8	187·6	102·8	98·2	107·0	104·6	97·9†	115·3†
1978	109·7	233·0†	103·5†	105·3†	109·9†	106·6	98·2	121·2
Qtrs 1	107·0	209·5	102·2	101·9	107·7	105·2†	98·8	116·2
2	110·7	229·5	104·5	107·3	112·0	107·8	98·2	122·4
3	111·4	236·8	104·9	107·2	112·7	107·6	98·8	123·2
4	109·6	256·3	102·5	105·0	107·2	105·8	96·2	123·0
Mths O	108·5	243	101·7	—	106	105	96	121
N	109·4	261	102·3	—	103	106	96	122
D	111·0	265	103·4	—	112	106	97	126

* All industries other than construction.
† Provisional.

Source: Economic Trends No.305

that not merely was the response very slow but that a number of prosecutions arose from failure to make the statutory return. Despite the great efforts made to ensure the co-operation of the traders, many were suspicious of the authorities' intentions and unwilling to co-operate. In consequence, the accuracy of some of the returns must inevitably be a matter for speculation.

Before the forms could be distributed it was necessary to carry out a Census of the distributive and related service trade establishments in the country. This was done during May to October 1950; enumerators all over the country listed the names and addresses of traders apparently falling within the scope of the Census – note – 'as far as could be judged from the outside of trading premises'. This is an interesting example of the difficulties encountered when a sampling frame is either non-existent as in this case and has to be built up, or is seriously defective. In this particular example the funds were made available for a complete enumeration before the Census. The enumerators distinguished between shops, stalls, yards, depots and other types of premises. It should be noted that the enumeration staff had instructions not to enter the premises or question traders or their employees; the basis of their description as indicated above, was visual.

The purpose of the Census – as distinct from the enumeration which preceded it – was to provide:

(1) Information about the number and size of wholesale and retail outlets and other establishments providing consumer services.

(2) Information regarding the value of the services rendered to enable more accurate estimates of the national product to be made.

(3) A measure of the relative efficiency of the distributive system as between different regions in the country, *e.g.* which areas have the most shops of certain kinds per head of the population and what is their turnover.

Apart from the above information which was primarily of interest to the government in respect of its economic policies, the Census was to provide further information which would be of interest to traders and their trade associations. Quite apart from their natural concern with the distribution of various types of shops throughout the country, they would have an interest in the turnover, wage bills, level of stocks maintained and methods of delivery employed.

The data assembled as a result of the pre-Census enumeration are reproduced in a publication entitled *Britain's Shops* and a detailed account is given of the enumeration, its difficulties and methods in the introduction to that report, which is better described by its sub-title, *A Statistical Summary of Shops and Service Establishments*. This particular report is quite distinct from the 1951 Census of Distribution reports themselves. There are, of course, differences in classification and of coverage. For example, the Census proper obtained a 91 per cent response (of all the outlets enumerated in the above enumeration) which was estimated to cover 95 per cent of the total trade of the retail establishments enumerated.

The Verdon Smith Committee on the Censuses of Distribution and Production had recommended in 1954 (*Cmnd. 9276*) among other things, that full Censuses of distribution should be taken every 10 years and that sample surveys should be taken from time to time in the interval between Censuses. The first of these sample surveys was taken for 1957 and the preliminary results published early in 1959.

One of the most interesting features of this survey was the manner in which the sample was selected. The aim was to include all traders with an annual turnover of over £100,000. These included all multiple retailers, all except the smallest cooperative societies, department stores, etc., but while it is fairly easy to enumerate all these larger traders with reasonable accuracy, there was no way of obtaining an up-to-date list of all other smaller independent traders. This object could only be achieved as in 1950 by enumerating them in a special Census for that purpose. The remainder of the sample covering these independents was therefore taken on a geographical basis as follows:

(i) New Towns, Central London and a few special areas where great changes were thought to have occurred since 1950; all retail trades were enumerated and a sample of one in five taken.

(ii) Greater London: a sample of electoral wards stratified by size was taken, distinguishing between shopping and mainly residential areas, and all shops in the selected wards were included in the survey.

(iii) Large towns (population 100,000 or more): a sample of streets stratified by size, *i.e.* number of shops in 1950, was taken.

(iv) Other towns were sampled by taking a cross-section of the local authority areas and sometimes stratifying the areas by size, by sales in 1950, and by population change since 1950.

(v) Rural Districts were also sampled by region after stratifying by size, either by population density or by population change since 1950.

The Census was carried out by post with a very energetic follow-up which gave an 89 per cent return from independent retailers, compared with a 96 per cent response from the larger traders, *i.e.* multiples, etc. So thorough was the follow-up that returns were obtained from 75 per cent of street traders, pedlars, hawkers and itinerant market traders! The 1957 totals were estimated by compiling 1950 as well as 1957 figures for the sample and calculating the ratio of 1957 to 1950 figures. These ratios were applied to the known 1950 totals to give the 1957 estimates. The information obtained in the Census included the number of establishments, turnover and number of people engaged in the establishments. All this information was analysed both by the form of the organisation and the kind of business.

Since the 1957 survey results were based upon sample data, the published statistics are subject to sampling errors. These have been calculated for each figure under the general classification of 'independent traders', *i.e.* Turnover, Number of establishments and persons engaged, for each category of business or trade. Allowance for the effect of the error on the total results, *i.e.* independent plus large-scale retailers, is also made in the corresponding figures for 'all traders'. However, for all the industry an error of less than half of one per cent is given. The error is larger than this for individual items but considering that the sample was one of 12 per cent, *i.e.* covering about 57,000 establishments out of a total of 480,000, the accuracy seems reasonable and quite adequate for administrative and statistical needs.

The 1957 sample survey covered the retail trade only and, to bring the picture of the distributive field up to date, in 1959 an enquiry was carried out into the wholesale trades. The main purpose of this enquiry was to obtain substantially complete figures of stocks and capital expenditure in the wholesale trades as new starting points for subsequent annual and quarterly estimates, rather than to provide a detailed analysis of wholesale trading. To avoid the considerable cost of listing every wholesale business, the register for this enquiry was compiled from the register of companies, known undertakings employing more than five people and other sources such as marketing boards, cooperative societies, etc. It is estimated that companies amounting to only 5·4 per cent of the total activity were excluded. Estimates for non-response and unsatisfactory returns accounted for a further 1·7 per cent. The information collected was limited to figures of receipts and stocks and capital expenditure, together with the particulars necessary for classifying returns by kind of business.

Full Censuses of Distribution have since been taken in 1961 and 1971 with a sample survey in 1966. The 1971 Census of Distribution and Other Services collected data on the following from retailers:

(*a*) the nature of the business, *e.g.* was it part of a retailer's buying group, was it self-service or mail-order;

(*b*) turnover;

(*c*) purchases;

(*d*) number of employees;

(*e*) wages and salaries;

(*f*) stock;

(*g*) capital expenditure;

(*h*) sales on hire purchase or instalment credit;

(*i*) book debts;

(*j*) transport costs; and

(*k*) floor space.

The service trades were asked to supply a more limited range of information. The results of the Census were published in 13 parts. Part 1 gave overall results for Great Britain; Parts 2-12 gave results by regions, towns and principal shopping centres; Part 13 gave data analysed by the nature of the business.

Overleaf is an extract of a summary table from the *Annual Abstract of Statistics* that compares some information obtained from the 1966 sample Census with the 1971 full Census.

It may be thought that a gap of some years between the transactions recorded and the publication of results of a Census is an unnecessary length of time, and it is worthwhile explaining this apparent delay. The first part of the explanation is that with an operation of this magnitude, a half-million retailers are involved, it takes many months for the returns to come in. The returns in the Census for 1961 were not all in 20 months after the end of 1961. In all, returns were received from 87 per cent of the establishments for 1961 and 78 per cent for 1971.

Secondly, it cannot be assumed that the information given on every return received is complete and correct. Where errors are found in returns, and the causes thereof are not obvious, it is necessary to write and ask for corrections to be made. This absorbs a good deal of time. A still greater volume of correspondence arises from letters written to the Department of Trade by traders, asking questions about the Census forms and their completion.

Apart from dealing with correspondence, there are a number of processes to be carried out on all Census of Distribution returns before any results can be compiled. The first of these consists of a quick examination to see that the returns are complete, and made on the appropriate form; it is at this stage that queries are raised if, for example, turnover figures are missing. The next stage is to assign numerical codes for certain items of information as a preparation for mechanical analysis; in addition to the area codes incorporated in the reference numbers, codes are assigned, for example, for the year of return, legal status, membership of buying groups, and special methods of trading such as by self-service. Additional coding is

TABLE 86
ALL ESTABLISHMENTS: GREAT BRITAIN

	1966			1971		
	Number	Turnover £ thousand	Number of persons engaged	Number	Turnover £ thousand	Number of persons engaged
Total retail trade		11,757,314			16,685,462	
Retail shops[1]	504,412	11,131,816	2,555,737	472,991	15,610,730	2,541,430
Co-operative societies	26,684	1,015,938	173,458	15,413	1,107,999	132,204
Multiples[2]	73,852	3,837,244	741,833	66,785	6,083,560	814,666
Independents[3]	403,876	6,278,634	1,640,446	390,793	8,419,171	1,594560
Grocers and provision dealers	123,385	2,907,655	522,343	105,283	4,156,487	542,676
Other food retailers:	104,359	2,081,314	459,358	92,524	2,614,683	418,437
Dairymen	4,456	442,342	67,320	3,853	563,190	59,287
Butchers	38,351	727,972	139,073	33,939	894,174	123,614
Fishmongers, poulterers	5,466	80,402	20,331	4,678	82,456	15,481
Greengrocers, fruiterers (including those selling fish)	27,172	314,180	89,195	23,318	383,058	85,917
Bread and flour confectioners	18,099	292,629	114,778	17,299	332,598	106,421
Off-licences	10,815	223,789	28,661	9,437	359,207	27,717
Confectioners, tobacconists, newsagents	63,333	1,045,572	297,762	52,064	1,305,875	275,458
Clothing and footwear shops	83,095	1,719,336	410,503	81,279	2,371,766	403,744
Footwear shops	13,519	258,909	65,229	13,445	349,347	68,661
Men's and boys' wear shops	15,099	350,246	72,153	14,619	482,527	71,046
Women's and girls' wear, household textiles and general clothing shops	54,477	1,110,181	273,121	53,215	1,539,891	264,037

[1]Excluding Electricity and Gas Board showrooms.
[2]Organisations, other than co-operative societies, with 10 or more branches.
[3]Organisations, other than co-operative societies, with less than 10 branches.

Source: Business Statistics Office

required in respect of branch shops of multiple organisations, each of which must be given the appropriate area code among others. Classification to one of 69 different kinds of business is carried out as a separate operation, and though the classification rules have been somewhat simplified, they are still quite complex.

Once the data are classified, the information is fed into computers, and is then ready for processing. Preliminary to the final processing, once a sufficiently large batch of returns is available in each kind of business, an analysis is made of certain key ratios, *e.g.* turnover per person employed. The object of this analysis is to determine the distribution of these ratios and to determine the limits outside which queries will be raised regarding the validity of individual returns. In other words, the statisticians provide themselves with basic standards against which they can judge the validity of their informants' data.

Delays in publication and a revision of the old system of large infrequent Censuses have resulted in the introduction of a new sequence of annual sample surveys. The first of these annual surveys was carried out in 1977 in respect of 1976. The new scheme takes advantage of the information about businesses obtained through the Value Added Tax system and sampling procedures will reduce the burden of form filling upon a large number of smaller retailers. The sample design means that fewer than 30,000 out of a total of some 300,000 have to fill in forms at all, 6,000 retailers only have to fill in the full Census forms, while the remaining 24,000 complete only a shortened version of the form. The data collected include total turnover, capital expenditure, stocks, purchases for resale, V.A.T. charged, credit sales and outstanding debts. It was originally intended to include a rotating list of questions to be asked some years but not in others. This idea, however, has been shelved for economy reasons.

A large scale enquiry into wholesaling was carried out in 1965 and again in 1974. The information collected was similar to that asked of the retailers.

Information arising from the enquiries mentioned above, together with monthly samples of retail sales, stocks and related topics are all published first in the Department of Trade's weekly journal now known as *Trade and Industry*. As will be seen below much of this information is converted into index numbers. This is partly for ease of comparison but it also underlines that the monthly sample data are much more important for policy and certainly more reliable in terms of indicating basic trends over several months than in measuring absolute changes from month to month.

National Income

The national income may be defined as the money value of the nation's output of all goods and services in a given period, usually a year. This aggregate is also referred to as the national output, since these incomes represent the cost of producing the output of goods and services. It follows, therefore, that there are two ways of measuring the national income; either all the incomes of the factors of production, or the values of each industry's output, may be aggregated. Before discussing the various problems that arise in measuring these aggregates, it is important to understand their purpose. It is clearly desirable to know what the nation's economy is producing in any year, as well as comparing one year with another to ascertain the rate of economic progress. All production is intended ultimately to satisfy consumer needs. The more that is produced, the more the community may consume, *i.e.* the higher its standard of living. Aggregate consumption is not the only measure of living standards. How hard and in what conditions does the population work in order to achieve a given output of goods? Consumption can be increased in the short run merely by living off capital. Is the community 'better off' if instead of 10,000 new houses it produces 50,000 new cars? In the sum of the national product these will represent about the same money value. It is also important to note the definition of national income used by the statisticians in different countries. For example, in an under-developed rural economy food grown and consumed on peasant holdings would represent a significant part of the national product. In the United Kingdom economy vegetables grown in gardens and allotments are not counted in national income estimates. Another important omission is the money value of housewives' services in the home which are unpaid. If they were valued in money terms, the national income in money terms would rise by at least 20 per cent. Colin Clark has attempted a more detailed estimate of the value of housewives' services. A full account of this estimate is published in the Bulletin of the Oxford Institute of Statistics.* Alternatively, if the housewives went out to work and paid some of the present factory or office workers to do their housework, although the real national income would not have changed, it would have increased considerably in money terms. Much the same conceptual problem arises with work for which no payment is received. Thus, a man working an allotment and consuming the produce at home adds nothing to the 'national income'. If, however, he and his neighbour sold each other their respective produce, the value of the produce added should, in theory, be added into the national income. Other problems arise in connection with the services of government, *e.g.* should the salaries of civil servants be included since they add nothing tangible to the national product? The same argument can perhaps be applied with more justice to the payments to members of the armed forces in peace-time.

These conceptual differences as to what should be included in the 'national income' make international comparisons extremely difficult, *e.g.* valuation of home-produced food in an agrarian economy. There have been several conferences under the auspices of U.N.O., with the purpose of standardising practice. Apart from these problems the differences in the reliability of various statistical data in different countries pose a problem which will probably not be solved for many years yet. Any published international comparisons should be scruti-

*Vol. 20, No. 2, May 1958.

nised with these considerations in mind, particularly estimates made of the annual rate of economic 'growth'.

The national income estimates are so prepared and presented, that they offer a comprehensive picture of the operations of the economy and the inter-relationships between various sectors. To the extent that the statistical data assembled in the annual Blue Book on the National Income and Expenditure are complete and accurate, overall economic planning is greatly facilitated. National income estimates for this purpose were first prepared officially by the Treasury in 1941, and used by the Chancellor as a background to the Budget statement in that year. In each of the next ten years a White Paper on these estimates was published a short while before the Budget statement. Since 1952 a Blue Book, which appears in the autumn, has appeared annually. The pre-Budget document is a short White Paper containing preliminary estimates of the main aggregates. Before 1941 there had been several private estimates of the national income or output. Various methods were used to arrive at these estimates. Unfortunately the accuracy of the figures was greatly impaired by the shortcomings of the data then available. Despite great improvements, even now the limitations of the data are such that in each year the successive Blue Books contain amended figures for previous years. The volume of data on which these estimates may be based has been considerably expanded and their quality improved, but even 23 years after the first White Paper appeared, several of the more important aggregates remain little more than approximations.

As indicated above, the origins of the national income accounts, as they are termed, derive from the efforts to apply the theories of employment evolved by Keynes just before the war. Since then, the national income accounts have formed the statistical basis of national economic planning, which is concerned with estimating the prospective levels of consumer expenditure, investment, exports, etc. Although the deficiencies of the published data were remarked on above, this is a reflection of the complexity of the task of bringing together statistics, not just from one part of the economy, but from every sector, private and public, financial, overseas, as well as industry, both private and nationalised, etc. When one remembers that nowadays not merely annual accounts, but also quarterly accounts are produced within months after the end of the relevant period, the scale of the statistical exercise can be imagined. For example, Sir Claus Moser in his lecture* observed that data on retail sales come from some half a million shops which must be sampled, data on exports and imports of goods and services must be collected; the Family Expenditure Survey provides data on private consumption of

* Op. cit.

goods and services. The difficulties of obtaining data apply to every sector of the economy and, in these days of inflation, the statisticians working on the national income estimates have also to adjust the money figures on to a common basis to facilitate comparison over time. This particular exercise is known as 'price deflation' and, both conceptually and in practice, it raises very difficult problems.

The published data are based upon material derived from three main sources, although these must be supplemented by information culled from a wide range of other sources. Even so the coverage is in many cases incomplete, while further difficulties arise from the fact that much of the published data used has in fact been compiled for purposes other than national income estimates.

The three main sources of data are the statistics assembled by the Inland Revenue, the Censuses of Production and Distribution and lastly the accounts of the central government. The significance of the last mentioned source may be better appreciated when it is remembered that the government is responsible for the expenditure of over two-fifths of the national income. Of these data those derived from the Inland Revenue are the most complete and accurate; those compiled from the Census of Production the least reliable.

The national income can be visualised in three ways:

(i) as a sum of incomes derived from economic activity, *i.e.* from employment and profits;

(ii) as a sum of expenditure, *i.e.* consumption and investment;

(iii) as a sum of the net products of the various industries of the nation.

These three views of the national income tend to explain the ways in which the statistics are presented and the estimates compiled. Some of the more frequently employed aggregates are given in Table 87 below, which illustrates the income approach in practice, *i.e.* those countries with a well-developed fiscal system. The various types of income are given in the upper part of the table and they are largely self-explanatory. The *residual error* is the balancing figure between the two separate estimates of the gross national product, the one based on incomes and the other on expenditure. The sub-aggregate is described as the total domestic income before depreciation and stock appreciation. These items inflate all the above incomes except rent and income from employment. An adjustment is made to eliminate the element of stock appreciation which may be defined as the increase in money terms in the value of stock distinct from a change in its physical quantity. The figures given for this item are little better than guesses, 'hazardous approximations' is the official description. Nevertheless, as will be seen from Table 87 it is an extremely im-

TABLE 87

GROSS NATIONAL PRODUCT BY CATEGORY OF INCOME   £ million

	1967	1970	1973	1975	1977
Factor Incomes					
Income from employment	23,761	30,404	43,564	68,289	85,839
Income from self-employment[1]	2,835	3,735	6,800	8,818	11,608
Gross trading profits of companies[1,2]	4,625	5,930	8,932	9,762	14,813
Gross trading surplus of public corporations[1]	1,132	1,447	2,063	3,093	5,035
Gross trading surplus of general government enterprises[1]	110	151	139	177	194
Rent[3]	1,989	2,833	4,256	6,476	8,922
Imputed charge for consumption of non-trading capital	247	332	541	857	1,176
Total domestic income[1]	34,699	44,832	66,295	97,472	127,587
less Stock appreciation	−194	−1,038	−2,994	−5,520	−5,317
Gross domestic product (Income-based)	34,505	43,794	63,301	91,952	122,270
Residual error	420	−349	645	555	1,083
Gross domestic product (expenditure-based)	34,925	43,445	63,946	92,507	123,353
Net property income from abroad	378	556	1,220	763	438
Gross national product	35,303	44,001	65,166	93,270	123,791
less Capital consumption	−3,266	−4,434	−6,890	−11,091	−15,801
National income (i.e. net national product)	32,037	39,567	58,276	82,179	107,990

[1]Before providing for depreciation and stock appreciation.
[2]Including financial institutions.
[3]Before providing for depreciation.

Source: National Income and Expenditure 1967-77

portant item, more especially in periods of rapidly changing prices.

The figure described as the *gross national product* at factor cost should be distinguished from the total defined as the net *national income*. The difference between the net and gross figures is accounted for by the depreciation of capital equipment in the country. Unfortunately the data relating to depreciation or 'capital consumption' are unreliable and incomplete.

However, commencing in 1956 estimates of capital expenditure have been published in the Blue Book. The methods adopted in making the present estimates of capital consumption were first applied to United Kingdom data by Redfern. A paper describing these methods 'Net Investment in Fixed Assets in the United Kingdom 1938-1953' was published in the *Journal of the Royal Statistical Society* in 1955. The methods currently in use are a development of Redfern's ideas but do not depart significantly from his original conceptions.

Very briefly, there are three stages in arriving at a figure for capital consumption:

(i) estimate gross fixed capital formation in each past year for each class of asset separately distinguished;

(ii) a length of life of each class of asset is assumed and its capital value written down on a straight line basis (*i.e.* a constant amount is written off each year);

(iii) indices of building prices for each class of asset are applied to the estimates of gross fixed capital formation (in (i)) thus converting them from a current to a constant (1975) price basis.

Data for these estimates are derived from the following principal sources:

(*a*) census of production for investment by private industry in plant, machinery and buildings;

(*b*) statistics of road vehicle registration and of houses built for private owners;

(*c*) statistics of gross capital formation, but these are limited to a few large industries.

It will be appreciated that estimates for long-lived assets, *e.g.* houses, may have to be made for many years back. Hence, these are of very little validity.

Estimates of capital formation in stocks and work in progress were originally on an 'establishment' basis and on the 1948 Standard Industrial Classification. They are now on a 'business unit' basis and the 1968 Standard Industrial Classification.*

The second method of estimating the gross domestic income is given in Table 88. The correspondence between the value of the national product and national income was mentioned earlier. In this table the gross products of various industries and sectors of the economy are given for three years. Similar adjustments in respect of stock appreciation and the residual error are made in this table. Most of the data upon which these figures are based are derived from the censuses of distribution and production, but since these are held only at intervals, the reliability of the final results cannot be as great as could be wished. By carrying out sample surveys in the fields of both industry and distribution in the years between the full-scale Censuses, the Blue Book estimates for these years are much improved.

As can be seen from the table opposite to convert gross domestic income to national income the net property income from abroad must be added on and the capital consumption subtracted.

Table 89 shows the gross national product by categories of expenditure. This particular method can be the least satisfactory of the three, particularly in a country where data relating to consumer outlays on various commodities and services are extremely unreliable and subject to a considerable margin of error. The composition of the

* A business unit may consist of several establishments. For example, a company may operate several plants.

TABLE 88

GROSS DOMESTIC PRODUCT BY INDUSTRY[1]   £ million

	1967	1970	1973	1975	1977
Agriculture, forestry and fishing	1,105	1,246	1,957	2,541	3,447
Mining and quarrying[2]	675	634	818	1,535	3,627
Manufacturing[2,3]	11,194	14,207	18,805	25,641	35,279
Construction	2,373	3,043	5,136	6,819	8,062
Gas, electricity and water[2]	1,145	1,384	1,910	2,987	4,296
Transport	2,087	2,736	3,834	5,270	6,641
Communication	753	1,015	1,618	2,832	3,603
Distributive trades	3,910	4,573	6,676	9,253	12,657
Insurance, banking, finance and business services	2,137	2,871	5,152	6,612	9,171
Ownership of dwellings	1,672	2,368	3,569	5,593	7,787
Public administration and defence	2,247	2,934	4,374	7,323	9,159
Public health and educational services	1,779	2,353	3,702	7,183	8,786
Other services	4,416	5,768	8,329	12,015	14,546
Total	35,493	45,132	65,880	95,604	127,061
Adjustment for financial services	−988	−1,338	−2,579	−3,652	−4,791
Residual error	420	−349	645	555	1,083
Gross domestic product at factor cost	34,925	43,445	63,946	92,507	123,353

[1]The contribution of each industry to the gross domestic product before providing for depreciation but after providing for stock appreciation.
[2]The estimated contributions of the Energy industries [4] to the gross domestic product after providing for stock appreciation are as follows (£ million):

1968	1969	1970	1971	1972	1973	1974	1975	1976	1977
1,780	1,810	1,830	2,020	2,370	2,560	2,840	4,060	5,380	7,440

[3]Figures for individual industries for certain years are shown in Table 00.
[4]Comprising minimum list headings 101, 104, 261, 262, 263, 601 and 602 of the *Standard Industrial Classification, 1968.*

Source: National Income and Expenditure 1967-77.

aggregate in this table requires no explanation, except to point out that taxes on expenditure are the outlay taxes which inflate the prices of goods which are purchased by consumers and public authorities, so the sub-total of £182,814mn. defined as total domestic expenditure in 1977. To change 'market prices' to 'factor prices' outlay taxes must be deducted and subsidies added back. In connection with these data, it should be noted that the Blue Books contain detailed analyses of consumer expenditure over a period of years. To bring out more clearly the shifts in consumer outlays between different categories of goods and services, the annual money outlays are corrected for price changes.

The profits arising from the revised valuation of stocks held by companies and trading concerns inflate the annual trading profits for the relevant years, and tax was assessed on these profits. It is a moot point whether such 'income' should be included, but in view of other arbitrary decisions that have to be made in computing the national income, its inclusion in most years makes no significant difference.

The advantages of computing the national income totals by various methods are obvious. The numerous cross-checks which are thereby made possible, especially in the various sub-totals, are invaluable. The modern method of constructing the National Income accounts, known as 'Social Accounting', is simply the adaptation of double-

TABLE 89

GROSS NATIONAL PRODUCT BY CATEGORY OF EXPENDITURE   £ million

	Reference number	1967	1970	1973	1975	1977
At market prices:						
Consumers' expenditure	*1*	25,491	31,660	45,187	63,192	83,530
General government final consumption	*2, 3*	7,194	8,962	13,327	22,930	29,121
Gross domestic fixed capital formation	*4*	7,524	9,453	14,149	20,817	25,429
Value of physical increase in stocks and work in progress		353	533	1,724	−1,925	1,288
Total domestic expenditure		40,562	50,608	74,387	105,014	139,368
Exports of goods and services	*6a, 6b*	7,382	11,491	17,204	26,943	43,446
Total final expenditure		47,944	62,099	91,591	131,957	182,814
less Imports of goods and services[1]	*7a, 7b*	−7,823	−11,122	−18,965	−29,028	−42,354
Gross domestic product at market prices[2]	*8*	40,121	50,977	72,626	102,929	140,460
Net property income from abroad[2]	*9*	378	556	1,220	763	438
Gross national product at market prices	*10*	40,499	51,533	73,846	103,692	140,898
Factor cost adjustment:						
Taxes on expenditure	*11, 12*	5,997	8,416	10,122	14,162	20,440
Subsidies	*13, 14*	801	884	1,442	3,740	3,333
Taxes *less* Subsidies		5,196	7,532	8,680	10,422	17,107

[1]Excluding taxes on expenditure levied on imports.
[2]Including taxes on expenditure levied on imports.

Source: National Income and Expenditure 1967–77

entry book-keeping principles.* Its value lies in the fact that every sub-total appears twice in the accounts and if it does not 'fit' in with the expected value as indicated by the size of the other totals in that particular section of the accounts, there is presumably some error. The difficulty is that a system of statistics of national income and expenditure must be comprehensive to be of use and an estimate must be included for each item that appears in a balancing account. It is not possible to base all the estimates on accurately recorded facts nor is it possible to calculate statistical 'margins of error' of the kind derived from random samples. What is done, however, is to form very rough judgements of the range of reasonable doubt attaching to the estimates. Some standardisation is obtained by grading each of the major components as having a margin of error of:

A ± less than 3 per cent,

B ± 3 per cent to 10 per cent,

or C ± more than 10 per cent.

As far as the various methods of deriving the various aggregates are

*For an account of the construction of such accounts see *National Income and Social Accounting* by Edey and Peacock, Hutchinson.

concerned, the correspondence of the three aggregates of the national income, product and outlay, while not necessarily proving the accuracy of any one of them, would suggest that the errors are not such as to invalidate the overall results. It is certain, however, that the major aggregates are much more reliable than the numerous sub-totals in the analyses. There still exist several important gaps in the requisite information for any one of the three approaches. For example, wages in the income approach, distribution in the output data and items such as motoring and holidays in the analysis of current personal expenditure, must be interpreted with caution. The outstanding weaknesses in the over-all aggregates remain the deficiencies in the data from which estimates of the level of savings and net investment in this country can be made. Until more detailed information regarding not merely the volume of savings and investment, but in particular their distribution within the economy is known, economic planning must remain a highly speculative exercise.

Nevertheless, despite all the criticisms of the data as published, it is no exaggeration to state that the Blue Book on the National Income and Expenditure is the most important economic document of the year. The plans of the Government and all the major commercial, industrial and financial institutions are based on that information. Without them fiscal and budgetary policy would be mere guesswork. As the volume of statistical data assembled by the government increases, as it undoubtedly will, so the accuracy of these estimates will be improved.

The Central Statistical Office published in 1968 a very full account of the sources and construction of the statistics of National Income entitled *National Accounts Statistics: Sources and Methods.* The first chapters are probably the most useful for students as the remainder of the book goes into great detail. It is, however, an excellent source of reference. The notes which accompany the Blue Book on National Income consist of:

(1) definitions of items in the summary tables in the Blue Book;

(2) revisions made in the previous year's estimates; and

(3) changes in treatment and definition made since the publication of the Central Statistical Office study mentioned above.

An especially important development in the field of short-term forecasting has been the development of quarterly estimates of the national income. These started in 1957 with the publication of quarterly estimates of consumer expenditure and since then similar estimates have been made of factor incomes, *i.e.* wages, salaries, profits and rent. These have been published since 1958 and in the following year quarterly estimates of all forms of final expenditure and the G.D.P. were started to be followed by seasonally adjusted series of both factor incomes and consumer expenditure. In 1963 fuller information on the invisible items on the balance of payments made it possible to give quarterly estimates of the gross national product (G.N.P.) as well as the gross domestic product (G.D.P.). All these quarterly series are published in the Monthly Digest of Statistics and with appropriate commentary in *Economic Trends*. Bearing in mind that the annual series are themselves liable to revision after publication, it must be recognised that some of these quarterly series are at best tentative estimates. However, given the need for economic planning, even such data are worthwhile.

One important application of data forming national income and expenditure statistics is the construction of *input-output* tables. The idea behind the tables is part of the general theme of viewing data as flowing through the economy. Thus the steel maker starts with raw material and sells his steel bars to the screw manufacturer. When the screws are made they may be sold to a car constructor. Thus, there are two cases in this small example where the output of one industry is the input of another. It is, therefore, very important to understand how goods and services flow through the economy if one wishes to know what the effects are of changes in any one element in the economy.

The social accounting matrix developed by the Department of Applied Economics at the University of Cambridge formed the basis of sets of tables published annually in the Business Monitor series, PA1004, of *Input-Output for the United Kingdom*. The data for these tables comes from the annual sample Census of Production and distinguish nearly 60 industry and commodity groups. Summary input-output tables are published in the National Income and Expenditure Blue Book. Sir Claus Moser referred in his lecture* to the 'enormous labour' which goes into the construction of such tables; the 1963 tables, for example, were not completed until 1969. The time required for collection is no longer as great, it is now possible to up-date the tables annually although, given the volume of the data, it should be recognised that many of the figures used are provisional or estimated. Quite apart from the value of input-output tables for studying the inter-dependence of the economy, a particular merit is that they facilitate the reconciliation of various figures in the national income accounts, *i.e.* the former provides a series of cross-checks on the various industry and sectoral totals which have been compiled independently.

In the longer term the idea of social accounting matrices is being developed to give a deeper understanding of the working of the

*Op cit.

economy. More attention is being given to the development of models of individual industries or sectors of the economy, *e.g.* the household sector (a process referred to as *dis-aggregated* analysis) than the concept of fitting detail into an overall economic model (known as macro-analysis).

REFERENCES

Annual White Papers and Blue Books on National Income and Expenditure.
Studies in Official Statistics No. 13.
Guide to Public Sector Financial Information No. 1, 1979. (Central Statistical Office).

Retail Sales Indices

For more than 40 years there have appeared monthly in the *Board of Trade Journal* (now *Trade and Industry*) indices reflecting changes in the level of retail trade. The primary purpose of these indices is to provide up-to-date information on the short-term trends in the trade of retail establishments. Inevitably, over this long period these indices have been subject to several revisions; 1952, 1959, 1963 and 1966. On the occasion of the latest change, the base year of the index was altered to 1971. One other important change which should be noted if longer period comparisons are to be made was the change made in 1955. This involved a change in the basis of presentation of the indices from a *commodity* basis, *i.e.* sales of furniture, groceries, etc., to the present *kind of business basis*, *i.e.* the sales by furniture shops, grocers, etc.*

With only a few exceptions, *e.g.* coal merchants and florists, the whole field of retail trade in Great Britain is covered. Retail establishments are divided into four groups: independent retailers, multiple retailers, *i.e.* those with chains of ten or more branches, cooperative societies, and general department stores. These traders contribute a voluntary monthly return of their sales, inclusive of Value Added Tax, to the Department of Trade. To this extent, *i.e.* that the returns are made voluntarily, it is arguable that the sample is not completely random. In fact, the coverage of the index reflects the bulk, particularly that of large-scale retailers, of retail trade in Great Britain. The panel of independent retailers numbers some 3,900 contributors and the large scale retailers account for about 80 per cent of the total trade of their class. Continuing attempts are being made to improve the representativeness of the panel of retailers which constitutes the sample.

The indices are compiled using a ratio method, *i.e.* linking the monthly sales of the current year with the sales of the corresponding month in the previous year. The calculation of the index consists of dividing the total sales in any one category of shops in the current period by their total sales in 1971, the base year, and multiplying the

*An article in *Trade and Industry* on 5th October, 1972, outlined the method of compiling the retail sales statistics.

result by the total sales of all shops in that category in 1971. The latter data are derived from the Census of Distribution. The following formula illustrates the basis of construction of the index for all classes of retailer, the retailers being first classified by size of turnover.

$$\text{Index of the sales in October 1977} = \frac{\text{Sales of the sample in October 1977}}{\text{Sales of the sample in 1971}} \times \text{Sales of all shops in 1971}$$

The data collected include sales of goods and services (for example, repairs and rentals) for both cash and credit. The results are published monthly in *Trade and Industry* as two indices; one relating to volume and the other to value. Parts of the published tables are reproduced opposite in Tables 90 and 91.

Deficiencies in the information available and some changes in the character of the trade of some of the contributory shops have affected the representativeness of the panel. Bearing in mind the limitations of these data, considerable caution is required in interpreting month-by-month movements in the index. It is probably safest to take note only of marked longer run trends shown by the index.

Wholesale Price Indices

Between 1951-5 the Board of Trade was producing two indices of wholesale prices. The first, which was the revised version of its original 1921 index, was finally discontinued in 1955. Classified into 200 commodities, *i.e.* some commodities being quoted several times to obtain an average, the weighting in the index was effected by including in each of the groups of commodities several quotations for particularly significant commodities. The object was that each commodity should be weighted in proportion to its significance in the overall net value of all manufactured goods produced in the United Kingdom as given by the 1930 Census of Production. Each month's average of prices was compared not with that of the preceding month, but with the average of the same month in the preceding year. This ensured that the changes in prices shown by the relatives each month were between the same goods, since many products, for example fruit, are seasonal. The index for the year was the geometric mean of the 12 monthly indices. In other words, the index was of the chain base variety and this fact enabled considerable variations in the constituent items to be made, whilst ensuring that in the short period at least the changes indicated by the index were between comparable sets of prices.

The old index was to be a means of answering the question 'what is the average change in the value of money relative to other things?'; a reflection of the acceptance of the then current quantity theory of

TABLE 90

VALUE OF RETAIL SALES SEASONALLY ADJUSTED

Index numbers of value of sales per week (current prices)

1971 = 100

(Sales in 1971 £ million Provisional estimates)	All kinds of business (15,895)	Food shops (6,693)	Non-food shops Total (9,202)	Clothing and footwear shops (2,314)	Durable goods shops (1,801)	Other non-food shops[2] (5,087)
1971	100·0	100·0	100·0	100	100	100
1972	112·0	108·9	114·2	112	118	114
1973	126·9	122·8	129·9	128	136	128
1974	146·7	144·5	148·2	149	143	150
1975	174·5	174·6	174·4	172	166	178
1976	200·3	204·4	197·3	190	186	205
1977 1st qtr	217·1	222·4	213·2	207	190	224
2nd	221·6	230·1	215·6	203	196	228
3rd	235·7	239·4	233·1	225	213	244
1976 Nov.	212·9	217·5	209·6	198	199	218
1977 February	218·1	224·3	213·6	206	194	224
April[1]	219·5	226·0	214·8	200	201	226
June[1]	223·2	233·5	215·8	202	195	229
August	237·6	240·4	235·5	232	208	247
Sept.[1]	236·6	240·9	233·5	232	217	245
October	234·4	239·3	230·8	217	213	243
1977 Aug.-Oct.	236·2	240·3	233·3	224	213	245
Percentage increase	4·7	3·0	5·9	7	7	5

[1] Five-week period.
[2] Including department stores and mail-order businesses.

Source: Trade and Industry, 9th December, 1977.

TABLE 91

VOLUME OF RETAIL SALES SEASONALLY ADJUSTED

Index numbers of sales per week (average 1971 prices)

1971 = 100

(Sales in 1971 £ million Provisional estimates)	All kinds of business (15,895)	Food shops (6,693)	Non-food shops Total (9,202)	Clothing and footwear shops (2,314)	Durable goods shops (1,801)	Other non-food shops[2] (5,087)
1971	100·0	100·0	100·0	100	100	100
1972	105·8	101·5	109·0	105	115	109
1973	110·7	101·0	117·7	109	127	118
1974	109·9	101·8	115·9	107	123	117
1975	107·9	99·3	114·2	108	121	115
1976	108·1	99·1	114·6	108	124	114
1977 1st qtr	105·0	94·9	112·3	108	118	113
2nd	103·9	95·3	110·0	103	119	110
3rd	106·8	94·8	115·5	110	125	115
1976 Nov.	109·2	97·9	117·4	108	130	117
1977 February	105·7	95·5	113·1	107	120	113
April[1]	103·4	94·6	109·8	102	121	109
June[1]	103·8	95·5	109·8	101	119	111
August	107·2	94·9	116·1	113	122	116
Sept.[1]	106·2	95·0	114·4	108	125	114
October	105·4	94·7	113·1	105	124	113
1977 Aug.-Oct.	106·3	94·9	114·5	108	124	114
Percentage increase	1·2	-0·3	2·2	3	2	2

[1] Five-week period.
[2] Including department stores and mail-order businesses.

money. The new index is based on an entirely different conception of the functions which the index should perform. The new indices reflected the view that there is no such thing as *the* price level. At best the majority of prices move in the same direction, but always in varying degrees. The indices were to be related to major economic groupings, for example, industries, and constructed 'as far as possible so that they may be of direct help to the government, to industry and to economists in studying the effects of price changes'.*

A new index was introduced in 1951 and the base date was subsequently revised several times. The current index based on 1975 was introduced and described in some detail in the *Trade and Industry* of 22nd September, 1978, and is in fact a collection of index numbers which have been classified into three main groups. First, there are price indices of commodities and materials which are important in the production processes of certain industries. These commodity price indices relate to materials such as aluminium, brass and copper among metals. Among the staple fibres there is an index for raw cotton. The second group of index numbers are to a certain extent based upon the first group; they are termed indices of basic material prices. Among the first of these indices to be produced were those based on the prices of materials used in the mechanical engineering industry and building and civil engineering respectively. It was intended that these particular indices would be sufficiently reliable to permit price revision clauses to be inserted into contracts for public works, whereby an agreed basis for adjustment of prices would be available to the contractor and the authority placing the order. The last of the three groups of indices are designed to reflect the price movements of the total output of certain important industries. For example, there is an index for the china and earthenware industry, for iron and steel (tubes) and for tinplate. Examples of the indices taken from each of the three groups are given in Table 92.

These index numbers are calculated from the price movements of some 11,000 closely defined materials and products representative of goods purchased and manufactured by United Kingdom industry. The index for an individual commodity is its current home market price expressed as a percentage of its annual average price in the home market in 1974. In compiling group indices the percentage changes are combined in proportion to the value of purchases or sales of the individual commodities in 1974 when a major price enquiry was undertaken. The data for weighting the constituents of the group indices are culled from the Census of Production, other short-term production indices, the Trade and Navigation accounts, together with information supplied by trade and industry. The base date for all

*Board of Trade *Journal* 19.5.51

the indices is 1975=100. The indices are arithmetic means of the percentage changes in the prices that have taken place since the base date. 1975 was taken as the base year in accordance with national accounts practice and international recommendations.

The prices used in the calculation of these indices are the 'ex-works' prices of the commodities. If the practice for the industry is to quote the price for the commodity 'delivered', then that quotation is used. The weighting is determined by the information derived from the Census of Production, although supplementary information (the source of which cannot apparently always be disclosed) has also been utilised to obtain correct weighting.

The price indices of output of broad sectors of industry (group 2) derive their weights from data relating to the sales of the product by the corresponding sector of industry in 1974. For example, the price index of the output of the iron and steel industry is based upon the combined prices of the commodities contained in the list of commodity price indices, *i.e.* iron castings, sheets, tinplate and tubes. It should be noted that the prices and weights of the materials used in this particular index, *i.e.* product of broad sectors of industry (group 2), relate only to the output sold outside the industry and not to that sold between firms within the same industry.

The monthly indices are published in *Trade and Industry* which also reviews longer-term trends in wholesale prices.

A selection of the more important indices in each of the three groups is published in the *Monthly Digest of Statistics*. As with so many other economic series these indices have been subject to periodic revision since they were first introduced in 1955. The number of prices included has been increased from 5,000 to 11,000, while the two revisions of the Standard Industrial Classification have meant that pre- and post-1968 indices for certain industries and trades may not be comparable. Before using these data the notes in *Trade and Industry*, which accompany the longer-term analyses, should be studied.

Overleaf are some examples of the indices as they appear in *Trade and Industry* reproduced in Table 92.

Overseas Trade

Statistics of overseas trade are among the oldest to be prepared in the United Kingdom. They date from the establishment in 1696 of the office of 'The Inspector-General of the Imports and Exports'. Their origin was to be found in the need to collect revenue and even today, despite the considerable changes and improvements, the classification still bears traces of this purpose. The statistics as compiled at the present time effectively start in 1871 when the statistics were based

TABLE 92

INDEX NUMBERS OF WHOLESALE PRICES

1975=100

Monthly averages

	Materials and fuels purchased by			Price indices of materials purchased by broad sectors of industry				Materials and fuels purchased by the						
SIC Order or MLH	Manufacturing Industry	Manufacturing other than food, drink and tobacco	Food drink and tobacco manufacturing industries	Food manufacturing industries	Food manufacturing industries (excluding animal and poultry foods)	Chemicals and allied industries	Steel industries	Nonferrous metals industries	Mechanical engineering industries	Electrical engineering industries	Electrical machinery industry	Insulated wires and cables industry	Radio and electronic components industry	Domestic appliances industry
	III to XIX	IV to XIX	III	211 to 229	211-229 excl. 219	V	311 and 312	321 to 323	321 excl. 342	IX	361	362	364	368
1975	100·0	100·0	100·0	100·0	100·0	100·0	100·0	100·0	100·0	100·0	100·0	100·0	100·0	100·0
1976	127·0	126·8	124·4	126·7	124·3	122·1	123·9	129·2	121·0	122·6	119·8	127·4	118·8	119·5
1977	145·6	141·8	149·2	152·3	151·7	146·3	140·3	143·5	140·2	140·3	138·6	140·9	138·5	140·9
1978	144·6	139·0	155·5	157·2	157·2	152·7	145·6	145·0	153·9	149·5	150·8	143·5	150·0	153·8
1977														
January	143·1	139·8	144·2	147·1	145·4	138·6	134·2	142·8	135·4	136·2	132·8	140·5	132·5	133·5
February	144·3	140·5	146·0	149·4	147·9	140·1	134·9	146·7	136·1	138·1	134·1	143·3	134·1	135·2
March	147·0	141·9	150·5	154·9	154·0	142·1	139·4	151·2	137·0	140·4	135·7	147·4	135·8	138·7

upon importers' and exporters' declarations of value (as well as of quantity) collected by Customs Officers at the ports and transmitted to the Customs Statistical Office for compilation. It is of some interest to note that since 1871 these data have been affected by two major changes only; the inclusion of exports of ships and boats as from 1899 which then represented about $3\frac{1}{2}$ per cent of the total value of exports and again in 1923 when the Irish Free State was created and trade with that country then became part of the United Kingdom external trade. The only other changes concerned classification; in particular, of countries due to changes in their frontiers.

The statistics of United Kingdom overseas trade are based upon the official certificates or declarations which must be made by both importers and exporters. These certificates give details of the nature of the merchandise together with figures of quantity and value. Imports are valued c.i.f. and exports and re-exports are valued f.o.b. The first abbreviation means 'carriage, insurance and freight'; the practice of including these items with the cost of the commodity imported follows logically from the definition of the value of imports required by the Customs; *i.e.* the 'open market' value or price inclusive of all costs of importation, which the merchandise would fetch if sold on the open market at time of entry into this country. The valuation placed upon exported merchandise represents the cost of the goods packed and delivered to the ship, *i.e.* f.o.b. The c.i.f. basis of valuing imports is something of an anachronism; it started as a result of the 1932 *Import Duties Act* which created a general *ad valorem* tariff, *i.e.* a tax on imports based upon the value thereof and clearly some standard method of valuation was needed. Actually this method did not differ greatly from the mode of valuation employed up till 1932, which was the cost to the importer including freight, insurance, etc. Nowadays about 85 per cent of the imports are duty free and the need for precise valuation in accordance with the formula is weakened. In practice, it is the cost price, *i.e.* the price actually paid for the goods to the port of entry, which the importer records on his certificate. This may differ substantially from the 'open value' price if, for example, a devaluation takes place and goods are imported at their cost before the devaluation occurred. For the dutiable goods, the authorities are satisfied that the total values reflect fairly accurately the actual c.i.f. cost of imports.

The statistics are first published about two weeks after the end of the month to which they refer in a press notice on *The Current Account of the U.K. Balance of Payments*. Imports, exports and re-exports which equal overseas visible trade form only part of the current account of the balance of payments. More detail is given in the section on Balance of Payments on p.583. The press notice on

The Current Account of the UK Balance of Payments is reproduced in the next issue of *Trade and Industry*.

About four weeks after the month to which they refer, a detailed series of tables, entitled the *Overseas Trade Statistics of the United Kingdom* are published. These statistics are compiled from the declarations made to H.M. Customs and Excise by importers and exporters analysed to conform to the second revised version of the United Nations Standard International Trade Classification (SITC(R2)) in some tables and the Brussels Tariff Nomenclature in others. The former classification gives data that are useful for broader economic analysis of trade flows, while the Brussels Tariff yields much more detailed information, of considerable use to the individual trader. Full details of the analyses are given in *Guide to the Classification for Overseas Trade Statistics* for (SITC(R2)) and Tariff and Overseas Trade Classification for Brussels Nomenclature. The tables in the monthly publication *Overseas Trade Statistics* are as follows:

Table 1A:

imports and exports by months and cumulatively for the year;

Table 1B:

total trade by area and country for the particular month and cumulatively;

Tables II and V:

SITC(R2) analyses by country of imports and exports;

Tables III and VI:

SITC(R2) analyses by some 1,300 commodity headings of imports and exports;

Tables IV and VII:

Brussels Tariff analyses of imports and exports;

Table VIII:

trade in gold.

Excerpts from the overseas trade figures by year and quarters as published in *Trade and Industry* are shown opposite.

The *Annual Statement of the Overseas Trade of the United Kingdom* is published in five volumes. It gives revised figures and greater detail than that which appears in the Overseas Trade Statistics, as follows.

Volume I gives summaries of imports and exports by commodity and area on an SITC(R2) basis.

Volumes II and III give highly detailed information of imports and exports by commodity on a tariff basis.

Volume IV gives detailed information of trade by country on an SITC(R2) basis.

Volume V gives detailed information of traffic by commodities

TABLE 93
EXPORTS BY COMMODITY (SUMMARY)
Overseas trade statistics basis

Seasonally adjusted values

£ million fob

	Total	Food, beverages and tobacco	Basic materials	Fuels	Manufactures							Miscellaneous
					Total	Machinery and transport equipment			Chemicals	Textiles	Other manufactures	
						Total	Machinery	Road motor vehicles				
1970	8,076	514	273	207	6,806	3,301	2,221	834	784	396	1,366	276
1971	9,187	588	278	236	7,825	3,871	2,593	988	884	426	1,639	260
1972	9,759	660	321	239	8,257	4,014	2,716	915	962	445	1,821	283
1973	12,505	876	433	370	10,455	4,774	3,221	1,100	1,272	590	2,509	371
1974	16,600	1,063	576	767	13,685	6,059	4,215	1,304	2,144	745	3,025	509
1975	19,922	1,428	561	814	16,459	8,233	5,782	1,736	2,179	699	3,511	660
1976	25,769	1,692	776	1,255	21,338	10,125	7,060	2,226	3,045	934	4,890	709
1977 1st qtr	7,588	504	251	480	6,169	2,764	1,951	623	899	287	1,527	218
2nd	8,332	538	227	542	6,727	3,043	2,071	666	953	284	1,751	248
3rd	8,638	583	232	595	7,046	3,355	2,359	686	1,031	296	1,583	242
Percentage change Q3/Q2	+3¼	+8½	+2½	+9½	+4½	+10	+14	+3	+8	+4	−9½	−2½

Source: Trade and Industry 1977

throughout United Kingdom ports and airports.

In passing, it should be noted that details of volume and quantity are available for about 98 per cent of all imports (by value) and 90 per cent of exports. This is important since such data enable index numbers to be calculated which permit the money aggregates over a period of years to be adjusted for changes in both price and quantity. The difficulties arising from changes in quality and type of product cannot be completely overcome by an index, hence it is sometimes difficult to be sure that one is comparing like with like. For example, the value of machinery, which is adjusted by reference to its weight, will be affected by the growing use in recent years of lighter alloys for its construction. (See sections below on these indices.)

So brief an account of the statistics of overseas trade can do little more than warn the reader who anticipates consulting any of the references given that the utmost care in extraction of figures is necessary. Comparability over a period of years is often more apparent than real and the notes to the various Tables and Accounts must be examined for changes, especially in classification. The difficulties of the student are intensified by the importance of the balance of payments problem; it is tempting to regard the statistics of overseas trade as a means of interpreting the balance of payments. This is far from being the case; the quarterly and annual figures on the balance of payments are very different from the publications discussed above. In fact, not even the expert can reconcile the documents since they are compiled on different bases. A major difficulty to which reference is sometimes made in the press discussions of monthly trade accounts, is the problem of adjusting the cost of imports from the c.i.f. valuation to that for the goods themselves, *i.e.* ex insurance and transport costs. These costs are estimated to represent between 10 and 13 per cent of the total c.i.f. value, but the percentage varies as between the various commodities and as between different countries. At best the correction can only be approximate.

Import and Export Unit Value Indices

Since 1946 the *Board of Trade Journal* now *Trade and Industry* has published a series of monthly indices which are used to measure the short-period changes in the United Kingdom's terms of trade. The 'terms of trade' is simply the ratio of import to export prices; if the former are rising more rapidly than the latter, then the terms of trade are said to be moving against the United Kingdom. In other words, the United Kingdom is receiving a smaller quantity of imports for a given volume of exports. In view of the nation's balance of payments problem this particular index is quoted regularly in discussions of the overseas trade statistics. The indices are designed to measure the monthly changes in the aggregate value of a *fixed* but representative selection of imports and exports. The basic data used in the construction of the indices are published in the *Overseas Trade Statistics*.

One of the weaknesses of the data, however, is that some of the commodity headings used relate to products which are not closely homogeneous. This results in certain fluctuations over a period of time which are not true price movements and the accuracy of the indices is consequently reduced. It should be noted that the indices are called 'unit value' indices to distinguish them from price indices which are normally constructed from data on suppliers' price quotations for closely defined products.

The commodity headings in the *Overseas Trade Statistics* are selected for use if their behaviour over a period of time leads one to suppose that they are reasonably homogeneous. The headings used cover some three-quarters by value of the total imports and two-thirds by value of the total exports.

Although the basis of selection of the headings used in the indices is that they are reasonably comparable over a period of time, there arises occasionally sizeable fluctuations that would not cancel out in aggregate. Such fluctuations are usually smoothed by discounting half or more of the price change if it represents a change of more than 0·1 per cent in the total unit value index. Similarly, if a product of a marked seasonal trade is used where for some months no quantities enter into trade, the usual practice is to repeat the unit value of a month in which trade of reasonable proportions did take place.

The selection of the unit values under each heading is so devised that a collection of commodities for both indices is derived which is representative of the current pattern of trade. The weights employed are 'fixed' base-year weights, determined by the pattern of trade in 1975. Thus the weighting employed for the indices in 1976 and later is given by the pattern of goods trade in 1975. The index itself is derived by calculating the geometric mean of the products of the unit values and their respective weights. In other words, the resultant indices measure the change from period to period in the value of a fixed selection of commodities, regardless of the fact that the composition of the goods traded in any period differs from that in others. This weighting system is therefore adequate only for as long as the pattern of commodity trade remains constant from year to year. If in any particular year there are marked changes, the use of the weights based upon the 1975 pattern will distort the indices in the later period.

Although the price indices are published monthly, separate indices – based on the monthly data – are published for successive quarters and for each year. A selection is given in Table 94 for both imports

TABLE 94

INDICES OF VISIBLE TRADE

	Seasonally adjusted 1975 = 100		Unadjusted 1975 = 100				1970 = 100	19th December 1971[2] = 100
	Volume indices[2]		Unit value indices[3]			Export price competitiveness index[5]	World commodity prices index[6]	Sterling effective exchange rate
	Exports	Imports	Exports	Imports	Terms of trade[4]			
1970 *1*	80·8	78·8	50·0	42·0	119·0	103·9	100	—
2	79·9	83·9	50·6	42·3	119·4	103·8	100	—
3	75·3	81·5	51·6	42·5	121·4	104·8	100	—
4	84·5	85·8	51·9	42·5	122·0	105·7	100	—
1973 *1*	94·1	104·9	60·5	52·0	116·3	101·5	141	88·8
2	96·2	106·5	62·3	56·0	111·4	101·1	153	89·3
3	99·8	109·5	64·9	62·1	104·5	94·3	174	84·2
4	101·2	114·0	68·1	68·2	99·9	93·4	205	83·0
1975 *1*	100·9	102·0	95·2	96·4	98·7	99·5	287	81·7
2	97·0	95·7	97·5	97·0	100·5	99·1	284	79·1
3	98·0	102·5	101·6	100·8	100·8	100·3	306	75·2
4	104·1	99·7	105·7	105·7	100·0	101·2	324	73·0
1977 *1*	115·8	109·4	135·7	137·2	98·9	97·9	440	61·8
2	118·0	109·6	141·4	141·0	100·3	101·6	450	61·6
3	124·4	106·6	145·2	143·7	101·0	103·3	432	61·8
4	117·6	102·7	147·3	143·8	102·4	107·0	412	63·3
1978[4] *1*	119·9	114·1	149·6	142·6	104·9	110·0	394	65·4
2	122·2	109·6	153·7	147·1	104·5	—	416	61·5

[1]Provisional.
[2]Date of the Smithsonian Agreement. Monthly figures are trade-weighted averages of daily rates. A methodological article on the effective exchange rate was published in the June 1974 issue of *Economic Trends*.
[3]On a balance of payments basis.
[4]Unit value index for exports expressed as a percentage of unit value index for imports.
[5]The ratio of U.K. to weighted average export (dollar) prices for major competitors in respect of manufactured goods.
[6]Weighted average, in sterling terms, of United Nations index numbers for primary commodities and non-ferrous metals.
Source: Economic Trends, Annual Supplement 1979

and exports. The differences in both unit value and volume over the period are comparatively small and are largely explainable by the change in the pattern of trade.

Import and Export Volume Indices

Index numbers which measure the changes in the *volume* of both imports and exports are also prepared by the Board of Trade. They are published monthly in *Trade and Industry*. The indices are designed to show the variations in imports and exports after eliminating price variations, *i.e.* volume changes only. This is done by recalculating the value of the imports (or exports) for any quarter at the average prices of the year 1975. By expressing the corrected value of imports (or exports) as a percentage of the 1975 value an index of *volume* change is derived.

The monthly figures used in calculating the index are derived from the *Overseas Trade Statistics*. As with the import and export unit value indices, adjustment of the contents of various headings is necessary. For those items for which only value and not voluume is given in the statistics, estimates of the probable changes are made by assuming that they move in the same manner as do related items for which both value and volume figures are available. This procedure is adopted to a rather greater extent for the export index since a larger proportion of total exports are given in value terms only. Both volume and value figures are available for all but 3 per cent of imports (by declared value).

These indices have been published for many years but, since in the view of the Department of Trade a change in both the base year and structure of the index should be made at least every five years (owing to the changes in the pattern of overseas trade) the index is not comparable as between different base years, except where the change of base has been accompanied by a revision of indices for the earlier years. The latest base year is 1975 to which the index was revised from 1970 in January 1978. At the same time the weights were revised on the basis of the average prices ruling in 1975 instead of 1970. In the current index the weights are based on the relative values of the individual categories of goods comprising the total value of trade in the year 1975.

The volume indices are given for the same sub-headings, *i.e.* raw materials, manufactures, etc., as the import and export *price* indices, which were discussed earlier. Like the monthly price indices the volume indices are separately calculated for each month, quarter and for each year.

They are reproduced in a summary form with a longer run of figures in the Annual Supplement to *Economic Trends*. As will be seen from the excerpt in Table 95 overleaf they are given both in an unadjusted and seasonally adjusted form. Also given are indices of the terms of trade and world commodity prices defined in the footnotes to the table.

The Balance of Payments

The Balance of Payments accounts provide a summary financial record of the overseas trading activities during the past year. Until 1939 it was based upon the data provided by the Customs Statistical Office, *i.e.* the Trade Accounts described above. With the introduction in 1939 of Exchange Control, a new basis for these statistics became available. An importer requiring foreign exchange to pay for goods had to make a detailed application to the authorities for the currency. Similarly, the exporter had to account for the proceeds in foreign currency of any exports. The authorities found themselves in possession of far more detailed and accurate data about the nation's overseas financial transactions than ever before. Since actual payment for goods usually takes place after receipt or despatch of the goods concerned, the Balance of Payments account before 1939 was

TABLE 95

EXPORT VOLUME INDEX NUMBERS

1975 = 100

	Total	Food, beverages and tobacco	Basic materials	Fuels	Manufactures							
					Total	Machinery and transport equipment			Chemicals	Metals and miscellaneous metal manufactures	Textiles	Other manufactures
						Total	Machinery	Road vehicles				
SITC Section or Division (Rev. 2)	0 to 9	0 and 1	2 and 4	3	5 to 8	7	71 to 77	78	5	67 to 69	65	Rest of 6 and 8
Weights	*1,000*	*71*	*28*	*41*	*823*	*417*	*286*	*92*	*106*	*92*	*36*	*172*
1975	100·0	100	100	100	100	100	100	100	100	100	100	100
1976	108·7	103	117	120	109	101	99	104	124	109	117	116
1977	118·7	111	126	165	118	106	102	105	141	116	120	134
1978	124·0	132	134	209	120	105	101	112	155	117	117	139
Unadjusted												
1978 1st quarter	119·5	132	128	175	117	104	101	106	144	111	118	134
2nd quarter	129·1	129	145	200	127	113	106	132	163	124	120	139
3rd quarter	119·5	124	122	236	115	99	95	108	151	109	108	135
4th quarter	128·1	144	142	224	122	102	101	102	159	122	122	147
1979 January	117·1	105	127	289	110	100	96	100	139	102	100	125

Source: Monthly Digest of Statistics, No. 401

in the nature of a revenue and expenditure account with debits accrued and credits outstanding. When the Exchange Control data became available the account became in effect a cash account, reflecting the timing of the payments rather than the actual movement of the goods giving rise to payments and receipts. From 1951 onwards the Exchange Control regulations were gradually simplified, significantly reducing the value of the regulations as a source of data. Consequently, the Overseas Trade Statistics were adopted as the basis for balance of payments figures of all imports and exports. At the same time increasing use was made of direct inquiries from industry as a source of data on invisible transactions (*e.g.* sales of services such as transport and insurance) and private long-term capital movements. In the main, the changes tended to alter the nature of the data to a 'flow of resources' basis which is more fitting for an analysis of economic change.

The main source on the principles of the accounts, the terminology and the methodology is given in the *United Kingdom Balance of Payments* published annually in September (provisional estimates are published in the preceding March). Extensive notes can also be found in *National Accounts: Sources and Methods* which is brought up to date by the annual Blue Book *National Income and Expenditure*.

The data are published in an expanded form in *Economic Trends* for March, June, September and December and the *Economic Trends: Annual Supplement*. They are also reproduced in *Financial Statistics*, the *Monthly Digest of Statistics* and the *Annual Abstract of Statistics*. The primary source of annual figures is the *United Kingdom Balance of Payments* which gives considerable detail over a period of 11 years.

The Balance of Payments is a series of accounts which summarise the transactions between the United Kingdom and other countries. The balance of payments account summarises the more detailed accounts of different aspects of the United Kingdom's international trade and financial activities. Among these individual accounts there is that dealing with visible trade, which covers the imports and exports of goods but excludes freight. The second major account is that which deals with the so-called invisible items. The invisible account incorporates all payments and receipts in respect of services as distinct from goods, such as shipping and air freights, insurance and tourism. They include all interest and profits received from United Kingdom investment overseas, as well as that paid to overseas owners of investments in the United Kingdom, together with expenditure on the armed forces overseas, and aid to underdeveloped nations in the form of grants (but not loans). The two accounts described above, *i.e.* visible and invisible transactions, when amalgamated produce what is known as the balance on current account.

This 'current' account is supplemented by tables which estimate the balance of long-term capital transactions. The long-term capital account includes payments and receipts of a capital nature, such as investment by United Kingdom firms overseas, or by overseas firms in United Kingdom industry; government loans and repayments, and borrowing by overseas governments on the London market. As will be seen from Table 96 which incorporates the figures for most of these items, the accounts are extremely complex. The major complicating factor in the compilation of these accounts is the inadequacy of some of the basic data. Thus, even in the current account, information relating to the invisible items is incomplete and in some cases inaccurate. It is the official view that these inadequacies lead to an understatement of the true position, *i.e.* in all probability the country has done better than the recorded figures suggest. The data in the capital account have been greatly improved in recent years, primarily as the result of the Department of Trade's special enquiries into capital movements, prompted by the recommendations of the Radcliffe Committee. Nevertheless, as will be seen from the table on p.587 there is a substantial 'balancing item' for each year. In fact, the balancing item is often larger than the surplus or deficit on the overall account. This balancing item reflects the net total of errors and omissions in the various figures which make up the balance of payments account. In the view of the official statisticians, the item is normally positive, *i.e.* indicating a net unrecorded inflow. In other words, the position of the United Kingdom overseas payments account is probably better in any year than the recorded figures would suggest.

The current and capital accounts are supplemented by a final account which is referred to as 'monetary movements'. Most transactions, whether current or capital, give rise to corresponding movements of funds affecting, in particular, the United Kingdom gold and foreign exchange reserves, or the overseas residents' holdings of sterling. The balance of monetary movements reflects the changes in these funds; a minus sign in front of the figure indicates a favourable change in the United Kingdom's position, and *vice versa* for a plus sign. The official view is that the balance of monetary movements has been a better measure of the United Kingdom's overseas trading and financial activities than the balance of the current and capital accounts. Unfortunately, in some years there have been substantial unrecorded short-term flows, so that if the balancing item has been exceptionally large and positive, the balance of monetary movements has given too favourable an impression. On the other hand, if the balancing item has been unusually small, and positive, or even negative, the balance of monetary movements gives too unfavourable an impression.

TABLE 96
UK BALANCE OF PAYMENTS

£ million

			1976				1977		
	1975	1976	1st qtr	2nd qtr	3rd qtr	4th qtr	1st qtr	2nd qtr	3rd qtr
								Seasonally adjusted	
Current account									
Visible balance	−3,203	−3,571	−538	−907	−1,144	−982	−930	−698	−50
Invisible balance	+1,556	+2,344	+473	+557	+698	+616	+414	+418	+449
CURRENT BALANCE	−1,647	−1,227	−65	−350	−446	−366	−516	−280	+399
								Not seasonally adjusted	
Current balance	−1,647	−1,227	−148	−352	−344	−383	−592	−345	+528
Investment and other capital transactions	+203	−2,819	−544	−1,837	−519	+81	+1,949	+339	+1,373
Balancing item	−21	+418	+14	+234	+1	+169	+556	+914	+709
BALANCE FOR OFFICIAL FINANCING	−1,465	−3,628	−678	−1,955	−862	−133	−1,913	+908	+2,610
Official financing									
Net transactions with:									
I.M.F.	—	+1,018	+580	+438	+309	—	+682	+217	+214
Other monetary authorities*	—	−34	—	+581		−924			
Foreign currency borrowing:									
by H.M. government*	+423						+584		+287
by public sector under exchange cover scheme	+387	+1,791	+276	+582	+492	+441	+18	+33	+116
Official reserves (drawings on, +/additions to, −)	+655	+853	−178	+354	+61	+616	−3,197	−1,158	−3,227

*Drawings on two Euro-dollar facilities for the government to borrow $2,500 million and $1,500 million respectively.

Source: Trade and Industry, 16th December, 1977

The foregoing cursory description of what are probably the most important economic data produced by the Central Statistical Office makes two points clear. First, these accounts are extremely complex and subject to a margin of error which may at times prove seriously misleading to anyone not familiar with the statistics. In particular, any assessment of the United Kingdom's overseas payments position should not be made without studying all aspects of these accounts. The second point to note is that these figures have been subject over the past three decades to extensive revisions and amendments as new data have become available. It is essential to consult the explanatory memoranda which accompany the published tables whenever these figures are quoted.

Hire Purchase Statistics

In recent times hire purchase has come to play an increasingly important part in the national economy. By 1978, credit outstanding amounted to over £6,200m. In consequence of this rapid expansion and its impact on the economy, it has become necessary to find some measure of the changes in both the volume and character of hire purchase debt. The Department of Trade publishes statistics monthly which cover the period since October 1955. These relate to the hire purchase trade of retailers in kinds of businesses where substantial sales of goods on hire purchase terms are made (*e.g.* furniture, radio and electrical shops) as well as to the hire purchase business of finance houses.

The estimates for retailers are based on the results of the 1971 Census of Distribution projected by means of monthly returns from a stratified panel of retailers. The panel comprises some 4,800 contributors; the large-scale retailers which contribute account for nearly 80 per cent of total retail sales. The estimates for finance houses which specialise in credit financing are based on the results of an enquiry taken of business transacted in 1965. The results of the enquiry are projected forward by monthly returns from a panel of finance houses comprising the largest houses and a sample of the smaller ones.

Data are collected on a voluntary basis and are subject to possible errors of bias, *e.g.* the sample is not random; some shops with a lot of hire purchase business may not bother to make a return. Consequently too much significance must not be attached to any particular figure but generally the trends in the volume of business are fairly indicated.

The monthly figures in terms of absolute sums of new credit advanced and outstanding debt and in the form of indices of average weekly sales are published in full in *Trade and Industry*. Summaries

TABLE 97
HIRE PURCHASE AND OTHER CREDIT
Great Britain

£ million

	Total debt outstanding to finance houses, other consumer credit grantors and retailers[1]		Total		Finance houses and other consumer credit grantors[1]		Retailers[2]	
	Unadjusted				Seasonally adjusted			
	Increase	Amount at end of period	New credit extended[3]	Increase in debt	New credit extended[3]	Increase in debt	New credit extended[3]	Increase in debt
Debt outstanding at 31st December, 1978 (unadjusted)				6,211		4,804		1,407
1976	—	3,856	3,688	—	1,835	—	1,853	141
1977	934	4,790	4,644	1,077	2,552	882	2,092	125
1978	1,421	6,211	5,998	1,561	3,563	1,370	2,435	191
1979 1st quarter	216	6,427	1,586	354	934	258	652	96
1979 January	25	6,236	525	119	300	73	225	46
February	80	6,316	531	127	311	98	220	29
March	111	6,427	530	108	323	87	207	21

[1]Direct business only; *i.e.* excluding agreements block discounted with finance houses by retailers. This series has been revised and rebased on results of the inquiry to Consumer Credit Grantors for 1976. For further details see *Trade and Industry*, 12th April, 1979.
[2]Durable goods shops, department stores (including co-operative societies), other general stores and general mail order houses.
[3]Excluding charges.

Source: Monthly Digest of Statistics, No. 401, Department of Trade

are published in the *Monthly Digest of Statistics* (an extract from which is shown overleaf); *Financial Statistics* and eventually in the *National Income and Expenditure* Blue Book.

Security Prices

Fluctuations in share prices and the level of stock market activity may be used as indicators of changes in the level of economic activity and business confidence generally. At the present time, there are no adequate published data relating to the volume of business undertaken on the stock exchanges, either London or provincial. The published figure of daily bargains in London is based on voluntary returns made by members and, quite apart from the fact that not all bargains are recorded, no indication is given of the size of the bargain struck. Movements in share prices are faithfully recorded in the daily Stock Exchange Official Lists and the columns of the financial press. These prices are used for purposes of compiling indices of share movements.

The two best-known indices at the present time are *The Times* Index of Industrial Ordinary Shares, and the *F.T.-Actuaries* Share Indices. Detailed accounts of the construction of both these indices are available.* *The Times* index number is a weighted arithmetic average of the prices of all shares included in the index. The index covers 150 shares of all classes, 50 large companies, large being defined as those with over £30m of capital at market prices, and 100 smaller companies. There are additional indices for capital goods and consumer goods industries, based on 43 companies apiece which produce wholly or mainly capital goods or consumer goods respectively. The weight given to each share in each index is proportionate to the average market value of the issue on two dates, on 1st July 1958 and 27th October, 1959. The base date for each index number is 2nd June, 1964. It should be noted that the monthly indices are the average of working dates.

The *F.T.-Actuaries* Index is, strictly speaking, a series of 50 price indices based upon about 650 securities quoted on the London Stock Exchange. The two main equity price indices are '500-industrial' and an 'All-Share' index of 594 equities. The 500-industrial and the index of the financial group, when combined form the above 'All-Share' index. Other than these indices there are commodity share group and fixed interest indices. The object of the price indices is mainly to reflect the performance of the ordinary share market of the London Stock Exchange as a whole. According to the official account, changes in the indices record how much better or worse off investors are as a whole. At 10th April, 1962, which is the base date, the market

The Times daily index number of Stock Exchange security prices (The Times Publishing Co. Ltd.) and *Guide to the F.T.-Actuaries* Share Indices.

TABLE 98
SECURITY PRICES AND YIELDS

	British government securities					Company securities					
	Calculated gross redemption yields[1]			2½% Consols[2]		FT-Actuaries share indices[3] 10th April, 1962 = 100					
						Debenture and loan stocks		Preference stocks		Industrial ordinary (500 shares)	
	Short-dated (5 years)	Medium-dated (10 years)	Long-dated (20 years)	Net price	Flat yield	Price Index	Redemption yield[4]	Price index	Dividend yield	Price index	Dividend yield
1973	10·45	10·65	10·78	23·2	10·85	65·48	11·40	71·45	10·97	185·26	4·10
1974	12·51	14·21	14·77	16·8	14·95	45·31	16·44	54·55	15·00	108·84	8·00
1975	11·48	13·18	14·39	17·1	14·66	46·25	15·95	61·95	15·28	135·97	6·70
1976	12·06	13·61	14·43	17·6	14·25	48·68	15·19	65·48	14·48	162·91	6·16
1977	10·08	12·02	12·73	20·4	12·32	55·58	13·41	71·71	12·81	208·79	5·50
1978	11·32	12·12	12·47	21·0	11·92	58·32	12·75	72·70	12·68	235·27	5·48
1979 January	13·48	13·61	13·68	20·0	12·51	54·54	13·59	72·09	12·98	242·66	5·66
February	13·33	13·80	13·94	19·8	12·63	52·11	14·21	68·63	13·69	243·91	5·70
March	11·32	12·07	12·35	22·0	11·36	55·71	13·32	70·80	13·24	276·79	5·08
April	10·62	11·41	11·68	23·4	10·68	60·27	12·33	74·06	12·63	294·02	4·85

[1] Derived from yield maturity curves fitted mathematically. Figures revised from January 1973 and a further modification in the method of calculation was introduced in June 1976: an explanation of the changes appeared in the *Bank of England Quarterly Bulletin* December 1972, September 1973 and June 1976. The yearly figures are averages of monthly yields. The monthly figures relate to averages of Wednesdays.
[2] Average of working days based on the mean of the middle opening and middle closing prices each day, excluding gross accrued interest; tax is ignored.
[3] Averages of daily figures calculated from middle market closing prices.
[4] Averages of daily figures calculated from middle market closing prices. Gross redemption yields of 15 stocks so combined as to give a yield average for a constant 20-year term.

Source: Bank of England, *Financial Times*, Institute of Actuaries, Faculty of Actuaries, *Monthly Digest of Statistics No. 401*

valuation of the 594 shares included in the 'All-Share' index was £18,170m. This was approximately equal to 60 per cent of the value of all quoted equities in the sections covered by the index. The calculation of the index is basically simple, since it is merely the total current market valuation of the shares included in each index related to the corresponding aggregate valuation of the same shares at the base date.

The '500-industrial' share index comprises three main groups of companies: those producing capital goods, consumer durable goods; and consumer non-durable goods, together with chemical, oil, shipping, and miscellaneous groups. Separate indices are calculated for each group. The remaining 94 quoted shares, which are added for purposes of the 'All-Share' index, relate to financial and property companies. In view of the size of this index, the daily computations are performed on a computer. The results are published daily in the *Financial Times* and the Institute of Actuaries supply subscribers with further details thereof.

Summaries of the indices are published in *Financial Statistics*, the Bank of England's *Quarterly Bulletin* and the *Monthly Digest of Statistics* – an extract from which is given overleaf. Brief descriptions of the indices are given in *Notes and Definitions to Financial Statistics*, while the *Guide to Financial Times Statistics* published by the *Financial Times* gives more detail.

Statistics of Transport

Since 1957 the Department of Transport has carried out a series of surveys of inland goods and passenger transport. Prior to 1957 rail transport was quite well documented but information on road transport was limited to the number of vehicles available but not the work that they were performing.

Road Transport

The surveys included one of goods operators in 1958 and another in 1962; a private motoring survey in 1961 and a National Travel Survey in 1965 and 1972-73; a series of National Road Condition Surveys in 1976, 1977 and 1978.

In the intervals between such surveys, a system of traffic counts is employed. Traffic counting was inaugurated in January 1958, on both a manual and automatic basis. In other words, in some cases an automatic counting device which recorded the passage of a vehicle was used, and elsewhere enumerators kept records of the vehicles which passed them. The information derived from these counts is used to measure the developments since the latest survey. One of the limitations of this use of traffic counts as an estimate of the volume

TABLE 99
Goods Transport in Great Britain

	1967	1968	1969	1970	1971	1972	1973	1974	1975	1976	1977
Total tonne kilometres (thousand millions)	123·2	129·5	135·1	138·1	135·3	135·8	141·4	139·6	143·1	144·5	129·7
Road	74·6	79·0	83·4	85·0	85·9	87·5	90·4	89·9	95·3	95·6	98·0
Rail[1]	22·3	24·0	25·3	26·8	24·3	23·4	25·5	24·2	23·5	23·1	22·8
Coastal shipping[2]	24·9	24·5	24·2	23·2	21·4	21·3	20·6	20·4	18·3	20·0	—
Inland waterways[4]	0·2	0·2	0·1	0·1	0·1	0·1	0·1	0·1	0·1	0·1	0·1
Pipelines[3]	1·2	1·8	2·1	3·0	3·6	3·5	4·8	5·3	5·9	5·7	8·8
Total (million tonnes)	1,939	2,007	1,964	1,916	1,882	1,904	1,977	1,819	1,877	1,794	1,720
Road	1,651	1,707	1,658	1,610	1,582	1,629	1,672	1,538	1,602	1,516	1,422
Rail[1]	204	211	211	209	198	178	199	176	175	176	170
Coastal shipping[2]	52	52	52	51	47	47	53	51	44	44	49
Inland waterways[4]	7	7	7	7	6	5	5	4	4	5	4
Pipelines[3]	25	30	36	39	49	45	50	50	52	53	75

[1]British Rail only prior to 1973, excluding freight tonnes by coaching train. Excluding net tonne kilometres by coaching train throughout. Excluding all free-hauled traffic. From 1969 onwards, including estimates for former freightliners and sundries traffic by rail now handled by Freightliners Ltd and NCL.
[2]The survey on which coastal shipping figures were previously based has been discontinued. Tonnages are from an alternative source which does not give tonne kilometres, for which the older source has been used up to 1976.
[3]Excluding movements of gases by pipelines. All pipelines of less than 16 kilometres were excluded.
[4]British Waterways Board only.

Source: Department of Transport

TABLE 100
Passenger Transport in Great Britain: Estimated Passenger Kilometres

Thousand million kilometres

	1967	1968	1969	1970	1971	1972	1973	1974	1975	1976	1977
Total	363·9	374·3	382·6	399·5	420·4	434·7	451·5	438·4	441·3	447·3	459·7
Air[1,5]	1·9	1·9	1·9	1·9	2·0	2·2	2·4	2·3	2·2	2·3	2·1
Rail[2]	34·0	33·4	34·7	35·6	35·4	34·5	35·1	36·1	35·1	33·0	33·6
Road:											
Public service vehicles[3]	61·0	59·0	58·0	56·0	56·0	55·0	54·0	54·0	54·0	53·0	53·0
Private transport[4]	267·0	280·0	288·0	306·0	327·0	343·0	360·0	346·0	350·0	359·0	371·0

[1]Domestic scheduled services, including Northern Ireland, Isel of Man and Channel Islands.
[2]Including British Rail, London Transport and other railway systems. The basis of calculating London Transport railways' Passenger kilometres has been revised from Passenger kilometres paid for to Passenger kilometres travelled.
[3]Calculated from operators' returns of numbers of passengers carried, using estimates for average length of journey.
[4]Based on statistics of vehicle mileage derived from the traffic counts and estimates of average numbers of persons per vehicle, derived from the Motoring and National Travel surveys.
[5]1977 figures are provisional.

Source: Department of Transport

of goods transported by road, is that it necessarily assumes that ton mileages change between one point and another in the same proportion as does the vehicle mileage. However, by the use of such traffic counting methods, it is now possible for the Ministry of Transport to prepare monthly estimates of the volume of inland road transport. Furthermore, a monthly index of inland goods transport is prepared for both road and rail, the rail figures being prepared with the aid of information produced by British Railways. The index is published monthly in the *Monthly Digest of Statistics.*

The collection of data on the number of vehicles of all kinds has been greatly simplified since the opening of the Driver and Vehicle Licensing Centre at Swansea in 1974. Prior to this date data had to be collected separately from each registration and licensing authority.

Rail and Waterways

As the rail and waterways systems are controlled by single national authorities it is now relatively easy to obtain detailed information about the amount of work performed by the systems.

Civil Aviation

Although the system is a mixture of nationalised and private operators, because of the nature of operation of the system there is ample documentation of the principal operations.

The main published sources of data on transport are the *Monthly Digest of Statistics* which gives monthly and quarterly figures, the *Annual Abstract of Statistics* which provides summaries of the operating statistics of all the main areas of transport (an extract of which is given overleaf) and the principal reference document *Transport Statistics Great Britain* published annually.

Business Statistics Office

A major development in the field of economic statistics was the formation in the New Year 1969 of the Business Statistics Office (B.S.O.). This followed the recommendations of a House of Commons Select Committee for the centralising of business data collection which, at the time, was largely in the hands of the Board of Trade Census Office which, as the name suggests, was responsible for the Censuses of Production and Distribution. A feature of the new department was that, although still nominally a part of the then Board of Trade, its activities were to be directed by an inter-departmental committee under the chairmanship of the Director of the Central Statistical Office. It was intended that the B.S.O. should become the main agency for the collection and publication of industrial and commercial statistics. In particular, it would maintain a central register of all businesses, *i.e.* a large sampling frame, to ensure reliable samples for its various sample surveys and Censuses. In 1972 the B.S.O. was moved to Newport, South Wales, where its main offices with over 1,000 staff are now located.

In the words of the B.S.O.'s first Head, Mr Martin Fessey, the B.S.O. is a 'statistics factory'. The scope of its enquiries is impressive and can best be illustrated by reference to some of the recent enquiries undertaken. Thus, that on engineering industry sales and orders is done on a monthly basis and involves a sample of 25,000 firms; that on the purchases of fuel by large users is a quarterly enquiry and covers some 3,000 large companies; the annual Census (strictly speaking, a sample) of production among manufacturing firms as well as a similar enquiry among construction firms collect information from 33,000 firms in the former industry and about 13,000 in the latter. Quite apart from the Census of Production, the enquiries into the distribution and service industries cover even more firms. Thus, the monthly survey of retail sales involves some 60,000 firms, while a quarterly enquiry among wholesalers to ascertain the volume of stocks held covers a sample of 2,700 such undertakings. In contrast, the annual enquiry into capital expenditure in both the service and the distributive trades is carried out among some 56,000 firms.

Such information is not conjured out of thin air. It is provided by firms listed on the B.S.O. register and which receive questionnaires which have to be completed and returned. In 1975 the B.S.O. distributed nearly 640,000 such forms; in the following year the total was reduced to 546,000 and in 1977 to 475,000.[1] The recipients of these forms are not always grateful! When the Bolton Committee, which had been set up to investigate means of assisting small firms, took evidence there was no lack of complaints about the 'burden' and 'time wasting' of 'form filling' for the government![2] The B.S.O has tried very hard to gain the willing co-operation of firms in this respect. New enquiries are only started after consultation with the industry concerned or with trades and industrial associations such as the Confederation of British Industry. Also, in devising forms which cover 160 industries there are questions which do not apply to all, but this is inevitable if any degree of standardisation of the general purpose questionnaires is to be achieved. It would be possible to devise special questionnaires appropriate to each individual industry, but that would be expensive. The B.S.O. has also had the co-operation of the Market Research Society and the Industrial Marketing Research Association, not to mention professional societies such as the accountancy bodies to devise suitable questions and forms for various

[1] Figures given in *Trade and Industry*, 2nd June, 1978.
[2] *Small firms*. Cmnd 4811. H.M.S.O. 1971.

industries. The point was made earlier that even with statutory enquiries it is essential to get the maximum co-operation from those approached for information, if the information is to be of any value. Because the larger firms are better staffed to complete the various questionnaires sent out, many surveys rely heavily upon a sample of such firms. Reference has already been made (in the sections on the Censuses of Production and Distribution) to the limited information which is collected from smaller firms and the fact that, for the smallest firms, estimates are made of their aggregate output since they are excluded from the sample enquiry. The advantage of this system is that it then becomes possible to process the smaller number of questionnaires more quickly and the results can be published sooner than would be the case with a larger sample and many firms dilatory in their replies. In recent years the time required to process the returned forms has been reduced and the results, in many cases, are published within three to four months of the despatch of forms from the B.S.O. For the production of statistics such as the index of industrial production speed is important and this is usually published within six weeks after the initial enquiry for data.

Of the half-million questionnaires which the B.S.O. sends out each year about three-quarters are returned in time for incorporation in the provisional results. About nine-tenths of the forms are available in time for inclusion in the preparation of the final figures. Bearing in mind that these enquiries are statutory, this can still be regarded as a good response. But, the truth of the matter is that the statisticians would like a better response rate. In his paper to the Royal Statistical Society* Mr Fessey observed that American businessmen are even more 'burdened' with statistical forms but, perhaps because they appreciate more the value of the data which are produced as a result of such enquiries, their response rate is better than that in the United Kingdom. The same, for various reasons, is apparently true of both France and Germany while, so Mr Fessey recounted, the Polish government has no difficulty in ensuring a complete response. He quoted a Polish statistician to the effect that 'all returns are made by telephone to us on the Thursday afternoon following the end of the month'! The issue was nicely summarised by the former Head of the B.S.O. when he observed that, while *laisser faire* might not be the right description of the attitude towards form filling in Britain, *laisser attendre* is fairly common as an attitude to statistical form filling.

The ultimate test of all statistics is their reliability for, as Mr Fessey observed on this issue, 'accuracy' is not a word statisticians should use in the context of B.S.O. enquiries. Inevitably there are sampling

*Business Statistics J.R.SS. 1978 Part 4.

errors; there are also errors and omissions from the register of firms in the production, distribution and service industries which constitute the sampling frame for most enquiries. And, it should be remembered, there are also the mistakes made in completing the form as well as the occasional slip in processing the data for publication. As far as reliability is concerned, not surprisingly the large aggregates are more soundly based than are the detailed headings which make up the aggregate. A particular problem is the reliability of provisional figures which, it will have been noted in some of the tables reproduced in this chapter, are published before the final figures are ready. The experience of the B.S.O. is that there can be substantial differences between the final and provisional figures. For example, the estimates of net capital expenditure in 1972 differed by 10 per cent. Not surprisingly, given such differences the question is sometimes asked whether provisional estimates should be published at all. On balance, the case is made out for publication since they are the best available guide to current trends. Furthermore, if such differences between the provisional and final figures do arise, then the matter can be examined jointly by the statisticians and people in the industry concerned to find out the cause and, that done, future estimates should be more reliable.

The main reason for publishing provisional estimates is to provide industry with the best available guides to current trends as quickly as possible. However accurate a statistic may be, it is of little value in the industrial decision-making process if it is not available until months after the decision has to be taken. Since 1976 a series of *Business Monitors* – discussed below – relating to some 160 industries has been published to provide industry with the latest available data. Some information is thus made available within about 12 weeks from the time it was collected. But, the record is not always as good. The volumes of the Census of Production on individual industries and the summary volumes for 1973 have been, according to Mr Fessey, 'unconscionably late'. The particular cause of this delay is that the results are to be published on the basis of two different classifications. The first is the U.K. Standard Industrial Classification and the second is that used by the Statistical Office of the European Economic Community. Plans to adjust the British classification to the E.E.C. basis have been formulated but their implementation has been delayed by shortage of staff and funds.

Most of the information collected from the manufacturing, extractive, distributive and service industries is published in the series of *Business Monitors*. These are a series of monthly, quarterly and annual publications published through H.M. Stationery Office. There are three main series of monitors; *production* monitors which appear monthly and quarterly referred to as the PM and PQ series; *service and distributive* monitors referred to as the SD series and lastly the *miscellaneous* monitors, or the M series. The production monitors comprising the first series also include the annual Census of Production monitors known as the PA series. The first series of quarterly monitors give up-to-date and detailed sales figures for over 4,000 products manufactured by firms in some 160 industries. Where the information is available, data on imports and exports, employment, prices, etc. are also given. The monthly series is more limited in coverage providing only summary figures designed to indicate aggregate movements and trends in contrast with the detail in the PQ series. The service and distributive monitors are of two kinds. The first group provides indicators of short-term trends in these sectors such as index numbers of sales, new credit extended, etc. The other group reports the results of the major annual or periodic inquiries. The information contained in these monitors relates to the types and number of businesses, numbers employed, turnover by commodity and purchases, stocks, credit sales, book debts and capital expenditure. The bulk of these data come from the periodic Censuses and, inevitably, the data relate to the industry structure of some years ago. For example, some such information about the wholesale trade in 1974 was published in 1978. The last group of miscellaneous monitors include topics not covered in the two main series such as new vehicle registrations, on overseas travel and tourism at one extreme to acquisitions and mergers of companies at the other. One of the more interesting and significant sets of data in this series relates to the extent of import penetration and export sales ratios for manufacturing industries.

It is probably too early to judge the success of the *Business Monitor* series in briefing businessmen about the state of their own industries, or helping them to make some assessment of the performance of their own firms in relation to the industry as a whole. There is no doubt, however, as soon as the full value of the data provided is appreciated by those who provide it, the less difficulty the B.S.O. and other government departments will have in persuading the business community to participate readily in their periodic enquiries. To encourage such co-operation and to publicise the usefulness to the business community of the information published by the B.S.O., the Central Statistical Office has produced a booklet entitled Facts from *your* Figures available from the Press and Information Service of the C.S.O. To quote the foreword, 'this booklet is dedicated to all those conscientious people who fill in statistical forms but sometimes wonder why . . .'. It is, in fact, a well-written and interesting publication in which a series of questions are put and answered on the usefulness of particular statistics, *e.g.* the monthly index of average earnings of employees or the retail sales index, to quote only two of those which are described and explained. Every student of official statistics in the world of business should read it. The same office also distributes a small booklet entitled *Government Statistics: A brief guide to sources* which is revised annually. It lists all the major publications and main statistical departments.

Statistical Sources

By this time the reader will need no reminder that the government, through the Central Statistical Office and the various departments, is the largest generator by far of statistical data. A very large proportion of the published data, more especially that prepared by government departments, is the by-product of the administrative actions of the department. Thus, the Department of Education and Science produces figures of children at school; the Department of the Environment compiles statistics of cars licensed; the Department of Health and Social Security prepares the figures of the numbers of recipients of various social security payments such as pensions and sickness benefit. A considerable body of statistical information comes from special and periodic enquiries such as the various Censuses or major surveys such as the *General Household Survey* or the *Family Expenditure Survey*. In addition, there are the reports of various *ad hoc* or official bodies, such as Royal Commissions, which compile still more statistics. In many ways it is fair to assert that, as far as many areas of the economy are concerned, there is an *embarras de richesse* of statistics.

There are, of course, gaps and for the specialist such gaps may be especially irritating. But, for most people needing any statistical data, unless they are familiar with the area in question, the problem is how to find out what is available and where it is published. The primary medium for locating any published official statistics is the C.S.O.'s *Guide to Official Statistics*. The second and latest edition of this very substantial publication appeared in 1978.

The *Guide* contains descriptions of all the published data from some 2,500 statistical sources which cover about 800 different topics. For each topic there are references to any publications which contain relevant information including journals such as *Trade and Industry*, the *Gazette* or *Statistical News* as well as any special reports which may have been published during the past decade. This should not be interpreted as indicating that every subject on which some statistical data are available is included in the *Guide*. But, the detail of the index is such that it should be possible to find under one or other related headings references to the special interest of the enquirer which will then lead to the relevant publications. Also, within each section there is included a short introductory note on the data available. This not only describes briefly the information available, but also provides relevant cross-references. Occasionally there is a reference to unpublished data and it is sometimes possible, with the co-operation of the government department concerned, to obtain such information for a modest fee.

At the beginning of the previous chapter a list of major reference works was given. It may be helpful, now that the reader has gained some impression of the published information, to consider which are the most helpful for the general reader. As a general source book for all kinds of statistical data including social and economic, the *Annual Abstract of Statistics* is probably the most comprehensive and, for a limited over-view of the main data, very useful. In the field of social statistics, as the reader will have grasped already, there is no more useful compendium than *Social Trends*, the last volume to appear being No. 10 in 1979. A particular virtue of the latest edition of this publication is an extended index which gives references to all previous issues since the same tables are not produced each year. In the economic field, *Economic Trends* is the most useful for general economic affairs. This monthly publication offers not only the major series of key economic variables but also includes important articles describing existing or proposed series of economic data. For industrial data and more detailed information than is given in *Economic Trends* for many subjects, the most important is the *Monthly Digest of Statistics*. For the reader who wants a useful sourcebook of economic data the *Annual Supplement to Economic Trends* is invaluable. A feature of this publication is the section devoted to notes on many of the major tables as well as definitions of important variables making up particular series.

While such statistical compendiums are of the greatest value, the working statistician who needs the most up-to-date information available cannot do without either of the two leading departmental journals to which frequent reference has already been made. The Department of Employment *Gazette* is the primary source of all statistics dealing with labour, prices and earnings. The Department of Trade's weekly journal *Trade and Industry* covers a very wide range of statistical information indeed. Almost any economic statistic which could be relevant to the businessman or industrialist finds some place in its pages. Both of these journals contain frequent and regular articles on the latest statistics, including any changes actual or proposed in such data. Neither of these journals is for the general reader but any student who is interested in economic or labour affairs should be familiar with the range of data which these publications provide. A particularly valuable publication is the C.S.O.'s quarterly journal *Statistical News*. This is primarily for specialists but the *Guide* includes many references to useful articles which have appeared in the *Statistical News* on particular topics, usually by the statisticians working in that area. If any work or study is proposed in a particular area of statistics, reference to the *Statistical News* for any relevant article is essential.

Conclusion

Any reference to statistical source material would be incomplete without a final warning. Readers of the last two chapters in particular will have noted the frequent footnotes to the tables and the references to changing definitions which recur in the text accompanying such tables. It is all too easy to extract published statistics and then make unjustified comparisons with other series. At all times when consulting published data, check on the sources and especially upon the definitions. Check also that the series has not been revised in recent times. For example, a line across the table or even in a single column of published figures usually denotes changes in the compilation of the series which make comparison of the years or period before the break and after the year in question impracticable. In recent years, especially with the C.S.O. seeking to co-ordinate the statistics produced by the various departments, always check whether the data relate to England and Wales, Great Britain or the United Kingdom. Most of the major economic and social statistical data are based upon sample enquiries. Information upon the relevant sample survey, its problems, etc. is usually published somewhere in the flood of statistical journals. If any work is to be done with such data, it is gross negligence not to read up the account of the method of collection and such comments thereon as may have been made. Particularly in the field of index numbers, of recent years there is not an index which has not been revised, modified or altered so as to affect comparability with earlier figures. Information on such changes is always published, usually in some detail.

Just in case any reader still labours under the illusion that the printed figure has some peculiar virtue of accuracy, despite all that has been said in the previous chapters, let him consider the following quotation from the Mercantile Credit lecture delivered by Sir Claus Moser:*

'The catalogue (of defects and deficiencies in official economic statistics) is daunting but it is no cause for taking fright. To a physicist it might be final confirmation of the weakness of statistics that we have to deal with such inexact data, but to a statistician it is

*Op. cit

the meat and drink of his trade. This is what we are skilled at; to measure and estimate things which are themselves inexact and volatile. We try to introduce new and better series, either to fill gaps or to replace existing measures. We keep our concepts and definitions under review and look out for improvements in methodology. We try to improve basic lists from which we draw samples and to develop improved methods of interpretation from incomplete data . . . In short, improving statistics is part and parcel of the work of every statistician.'

CHAPTER XIX

STATISTICS IN BUSINESS AND INDUSTRY

The efficiency of any industrial or commercial undertaking depends ultimately on the quality and efficiency of its management. To function properly, management must have available to it, as and when required, all information which is relevant to the conduct of the affairs of the undertaking. These range from the state of the labour force or the cash requirements of the firm to the results of the latest market research survey for a new product. If the firm depends upon raw materials from overseas, then it will have an interest in the state of world trade and its effects upon commodity prices and, if it operates overseas, it will need to know something about economic conditions in the countries where its subsidiaries and associated firms are situated. With the tendency for industrial and business organisation to expand, not least through the medium of subsidiary and ancillary undertakings, the time has long since passed when the manager not only knew the name and face of every workman on his staff, but his every customer as well. In the modern large-scale industrial or commercial undertaking, the statistician can serve in two ways. He can feed management with data and information relating to its commercial activities, *i.e.* its selling costs and the distribution of its markets, and in the industry he can help achieve the maximum efficiency on the production side. These various aspects of the statistician's work can now be discussed separately.

Desk Research

It is a commonplace that many firms maintain only the minimum of records sufficient to satisfy their accountants and auditors. Relatively few use such material to break down their turnover according to the size of individual orders, periodicity of re-ordering by the larger customers, the distribution of orders in the home and/or overseas markets, etc. On the labour side few records are kept regarding absenteeism and sickness. Admittedly, the maintenance of such records entails expenditure, but if the expenditure of a few thousand pounds per annum can achieve either savings in costs of production or increase efficiency amounting to many more thousands of pounds, then clearly the expenditure is fully justified. Most industrial consultants called in to examine the affairs of an undertaking invariably start by learning all there is to learn about its affairs from its internal records, *i.e.* costs, sales, etc. Their recommendations are often based on the facts to be found in the data already available to management!

The Z Chart

Graphical methods are especially valuable in business as a means of conveying information to management.

A type of graph which enjoys a considerable vogue in business rather than in statistical circles, is that known as the Z chart. It derives its name from the form made by the lines on the graph, as will be seen from a scrutiny of Figure 26. The Z chart is merely a method of graphing a time series in such a way that the totals for successive periods are plotted and in addition the cumulative total and a moving annual total.

TABLE 101

ABC COMPANY LTD SALES RECORD 1978

Month		Monthly Sales	Cumulative Monthly Total	Moving Annual Total
January	..	£	£	£
February	..	9,378	9,378	138,680
March ..	..	7,624	17,002	138,827
April ..	..	9,310	26,312	138,965
May ..	..	12,851	39,163	139,633
June ..	..	14,394	53,557	140,172
July ..	..	17,839	71,396	142,619
August ..	..	15,674	87,070	142,206
September	..	15,301	102,371	141,977
October	..	12,219	114,590	143,869
November	..	10,046	124,636	144,705
December	..	8,917	133,553	144,147
		11,463	145,016	145,016

The data on which the graph is based are given above in the table, showing the sales of ABC Co., Ltd. The first column gives the monthly turnover, and the second the cumulative total as from January. The final column provides the annual total of sales for the twelve months ended in any month of the current year. Thus against June the figure in the third column is £142,619, *i.e.* the total sales for the twelve months ended 30th June 1978. The total for the period ended 31st July is £142,206, which is smaller than the preceding figure by £413. Since the sales for the current August were £15,301, the sales for the August in the previous year were £413 greater, *i.e.* £15,714. The figures for all the months for the preceding year can be so computed if necessary from the table, except for January. The real value of the moving annual total is that it indicates the trend of sales relatively to the preceding year's experience. If the moving annual total line is rising, it indicates that each month this year is an improvement on the same month of the preceding year. If required, a series of such charts for successive years can be set side by side for comparative purposes.

Figure 26

Z CHART

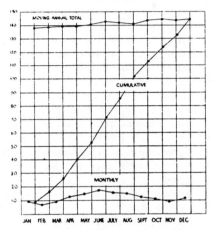

Sales record of ABC Company Limited 1978

External Statistics

Quite apart from the information relating to the operation of the business, every business undertaking has some interest in the overall state of the economy and, in all probability, in particular parts thereof. For example, an engineering firm would be interested in the trends in prices of particular metals, of machine tools and small parts. Likewise, the level of unemployment in the country has a direct effect upon the availability of labour, and not least upon its cost. While the value of an exchange of views on the state of the economy and its immediate prospects with other businessmen may be interesting and even informative, there is really no adequate substitute for a careful appraisal of all the relevant facts, as presented in documents such as the *Economic Survey*, the Department of Trade industrial returns on capital expenditure, hire purchase, etc. Likewise, for firms interested in overseas markets, the study of market reports such as appear regularly in the journal *Trade and Industry* is essential for the efficient conduct of business.

Closely related to the collection of information on the state of the economy, many firms also conduct either through the medium of their own research department, or by the services of a market research agency, market research surveys. Such research is not restricted to consumer goods. In recent years the many producers of capital goods such as large machines and equipment, have been using market research to ascertain the views of users, both actual and potential, of their products on the desirability of changes, adaptation to different requirements, etc. Such surveys are not only informative but, if they are undertaken at fairly regular intervals, changes over time may be more indicative of the future of the undertaking than a mere snapshot of its market at a particular point of time. Indeed, most market research consultants complain that some firms regard their function in much the same light as people regard their doctors, *i.e.* to be called in only when there is trouble. As long as all seems well, the firms are happy to drift along. Yet only by periodic surveys is it possible to assess how well a firm is doing. For example, in a growing and expanding market, while a single firm's sales may be increasing very satisfactorily, it may be steadily losing ground to a competitor whose share of the market is growing even more rapidly. Without continuous or at least periodic surveys such facts may be overlooked, with dire consequences in the long run.

Some market research agencies maintain consumer panels, which are used to test their client firms' new products. Such panels are, at least in theory, random samples of households or consumers who at intervals receive samples of a product and return a pre-paid business card indicating their views on the product. The services of such a consumer panel can be obtained more cheaply than a full-scale survey, since once established, the survey organisation can keep the panel busy on behalf of a number of client firms. The main problem of such consumer panels – and it is for the survey organisation to meet this problem – is that first, members become conditioned to acting as guinea pigs and that second, the membership tends to fluctuate. Thus the members no longer tend to behave as would the average consumer while to the extent that the composition of the panel changes, the substitute may not exactly match the unit it replaces, and thus the representativeness of the panel may be adversely affected. The results of such enquiries are a valuable counter to the director who has a penchant for arguing dogmatically from a sample of one. We have all heard the individual who knows a friend who knows someone else whose experience is then used to reflect the state of current opinion on a particular topic.

As has been shown in the preceding chapter and elsewhere in this book, there is no real shortage of information relating to the state of the economy, trade internal and external, industry or distribution in this country. Admittedly the data required for the use of a particular firm or undertaking may not be available in just the form it would like, but substitute data or series can usually be found. The real problem confronting the economic statistician is not usually, however, a shortage of data, so much as the plethora of published statistics from which he must choose those most suited to his needs. The statistician soon learns in industry and business that the fewer figures he can present to his board the better. He learns too that the more conviction with which he can support his conclusions, the shorter will be the discussion thereof. As every statistician in business knows, his biggest problem is the man who wants 'facts', and not intelligent deductions from the available evidence. There are times when the conclusions from the available data must be qualified, and great care is required on the part of the statistician in the manner he qualifies his evidence. On the other hand, he should not allow himself to be bulldozed into statements which he knows cannot be substantiated. For example, in making estimates of the future trend of sales, he is at best making an informed guess, and it is important that this point be got across to the board without at the same time, however, implying that any damn fool's guess is as good as his own.

In short, the problem of the statistician in industry or commerce is not so much statistics, as the need to be able to present to his colleagues and superiors the information he has collected in such a way that it is clear and capable of only one interpretation. In this respect, diagrams are an especially valuable adjunct. Overloaded tables must be avoided.

One last point is worth making since it tends so often to be overlooked. Generally speaking, the value that a firm derives from its statistician, particularly if he is the first appointment, is dependent on the statistician's own efforts. Usually he can expect little guidance as to what is required from him. It is up to him to decide what information is most likely to help in the formulation of policy and, as already stated, what manner of presentation will find readiest acceptance.

Business Forecasting

One of the most interesting applications of statistical techniques in business is known as forecasting. It is a commonplace that anyone who can predict the future accurately will soon make a fortune for himself and those associated with him. The mere fact that there are so few millionaires in this world makes it clear that there are few such people. However, some estimates of future trends of sales, consumer wants, etc., have to be made. There are various types of forecast, ranging from the hunch of the businessman that prices are going to rise, to the rather more sophisticated efforts of the statisticians at the National Institute of Economic and Social Research and the Central Statistical Office, whose labours are directed to the determination of short-run forecasts. These techniques are directly related to economics and are described as econometrics. Between these two extremes, forecasts can be made on the basis of extrapolating trends either by sketching in a freehand line following the path of the trend on a graph or by more complicated mathematical methods on the lines of those discussed in Chapter XI.

Nevertheless, for all the energy and thought expended in this particular field of study, it can hardly be asserted that the achievements of statistical forecasting have added any laurels to the subject of statistics. While the hunch is a plain, undiluted guess, the complex econometric model is also ultimately dependent upon numerous hunches, in so far as one must make guesses or estimates about the relationship between and the magnitude of certain key variables in the economy.

Modern economic planning or forecasting depends largely on the development of an economic 'model' which enables the workings of the economic system to be simulated in such a way that the consequences of given policies, e.g. a Budget surplus, or import surplus, can be predicted. The accuracy of the prediction depends, of course, on the extent to which the model can reproduce the manifold complexities of the economic system. How far is this a practicable proposition?

The basis of any economic model is known as a 'social accounting matrix' produced by a group of economists under Professor J. R. N. Stone working at Cambridge graphically referred to as SAM. This is being used by the National Economic Development Council and takes the form of drawing up a set of accounts on double entry principles for each main sector of the economy, e.g. agriculture, constructional trades, public authorities, exports, etc. The object of this set of accounts, i.e. SAM, is to reproduce the inter-relationship of each sector, e.g. the output of the mining and quarrying industry is the input of the building and constructional industry among others.

Once such a social accounting matrix has been devised, it is possible to follow through the effects of changes introduced in one sector of the economy and their consequences on other sectors. This is done by setting up a system of simultaneous equations which reflect these inter-sector relations. The electronic computer into which these data are fed enables the economists to simulate a whole range of situations which might emerge given various conditions and responses. Unfortunately, the reliability of the predictions, i.e. the behaviour pattern of the economy reproduced in the model, depends on the quality of the information put into the matrix and the computer. While a computer can perform miracles of high-speed sorting of facts or calculations, it cannot 'think'. It can only work on the information fed into it by its operators.

With economic model building there are two basic problems. The first is to know exactly how the economy works and the precise nature of the inter-relationship between different sectors of the economy. For example, if the U K has a budget deficit what would the results be for prices, capital investment, saving, on imports, on exports, etc.? While it is true to state that the modern economist knows a great deal about the working of the economic system, and his knowledge is continually expanding, it has not yet reached the stage at which he can talk of economic relationships which approximate to the laws of physics or chemistry. There are so many influences in the economy, from the state of business confidence, the state of the world markets, to the volume of bank credit and even political considerations, that it is quite impossible to predict with any degree of confidence their consequences in a given framework of economic facts.

Apart from deficiencies in our knowledge of the precise workings of the economic system, our statistical information is, as was indicated in the previous chapter, still limited. When Mr Macmillan presented his 1957 Budget he complained that formulating his budget policy with the then available statistical indicators was akin to looking up this year's trains in last year's Bradshaw. Since then, there has been a very real improvement both in the quality and coverage of official statistics. But there are still gaps and, more to the point, the statistics often appear long after the events they describe.

'Forward-looking' Statistics

Because of the difficulties of making reliable forecasts, usually on the basis of extrapolating, *i.e.* projecting, the experience of the past, recent years have witnessed an attempt to collect what are sometimes called 'forward-looking' statistics. These data are based generally on surveys of consumers' and industrialists' expectations and intentions regarding the future. In the United States such surveys are frequent, but they are relatively new in the U K. One of the best known is the Department of Trade's sample survey among large industrial undertakings to assess their intentions in the field of capital expenditure. The results of the survey, are published quarterly in the Department of Trade *Journal*.

Directly related to the Board of Trade survey is the Confederation of British Industry's four-monthly survey, which seeks to evaluate industrialists' views regarding their short-term prospects, regarding output, orders and exports. (A copy of the Schedule used in this survey is reproduced on pp. 32-3.)

An official description of the methods of short-term economic forecasting makes the point that 'while the relationship between forecast and out-turn has varied very much from company to company it has been found that, in the aggregate, firms' forecasts are in excess of actual expenditures in a fairly systematic way'.* Thus it is possible to make reasonably reliable assessments of future trends even if the basic information is biased but, of course, the bias must be consistent in direction!

Linked to this field of enquiry is the considerable improvement in the quality and coverage of statistics with special reference to industry. An important point here is the need for early publication. Thus, the index of industrial production is published monthly, with a time lag of only six weeks, and this is increasingly used as an indicator of trends. The index numbers of the volume of Output and Orders (by adjusting money values to 1975 prices) from a wide range of industries where the production process takes a certain time, e.g. engineering, textiles, clothing industries, are valuable short-run indicators of activity. The journal *Trade and Industry* publishes such indices shown in Table 102 relating to the engineering industries for both home and export markets. The Department of the Environment collects statistics of new orders obtained by the constructional industry. Likewise, the Department of the Environment carries out a half-yearly enquiry into builders and property developers' intentions concerning private house building. A tremendous amount of working capital is tied up in stocks held by British industry and firms engaged in wholesale and retail trade. Important data are collected thereon by the Census of Production and the Census of Distribution. In addition to these, however, figures are collected each quarter from a sample of manufacturers, wholesalers and retailers whose total stock represents about two-thirds of the national stocks, and the results are published periodically in the Department of Trade *Journal*. Table 103 illustrates the type of information collected and its mode of publication. These figures do not show the absolute value of the stocks held (although an indication thereof is provided by the end-December 1977 book value at the top of the table), but only quarterly changes in volume measured in terms of 1975 prices. A description of the sources of information on manufacturers' and distributors' stocks is given in the annual supplement to *Economic Trends*.

In themselves, such series and data may not provide a complete answer to the problem of economic forecasting. However, in so far as

*Short-term economic forecasting in the UK, *Economic Trends*, August 1964.

TABLE 102

ENGINEERING AND CONSTRUCTION: OUTPUT AND ORDERS

Seasonally adjusted volume index numbers

	Engineering industries[1]							Construction (GB)	
	Total			Home market		Export		Output[3,4]	Orders received
	Sales	Orders on hand end of period	New orders[2]	Orders on hand end of period	New orders[2]	Orders on hand end of period	New orders[2]		
	1975 average monthly sales = 100	Average 1975 = 100	1975 average monthly sales = 100	Average 1975 = 100	1975 average monthly sales = 100	Average 1975 = 100	1975 average monthly sales = 100	1975 = 100	1975 = 100
1973	98	113	116	120†	121†	100	105†	118·6	141·4
1974	102	114	103	115	102	112	106	106·3	101·1
1975	100	88	84	87	83	94	84	100·0	100·0
1976	97†	81	92	74	87	94	104	98·5	105·5
1977[5]	97	83	98	75	94	100	109	98·0	94·6
1978	99	90†	103	84	101	100	106	104·9•	102·9•
1976 1	96	84	85	83	83†	86	90	100·3	112·6
2	97	80	87	79	86	82	89	97·6	114·5
3	96	80	97	77	90	87	114	96·3	99·7
4	97	81	100	74	90	94	123	96·3	95·2
1977• 1	97	82	93	74	95†	97	109	99·9	91·0
2	96†	82	97†	73	89	97	116†	96·1	93·3
3	97	83	97	73	93	100†	105	96·5	96·1
4	96	84†	99	75	97	100†	105	98·5	98·1
1978• 1	99	83	99	75	95†	101	110	100·7	102·2
2	98	84	95	75†	94	98	97	101·5	99·0
3	100	90	103	84	100	100	110	107·1	106·9
4	98	83	113	76	116	100	108	106·6	103·4•
1978• J	97	83	99	76	104	96	88	104·4•	95·0
A	100	84	101	75†	96	97	113	—	111·7
S	102	84	107	76	99	100	128	—	114·0
O	96	88	99	83	99	99	99	—	109·5
N	97	90	130	84	139	100	107	—	96·5
D	102	90	112	84	109	101	117	—	104·2•
1979• J	83		83		81		88	—	85•,•

[1]Mechanical, instrument and electrical engineering (SIC Orders VII, VIII and IX).

[2]Net of cancellations.

[3]This index is based on an output series which includes repair and maintenance estimates of unrecorded output by small firms and self-employed workers and output by the direct labour departments of the public sector.

[4]Details of the method of deflation to constant prices are given in Economic Trends, No. 297, July 1978.

[5]Estimates based on orders reported by major contractors.

•Provisional.

†Revised figures.

Source: Economic Trends, No. 306

TABLE 103

STOCK CHANGES

Seasonally adjusted

£ million, 1975 prices

Book values end-December	All industries	Manufacturing[1]				Distribution			Other Industries
		Total	Materials and fuels	Work in progress	Finished goods	Total	Retail	Wholesale	
1977²	34,469	19,995	7,277	7,321	5,397	7,722	3,181	4,541	6,752
1976 I	− 88	− 13	− 88	42	34	50	7	43	− 125
2	− 74	− 29	− 47	38	− 20	− 76	− 67	− 9	31
3	163	99	48	37	14	127	46	81	63
4	259	259	23	104	131	43	27	16	43
1977 1	430	234	92	123	21	199	117	82	3
2	293	97	38	69	204	184	4	180	12
3	− 70	− 5	− 23	− 33	50	− 139	− 59	− 80	74
4	325	116	− 47	174	− 11	51	− 33	84	158
1978 1	291	38	− 26	17	48	143	62	81	110
2	280	272	15	128	158	66	128	62	− 58
3	302	175†	20	102†	52†	99†	54	45†	28
4	89	111	9	199	− 97	10	89	− 79	32

[1]Differences between totals and the sum of constituent parts of manufacturing are due to rounding.
²Unadjusted 1975 price stock levels.

Source: Economic Trends, No. 306

they are published relatively quickly after the events they describe, and to the extent that experience shows some inter-relationship between changes in these forward-looking data, there is every possibility that a valuable tool may be devised which will improve the accuracy of short-run predictions. At least, if the interpretations of these data and the findings of the more sophisticated techniques such as the econometric model of the United Kingdom and its quarterly forecasts, coincide, then it is a reasonable assumption that the findings are reliable. Always assuming, of course, that the model is not based on the same data as are the other estimates.*

Government economic policy is based upon short-term forecasts which are themselves formulated on the basis of two main sets of economic data. The first stage in the formulation of a forecast is the diagnosis of recent trends. The statistical evidence for this is derived from a variety of economic series, in particular those relating to the labour situation such as the number of registered vacancies and unemployed, together with figures of wage rates. In addition, retail sales, which account for some 50 per cent of personal consumption, new car registrations, hire purchase transactions, as well as export and import data, are all examined to assess the volume of demand for the economy's resources. The second branch of the exercise is based upon the predictive data available. Such information is derived from two main sources, surveys of intentions such as those described above and the programmes of planned and scheduled expenditure developed by government departments and public boards, *e.g.* the nationalised industries. These predictive data are then linked with other estimates, *e.g.* the quarterly figures of the Gross Domestic Product which then enable preliminary forecasts of all expenditure other than personal expenditure to be estimated.

Estimates of prospective personal consumption are built up by making individual forecasts of all the main components of personal income, direct taxes, consumer prices and personal savings. Such estimates are then reconciled with estimates of the aggregate expenditure and income derived by estimating total personal income from the prospective total of national output. This is possible because the level of factor incomes is obviously directly linked with the volume of output. A key figure in the estimate of prospective income is that for wages and salaries which together account for almost two-thirds of total personal incomes. This is based on estimates of rates of change in wage rates which are themselves estimated in the light of recent trends. This is not as haphazard or arbitrary as it may appear since wage bargaining processes are considerably

*The cynic would, however, argue that the mere fact of several economists agreeing on the significance of a set of data is in itself conclusive!

influenced by habit and convention.[1] Hence past experience is a reliable guide, although special attention must be paid to the trend of prices which can affect the pattern of wage bargaining. These estimates of wage rates and earnings are then linked up with the estimates of prospective demand for labour.

The pattern of price movements is a fundamental factor in any economic forecast. The trend of consumer prices is evaluated from a break-down of the goods and services which are included in the retail price index. Thus the future movement of food prices which are sensitive to changes in domestic supplies are evaluated independently of changes in rents and rates, as well as of other goods and services. Of these, the official report notes that United Kingdom businessmen generally fix their prices on the basis of a standard, or normal degree of capacity working. In other words, given the cost of labour, short-term variations in the level of output make little difference to prices charged.[2]

The entire structure of the forecasts relating to the internal domestic economy is dependent upon changes in the balance of payments. For this purpose exports are estimated by breaking down the aggregate for the main markets. For example, United Kingdom exports to the United States are correlated with changes in the United States gross domestic products. There is a similar breakdown of imports, in this case by class, *e.g.* foodstuffs, commodities and materials plus manufactures. For each class an estimate is made on the basis of price trends and demand.

For all the apparent comprehensiveness of this approach to economic planning, the fact remains that all the component estimates are no more than informed guesses. In addition, a serious error in any one major component, *e.g.* the balance of payments, can vitiate the results of the entire exercise. Nevertheless, the techniques and information available are being continually improved.

Industrial Statistics

So far the discussion has concentrated primarily upon what has been called earlier in this book 'descriptive statistics'. Generally speaking, particularly in commerce and even in industry, a large volume of the statistics collected and prepared are of this type. Sometimes, where sales forecasting is an important part of the work, more refined statistical techniques will be used. Generally speaking, however, a familiarity with statistical sources, the presentation and interpretation of such data are the prerequisites of a competent statistician. In industry, however, at least on the production side, the

[1]Op. cit. *Economic Trends*, August 1964.
[2]Op. cit.

main emphasis is laid upon statistical techniques. In recent years the importance of these techniques has been growing apace, and there is, as will be seen, tremendous scope for the mathematical statistician in industry, who is interested in the growing field of operational research.[1]

Quality Control

Probably the most widely known of all statistical techniques employed in industry is statistical *quality control*. This is a simple application of the theory based on the Normal curve (see Chapter XIII). Modern mass production techniques involve ensuring that each item of output has standard dimensions or other physical properties within certain limits of a predetermined ideal standard. In theory, the product can be checked when it comes from the machine. But at this stage the damage may have been done. It is far more economic to try to check any fault in the production process at the earliest possible moment, and statistical quality control, because it draws attention at an early stage to a situation in which the quality of production is beginning to deteriorate, is extensively employed. The basis of the technique is illustrated in Figure 27, which shows two charts, the Mean Chart and Range Chart. Time is measured along the horizontal axis, while the variation in specifications of the product is measured along the vertical axis. The so-called process average or mean range represents the approximation to the standard product which experience with the manufacturing process has shown can be achieved. Furthermore, on the basis of past production experience, the variation about this standard quality has been measured and is indicated by the addition on both charts of two further lines referred to as the inner and outer limits. These limits, usually referred to as control limits, are equal to 1·96 and 3·0 standard errors of the sampling distribution. Once the production process is under way, samples of output are taken at fixed intervals and the average dimension of the sample and the range of dimensions thereof are plotted on the two charts. If either the average or the range begin to drift outside the control limits, this signifies that the production process is tending to go out of control. If left unchecked, therefore, the process will begin to produce defective components. The size of the sample and the periodicity of the sample taken depends on the process, and must be determined by the statistician in conjunction with the engineer. The reader will doubtless appreciate the reasons for using two charts for this particular technique. Successive samples may in fact produce the same mean size, but as was shown in the discussion of averages, it is possible for two samples to have the same means but very dif-

[1]Some of the methods are outlined below.

Figure 27

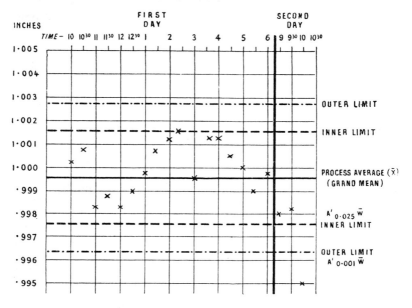

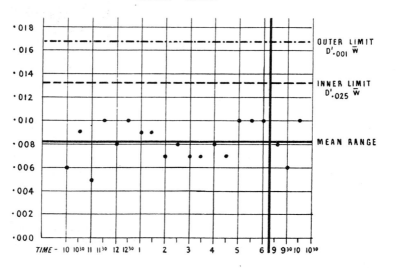

ferent dispersions. Thus, one could have a situation in which the sample mean was within the inner control limits, and yet every one of the items in the sample was defective, since it fell outside the limits set on the range chart. The great advantage of this particular system is not only that it draws attention almost immediately to a situation in which the production process is getting out of control, but once installed, it can be operated by relatively unskilled workers, provided they adhere strictly to the rules laid down by the statistician

The foregoing example illustrates the simplest type of quality control. In recent years, however, there have been extensive adaptations of this system to all kinds of industrial processes and the study of industrial quality control forms an important part of the application of statistical theory.

REFERENCES

Quality – Its Creation and Control, Institution of Production Engineers.
Quality Control, G. Herdan, Nelson.

Operational Research

The major benefit in the statistical field which industry and business have derived from the introduction of the computer, apart from the savings on routine clerical work, is the application of operational research techniques to their problems. Evolved during the last war, O.R., as it is often termed, has been adapted to assist management in two ways. First, it can help management in arriving at policy decisions in the light of all the known facts, and with the full knowledge of the consequences of the alternative policies available to the management. Second, it can assist management to secure better methods of carrying out existing operations. The significance of the computer lies in the fact that operational research uses mathematical models in the study of industrial and commercial problems. These models are often difficult to construct and invariably involve innumerable calculations which, without a computer, could not be resolved in any reasonable time. The basic principle underlying O.R. is the mathematical model based upon a set of equations which reflect different aspects of the working of the system. For example, in problems concerning the level of stock of component parts which a manufacturing firm should hold, the size of its stocks at any time determines the amount of working capital tied up in this way. Likewise, the cost of running out of the stock of a given component in terms of production delays can be calculated and expressed in the form of an equation. Thus, these mathematical models comprise a number of such equations, to which an optimum solution may be derived. The optimum solution in question may be in terms of that allocation of resources which yields a manufacturer the highest profit. Or it may, in another set of circumstances, be the solution which reduces to a minimum delays in the production process. The essence of O.R. techniques, the mathematics apart, is precise information and data relating to the problem concerned. Whether the problem be one of stock levels, transport, or production, the first stages must be to define the problem and obtain sufficient information relating to the relevant variables in order to construct the model, *e.g.* cost of resources used. One of the major virtues of O.R. is that before any mathematical work can be started, the team and management are forced to consider all aspects of the problem and what its solution may entail. Such detailed analyses of given situations are in themselves very useful in clearing the mind! Reference is occasionally made in literature on this subject to the 'O.R. team', and it is important that the reader should appreciate that operational research is essentially inter-disciplinary. It uses the skills and techniques of mathematics, statistics, economics, engineering, and other sciences, so that whatever the type of problem encountered, the skills are available to analyse it.

Linear Programming

One of the earliest and the most widely applied O.R. techniques is known as *linear programming*. This is a technique for allocating limited resources among a number of competing demands in such a way as to maximise the output or minimise costs. The complication here lies in the fact that alternative uses exist for the limited resources. Furthermore, there are substantial costs involved in allocating these resources more to one use than to another. The computer is eminently suited for this type of problem involving factors which can vary within specified limits. The machine repeats the calculation over and over again, varying each factor by pre-determined amounts, and an optimum solution is derived. One of the earliest applications of linear programming has been that used by the National Coal Board to determine the best policy of marketing coal. The facts are that a number of different grades of coal can be produced from a number of different coal mines and are required in varying quantities by a number of different customers. Linear programming techniques enabled the decision to be made as to which grade of coal should be produced from which coal mine, and sent to which customer in such a way, either that output from some of the mines is maximised, or that output and transportation costs are minimised.

Transportation problems lend themselves especially well to linear programming. Thus, a large undertaking which maintains depots in different parts of the country in order to meet the needs of its various customers in those areas, can by the use of linear programming determine whether these depots are the best-sited to keep transportation costs to a minimum yet satisfy their customers' requirements with the minimum delay.

Queueing Theory

One of the most interesting applications of O.R. is that known as *queueing theory*. Motorists are accustomed to delays at toll bridges or ferries; many of us are familiar with the delays on a busy telephone switchboard; with waiting in canteen queues for lunch, etc. The general issue dealt with in this particular type of problem is how to reduce waiting time to the point at which the costs thereof are minimised. One of the simplest illustrations concerns a post-war study of ore handling in British ports, where substantial imports of ore were handled by special equipment. The ideal situation would be, of course, that ships would arrive at regular intervals, come straight into port, be unloaded immediately and allowed to depart. Furthermore, the intervals of arrival should be such that at no time was any of the unloading equipment in the docks idle. In practice, the situation is of course rather different. Ships arrive at irregular intervals and often have to wait because there is no berth available. This is an expensive process, since the ship is thereby losing revenue. On the other hand, to expand the port facilities to meet any feasible number of ships arriving more or less at the same time so that none of these ships shall be delayed, would be extremely expensive and would mean that the port facilities would be under-utilised for long periods of time. O.R. techniques enabled a considerable amount of information relating to costs of the ship's time, as well as the operation of unloading equipment, to be calculated. It was possible to estimate the minimum discharging capacity that needed to be made available in order to keep waiting time of ships at a minimum. In other words, this type of queueing problem illustrates the classical problem of conflicting interests between the two parties; the port operator who wishes to see all his berths occupied and busy, and the ship owners or charterers who wish to ensure that their ships are never kept waiting to turn round.

The same techniques can be employed in the designing of landing facilities at airports, of taxi parking areas, the movement of travellers through customs, or out-patients at a hospital; and even the timing of traffic lights to facilitate movement of traffic in such a way that queues do not pile up on either side of the intersection.

Stock Control

Most business organisations, whether they are manufacturers, wholesalers or retailers, carry a stock both of components and raw materials for production purposes, or finished goods for supply on demand from their customers. The published statistics available on stocks by firms in the United Kingdom suggest that the value of such stocks represents many thousand millions of pounds of working capital. As any accountant knows, a firm which is short of working capital can usually meet part of its needs by running down its stocks. The essence of stock control, with which is usually linked the buying policy for stock, is to evaluate on the one hand the relative costs of maintaining so large a stock that there is no danger whatsoever of being unable to satisfy demand, whether that demand be from the producer or a customer, and on the other hand the cost in terms of tied-up capital, factory space, etc. An optimum solution to this type of problem can be obtained by an analysis of information relating to stocks and withdrawals from them, as well as the annual cost of providing storage space, of interest on capital tied up in stocks, loss arising from obsolescence or deterioration, and the risk of loss due to falling prices. On the other hand, with a large stock advantages may accrue from the elimination of the danger of run-outs; possibly lower prices from suppliers in the case of raw materials where a regular order is placed and, in the case of the manufacturer, the risks and cost of failing to meet his customers' requirements on demand. Linked with the problem of what level of stocks should be held to balance the relative costs of the two extreme policies, is the problem as to when new orders for the replacement of stock should be made. The problem here arises because if there is a sudden demand for a particular component, and stocks are depleted, production may be held up since there is always some delay before new materials can be ordered and delivered. Furthermore, an examination of this particular problem will also bring to light the problems of ensuring that the person in charge of stock is kept fully aware of the position of each component or type of stock held. Where the stock consists of a wide range of heterogeneous products, it is all too easy to overlook that some stocks are near run-out. Thus, by ascertaining the optimum size of stock to be held and the point at which a re-order should be placed for such stock, substantial savings may be made in a firm or organisation where stocks are high. For example, Mr R. A. Ward reports on the basis of practical studies carried out over three years, 'In most of the stores at least 20 per cent of the commodities stocked were found not to have been issued in the preceding 12 months and those in charge of the store had not realised that so high a proportion of the stock had remained static'.* He goes on to add that the results achieved by such methods indicate that between 2 and 4 per cent of the annual value of the store's turnover can be saved.

*Operational Research in Local Government, R.I.P.A.

Critical Path Analysis

Towards the end of the 1950s, both in Britain and the United States a new management technique was evolved which, unlike most of the O.R. methods, does not necessarily entail the application of mathematical statistics. In practice, however, the more complex problems necessitate such techniques and a computer! This technique, known as *Critical Path Analysis*, has been used with especial success with large contracts where the basic problem comprises the organisation of a large number of interrelated jobs in such a way that one part of the work cannot always be started until another is finished, and where there is a fixed point of time at which the entire project must be completed. An obvious example would be a large construction project, *e.g.* an oil refinery or electricity generating station, and the U.S. Navy used this technique in the construction of the Polaris submarine. The essential principle of critical path analysis is the setting down in simple graphical form – in the form of a network of 'paths' – all the available information relating to the project in such a way that the time required for each single stage of the project is evaluated. The chart shows the interdependence of each stage and, given the precedence of the various sections of the work, an estimate can be derived of the probable minimum time required for the project. The sequence of events required to minimise the time required is known as the critical path. The term critical path analysis (C.P.A.) stems from the fact that by continually checking the progress of the work, if at any point any of the sections of the work take longer to complete than anticipated, then the original schedule will be thrown out. By use of a computer, which is fed continuously with the latest information on progress achieved, the model can be revised in the light of such unexpected changes and a new plan of operation formulated to minimise the time needed to complete the job. If, however, the time taken on particular sequences of the job is reduced, then it may prove possible to follow a slightly different schedule, dependent on the revised programme put out by the computer, which will have the effect of reducing the overall time for the entire project. This will mean that a new sequence of work becomes relevant and hence critical.

The main advantage of this technique is that it enables the productive efforts to be concentrated on those points where the maximum benefit in terms of time saving is likely to be achieved. A more sophisticated application of the same technique developed in the United States is known as *project evaluation and review technique* (known as P.E.R.T.). In this case three separate time estimates are submitted for each activity or section of the work, the most optimistic, the most likely, and the most pessimistic. As the project proceeds, information relating to progress is assembled, and the probability of achieving the target dates is then reviewed. The obvious advantage of using three estimates of the time required for each section of the work is that it avoids the situation in which the engineer or technician in charge plays safe if he only has to give one estimate of the time he will require. An offshoot of the same technique is the so-called least-cost programme, wherein both the normal time and cost for a given project are estimated and in addition a 'crash' time and cost are submitted for each activity, so that in the event of any unexpected delay on a particular section of the work, the relative advantages of expending more money on a crash effort to offset the delay and the consequences of deferring the final completion date may be compared.

Apart from the foregoing O.R. techniques there are many others, such as the Monte Carlo method, replacement theory, and dynamic programming. The theory of games is a relatively new development, which undoubtedly has a future as an aid to business decision-making, but some of the theoretical problems involved are highly complex and as yet commercial application of this technique is limited. However, the essence of all O.R. techniques is that they are primarily mathematical in character. The foregoing sections have sought merely to indicate in very brief outline the nature of the problems which such techniques may help resolve. The management trainee or accountant who has some mathematical ability, *i.e.* at least Additional Maths at 'O' Level, preferably 'A' Level Pure Maths, can consult with profit and interest some of the references given hereunder. For the student, however, whose mathematics is merely sufficient to acquaint him with the elementary statistical methods outlined in the earlier part of this book, the only solution is to read one of the simpler introductions to O.R. in the hope that he will at least understand what his statistical colleagues are talking about.

REFERENCES

One of the least technical introductions to O.R. is *A Manager's Guide to Operational Research* by Rivett and Ackoff (John Wiley and Sons). This is completely non-mathematical and eminently suited to the non-mathematician. A slightly more advanced introduction is *A Guide to Operational Research*, by E. Duckworth (Methuen). This contains a number of simple illustrations of various techniques with no more arithmetic than the average 'O' Level candidate can understand. At about the same level, *An Introduction to Critical Path Analysis*, by K. G. Lockyer (Pitman) deals with this one particular technique.

For the reader with some mathematics, *Management and Mathematics* by Fletcher and Clarke (Business Publications) is a useful introduction to the various O.R. techniques referred to above. All these works provide references to further and more advanced reading, of which there is a growing quantity, particularly from the United States.

Acceptance Sampling for Accountants

Every accounting student will be familiar with test checks on the books and vouchers of client firms. The principle underlying test checking is the same as that underlying sampling. But, whereas in statistical sampling the sample is selected in such a way as to ensure that the choice of population units is random, with the conventional test checks everything depends on the auditor's own judgement. For example, he may decide to vouch two or three months' purchase invoices and a different two months of sales invoices, and perhaps one month of the petty cash vouchers. In other words, a very large element of intuition and subjective judgement determines the actual scope of the audit.

In recent years, statistical sampling techniques have been evolved to assist auditors and accountants who are confronted with large quantities of checking, as for example in the records of a large organisation. One of the most generally used techniques is known as *acceptance sampling*. This is a statistical approach to the problem of controlling the accuracy of clerical work by means of sample inspection of the records. The results of the inspection are then compared with a previously determined objective standard, and in the light of the results of that comparison, the decision is made as to whether or not more checking is necessary.

The basic problem, as with any significance test, is to decide at what level of confidence the auditor may accept the sample and thus run the risk of accepting an unsatisfactory population. Alternatively, if he rejects the sample, he runs the risk of rejecting a satisfactory population.

The basic principle underlying all acceptance sampling methods is to achieve a balance between two extremes, *i.e.* a complete checking of all items, which is largely unnecessary and expensive to the client or the organisation concerned, or a sample enquiry which can in theory be so small that a considerable risk is run of serious errors being overlooked. Since these errors will cost the organisation money, they may considerably outweigh any savings achieved by the reduced audit.

The application of acceptance sampling necessitates certain information before a sampling scheme can be devised. First, the size of the population of vouchers, invoices, etc., must be determined.* This may seem to be at cross-purposes with what has been written earlier about sample sizes being independent of the population size. These auditing techniques involve the use of specially prepared tables (see below) based upon a formula which uses the population size to provide the auditor with the sample size appropriate to the expected proportion of errors in the population and the level of confidence at which it will be decided to accept or reject the sample. The actual

---

*Acceptance sampling can, of course, be applied to documents other than vouchers. It can also be applied to postings, costings, the castings of cash books, ledgers, etc.

choice of the sample units, once the size has been determined by reference to the specially constructed tables, is best carried out by normal systematic sampling, *i.e.* a random starting point and every *nth* item selected. In drawing his sample, the auditor will probably stratify his population, deciding to take a small, *e.g.* 2 per cent, proportion of the very small invoices, and a slightly larger proportion of the invoices for larger sums. The acceptance level is simply the highest number of errors which can be accepted without rejecting the sample.

Second, an estimate must be made of the relative quality of the vouchers, *i.e.* what proportion are likely to contain errors. This can normally be estimated on the basis of past experience of that particular audit. Thus, if the client has his own internal audit it is reasonable to assume that the chances of errors are less than in a firm where financial control is less satisfactory. Next, the auditor must determine what is defined as an *acceptable error risk*.[1] This is merely a guide to action in the sense that once this predetermined number or proportion of errors has been detected in the sample the decision is made to extend the audit. In practice, however, the accountant uses one of the published sets of tables[2] to guide him as to the appropriate sample size, given the population and the acceptance rate for that population that he considers appropriate.

The foregoing technique may be illustrated by a simple example. Let it be assumed that the bought ledger comprises some 4,800 accounts with balances of varying sizes. Let us assume, further, that the population can be divided into two strata, one of 4,000, another of 800, the former containing relatively small accounts, and the other rather larger balances. It may be assumed, further, that experience shows that the expected rate of errors in both strata will be 3 per cent and 2 per cent respectively. The auditor would be prepared to accept a variation about this expected error rate of 2 per cent, and he is prepared to accept or reject the sample subject to this degree of precision at the 95 per cent level of confidence. A reference to the appropriate tables shows that a sample size in the case of the 4,000 population will be 261, and in the case of the 800 population a sample of 152 will be required. Thus a total sample of 413 out of the 4,800 balances in the population will need to be checked. The samples are then drawn by some systematic method of sampling from the strata, and the balances verified. Provided the errors detected do not exceed 5 per cent in the case of the smaller accounts and 4 per cent in the case of the larger accounts, the auditor will be prepared to pass the bought ledger. If, however, the error rate detected is in excess of the limits set, then further work will be required.

[1] Some writers in this field use the term *acceptance quality level*.
[2] *Sampling Inspection Tables*, by Dodge and Romig (John Wiley & Sons), 1944, or *Sampling Tables for Estimating Error Rates or Other Proportions*, R. G. Brown and L. L. Vance (University of California), 1961.

There are three main types of sampling techniques employed in this field. First, the single sample characterised by a fixed sample size and single acceptance number. Second, a double sample where the sample is divided into two parts and the second part is examined only if a clear decision cannot be arrived at upon the results derived from the first sample. Third, sequential sampling where, instead of choosing a sample of fixed size, the population is sampled item by item, the work being terminated as soon as there is sufficient information for a significant conclusion, *i.e.* that the records are so accurate that no more work need be done, or so inaccurate that a detailed investigation is necessary. Sequential sampling may take some considerable time, and consequently modifications of this technique have been evolved. Basically the method consists of taking a sample of a fixed size and then, dependent upon the number of errors found in that sample, the decision is made whether to accept the entire population or whether to take another sample.

Where double sampling is used, the tables again are consulted to determine the appropriate sample size given the acceptable error rate. Double sampling is sometimes preferred to single sampling, because a smaller size of sample can be used since there is the possibility of further check. Since in practice it is often not required, the amount of checking to be done is kept to a minimum. In the case of double sampling, however, it is generally agreed that the quality of the sample must be much higher, *i.e.* the proportion of errors detected in the first sample must be much lower, than with single sampling. What that level should be, if a second sample is not to be used, must be determined in advance.

Acceptance sampling, whether single or double sampling is used, only enables the auditor to decide in the light of pre-determined criteria to accept or reject the population as satisfactory or unsatisfactory. It does not enable him to decide how satisfactory or inaccurate any work is. For this purpose, a technique known as *estimation sampling* is used. This involves the taking of a sample to estimate the average characteristic of the population, which when taken together with the standard deviation will give an estimated value of the whole with a degree of probability of its accuracy. Estimation sampling is especially useful, for example, in stock valuation, particularly if there are numerous items. A relatively small sample thereof will enable a reliable estimate to be made of the whole, the size of the sample selected for purposes of estimation clearly depending on the limits within which any acceptable estimate of the population parameter must fall.

REFERENCES

Statistical Sampling for Auditors and Accountants, L. L. Vance and J. Neter.
Introductory Chapters to Sampling Tables, op. cit.

INDEX